Sima Eliovson

THE COMPLETE GARDENING BOOK

Other books by SIMA ELIOVSON:

Flowering Shrubs, Trees and Climbers for Southern Africa.
South African Wild Flowers for the Garden.
Discovering Wild Flowers in Southern Africa.
Proteas for Pleasure.
Bulbs for the Gardener.

Published by

HOWARD TIMMINS

A well-cared-for lawn is a perfect foil to flower borders, trees and shrubs. Feed it adequately each growing season.

THE
COMPLETE
GARDENING BOOK

SIMA ELIOVSON, F.R.H.S.

HOWARD TIMMINS
CAPE TOWN
1968

First Published November 1960

Second Edition February 1962

Third Edition March 1964

Fourth Edition January 1966

Fifth Edition June 1968

Citadel Press, Lansdowne, Cape

"Flowers—are a proud assertion that a ray of beauty outvalues all the utilities of the world."

RALPH WALDO EMERSON

DEDICATED TO ALL FLOWER-LOVERS

CONTENTS

LIST OF BLACK AND WHITE ILLUSTRATIONS

LIST OF COLOUR ILLUSTRATIONS

INTRODUCTION

THE JOYS OF GARDENING

The aim of this book is to help the amateur to make gardening a joy and not an anxious problem; to suggest ways of furnishing the garden with plants that give colour throughout the year; to enumerate easy and common-sense methods of pruning, compost making and other essential tasks and to try to stimulate the imagination so that each gardening task will be approached with economy of effort and confidence that success will follow.

Above all, it will indicate a plan of how to commence. Nothing can equal the joy of the amateur who has built up his own garden and knows that every tree and flower is there by his own planting. An early Japanese landscape gardener once expressed his satisfaction with his small garden by saying that there was "no greater pleasure than the soil brought with my own basket and the stone shaped by my own hand". There is also nothing more irritating for the amateur than to find later that had he known where to place his plants and how to care for them they might have thrived and been a greater success. "It's easy when you know how" is a phrase often heard and "know-how" has been stressed in this book as a means to an end—the enjoyment of gardening and of the garden.

The special problems of the gardener have been detailed, including gardening in the shade, at the seaside or in dry localities inland, in cold frosty places and in the sub-tropics. Instructions have been given on how to grow the popular garden plants, like Roses, Iris, Lilies, Sweet-peas and Delphiniums, as well as many fruits and vegetables, trees and shrubs. Little space has been taken up with descriptions of plants in this book, even though numerous plants are suggested for different purposes. Many of these have been amply described in two previous books* by the author and all the others will be found either in seedsmen's catalogues or in standard gardening dictionaries and encyclopedias.†

Many people who live in flats have an urge to grow things and their wishes may be satisfied by growing house-plants or miniature trees, while they might be interested in methods of growing plants without soil. Both these

and the hobbyists who wish to grow mushrooms or orchids have been remembered in this book which seeks to point out to all the joys of gardening.

One of the most pleasant remarks that one can make to a gardener is to tell him that there is always something interesting and colourful in his garden. Collecting a variety of plants will give one that pleasure and supply a well-furnished garden that is easy to care for. The demands of modern life are such that the gardener cannot spend all his leisure time working in the garden, while comparatively few people are able to employ sufficient garden labour. There are many ways of reducing maintenance while making the garden interesting and beautiful, and many suggestions of how to do this have been given in the following pages.

What is there about gardening that appeals to everyone? Part of the pleasure lies in appreciating the beauty of the lay-out with its background of foliage and green lawn and its interesting features such as ponds and winding pathways. Even those who do no gardening can enjoy this. Part of the pleasure lies again in the peacefulness that comes over one when walking around the garden, noting the development of one's plants and considering the work to be done. This might be tempered with frustration, of course, when one sees more work than one can manage, but the peacefulness returns as soon as any part of the work is tackled. When armed with the pruning shears, it is almost impossible not to concentrate on each woody twig to the exclusion of business worries and many men find gardening a panacea. The combination of busy hands and a peaceful, though attentive, mind will make solitude creative.

The ultimate joy of gardening is the interest taken in nature. Even a child can appreciate the fascination of unfurling leaves or blossom in spring and be amazed at the growth of a seedling. Although nature makes plants grow, the gardener cannot help feeling a sense of pride in anything he has grown. He feels that it is his placing of the seed in the soil that has brought it to life and that it is his care that has brought it to fruition.

It is said that plants do well if they are loved. This is a sentimental way of expressing the fact that if one is sufficiently interested to find out their needs, one cannot help making them thrive. "Greenfingers" is the title that

---

*Flowering Shrubs, Trees and Climbers for Southern Africa; South African Wild Flowers for the Garden by Sima Eliovson.

†Manual of Cultivated Plants, 1949, by L. H. Bailey; The Royal Horticultural Society's Dictionary of Gardening.

the veriest amateur can have if he turns his attention to the essentials that are needed and is not frightened off by those who make a pretence of secrets. It is in this way that gardeners are made. If one adds imagination to the interest, then one cannot help but make a beautiful garden.

The essential attribute for a successful and happy gardener is imagination. Without imagination and good taste it is not possible to plan a lovely garden. The imaginative gardener envisages the display he can have in the garden by studying a seed-catalogue and visualises the effect of his flowers when he plants out the seedlings.

Gardening has been called a combination of art, craft and science. Up-to-date scientific information is a great help to the modern gardener. A modern material like polythene film can be put to good use in many well-tried gardening practices such as the propagation of plants. The study of chemicals and fertilizers used in gardening is a fascinating subject of research for the scientific-minded.

Gardening, therefore, has something for everyone and can be a creative hobby which gives one great satisfaction. It is hoped that this book will be an inspiration and a practical help to the beginner and create new interest for the veteran.

During the preparation of this book, I have drawn not only on my own gardening experience, but on that of many gardening friends and acquaintances in different parts of the country as well as overseas. I have had the benefit of up-to-date scientific information from government research departments and several commercial growers. To these people, too numerous to mention by name, I offer my sincere thanks.

SIMA ELIOVSON,
November, 1960.

CHAPTER ONE

TROUBLE-FREE GARDENING

Everyone who makes a garden is prepared to spend some time and energy on its lay-out and upkeep, whether this is of one's own effort or that of hired help. It is easier to make and maintain a garden where the climate is good than where there are difficulties that discourage gardeners, particularly those who begin new gardens.

There is no really perfect climate, however, for each has some limiting factor that influences the plants that do well and those that do not thrive. Frost in winter, excessively strong winds, tropical heat, long periods of drought—these are the problems that challenge the gardener, apart from the question of the quality of the soil or local shortages of labour. The quality of the soil can be improved with diligence and the shortage of labour can be met by planning a garden of easy maintenance, but climatic conditions must be understood if one wishes to make a success of gardening in any given area.

People want to see their plants thrive and are disappointed when they succumb to the elements. Rather than battle against odds, they tend to plant only what they see does well in neighbouring gardens and to be content with very little variety. This leads in turn to lack of interest in garden design, for attractive lay-outs need many different plants to provide colour, variation, foliage contrasts or interesting shapes of trees and shrubs.

Knowledge of the plant materials that will thrive in different conditions is of the greatest importance in creating a well-filled yet trouble-free garden. People who live in large progressive cities can visit well-known nurseries and purchase numerous plants that will grow in their area, but those who live in places where gardens are not well developed or in country towns are severely limited in their choice of plant material. Local nurseries usually stock those plants which grow well in their area, but they cannot be expected to offer every single plant that will be successful, for economic or other reasons.

This book will provide numerous lists of plant materials suitable for different conditions, as well as plants for different purposes, at the end of each relevant chapter, including this one. All these plants are obtainable in South Africa. As an extra aid, however, the following pages will be devoted to a discussion of the chief climatic areas found in Africa south of the Equator and some

general remarks on how to plan gardens in those areas, with particular reference to local problems.

Africa south of the Equator has its summers at Christmas time and its winters during June and July. Its climate varies from tropical to sub-tropical and temperate. There is a summer rainfall over all but the south-western Cape, which has its rains in winter. There are many semi-desert areas, notably that of the Karroo and the northern Cape, where as little as five inches of rain falls each year, while the mountain areas of the Drakensberg receive up to a hundred inches of rain in a season.

Each of these areas has a quota of plants that grow with ease and the gardener should start with these. Once having established the backbone of the garden and its lay-out, the enthusiastic gardener will experiment further and probably be amazed to find that nearly everything he plants will grow if it receives correct care. One can grow Lilac in Durban or Frangipani in Johannesburg if one makes an effort, but these exceptions do not make a garden, which should consist basically of healthy, strong-growing plants that thrive with ease.

GARDEN PLANNING IN THE CAPE PENINSULA AND SOUTH-WESTERN CAPE

The south-western Cape has a Mediterranean climate similar to that of S.W. Australia and parts of California. It has an extremely wet winter and a long dry summer, almost rainfree from November to March. The countryside itself is a veritable garden in September and October when thousands of wild spring flowers carpet the fields and mountain areas. Even the west coast, which is a semi-desert in the Namaqualand area, is covered with tracts of brilliant wild flowers that bring people from all over the world to see them when they bloom from mid-August to mid-September.

What glorious feasts of colour the gardens should be in the Cape at this time, when with a little extra care, the choicer wildings could be disciplined into herbaceous or annual borders and bulb beds. (See *South African Wild Flowers for the Garden* by Sima Eliovson.) Other spring-flowering plants which benefit from winter's rains also grow with the greatest of ease. Modern irises with their remarkable colour range, roses, countless flowering shrubs and trees as well as bulbs like English bluebells, perennials

1

like Geraniums and annuals like Primula grow almost without attention.

Perhaps it is this extravagant ease with which the spring garden flourishes that makes the average Cape householder do so little for his garden during the long dry summer. Few people spend much time in their gardens in summer as they are lured away to the beaches and the glorious beauty spots that abound within easy driving distance of their homes. Shortage of labour makes it difficult to keep the garden well watered and no amount of artificial watering really equals a good soaking rain. Nevertheless, the humidity near the coast keeps many plants growing vigorously, for these would shrivel if they were not heavily watered in inland gardens. Cannas, which need plenty of water in summer, thrive at the Cape and are undoubtedly helped along by the unseen humidity in the air.

On the whole, the Cape gardener should choose drought-resistant plants for his summer garden. These plants may not necessarily be drought-resistant inland, but will thrive at the coast. A list of suitable plants will be found at the end of this chapter. A large selection of these will make the gardens easy to maintain without sacrificing the interest of a well-planted garden. One sees in the smaller gardens, all too often, a neat square of lawn with little but a line of beautiful hydrangeas against the house—delightful, but not sufficient to make a garden of interest and real charm. Garden design is particularly important in areas where choice of plant material is restricted and Cape gardens should make up in lay-out what they lack in variety of plants during summer.

During the hot dry months the backbone of the garden should comprise numerous interesting flowering shrubs which will grow without too much trouble. One should rely for colour on the more common, heat-resistant annuals like Zinnias, Phlox and Marigolds and group these effectively in the lovely separate colours that may be obtained from seedsmen nowadays. Seed may be sown in September, but as this is usually a cool and rainy month at the Cape and the weather does not really warm up until the middle of October, it may have to be planted in a seed-frame. (See Chapter 20.) Seedlings are generally planted out in October and seed may also be sown then, in which case it will frequently only reach its peak of flowering in January or February.

Strong south-westerly winds blow at the end of winter and well into the first half of summer, making life difficult for the gardener who lives right on the coast, such as at Fish Hoek or Muizenberg. Many gardeners complain that their seedlings are blown right out of the soil during early summer. There are many colourful perennials and shrubs that grow easily and resist the wind at the sea

coast, however. These will be listed at the end of this chapter. (See also the section on "Garden Planning in the Port Elizabeth area".)

Many sea-coast gardens at the Cape are built on rocky slopes and have little soil. One can construct rocky pockets containing soil, but it is also advisable to put in plants which will grow well in shallow soil and which will drape over the rocks. Many succulents do very well in these conditions and should be grouped together to make a striking feature in the garden. Constructed features such as rocky steps, paved areas, garden seats, pergolas or ponds are especially valuable to create interest in the sea-coast garden where choice of plant material is limited because of the climate. It is important to plan the general shape of the garden and not merely put in the easily-grown plants haphazardly.

Lawns should be kept to a minimum in Cape gardens, for they require labour in feeding and mowing. They generally require a good deal of weeding during winter and watering during summer droughts. The lawns used are coarse Buffalo Kweek and Kikuyu, while Royal Cape is finer. The coarse Kikuyu is not as rampant as it is in summer rainfall areas, for growth is slower in summer and the lawn may be more easily controlled. Mowing once a week is sufficient, but it must be done regularly.

Frost does not trouble the gardener in the south-western Cape and the winter rains enable him to have an evergreen garden. Almost anything will grow in the Cape with a certain amount of trouble, while there are countless garden plants which will grow without much attention. With a long list of trouble-free plants and the will to include numerous native plants,* following Kirstenbosch as a splendid example, Cape gardeners could have outstanding gardens, no matter how small, against a setting as beautiful as any in the world.

GARDEN PLANNING IN THE PORT ELIZABETH AREA

The triangle of land which stretches from Grahamstown in the north to Plettenberg Bay in the south, with Port Elizabeth as its peak, has a trying climate which challenges and often defeats the gardener who tries to lay out a garden of everyday plants.

The winters are mild, frost-free and rainy, but the summers are hot and very dry. The soil is poor and sandy and what little water reaches it is apt to disappear in a short while. Water restrictions plague the citizens of Port Elizabeth, but their chief trouble is the wind. At the end of winter, the winds tear around the corner of

---

*See *South African Wild Flowers for the Garden* by Sima Eliovson.

South Africa, trying their best to uproot garden plants and bending the trees that grow along the sea front almost double. Strong winds blow for at least three months in the year, yet there are very few gardens in the area which have more than a small selection of wind-resistant shrubs in them.

People, however, are discouraged too easily and are apt to give up before they have tried. The secret of successful gardening in this area is to plant those shrubs and trees which are known to grow easily and to concentrate on annuals and perennials which will succeed without too much attention. One should plant a minimum area of lawn and substitute groundcovers. (See Chapter 10.) A list of suitable plants for this area will be found at the end of this chapter.

One should also count one's blessings and realise that all is not what it appears to be. A study of the humidity at the coast will surprise many people. Quite frequently the humidity which develops during the night in summer will reach 90 per cent, but will go down to zero by midday. This means that the plants will have received some moisture at night to keep them alive even without artificial watering. Also there is no winter frost, which cuts down many plants in other parts of the country. The Port Elizabeth gardener can have an evergreen garden and grow a larger selection of tropical plants than his inland associates.

Many beautiful wild plants grow in the area around Port Elizabeth and are cherished by gardeners in other parts of the world. *Strelitzia reginae* is used as the city flower of Los Angeles, California, and is freely planted in all the streets. These magnificent plants grow wild amongst the scrub on the sea coast and should be represented in every garden in this area. *Schotia afra*, the Cape Boerboon, is a shrub which should rear its cerise flower clusters with pride in the garden. It grows easily from seed, which may be gathered from the rather straggly plants seen in the wild. *Tecomaria capensis* (Cape Honeysuckle) in orange and yellow, and *Plumbago auriculata* in palest blue, are rambling shrubs from the area which have already found their niche in cultivation, yet they are not planted as freely as they should be. The fine wild flower plantings in Settlers' Park should be an example and inspiration to all.

Port Elizabeth and the hinterland which extends into the semi-desert around Jansenville and the Little Karroo, is the home of many succulents, some of which have glorious flowers. The Red Crassula (*Crassula falcata*) and many colourful Aloes such as *Aloe striata* are found there and should be planted in massed groups in the garden.

Apart from native plants of the area, there are many plants from other lands which thrive in the same conditions. The flowering gums of Australia, the Hibiscus of Asia and the Oleanders of the Mediterranean region are some of the colourful plants that are commonly seen. There are hundreds more that will thrive as well, however, if only one knows which to plant. It is hoped that the plants suggested at the end of this Chapter will help to make the gardener's task easier and more interesting.

When laying out a new garden the first task is to plant wind-resistant trees and shrubs around the boundaries, which will shelter the smaller plants within the garden and enable one to plant other things that are not quite so wind-resistant. If the garden is more than half an acre in size, it is advisable to plant two rows of trees and shrubs to form a thick barricade. Alternate the larger trees so that there is no stiffness in the planting and try to contrast foliage and flower colours.

The second task is to improve the soil. Before planting each tree or shrub make a large hole at least 2 feet square and deep and fill it with the top soil and well-rotted compost containing manure. Compost made with activators other than manure is also valuable. Compost making is of the utmost importance to the Port Elizabeth gardener and it should be made in quantity. (See Chapter 17.) Its continual use will enrich the soil and help to conserve moisture, besides promoting healthy and more rapid growth. Vegetables grown in soil well mixed with compost will grow well and be full of nutrition, as well as more blight-resistant.

Port Elizabeth gardeners should pay great attention to garden planning and make up in lay-out what they lack in tremendous variety. To use the common plants to the greatest advantage is an art that will excite admiration. Learning to group smaller plants in clumps and grow similar types of plants near one another is something which every modern gardener strives to do. If one grows succulents, try to make a feature of them instead of dotting them around the garden in the more arid spots. Arrange an artistically shaped bed in a flat garden and plant it closely with groups of succulent plants, contrasting the bluish-grey smooth leaves of *Aloe striata* or *Sempervivum* with the mounds of light green rosettes of *Aloe arborescens*, or a spreading mat of "Mesembs". A rockery is the ideal place for a collection of succulents and the rocks can be softened by the use of many spreading plants like *Gazania uniflora*, *Convolvulus mauritanicus* and *Lantana montevidensis*.

The lawn should be a neatly sculptured shape according to the size of the garden. (See Chapter 24 on Lawns.) Evergreen lawns are used in Port Elizabeth, mainly the natural kweek (*Cynodon dactylon*) or the coarser Kikuyu grass. They will have to be watered in summer so that the area should not be large. Make use of Lippia grass as a groundcover, which needs no mowing and grows on poor soil with little moisture. It is the best lawn-substitute for dry areas. The tiny flowers which attract bees in spring may be removed with an ordinary lawn mower, if desired. Extend the restful effect of a lawn by means of various groundcovers planted in large green patches around the lawn area and blending into the surrounding shrubs. (See Chapter 10 on Ground-covers.)

Flower beds should be limited in size in the Port Elizabeth garden. Form the habit of planting all one's annuals in the same bed to create the maximum concentrated effect. Choose common, heat-resistant summer annuals like marigolds, zinnias, petunias, alyssum and ageratum and use them as an artist uses colour. Modern plant hybrids come in such beautiful colours that one can obtain remarkable results with them. Purchase seed in separate colours instead of mixing them and derive more interest from ordinary plants. A patch of blue ageratum placed beside orange dwarf marigolds and flanked by white alyssum creates a satisfying garden picture which is not based on the rarity or difficulty of growing them. The impact of tall red zinnias behind white candytuft which is bordered by low-growing purple alyssum will long be remembered even if other parts of the garden are not colourful.

Mixing these common annuals in a mixed border with easily grown perennials such as geraniums and rudbeckia is an ideal way of concentrating colour in the garden, while the rest of the garden is covered by shrubs, lawns, rose beds, irises, vegetables, succulents and other features. It will be easier to water the smaller plants during restrictions if they are all kept together. Shrubs and trees need only be watered once or twice a week with the watering can, while the hose can be reserved for spraying the bed of annual and perennial plants.

The spring garden will give the Port Elizabeth gardener much more scope because of the winter rains and mild temperatures. The planting season should commence in March by putting in a large variety of spring flowering bulbs (see Chapter 27), while seed of numerous bright annuals like Namaqualand daisies, Nemesia and Arctotis should be sown towards the end of March. (See Chapter 25.) Annuals with delicate flowers should be placed in sheltered positions where the spring winds will not damage them unduly.

In these areas which have hot dry summer months, it is advisable to introduce water into gardens, even if this takes the form of a tiny shallow pond which can be filled with a watering can. It will create a cool feeling in the garden on hot days and may be surrounded by easily grown sword-ferns and drought-resistant acanthus. In order to prevent too great evaporation, place the pond under the shade of a tree.

Shade should be sought after and small shade trees planted in the garden inside the windbreak. *Trichelia emetica* (Natal thunder tree) is an excellent shade tree and *Melia azedarach* should prove successful. A circular pergola covered with strong-growing climbers like Bougainvillea, Honeysuckle (*Lonicera*) or Port St. John's Creeper (*Podranea ricasoliana*) will provide a thick curtain of shade and a place to grow small, shade-loving plants as well as protect them from the wind.

One can see by the above suggestions that it is quite possible to create a garden in the Port Elizabeth area which is a haven of beauty and restfulness. The main thing is to conquer apathy and defeatism by developing the knowledge of which plants will help the gardener to combat the elements and then to give these plants the best attention possible. The lists at the end of this chapter will be found useful in choosing plants that will grow easily in the Port Elizabeth area. Many others will also grow in the area once the easily grown plants provide them with shelter.

GARDEN PLANNING IN THE EASTERN CAPE — FROM GRAHAMSTOWN TO EAST LONDON

When travelling by car on the main road northwards from Port Elizabeth, one sees the countryside covered with Euphorbias and other drought-resistant plants. Nearing Grahamstown, one enters a series of wooded hills and then descends into the old city of Grahamstown. Northwards from here to King William's Town and eastwards to East London, the Euphorbias disappear and one travels mainly through grassland. This is a visual indication of how the climate changes, becoming less arid and so making life easier for the gardener. Although it can be very dry in Grahamstown, rain occurs at intervals throughout the year. Summers are hot, cooled by sea-breezes from the coast only 36 miles away, but winters are mild and sub-tropical plants thrive.

East London has the advantage of humidity from the sea, but its chief problem is that of wind. All sea-coast gardens naturally endure a certain measure of wind and the gardener is advised to plant many wind-resistant shrubs and trees, particularly on the boundary, to shelter the garden interior.

In general, it may be said that one can grow most things in East London gardens, as is manifest in the large selection of plants to be seen there. The accent should be on evergreen plants that enjoy a sub-tropical climate, rather than on deciduous plants from cold winter areas. The gardener is advised to read the section on Durban coast gardening, except that the range of plants to be grown may be enlarged as the climate is not so hot or so humid. Similarly, the chapter on gardening in Port Elizabeth may be read yet modified because of the more benign climate. Certain aspects of gardening in both these areas apply to the gardener in East London. The Grahamstown gardener must endeavour to make a garden that will also include drought-resistant rather than wind-resistant plants. (See lists at the end of this Chapter.)

GARDEN PLANNING IN THE TRANSVAAL

The Transvaal covers an area larger than the British Isles and it is not surprising that there is a large variation in its climate. The whole area enjoys a summer rainfall and a dry winter, which varies from cold to mild in the different parts.

Johannesburg is the largest city in the Transvaal, as well as in South Africa, with a huge proportion of beautiful gardens which are among the finest in the world, particularly for the size of its population. Conditions vary from those of the capital city of Pretoria, only 30 miles further north but 1,200 feet lower in altitude, so that it is best to discuss these two large gardening areas separately. Johannesburg is situated on the highveld at an altitude of 6,000 feet and there are many other highveld areas of the Transvaal, extending from Ermelo and Volksrust in the east to Klerksdorp in the west, with a similar climate. If anything, their winters are colder and gardeners will have to select very hardy shrubs and trees as wind-breaks to give protection to their other plants. For the rest, they can follow the procedure of the Johannesburg gardener.

Johannesburg is fortunate in having an ideal climate for gardening. It is hot enough in summer to grow many sub-tropical plants, yet cold enough in winter to grow many beautiful deciduous trees and shrubs which come from the colder parts of the world. Perhaps its greatest disadvantage is that it suffers from some sharp frosts in winter, which are severe enough to kill many tender plants, but the gardener can create protected corners for some of them and there are so many plants that do well in Johannesburg that there is no garden large enough to contain them all. Tender plants can be grown more successfully in older gardens than in newly established ones. Protection from the cold south winds in the form of hedges or hardy trees will warm the garden considerably as they grow and provide sheltered nooks in which to place more delicate plants.

Gardens look bare during winter when lawns turn brown and the majority of trees lose their leaves. Nevertheless, one can have a bright winter and spring garden— some think that the spring gardens are lovelier than the summer gardens—for there are many mild sunny days to be enjoyed during the winter months. Spring annuals and bulbs can be concentrated in large beds near the house, where a mixed herbaceous border effect will be obtained. Evergreen shrubs, too, can be planted where they will be most appreciated in winter, in order to prevent a bare look. The gardener must remember to water all evergreen shrubs and trees as well as the annuals regularly during winter, for rain seldom falls. Plants from the winter-rainfall area of the Cape, such as Proteas, do extremely well, responding to the winter sunshine, but must be watered about twice a week if they are to flourish.

Following on winter, the spring months from mid-August to mid-October are very hot and dry. This is a time when regular watering is most important in the highveld garden. Azaleas and spring bulbs must not be allowed to dry out or they will shrivel, for the inland air is very dry. They should be grown in shady places in Johannesburg and other inland places so that their delicate flowers will not dry out under the hot spring sun, whereas these same plants can grow out in the open sun at the coast, where the humidity in the air will sustain them.

Summer rains are often good but erratic and everything dries out rapidly. Watering is one of the gardener's most important tasks, not only in Johannesburg, but in the whole Transvaal, Orange Free State and Natal except in the mountains or on the coast.

Lawns are beautiful when there are good rains, but turn yellow quickly when there are hot dry periods. Lawns should not be as extensively planted as they are (see Chapters on Lawns and Groundcovers) unless one has the labour, water and power tools to care for them scrupulously. Deciduous lawns which turn brown in winter are most commonly and advisedly used and there are many types. (See Chapter 24 on Lawns.) Evergreen lawns must, unfortunately, be watered regularly during winter and this is uneconomical as well as unsuitable, for their wetness prevents their being used to the fullest extent. Semi-evergreen Kikuyu grows so easily that it is difficult to control and is best excluded from the average garden in the summer rainfall area.

Although Johannesburg gardens are generally large, with a great variety of plants of good quality, many could be improved in lay-out and design. The progressive and enthusiastic Johannesburg gardeners, however, are fast following modern trends and their gardens are becoming more beautiful with the months. The Johannesburg gardener should make a choice of hardy or drought-resistant shrubs and trees and note tender plants in the lists at the end of this chapter and elsewhere in the book.

The Pretoria Area. All that has been said of Johannesburg gardens applies to those of Pretoria, but the summers are hotter and the winters milder. It is possible to grow many more sub-tropical plants in Pretoria, particularly in those gardens which have a northern aspect on the hills surrounding the city. Frost also strikes during winter, but the same precautions may be taken in providing shelter for tender plants as in Johannesburg.

The heat in summer discourages many gardeners, but there is no special problem except that of keeping plants adequately watered. Shade should be sought after and a feature made of shade-loving plants. The spring garden is so hot, however, that many plants must receive extra care at this time. Semi-shade should be provided for spring bulbs or plants like Azaleas and great attention must be paid to watering. The leaves of moisture-loving shrubs should be sprayed with the hose in order to prevent drying out. An overhead sprinkler attachment is a necessity.

The Northern Transvaal. The area north of Pretoria to the Zoutpansberg becomes increasingly warmer and more sub-tropical. In spite of the fact that it has occasional frost in winter, the winters are mild and one can grow a large variety of plants. I have seen a well-watered garden in Louis Trichardt boasting multi-flora sweetpeas with 16 flowers to a stem, eight of them in bloom with the remainder in bud. Side by side with these cool-weather flowers one sees fiery Kaffirboom (*Erythrina lysistemon*), tropical Potato trees (*Solanum macranthum*), the feathery plumes of *Iboza riparia* and other beautiful plants that make this an ideal gardening area.

The Mountain Areas of the Northern and Eastern Transvaal. Lucky gardeners live in the mountain areas of the northern and eastern Transvaal where summer rains are heavy and everything grows in abundance. Although winters can be very cold, the mountains collect moisture in the form of cloud mists and the moisture in the atmosphere reduces severe frost damage, so that one can grow many half-hardy plants in the open. Conditions vary with the altitude and the higher one ascends the easier it becomes to grow all those European plants liking cooler winters. Perhaps the only physical handicap in this area is the need to provide good drainage for those plants that prefer drier conditions. Rockeries will allow one to find places for succulents and other plants that need good drainage. Mountain gardeners can devote themselves to the art of creating gardens of good design and incorporate many features that make a garden interesting.

The Lowveld. The eastern strip of the Transvaal, running from the foot of the Zoutpansberg southwards through Tzaneen, Sabie and Nelspruit to Barberton, constitutes the lowveld. Here lie some of the best gardening areas in the Transvaal. Mild dry winters and very hot summers, up to 100 degrees in the shade, encourage the growth of sub-tropical plants and fruits. Moisture is the key that unlocks the secret of gardening in these areas. Rain falls heavily in some parts, but water must be given regularly during dry spells.

Gardeners in these hot areas should make a feature of shade in one part of the garden. I have seen a beautiful garden with a shady haven that was a riot of tropical colour. Several large spreading evergreen trees gave almost complete shade and the whole area was banked with *Impatiens holstii* with its small flat flowers in many shades of scarlet and rose; tall begonias with pendant sprays of crimson, while cascades of large *Monstera* leaves and *Colocasia* (Elephant's ears) lent a verdant air to this hothouse atmosphere. A narrow slate path led one into this retreat and a tiny rivulet, bordered with mossy stones, gave the final touch of cool luxuriance. The gardener had used the advantages of the sub-tropical climate intelligently to grow plants that thrive in these conditions, instead of struggling to grow plants from cool countries.

Water in the garden, in the form of a pool or tiny stream, is most valuable in hot areas. Even if one fills it from time to time with the hose, it creates a cool atmosphere that encourages the people of the house to sit and rest in the garden.

Showy flowering trees, shrubs, climbers and perennials, many of them suited to tropical climates, will thrive in these areas and make for less effort in gardening. (See lists at the end of this Chapter.)

The nearby hillsides abound with showy indigenous plants such as the Kaffirboom (*Erythrina lysistemon*), Pride-of-de Kaap (*Bauhinia galpinii*), *Sutera grandiflora* and the Burning Bush (*Combretum microphyllum*). Numerous Aloes grow wild in the area and bear their striking flowers in winter and spring. Portions of the garden devoted to succulents will be useful and drought resistant. The lowveld gardener should plant these indigenous subjects in abundance to lend colour to the garden without difficulty. (See *South African Wild Flowers for the Garden* by the author.)

GARDEN PLANNING IN THE ORANGE FREE STATE

The largest part of the Orange Free State consists of dry grasslands which are bitterly cold in winter and excessively hot in summer. A smaller portion to the east near Ficksburg borders on the Lesotho mountains. Although this area is even colder than the central plains, it receives more rain in summer and autumn.

The central plains are plagued by strong winds that tear across them in steady gales at all times of the year. Fires were prevalent in the early days, fanned by the wind. Winter's cold and the lack of summer moisture, together with the devastation of fires and wind, have prevented large woody species of trees from colonising. Some small indigenous species like the Wild Olive and the Karree have been found within the protection of the koppies, but the Free State plains have been naturally treeless within the memory of history. Attempts to plant trees by farmers were discouraged because of the winds and lack of fresh water, for most of the water which exists in the high water table a few feet below the surface of the soil, was found to be brack.

For many years, gardening in the Orange Free State was at a low ebb. In the last few years, however, it has been proved that, given protection while young, one can plant trees in this area and create beautiful gardens where there was once a dust bowl. The establishment of new gold mines at Welkom prompted the Chamber of Mines to start a tree-planting scheme and over a million trees have been planted there to date, with the help of a well-known landscape gardener. All types of hardy trees and shrubs have been tried with success. The method used in establishing them was to water them with fresh water for the first two or three years and then leave them to fend for themselves. Once they had grown, they would manage to exist in spite of any brack water in the soil. Wind-resistant trees were planted first and then numerous other trees succeeded within their shelter. In sheltered north-facing corners made by walls, it was found possible to grow even tender plants such as Poinsettia and Hibiscus.

This success has prompted farmers and gardeners in neighbouring towns, with similar drawbacks, to do the same. Gardens in Sasolburg, for example, boast numerous plants that never would have been tried formerly and nothing seems impossible. The high water table, in fact, enables moisture-loving trees to thrive, trees which one might not otherwise attempt to plant, judging only by the hot, dry climate. The Swamp Cypress (*Taxodium distichum*) does extremely well, while berrying Hawthorns and Crab-apples are thoroughly at home. All manner of Oaks do well as street trees and grow surprisingly quickly.

The first task of the Free State gardener is, therefore, to create a windbreak chosen from wind-resistant trees. Evergreen shrubs like Euonymus and Pyracantha are particularly useful as stop-gaps against wind. The evergreen trees and shrubs should be placed so that they will grow to touch one another along the boundaries, thereby creating a calm haven inside the garden. Evergreens should be planted outside and deciduous shrubs inside, for privacy. These trees and shrubs must be frost-hardy to shelter the less hardy plants which may be planted later. The owner of a small garden should endeavour to choose only hardy shrubs in order to prevent disappointment. (See list at the end of this Chapter.)

Good garden design and grouping of plants for ease of maintenance should be the chief aim. Easily-grown annuals for summer and winter will provide colour. Permanent plants should be chosen to furnish the garden and make it luxuriant with the least amount of trouble. (See Chapter 11.) A feature should be made of summer flowering bulbs that are dormant in winter. There are also many spring bulbs that will succeed if they are watered regularly. Window-boxes and large tubs on a sheltered verandah will enable one to grow many plants that require warmth and protection from cold winds, such as the Shrimp Flower (*Beloperone guttata*).

The gardener from the eastern Free State should capitalise on the fact that the intense cold, accompanied by copious rains in March, produce beautiful autumn colours in the leaves of deciduous trees. Everyone is familiar with the huge old Lombardy poplars on farms in the Free State that become living columns of gold before the leaves fall. Nowhere have I seen a more vividly scarlet True Virginian Creeper (*Parthenocissus quinquefolia*) than on the walls of a simple home in Ficksburg, nor more gloriously yellow planes in the countryside nearby. Gardeners in these areas should make a feature of collecting trees and shrubs with red and gold autumn foliage (see lists in Chapter 29) so that their gardens will become famous for their autumn display. Berries of all kinds and many spring-flowering deciduous shrubs will also thrive. There are many hardy evergreens to be found amongst trees and flowering shrubs, and these should be the backbone of the cold Free State garden. Colour may be provided by any number of annuals and perennials in summer and there are also many annuals and bulbs which enjoy cool climates that will provide a beautiful show in the spring. (See lists at the end of this Chapter.)

KARROO GARDENING

A vast tract of land in the central and northern Cape is known as the Karroo. This is a semi-desert with strange flat-topped hills, treeless for hundreds of miles. The days are fiercely hot and the nights are very cold, icy in winter. The natural covering of this area consists of low scrub and hundreds of succulents which are well able to withstand the dryness, for the rainfall is low, occurring mainly during the autumn, winter and spring. In September, the traveller through the Karroo will see glittering patches of colour from purple and yellow Mesembs and the glowing terra-cotta and golden Gazanias as well as many taller, drought-resistant, yet beautiful shrubs.* These plants exist only on the rainfall, so that it is not difficult to imagine how gloriously the gardens could bloom provided that they had sufficient water.

The Karroo gardener should endeavour to collect drought-resistant plants for his garden, certainly including as many of the indigenous plants as possible. Grown in a garden, without being trampled on or nibbled at by sheep, they will bloom even more spectacularly than they do in the wild. Drought-resistant trees from other lands, like Tamarisk, also do well and should be planted extensively.

The cold winters make it imperative to choose hardy trees and shrubs that will endure frost and wind. Deciduous fruit trees like pears do extremely well and some beautiful old specimens may be seen lining the streets of Beaufort West and Graaff-Reinet, for example. Berrying shrubs, including evergreen ones like Pyracantha, will grow quite well.

One must first establish a windbreak of shrubs or trees, depending on the size of the garden, before starting to plant the interior. A shade tree, too, is very important in this hot climate. Owing to the fact that the gardens receive very little rainfall and that annuals require constant watering, it is advisable to grow as many perennials as possible, rather than annuals, and to confine the latter to a small bed where they can be cared for together. A simple design should be made before planting, so as to avoid the depressing oblong beds so often seen in country gardens. A wide undulating border around the garden, planted with shrubs as a background, with perennials and colourful annuals in the foreground, acts as a simplified herbaceous or mixed border.

Lawns may be planted, but where these are too difficult to maintain, the areas may be paved or covered with ground covers. Lippia grass is especially recommended. A large chequered garden floor in place of lawn can be very attractive and is very easy to maintain. The ground is divided into squares, each about 3 or 4 feet square. These are filled individually at random, some with cement studded with pebbles, some with beds of

*See *South African Wild Flowers for the Garden* by the Author.

creeping thyme, some with closely-planted succulents, others with slate or flat stones and some with a patch of ordinary green grass. (See Chapter 10 on Ground-covers.) An occasional watering will keep these patches growing well. Allow the plants to spill over the edges of the cement for an informal effect, but the edges may also be trimmed.

On the whole, the Karroo gardener should follow the same plan as the gardener in the Orange Free State, but modify his choice of plants where sufficient water is not obtainable for gardening purposes. (See lists of drought-resistant and hardy plants at the end of this Chapter.)

GARDEN PLANNING IN NATAL

Natal is divided into three gardening areas, namely the sub-tropical coastal belt around Durban and the South Coast, the mild warm area around Kloof and Pieter-maritzburg, and the colder Natal highlands which have a climate very similar to that of Johannesburg. Those who garden in these highlands are advised to read the chapter on gardening in the Transvaal, with special reference to Johannesburg, for it would be redundant to discuss their problems here.

Although Kloof is only 20 miles from Durban, it is 2,000 feet higher and this makes gardening much easier. Durban, at sea-level, has to cope with the winds from the sea and the high humidity which is ever-present. This makes the heat seem even more intense than the temperature would indicate and it becomes positively tropical in January, February and March. The humidity, however, has its advantages in the garden as it prevents many plants like Azaleas and Hydrangeas from drying out rapidly in hot weather and helps shrubs to resist drought. The flat strip at sea-level, where the Botanic Garden is situated, has slightly brack soil, and seed beds must be raised in order to prevent the salt from reaching the seedlings. Countless plants seem to thrive, nevertheless, so that the gardener need not be discouraged. One need only take note of the plants that thrive in Durban North to realise just how many plants will grow well—far too many to be included in any one garden. I have seen a garden in Durban North where everything flourishes, from roses and lilacs to bananas and pawpaws, so that where there is interest and energy, almost anything can be attempted.

Plants grow so easily in Durban, that this, strangely enough, is the downfall of the average gardener. He is so accustomed to shrubs growing without attention, barring occasional watering, and seed like Zinnias sprouting overnight, that other plants are overlooked and the gardens have too little variety. One never knows what can thrive unless one tries. Fifty years ago there was not a Hydrangea to be seen in Durban, but now there is scarcely a garden without great patches of these lovely blooms that grow so easily. Even so, there is too little selection of colours and the plants are pruned indiscriminately, secure in the knowledge that the luxuriant climate will conjure forth flowers in the summer. (See Pruning of Hydrangeas, Chapter 31; Section III.)

Durban is a spectacular sight to the visitor, with its street trees of scarlet Flamboyants in summer and Spathodeas in winter; with great banks of pink and purple Bougainvillea spilling over boundaries and flaming hedges of Poinsettia (*Euphorbia pulcherrima*) and Christ-Thorn (*Euphorbia splendens*). The gardens, however, should have a far greater selection of flowering shrubs than are evident, for many will grow with as little trouble as those that are commonly seen. (See *Flowering Shrubs, Trees and Climbers for Southern Africa*, by the author.)

The garden design should be a little more complicated in order to find room for extra specimens. There is a limited number that can be planted along a boundary or around the house. Shrubs should not be dotted about in the lawn, but planted in an undulating band like a herbaceous border. This will also ensure more privacy, for most gardens may be seen in their entirety from the street, which makes them immediately appear smaller and less interesting. A garden which can be seen at a glance does not induce the feeling of wanting to explore and wander around it.

A shade tree should be situated in the garden, since Durban is an ideal place for outdoor living, particularly during the rainless, mild winter months. A semi-circle of evergreen, wind-resistant shrubs should be planted to provide shelter from the wind in order to encourage the people of the house to sit in the garden.

"Natal fever" is the term jokingly applied to the lassitude which overcomes people who lack energy in the heat and makes them loath to attempt more than the essential daily tasks. As far as gardening is concerned, the garden must be planned in recognition of "Natal fever" and made as easy to maintain as possible, particularly as labour is not easily obtainable and is mostly very unskilled. Energy must be spent on collecting suitable plants, however, and improving the condition of the soil.

The soil must be improved as Durban and coastal soils are very sandy and poor. Compost making should be essential in every garden, no matter how small, and plenty of compost added in the form of continuous dressings all over the garden. (See Chapter 17.) The Municipal Botanic Garden sells compost for those who find it impossible to make it themselves, but this is, naturally, more costly as one can never have enough. Manure on its own is a valuable food for hydrangeas and other greedy feeders, and is worth the expense entailed in purchasing it. The fact that the coastal soil is sandy has the advantage that it is naturally well-drained and few plants die from "wet feet".

Lawns should be kept to a minimum, so that they may be cared for thoroughly. They need good feeding and renovation every few years as they deteriorate rapidly in the poor soil. The evergreen indigenous types like Kweek and Buffalo Grass are best. (See Chapter 24 on Lawns.) It is better to have a small area of perfect lawn than to use lawn to cover every bare piece of ground in the garden. Groundcovers like Periwinkle and Tradescantia have the greatest value in Durban gardens, especially as they grow in the shade. They require little maintenance and add the restful green tranquillity that is usually provided by a lawn. (See Chapter 10 on Groundcovers.)

A Durban garden is an evergreen garden. The lawns, shrubs and trees are mainly evergreen, for most deciduous shrubs and trees are not happy in the year-round warm, moist atmosphere. Deciduous fruits like peaches and cherries do not grow successfully, but there are many sub-tropical fruits like mangoes and avocado pears that compensate the gardener. Many deciduous, spring-flowering shrubs like the Purple Magnolia, *Magnolia soulangeana*, will not thrive, but the evergreen *Magnolia grandiflora* with its immense, waxy, white flowers will grow superbly. The gardener should not attempt to grow deciduous shrubs from cool countries that survive with difficulty and are not happy in the heat, but rather seek a selection of beautiful flowering evergreens that others in colder climates would give anything to own.

Many deciduous plants, like Roses, have woody stems which are attacked by termites and these had to be planted in raised beds or drums if they were to be grown without too much trouble, but the use of modern insect repellents in the soil has made it possible to grow roses successfully in the open ground. (See page 255.)

There are some tropical plants that drop their leaves in winter for a short dormant period, like Frangipani (*Plumeria*) and Pride of India (*Lagerstroemia*), but these are the exceptions rather than the rule, and they have their origins in the hotter countries of the world. As a general rule, the evergreens do better than deciduous shrubs and trees in sub-tropical areas. Certain plants which are deciduous inland in cold areas remain almost evergreen at the coast, such as Jacaranda and the Orchid Tree (*Bauhinia variegata*), so that one must study each plant individually. (See list of plants for hot or sub-tropical areas at the end of this Chapter.)

GARDENING IN THE PIETERMARITZBURG AREA

Fortunate indeed is the person who owns a garden in Pietermaritzburg and its surrounding area. It has been called the Garden City of Natal and is blessed with a wonderful climate for plants. The summers are hot with a high rainfall and the mild, frost-free winters have mists that may be a menace to motorists, but are a boon to Azaleas. One can grow most of the tropical shrubs, trees and other plants that grow in Durban, but one can also grow deciduous shrubs like Viburnum that are not happy at the coast. Without the buffeting coastal winds, it is possible to grow all manner of delicate annuals that dislike wind. The soil is good and the only thing to stand in the way of a lovely garden is the human element.

Too much rain in summer might cause spring bulbs to rot in the ground and the gardener is advised to lift and store them in a cool place during the summer months. A very well-drained position will offset this danger to a certain extent.

On the whole, the Pietermaritzburg gardeners would be advised to concentrate on plants which thrive in sub-tropical areas rather than in cold areas, both from an aesthetic point of view and because they do so well.

Places like Kloof, which is almost half-way between Durban and Pietermaritzburg, have a climate which resembles the latter rather than that of the coastal strip. They combine some of the problems of Durban with the less exacting climate of Pietermaritzburg and also have some of the finest gardens of Natal in the area.

GARDEN PLANNING IN RHODESIA

Rhodesia has a climate similar to that of the northern Transvaal, while it becomes ever-increasingly tropical as one proceeds northwards. Altitude affects the type of plants one can grow in this normally sub-tropical region. In the mountainous region near Umtali one can grow many plants from the cooler climates of the world that will not be so happy at lower altitudes.

Much that has been said about gardening in the northern Transvaal and in the Durban area applies to gardening in Salisbury, the largest city of Rhodesia. It has a combination of climates in so far as the vegetation is as tropical as that of Durban, but the dry inland atmosphere and altitude makes the summers less hot. The winter nights can be very cold, but there is none of the intense cold and frost of the Transvaal highveld. This increases the range of plants that can be grown out of doors and, in Salisbury, one can grow evergreen Spathodeas (Nandi Flame) and Hibiscus hedges that are the envy of those from colder climes.

It is best to plant evergreens or deciduous trees that enjoy a hot climate. Some evergreens that have their origins in cool climates, like Cotoneasters, will grow but seldom bear berries as freely as they do in places with cooler climates, so that they should not dominate the garden scene. Plant these on south walls and in cooler parts of the garden for best results. Deciduous trees grow satisfactorily, although it is wiser to choose those which will withstand the long, dry winter and spring, like Jacaranda, than those that require plenty of moisture like the Pin Oak (*Quercus palustris*) and the Tulip Tree (*Liriodendron*). Roses will grow well if they are given attention, some thriving better than others.

The climate of Bulawayo is very much the same, but is if anything, slightly cooler in winter yet drier and hotter in summer. It is possible, however, to grow tender trees like Flamboyant (*Delonix regia*) and Frangipani with a little protection in the early stages.

The chief problem of the Rhodesian gardener is probably that of heat combined with lack of water. The heavy summer rains help the garden from October to March but the spring is hot and dry and can be a trying time for the gardener who has nursed spring-flowering plants through the mild winter or who is putting in summer seedlings. The garden needs plenty of moisture at this time and one's chief concern is to water copiously and regularly soaking the ground with a sprinkler. The addition of plenty of compost and peatmoss to the soil will aid water retention as well as improve the soil.

Spring flowers with delicate blooms that will dry out in the hot sun, like daffodils and tulips, should be given semi shade in Rhodesian gardens. This is a problem common to the whole of the inland, summer-rainfall area in southern Africa. (See sections on Johannesburg and Pretoria.) It will be found easier to grow annuals during winter than during summer in the hotter areas, when one should concentrate on heat-resistant annuals.

Those who live in areas that experience long droughts should concentrate on planting a large number of drought resistant plants. Sections for showy succulents should also prove valuable. Those plants which require more moisture should be placed near the house, where they cannot be overlooked in the daily round. Lawns may be kept to a minimum where one cannot water them during hot, dry periods. (See Chapters on Lawns and Groundcovers.)

All gardens in hot areas should have shade trees cool the garden and to provide areas for outdoor living. Some water in the garden will also give an impression of coolness.

It may be seen, therefore, that the amount of water available will influence the type of garden one can create in this otherwise excellent climate for gardening. One should strive to obtain as large a selection of plants as possible order to add to the variety obtainable. Being a horticulturally young country, the range of plants could be extended with benefit to all concerned. (See lists of suitable plants at the end of this Chapter.) The Rhodesian gardener is advised to read the foregoing sections on the Transvaal and Natal in order to avoid repetition here.

GARDENING IN THE TROPICS

The vast countries in Africa south of the Equator include Zambia, Malawi, Tanzania, Angola, Moçambique, the Congo and part of Kenya and Uganda.

It is impossible to generalise about gardening in areas as large as these except to say that they are mainly tropical. The long dry winter is mild and warm, while the summers are exceedingly hot with a very high rainfall, falling almost every evening, in the way of the tropics. Yet differences in altitude make it possible to grow almost any plants that may be grown elsewhere in the world. At altitudes of 4,000 feet, it is possible to grow the deciduous trees of Europe that are not happy in lower, hotter regions.

To go into detail about each area and altitude would be to repeat nearly everything that has been covered in the preceding sections. The gardens of these tropical countries resemble most closely those of Rhodesia and of Durban. Like these, the gardens are chiefly evergreen, except where high altitudes make the climate more temperate. Tropical plants and fruits like mangoes and bananas flourish. At the same time, one can grow many evergreens from cooler climates and the choice is enormous. Plants which are usually grown indoors or in hot-houses in cooler climates flourish out of doors where there is sufficient shade and moisture.

There are many perennials and annuals to choose from in the garden, particularly amongst the heat-resistant types. (See lists at the end of this Chapter.) Perennials are easier to grow than annuals and these should, perhaps, be given preference in the garden, but annuals are essential to give colour. Dahlias and cannas are outstanding examples of perennials that thrive in hot places as well as cool. Petunias and marigolds are annuals which grow so well that they should be included in every garden. Cool-weather annuals that may be planted during the winter months, like sweet-peas, grow magnificently and impress one with the adaptability of plants that can grow almost everywhere in the world.

Flowering shrubs and trees should be the backbone of the tropical garden as well as of the temperate garden, and where climates are hot, will furnish the garden with little effort. The selection is tremendous. (See *Flowering Shrubs, Trees and Climbers for Gardens in Southern Africa* by the author.) Shade trees are very important in hot climates and

there are many plants that will thrive under these. (See Chapter 9 on Gardening in the Shade.) Flower beds should be planned to incorporate those plants which grow easily, both annual and perennial, in a mixed border against a background of shrubs. The use of water to induce a feeling of coolness, in the form of ponds or tiny streams rippling over stones, is to be recommended. These must not be neglected so that they become breeding places for mosquitoes, however.

The gardener must endeavour to make compost and add organic manures to the soil. In places where water is expensive, one should plant drought-resistant plants that are suited to hot climates (see lists below).

THE WORLD IN YOUR GARDEN

There are parallels to gardening in many parts of the world and the climate of southern Africa may be compared to that of countries like Australia, New Zealand, California, the southern States of America and South America. It is fascinating to compare the climates of these places and to realise that one can grow plants from these countries without difficulty in southern Africa and that the native plants of southern Africa will grow there in reciprocation.

The winter rainfall area of the Cape, with its long dry summer, is similar to that of the Mediterranean, and this is shared by California, S.W. Australia, around Melbourne and Perth, and Chile. All these places have a chiefly evergreen natural vegetation with the main period of bloom in spring. September and October are the best months in which to see the natural spring flora of the Cape, Chile and S.W. Australia, while April and May are the best flowering months in California, being spring in the northern hemisphere. Cape wild flowers flourish in California, however, and South African wild flowers are grown there successfully and in profusion.

The sub-tropical areas around Durban in South Africa have their counterparts in eastern Australia, south of Brisbane and the Southern States of America, as well as in parts of South America. The rich treasure house of plants found in South America include notables like Fuchsia, Tibouchina, Hippeastrum, Jacaranda and the Cape Gooseberry, which have found their way into gardens all over the world. Although most of South America is regarded as tropical or sub-tropical, cool areas exist at high altitudes and to the south, while Chile has a winter-rainfall area similar to that of California and the Cape.

It should be noted, therefore, that the advice in this book can be applied elsewhere in the world, especially in the southern hemisphere continents of Australia, New Zealand and South America, but also in the temperate countries of the northern hemisphere, such as California, the southern States of America and southern Europe.

Gardeners all over the world have similar problems in choosing plants that will resist wind, salt spray, drought and cold. The plants listed below will do well in similar conditions in countries other than in southern Africa. It should be noted too that principles of garden planting are universal, as is the knowledge of growing plants that are cherished by gardeners everywhere.

TROUBLE-FREE PLANTS FOR DIFFICULT CLIMATIC ZONES

Some Plants for the Sea Coast

These must resist wind and salt spray. Most of these may be planted near the edge of the ocean, but may become dwarfer as a result of wind. Some will grow in sandy soil, but try to improve the soil as much as possible. All will grow in good soil close to the sea. Many are drought-resistant at the coast. Plant large specimens of trees and shrubs if possible. Those marked T are tender and are more suitable for the warm east coast than the cooler south-western Cape.

Trees

Acacia (Wattles) in variety.
Araucaria (Monkey Puzzle).
Calodendrum capense (Cape Chestnut).
Cassia javanica (Pink Cassia) T.
Castanospermum australe (Moreton Bay Chestnut).
Casuarina.
Citharexylum.
Delonix regia (Flamboyant) T.
Erythrina caffra (Coast Kaffirboom).
Eucalyptus ficifolia (Flowering Gum).
Eugenia paniculata (Brush-Cherry).
Grevillea banksii (Scarlet Grevillea).
Grevillea robusta (Silky Oak).
Hakea saligna (Willow Hakea).
Hibiscus tiliacus (Tree Hibiscus) T.
Jacaranda acutifolia (Jacaranda).
Lagunaria (Pyramid Tree).
Leptospermum laevigatum (Small-leaved Myrtle).
Leucadendron argenteum (Silver Tree).
Melia (Syringa or China-berry).
Melaleuca nesophila (Tea Myrtle).
Metrosideros (New Zealand Christmas Tree).
Millettia grandis (Umzimbiti).
Myoporum insulare (Boobiyalla) and *M. laetum.*
Oreodoxa regia (Royal or Bottle Palm) T.
Paulownia.
Phoenix canariensis (Canary Date Palm).
Pinus pinea (Stone Pine).
Pittosporum, all kinds.
Plumeria (Frangipani) T.
Schotia afra. Cape Boerboon.

Spathodea (Nandi Flame) T.
Stenocarpus sinuatus (Firewheel Tree).
Strelitzia nicolai (Wild Banana).
Tabebuia pallida. T.
Tamarix (Tamarisk).
Thevetia peruviana (Yellow Oleander) T.
Trichelia emetica (Thunder Tree).
Virgilia oroboides (Keurboom).
Washingtonia robusta (Fan Palm) T.

Shrubs

Abelia (Glossy Abelia).
Acalypha (Copperleaf) T.
Abutilon (Chinese Lanterns).
Allamanda. T.
Aster filifolius.
Bauhinia (Camelsfoot).
Breynia nivosa (Snow-bush) T.
Buddleia (Butterfly Bush).
Burchellia (Wild Pomegranate).
Carissa (Natal Plum) T.
Cassia in variety.
Chaenomeles (Flowering Quince).
Chamaelaucium (Geraldton Waxflower).
Chrysanthemum frutescens (Yellow Daisy Bush).
Cistus (Rock-Rose).
Codiaeum (Croton) T.
Coleonema (Confetti Bush).
Cotoneaster.
Crotolaria (Bird Flower).
Daphne.
Datura candida (Moonflower).
Diplacus (*Mimulus*) (Monkey Flower).
Duranta (Forget-me-Not Tree).
Echium fastuosum (Pride of Madeira).
Elaeagnus.
Erica (Heath).
Erythrina humeana.
Escallonia.
Euonymus (Spindle Tree).
Euphorbia pulcherrima (Poinsettia).
Euphorbia splendens (Christ-thorn).
Euphorbia fulgens (*E. jacquiniflora*) and others.
Gardenia, many kinds.
Hebe (*Veronica*).
Hibiscus rosa-sinensis (Chinese Hibiscus).
Holmskioldia (Chinese Hat).
Hydrangea macrophylla.
Iboza riparia, T.
Ilex (English Holly).
Ixora. T.
Jasmines.
Lagerstroemia (Pride-of-India).
Lantana.
Lavandula (Lavender).
Leonotis (Lion's Ear).
Leptospermum (Tea Tree).
Leucospermum (Pincushion Flower).
Mahonia aquifolium (Holly Mahonia).
Nerium oleander (Oleander).
Ochna atropurpurea (Carnival Bush).
Pittosporum, all kinds.

Plumbago.
Poinciana pulcherrima (Peacock Flower) T.
Polygala.
Protea, many kinds.
Psoralea pinnata.
Pyracantha (Firethorn).
Raphiolepis (Indian Hawthorn).
Quisqualis indica T.
Romneya coulteri.
Rose, "Mermaid" and others.
Rosmarinus (Rosemary).
Russelia (Coral Bell Bush) T.
Solanum rantonettii.
Spartium junceum (Spanish Broom).
Strelitzia reginae (Crane Flower).
Streptosolen (Marmalade Bush).
Symphoricarpos (Snow-berrry and Coral-berry).
Tecomaria (Cape Honeysuckle).
Viburnum tinus (Laurestinus).
Wigandia macrophylla.

Climbers

Aristolochia (Dutchman's Pipe).
Bignonias.
Bougainvillea.
Ipomoea tuberosa (Wood-rose).
Parthenocissus (Virginian Creeper).
Petrea volubilis (Purple Wreath).
Podranea (Port St. Johns or Zimbabwe Creeper).
Solandra (Cup-of-Gold).
Solanum (Potato Creeper).
Sollya heterophylla (Bluebell Creeper).
Trachelospermum (Star-Jasmine).

Annuals and Herbaceous Plants

Acanthus (Grecian Leaf).
Agapanthus.
Agave.
Aloe arborescens and others.
Alyssum.
Arctotis.
Aristea.
Armeria.
Bamboos.
Canna.
Centaurea, grey-leaved.
Convolvulus mauritanicus.
Dahlia.
Diascia.
Dietes (Wild Iris).
Gazania uniflora and others.
Gaillardia.
Gaura.
Geranium incanum and others.
Gerbera (Barberton Daisy).
Godetia.
Lavatera (Mallow).
Limonium latifolium (Statice latifolia).
Limonium roseum (Sea Lavender).
Lobelia.
Marigolds.

Mesembs (Fig-Marigold, Vygies).
Nasturtiums.
Nierembergia.
Orphium frutescens.
Osteospermum ecklonis (Blue-and-White Daisy Bush).
Pelargonium, many kinds.
Salvias.
Scabious.
Vinca rosea (Lochnera rosea) T.
Watsonia, many kinds.
Yucca Lily or Adams-needle.

Drought-Resistant Plants for Dry Areas Inland

Most of these will also grow in dry places at the coast, as will many of the sea-side plants listed above. Water these plants regularly in the garden if possible, especially when young, but they will survive periods of drought and heat.

Trees

Acacia (Wattles).
Brachychiton (Flame Tree, Kurrajong and Queensland Lacebark).
Casuarina.
Cercis siliquastrum (Judas Tree).
Crataegus (Hawthorn).
Cupressus macrocarpa.
Cussonia (Cabbage Tree).
Dodonaea viscosa (Sand-Olive).
Dombeya rotundifolia (Wild Pear).
Erythrina (Kaffirboom, Coral Trees).
Eucalyptus (Flowering Gums and others).
Fraxinus (Ash).
Gleditschia (Honey Locust).
Greyia (Mountain Bottlebrush).
Hakea saligna (hedge).
Jacaranda (Jacaranda).
Koelreuteria (Goldenrain Tree).
Ligustrum (Privet).
Melaleuca nesophila (Tea Myrtle).
Melia azedarach (China-berry).
Parkinsonia.
Phoenix canariensis (Canary Islands Date Palm).
Pittosporum tenuifolium (P. nigricans).
Prunus cerasifera (Brown-leaved Plum).
Prunus persica (Flowering Peach).
Rhus erosa (Besembos).
Rhus lancea (Karee).
Rhus succedanea (Wax Tree).
Robinia pseudacacia (Black Locust).
Schinus molle (Pepper Tree).
Schotia brachypetala (Tree Fuchsia).
Tamarix (Tamarisk).
Tipuana tipu.
Ulmus (Elm).

Shrubs

Adenium obesum multiflorum (Impala Lily).
Berberis (Barberry).

Buddleia (Butterfly Bush).
Callistemon (Bottlebrush).
Cassia.
Cestrum.
Chaenomeles (Japanese Flowering Quince).
Clianthus sp.
Cotoneaster.
Crotalaria (Bird-flower).
Daubentonia (Sesbania).
Diplopappus filifolius. (Wild Aster)
Echium (Pride of Madeira).
Encephalartos (Cycad).
Erythrina zeyheri.
Escallonia macrantha.
Euphorbia splendens (Christ-thorn).
Euryops athanasiae (Clanwilliam Daisy).
Greyia (Mountain Bottlebrush).
Iboza (Misty Plume Bush).
Jasminum (Jasmines).
Lagerstroemia (Pride-of-India).
Lantana hybrids.
Leonotis leonurus (Lion's Ear).
Leptospermum (Tea-Tree).
Lonicera (Honeysuckle).
Nerium oleander.
Nymania capensis (Chinese Lanterns).
Pittosporum tobira (Japanese Pittosporum).
Poinciana gilliesii.
Portulacaria afra (Elephant's Food).
Punica granatum (Pomegranate).
Pyracantha (Firethorn).
Rhigozum obovatum (Karroo Gold).
Ricinus communis (Castor Oil).
Robinia hispida (Rose Acacia).
Romneya coulteri (Tree Poppy).
Sutera grandiflora (Wild Phlox).
Sutherlandia (Balloon-Pea).

Climbers

Bougainvillea.
Dolichos (Hyacinth Bean).
Doxantha (Cat's Claw Creeper).
Plumbago.
Podranea (Zimbabwe Creeper).
Polygonum aubertii (Silver Lace-Vine).
Pyrostegia (Golden Shower).
Senecio tamoides (Canary Creeper).
Solanum (Potato Creeper).
Tecomaria (Cape Honeysuckle).

Other Plants

Acanthus (Grecian Leaf).
Agave (Century Plant).
Aloe, many kinds.
Amaranthus.
Arctotis, many kinds.
Asparagus Ferns.
Boophane (Red Posy).
Bulbine (Cat's Tail).
Cerastium (Snow-in-Summer).
Ceratostigma.

Cissus (Wild Grape).
Crassula, many kinds.
Crinum moorei.
Cuphea, several.
Dietes (Wild Iris).
Dorotheanthus (Bokbaai Daisy).
Euphorbia marginata (Snow-on-the-Mountain) and others.
Eschscholzia (Californian Poppy).
Gazania uniflora and others.
Geraniums.
Gerbera (Barberton Daisy).
Helichrysum (Everlasting).
Lippia repens (Lippia grass).
Mesembryanthemum family (Mesembs).
Nerines.
Pelargoniums.
Portulaca.
Phalaris (Ribbon Grass).
Saponaria (Bouncing Bet).
Sansevieria.
Scilla natalensis.
Sedum.
Sempervivum.
Tulbaghia.
Vinca rosea (*Lochnera rosea*).

Hardy Plants for Cold Areas

The larger specimens will be useful as windbreaks to shelter a large garden.

Trees

Acacia (Wattles).
Acer (Maples).
Aeschylus (Horse Chestnut).
Arbutus unedo (Strawberry Tree).
Betula (Birch).
Castanea sativa (Spanish Chestnut).
Catalpa.
Cedrus deodara (Deodar).
Celtis africana (Camdeboo Stinkwood).
Cercis siliquastrum (Judas Tree).
Crataegus (Hawthorns).
Cupressus macrocarpa (Monterey Cypress).
Cupressus sempervirens stricta (Pencil Cypress).
Dais cotinifolia.
Eucalyptus (Gums).
Fagus (Beech).
Fraxinus (Ash).
Gingko biloba (Maidenhair Tree).
Gleditschia (Honey-Locust).
Grevillea robusta (Silky Oak).
Hakea saligna (Willow Hakea).
Ilex aquifolium (Holly).
Koelreuteria (Goldenrain Tree).
Liquidambar (Sweet Gum).
Liriodendron (Tulip Tree).
Malus (Crabapples).
Melia (China-berry).
Paulownia.
Pinus (Pines).

Platanus (Plane).
Podocarpus (Yellow-wood).
Prunus (Flowering Peaches, Plums, Cherries, Almond).
Quercus (Oaks).
Salix (Willows).
Sambucus (Elder).
Sophora japonica (Pagoda Tree).
Tamarix (Tamarisk).
Tipuana tipu.
Taxodium distichum (Swamp Cypress).
Ulmus glabra (Wych Elm).

Shrubs

Abelia grandiflora (Glossy Abelia).
Azalea indica (*Rhododendron indicum*).
Berberis, several.
Buddleia (Butterfly Bush).
Callistemon (Bottlebrush).
Camellia japonica.
Ceanothus.
Chaenomeles (Japanese Flowering Quince).
Coleonema (Confetti Bush).
Cotoneaster, numerous.
Cydonia oblonga (Quince).
Deutzia (Bridal Wreath).
Diospyros (Persimmon).
Diplopappus (Wild Aster).
Elaeagnus pungens.
Erica (Heath), numerous.
Erythrina acanthocarpa (Tambookie Thorn).
Erythrina zeyheri (Prickly Cardinal).
Euonymus (Spindle Tree).
Exochorda (Pearl Bush).
Forsythia (Golden-bells).
Gardenia jasminoides.
Hamamelis mollis (Witch-Hazel).
Hibiscus syriacus (Syrian Hibiscus).
Hypericum (Gold Flower).
Lagerstroemia (Pride-of-India).
Lantana hybrids.
Lavandula (Lavender).
Leonotis leonurus (Lion's Ear).
Lippia citriodora (Lemon-Verbena).
Magnolia, numerous.
Mahonia aquifolium (Holly Mahonia).
Nautochilus (Shell Bush).
Nerium oleander.
Philadelphus (Mock-orange).
Pittosporum, several.
Punica (Pomegranate).
Pyracantha (Firethorn).
Rhigozum obovatum (Karroo Gold).
Rhododendron, numerous.
Rhus, several.
Robinia hispida (Rose Acacia).
Romneya coulteri (Matilija Poppy).
Rosmarinus (Rosemary).
Spiraea (May), several.
Sutherlandia (Cancer Bush).
Symphoricarpos (Snowberry, Coral-Berry).
Syringa (Lilac).

Viburnum (Snowball Bush, Laurestinus).
Weigela (Fairy Trumpets).

Climbers

Asparagus fern.
Bignonia capreolata.
Campsis radicans.
Clematis hybrids and *C. montana.*
Clytostoma (Mauve Bignonia).
Ficus pumila (Creeping Fig).
Hedera (Ivy), several.
Jasminum officinale (Jasmine).
Lathyrus (Perennial Pea).
Lonicera japonica (Japanese Honeysuckle).
Parthenocissus (Boston Ivy and True Virginian Creeper).
Podranea ricasoliana (Port St. John's Climber).
Polygonum aubertii (Silver Lace-Vine).
Solanum jasminoides (Potato Creeper).
Trachelospermum (Star-Jasmine).
Wistaria.

Other Plants, including bulbs and herbaceous plants.

There are too many perennials and annuals to enumerate here. Seek further examples in the relevant chapters.

Agapanthus.	*Nerine,* numerous.
Aristea.	*Ornithogalum.*
Anemones.	Pansy.
Astilbe.	Peony.
Bulbinella.	Poppy.
Canna.	*Ranunculus.*
Crinum.	Stock.
Daffodil (*Narcissus*).	*Tigridia.*
Dahlia.	*Tulbaghia.*
Dierama.	Tulip.
Dimorphotheca.	*Ursinia.*
Eucomis.	*Venidium.*
Galtonia.	*Viola.*
Hemerocallis (Day-Lilies).	*Wachendorfia.*
Iris.	*Watsonia.*
Muscari (Grape Hyacinth).	*Zantedeschia.*

Plants for Hot or Sub-Tropical Areas

Many may be grown inland as well as at the coast. They will stand the wind, heat and high humidity of the east coast.

Trees

Acacia podalyriaefolia (Pearl Acacia).
Araucaria (Monkey Puzzle; Norfolk Island Pine).
Bauhinia variegata (Orchid Tree).
Bolusanthus (Wistaria Tree).
Brachychiton (Flame Tree; Queensland Lacebark).
Calliandra (Shuttlecock Flower).
Calodendrum capense (Cape Chestnut).
Cassia fistula (Pudding Pipe Tree).
Cassia javanica (Pink Cassia).
Castanospermum australe (Moreton-Bay Chestnut).

Chorisia speciosa (Floss-Silk Tree).
Cinnamomum camphora (Camphor Tree).
Cupressus sempervirens stricta (Pencil Cypress).
Delonix regia (Flamboyant).
Erythrina (several Kaffirbooms, Coral Tree).
Eucalyptus ficifolia (Flowering Gum)
Firmiana simplex (Chinese Parasol Tree).
Grevillea banksii (Scarlet Grevillea).
Jacaranda acutifolia.
Magnolia grandiflora (White Laurel Magnolia).
Millettia grandis (Umzimbiti).
Plumeria (Frangipani).
Pterocarpus rotundifolius (Round-leaf Kiaat).
Solanum macranthum (Potato Tree).
Spathodea campanulata (Nandi Flame).
Stemmadenia galeottiana (White-Bell Tree).
Tabebuia pallida.
Thevetia peruviana (Yellow Oleander).
Tipuana tipu.
Trichelia emetica (Thunder Tree).

Shrubs

Abutilon (Chinese Lanterns).
Acalypha (Copperleaf).
Adenium (Impala Lily).
Alberta.
Bauhinia galpinii (Pride-of-de Kaap).
Beloperone (Shrimp Flower).
Bixa.
Bouvardia.
Breynia (Snow-bush).
Brunfelsia (Yesterday, Today and Tomorrow).
Callicarpa (Beauty-Berry).
Carissa grandiflora (Natal Plum).
Codiaeum (Croton).
Coffea arabica (Coffee).
Datura candida (Moonflower).
Dombeya calantha (Pink Dombeya).
Duranta repens (Forget-me-not Tree).
Erythrina humeana (Hume's Kaffirboom).
Euphorbia pulcherrima (Poinsettia).
Euphorbia fulgens.
Euphorbia splendens (Christ-thorn).
Gardenia globosa (September Bells).
Hibiscus rosa-sinensis (Chinese Hibiscus).
Hibiscus schizopetalus (Fairy Hibiscus).
Hydrangea macrophylla.
Holmskioldia (Chinese Hat).
Ipomoea arborescens (Tree Convolvulus).
Iboza riparia (Misty Plume Bush).
Ixora coccinea.
Lagerstroemia (Pride-of-India).
Leptospermum (Tea Trees).
Leucospermum (Pincushion Flowers).
Malvaviscus mollis (Fire-dart Bush).
Michelia (Port Wine Magnolia).
Mussaenda frondosa (White Flag-bush).
Nerium oleander (Oleander).
Plectranthus (Spur Flower).
Poinciana pulcherrima (Peacock Flower).
Protea, several.

Reinwardtia indica (Yellow Flax).
Rhododendron indicum (Indian Azalea).
Ricinus communis purpureus (Mahogany-leaved Castor-bean).
Russelia (Coral-Bell Bush).
Solanum mammosum (Pig's Ears).
Strelitzia reginae (Crane Flower).
Streptosolen (Marmalade Bush).
Tecoma stans (Yellow Bush Tecoma).
Tibouchina (Brazilian Glory Bush).
Wigandia macrophylla

Vines and Rambling Shrubs

Antigonon (Coral Vine).
Allamanda.
Beaumontia (Giant Trumpet Climber).
Bougainvillea, numerous.
Clerodendrum splendens.
Clerodendrum thompsoniae (Bleeding Heart Clerodendron).
Cryptostegia (Rubber Vine).
Ipomoea horsfalliae briggsii (Crimson Wax Trumpet).
Ipomoea tuberosa (Wood-rose).
Jasminum sambac (Arabian Jasmine).
Petrea volubilis (Purple Wreath).
Phaedranthus (Mexican Blood Trumpet).
Pyrostegia (Golden Shower).
Quisqualis indica (Rangoon Creeper).
Senecio tamoides (Canary Creeper).
Solandra nitida (Cup-of-Gold).
Stigmaphyllon ciliatum (Golden Vine).
Thunbergia grandiflora (Bengal Trumpet Vine).

Other Plants
Perennials and Herbaceous Plants

Aloe. Drought resistant.
Agapanthus. Regular water.
Asparagus Ferns. Summer moisture.
Aster (Michaelmas Daisy). Summer water.
Begonia semperflorens and others. Shade, moisture.
Browallia. Shade, moisture.
Canna. Summer water.
Carnations. Regular water.
Centaurea cineraria.
Chrysanthemum frutescens (Yellow Daisy Bush) and other Drought-resistant.
Chrysanthemum maximum (Shasta Daisy).
Clerodendrum speciosissimum. (Scarlet Clerodendron). Shade, moisture.
Coreopsis.
Dahlia. Summer water.
Dichorisandra thyrsiflora (Blue-flowered Bamboo). Shade summer moisture.
Fatsia papyrifera (*Tetrapanax*). Drought-resistant.
Gerbera (Barberton Daisy). Summer moisture.
Gazania, many kinds.
Grasses (*Briza, Coix, Phalaris* and others).
Hedychium (Ginger-Lily. Summer moisture.
Hemerocallis (Day-Lily). Regular moisture.
Hippeastrum (*Amaryllis*) Summer moisture.

Graceful curved lines for lawn edges and beds can be used in even the smallest garden, adding to the effect of spaciousness.

Any type of plant may be grouped attractively in a bed with curved lines. Here a collection of large succulents, chiefly Aloes and cacti, is bold and effective.

Distinctive perennial plants mellow stark lines between house and patio. Tall Plume Poppy (*Bocconia cordata*), with large, distinctive leaves, and creeping *Plectranthus* in the foreground, provide luxuriant foliage.

Long-flowering shrubs adorn the walls of the house. Chinese Hibiscus (*H. rosa-sinensis*) thrives on the warm north wall and the Shrimp Flower (*Beloperone guttata*) will bloom constantly in a pot on the verandah if it is fed occasionally with a concentrated fertilizer.

Impatiens. Shade, moisture.
Kalanchoe. Shade, drought-resistant.
Kniphofia, Red Hot Poker.
Lippia repens (Lippia Grass). Drought-resistant.
Monarda (Bergamot).
Pelargoniums. Drought-resistant.
Phlox paniculata (Perennial Phlox). Summer moisture.
Salvias. Summer moisture.
Sansevieria. Shade, drought-resistant.
Tigridia (One-Day Lily). Summer moisture.
Vinca rosea (*Lochnera rosea*) Drought-resistant.
Zantedeschia pentlandii (Yellow Arum Lily). Summer moisture.

Some Heat-resistant Summer Annuals

Need regular watering.

Ageratum.
Alyssum.
Calliopsis.
Celosia.
Cleome.
Cosmos.
Cuphea, Firefly.
Eschscholzia.
Euphorbia marginata.
Gaillardia.
Gomphrena.

Helianthus (Sunflower).
Marigold.
Nasturtium.
Petunia.
Phlox.
Poppy, Shirley.
Portulaca.
Salvia, Red.
Tagetes.
Tithonia.
Zinnia.

CHAPTER TWO

ADVICE TO THE NEW GARDENER

One of the amateur gardener's small moments of triumph comes when he can turn around to the so-called expert or veteran, who always seems to know the right thing to do, and tell him that his plants have grown successfully in defiance of the well-known rules. He makes a point of announcing gleefully that a shade-loving plant has done better in the sun, that he doesn't find it necessary to give other specified plants a rich soil or that he plants his seeds at least two months earlier or later than the prescribed time. This news, however, will never dismay the experienced gardener, for none knows better than he the magic of plant behaviour; how really impossible it is to lay down fixed and scientific rules for plant growth in most cases, and how difficult it really is to make serious mistakes about caring for plants. One has only to see how plants seed themselves freely in the garden to become aware of the tenacity and indestructibility of seemingly delicate seeds and plants.

This realisation should not cause the gardener to throw all his knowledge to the winds and perform his tasks without method, but it should serve to encourage the amateur who really does not know how to begin, much as he longs to master the art of gardening. There are some amateurs who set out to work according to a precise formula, who use a ruler to measure the distances between their bulbs when they are planting, who fret unless they are told how many ounces of manure should be incorporated to the square foot of soil and also the exact date when they should plant their seeds. These people will lose a great deal of the pleasure of gardening until they become more relaxed and less afraid of their plants. Given average good conditions, most plants will thrive and it is only a comparatively small proportion of plants which require specialised conditions in which to grow.

Experienced growers have found, however, that most plants do particularly well when they are planted in special situations. In striving to obtain the best display from our flowers, we seek the best situations in the garden as well as the best soil conditions. From observations culled from nature, from assessing why plants do well in certain climates and for a host of other reasons, the well-informed gardener has been able to draw many conclusions. Much of this knowledge would be wasted if gardeners did not discuss their experiences and results

with one another, and since this has been the case for many years, both in the matter of the spoken as well as the written word, there has accumulated a vast storehouse of knowledge about placing plants in special positions, which can be adapted for one's own special purpose and climate.

In this way, rules can be formulated about which plants will grow better in the shade, which in the sun, which in poor soil, which in boggy places and in many other situations and conditions. These rules do not mean that the plants will not thrive in any other place and that the gardener should be discouraged from planting them if he does not have the ideal place. A plant which grows in a boggy place, for example, will grow quite successfully in the garden if it is given good soil and plenty of water. One of the reasons why we try to place our plants in ideal situations is that it saves us so much time and trouble. If the bog-loving plant is placed in soil which is constantly moist from a dripping tap, this will save us remembering to water it constantly, as we would have to do if it were planted in dry soil. If we go away for a holiday, we can rest assured that it will not die for lack of water in case it is forgotten by those who do not know its needs. Conversely, plants which dislike wet conditions can be planted in a raised rockery or sloping bed so that excess rain-water does not settle on them and kill them. This happens frequently to shrubs such as the Blushing Bride (*Serruria florida*) which succumb from a too heavy summer rainfall if they are not in an exceedingly well-drained position. That is also the reason why it is customary to lift bulbs and store them during their dormant season in places where heavy rain falls while they should be kept dry.

All these points may seem bewildering to the amateur gardener and probably both the amateur and experienced gardener would like to have some tabulated guidance as to which plants will thrive best in special situations. It often happens that one may have a difficult situation in the garden such as a hot west wall, a cold south-facing position or a large bare expanse of shade under trees, and it would also be useful to have lists of plants which are suitable for these situations. Most of us know a few plants that grow in such spots, but it makes the garden far more interesting if we can plant numerous specimens and contrasting groups of plants in such places in order to increase variety in the garden.

The following chapters will all have lists of suggested plants for different situations and the gardener should endeavour to study them and try plants with which he is not familiar. Do not be afraid to try new plants that are not necessarily grown by friends and neighbours and so add to the interest and wider experience of the neighbourhood as well as of your own garden.

Remember that "the eye of the master makes the horse grow fat" and always direct the work in your garden even if you do no physical work yourself.

CHAPTER THREE

DESIGNING A GARDEN

No two gardens can be alike, even if the same person designs them, as each piece of ground has its own shape and style of house, as well as surrounding buildings that may have to be hidden. Most plots have slightly sloping ground that can be made delightfully interesting or ugly, according to their treatment. (See Chapter 5 on "Hillsides and Sloping Gardens.")

The size of one's garden need not prevent one from making it beautiful and interesting. Japanese principles of garden design should be adapted for small gardens. Dwarf trees and plants, small-scale arrangements of rocks, tiny pools and miniature hillocks can make a small space of 20 feet square as interesting as a broad landscape. Interest in garden design has nothing to do with the size of one's property. There is a garden in an eastern Transvaal town which started out as nothing but a six-foot strip between the house and the fence, completely shaded by a street tree. The owner created a cool green haven with stepping stones in a "lawn" of Helxine (Baby's Tears) with numerous ferns, fuchsias and pot plants giving it the air of a natural conservatory.

The large garden of half an acre or more is possibly more of a trial to the new owner, who can visualize it only as a flat stretch of lawn bordered by a hedge. One can, however, break up a garden into sections or "rooms" in order to make it more interesting, carrying out in a small way the principles of dividing the famous landscape gardens of the past. Great English gardens on large estates consisted of many gardens within gardens, merging and leading gracefully into one another. They had separate rose gardens, water-gardens, wild-gardens, formal gardens, pot-gardens, kitchen gardens and orchards. We can today, even in a small garden, devote special areas to the rose garden, enclose a portion devoted to a collection of plants with grey foliage and white flowers or a collection of scented plants, flowers and herbs. One can tend certain plants like Roses, Bulbs, Dahlias, Proteas, Heath and Aloes more successfully by grouping them according to their needs and designing their situation attractively.

A long walk between a double herbaceous border serves to divide a garden and give it interest. The swimming pool can be treated as a special area encircled by a low hedge or decorative fencing, as can the children's play area. (See Chapter 6 on "Construction.") One can use shrubs, different levels or walls to divide the garden and create vistas by leaving spaces between them. Division makes a garden seem larger and tempts one to walk and see what is around the corner in another section. A garden full of nooks and crannies made by shrubs and permanent plants which almost take care of themselves is even less trouble to look after than a dull, flat garden filled only with straight beds of annuals, no matter how colourful or well grown.

The tendency today is towards informality in gardens. This can be achieved by using flowing curved edges to beds and paths, simple types of construction and the clever use of plant materials to give a softening or woodland effect. On the other hand, a little formality, provided that it is tasteful in spirit, can be refreshing and have great beauty. Architectural elements like well-made walls and steps can give good design to the garden, especially near the house. Brick-paved patios, garden walls and fences, as well as small, formal enclosed gardens for special plants can be delightful. A tiny city garden treated on formal lines with walls and paving can have as much charm as a large rambling garden.

How to Reduce Maintenance in a Garden

When planning the garden, consider the initial cost in proportion to the ultimate maintenance which your garden will require. The three elements which require most time and labour are the care of the lawn, the clipping of hedges and planting of flower beds.

Grass is the cheapest and quickest groundcover, but there is plenty of work entailed in mowing, clipping and feeding it, not to mention watering it during dry periods. Large paved areas are more costly at the beginning, but are paid for over the years in reducing labour expenses. In any case, areas which have continual wear, such as paths or "out-door living rooms" should have hard, quick-drying surfaces. (See Terraces in "House and Garden," Chapter 4.) One cannot expect grass to grow everywhere, so that one should make use of groundcovers on slopes or beneath trees where lawn is difficult to establish. (See "Groundcovers," Chapter 25).

Hedges are necessary for privacy, but in a small garden a careful choice of evergreen shrubs and trees will eliminate the labour of clipping. This is worth doing even though the initial cost of buying the plants is higher. One can use fences and screens in conjunction with shrubs to obtain quick effects. (See Chapter 6 on "Construction.") Plant quick-growing creepers or rambling shrubs over a wire boundary fence in order to give privacy and colour while one's shrubs and trees grow.

Limit the number of flower beds devoted to seasonal or time-consuming annuals which may have to be replaced twice a year. Concentrate on planting shrubs and "permanent" herbaceous plants in these areas. Make a study of bright annuals which can be grown from seed thrown into the ground each season to create colourful displays. (See "Growing Annuals for Display," Chapter 25.)

HOW TO START AND PLANT A NEW GARDEN

When one is confronted with a large piece of virgin ground, one must do the most important things first, so as to avoid being discouraged by the thought of everything that is to be done in the future. First site the house. Cut down all tall weeds and grass and pile them into compost heaps along the back boundary, so as not to take up too much space. If it is autumn, burn them and scatter the ash over the soil, especially if there are noxious weeds amongst them like Khaki-weed or Black-jacks.

Remove all trees which are likely to prove troublesome in the future, such as Poplars, giant Gums and Black Wattle, using chemical weedkillers if necessary. Eliminate old misshapen trees with broken branches from which new growth has sprung, as these will never grow gracefully. Do not be sentimental about unsuitable trees as these can be replaced with quick-growing new trees that will be shapely and grow up together with the garden. Save all indigenous trees that are growing well and would be hard to replace, like *Protea caffra*. Trees on empty land that are not indigenous are bound to have been neglected, so that one should clean the area around them and fertilize them (See Care of Trees, Chapter 29.) Cut out any dead wood and trim to make them shapely.

The feelings of a home-owner who has completed his home and then turns his attention to the lay-out of the garden are bound to be a mixture of excited anticipation and dread. The essential requirement is speed. He must hurry to cover up the dust and lumps with a smooth lawn, quickly produce some colourful flowers, rapidly plant a tree for shade and a hedge for privacy. All these things must be done, but an interesting garden is often lost to the future in the anxiety for neatness and tidiness. There are so many things to think about at the same time, the natural condition of the soil, the choice of plants, the desire to make the garden easy to maintain, plus the inadequate feeling of not knowing exactly what to do about everything. These thoughts make the gardener feel that, at all costs, the primary lay-out and planting of the lawn must be accomplished as soon as possible. The result is, generally, a perfectly flat garden made up mainly of lawn, bordered timidly with a row of shrubs interspersed with a few perennials and annuals. One or two flower beds may be dotted about in the larger spaces. There will be very little change in such a garden after about 5 years, except that the shrubs and trees will now take up most of the border around the lawn and little narrow beds will have appeared along the edges of paths to accommodate the ousted annuals and perennials. Once the natural differences in the landscape are ironed out in order to cover the garden with a lawn, it is very difficult to make changes later, partly because they no longer seem necessary and partly because it is difficult to visualize the potentialities of what can be done. (See Chapter 5, "Hillsides and Sloping Gardens.")

How to avoid these results at a stage when the gardener is probably new to gardening and shaky about practical details and knowledge of plants, involves earnest thought and sketching rough plans on paper. The most important thing is not to attempt too much at the same time. Work on one portion of the garden at a time, starting with the area immediately in front of the house. This will appease the family while the side parts or the furthermost half are being developed later. If one is undecided about how to design the garden, one should seek the advice of a landscape gardener.

BOUNDARY TREES AND SHRUBS FOR HEDGES

These take longer to grow than any other plants and are need for privacy. They can be put in even before the house is built so that they can start growing while the rest of the garden is taking shape. It is usually not necessary to level the ground along the boundary, for trees and hedges can be planted on the natural soil level. Levels can be altered in the main body of the garden later and made to slope up or down towards the trees. This will give added interest to the terrain.

Do not crowd large forest trees along the boundary as their shapes will be spoilt in future years. Find out how much a tree will spread and give it sufficient space. Plant at a distance from the fence so that the branches will not overhang it when fully grown, but simply tip it. Avoid straight lines and stagger trees and shrubs irregularly so that they will have a natural appearance when mature.

Plant evergreens on the outer borders for privacy and

windbreaks. Deciduous trees can be chosen later and planted on the inner borders. Do not choose large forest trees if the garden is less than half an acre in size, but make your choice from medium-sized trees that will create the same effect. (See Chapter 29 on "Shrubs and Trees.")

Always prepare the soil well for trees, shrubs or hedges. (See Chapter 17 on "The Fertile Soil," and under "Hedges" in Chapter 6 on "Construction.")

THE AREA AROUND THE HOUSE

Level the area around the house first. If the ground slopes down towards the house, one must excavate in front of the house so that the area immediately in front of the house is perfectly flat. Ideally, one should make a level area of at least 20 feet away from the front of the house in order to give one a sense of spaciousness and show the house off to best advantage. Anything less than 6 feet away is ugly and useless for planting. If the ground slopes sharply away from the house, try to build up a level area at least 20 feet wide in the front, or the house may appear to be settled awkwardly on a mound. For treatment of the banks formed by excavating for filling in to make a level area see Chapter 5 on "Hillsides and Sloping Gardens."

Plant a few shrubs and climbers against the walls, preparing the soil well. (See Chapter 4 on "House and Garden.") If there is any paving to be done, finish it before planting any lawn in front of the house. Finish off the edge of a paved terrace with a curved line and plant the lawn from that point if the rest of the ground is flat. Otherwise it must be finished with a retaining wall or a drop. (See Chapters 5 and 6.)

LAYING OUT THE GARDEN IN PORTIONS

Aim to plant an expanse of lawn directly in front of the house, but not as far as the edge of the property if the garden is large. The position of the driveway will influence the area of lawn to be planted. (See section below.) Mark the perimeter of the lawn in a definite shape, using a hose-pipe laid on the soil to judge the effect. The edge of the lawn should also form the edge of a bed which can be made into a wide herbaceous border backed with shrubs. Treat this as a nursery bed to begin with, putting all the perennial plants that one collects from friends into it until one can replant them at a later date. Plant the shrubs as soon as possible to serve the double purpose of acting as a background for one's plants and screening the un-made portion of garden behind it.

If the house is near the street, the border will be more or less near the boundary, but if there is more than eighteen yards between the front of the house and the bound-ary, the border can be used to divide the lawn into two areas. This is an ideal way of marking different levels in a sloping garden, but it can also be done if the garden is flat. Make the border arch from one or both sides into the centre of the garden, but leave a wide opening between the "horns" so that one can see through to the second half of the front garden, if necessary down a flight of steps. This will make the garden appear larger than it really is and mark a natural limit to the amount of work to be done in the first season. If the garden is broad and more or less divided by the driveway, plant the portion in front of the house first and do the sides later. The advantage of delaying the planting of a second area until the next season, is that it enables the new gardener to develop confidence and a knowledge of what he wants after working in a garden for a time and seeing that the problems are not really as great as were first imagined.

Works of construction like rockeries and rose-gardens should be undertaken during winter so that they can be completed in time for spring planting.

PLANNING THE DRIVEWAY

For suggestions of materials for driveways see Chapter 6 on "Construction". Also see plans below. The shape of one's ground and the placing of the house will limit the position of the drive. Houses which are built with their garages close to the street present very little problem as the drive is short and does not interfere with the lay-out of the main garden in front of the house. North-facing houses placed at the back of the stand with the whole garden in front of them will have a longer and more prominent driveway. Try not to allow the drive to cut the garden in half, yet do not place it right up against the neighbouring fence. Allow a little space on either side so that plants can be used to detract from its essential hardness.

Try to curve the drive slightly, but do not allow the driveway to sweep across the garden in front of the house and over to the other side. This will only be pleasing if the garden is very large and the drive is kept well away from the front of the house. It is far more restful to look out on to a lawn and shrubs than on to any path or drive-way.

SHADE TREES NEAR THE HOUSE

A shade tree may be planted on the edge of the paving or in the grass at least 20 feet from the house. Do not allow it to keep the light out of the rooms. A deciduous tree is preferred as it will give shade in summer but allow maximum sunlight to reach the house in winter. The tree should have width rather than height and not be too large. Aim to have a shade tree in a strategic position in the garden as soon as possible. (See Chapter 29 on "Shrubs and Trees.")

TAPS IN THE NEW GARDEN

Put down as many taps as possible while constructing the new garden. Try to have one tap for every 90 feet of level garden, so that one can reach every part of it with a 100-foot hosepipe and sprinkler. Each level should have its own tap in order to prevent knocking over plants with the hosepipe. When placing taps near the boundaries, place them at least 6 feet from the hedge or you will not be able to reach them easily. Taps can be placed near steps or gateways.

Camouflage taps with plants, for there is nothing uglier than a bare tap poking out of the lawn. Plant a group of evergreen Watsonias beside it, or make it an excuse for planting a moisture-loving tree like a Pussy-Willow, flanked by leafy perennials like Acanthus. Plant only at the back and sides of the tap so that one can approch it easily. Place a piece of slate beneath it so that one can step on it instead of on muddy soil. A tap alongside a bed of flowers can make a wet place for bog-loving plants like Japanese Irises.

RE-DOING AN OLD GARDEN

It is much easier to lay out a new garden than to re-do an old one. One is so influenced by the lay-out that exists that it requires real imagination to sweep aside the barriers and make something new and attractive out of it.

In addition, the soil in old gardens is often neglected and hard, seeming to defy all thoughts of making it fertile again. Before digging compacted soil, water it thoroughly and deeply, but do not dig it until the following day when it will have dried a little. It is not easy to dig wet soil and the ground will be further compacted by treading on it while wet.

All that applies to a new garden can be adapted to an old one. Do not attempt to change everything all at once, but work away from the house and re-do a portion each season.

Do not pull out shrubs and trees before deciding on whether they can fit into the new plan. It is an asset to find mature trees and shrubs in a garden, but one should be ruthless if a shrub stands in the way of what would make a pleasant open place. Some beautiful slow-growing trees like Eugenia or Magnolia should be kept even if the garden has to flow around them. It is easy to make a narrow neck of lawn opening out into a balloon-shaped portion behind. (See sketch.) The little nook thus created will afford added interest and a bench or birdbath placed in it will provide an excuse to visit it.

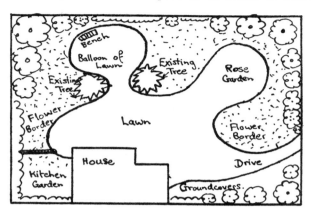

Eliminate narrow beds and pathways that cut up the garden. Always aim to have an expanse of lawn, edged with borders of shrubs and other flowers, as described above.

An old garden is usually shady with bald patches in the lawn under trees. Do not attempt to replant the lawn, but dig and improve the quality of the soil and plant groundcovers to take its place. (See Chapter 10.) One can pave part of the area around an old tree and make a raised bed around another portion, containing rich soil for delicate plants. One can place tubs of hydrangeas or fuchsias on the paving. (See sketches of "Treatment of the area under Shade Trees," Chapter 9.)

CHOOSING PLANTS FOR A NEW GARDEN

Resist the temptation to grow annuals in the first season, except for a few which can be raised by "throwing in" seeds. (See Chapter 25.) Purchase as many shrubs as possible so that one can start off by achieving "a permanent garden" from the beginning. Trees and shrubs form the skeleton of the garden. See paragraph on "Boundary Trees" above and the Chapter on Shrubs and Trees as well as several other Chapters in this book. Start collecting perennials and bulbs of a permanent nature so as to reduce future labour. Lastly, plan to grow annuals and vegetables.

When choosing plants for a new garden, think ahead and not only of the immediate appearance. Shrubs with precious flowers like Magnolias or trees with beautiful autumn tints should not be avoided because they are slow-growing. Avoid disappointments by choosing plants which suit one's climate and do not insist on growing tender things where winters are cold or planting spring-flowering deciduous shrubs in sub-tropical areas. When the trees have grown to create shelter from the wind, one will be able to grow sensitive or tender plants which would not succeed so well in a new garden.

Consider how much care you are prepared to give your plants before choosing them. If one has dry or rocky soil, make a feature of easily grown succulents or plants which grow and spread easily. Plant moisture loving plants in rich soil in shady places. One can change the soil and alter conditions if one is prepared to give one's plants extra care. Always prepare the soil properly before planting anything as it will then grow more quickly.

Variety. Avoid a repetition of the same plants all over the garden. It becomes quite boring to find the same mixture of annuals and perennials edging all the beds in a garden from the front gate to the far corners, even though they are well-grown and charmingly arranged.

When choosing plants try to obtain a large variety. Acquire different plants so that there will always be something in bloom all through the year. Shrubs and perennials which flower during transition periods when the normal display of annuals is over are especially valuable. Although it is a good principle of garden design to plant shrubs in groups of one kind for effect, this can only be done in a very large garden. One can plant groups of small shrubs instead, but should plant as many differing large shrubs and trees as possible. Aim to collect leafy plants that may not be spectacular in themselves, but help to make a garden mellow with their creeping or luxuriant foliage. (See "The Beauty of Foliage," Chapter 12.)

Colour Schemes. It is pleasant to plan colour schemes which can be varied from year to year. Try a bed of blue and white flowers or a yellow and white border, but do not develop a fad about having only one or two colours in the entire garden or it will become boring. If one is fond of white flowers, for example, set aside a special area devoted to a white garden and make it a feature. Place a bench in it, surround it with white flowering shrubs and roses and place it where it can be seen in the evening when the light flowers show up well. If one collects plants with grey leaves, plant a walk with them, but try to place contrasting foliage beside them, such as bronze-leaved plums, Ajuga or *Lobelia cardinalis*, or they may look insipid on their own.

It is a thrill to see a planned colour scheme come to life. Look upon common flowers as colour notes and do not be a snob about planting easily grown, ordinary plants like Ageratum, Cannas or Pelargoniums in order to obtain a showy effect.

Fashions in Plants. Half the fun of growing plants is to find something that is different. That is why hybrid-ists are continuously bringing out plants in new colours and forms. One is often tempted to plant something only because it is different and not because it is any better. Blue roses and black tulips may be desired because they are novel, but may not be as beautiful as the colours which are obtainable.

Avoid trying to obtain plants that do not exist, such as a scented Bignonia. A beautiful plant is often overlooked because it is common. Many plants that grow too easily in some climates are rejected, although they are highly prized elsewhere. One must, therefore, keep an open mind about plant materials and try to use them in suitable places without developing any prejudices against them.

Collecting Plants. Once the initial stages of laying out the garden have passed, it is almost inevitable that the enthusiast becomes a plant collector. This interest, however, should not be allowed to spoil the general appearance of the garden. Do not overcrowd the garden at the expense of good design. If one specialises in growing one type of plant like Aloes, Daylilies, Proteas or Roses, try to group them into a pleasing arrangement instead of merely growing them for their own sake and dotting them about thoughtlessly or regimenting them into straight beds.

The collector of precious bulbs that need to be raised or kept in pots should group the pots on a paved area under a tree near a tap, so that they can be cared for properly and visited by people who like to see plants of special interest. Such a spot can be used for keeping shrubs and cuttings that are waiting their turn to be transplanted into the garden.

Change your collections every few seasons rather than try to grow a little bit of everything all over the garden at the same time. This will widen your gardening interests even if you are compelled to leave out some things to try in another season.

SIMPLIFIED GARDEN PLANS

Each piece of ground must be planned differently according to its special needs and it is unlikely that the following plans could be used without alteration to suit different plots as well as the requirements of the trees and shrubs to be planted. The following plans show only rough outlines, indicating how to divide the garden into areas for growing special plants or for recreation. Features such as swimming pools and rose gardens can be left out without affecting the design. The basic shapes of plots have been chosen as examples for suggested lay-outs, but many alternatives exist, too numerous to be shown here.

BROAD PLOTS

I. LARGE AREA—NORTH ENTRANCE

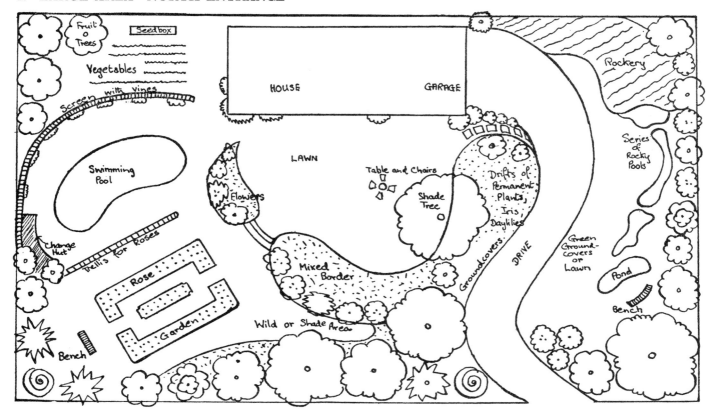

II. LARGE AREA—SOUTH ENTRANCE

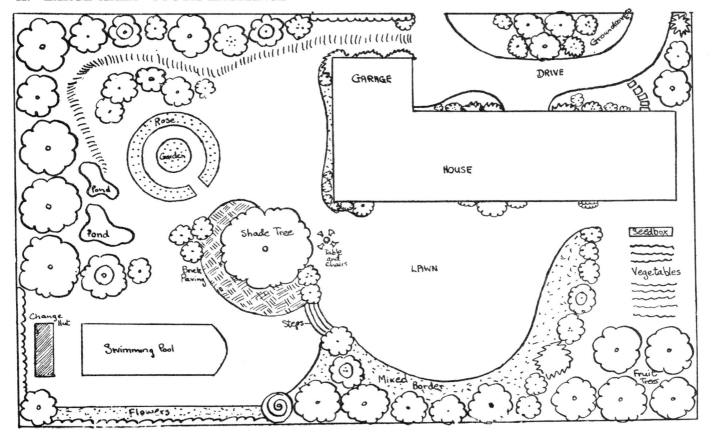

BROAD PLOTS

III. SMALL AREA—NORTH ENTRANCE

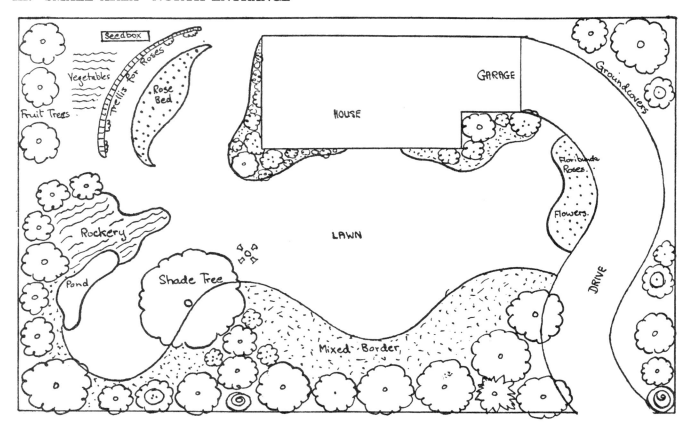

IV. SMALL AREA—SIDE ENTRANCE

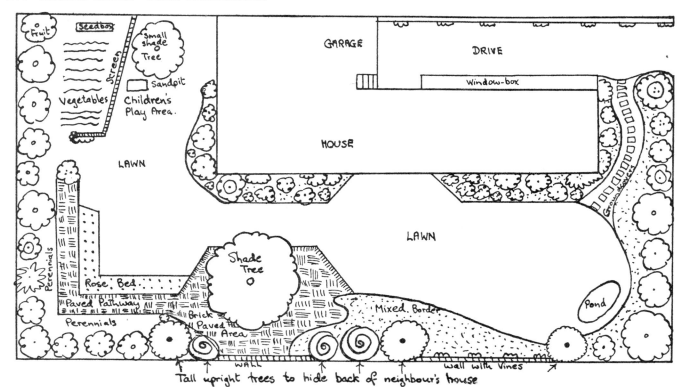

I. SMALL AREA—SOUTH ENTRANCE

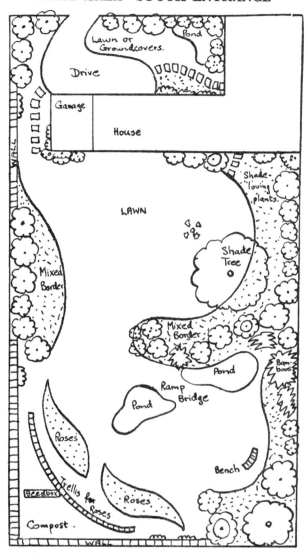

TINY SQUARE PLOT—SIDE ENTRANCE

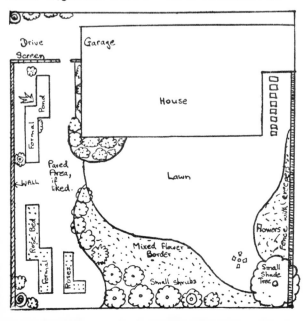

LONG PLOTS

II. LARGE AREA—NORTH ENTRANCE

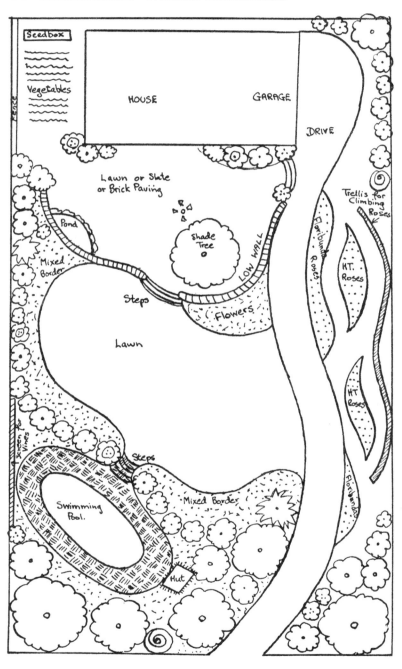

SQUARE PLOTS

**I. LARGE AREA—
     NORTH ENTRANCE**

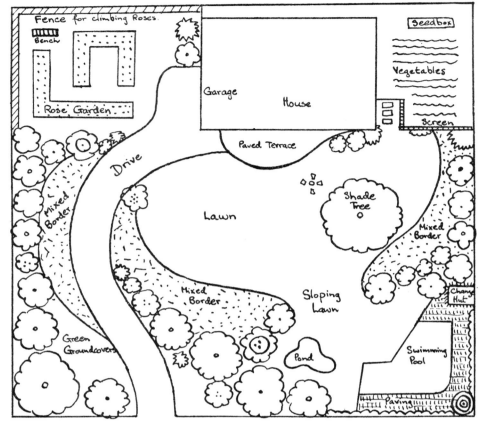

**II. LARGE AREA—
      SOUTH ENTRANCE**

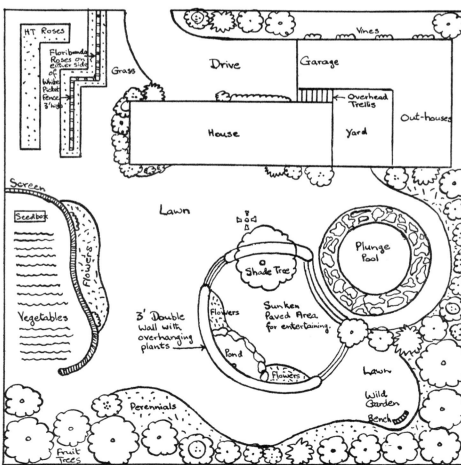

CHAPTER FOUR

HOUSE AND GARDEN

Plants can work miracles for houses, softening bare walls, mellowing a newly built house, camouflaging faults and ugly features or complementing beautiful lines. Plants accentuate the character of a house. Tall plants like the palm-like Cordyline or Cereus Cactus can create atmosphere around a Spanish or contemporary ranch-style house. Plants with bold leaves like Fatsia or Castorbean suggest tropical luxuriance. Plants like Wistaria and flowering Cherries create graceful oriental lines. A large tree growing up behind a house provides a softening background, while a tall narrow tree like Pencil Cypress planted beside a low roof gives it balance. Tall accent plants and trees used near a house can also be used in the garden to mark the top of a flight of steps or in a far corner to lead one's eye to a vista.

Plants should never be grouped so thickly along the foundations of a house that it appears to rise from a green nest. Strategic placing will offset spaces and will not break the basic design. Plant low-growing bushes under windows and only place tall shrubs on blank walls. Tubs or pots containing small shrubs can be placed on terraces and verandahs. Many houses have built-in window-boxes which can be changed about with colourful plants. As a general rule, one should plant only the choicest flowering subjects around a house, choosing them for permanence and giving preference to evergreens. Choose plants with strong-coloured flowers for white walls, but reserve pale yellow, pink, blue or white flowers for red or yellow brick walls. A cerise-flowered climber like Mexican Blood Trumpet (*Phaedranthus buccinatorius*, formerly *Bignonia cherere*) will look spectacular against a white-washed or pale pink wall, but is not as pleasing against golden face brick, where the terracotta *Campsis* Madame Galen would be more harmonious.

When planting against the walls of the house, one must consider climatic problems. The west wall is always hot, the south wall cold and draughty with little sunshine. East walls are chilly in winter so that plants growing there should be able to stand frost. Plants which like cool conditions do best on an east wall where they receive morning sun and are shaded from the fierce western sun. The north wall is best as it is warmest in winter and cooler than the west wall in summer. It provides shelter for tender plants in cold areas, while the north-west corner is even better, shielding plants like Poinsettias from being cut down in winter by early morning frosts. Even in frost-free or sub-tropical areas, the north wall should be reserved for the slower-growing, spectacular plants that require full sun.

Climbers on walls make a house mellow and "friendly". They grow fairly large and one should not smother the house by planting too many different kinds. Rather make a feature of one or two on one wall and choose colours that complement one another, such as royal blue *Petrea* and pale pink *Bougainvillea natalia* or the cerise Coral Vine (*Antigonon leptopus*). Climbers can be used to cover outhouses, unattractive trees, fences, pergolas and bowers made of wire fencing. They also make excellent groundcovers on sloping banks or rubbly ground.

Climbers generally need the support of a wooden trellis (treated with wood preservative) or a wrought-iron framework. This can be made to run horizontally along the wall as it is not always necessary for the plant to climb upwards. Cut back creepers to within 3 feet of the eaves to prevent rats from entering the roof. One should erect a trellis about 6 inches from the wall and place the plant a foot from the wall, enriching the soil with compost and bonemeal. Support the plant with a small cane for the first two years and give it plenty of moisture. One can knock nails or iron eyelets into walls to which one can tie string as a support for roses and other climbers, but these may be wrenched out by the weight of the plant so that one should do this only to rough garden walls. Very few climbers are self-clinging, but should always be used when it is necessary to cover a large blank wall, especially on a double-storey building. They cling by means of little rootlets and need only occasional clipping.

A garden is the extension of the house and our climate is ideal for entertaining on terraces within easy access to living rooms or kitchen. The modern trend of building a house to enclose a patio or atrium encourages one to seek small-scale plants and trees that will grow in semi-shade and create a leafy haven. One can build walls or erect fences in conjunction with the house to form secluded terraces leading off bedrooms and living rooms or even kitchens to form a children's play area. In this way one can create little pockets of climate that make it possible to grow plants that would not usually grow in one's own locality. Here one can make a suntrap, a wind-shelter, or a shady nook with the help of shrubs, fences, trees and vines, as well as lath or even plastic roofs to keep out the rain.

Terraces should be paved for cleanliness and in order to reduce maintenance, but beds and spaces should be left open for plants and trees. Paving materials like slate or old brick laid on its side in block or herring-bone patterns are delightful, while cement can also be made to look more attractive if it is decorated. This may be done by letting in other materials like pebbles, mosaic or bricks here and there in the surface, or scratching it with a wire brush when wet. Paving slabs interplanted with Dichondra or Lippia grass, which do not need mow-ing, are also pleasant. Textures of paving materials can be mixed to enhance one another and spreading plants may be used to soften hard edges.

Paving around the house in the form of a 3-foot path-way can be made of brick or slate as above, with spaces left for shrubs and climbers. This keeps the walls clean and prevents too much moisture collecting near the foundations. Beds for flowers can be made at the edge of the paving so that the plants will hide the edge, or lawn can be grown up to the edge. Portions of this path can be widened to form a large, irregularly shaped ter-race.

SUGGESTED PLANT MATERIALS

DRAMATIC ACCENT PLANTS OF ARCHITECTURAL VALUE

Agave americana (Century Plant).
Alpinia speciosa (Shell Ginger).
Bamboo—many varieties.
Ensete ventricosum (Wild Banana).
Fatsia papyrifera (*Tetrapanax*).
Hedychium (Yellow or Red Ginger Lily).
Heliconia psittacorum (Lobster Claw).
Melianthus major (Kruitjie-roer-my-nie).
Mahogany Castorbean (*Ricinus*).
New Zealand Flax (*Phormium tenax*).
Pampas Grass (*Cortaderia*).
Sparmannia africana.
Strelitzia nicolai (Wild Banana or Blue and White Strelit-zia).
Strelitzia reginae (Crane Flower).
Wigandia macrophylla.
Yucca filamentosa (Yucca Lily).

UPRIGHT TREES FOR VERTICAL ACCENTS

Cabbage Tree (*Cussonia paniculata*).
Flame Tree (*Brachychiton acerifolium*).
Florist Gum (*Eucalyptus cinerea*).
Golden Cypress (*Chamaecyparis*).

Hymenosporum flavum.
Lombardy Poplar (only for huge gardens).
Maidenhair Tree (*Gingko biloba*).
Palm Lily (*Cordyline australis*).
Pencil Cypress (*Cupressus sempervirens stricta*).
Pin Oak (*Quercus palustris*).
Pompon Tree (*Dais cotinifolia*).
Pyramid Tree (*Lagunaria patersonii*).
Silver Tree (*Leucadendron argenteum*).
Tulip Tree (*Liriodendron tulipifera*).
Yellow-wood (*Podocarpus henkelii*).

PLANTS FOR WINDOW BOXES

Compact or Upright. *Ageratum, Alyssum, Dorothean-thus,* bedding Dahlias, *Linaria,* dwarf Marigolds, Pansies, *Primula malacoides, Portulaca,* dwarf Stocks, dwarf Zin-nias, Violas, Wallflowers, Fairy Roses, Ornamental Peppers (*Capsicum*), Succulents which are suitable for growing in pots. (See Chapter 28.)

Hanging. *Asparagus sprengeri, Cineraria saxifraga, Gazania uniflora, Geranium incanum* and Ivy Geraniums, *Lantana montevidensis,* hanging *Lobelia,* Nasturtium, *Petunia, Verbena,* Succulents like *Sedum.* (See Chapter 28.)

SELF-CLINGING VINES

These will climb up smooth walls without support, but some will cling to rough walls, marked *. Those which do not cling but are woody and "lean" against the wall are Bougainvillea and Petrea.

Bignonia capreolata. Bronzy-yellow.
Campsis radicans and hybrid Mrs. Galen. Terracotta, orange and yellow bignonia-flowers.
Clytostoma callistegioides (*Bignonia speciosa*). Mauve Bigno-nia.
Doxantha unguis-cati. Cat's Claw Creeper. Yellow flowers.*
Distictus riversii. Purple bignonia-flower.*
Ficus pumila (*F. repens*). Creeping Fig. Small, round leaves. Clip back large-leaved growth.
Hedera helix. English Ivy. Dark green leaves.
Hedera helix var. *minima.* Small creepers with small green or variegated leaves.
Hedera canariensis variegata. Variegated Canary Islands Ivy. Green and white large leaves.
Hydrangea petiolaris. White flowers. Tall, but slow.
Parthenocissus quinquefolia (*Ampelopsis quinquefolia*). True Virginian Creeper or Five-leaved Ivy. Red autumn leaves. Five leaflets, centrally jointed.
Parthenocissus tricuspidata (*Ampelopsis tricuspidata*), Japa-nese or Boston Ivy. Broad, three-lobed leaves. Variety *veitchii* has smaller leaves. Autumn tints.
Phaedranthus buccinatorius (*Bignonia cherere*). Cerise.*

WHAT TO PLANT ON THE WALLS OF THE HOUSE

North Wall

Shrubs. Shrimp Flower (*Beloperone*); *Brunfelsia*; *Bou-vardia*; Chinese Hibiscus (*Hibiscus rosa-sinensis*); *Eupatorium; Euphorbia fulgens; E. splendens* (Christ-thorn); *Euphorbia* *pulcherrima* (Poinsettia); Heath (*Erica*); *Iboza; Ixora; Protea cynaroides; Streptosolen* (Marmalade Bush); *Strelitzia reginae* (Crane Flower).

Small Trees or Large Shrubs. *Sparmannia africana; Tibouchina semidecandra;* Pompon Tree (*Dais cotinifolia*); Silver Tree (*Leucadendron argenteum*).

Climbers. *Antigonon* (Coral Vine); *Bougainvillea,* tender species; Purple Wreath (*Petrea*); Mexican Blood Trumpet (*Phaedranthus buccinatorius,* formerly *Bignonia cherere*); Potato Creeper (*Solanum wendlandii*); Scarlet Honeysuckle (*Lonicera sempervirens*); *Stephanotis; Solandra nitida* (Cup-of-Gold).

EAST WALL

Shrubs. *Acer palmatum* (Japanese Maple); *Buddleia; Ceanothus; Cotoneaster* (*C. microphyllus* and *horizontalis*); *Cuphea; Exochorda* (Pearl Bush); *Hebe* (Veronica); Lavender; Lilac; Lemon-Verbena (*Lippia*); Mock-Orange (*Philadelphus*); Tea-tree (*Leptospermum*); Rosemary; Spanish Broom (*Spartium junceum*); Syrian Hibiscus (*Hibiscus syriacus*); *Spiraea* (all kinds); *Weigela; Viburnum* (*V. opulus,* Snowball Bush and *V. tinus,* Laurestinus).

Small Trees or Large Shrubs. *Photinia; Pittosporum; Pyracantha* (Firethorn); *Cotoneaster glaucophyllus; Callistemon viminalis* (Weeping Bottle Brush).

Climbers. *Clematis montana* and hybrid Clematis; Cat's Claw Creeper (*Doxantha*); *Hardenbergia comptoniana; Jasminum polyanthum;* Japanese or Pink Honeysuckle (*Lonicera; Mandevilla; Polygonum aubertii;* Roses; *Senecio tamoides* (Canary Creeper); Wistaria.

WEST WALL

Shrubs. *Abelia; Brunfelsia; Camellia; Cantua buxifolia; Cestrum,* red or pink; *Cotoneaster; Cuphea; Escallonia langleyensis; Feijoa; Greyia sutherlandii; Leonotis leonurus;* Moonflower (*Datura candida*); Tea-tree (*Leptospermum*).

Small Trees or Large Shrubs. Bottle-brush (*Callistemon*); Castorbean (*Ricinus*); Forget-me-not Tree (*Duranta*); *Grevillea banksii; Oleander;* Pomegranate (*Punica*); *Poinciana gilliesii* (Bird-of-Paradise); Pride-of-India (*Lagerstroemia*); *Pyracantha* (Fire-thorn); *Wigandia.*

Climbers. *Aristolochia* (Dutchmans-Pipe); *Beaumontia; Cobaea scandens; Hardenbergia* (Lilac Vine); Cat's Claw Creeper (*Doxantha*); Canary Creeper (*Senecio tamoides*); *Distictus riversii;* Golden Shower (*Pyrostegia ignea*); *Lonicera* (Honeysuckles); Mexican Blood-Trumpet (*Phaedran-*

thus); Potato Creeper (*Solanum jasminoides*); *Phaseolus caracalla* (Snail Vine); Star-Jasmine (*Trachelospermum jasminoides*); Wood-Rose (*Ipomoea tuberosa*); Wonga-Wonga vine (*Pandorea pandorana,* formerly *Tecoma australis*).

SOUTH WALL

Plant bulbs of many kinds and shade-loving plants here. (See Chapter 9 on "Gardening in the shade.")

Shrubs. *Azalea; Abutilon; Abelia; Berberis; Camellia; Cestrum,* Red; *Forsythia; Fuchsia;* Holly (*Ilex*); *Hydrangea; Hypericum* (Gold Flower); *Jasminum officinale, J. stephanense* and *J. polyanthum;* Japanese Flowering Quince (*Chaenomeles*); *Kerria japonica* (Globe Flower); Lilac; Lemon-Verbena (*Lippia*); *Spiraea,* all kinds, Snowball Bush (*Viburnum opulus*); Witch-Hazel (*Hamamelis mollis*).

Small Trees. Laurestinus (*Viburnum tinus*); Spindle Tree (*Euonymus*); Winter-Sweet (*Chimonanthus praecox*).

Climbers. Asparagus Fern; Cascade Creeper (*Polygonum aubertii*); Creeping Fig (*Ficus pumila*); English Ivy; Canary Islands Ivy; Japanese Honeysuckle; Virginian Creeper; Boston Ivy (*Parthenocissus tricuspidata*).

PLANTS FOR INSIDE GARDENS, PATIOS, ATRIUMS

Small Trees. Small Citrus Trees like Kumquat; *Daubentonia* (*Sesbania*); *Calliandra;* Loquat; Strawberry Guava; Pride-of-India; *Bauhinia variegata; Ficus elastica;* Kentia Palm; Tree Ferns (Shelter, moisture); Frangipani; *Photinia; Cercis canadensis; Koelreuteria paniculata.*

Shrubs. *Gardenia; Hibiscus; Plectranthus; Brunfelsia;* Shrimp Flower (*Beloperone*); *Elaeagnus pungens; Azalea; Camellia; Plumbago.*

Herbaceous Plants. *Acanthus; Agapanthus;* Bamboo; Elephant's Ear (*Colocasia*); *Fatsia,* Ferns; Shell Ginger and Ginger-Lily; Banana; *Strelitzia.*

Vines. *Ficus pumila; Hardenbergia* (Lilac Vine); English or Canary Islands Ivy; *Clerodendrum; Solandra* (Cup-of-Gold); Star-Jasmine; *Jasminum polyanthum;* Philodendron, Monstera, *Fatshedera lizei.*

Groundcovers. *Helxine soleirolii* (Baby's tears); Lily Turf (*Liriope*); *Ajuga reptans* (Carpet Bugle); *Dichondra* (Lawn-Leaf); *Lamium* (Dead-Nettle); Japanese Spurge (*Pachysandra*); Wandering Jew (*Tradescantia* and *Zebrina*); Ground Ivy (*Nepeta hederacea*); Strawberry saxifrage (*Saxifraga sarmentosa*).

CHAPTER FIVE

HILLSIDES AND SLOPING GARDENS

Slightly sloping ground is an advantage, for it can make a garden more interesting than if it were perfectly flat. Steep natural hillsides, however, as well as steep banks cut into the ground by the builder when levelling the site for the house, present a problem which involves thought, labour and, often, expensive construction. Modern architects who fit the house on to the slope, make things easier for the new owner, who is not left with a steep bank after "cutting and filling". A steep bank, however, can be made to look attractive and there are several advantages in having one. It can provide privacy and form a windbreak more quickly than trees. Furthermore, trees grown on top of it can shut out any undesirable view. A north-facing slope is warmer than a flat garden which is exposed to wind and one can grow many tender plants against it that could normally not be grown in one's own climate.

Nevertheless, every slope creates a problem and one must use imagination in order to make the most of it. There are many ways of treating sloping ground, depending on whether the garden is large or small or whether the slope is slight or steep. Whatever the slope, try to make a level area of at least 20 feet in front of the house, so that it can be seen at its best. (See Chapter 3, "Designing a Garden.")

A Gentle Slope. A shallow slope can be turned into a series of two or three level areas, irregular in size, with low banks between, or can be levelled into one large area with one steeper bank, preferably near the back.

The entire garden can be allowed to form a gentle grassy slope, but one must break it here and there with small level areas and features like low retaining walls, or one will have an uncomfortable feeling of being unable to linger and rest in such a garden. This can be done quite informally by using several methods. Build a semi-circular low slate wall into any portion, levelling out the area in front, possibly for a bench, and use it as a focal point for planting overhanging plants at the top of the wall. Scoop out a bay anywhere down the slope and group a mass of rounded or rambling shrubs on the flattened portion, allowing some to tumble down from the top, like Cape Honeysuckle (*Tecomaria capensis*) or Plumbago, as well as several creepers. The sides of this bay of

shrubs will merge into the grassy slope. Small rock outcrops can be fitted into parts of the slope and planted with colourful flowers or spreading shrubs.

A gentle slope is ideal for a narrow stream trickling down the side to fill a pond near the bottom, or a series of rocky pools planted most attractively. (See Ponds, Chapter 6.) Instead of walking up the grassy slope, one can put down a ramp-like path which consists of long, shallow steps. These can be made of blocks of brick. Each block can be edged with a strip of *Ajuga* (Carpet Bugle) and the next step can be put down a little higher than the last. Such a path can also be made of slate. Be careful to break it with plants and arrange the next level like a step, as a continuous ramp is tiring and can be dangerous.

A Medium Slope. This should be divided into a series of levels held by low retaining walls, rockeries and other methods. Change the level in parts rather than cut the ground into large, level, equal areas. A medium slope can be treated in some parts like a shallow slope and in some parts like a steep slope. If one is forced to level the whole area, then make two steeper banks, one behind the house and one in front. Plant shrubs and trees on top of the banks as a windbreak.

A Steep Slope. This must be controlled in order to prevent erosion. One can cut and fill to obtain some large level areas. Leave the natural slope on other parts and pack the ground with shrubs and groundcovers. Hold the banks between levels in different ways described below. Build in curving paths or ramps between levels.

Avoid formal square terraces built like a series of giant steps going down a steep hillside. Rather have one broad terrace, then a series of two or three smaller terraces of different sizes, or even a steep bank held by a rockery. Try to curve retaining walls in order to avoid a stiff look. If the wind is troublesome, plant small trees at the top of each level.

For a steep slope in a small garden make numerous small terraces which can be treated as flower beds. Cover the low retaining walls with overhanging plants. Try to vary the size of the terraced beds and do not let them be too straight. One must have narrow winding paths

A curved stone retaining wall, overhung with plants, holds the drop between two levels of lawn with efficiency and good design.

A sloping garden can be relieved by scooping out a level area on the lawn, without expensive construction, and filling it with spreading shrubs and perennials.

Sloping banks can be held with outcrops of rock and give one extra planting space. Inlets of lawn coming up from a lower level allow for free movement.

Beautify and partly conceal a tap on the lawn with plants like *Tetrapanax*, *Papyrus* or *Erica* (Heath) and a few casually placed rocks.

When a slope has been altered so that the ground level is raised around trees, build a "tree-well" to prevent the earth from touching the bark. (See Chapter 5.)

A tap my be concealed by planting a moisture-loving Pussy Willow and graceful Grecian Leaf (*Acanthus*) alongside it. (See Chapter 3.)

between the terraces in order to tend or examine the flowers.

Changing the Level Around Established Trees

If the slope must be lowered, do not remove the soil around the tree's roots, but dig down from the outer perimeter of the branches. Build a circular wall to retain the soil around the roots. One can use the area under the tree as a bed for growing Fuchsias and other shade-loving plants and can grow overhanging wall plants around the edge. Part of the wall can be used as a seat.

If the slope must be raised above the level of an old tree, one must build a "well" of stones or brick around it. Leave at least 18 inches of air space around the trunk to allow for ventilation, watering and for further growth. In order to prevent anyone stumbling into the well one can build a low circular "window-box" for plants around the top or a circular garden seat.

How to "Landscape" a Bank

A long high bank can be treated differently in sections, provided that the total effect is harmonious. One can move the soil, with the aid of machinery if necessary, so that parts of it are made broader and shallower than others. The steeper parts can be held by means of walls or rockeries, while the more gradual slopes can be held by plants or grass. One can divide a bank into two or three level terraces, at least 6 feet wide, and plant them thickly with shrubs and creeping plants to overhang the retaining walls. This will give the effect of a bank of greenery. Once one has walls and rock to check erosion, one can plant almost anything on a bank, but if there is no hard material to hold the soil, it is possible to knit the soil with the roots and creeping stems of suitable plants. This is known as saturation planting. (See below.)

HOW TO HOLD THE SOIL ON A BANK IN DIFFERENT WAYS

I. Rockeries form the most natural and appealing way to hold the soil on any slope, steep or gentle. Try not to overdo them, however, and reserve them for one bank only if possible. Try to treat other banks in one of the ways described below. Rockeries can be used in conjunction with grass and other plants, as well as steps and waterfalls. (See Chapter on Rockeries.)

II. Grass has long been used to hold banks in the form of rolling lawn. This is most satisfactory on a gentle slope for there are difficulties in mowing, watering and feeding grass on a steep slope. If lawns are planted to intersperse rockeries, there is the added labour of clipping the grass near the rocks. Make use of ground-covers which will hold the soil as well as lawn, but require no clipping. (See recommended list below and Chapter 10.)

III. Construction. A certain amount of construction can be done to give interest to a bank. Changes in level can be finished off in many ways. Retaining walls of many kinds, fencing and steps can be used on their own or in conjunction in order to hold the soil on a bank.

(a) Retaining Walls. A low wall can be built at the foot of a slope to give the effect of a raised bed. This gives a neatly finished look to a garden and can be overhung with many delightful plants. (See list in Chapter 6.) Always try to curve the wall like the edge of a herbaceous border and use decorative materials like stone, slate or old brick.

The low wall can take the form of a long garden seat, topped with wood if liked. Such a bench can also be built with a back made of stone to take care of a 3-foot drop. The soil at the top can be sloped back or it can be edged with plants like a window-box.

Medium retaining walls can take the form of a double wall or a dry wall, which permits free drainage. (See Chapter 6.)

Steep retaining walls are hard-looking, but can be softened by planting large creepers like Golden Shower at the top and allowing them to curtain the wall. Steep walls can be made more interesting by building them in the form of long window-boxes or double walls for growing plants up the wall. This is worth doing if the garden area is small, for it gives one more space to grow plants.

(b) Steps make changes of level interesting and can be formal or informal. (See Chapter 6.) Steps always lead to problems of how to retain the soil at the side. Informal steps are best edged with rocks. Formal steps should be edged with low walls over which plants can be grown to soften the edges.

Long steps can be made along the whole length of a bank and covered with grass, but are laborious to tend. Long steps made of materials like slate or brick can be broken by informal planting. Construct all the risers along the bank, but only fill in the treads in two or three places, leaving the rest open in large portions. Fill these in with a mixture of plants like tall rounded Daisy Bushes or spreading plants like *Senecio leucostachys* or Gazanias, as well as hosts of graceful plants like Agapanthus. (See illustration.)

(c) A fence of stout planks can be used to hold up the base of the bank and overgrown with climbing roses.

IV. Saturation Planting. One aims to plant broad-leaved evergreen shrubs and spreading groundcovers in sweeping masses following the contour of the bank to create a mass of luxuriant greenery. This can be very effective on a hillside. It can be done on a low bank as well. Saturation planting is most successful if the ground slopes back at an angle of at least 45 degrees or preferably 30 degrees. Try not to overplant with too much of a mixture or a jungle will emerge later. Choose shrubs which are not too rampant or there will be too much pruning afterwards. Spreading plants are excellent, but one must know how much space they ultimately require. One can plant slow-growing shrubs and fill the spaces between them with numerous, easy-to-propagate plants which can be pulled out alternately as the shrubs mature. A few high-headed trees will relieve the planting and provide privacy. These can be under-planted with shade-loving shrubs edged with low evergreens. Choose plants that do not need coddling and will stand up to possible droughts. Wild plants, succulents and drought-resistant plants like *Plumbago* are suitable. (See lists below.)

How to Plant. Make contour furrows up the slope and plant out thickly for quick effect. Covering the ground closely, especially with groundcovers, prevents weed growth and erosion. Do not take cuttings of Ivies or Mesembs (Vygies) and plant them directly into the slope, but start them in flats so that they can develop strong roots first. Plants like *Nierembergia* or Wild Strawberry (*Duchesnea*) are also best started in flats. If plants are given a good start they will survive and grow more quickly in a difficult situation.

Evergreen shrubs should be transplanted from tins. Cut back into the soil on the slope and pack the soil in front to make a basin, holding it with a rock if liked. Place the plant in the centre and apply water slowly. On a steep slope insert a hollow pipe leading from the surface towards the roots and water through it. Plant heavy shrubs near the base of the bank to hold any slipping soil.

Introduce a few bursts of colourful annuals like Petunias or dwarf Marigolds to relieve the density of foliage. This is especially important in a small garden. The tops may be cut back at the end of the season, leaving the roots below to knit the soil, as well as aerate and feed it when decaying.

Water the bank by saturating it with a fine spray from a sprinkler. Control weeds by mulching. Careful attention to weeding and watering, as well as filling in soil that may have eroded, is important in the first year. Once the planting is established, it will require little further care.

SUGGESTED PLANTS FOR BANKS AND HILLSIDES

GROUNDCOVERS. (Also see Chapter 10.)

Establish plants and cuttings in flats first.

Flat Effects

Arctotis (Gousblom).
Arctotheca calendula
Ajuga (Carpet Bugle).
Alyssum.
Bulbine caulescens.
Cerastium (Snow-in-Summer).
Crassula, many kinds.
Dichondra repens (Lawn-Leaf).
Drosanthemum hispidum (Dew-flower).
Duchesnea (Wild Strawberry).
Gazanias.
Geranium incanum.
Hedera (Ivy).
Hypericum repens.
Lippia Grass.
Nepeta mussini (Catmint).
Nepeta hederacea (Ground Ivy).
Potentilla.
Polygonum capitatum.

Mounding and spreading plants

Crassulas.
Erigeron karvinskianus (*Vittadinia*).
Euphorbia myrsinites.
Hypericum calycinum (Gold Flower).
Iberis sempervirens (Perennial Candytuft).
Japanese Honeysuckle (*Lonicera*).
Japanese Spurge (*Pachysandra*).
Mesembs (Vygies).
Nierembergia (Cup Flower).
Salvia leucantha (Purple Salvia).
Sedums.
Stachys lanata (Lamb's Ears).
Vinca major (Periwinkle).

STRONG UPRIGHT PLANTS FOR SLOPES

Agapanthus, Evergreen Watsonias, hardy Ferns, Tulbaghias, Harebells (*Dierama*), Red Hot Pokers (*Kniphofia*), Barberton Daisies (*Gerbera*), Yucca Lily, New Zealand Flax, Day-Lilies and many others.

RAMBLING SHRUBS AND VINES

Plumbago, Cape Honeysuckle (*Tecomaria capensis*), Star Jasmine (*Trachelospermum*), *Bauhinia galpinii*, Golden Shower (*Pyrostegia*), *Bougainvillea*, Mexican Blood Trumpet (*Phaedranthus*), Cat's Claw Creeper (*Doxantha*), Japanese Honeysuckle (*Lonicera japonica*).

MEDIUM-SIZED AND SMALL SHRUBS

Acacia cultriformis. Knife-leaf Wattle.
Ceanothus. Not long-lived.
Cistus. Do not prune heavily.
Cotoneaster. Prostrate varieties, root along stems and bind soil.
Chamaelaucium uncinatum. Geraldton Waxflower.
Clianthus puniceus.
Daisy Bushes (*Chrysanthemum* species).
Diplacus (Bush Mimulus). Cut back after flowering.
Echium fastuosum. Pride-of-Madeira. Cut off flowers.
Escallonia macrantha. Roots along stems.
Elaeagnus pungens.
Erica. Heath. *E. glandulosa, E. densiflora.* Best on gentle slope.
Euryops athanasiae. Clanwilliam Daisy.
Hypoestes aristata. Ribbon Bush. Cut back at end of winter.
Grevillea rosmarinifolia.
Lantana montevidensis. Mauve Lantana. Cut back every year.
Leonotis leonurus. Lion's Ear. Cut back each winter.
Leptospermum scoparium. Tea Tree.
Leptospermum laevigatum. Seaside, sandy soil. Prune back.
Leucospermum nutans. Nodding Pincushion. Gentle slope.
Mahonia aquifolium. Holly Mahonia. Semi-shade, water.
Melaleuca lateritia. Robin Redbreast Bush.
Nautochilus labiatus. Shell Bush. Cut back at end of winter.
Ochna atropurpurea. Carnival Bush. Tender.
Osteospermum ecklonis. Blue-and-white Daisy Bush. Cut back after flowering.

Protea. Gentle slope. *P. cynaroides, P. barbigera, P. nana.*
Pyracantha. Cut back occasionally.
Romneya coulteri. Matilija Poppy. Spreads by suckers.
Rosmarinus officinalis prostratus. Creeping Rosemary.
Sutera grandiflora. Cut back at end of winter.
Symphoricarpos. Snowberry or Coral Berry. Hardy. Needs moisture.
Tamarix pentandra. Plant near top. Cut to ground every few years.

LARGE SHRUBS OR TREES

Large trees are best planted near the top.
Acacia podalyriaefolia. Pearl Acacia.
Arbutus unedo. Strawberry Tree. Needs water.
Calliandra. Tender, spreading shade.
Callistemon viminalis. Weeping Bottlebrush.
Erythrina crista-gallii. Coral Tree.
Eucalyptus cinerea. Florist Gum.
Eucalyptus ficifolia. Flowering Gum.
Grevillea banksii. Scarlet Grevillea. Tender.
Grevillea robusta. Silky Oak.
Hakea. Tough.
Lagunaria patersonii. Pyramid Tree.
Melaleuca nesophila. Tea Myrtle.
Nerium oleander. Oleander.
Parkinsonia. Light, sparse foliage. Tender.
Pittosporum. All kinds.
Prunus. Flowering Peach or Brown-leaved Plum.
Photinia. Upright.
Protea neriifolia. Oleander-leaved Protea.
Spartium junceum. Spanish Broom.
Wigandia. Large rough leaves. Suckering.

CHAPTER SIX

CONSTRUCTION

FEATURING BUILDING MATERIALS AND PLANTS

Garden Paths; Steps; Driveways; Walls, Fences and Screens; Hedges; Ponds; Swimming Pools;
Ornaments and Furniture

THE GARDEN PATH

Garden paths are necessary in rose-gardens, alongside shrub borders, cutting through long beds of flowers or leading one to a special feature in the garden, such as a pool. A footpath leading from the driveway to the house is necessary during wet weather, when one's shoes would be spoilt by walking over damp grass. A garden path need not be straight or ugly and is always more pleasant if it winds slightly.

Paths can be constructed of many materials. Gravel paths are simple, but are apt to look hard and barren. Grassy paths are attractive and cheap to put down, but require maintenance in the form of clipping, mowing and feeding. Building materials like brick and slate are more expensive, but are easy and quick to lay and no trouble to maintain. Old brick laid on its side in a bed of sand makes a good path. It is not necessary to lay the bricks in mortar unless one requires a large firm surface as on a terrace. Slate paths possibly have the most charm and the spaces between the slate can be filled with plants instead of cement. Paving slabs can also be planted up in the same way.

Simply level the soil and lay thick pieces of irregularly shaped pieces of slate on the surface, in the form of stepping stones or as a wide path of jigsaw pieces, leaving 2 or 3-inch spaces between them. Fill the spaces with a mixture of good soil and compost and plant them with *Dichondra* (Lawn-leaf) or Lippia grass which need no clipping. Crazy paving using ordinary lawn grass requires too much labour. In shady moist areas one could plant *Helxine* (Baby's Tears) or *Ajuga* (Carpet Bugle) between the stones. In sunny dry places one can use succulents like creeping Sedums and Crassulas. A mixture of tall and short flowering plants is informal and pleasant. These can include *Alyssum, Portulaca, Dorotheanthus,* Californian Poppy, *Nierembergia* and *Cerastium* (Snow-in-Summer).

STEPS

Steps are essential where the level changes in a garden and can be made in many ways, using slate, brick, stones, cement blocks, wooden railway sleepers or logs. Wood must be treated in places where white ants are troublesome. (See under Termites, Chapter 37.) The ideal garden step should have a tread of not less than 13 inches, but can be extended to several feet in the right setting. No garden step should be more than 6 inches high, the risers being preferably 4 to $5\frac{1}{2}$ inches in height.

Steps may be formal or informal in spirit. Informal steps may be made of slate, projecting slightly over brick or strips of stacked slate, using uneven sized treads. A staircase which has heavy traffic should be cemented in the joints, but in the average garden the soil can be left open so that plants can be placed in the crevices to match a slate path. (See above.) Deep steps in the form of a long ramp can be laid in brick or concrete blocks, broken by strips of low plants like *Ajuga* at the base of each rise. Logs can be laid horizontally to hold deep grassy steps in place.

Formal steps can be important and classically beautiful in the right setting, but should be kept low and broad, with landings made at intervals.

The treatment at the sides of the steps in order to hold the soil varies according to the general effect wanted. For this and other suggestions on steps to retain soil on different levels, see Chapter 5.

DRIVEWAYS

A driveway is important and can make or mar the general appearance of the garden. Wherever possible, the drive should be the main entrance to a garden, for a small gate with a separate footpath usually breaks it up unnecessarily. An ideal driveway should be 12 to 15 feet wide so that two motor cars can pass each other without damage to grass or plants. A single driveway should not be less than 9 feet wide. One should provide a turning area where one's friends can park and the minimum radius should be 27 feet.

Drives have a hard appearance which can be softened in several ways. Avoid a straight drive alongside a fence, but try to curve it slightly in such a way that there is a small portion of ground on which to plant shrubs, lawn or groundcovers. Materials for driveways create hard or soft effects, but must be chosen for their durability and ease of upkeep. Drives made of tarmac, concrete or slate are more expensive than gravel drives, but are cleaner and require no maintenance. A drive constructed of ordinary soil will only be successful if it is of a well-drained nature, but it will need to be rolled and dragged with a sack after rains and the hollows may have to be topped with fresh gravel from time to time. The surface can be hardened a little by rolling in coarse salt. Such a gravel drive is informal in appearance. A loose gravel topping in the form of coarse grey stones is neither attractive nor comfortable either for pedestrians or for motor cars.

Black tarmac is the easiest and quickest to lay, but looks harder than other materials, although sand may be spread on the freshly made surface, requiring only occasional sweeping. Concrete is generally ugly unless one can decorate it in some way with a pattern of bricks or stones or put it down in the form of random paving slabs. The most pleasing drives are constructed of slate, preferably in warm colours, provided that one can obtain it about 2 or 3 inches thick or it may break up beneath the weight of vehicles. Drives can be made to look less prominent by setting two 18-inch strips of slate or paving slabs into grass.

A gravel drive is the easiest for the amateur to construct. The area must be excavated to a depth of about 10 inches, of which the bottom 6 inches is filled in with broken bricks and stones. Place a 2-inch layer of gravel or smaller stones on top and finish off with 2 inches of heavy yet porous soil on top of this. It must be stamped down well. The best soil is a firm type of gravelly soil that binds well, yet has a porous texture to allow for drainage. The drive should be made with a slight camber, the centre being about 2 inches higher than the sides. If gutters are necessary, make them as low and inconspicuous as possible.

WALLS

Walls may be needed to support a terrace or to separate one part of the garden from another. For screening walls, see next section. These can be made of brick or stone and overhung with plants and creepers or one can construct double walls and dry walls. A high double wall is similar to a window-box and enables one to grow dwarf flowers which open at eye-level. Lower double walls can almost be treated as raised flower beds and can be curved to expose a large planting surface. All double walls can be filled in at the base with rubble which makes for perfect drainage.

A dry wall consists of large stones placed on top of one another without mortar, to form a retaining wall against a bank. It should lean back into the bank at an angle of about 30 to 45 degrees. The method of construction is to place the largest stones on the ground, dipping down towards the back. Then place a thick layer of good soil mixed with compost on top. Place the roots of the plants into the soil, allowing the foliage to hang out. Add each layer of stone in succession, interspersing the layers with soil and suitable plants until the wall reaches the required height. A dry wall is more successful in a moist than in a dry climate, although many drought-resistant plants and succulents can be used.

SUGGESTED PLANT MATERIALS FOR WALLS

Hanging Plants for a Garden Wall or Double Wall

*Arctotis acaulis.**
*Asparagus sprengeri.**
*Cineraria saxifraga.**
Convolvulus mauritanicus.
Dimorphotheca, Bloem Erf Beauty.
Fuchsias.
*Gazania uniflora.**
*Geranium incanum.**
Geraniums, Ivy-leaved.
Hedera. Ivy. Smaller trailing kinds.
Helichrysum argyrophyllum. Everlasting.*
Hypericum, creeping types.
Iberis sempervirens. Evergreen Candytuft.
Linaria cymbalaria. Creeping Linaria or Kenilworth Ivy.
Lobelia, Hanging.
Nepeta hederacea (Glechoma). Ground Ivy.
Nasturtiums.
Phlox subulata. Alpine Phlox.
Plectranthus, variegated.
Rosmarinus prostratus. Creeping Rosemary.
Senecio macroglossus.
Thunbergia alata. Black-eyed Susan.*
Trifolium pratense.
Vinca major (Periwinkle).
Zebrina pendula. Wandering Jew
Verbena. Many hybrids.

Plants for a Dry Wall

Alyssum saxatile.
*Asparagus sprengeri.**
Bulbine alooides and *B. caulescens.**

*See *South African Wild Flowers for the Garden* by Sima Eliovson.

Campanulas.
Cephalophyllum—Sour Fig.*
Convolvulus tricolor (Dwarf).
Crassula—many kinds.*
Dianthus (Pinks).
Duchesnea (Creeping Strawberry).
Erigeron karvinskianus (Santa Barbara Daisy).
Ferns. Hardy species.
*Gazania longiscapa.**
Gerbera jamesonii (Barberton Daisy)*
*Geranium incanum.**
Geranium, Ivy-leaved.
Hypericum, creeping forms.
Lampranthus (Mesembs).*
*Lobelia erinus.**
Linaria, Creeping (*L. cymbalaria*).
Nasturtiums.
Nepeta mussini (Catmint).
Plectranthus (shady places).*
Sedum.
Sempervivum.
Streptocarpus (shade, moisture).*
Trifolium repens (Creeping Clover).
Wallflowers (*Cheiranthus*).

FENCES AND SCREENS

Fences form quick screens which are less bulky than shrubs and require no maintenance. They can be used for many purposes. A fence around one's property is almost an essential. An ordinary wire fence can be overgrown with creepers to soften it. Decorative openwork fences can be used within the garden. These vary from an informal, ranch-type, low fence of gum poles, which is ideal for rambling roses or honeysuckle, to a precisely-made, white picket fence which can edge a driveway or enclose a swimming pool, forming a decorative background to a flower bed at the same time.

One can erect a high fence as a background to a flower bed and make use of the space behind it for storing garden tools. Short fences can be used to camouflage ugly parts of a house like bathrooms and water pipes. Fences can also be placed around a patio and may be movable if liked. (See below.) Fencing can be erected purely for decorative purposes, to enhance the shapes of graceful trees like flowering cherries or upright accent plants. When planting against fences, leave clean, open areas to contrast with planted areas. Portions of decorative fencing, used alternatively with groups of evergreen shrubs, can make an interesting boundary to the garden. Try to have curved lines in a fence if possible.

Materials for fences can be novel and have architectural value. Diagonal lattice placed against a plain wall or wooden fence provides interest and a support for

*See *South African Wild Flowers for the Garden* by Sima Eliovson.

climbers. Use closely interwoven, wooden panels to give complete privacy. One can use open trellis-work of many kinds. Erect upright poles about 6 feet apart and fill in the spaces with narrow wooden slats, broad planks, bamboo or wattle branches arranged in a diagonal rustic pattern. Glass can also be used as a screen, especially on top of a garden wall in order to provide a windbreak at the seaside without obstructing the view.

Movable screens may be made to give privacy in a new garden, later moving them to another part of the garden. These should consist of upright wooden frames, about 6 feet square, filled in with different materials as described above, or even plywood, plastic or glass. One can place tubs beside them containing Fuchsias, dainty Bamboos or light-growing climbers like *Mina lobata*, *Maurandia* or Black-eyed Susan.

Permanent walls which screen one from one's neighbours or divide the garden can be made into a striking feature. Curves, nooks and crannies in garden walls are delightful, while garden seats may be built into them. Walls can be built of brick or concrete blocks and whitewashed to make them more attractive. Most plants grow best on walls which have openwork to admit light and air. Climbers grow through the spaces. Honeycomb brick walls give ventilation yet privacy with chequered shade, while many types of sawn tiles may be used to make a similar pattern. (See illustrations of walls on page 64.)

HEDGES

Hedges are planted primarily to ensure privacy and should, therefore, be densely evergreen. Deciduous or semi-deciduous hedges should be used only as boundaries inside the garden. Choose evergreen shrubs that suit one's climate, checking whether they need to be frost-hardy or drought-resistant. Hedges must be able to stand constant clipping and one should choose a hedge that will not be too thorny or difficult to cut. Remember that trimming removes flowers and berries to some extent. In order to save the labour of cutting, one can plant evergreen shrubs all along one's boundary, but each must be given sufficient space in which to develop fully. Grow creepers on a wire fence as a temporary or permanent screen at the base. All hedges do best when bounded by wire netting 2 to 3 feet high. When planting individual shrubs, stagger them slightly and make separate holes for each.

When planting a formal hedge, prepare the soil well by digging a trench at least 18 inches deep and adding manure to the lower half. Try to add compost to the top soil. Allow the small plants to grow freely for a season and then cut them back to induce bushiness. In one's haste to obtain privacy, do not allow the hedge to become leggy. Hedges must be clipped regularly at least three or four times a year, removing a little foliage at a time. Cut the top narrower than the base so that the sun can shine on the lower portion of the hedge or it will become thin. If an old hedge has become thin, do not be afraid to cut it back severely as it will thicken out again when new growth starts.

Endeavour to water one's hedge deeply at least once a month during the dry period and when new growth starts in spring. Fertilize the hedge once a year with a mulch of manure and mixture 2 : 1 : 2.

Evergreen Hedges for Cold Districts

Abelia grandiflora. Glossy Abelia.
Acacia cultriformis. Knife-leaf Acacia.
Ceratonia siliqua. Carob—tall.
Cupressus macrocarpa. Monterey Cypress.
Escallonia macrantha.
Elaeagnus pungens.
Eucalyptus cinerea. Florist Gum—windbreak.
Hakea saligna—bronze young leaves.
Leptospermum laevigatum—Australian Myrtle.
Ligustrum (Privet). Green or golden.
Photinia. Large leaves.
Pittosporum tenuifolium (*P. nigricans*). Small leaves.
Pittosporum tobira. Japanese Pittosporum.
Prunus laurocerasus. Cherry Laurel.
Pyracantha. Firethorn.
Viburnum tinus. Laurestinus.

Evergreen Hedges for Warm, frost-free Districts

Abutilon. Chinese Lantern.
Bougainvillea. Woody climber.
Brunfelsia. Yesterday, Today and Tomorrow.
Carissa grandiflora. Amatungulu.
Coffea arabica. Coffee.
Duranta plumieri. Forget-me-not tree.
Euphorbia splendens. Christ-thorn. Dwarf.
Feijoa. Pineapple-Guava.
Hibiscus rosa-sinensis. Chinese Hibiscus.
Nerium oleander. Oleander.
Plumbago auriculata. Plumbago.
Portulacaria afra. Elephant's Food.
Tecomaria capensis. Cape Honeysuckle.
Thevetia peruviana. Yellow Oleander.

Evergreen Hedges for Coastal or Mountain Districts

Acalypha (frost-free).
Azalea (purple and white only).
Camellia, single.
Ceanothus.
Codiaeum. (Croton) (frost-free).
Coleonema album.
Duranta plumieri. Forget-me-not tree.
Erica caffra. Hedge Heath.
Eugenia paniculata australis. Brush-cherry.
Euonymus japonicus. Spindle Tree.

Gardenia, many kinds.
Hypericum sinense. Gold Flower.
Ilex aquifolium. Holly.
Oleander (*Nerium oleander*).
Myoporum insulare (Boobiyalla or Minitoca).
Pittosporum, all types.
Pyracantha. Firethorn.
Raphiolepis. Indian Hawthorn.
Veronica (Hebe).

PONDS AND WATER GARDENS

A little water in a garden creates a cooling atmosphere and should be an essential part of every garden in a hot climate. The tiniest pond, no wider than 2 or 3 feet across, can add charm to any garden, especially if it is backed by a diminutive rockery or a white-washed wall spouting water from a plaster mask. Small circular or rectangular formal pools can be outlined with brick and set into a terrace, surrounded by potted Geraniums and other plants. Try to leave spaces in the surrounding paving so as to enable plants like miniature Ivies to creep in and soften the edges of a formal pond. Plants growing in the water itself also have a softening effect.

Water trickling slowly down a slope in a narrow concrete furrow edged with stones and mounds of plants has interest and rustic beauty. It can look pleasing even when it is empty if it is artistically made. Many people are deterred from having trickling water by the thought of putting in an expensive pump to recirculate the water, but it is not necessary to pump the water back to its source or build in special pipes to lead the water to the top of a rockery or well. The water can be made to trickle out from any point with the aid of a plastic hose and one can arrange for the overflow to be turned into a bog-garden. Attach a piece of plastic hose to a nearby tap and bury it a few inches below the soil, guiding it to emerge at any height. Allow a tiny drop of water to trickle out, so that there is a constant drip. This can be turned off at night or whenever it is not wanted. Whenever the pond becomes full, the overflow can seep into a bed of good rich soil where plants which enjoy boggy conditions may be grown. (See list below.) This bed should be well-drained at the base, for the plants must not lie in stagnant water, nor should they be allowed to dry out completely. One can place rocky pockets in this bed in order to hold up plants which do not require too much water. Fish keep the water in the pond fresh while plants like *Lagarosiphon* discharge oxygen into the water and prevent stagnation.

Plants which grow in the water need soil and should be planted in tins or large flower pots so that they can be taken up each year for dividing if necessary. By confining their roots, one can prevent vigorous plants from overrunning the whole water garden. Never allow the plants to hide the water completely. They should not cover more than one third of the water's surface. Plant waterlilies in pots with their crowns at soil level in a rich mixture of soil and manure. Cover the soil with an inch-thick layer of clean river sand in order to prevent the soil from making the pool muddy. Sink the pot so that there is from 6 to 15 inches of water above the plant. Smaller bulbs which like moisture, like Crinums or Romuleas, can be grown in clay pots and stood on rocks with their rims just below the surface. They can be lifted out to dry off during the dormant period. Water hyacinths float and feed from the water, but multiply so rapidly that they choke out other plants if they are not kept in check. Most water plants need sun and air so that the pond should be placed in a sunny position and away from overhanging trees as their leaves may pollute the water, especially in a small pond.

Suitable plants must be chosen to surround the pond, both at its edges and to form a harmonious background. Try to choose plants with a leafy, luxuriant appearance for the edge of the pond. Creeping plants like Creeping Jenny (*Lysimachia*) and fluffy plants like *Geranium incanum* are ideal for hiding any ugly cement edges. An informal effect can be achieved by using plants with grassy leaves such as waving reeds, Harebells (*Dierama*) and evergreen Watsonias. Dramatic plants with large leaves like Elephant's Ear (*Colocasia*) or Ginger-Lily (*Hedychium*) add a tropical touch to the pond. Many plants that suit the waterside in appearance do not require wet soil and may be planted in drier soil surrounding the water garden, such as Pampas Grass and New Zealand Flax. (See lists of plant materials below.)

Ponds can be constructed very easily and simply, especially if they are small and fairly shallow. One can make two levels in a large pond to accommodate plants which like deep water and those which like shallow water. The deepest portion can be 2 feet deep and the shallow, near the edges, about 9 inches deep. Hollow out the soil in the desired shape and tamp it down well. Place a coping of flat rocks around the edge, arranging them irregularly to create a rustic effect. Make a waterproof concrete mixture as follows. Mix together 2 parts of sand to 1 part of fine gravel and 1 part of cement. Add silicate of soda, waterproofing grade (Trade names P84 and NU 84) at the rate of ⅓ gallon to a bag of cement. Pour the mixture into the base of the pond and smooth it towards the edges, making it about 2 inches thick. Large ponds must be thicker at the base and may be reinforced with wire mesh. Smooth the surface, keep it damp for two days and then fill the pond with water. Change the water after a week before putting in plants or fish.

SUGGESTED PLANT MATERIALS FOR PONDS

I. AQUATICS. PLANTS WHICH CAN BE GROWN IN THE WATER

Arrowhead (*Sagittaria*). Narrow or arrow-shaped leaves. Clusters of 3-petalled white flowers. Hardy. Shallow water.

Giant Water Lily (*Victoria regia*). Huge, platter leaves. Only for sub-tropical, frost-free places and large ponds. Deep water.

Lotus (*Nelumbium speciosum*). Large pink or white flowers on tall stems. Tender, beautiful seed pod. Deep water.

Papyrus grass (*Cyperus papyrus*). Also called Old Man's Beard. Tall, reed-like stems with tufted, grassy tops. *C. alternifolius* (Umbrella Plant) is shorter, with broader radiating leaves. Several other dwarf species.

Pickerel-weed (*Pontaderia cordata*) heart or arrow-shaped leaves and spikes of blue flowers. Shallow water.

***Small Yellow Water Lily** (*Limnanthemum thunbergianum*). Small yellow flowers with feathered edges. Round leaves float.

***Star-of-the-Marsh** (*Dipidax triquetra*). Spikes of starry white flowers in spring. Deep or shallow water.

**Romulea*. Dwarf. Starry colourful flowers open in spring sunshine. Sink pots just below surface and lift to dry in summer.

***Water Crinum** (*Crinum campanulatum*). Pink trumpet flowers in spring. Shallow water. Lift pot and dry out in summer, but can remain in water.

Water Hyacinth (*Eichhornia crassipes*). Leaves float on shallow or deep water without soil. Erect blue flowers. Keep in check. Will clog rivers.

Water lily (*Nymphaea*). Hybrids with red, pink, yellow or white flowers float on surface. The Blue Water Lily (*N. capensis*)* stands well above water. Deep or shallow.

Water poppy (*Hydrocleys*). Primrose yellow flowers about 2 feet across. Oval floating leaves. Shallow water.

***Water Uintjie or Cape Hawthorn** (*Aponogeton distachyus*). Forked white flowers, slightly scented, also rosy varieties. Shallow or deep water.

II. WATERSIDE PLANTS FOR MOIST, RICH SOIL—BOG-PLANTS

Medium-sized Plants

Alpinia (Shell Ginger).
Astilbe.
Arum, white (*Zantedeschia*).
Dwarf Glory Bush (*Dissotis incana*).
Elephant's Ear (*Colocasia*).
Ferns.
Ginger-Lily (*Hedychium*).
Gunnera (not common).
Japanese Anemone (*Anemone japonica*).
Japanese Iris (*I. kaemferi*).
Kniphofia multiflora (Bulrush Poker).
Monkey flower (*Mimulus*).
Orange River Lily (*Crinum bulbispermum*).
Primula pulverulenta.

---

*See *South African Wild Flowers for the Garden* by Sima Eliovson.

Red Lobelia (*L. cardinalis*).
Red-root (*Wachendorfia thyrsiflora*).
River Bells (*Phygelius capensis*).
River Lily (*Schizostylis coccinea*).

Low flat Plants

Ajuga (Carpet Bugle).
Dichondra (Lawn-leaf).
Helxine (Baby's Tears).
Hypericum, creeping types.
Lobelia, edging (*L. erinus*).
Lysimachia (Creeping Jenny).
Myosotis (Forget-me-not).
Tradescantia (Wandering Jew).
Zebrina (Wandering Jew).

Shrubs and Trees

Casuarina, several kinds.
Coast Tea-Tree (*Leptospermum laevigatum*).
Flax-leaf Paperbark (*Melaleuca linariifolia*).
Tree Hibiscus (*Hibiscus tiliacus*).
Italian Alder (*Alnus cordata*).
Swamp Cypress (*Taxodium distichum*).
Willows (*Salix*).

III. Waterside Plants for Drier Soil, but Water Regularly

Acanthus (Grecian Leaf).
Agapanthus (all kinds).
Aristea.
Azalea (*Rhododendron indicum*).
Bamboos, tall and short.
Begonias (shade).
Bocconia (Plume Poppy).
Crocosmia aurea (Falling Stars).
Drosanthemum (drape over rocks).
Eupatorium.
Ferns, hardy species.
Fountain Grass (*Pennisetum ruppelii*).
Geranium incanum.
Harebell (*Dierama*).
Heliconia (Lobster Claw).
Heliotrope (Cherry Pie).
Hemerocallis (Day-Lily).
Lantana montevidensis. Mauve Lantana.
Magnolias, all kinds.
Melianthus major (Kruitjie-roer-my-nie).
Mesembs. All kinds.
Nandina domestica.
New Zealand Flax (*Phormium tenax*).
Pampas Grass (*Cortaderia*).
Quaking Grass (*Briza*).
Red Hot Pokers (*Kniphofia*).
River Bells (*Phygelius*).
Senecio petasitis.
Shrimp Flower (*Beloperone*).
Spiraea, all kinds. (May).
Tecomaria (Cape Honeysuckle).
Watsonias, evergreen.

IV. Background Trees for Water-gardens

Deciduous

Flowering Cherries (*Prunus serrulata*).
Liquidambar (Sweet Gum).
Pin-Oak (*Quercus palustris*).
Tulip Tree (*Liriodendron*).

Evergreen

Weeping Bottlebrush (*Callistemon viminalis*).
Carob (*Ceratonia siliqua*).
Eugenia (Brush-Cherry).
Tarata (*Pittosporum eugenoides*).
Yellow-wood (*Podocarpus*).

Swimming Pools

Swimming baths or pools are frequently seen in inland cities like Johannesburg and can be fitted into large or small gardens. They need not be large, a large one being about 40 feet by 20 feet, while a plunge pool of half the size is adequate for cooling off on hot days. The gardener can plan an attractive shape that will fit into the general garden design, for a plain, rectangular pool is not essential. Do not overdo this and introduce too many curves. An informal shape with rocks placed on some of the edges has a natural look. Sculptured kidney shapes and circular pools are pleasing and may be built to lead off from a paved terrace near the house. It is generally best to place the pool away from the bedroom section of the house, within easy access of the kitchen.

Choose an open sunny situation so that the pool is not shaded by tall trees in the early afternoon. Place it below a bank so that the filter can be built against it and covered with soil and lawn or rocks and plants. A waterfall can be allowed to trickle over the rocks if desired.

A swimming pool is a feature of the garden that can make or mar its beauty. Make use of attractive garden walls to enclose the pool for privacy or as a safety measure for young children. A white picket fence with rambling roses as a backing for a flowerbed can be made to look charming.

Garden Ornaments and Furniture

Garden ornaments should not be overdone, but can be very attractive and interesting, often luring one to a far corner of a garden. Tastefully designed classical urns, shell-like bird baths, abstract forms or figures of animals and birds, like frogs or herons spouting water into a secluded pool, can complement dark green foliage. White or pale stone colours blend into the garden picture and one should avoid brightly painted crude figures.

Large terracotta or ceramic pots holding leafy or flowering plants are ornamental on paved terraces or verandahs and last longer than wooden tubs. They may be round or square in design. A small enclosed portion of the garden can be devoted to a collection of plants in pots. It can be classical in spirit or designed on informal lines.

Seats may be looked upon as ornaments which enhance garden walls and terraces, being built-in on occasion. Good structural features like seats give pleasure even when colourful annuals are over. Rustic seats consisting of two large stones spanned by a smooth-grained plank can fit into a nook in a large rockery or any other part of the garden. A well-designed garden bench can make all the difference to a graceful tree with a sprinkling of daffodils nearby.

Garden furniture must be durable enough to leave out of doors in all weather, yet attractive. Iron furniture lasts longer than wooden or cane furniture if it is left out in the garden, for wooden legs may be destroyed by termites (white ants), while rot may affect wooden joints after a number of years. Wooden tops can be placed on iron legs and should generally be painted annually to preserve both wood and iron. White is the most pleasing colour for garden furniture. White wrought-iron chairs and tables can be imaginatively designed and delightful. Table tops may be made of white marble or durable glass mosaic in one or more shaded colours. Chair cushions may be made of foam rubber and covered with plastic so that they can be left out of doors, or they will have to be carried inside, leaving the furniture in the garden.

CHAPTER SEVEN

THE HERBACEOUS OR MIXED BORDER

The herbaceous border in the garden can be likened to a mixed bowl of flowers in the house. One can combine a little of all sorts of flowers, common or choice, even clashing in colour sometimes, yet the whole effect is charming and distinctive. No two mixed bowls are ever alike and no two herbaceous borders are ever alike, for both depend on the whim of the person who arranges them and the happy knack of planning colour combinations that "come off". Some people's borders will always be magnificent affairs, combining great artistry with skill in growing special plants. But the amateur should never be afraid of planting a border, for one can obtain a pleasing effect far more casually and with less risk of failure than when planting out a formal bed of one kind of plant.

The great herbaceous borders, made famous by English gardens, limited their plant materials to herbaceous perennials, which reached their peak during summer, but died down completely during winter. Today, the herbaceous border is much more of a large bed where one can put all one's eggs in one basket and obtain an impressive display with comparative ease. It should really be called a mixed border. If we limit our borders to perennials only, we find that the total effect is not striking enough during our hot, bright summers, so that we must include colourful patches of annuals towards the front of the bed. These can be conveniently replaced with annuals which grow during winter and bloom in spring, detracting from the dormant perennials which rest inconspicuously at the back of the bed. Few gardens are large enough to let the dormant perennial border lie completely bare during winter, as it is usually placed in a noticeable position, so that this method of alternating the annuals is practical in the average garden.

There are no hard and fast rules about planning the herbaceous border, but it should be as large as possible in order to create the best effect. The border can run along the whole length of a garden and be so dominant that it provides nearly all the colour in the garden. The rest of the garden can be devoted to shrubs, lawns, rockeries, roses and various permanent leafy plants. The ideal border is meant to be seen while walking sideways down its length, and a double border can be planted on either side of a pathway. The border can be placed on one or both sides of the main drive, so that visitors can see it as they enter, while the rest of the garden can be green, tranquil and unchanging. The border should also be as deep as possible from front to back, so that at least four rows of plant groups can be arranged in it. The minimum depth for the border should be 6 feet, while an ideal depth is 12 to 14 feet. Such a border can be from 20 to 30 feet in length or two or three times as long.

Herbaceous plants show off best when there is a neutral green background of leafy shrubs, a hedge or distant trees. Allow at least 3 feet of space between the back of the bed and the shrubs so that they do not deprive the plants of sunlight and root-room and so that one can walk between them in order to tend the border. A wide border on the edge of a drive can be planted so that it can be viewed from the house as well. When planting a border to be viewed on both sides, one must not have a background, but endeavour to place the tallest plants near the centre of the bed, grading down towards both edges.

The most artistic herbaceous borders usually have a curve in them. These vary from a simple semi-circle or kidney-shape to a long bed with an undulating front edge. Try to make one part of the border broader than another, so that one must sometimes walk around a curve while viewing it. These undulations are more successful when the border is really long and should never be overdone. The easiest way of marking the front edge is to place a long hose-pipe on the ground and move it about in gradual curves so that one can see the final effect. When the shape is finally decided, mark it firmly with a spade.

There are many ways of carpeting the approach to the herbaceous border. Most borders are set on the edge of the lawn and the edges must be carefully clipped to keep the shape constant and neat. One can neaten the edge with unseen barriers like aluminium strips or bricks sunk into the soil below the edge of the lawn. Paving of various kinds can be used with great success. A row of slate stepping stones can be placed on the edge of the bed, separating it from the lawn, while the paths between double borders can be paved with old brick, crazy paving or simply made of grass.

Border plants generally need full sun and are seen at their best when viewed from the north. The best view is obtained when the border runs from east to west and faces north, but if this is not possible, run the border from north to south, facing east. Afternoon shade from the background shrubs is better for one's plants than morning shade. A south-facing border is successful in summer, but might be too cold for winter planting as the shadows lengthen over the bed. Also, many plants will turn towards the sun and may not be seen at their best by the viewer.

The soil for the border should be deep and well-drained. It is no use trying to establish a border on rocky outcrops or in a position where rain-water collects without draining off. If one could place the border on a terrace which has been built up over a layer of rubble, no better place could be found to grow all manner of plants with success. Prepare the soil well as one will not have to do this again for at least two seasons. Some plants, like Agapanthus, can be left undisturbed for four or five years, while others, which multiply rapidly, like Michaelmas daisies, should be taken up and divided annually or every second year, according to how over-crowded they have become. The plants should be given good rich soil and one can add plenty of manure or compost while preparing the bed. Remove the topsoil to a depth of 5 inches, then loosen the subsoil a further 6 inches. Spread a thick layer of manure over this and mix it in thoroughly with a large fork. Replace the good topsoil. Spread a layer of well-rotted manure or peat-moss over this and gently fork it into the top 2 inches. This soil preparation can be done towards the end of winter, a week or two before one is ready to divide and plant out one's perennials.

Some people prefer to replant an established herbaceous border in autumn. This is a good idea in some cases where it is important to know the subtle colours of plants like Cannas which one might forget if they were merely labelled. It may also be done for the sake of convenience if one will be away or too busy in the spring. Otherwise, it is preferable to replant the border in early spring, during the month of August, when new growth begins. (See how to divide perennials in Chapter 26, "Cultivation of Perennials".) Always plant tiny pieces of perennials, which will flower more successfully than large clumps and will grow rapidly into new clumps during the season.

In order to plant one's perennials in a natural manner, do not arrange them in stiff rows. Draw a rough circle about 3 or 4 feet in diameter on the ground and fill it with the plants, spacing them from 8 to 15 inches apart according to the size of the mature plant. Do not make all the circles the same size or the border will look monotonous. Place the taller plants at the back and the short ones in front, but do not grade these evenly. Bring taller plants deliberately towards the front here and there, provided that they do not obliterate the background.

It is important to include only one kind of plant in each group and to select it in one colour only. Mixed colours create a spotty appearance, although they may be used occasionally for variety. Regard all your plants mainly for their colour and do not exclude them even if they are common or easily grown. Try not to place strong, bright colours like scarlet and orange side by side, although this is a matter of taste. Separate such colours with white, blue or pale tones. Always try to combine harmonious colours side by side and the bright ones will merge into the whole. Some people try special colour schemes like a border composed only of blue and white flowers. These can be amusing for a change.

Variation in plant form is also necessary. Plants which grow into spires, like *Delphinium*, contrast effectively with rounded masses formed by *Achillea* or *Monarda*. Introduce plants with spiky leaves, like *Iris* or *Tigridia*, to provide an accent between low, spreading plants like petunias, but keep them away from the edges.

One could use almost any garden plant in the border. It is an excellent place to grow clumps of tall lilies which benefit from being shaded at the root. Bulbous-rooted plants like Day Lilies and Red Hot Pokers provide permanent leafy clumps that finish off the sides and add their dividends of flowers from time to time. Such subjects are really only suitable for the really large border, as the smaller border needs longer-flowering plants. Cannas in groups of one colour make excellent long-flowering, solid masses at the back of any border, while dwarf kinds may be planted near the front. Dahlias provide good colour notes, but should be used with restraint in occasional groups of about five plants of one colour. Bishop of Llanduff has decorative bronze foliage as well as dark red blooms. Dwarf types like Coltness hybrids can be planted near the front. Groups of three to five floribunda roses like Fashion or Ma Perkins lend interest to the border. Keep roses to the front or sides so that one can reach them in order to remove faded flowers.

Flowering shrubs can be used towards the sides and centre-back to introduce unusual colour notes like blue-flowered *Ceanothus* and *Echium* or bronze-leaved *Berberis*. Medium-sized, shrubby plants like grey-leaved Centaureas and *Senecio leucostachys* as well as daisy bushes are excellent in a large mixed border. Annuals in separate shades must be used to accentuate the foreground with brilliant colour. Petunias in pink, white, red or purple are a great standby, while Ageratum and dwarf Marigolds make valuable edgings. Tall Marigolds and Celosia make bold accents for the centre and Zinnias near the back are magnificent foils for graceful plants.

Try to make the border colourful for as long as possible during summer and autumn and do not worry if some perennials flower at different times. Do not overdo any one kind of plant and change one's arrangement each year in order to stimulate interest. One can obtain an artistic effect, especially in a very long border, by repeating the same plants two or three times at intervals. Be aware of vigorous plants that tend to encroach on the others, like *Physostegia* or Sea Holly (*Eryngium*), but annual division will keep these in check. The majority can be left for two or three years without division, others for five or six years, while some resent any disturbance at all. (See under "Cultivation of Perennials".)

The following lists of useful perennials and summer annuals for borders are grouped according to colour. A suggested plan for an effective but simple herbaceous border appears below. This can be changed endlessly and either simplified or elaborated.

TEN PLANTS OF EACH COLOUR FOR THE BORDER

RED FLOWERS

Perennial. *Salvia* (tall and dwarf).
Canna (tall).
Tigridia (medium).
Monarda (medium).
Fuchsia fulgens (medium).
Lychnis (low).
Verbena (low).

Annual. *Celosia* (medium).
Petunia (low).
Phlox, Tetra red (low).

PINK

Perennial. *Salvia* (tall).
Canna (tall).
Echinacea purpurea (pink Rudbeckia) (medium).
Monarda (medium).
Perennial *Phlox* (medium).
Diascia (low).
Dianthus (low).

Annual. *Cleome* (tall).
Lavatera (tallish).
Petunia (low).

WHITE

Perennial. Shasta daisy (medium) (double, single).
Delphinium (medium).
Gaura (medium).
Achillea (low).
Perennial *Phlox* (medium).
Erigeron karvinskianus (low).

Annual. Candytuft (medium).
Petunia (medium).
Alyssum (low).
Ageratum (low).

BLUE

Perennial. *Delphinium* (medium-tall).
Salvia patens (medium).
Salvia farinacea (tallish).
Agapanthus (medium).
Eryngium (medium).
Anchusa (medium).
Veronica (low).
Stokesia (low).

Annual. Butterfly *delphinium* (low).
Cynoglossum (tall).

ORANGE

Perennial. *Leonotis leonurus* (tall).
Dahlia (tall).
Lilium henryi (tall).
Lilium davidii (medium).
Alstroemeria aurantiaca (medium).
Canna (tall and medium).
Hemerocallis (medium).

Annual. Marigold (tall and dwarf).
Zinnia (tall).
Zinnia linearis (low).

LAVENDER AND ROSY MAUVE

Perennial. Michaelmas daisy (medium).
Salvia turkestanica (medium-tall).
Physostegia (medium).
Perennial *Phlox* (medium).
Mauve *Penstemon* (medium).
Rehmannia alata (medium).
Erigeron hybrids (low).
Nepeta (low).

Annual. *Petunia*.
Ageratum (lavender blue, low).

DEEP PURPLE

Perennial. *Campanula* (medium).
Purple *Monarda* (medium).
Perennial *Phlox* (medium).
Gay-Feather (*Liatris*) (tall).
Chrysanthemum (medium).
Dahlia (tall).

Annual. *Petunia* (medium).
Phlox (low).
Alyssum (low).
Scabious (tall).

YELLOW

Perennial. *Rudbeckia* (tall).
Helenium (tall).
Helianthus (tall).
Canna (tallish).

Solidago (medium).
Achillea, canary and sulphur (medium).
Coreopsis (medium-low).
Yellow Marguerite (low).

Annual. *Zinnia* (tall).
Dwarf marigold (low).

BRONZE TONES

Perennial. *Rudbeckia* (medium).
Chrysanthemum (tall, medium, dwarf).
Gaillardia (medium).

Mahogany Castorbean (very tall, shrub-like).
Purple-leaved *Berberis* (medium, a shrub).
Hemerocallis (medium).

Annual. *Zinnia* (tall).
Rusty red marigold (dwarf).

MIXED COLOURS

Perennial. Dahlia, Coltness hybrids (low).
Tigridia hybrids (medium).
Penstemon (medium).
Bearded Iris.

PLAN FOR A SIMPLE HERBACEOUS BORDER
12 FEET DEEP AND ABOUT 30 FEET LONG

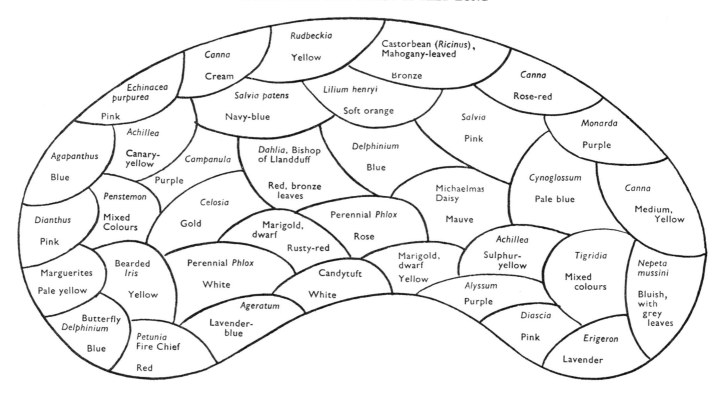

CHAPTER EIGHT

ROCK GARDENS

If possible, every garden should have some rock somewhere. The appearance of weathered stone or rock is a charming feature in any landscape and the combination of plants and rocks somewhere in the garden creates an interest apart from the neatness of flowerbeds and borders. In gardens of today especially, where a natural appearance is required, the addition of a few rockery pockets will help to achieve informality. Rock is available in most parts of southern Africa and can be ordered in bulk from contractors. Souvenirs of weathered rock can be brought home generally from the shortest motor trip, although this is naturally a very laborious way of making a collection.

Apart from the artistic necessity for having a rockery, there are many practical reasons for building a rockery, no matter how small. Certain beautiful and valuable plants like Cape Heath and Protea or Australian Leptospermum, require the good drainage that always occurs in a rockery, for the rockery is generally raised above the ground and the water can then trickle down to a lower level. In addition, the very fact that the rockery beds are raised makes the rockery easy to tend, both for old and young.

The rockery is a place where the gardener can find a little mental relaxation in that he does not always have to consider colour schemes as he does in the border. One can have a brilliant show in a rockery which has the effect of a mixed bowl of flowers and yet one can find room for many less showy treasures culled from friends' gardens, which might otherwise be lost in a general bed or create a spotty effect. The rockery becomes the store-cupboard for many pretty little plants without looking untidy, for one can always find a little nook amongst the rocks for the odd bulbs of which one only has a few— those extra special colour forms of Barberton daisies, Potentillas or Alpine phlox, a clump of Bulbinella or Japanese anemones and the succulent Crassulas and Aloes which look their best amongst the rocks, to mention only a few plants which one could plant in the rockery.

The rockery enables one to grow many species of plants in a small area. If one had to plant out all the interesting plants one owned into a bed, the result would be a hotchpotch and the plants might not even do well, but in the rockery those same plants will look their best, enhanced by the rocks and the general shape of the rockery much as jewels in the right setting.

WHERE TO BUILD A ROCKERY

The site for the rockery is most important as it is a permanent feature and should be planned with a great deal of care. One should always choose a sunny position if possible. It will not matter if a small portion of the rockery is shaded by trees as this can be filled with shade-loving plants, (See Chapter 9 on "Gardening in the Shade") but it is a mistake to have the whole rockery in the shade as this immediately limits the type of plant one can grow and makes it exceedingly difficult to create any show of colour.

It is best to view the rockery from the north side in the southern hemisphere. Plants will flourish much better in a rockery facing north or north-west than in a southerly direction, even though the rockery may be placed in the centre of the garden.

The rockery should be situated on a natural slope of ground. This will make it easier to construct and the drainage will automatically be better. Do not choose a low or sunken spot in the garden or it will be too damp in rainy weather and drainage will be poor. If there is no natural slope in the garden, one can easily construct one by excavating one area and creating a higher level by banking up the soil behind it. The drop need not be greater than two feet in order to construct a very attractive rockery. A rockery on a shallow slope is often more successful than one on a steep drop, where it often becomes very large and too overpowering. Do be careful not to bury the topsoil of the higher level when building up a bank. Remove it and fill the base with rubble before piling up the soil, then spread the topsoil over the top, or better still, save it to fill the pockets when the rocks have been placed in position. If the slope is not too steep one can plant grass on portions of the bank between rocky outcrops. If one does not wish to mow grass on a slope, use lawn substitutes like Ajuga, Dichondra or Lippia grass.

One should always plan to create some background for the rockery in the shape of large shrubs. This depends on the position from which the rockery will be viewed. In an ideally situated, north-facing rockery some larger shrubs may be planted behind the top edges of the rocks. They should be planted several feet from the rocks and not in a straight line, but in groups. Spaces must be left so that one can look up and beyond the rockery if there is a vista. One taller shrub can be used to form an accent. A winding path could lead through one portion of a large broad rockery to an opening between the shrubs at the top. A small rockery could have small evergreen shrubs in the top pockets, which give it body and add their beauty of form to the rock planting.

How to Build a Rockery

When choosing stone or rocks to build a rockery, try to use only one type of rock. This will give a more pleasing and natural effect than using different types and colourings. Use large pieces of rock rather than fragments. It is better to use a few large rocks for a bed than numerous small ones.

When one has finally decided on the right position and collected one's rocks together, it is no easy matter to assemble soil and stones into an artistic yet practical

SOME ROCKERY OUTLINES

The outline of the front edge of the rockery should flow in and out in gentle curves, using the interest of the rocks to prevent a hard-edged look. There should not be so many bays that they become fussy repetitions and lack general shape.

One should mark out the lower edge of the rockery on the soil with a sharp stick, then dig a broad band all along this line, so that one can manoeuvre the rocks into the soil more easily. Starting from one side, place four or five rocks along the front edge. Show the most decorative side of each rock and bury the ugly edge. Tip each rock slightly backwards in order to help the rain soak down towards the roots of the plants. Insert the rocks well into the ground. In some cases, at least half of the rock should be buried. The rock should come out of the ground at an angle of about 45 degrees as if it is protruding from a natural outcrop.

It is always best to place the rocks horizontally along the ground and not have them jutting up into the air like

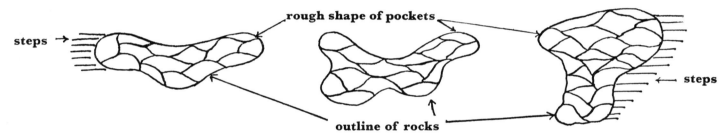

rockery. It is a great temptation to mound the soil into a slope and stick rocks into it here and there, hoping to cover any discrepancies with trailing plants. This is an unsatisfactory method of making a rockery as it does not hold the soil properly and the top soil will eventually be washed down between the rocks, leaving the roots of the plants bare. The water might also run off too quickly and not be able to reach the roots of the plants, so that they will not grow well. In addition, such a rockery will resemble a raisin bun until the plants have covered it completely.

First of all, one should plan out the general outline of the rockery. This should never be absolutely straight, but have some curve in it somewhere. The lower edge of the rockery is the most important to consider and this can either form a large bay or curve inwards in a kidney shape. It is always more artistic to have one part of the rockery deeper from front to back than another. A small rockery can be set in a sloping lawn and be given an irregular outline, which may be broad at the top and tapering to the base or vice versa.

milestones. The front of the lowest rocks should rest on the ground and the back should go down below the surface. Stand with one's weight on the rock to make sure that it is firm. Arrange some rocks with their flat surfaces uppermost so that one can use them as stepping stones when picking flowers or tending to one's plants.

After a few rocks have been securely placed, complete the pocket by placing other rocks, of a similar size, around the sides and the back. These back ones should rest firmly on the ground and not be buried as deeply as the front ones. Their base should be approximately at the height of the front rocks. Now fill the front pocket with soil, tamping it down firmly between the rocks. If there is a gap between the front rocks where the soil is likely to be washed out, place a smaller rock in the gap on the inside of the pocket to act as a rough plug before filling up with soil. Never use cement as this will prevent drainage.

Work slowly along the front edge of the rockery, completing many of the lower pockets and achieving different levels by using larger and smaller-sized rocks. Vary the

A straight grassy path, flanked by borders of perennials and Silver Trees (*Leucadendron argenteum*), leads to a formal pond.

A curved border of blue and white perennials and annuals screens one part of the garden from another.

Paths can be made easily by embedding large pieces of slate on good soil, leaving spaces between for planting.

Here *Dichondra repens* (Lawn-leaf or Wonder-Lawn) fills the spaces between the crazy paving, needing no cutting and thriving in the shade.

Step designs can be interesting. Slate can be set with cement (above) or interplanted (below) with creeping groundcovers like Carpet Bugle (*Ajuga reptans*).

Steps with a cement base can be set with flat stone chips to give an interesting finish.

size of the pockets, but endeavour to make them as large as possible. With the lower pockets filled, it is now an easy matter to proceed higher. Fill in the soil behind the first pocket and place more rocks at the sides and back to form a higher pocket. Vary the size and shape of the different pockets and try to achieve a natural look. Always strive to give the impression that the rocks grow out naturally from the slope. It is best to arrange the pockets so that there is not a big drop between them, but a gentle gradation of levels.

When one finally reaches the top level of ground, it will be necessary to place rocks along the top edge of the rockery. These should be deeply set into the ground and protrude only a few inches. As always, let some rocks stand up higher than others for interest. Quite a big boulder might make an occasional pleasant feature. Try to place the top rocks in an irregular line, finishing off the top pockets individually.

PREPARATION OF SOIL

When the rocks are finally in place, the soil should be filled up to the top of each pocket. During construction, quite a lot of soil will have been placed in each pocket, but this may only be gravelly or poor subsoil. The more gravelly the soil beneath the rockery, the better the drainage will be. The soil inside each pocket, however, should be very good, to a depth of at least 1 foot. Remove some of the poor soil in the pocket and fill up with a mixture of good top soil and loam. The more loam in the form of well-made compost that you can incorporate, the better. It is not necessary to add manure, for many rockery plants do not like manure. The manure which has been well-rotted and become part of the compost, will be more than satisfactory. The fibrous matter in the loam will retain moisture yet also aid drainage.

WHAT TO PLANT IN A ROCKERY

It might seem presumptuous to give advice on what to put into a rockery, for the subject is vast and the number of plants one could grow there are unending. So much depends on the taste of the gardener and the desire to have either a brilliant show or merely a collection of interesting foliage plants. At the same time, however, there are so many plants that are seen in rockeries which do not belong there, that it might be as well to first mention those that are not suitable.

It is a good idea to start with easily-grown plants so that one can have a well-grown look in a fairly short time, but one should beware of plants that grow so easily that they take over the whole rockery, multiplying freely and finding a firm roothold in between the rocks so that they are very difficult to eradicate or keep in check. Most

of the common garden perennials fall into this category and, in any case, belong chiefly to the herbaceous border and rob the rockery of its essential character. They smother the rocks in a very short time and the rockery merely resembles a sloping herbaceous border. If these same perennials are also used elsewhere in the garden then the rockery will simply become boring in its repetition of plants.

Rampant perennials which are seen in rockeries and should not be planted there are subjects like *Gaura*, Shasta Daisies, Blue *Salvia*, *Achillea*, *Cuphea micropetala*, Campanula (except for Canterbury Bells), Cannas, Coral Bells (*Penstemon barbatus*) and many others. There are so many really suitable plants for rockeries that even the less rampant common perennials like *Geum*, *Erigeron* and bearded Iris should be omitted. Some bulbs like Gladioli, particularly the common African Gladiolus (*G. psittacinus*) or Garden Montbretias (*Tritonia* hybrids) should never be planted in the rockery as they multiply so easily that they become a pest. They send runners under the rocks and it is virtually impossible to eradicate them.

Perennials such as Barberton daisies, Agapanthus and Red Hot Pokers are very suitable in the rockery, not only because their spread can be checked, but because their appearance suits the rocky setting. Creeping perennials like Wild Strawberry (*Duchesnea*), *Cerastium* (Snow-in-Summer), Santa Barbara Daisy (*Erigeron karvinskianus*), Pelargoniums and Mesembryanthemum are also suitable, but must be kept in check carefully. Try to confine each of them to one spot and do not allow them to spread beyond their allotted area. Weed them out ruthlessly if they begin to smother nearby plants.

Bulbs such as Yellow Arums, Pineapple Flowers (*Eucomis*), *Tulbaghia fragrans*, Daffodils, Ranunculus, Anemones and many others are suitable as they do not spread too freely and can be lifted easily when dormant.

Shrubs are very suitable and it is amazing how many small shrubs can be found to dress the rockery. Use as many evergreens as possible, for they prevent a bare look in winter. Plants like Heath and Strelitzia are extremely successful. Shrubs which drape themselves over rocks, like Purple Lantana or Flame Pea (*Chorizema*) are delightful. It is advisable to plant several tall shrubs or small trees in the larger rockery in order to give it an interesting form. Choose trees that do not spread too much and cover the rocks unless one has an extremely large rockery. Small trees with slim trunks and a fairly narrow habit, such as *Dais cotinifolia*, Weeping Bottlebrush, *Cussonia paniculata* (Cabbage Tree) and Tamarisk are best. Shrubs with a suckering habit like *Kerria japonica* (Globe Flower) and *Rhus typhina* should not be planted, for they behave like rampant perennials.

Climbers are valuable in a large rockery. *Bougainvillea* or Canary Creeper (*Senecio tamoides*) can be very attractive spreading over stones and slopes.

Succulents are ideal plants for the rockery, for they thrive in conditions where drainage is good and usually grow amongst stones in nature. Crassulas are particularly attractive as they generally have showy flowers. Here again, the rampant growers like *C. multicava*, which spreads so easily in the shade, must be weeded out periodically, but it can be controlled easily. Beautiful species like *C. falcata* and *C. portulacea*, however, do not spread very much and are ideal where conditions are suitable.* The American Sedums (Stonecrops) are ideal for planting amongst rocks and the dwarf species will grow in the poorest soil, but must be kept in check constantly. Aloes are perfect succulents for the rockery, for they grow amongst rocks in nature and there are scores from which to make a choice.

Cacti make striking plants in a rockery, but do not blend well with ordinary garden flowers and should be planted almost as an architectural feature to complement the house. They are mainly of interest for their grotesque forms, not for their flowering habits, and are of special interest to collectors.

Annuals. Amost any annual can be planted in the rockery, but the best ones are of the type that create a massed display of colour, like Namaqualand daisies, rather than the type that sends up a slender stem, even though the flower itself is beautiful, like Clarkia or Godetia. The massed bushy flowers fill the rock pockets gracefully and overflow the edges of the rocks in a natural manner. Stiff, spiky annuals are apt to look rather prim and out of place. On the other hand, some of the common annuals like the taller Petunias are too spreading in growth and should be avoided, particularly in a small rockery. The ideal annual for the rockery should be fairly compact and not sprawl untidily like Echium Blue Bedder.

Low-growing annuals, like *Ageratum* and *Dorotheanthus*, are particularly valuable for the front of the rockery. Be careful of annuals like Marigolds that seed themselves so freely that they overrun everything. They must be scrupulously weeded out in the following season.

One should plant the type of annual which is used more for display than as a cut flower, so that one is not tempted to cut the blooms for the vase. Members of the daisy family are particularly suitable.

*See *South African Wild Flowers for the Garden* by Sima Eliovson.

HOW TO PLANT THE ROCKERY

Having decided on the plants to use, one must try to avoid a spotty effect by planting one of everything irrespective of its size. Group several plants of one kind in each pocket as a start. One pocket can be filled with dozens of one type of annual such as *Nemesia*, and another filled with two or three small shrubs of a kind, like *Strelitzia* or Cape Heath. Larger plants like Pride-of-Madeira (*Echium fastuosum*) can be represented by single specimens. Even though the pocket is filled mainly with one type of plant, other plants can be placed at the corners of the pockets to avoid a too formal look and appear as if they overflow from one bed to the next. Barberton daisies (*Gerbera*) or *Bergenia* are particularly suitable as they love the cool root run under the rocks, while their pretty foliage softens the stone without hiding it completely.

Most of the decorative rock surfaces should continue to show when the plants are fully grown, for if they are completely overgrown, the character of the rockery will be lost.

One should put in as many permanent plants as possible and arrange a few beds of annuals here and there for a brilliant show. Quick-growing annuals, like Phlox, can also be used to dress the rockery until the slower, more permanent shrubs have grown. It is better to rely on the display of annuals at first than to overplant with specimens of a permanent character.

In general, the larger plants should be planted at the back of the rockery, that is, in the top pockets, while dwarf plants should be planted in the lower pockets, so that they can be viewed easily. In some portions, however, bring taller plants to the fore or the planting will become monotonous.

MAINTENANCE OF THE ROCKERY

The well-built rockery requires very little maintenance, but weeds and grass should not be allowed to gain a foothold in the rocks. Do not allow the lawn to grow right up to the rocks in the front as it will be very difficult to mow and require a great deal of hand labour to keep it from growing up into the crevices of the rocks. The lawn should be trimmed with a neat edge following the curve of the rockery at least one foot away from the rocks. This narrow bed can be filled with many small plants which look well against the rocks and help to link the rockery to the rest of the garden.

Water the rockery regularly and allow the spray to soak well down into the soil. It will be found necessary to water the rockery only about twice a week if this is done thoroughly. Rockeries devoted to succulents need be watered less frequently, particularly when they are accustomed to have a dry period in nature. This will depend on whether they come from a summer or winter-rainfall area.*

Snails are fond of making their home in the damp areas under the rocks and must be kept in check before they can damage small plants. Use snail bait early in spring to prevent these pests from multiplying.

Do not allow trailing shrubs like *Lantana montevidensis* or shrubby perennials like certain Bush Salvias to become straggly. They may be cut back after flowering or during winter and will make neat growth in the spring. In all cases keep the rockery neat and check the spread of the same type of plant everywhere. A small pocket of wild strawberry is delightful, but it soon becomes a pest if it is allowed to be introduced into every part of the rockery and form a carpet for Aloes and other plants out of character.

LISTS OF PLANTS SUITABLE FOR THE ROCKERY

The following lists have been drawn up to assist the gardener in making a choice of a large variety of interesting and suitable plants for the rockery. Dwarf plants generally grow up to three or four inches and are suitable for edging, short plants are up to about 12 inches in height, medium from 18 inches to 2½ feet and tall about three feet or more.

Annuals

A few of these are perennials which are best grown each year from seed.

Ageratum. Bluish-mauve, dwarf, summer.
Alyssum. White or mauve, dwarf, summer.
Anchusa. Blue, medium, spring or summer.
Arctotis acaulis. All colours, trailing, spring.
Brachycome iberidifolia (Swan River Daisy). All shades, dwarf, summer, spring.
Chareis heterophylla. (True Blue Daisy.) Blue, dwarf, spring.
Chrysanthemum, Annual. All colours, short, summer.
Convolvulus minor. Blue, trailing, summer.
Cotula. Yellow, dwarf, spring.
Cuphea miniata (Fire-fly). Reddish, short, summer.
Cynoglossum. Blue, medium, summer.
Dahlia, Coltness Hybrids. Bright colours, short, summer.
Dimorphotheca sinuata (Namaqualand Daisy). Orange and yellow, short, spring.
Dorotheanthus bellidiformis (Bokbaai Vygie). Bright colours, dwarf, spring.
Eschscholtzia californica (Californian Poppy). Orange and mixed hybrids, short, summer.
Felicia bergeriana (Kingfisher Daisy). Blue, dwarf, spring.
Gaillardia. Orange or red, short or medium, summer.

Heliphila. Blue, short, spring.
Linaria—Fairy Bouquet. All colours, short, spring, summer.
Linum grandiflorum (Flax). Red, short, summer.
Lobelia erinus (Edging Lobelia). Blue, dwarf, spring and summer.
Lychnis. Pinks, reds, short, summer.
Matricaria. Yellow, white, short, summer.
Marigold. Yellow, orange, dwarf types, summer.
Myosotis (Forget-me-not). Blue, pink, dwarf, spring. (Shade).
Nemesia strumosa (Cape Jewels). All colours, short, spring.
Nemophila. Blue, short, summer.
Oxypetalum. Blue, short, summer.
Petunia. All shades, medium, summer.
Phacelia. Blue, medium, summer, spring.
Phlox drummondii nana. All shades, short, summer.
Portulaca grandiflora. All shades, short, summer.
Sanvitalia procumbens (Creeping Zinnia). Orange, dwarf, summer.
Schizanthus (Poor Man's Orchid). Pale shades, medium, spring.
Senecio elegans. Mauve, medium, spring.
Tagetes (Marigold). Orange, dwarf, summer.
Torenia fournieri (Wishbone flower). Blue, dwarf, summer. (Shade).
Tropaeolum majus (Nasturtium). Orange and yellow, trailing, summer.
Ursinia anethoides. Orange, short, spring.
Venidium fastuosum (Double Namaqualand Daisy). Orange, tall, spring. (Large rockery).
Verbena. All shades, short, spreading, spring.

Perennials for the Rockery

Arctotis squarrosa. Orange flowers, spreading, spring.
Alyssum saxatile. Golden yellow flowers, grey foliage, short, spring or summer.
Anemone japonica (Japanese Anemone). Pink, white, tall (Shade).
Bergenia (Megasea or Saxifraga). Pink flowers, spreading, winter or spring.
Cerastium tomentosum (Snow-in-Summer). White flowers, grey foliage, dwarf, spreading, summer.
Chironia baccifera. Pink flowers, red berries, short, summer and autumn.
Cineraria saxifraga. Yellow flowers, trailing, spring, summer and autumn.
Dianthus caesius (Cheddar Pink). Pink flowers, grey foliage, short, spring.
Diascia integerrima. Pink, short, spring and summer.
Echinacea purpurea (*Rudbeckia purpurea*). (Pink Coneflower), pink flowers, tall, summer.
Erigeron karvinskianus (Santa Barbara Daisy). White dwarf, summer, keep in check.
Felicia rotundifolia. Blue, medium, spring and summer.
Gazania longiscapa. Yellow, orange, red, buff, short, spring or early summer.
Gazania pavonia. Terracotta flowers, dwarf, spring.
Gazania uniflora (Trailing Gazania). Yellow flowers, grey foliage, spring and early summer.
Geranium incanum. Mauve flowers, spreading, summer.

*See *South African Wild Flowers for the Garden* by Sima Eliovson.

Gerbera jamesoni (Barberton Daisy). All shades, short, spring and summer.

Helichrysum argyrophyllum. Golden everlasting flowers, silvery foliage, low, spreading, autumn, spring.

Hemerocallis (Day-Lilies). Yellow or reddish flowers, tall, summer.

Leonotis leonurus (Lion's Ear). Orange, very tall, shrub-like, autumn.

Limonium latifolium (*Statice latifolia*). Lilac flowers, medium, winter, summer.

Limonium roseum (Sea Lavender). Pink, medium, summer.

Lychnis coronaria (Rose Campion). Cerise flowers, downy leaves, medium, summer.

Nepeta mussini (Catmint). Mauve flowers, grey foliage, short, spreading, summer.

Nierembergia. Mauve, short, early summer.

Osteospermum ecklonis. (Blue-and-White Daisy Bush). White flowers, blue centres, tall, winter and spring.

Pelargonium (all species). All colours, tall, spreading, spring, summer.

Plectranthus (all species). (Spur Flower.) Blue and pink flowers, tall, spreading, summer and autumn (shade).

Potentilla. Yellow and red, low, spreading, summer.

Pyrethrum. All colours, short, summer.

Streptocarpus. All colours, short, shade-loving.

Sutera grandiflora (Wild Phlox). Mauve, very tall, spring to autumn.

Sutherlandia frutescens (Balloon-Pea). Red flowers, green pods, tall, winter and spring.

Ursinia sericea. Yellow flowers, grey foliage, medium, spring.

Small Shrubs for the Rockery

Barleria obtusa. Mauve flowers, spreading, 2 to 3 feet, autumn.

Ceratostigma. Blue, 3 feet, summer, deciduous, cut back each year.

Chorizema cordatum (Flame Pea). Orange and purple flowers, 2 feet, spring, evergreen.

Coleonema pulchrum (Confetti Bush). Pink, 4 feet, winter, evergreen.

Diplopappus filifolius (Wild Aster). Pinkish-mauve, 3 feet, spring, evergreen.

Encephalartos (Cycad). Dwarf forms, 3 to 6 feet, evergreen foliage.

Erica (all species). (Heath.) All colours, every month of year, evergreen.

Erythrina acanthocarpa (Tambookie Thorn). 4 feet, red and greenish flowers, spring, deciduous.

Euphorbia fulgens (*E. jacquiniflora*). Scarlet. 3 feet, spring, evergreen, tender.

Fabiana imbricata (Chile-heath). White, 5 feet, spring, evergreen.

Gamolepis chrysanthemoides (Daisy Bush). Yellow flowers, late summer, 4 feet, evergreen, cut back after flowering.

Hebe speciosa. Pink, mauve, purple, 3 feet, winter and spring, evergreen.

Lavandula (Lavender). Grey foliage, 3 feet, spring, evergreen.

Leucadendron grandiflorum (Rose Cockade). Rose bracts, 4 feet, spring, evergreen.

Leucospermum nutans (Pincushion Flower). Orange, 4 feet, spreading, autumn to spring, evergreen.

Mackaya bella. Mauve, 4 feet, spring, evergreen. (Shade).

Mimetes lyrigera. Red bracts, 4 feet, spring, evergreen.

Ochna atropurpurea (Carnival Bush). Yellow, 6 feet, spring, evergreen.

Podalyria sericea. Mauve, 3 feet, autumn, silvery foliage, evergreen.

Protea cynaroides (King Protea). Pink, 4 feet, winter and spring, evergreen.

Protea nana (Mountain Rose). Red, 3 feet, spring, evergreen.

Punica granatum nana (Dwarf Pomegranate). Red, 18 inches, summer.

Reinwardtia indica (Yellow Flax). Yellow, 3 feet, winter, evergreen.

Serruria florida (Blushing Bride). Pink, 4 feet, winter, evergreen.

Spiraea, Anthony Waterer (Red May). Red, 3 feet, spring. deciduous.

Spiraea arguta (Garland May). White, 3 feet, spring, deciduous.

Strelitzia reginae (Crane Flower). Orange and blue, 3 feet, spring, evergreen.

Large Shrubs and Small Trees for the Large Rockery

Berzelia species. White, 6 feet, winter and spring, evergreen, moisture.

Brunia species. White or red, 6 feet, winter and spring, evergreen.

Callistemon viminalis (Weeping Bottlebrush). Scarlet, spring, 10 feet, evergreen.

Callistemon speciosus (Tree Bottlebrush). Scarlet, spring, 10 feet, evergreen.

Chamaelaucium uncinatum (Geraldton Waxflower). Pink, 8 feet, spring, summer, evergreen.

Cussonia paniculata (Cabbage Tree). Grey foliage, 10 feet, semi-evergreen.

Daubentonia (*Sesbania*). Orange, 8 feet, early summer, deciduous.

Dais cotinifolia (Pompon Tree). Pink, 12 feet, early summer, deciduous.

Erythrina crista-gallii (Coral Tree). Red, 10 feet, summer, deciduous.

Erythrina humeana (Hume's Kaffirboom). Red, 8 feet, summer, deciduous.

Greyia sutherlandii (Mountain Bottlebrush). Red, 8 feet, spring, deciduous.

Iboza riparia (Misty Plume Bush). Mauve, 6 feet, early spring, deciduous.

Leptospermum species (Tea Tree). Pink or white, 8 feet, winter, evergreen.

Leucadendron argenteum (Silver Tree). Silver leaves, 20 feet, evergreen.

Leucadendron salignum (Geelbos, Gold-tips). Yellow bracts, 6 feet, spring, evergreen.

Nymania capensis (Klapperbos). Pink pods, 9 feet, spring, evergreen, needs dry summer.

Rhigozum obovatum (Karoo Gold). Yellow flowers, 8 feet, spring, evergreen.

Schotia brachypetala (Weeping Boerboon). Crimson, early summer, 10 feet, semi-evergreen.

Succulents for the Rockery

Aloe, all species. All through year, dwarf to tall, evergreen, scarlet, orange, yellow.

Bulbine, several. Yellow, summer, low, spreading, evergreen, endures poor soil. (Shade.)

Cotyledon species. Grey or green leaves, coral flowers, medium, evergreen.

Cissus juttae. Red grape-like fruits, 4-foot trunk, autumn deciduous.

Crassula falcata (Red Crassula). Red flowers, grey leaves, 2 feet, summer, evergreen.

Crassula portulacea (Pink Joy). Pink, 6 feet, autumn and winter, evergreen.

Lampranthus species (Mesembs). All colours, low, spreading, spring, evergreen.

Rochea coccinea (Red Crassula). Red, 18 inches, summer, evergreen. (Shade.)

Echevaria. Grey rosettes, low, spreading, evergreen.

Euphorbia, many varieties.

Sedum (Stone Crop). Evergreen, low, spreading mats of leaves, pink or red flowers, foliage colours often red in winter.

Sedum spectabile. Mauve flowers, bluish-grey leaves, 2 feet, autumn. (Shade.)

Stapelia. Carrion Flower. Curious flowers, low foliage good for dry corners between rocks.

Bulbs for the Rockery

Agapanthus. Blue, white, deciduous and evergreen, summer.

Aristea. Blue, evergreen, spring and summer. (Shade.)

Babiana. Short, all colours, spring, deciduous.

Billbergia. Cerise, winter, evergreen, low.

Bulbinella. Yellow, winter, deciduous, 2 feet.

Clivia. Orange shades, medium, summer, evergreen. (Shade.)

Crinum moorei. Pink, tall, summer, deciduous. (Shade.)

Cyrtanthus (Ifafa Lilies). Pink, yellow, white, short spring, semi-evergreen.

Dierama (Harebells). Pink and mauve, tall, summer, evergreen.

Dietes (Wild Iris). White, yellow, tall, summer, evergreen.

Eucomis (Pineapple Flowers). Green, summer, tall, deciduous.

Galtonia (Summer Hyacinth). White, summer, tall, deciduous.

Haemanthus (Torch Lilies). Red, spring, summer and autumn, short and medium, deciduous, shade-loving.

Kniphofia (Red Hot Poker). Scarlet, orange, summer and winter, tall, evergreen.

Moraea spathulata. Yellow, spring or autumn, medium, evergreen.

Nerine filifolia. Pink, autumn, short, evergreen.

Nerine masonorum. Pink, autumn, short, evergreen.

Ornithogalum saundersiae. White, summer, tall, deciduous.

Ranunculus. All colours, spring, short, deciduous, moist soil.

Scilla natalensis. Blue, spring, tall, deciduous.

Tulbaghia fragrans (Sweet Garlic). Mauve, winter, short, semi-deciduous.

Tulbaghia violacea (Wild Garlic). Mauve, summer, short, evergreen.

Watsonia, all colours. Summer and autumn, tall, evergreen.

Zantedeschia pentlandii (Yellow Arum). Yellow, medium, summer, deciduous.

Zantedeschia rehmannii (Pink Arum). Pink, short, early summer, deciduous.

CHAPTER NINE

GARDENING IN THE SHADE

Those with new gardens to lay out seldom have shady places and do not have the older gardener's problem of what to plant in the shade. The need for the knowledge of which plants will thrive in the shade, however, grows with one's trees. It is as well to realise what will happen when these are grown and to have an idea of what to plant there in the future.

It is a distinctive feature of most Southern African homes to boast a line of Hydrangeas along the shady south wall. Although these are very beautiful during summer, one often wishes that they would not be used so inevitably along the south wall as well as in most other shady spots in the garden. It adds considerably to the interest of the garden if one has a long list of plants to choose from when considering what to plant in a shady spot.

This chapter will be devoted to lists of plants which will grow in the shade, but it is first necessary to describe the type of shade one finds in a garden and also the requirements that the plants will need for successful cultivation.

How to Tell which Plants are Shade-Lovers

Sunlight is the chief requirement of plants, which use it to build up energy and grow vigorously. Most plants need sunlight for at least half the day, particularly before midday, when they are building up a new supply of sugar for the day. It is not known scientifically why some plants can thrive with less sunlight than others. Many shade-lovers, like *Impatiens*, have comparatively broad thin leaves which are spread out to catch the light, while others have tough thick leaves, like *Rhododendron*. On the whole, they have broad leaves, but when one thinks of the numerous sun-loving plants with broad leaves like Poinsettia, then one realises that there are no hard and fast rules to follow in recognising those plants which will thrive in the shade. One has simply to depend on the experience of gardeners who have actually grown certain plants in shady places for generations.

A study of where plants come from in the wild and how they grow will immediately indicate whether they are shade-lovers or not. If they grow in nature in the woods or under rocks, then it can be presumed that they will enjoy shade in the garden. Sometimes, however, they need different treatment on being grown in a country with a different climate. Plants which grow happily in the open sun in countries which have soft sunshine and very few cloudless days will require a certain amount of shade in warmer and drier countries. For example, tulips grow in the open in Holland, while they need a certain amount of shade in the hotter parts of South Africa if they are to do well. In the south-western Cape, again, they will do perfectly well in the open, for there is less sunlight available during the rainy winter there than there is during the sunny winters of the Transvaal and Rhodesia. In addition, these delicate flowers bloom in spring, when the dry heat of the highveld or the Rhodesian spring would shorten their flowering period considerably or wither their blooms. Tulips are now especially treated to resist heat.

The necessity for shade and moisture are often irrevocably bound together, for shade prevents those plants which need plenty of moisture from losing it too rapidly from their leaves. Plants which grow out in the open sun on the seacoast where there is humidity, will often require to be grown in the shade in hot dry places inland. Hydrangeas and Azaleas, for example, will grow in the open sun at the coast in South Africa, but need shade in the dry inland districts, or they will flag within a few hours on a hot day. In fact, it is advisable to spray their foliage with water on hot and windy days, for the wind removes moisture rapidly from leaf surfaces.

Types of Shade. When we talk of shade in the garden, we do not mean black shade where very few plants of any consequence will grow. There are some notable exceptions to this rule, such as the spectacular flowered Clivia which is very tough and easy to grow. But this plant, too, will do better if it receives reflected light around it. Areas which receive no direct sunshine at all, but where there is light available, are described as having full shade. Plants like ferns and many others from woodlands, thrive in such areas with full shade.

Semi-shade is the term used to describe places which receive direct sunlight for about two or three hours during the day. Plants on the east or south-east side of a house will receive sun for a short period in the morning and be shaded for the remainder of the day, so that they are growing in semi-shade. Plants on a south-west wall will also receive some afternoon sunlight, but this will not be as beneficial, for it falls when the plant has already built up its daily supply of energy.

Semi-shade also describes the area under trees like *Melia azedarach*, which filters the sunshine through its light foliage on to the soil below. The sun may also strike the ground under tall dense trees like Pines for several hours, so that the plants growing there may also be described as growing in semi-shade. The lower branches of tall evergreen trees may be removed so as to allow more light to fall on the plants beneath them.

Most plants need sunlight in order to thrive and will become spindly in the shade. There are some, such as *Nicotiana* and *Campanula*, which will grow equally well in the sun or in subdued light and these are therefore valuable to the gardener as shade-tolerant plants.

Many of the plants listed below will grow perfectly well in the open sun, particularly if they are well watered, but it is found they can adapt themselves to grow in the shade and are therefore classed as shade-lovers. They should receive as much light and air as possible around them, even if they receive no direct sunlight. Some of the plants do better if they receive some sunshine and these have been classed as those requiring semi-shade.

It is an interesting fact that plants with gold and green variegated leaves generally lose their golden mottling in shady places. This is attributed to the fact that plants produce more chlorophyll or green matter in the shade in the effort to grow well. Chlorophyll converts sunlight into sugar and energy for the plant, and, the more chlorophyll the plant can produce, the more it can trap the meagre light it receives under trees and in other shady places. Oddly enough, there are certain variegated shrubs like the Snow-bush (*Breyia nivosa*) which must be grown in the shade and are popular as indoor pot-plants where they do not lose their white-tipped colouring. Thus one has to know one's plants before subjecting them to strict rules and regulations.

House-plants must of necessity be shade-tolerant, but will be listed in a separate chapter. (Chapter 34.)

CULTIVATION OF SHADE-LOVING PLANTS

Plants which grow in the shade generally grow under trees, so that they have not only to struggle for light, but have to compete with the tree roots for moisture and soil nutriments. It follows, therefore, that the gardener must take care to provide a good soil and plenty of moisture if he wants to grow his plants successfully.

When first preparing a shady spot, one must loosen the soil to a depth of anything from 9 inches down to 2 feet, depending on the size of the plants to be used. Remove some of the soil if it is poor and then add as many barrow-loads of humus as one can. Well-rotted leaf-mould or compost made with manure is ideal. Fertilizers or manure on their own will not improve the quality of the soil and it is important that the ground should be softened so that the small plant roots can penetrate it easily. The fibrous loam will also be able to absorb moisture better and retain it longer. An examination of the soil in natural woodland, where shade-loving plants are found, will indicate how rich and loamy it is, as a result of the decay of continuously falling leaves. Woodland plants, therefore, need exceptionally good soil if they are to do as well in the garden as they do in the wild. Annual dressings of compost laid on the surface of the soil or lightly forked in, will continue to keep the soil in good condition.

Once the plants are in position they must be watered regularly and deeply. It is best to place a garden spray on the bed and let it soak down into the surface for a period of at least half an hour or more. This will provide adequate moisture for the trees as well as for the shade-loving plants. As a rule it is best to water again as soon as the soil begins to dry out near the surface, but one should not allow the area to dry out completely. As shade helps to conserve moisture, it should not be necessary to water more than twice a week, unless the weather is very hot and dry.

Some plants are more drought-resistant than others. Succulents, perennials or bulbs with large fleshy roots like Haemanthus or Agapanthus can do without water much more readily than fibrous rooted plants like Azaleas or delicate annuals like Primulas. Small plants must be watered more frequently than deep-rooting shrubs, but certain shrubs like Hydrangeas need constant moisture during summer in order to do really well. The gardener's own knowledge of his plants will indicate how often to water, but as a rule, none should be allowed to dry out completely in the shade or the tree roots will rob the smaller plants of all the available moisture. Try to group the types of plants which require plenty of moisture near one another and place those which are better able to resist drought in the further corners of the garden, where, if they are sometimes overlooked, they will not suffer unduly. If the soil is reasonably good, underplant trees with groundcovers like Wild Strawberry, Japanese Spurge or evergreen grasses like Kentucky Blue-grass. These will have to be watered regularly throughout the year and fertilized occasionally. If the soil is dry, poor or shallow, however, grow shade-tolerant succulents instead. (See list below.) Group the easy-to-grow plants in dense shade near the trunk of the tree and those which require more sunlight and, possibly, better soil, on the outskirts of the tree's shade.

Trees and Types of Undergrowth. Certain trees are better than others from the point of view of underplanting. On the whole, deep-rooting trees like Pines and Gums are better than surface-rooting trees like Oaks or Elms. The falling leaves and needles of evergreens can smother small plants, but should not be a problem if large shrubs or vigorous perennials are used.

One should choose plants with strong-rooting systems to place beneath or alongside trees like Virgilia, which has masses of spreading fibrous roots near the surface of the soil. Do not be afraid of planting under this type of tree, as it actually benefits the tree to have the plants around it. Fibrous-rooted trees are generally lovers of moisture and they enjoy the extra moisture they receive when the smaller plants are well watered. It is, therefore, of mutual benefit to trees and the plants around them to keep them well watered.

There are many trees which have root systems that do not interfere very much with the surface soil, particularly if the soil is good and deep. *Melia azedarach* is a particularly suitable tree to underplant, as it has light shade in summer and its roots do not lie at the surface of the soil. Small trees like the Weeping Bottlebrush (*Callistemon viminalis*), the Brush-Cherry (*Eugenia australis*) or Spring Tamarisk (*Tamarix gallica*) will provide light shade during part of the day and are quite useful for those plants requiring semi-shade.

One can avoid the roots of trees by sinking barrels or drums containing good soil into the ground where it is feared that tree root competition will eventually weaken the plants. Such containers eventually rot and one is then in the same position as before. One successful gardener I know prevents this by fairly unorthodox means, contriving to grow precious Rhododendrons beneath rampant Gum trees. He makes a "container" of concrete by scooping out a large deep hole, at least 4 feet across and lining it with a 3-inch wall of rough concrete and stone. This is filled with good soil mixed with peat and compost and the plants thrive happily in it. There is no drainage, so that this method would only be successful in places with a dry atmosphere as on the high-veld inland. Such a concrete trough can be made to create wet conditions for plants like Japanese Iris, but one must be careful not to overwater during the dormant period.

There should be no need to sink containers into the soil, however, if one has dug it well and is prepared to water and feed regularly. Most important of all, one should choose the correct plants to withstand the competition with tree roots.

Treatment of the Area under a Shade Tree. There are various ways in which one can make use of the shade

from trees without necessarily competing with their roots. This can be done by raising the surface of the soil by as little as 12 inches. One should not bury the tree trunk in soil or rot may set in and eventually result in the death of the tree.

The simplest way to avoid tree roots is to plant the tree at the foot of a rockery so that its spreading branches can shade the rockery while its roots spread freely on a lower soil surface. This surface can be covered by strong plants like Ivy or Periwinkle or even Agapanthus, while the delicate plants needing rich, light soil, like Heuchera or Japanese anemones, can be grown in the rockery pockets above.

One sometimes has an established large shade tree on a flat surface in the garden where one cannot construct a rockery, however. During the passage of years, the lawn has deteriorated due to the lack of light and one decides to underplant the tree with other plants. If one makes a large bed around the tree, filling it with strong plants, then one is deprived of a shady place where one can sit in the garden. The best thing to do is to construct a small raised portion curving around half the tree and to make a paved area on the other half. The paved area should be north or south of the tree, depending on whether one wants winter sunshine to fall on the north side or not.

Begin by arranging a tiny wall of stones half-way around the tree-trunk and about 12 inches away from the bark. Then build outwards as far as desired. The outside edge of this raised bed may be a formal wall of brick or thick strips of slate laid horizontally, or it may have the informal finish of rocks as in a rockery. The height of this raised bed can be anything from 6 to 18 inches. Low beds can be used for small bushy plants like *Begonia semperflorens* or Polyanthus Primroses, while higher beds can be used for taller drooping plants like Fuchsias or *Abutilon megapotamicum*, which will overhang the wall. If desired, a seat may be built into part of the wall.

If one wishes to surround the tree completely by a raised bed, then one should continue the internal wall right around the tree, but leave at least a foot of space all around the bark to form a small well. In this way, it is possible to make use of an established tree right in the centre of a new rockery which is being constructed from a higher to a lower level and which encompasses the tree. The tree will continue to grow and breathe freely without rotting. Remember to water the tree through this "well" occasionally, as well as soak the rockery.

If one must pave the area entirely around a tree, leave

PLAN

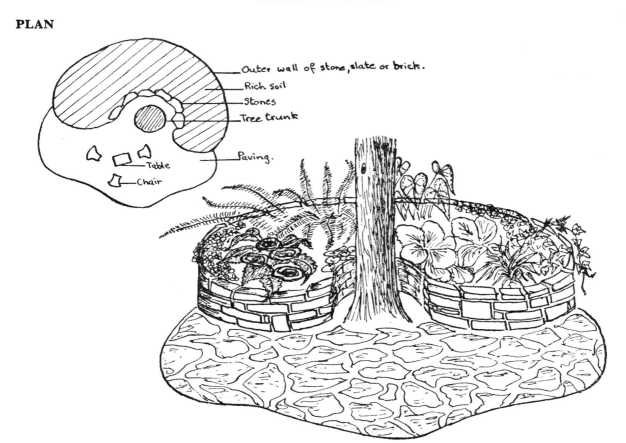

Outer wall of stone, slate or brick.
Rich soil
Stones
Tree trunk

Paving.

Table
Chair

a few feet open near the base of the tree and plant it with an evergreen groundcover. Sink a few wide vertical pipes into the soil for extra feeding and watering of the tree.

CHOOSING PLANTS FOR SHADY PLACES

Lists of plants which will grow in the shade also appear in the Chapters on "Groundcovers", "Trees and shrubs" and elsewhere. In order to make the choice easier, however, these plants are grouped here together with other plants, according to the type of soil they need and their ability to compete with tree roots. The plants are further divided into three sections, according to their ease of culture and maintenance. The following abbreviations are used to save space:

Ev = Evergreen. D = Deciduous. F = will grow in Full shade. S = Semi-shade. Fls. = Flowers.

Many of these plants will also grow in full sunlight, but this will not be noted here.

SECTION I

SHADE-TOLERANT PLANTS WHICH GROW EASILY IN SPITE OF ROOT COMPETITION FROM TREES

These may be planted under trees which have spreading fibrous roots near the surface, such as Elm or Virgilia. Water regularly. Some will tolerate dryness more than others.

Shrubs

Athanasia parviflora. Coulter-Bush. Ev. 6 feet. Yellow fls. S.

Berberis julianae. Wintergreen Barberry. Ev. 5 feet, Yellow fls. S.

Berberis stenophylla. Ev. 6 feet. Yellow fls. S.

Ceratostigma plumbaginoides and *C. wilmottianum.* 1 to 3 feet. Blue fls. S.

Cotoneaster horizontalis. D. 3 feet. Red berries. F or S.

Cotoneaster microphyllus Ev. 3 feet. Red berries. F or S.

Chaenomeles lagenaria. Japanese Flowering Quince. D. 6 feet. Red or white. F or S.

Lonicera heckrottii. Bush Honeysuckle. Ev. 4 feet. Pink fls. S.

Mahonia aquifolium. Holly Mahonia. Ev. 4 feet. Yellow fls. F or S.

Melianthus major. Honey-flower. 7 feet. Dies down if cold. Maroon fls. S.

Melianthus minor. 3 feet. Ev. if mild winter. S.

Spiraea. May. Most species. 3 to 6 feet. D. White, pink red. S.

Climbers. Use these as groundcovers if liked.

Asparagus asparagoides. Smilax. Ev. 6 feet. F or S.

Asparagus plumosus. Asparagus Fern. Ev. 10 feet F or S.

Asparagus sprengeri. Basket Asparagus. Ev. 5 feet. Red berries. F or S.

Hedera helix. English Ivy. Ev. Tall. F or S.

H. canariensis var. *variegata.* Variegated Canary Islands Ivy. Ev. S.

Jasminum officinale. Jasmine. D. 6 feet. White fls. F or S.

Lonicera japonica. Japanese Honeysuckle. Ev. 15 feet. White and yellow fls., F or S.

Parthenocissus tricuspidata. Boston Ivy or small-leaved Virginian Creeper. D. F or S.

Parthenocissus quinquefolia. True Virginian Creeper. D. F or S.

Trachelospermum jasminoides. Star-Jasmine. Ev. 6 feet. White. F or S.

Perennials

Ajuga reptans. Carpet bugle. Ev. Groundcover. Moisture. F or S.

Chlorophytum species. Hen-and-Chickens. Ev. Groundcover. 9 inches. F or S.

Hypoestes aristata. Ribbon Bush. D. 4 feet. Mauve fls. S.

Lamium maculatum. Dead-Nettle. Ev. groundcover to 10 inches. F or S.

Nepeta hederacea. Ground Ivy. Ev. flat groundcover. F or S.

Nepeta mussini. Catmint. 6 inches. Mauve fls. Grey lvs. S.

Nepeta nervosa. D. 1 to 2 feet. Blue fls. S.

Polygonum capitatum. Semi-ev. 6 inches. Groundcover. Pink fls. F or S.

Saponaria officinalis. Bouncing Bet, Soapwort. 1 to 3 feet. Pink fls. Dies down in winter. Can become a pest. F or S.

Tradescantia sp. Wandering Jew. Ev. Green foliage. Spreading. Tender. F or S.

Vinca major. Periwinkle. Ev. 1 foot. Groundcover. Blue fls. F or S.

Zebrina pendula. Wandering Jew. Ev. Purple, green and silver lvs. F or S.

Succulents. These will tolerate dryness, poor soil.

Bulbine alooides. Ev. Very shallow soil on rocks. Yellow fls. F or S.

Bulbine caulescens. Stalked Bulbine. Ev. 8 inches. Spreads. Yellow fls. F or S.

Crassula portulacea. Pink Joy. Ev. 6 feet. Pink fls. S.

Crassula multicava. Fairy Crassula. Ev. 4 inches. Pink fls. F or S.

Gasteria. Speckled tongue-shaped lvs. Pink fls. F or S.

Sedum spectabile. Ev. 2 feet. Mauve fls. Cut back. F or S.

Bulbous Plants

Agapanthus orientalis. Ev. 2 to 6 feet. Blue fls. Moisture all year. S.

Clivia, all species. Ev. 1½ feet. Orange fls. Moisture in summer. F or S.

Dietes vegeta. Ev. 3 feet. Blue and white fls. F or S.

Eucomis. Pineapple Flower. D. 1 to 6 feet. Hardy, moisture in summer. S.

Kniphofia. Red Hot Pokers. Ev. 3 feet. Orange fls. Moisture all year. S.

Liriope sp. Ev. 6 inches. Grassy leaves. Small whitish fls. F or S.

Ornithogalum caudatum. Ev. Insignificant fls., but grows easily under trees. Large bulb. 12 inches. F or S.

Sansevieria. Bowstring Hemp. Many sp. Ev. Poor dry soil under trees. F or S.

Scilla natalensis. Blue Squill. D. Blue flower spikes to 3 feet, moisture in summer. Good drainage necessary. Prefers rocks. S.

Scilla peruviana. Peruvian Squill. D. Low rosette. Blue fls. F or S.

SECTION II

SHADE-TOLERANT PLANTS NEEDING SLIGHTLY BETTER SOIL

These can be planted under deep-rooting trees like Grevillea or *Acacia elata.* Some will tolerate drier soils than Section III, but need regular watering.

Shrubs

Abelia grandiflora. Glossy Abelia. Ev. 4 feet. White fls. F or S.

Abutilon hybrids. Chinese Lanterns. Ev. 6 feet. Pink, orange, yellow. Moisture. F or S.

Burchellia bubalina. Wild Pomegranate. Ev. 10 feet. Red. Tender. S.

Carissa grandiflora. Natal Plum. Ev. 10 feet. White fls. red fruit. Tender. F or S.

Cestrum species. Semi-ev. 10 feet. Red, pink, purple, yellow. F or S.

Encephalartos villosus. Cycad. Ev. palm-like. 4 feet. Drainage. F or S.

Escallonia langleyensis. Semi-ev. 4 feet. Pink fls. Moisture. S.

Euonymus japonicus. Spindle Tree. Ev. 6 feet. Red berries. F or S.

Euonymus radicans. Winter-Creeper. Ev. Low. Green or variegated lvs. Moisture. F or S.

Feijoa sellowiana. Pineapple-Guava. Ev. 5 feet. Pink fls. S.

Forsythia. Golden-bells. D. 5 feet. Yellow fls. Moisture. F or S.

Hebe speciosa. Showy Hebe. Ev. 3 feet. Purple, red, pink. F or S.

Hypericum sp. Gold Flower. Ev. 4 to 6 feet. Yellow fls. F or S.

Ilex aquifolium. English Holly. Ev. 5 feet or more. Red berries. F or S.

Jochroma tubulosum. Blue Tube Flowers. Ev. 6 feet. Blue fls. S.

Kerria japonica flore-pleno. Globe Flower. D. 5 feet. Yellow fls. F or S.

Ligustrum. Privet. Ev. 8 feet. Green or variegated lvs. S.

Lippia citriodora. Lemon-Verbena. D. 6 feet. Scented fls. S.

Mackaya bella. Ev. 4 feet. Lilac fls. Tender. S.

Nandina domestica. D. 5 feet. Bamboo-like. Red berries. F or S.

Pittosporum, all species. Ev. 6 to 10 feet. Green foliage. S.

Plectranthus, all species. Ev. 2 to 5 feet. Blue or pink fls. Protect from frost. F or S.

Raphiolepis indica. Indian Hawthorn. Ev. 5 feet. Pink fls. S.

Sambucus. Elder. D. 5 feet. Suckering, finely cut foliage. S.

Climbers or Rambling Shrubs

Clytostoma callistegioides. Mauve Bignonia. Ev. Mauve fls. S.

Doxantha unguis-cati. Cat's-claw Creeper. Ev. Yellow fls. S.

Hardenbergia comptoniana. Lilac Vine. Ev. 6 feet. Purple fls. S.

Jasminum sambac. Arabian Jasmine. Ev. 5 feet. White fls. Tender. F or S.

Rhoicissus capensis. Wild Grape. Ev. 5 feet. Red fruit. Tender. S.

Senecio tamoides. Canary Creeper. Ev. or D. in cold places. Tall. Yellow fls. S.

Perennials

Many as in Section 1, *Ajuga, Asparagus,* Geraniums, etc.

Duchesnea indica. Wild Strawberry. Ev. groundcover. Red berries. F or S.

Erigeron sp. Ev. Dwarf, mauve fls. S.

Geum. Ev. 1 foot. Red or yellow fls. S.

Hemerocallis. Day-Lilies. Ev. 3 feet. Yellow or bronze fls. S.

Bergenia (Megasea, Saxifraga). Ev. 1 foot. Pink fls. S.

Billbergia. Ev. 18 inches. Cerise fls. Drought-resistant. F or S.

Campanula. D. 6 inches to 3 feet. Blue or white fls. S.

Pelargonium peltatum. Ev. Pink or lilac fls. Sprawling S.

Physostegia. Dragon's Teeth. D. 2 to 4 feet. Mauve. S.

Platycodon. D. 1 to 3 feet. Dark blue fls. S.

Rehmannia. D. 3 to 4 feet. Rose fls. Moisture. F or S.

Saxifraga sarmentosa. Strawberry Saxifrage. Ev. trailing. White fls. F or S.

Scabiosa africana. Wild Scabious. Semi-ev. 4 feet. Mauve fls. F or S.

Senecio petasitis. D. 6 feet. Large yellow heads. S.

Veronica sp. D. 2 feet. Blue or pink fls. S.

Vinca rosea (Lochnera rosea). Ev. 2 feet. Mauve or pink fls. Ever-blooming, sub-tropical. S.

Succulents

These are all evergreen and can grow right up against tree trunks. Shallow rooted, one should mix compost into the top 2 inches. They are drought-resistant, but need watering during the growing season. Drainage should be good. A slight slope is ideal.

Aloe thompsoniae. Ev. 10 inches. Orange fls. Moisture. F or S.

Crassula falcata and *C. perfoliata.* Ev. 1 to 3 feet. Red fls. S.

Kalanchoe. Many species. Ev. Tender. Red fls. F or S.

Oscularia caulescens. Scented Mesemb. 1 foot. Pale pink. F or S.

Rochea coccinea. Red Crassula. Ev. 18 inches. Crimson fls. S.

Bulbous Plants

Aristea. Ev. 1 to 3 feet. Blue fls. F or S.

Chasmanthe floribunda. Pennants. 3 feet. Dormant in summer. S.

Crinum moorei. Semi-ev. 3 feet. Pink fls. F or S.

Crocosmia aurea. Semi-ev. 2 feet. Orange fls. Dormant in winter. S.

Curtonus paniculatus. Pleated-Leaves. 3 feet. Dormant in winter. S.

Haemanthus, all species. Torch Lily, Snake-Lily, Paint-Brush. 6 inches to 3 feet. Scarlet or white fls. Mainly dormant in winter except for two from Cape. Good drainage. F or S.

Moraea ramosissima. 2 feet. Yellow fls. Dormant in summer. S.

Muscari botryoides. Grape Hyacinth. 6 to 9 inches. Dormant in midsummer. Blue fls. F or S.

Nerine sarniensis. Red Nerine. 1 foot. Dormant in summer, best in pots. F or S.

Nerine, all other species. 1 to 2 feet. Pink fls. Some evergreen, some dormant in winter. F or S.

Tritonia crocata, T. hyalina and *T. squalida,* Mossel Bay Kalkoentjies. 12 inches. Orange, salmon, pink. Dormant in summer, F or S.

Tritonia pottsii. Slender Tritonia. 3 feet. Dormant in winter. Red. fls. F or S.

Veltheimia viridifolia. Forest Lily. 18 inches. Semi-ev. Pink fls. F or S.

SECTION III

SHADE-LOVING PLANTS WHICH NEED GOOD SOIL AND MOISTURE

Many of these will grow under trees, but do well on the outskirts where the soil can be well prepared with plenty of compost. Permanent plants must have a layer of compost added annually. The plants listed below do well in shady rockeries or in the shade of the house. The tender plants can be grown in pots on the verandah. Some of these plants will tolerate drier conditions than others.

Shrubs

Acer palmatum. Japanese Maple. D. 3 to 5 feet. Pinnate foliage. Moisture. S.

Azaleas, Indian (*Rhododendron indicum*). Ev. 2 to 6 feet. Various colours. F or S.

Breynia nivosa. Snow-bush. Ev. 5 feet. Mottled foliage. Tender. F or S.

Camellia. Ev. 3 to 15 feet. Pink, red, white. Acidity. F or S.

Chimonanthus praecox. Winter-sweet. D. 8 feet. Yellow, scented fls. F or S.

Clerodendrum speciosissimum (C. fallax). Ev. 3 feet. Herbaceous. Tender. Scarlet. S.

Daphne odora. Ev. 4 feet. White pink. Acidity. Drainage. F or S.

Deutzia sp. Bridal Wreath. D. 5 feet. White fls. S.

Eupatorium sp. Giant Ageratum. Ev. 5 feet. Violet fls. Protect from frost. F or S.

Elaeagnus pungens. Ev. 5 feet. Also variegated gold and green lvs. F or S.

Fuchsia hybrids. Ev. 2 to 6 feet. Pink, purple fls. Protect in winter. F or S.

Gardenia, all species. Ev. 3 to 8 feet. White, waxy fls. Acidity. S.

Heliotropium. Cherry Pie. Ev. 2 to 4 feet. Purple or lilac. S.

Hydrangea macrophylla. D. 2 to 8 feet. Blue or pink fls. Moisture. F or S.

Jacobinia carnea (Justicia). Pink Jacobinia. Ev. 4 feet. Pink fls. Tender. F or S.

Michelia fuscata. Port Wine Magnolia. Ev. 5 feet. Wine fls. F or S.

Philadelphus coronarius. Mock-Orange. D. 8 feet. White fls. S.

Potentilla fruticosa. Ev. 4 feet. Yellow fls. S.

Prunus laurocerasus. English Laurel. Ev. 15 feet. Glossy lvs. S.

Rhododendron hybrids. Ev. 2 to 6 feet. Pink, purple, white. Acidity. Moisture. F or S.

Sparmannia africana. Ev. 15 feet. White fls. Tender. F or S.

Symphoricarpos albus. Snow-berry. D. 4 feet. White berries. F or S.

Symphoricarpos orbiculatus. Coral-Berry. D. 4 feet. Coral berries. F or S.

Syringa villosa. Late Lilac. D. 8 feet. Pink fls. F or S.

Syringa vulgaris hybrids. Lilac. D. 10 feet. Lilac, pink, white. Moisture. F or S.

Viburnum opulus. Guelder Rose. D. 10 feet. White flowers, red berries. F or S.

Viburnum opulus sterile. Snowball Bush. D. 10 feet. Large balls of white fls., no berries. F or S.

Weigela florida and hybrids. D. 5 feet. Red, pink, white. S.

Climbers and Trailing Shrubs

Abutilon megapotamicum. Ev. 5 feet. Drooping sprays of red and yellow fls. F or S.

Clematis hybrids. D. 9 feet. Large fls. Morning sun. S.

Clematis montana rubens. D. Root in shade, emerges above to flower in sunshine. Pink fls. S.

Clerodendrum splendens. Climbing Scarlet Clerodendron. Ev. 4-inch heads of scarlet fls. Tender. S.

Clerodendrum thompsoniae. Bleeding Heart Clerodendron. D. Drooping sprays of flowers, inflated white calyx and pendulous red fls. F or S.

Ficus pumila. Creeping Fig. Ev. Tiny round lvs., clings. F or S.

Hedera helix. English Ivy. Ev. clinging. Also small-leaved varieties. F or S.

Hedera canariensis variegata. Variegated Canary Islands Ivy. Green and white lvs. S.

Hoya carnosa. Wax Plant. Ev. Pink fls. Tender. Tub on verandah. F or S.

Lonicera sempervirens. Ev. Coral. Tender. S.

Maurandia barclaiana. Ev. purple fls. S.

Monstera deliciosa. Ev. slit lvs. Outdoors under trees in low-veld etc. otherwise indoors. F or S.

Podranea brycei. Zimbabwe creeper. Ev. Pink fls. Will climb up trees. S.

Stephanotis floribunda. Ev. White fls. Shelter from frost. S.

Sollya heterophylla. Bluebell Creeper. Ev. Blue fls. S.

Trachelospermum jasminoides. Star-Jasmine. Ev. Fragrant, white fls. F or S.

Perennials

Need good soil and moisture.

Anemone japonica. Japanese Anemone. 3 feet. Dormant in winter. Pink or white fls. F or S.

Acanthus. Grecian Leaf. 6 feet. Semi-dormant in mid-summer. Large leaves. Whitish fls. F or S.

Aquilegia. Columbine. 2 feet. All colours. Biennial. F or S.

Astilbe. 2 feet. Dormant in winter. Red, pink, white. Moisture. F or S.

Begonia coccinea. Ev. except in cold areas. Coral red fls., ever-blooming. Tender. F or S.

Begonia semperflorens and others. 1 to 6 feet. Pink, red, white, F or S.

Bellis perennis. English Daisy. 6 inches. Pink, white. Biennial, treat as annual. F or S.

Browallia major. 12 to 18 inches. Ev. in mild areas, pots in cold places. Blue fls. F or S.

Calceolaria. 2 to 3 feet. Yellow, tan. F or S.

Campanula. Canterbury Bells. Biennial. Blue or pink. F or S.

Cineraria hybrids. 18 inches, all colours. Biennial, pot or garden. F or S.

Cineraria saxifraga. Ev. spreading groundcover. Tiny yellow fls. S.

Coleus. Ev. ornamental coloured leaves. Outdoors in summer or pot plants. F or S.

Dicentra spectabilis. Bleeding Heart. 2 feet. Crimson fls. Moisture in summer. Dies down in winter. Shelter. S.

Dichorisandra thyrsiflora. Blue-flowered Bamboo. 6 feet. Dormant in winter. Pot plant in cold areas. F.

Digitalis. Foxglove. 4 feet. Biennial. Mauve, pink, white. F or S.

Fatsia papyrifera. (*Tetrapanax*) Ev. 6 feet. Large fig-like lvs. Suckers. S.

Ferns, Hardy. See under House Plants. F or S.

Gloxinia. 1 foot. Rich colours. See House Plants. F.

Helxine soleirolii. Baby's Tears. Mossy groundcover. F or S.

Heuchera. Coral-bells. 18 inches. Coral fls. S.

Impatiens. Zanzibar Balsam. 2 to 4 feet. Ev. in mild areas. Treat as summer annual in cold places. Moisture. Red shades. F or S.

Lilies. Grow during summer. Afternoon shade or sun.

Lobelia cardinalis. 3 feet. Scarlet fls. bronze lvs. Semi-dormant in winter. F or S.

Lunaria annua. Honesty. 2 feet. Biennial. Grown for silvery seed-pods, pink fls. unimportant. F or S.

Mimulus tigrinus. Monkey flower. Yellow or tan. Moisture. F or S.

Myosotis. Forget-me-Not. Blue fls. Treat as annual. Moisture. F or S.

Paeonia hybrids. Peony. 3 feet. Dormant in winter. Light shade, but prefers full sun. Pink, white, mauve. Do not plant deep.

Phlox paniculata. Perennial Phlox. 1 to 4 feet. White, purple, rose shades. Dormant in winter. Light shade or sun.

Phygelius capensis. River Bells. Ev. 3 feet. Red fls. May die down in cold winters. Moisture. F or S.

Potentilla sp. Pink or yellow fls. S.

Primula polyantha. Polyanthus Primroses. 6 inches. Mixed colours. Dormant in summer. Rich soil. S.

Primula obconica. 9 inches. Large mauve fls. Pot plant. F or S.

Saintpaulia. African Violet. Ev. Purple, pink. Pots. S.

Streptocarpus, species and hybrids. Cape Primrose. Some evergreen, others dormant in winter. Good on rocks or as pot plant. Pink, mauve, red fls. F or S.

Thalictrum dipterocarpum. Ev. 3 to 5 feet. Fern-like lvs. mauve fls. F or S.

Violets. Ev. 6 to 12 inches. Purple and pink and white. Moisture. F or S.

Annuals

Browallia elata. 1 foot. Blue, white. Summer. F or S.

Clarkia. 2 feet. Spring. Pink shades. S.

Cynoglossum. Chinese Forget-me-not. 1 to 2 feet. Summer. F or S.

Lobelia erinus. 4 inches. Blue. All year. F or S.

Nicotiana. Tobacco Flower. Continuously. Many colours. F. or S.

Nigella. Love-in-a-Mist. Blue or white. Moisture. S.

Pansy. 6 to 8 inches. Many colours. Winter to spring. S.

Primula malacoides. 9 inches. Winter to spring. F or S.

Schizanthus. Poor Man's Orchid. All colours. Winter to spring. Shelter. S.

Torenia fournieri. Wishbone Flower. 6 inches. Lilac and violet fls. Also pot plants. Summer in cold places. F or S.

Viola. 3 to 6 inches. Blue, apricot, yellow, maroon. All year from autumn. S.

Bulbous Plants

Anemone coronaria hybrids. 6 to 12 inches. Mainly blues and reds. Afternoon shade.

Alstroemeria. 1 to 3 feet. Pink, red, orange. S.

Begonias, tuberous. One to 2 ft. All colours, dormant in winter. F or S.

Cyclamen neapolitanum. Hardy Cyclamen. Miniature with pink fls. Under trees. F or S. Cyclamen hybrids are better indoors as pot plants.

Dierama, all species. Hare-bells. Ev. 1 to 3 feet. Pink, white, yellow, purple. Moisture in summer. S.

Freesia, all species. 1 foot. All colours. Plant in autumn for spring bloom. F or S.

Gladiolus, many spring-flowering species. 1 to 3 feet. Dormant in summer. S.

Gloriosa, all kinds. Flame Lily. Orange, red, yellow. Climb to 3 to 4 feet, need support. Dormant in winter. S.

Lachenalia, all kinds. Cape Cowslip. Purple, red, white, 3 to 9 inches. Dormant in summer. Good for pots. F or S.

Lapeyrousia laxa. Woodland Painted Petals. 6 to 18 inches. Red or white fls. Dormant in winter. S.

Liatris. Gayfeather. 4 feet. Purple or white. Dormant in winter. S.

Lilium. All Lily species and hybrids. 1 to 9 feet. Many colours. Grow above soil in summer. Sun or afternoon shade.

Littonia modesta. Climbing Bell. 4 feet. Yellow. Dormant in winter. S.

Narcissus (and Daffodil) hybrids. 4 to 18 inches. Many colours. Dormant in summer. Sun or semi-shade.

Ranunculus hybrids. 12 to 18 inches. All colours, dormant in summer. S.

Schizostylis coccinea. River Lily, Semi-ev. 18 inches. Red or pink fls. Moisture, especially in summer. F or S.

Scilla campanulata. English Bluebell. 2 feet. Blue or pink fls. Dormant in summer. F or S.

Sparaxis tricolor. Velvet Flower. 9 to 18 inches. All colours. Dormant in summer. S.

Tulbaghia fragrens. Sweet Garlic. Semi-ev. 15 inches. Lilac fls. Moisture in summer. F or S.

Tulips, modern hybrids. 2 feet. All colours. Dormant in summer. Afternoon shade inland, sunshine at coast.

Zantedeschia aethiopica. White Arum Lily. 3 to 5 feet. White fls. Moisture. F or S.

Grasses

Bent Grass (*Agrostis tenuis*). Moisture all year. S.

Berea Grass (*Dactyloctenium australe*). Warm climate. S.

Kentucky Blue-Grass (*Poa pratensis*). Moisture all year. F or S.

Richmond Grass (*Digitaria diversinervis*). Warm climate. S.

CHAPTER TEN

GROUNDCOVERS

Groundcovers are plants which have the ability to cover the ground with a low carpet of foliage in place of lawn. This carpet may be low and smooth or soft and thick. Groundcovers need not always be carpet-like. Some can form low mounds along the ground, others can be shrubby and create an undulating surface.

The plants should grow easily and require little upkeep or attention. They are generally evergreen spreading perennials that remain in place for many years or may even be climbers, low-growing shrubs or succulents. A list of plants which are suggested for groundcovers will be found at the end of this chapter in order to help the gardener make a choice.

WHY WE USE GROUNDCOVERS

American gardeners of today make the greatest use of groundcovers, for their gardens are planned for ease of maintenance. Few people there have large estates or employ permanent gardeners. Lawns are kept to a minimum, for these require so much attention in the form of mowing and edging. In Southern Africa, however, there are still numerous gardens of an acre or more to be found and there is usually a certain amount of labour available, even though this is mainly unskilled. Unless one is fortunate enough to own a power lawn mower, however, large stretches of lawn still occupy the major part of the gardener's time. These areas are usually too large to be cared for scrupulously and they seldom look their best, for a well-kept lawn needs care. (See Chapter 24.) In addition, lawn is planted too freely in places where conditions will not allow it to prosper—between shrubs, under trees, over banks, along paths and in all the out-of-the-way corners of the garden. A bare patch of ground is regarded as offensive by the landscape gardener who endeavours to cover every spot with greenery and can think only of grass as the medium with which to do this.

It would be better to reduce the size of the lawn to one carefully sculptured sweep and to use groundcovers in parts where one does not always walk. These evergreen plants will extend the restful appearance of the garden created by the lawn's low green carpet without adding to its upkeep, both in labour and money.

WHERE TO USE GROUNDCOVERS

(a) In place of Lawn

It is easier to clothe a sloping bank of soil with a neat groundcover like *Ajuga reptans* (Bugle) than to maintain and mow a lawn in that position. In addition to providing a closely knit green carpet, *Ajuga* produces, each spring, a mass of blue spikes resembling Grape Hyacinths.

Instead of making all pathways of lawn, it is better to put down a few flagstones to protect one's shoes while walking in wet weather and border them with plants like Snow-in-Summer (*Cerastium tomentosum*) or even the fluffier Catmint (*Nepeta*). The flagstones may be placed in a strip or thick, flattish stones may be used as steppingstones in a lake of greenery like Ivy.

The formal lawn is often bordered by trees and shrubs with strong-growing permanent plants beneath them. The edge of the lawn often undulates in and out and where it competes with the roots of the shrubs and the shade of the trees, it grows unevenly and not up to the standard of the central area. This is where groundcovers that tolerate shade and root competition can be used in combination with the permanent plants. They will create a soft charm by spilling out from beneath the trees into the open sun and so help to blend the edge of the lawn and the undergrowth into a luxuriant carpet of green. Textures of contrasting foliage and different colours of green or grey will also provide extra interest.

In the same way, groundcovers may be used instead of lawn along the border of a long driveway; low ones grouped in front, taller ones behind and then a background border of shrubs and trees. As an extra colour note, spring bulbs like Daffodils or summer-flowering Lilies can be planted beneath groundcovers like *Vinca major* (Periwinkle). The groundcover should not be so vigorous or tall that it strangles the bulb foliage. It will be necessary to give the bulbs plenty of water during their growing season and to be careful not to damage the groundcover when lifting the bulbs after one or more seasons. Certain groundcovers which do not get out of hand too easily, such as *Nepeta*, may be used in patches in a bed bordering the lawn, either by themselves or in combination with herbaceous perennials.

(b) In other parts of the Garden

Many houses have a paved area near their entrance, part of which may be used as a driveway. Groundcovers will soften the edges of gravel or concrete. Beds may be set into the paved area where one or several groundcovers may be used with different foliage textures and colours. Certain succulents like the stemless green "roses" of *Sempervivum* or the fleshy creeping Crassulas and bead-like Sedums contrast well with one another and may be planted in a pleasing design in a formal bed. Ground-covers like thyme and other herbs may also be planted in formal rectangles in combination with squares of gravel or paving stones to make an interesting garden "floor".

The hardy character of creeping "mesembs" like *Cephalophyllum* (Sour Fig) and *Drosanthemum* (Dew Flower) enables them to be combined with stone or slate and require very little watering. A steep incline may be walled with slate at an angle in order to hold the soil. This is a very hard finish which must be softened and the "mesembs" will hang down like a green curtain from the top, providing in addition, a blaze of purple or yellow in the spring. *Lantana montevidensis* (Trailing Lantana) is another groundcover which will form a curtain of foliage and purple flowers on a low slope.

Groundcovers can be used to soften any raw construction like low brick and stone walls, concrete retaining walls or steps. They may also be used to clothe the rocks on a large rockery or on a natural rocky outcrop. They may be planted between large logs of wood which are used longitudinally as steps or cut in cross-section and used as stepping stones.

A bed of low-growing groundcovers against the house can be used as a carpet for strong-growing plants with thin stems like Papyrus or shrubs with narrow trunks like Poinsettia. Colourful plants or annuals in large pots could also stand on such a green permanent base.

A civic-minded gardener may yearn to plant lawn on the pavement, but cannot spare the labour to keep it tended. Groundcovers like ivy or periwinkle may be used in a broad band against the hedge and clipped back once a year to prevent encroachment on the walking area. Low shrubby groundcovers against a fence can be edged with a narrow strip of lawn bordering the street in order to cut down on the area of lawn and yet create a well-groomed picture. A strip of plant material like *Cerastium* will provide a soft base to a split pole fence.

CARE OF GROUNDCOVERS

Primarily, groundcovers should not require very much care. They should be able to depend mainly on the rainfall for nourishment and should only be watered about once a fortnight in dry periods. Some never need to be watered at all if they are planted in areas where the seasonal rainfall coincides with that in their country of origin. Many ground-covers have low moisture needs, while some require a dry position as too much moisture will make them rot. A few require regular weekly or twice weekly watering or they will not grow vigorously.

Some groundcovers will thrive both in the sun or in the shade, while some require only the one or the other. These requirements will be noted in the lists at the end of the chapter.

Preparation of the soil before planting groundcovers is simple. The ground should be deeply dug if it is very hard and as much compost as can be spared should be mixed into the top few inches of soil. This will help the plants to become established easily and conserve moisture until they cover the ground and so provide their own mulch of foliage. An annual application of liquid manure or artificial fertilizer may be given, if necessary, to keep the plants growing vigorously. Regular watering will probably be quite enough for some.

Groundcovers are generally chosen from creeping or herbaceous perennials that remain in place for many years and seldom need dividing. They should only be divided if they cease to grow well through overcrowding. Certain shrubs and climbers can be used as groundcovers and these will remain permanently in position, never needing division.

Many climbers will spread over the ground and can be used as groundcovers, especially on sloping banks. The best examples are Bougainvillea, Golden Shower and Mexican Blood Trumpet (*Phaedranthus* or *Bignonia cherere*).

Many of the evergreen "permanent" plants listed in Chapter 11, like Agapanthus and Evergreen Watsonias, may also be used to cover the ground in large patches, but do not have the special attributes of the true groundcover. They also require more careful attention and do not belong to this chapter.

Most of the groundcovers listed below will keep their low appearance without trimming.

LIST OF LOW EVERGREEN GROUNDCOVERS

I. LOW GROUNDCOVERS FOR SHADY PLACES

Ajuga reptans. CARPET BUGLE. Amenable, trouble-free surface plant with green or bronze leaves, blue flower spikes in spring. Filtered shade or sun. Regular moisture, no cutting. Can be mown high if it becomes too billowy. For banks or level ground, stepping stones. Hardy.

Bergenia cordifolia (*Megasea* or *Saxifraga*). Large, round leathery leaves to 6 inches, pink flowers in mid-winter. Spreads slowly, needs shade, good soil and moisture.

Bulbine caulescens. STALKED BULBINE. Succulent foilage to 8 inches, makes dense mat in poor soil under trees like *Acacia elata*. Yellow flowers. Drought-resistant. Will also grow in full sun.

Chlorophytum. HEN-AND-CHICKENS. Green or variegated leaves in tufts. Drought-resistant. Spreads easily under trees.

Cineraria saxifraga. Light green leaves, tiny yellow flowers. Spreading plant will cover a 3-foot bank or wall.

Crassula multicava. FAIRY CRASSULA. Small 4-inch plant with round greyish leaves, pink flowers. Multiplies freely, forming cover on poor rocky soil in full or partial shade under trees. Drought-resistant.

Convolvulus mauritanicus. GROUND MORNING GLORY. Trailing green stems with small mauve flowers. Partial shade or sun. Drought-resistant, strong rooted, spreading to 3 feet wide. Good for banks, overhanging rocks and walls.

Dichondra repens. LAWN-LEAF. Known in this country as WONDER-LAWN. Lawn substitute. Mat of small green leaves which can be walked on. Needs moisture and fertilizer. Sun or filtered shade, but better in shade in hot, dry inland places. Cut with mower when in seed. Good on banks or between paving stones under trees. Grow from seed or plugs.

Duchesnea indica (*Fragaria indica*). WILD STRAWBERRY. Strawberry-like leaves and red fruit which is not edible. Best in cool, moist areas in good soil. Can be clipped if desired.

Hedera. IVY. Excellent strong quick cover for any soil or climate, sun or shade. Water once a week if rain does not fall. ENGLISH IVY (*H. helix*) is best in large areas under trees or steep slopes. Use small-leaved varieties for shaded, smaller areas. VARIEGATED CANARY ISLANDS IVY needs more sun.

Helxine soleirolii. BABY'S-TEARS. Also known as "Happiness-in-the-Home" and "Mind-your-own-Business". Tiny bright green leaves forming a moss-like covering in full shade. Invasive. Will grow between flagstones, over rocks and in shallow soil. Needs moisture.

Hypericum calycinum. GOLD FLOWER. Roots spread underground, stems to 1 foot high, yellow flowers. Best in partial or full shade with adequate moisture. Cut back in early spring.

Lamium maculatum. DEAD NETTLE. Perennial with trailing stems and attractive variegated green and silver leaves, yellow flower spikes, makes soft mat 9 inches thick. Full or semi-shade, moisture.

Liriope spicata. LILY-TURF. Tufts of strap-like leaves, 6 to 8 inches. Mauve flowers. Full shade.

Nepeta hederacea (*Glechoma*). GROUND IVY. Light, green, rounded, scalloped leaves on long, prostrate stems, invasive. Tiny mauve flowers in spring. Grows in full or semi-shade under trees like Jacaranda. Water regularly.

Ophiopogon japonicus. MONDO GRASS or LILY-TURF. Tufts of narrow leaves, 6 to 8 inches long, lilac flowers. Resembles Liriope. Makes evergreen groundcover if planted closely in semi-shade. Burns in hot sun, yet becomes too long in deep shade and falls over. Slow to cover, needs moisture. Do not mow. Propagate by division.

Pachysandra terminalis. JAPANESE SPURGE. From 6 to 10 inches high, making a soft mat of dark green, patterned foliage. Water regularly in places with dry atmosphere. Will grow in dense shade or partial shade, dislikes full sun. Hardy. Slow to establish.

Phalaris arundinacea picta. Short striped green and white grass. Grows in poor soil under shade of trees.

Polygonum capitatum. Spreading perennial with tiny pink balls of flowers and pinkish leaves with V-shaped bands. Forms neat mat to 6 inches, invasive. Needs moisture. Excellent for large areas under trees, in full or semi-shade as well as sun. If browned by frost, comes on in spring.

Saxifraga sarmentosa. STRAWBERRY SAXIFRAGE. Rounded, marbled leaves, multiply freely like strawberries, white flowers. Full or partial shade under trees, moisture and rich light soil. Use variety *tricolor* as an indoor plant.

Sedum spectabile. Succulent with bluish-grey leaves and flat heads of pinkish-mauve flowers in autumn. Plant in masses in poor dry soil under trees. Cut back each winter.

Vinca major. PERIWINKLE. Trailing, rooting stems, blue flowers. Also a variegated gold and green-leaved form. Best in full or semi-shade with moisture. Holds slope.

Tradescantia fluminensis. WANDERING JEW. Green trailing stems, fleshy leaves. Shade, moisture, tender.

Zebrina pendula. WANDERING JEW. Green and silver foliage, purple beneath, purple flowers. Best in shade protected from frost by overhanging branches.

II. LOW GROUNDCOVERS FOR FULL SUN

Several of the above list will also grow in full sun if they are watered regularly, such as *Ajuga*, *Convolvulus mauritanicus*, *Dichondra*, *Hedera* (Ivy) and *Polygonum*.

Alyssum saxatile. GOLDEN ALYSSUM. 9-inch plants with grey foliage, yellow flowers. Rockeries or sloping ground, regular moisture.

Arctotheca calendula. CAPE WEED. Creeping form with rough green leaves, yellow daisy flowers. Useful as a soil-binder. Blooms spring, summer and autumn.

Arctotis stoechadifolia. TRAILING ARCTOTIS. Flat, creeping perennial with greyish leaves, cream (or coloured) daisy flowers. Will cover large area of rock or poor soil. Drought and heat-resistant. Full sun.

Cephalophyllum. SOUR FIG. Thick-leaved, creeping succulent of *Mesembryanthemum* family which forms large curtain of coarse leaves for covering poor sandy banks or overhanging steep rocks. Occasional large flowers. Excellent for hot, dry places or sea-side. Needs very little moisture. Drainage must be good.

Cerastium tomentosum. SNOW-IN-SUMMER. Silvery-grey mat 6 inches high, tiny white flowers. Spreads easily on slopes or level ground. Water regularly but drainage must be good. Best in full sun, but will grow with sun for half the day.

Ceratostigma plumbaginoides. Dwarf soil-binder with dark blue flowers. **C. wilmottianum** is taller with lighter flowers. Cut back each winter. Good for banks. Seeds freely.

Dimorphotheca, Bloem Erf Beauty. Low, large spreading perennial with large mauve daisy flowers in spring. Drought-resistant, full sun, poor soil. Excellent for banks, walls, rockeries. Cuttings are slow to root.

Walls provide privacy as well as a background for many plants. Simple breeze blocks (above) can be given charm with a curve, a peep-hole, white-wash and luxuriant accent plants. Variegated Canary Islands Ivy (*Hedera canariensis variegata*) makes a graceful curtain over a stuccoed wall (centre).

A brick wall, in an easily-constructed honey-comb pattern, casts a chequered shade and provides a hold for dainty climbers like Zimbabwe Creeper (*Podranea brycei*) and Jasmine (*Jasminum polyanthum*).

A high shady boundary wall can be made interesting by constructing a wishing-well, fed by a dripping hosepipe, and planting ferns and fuchsias to give it woodland luxuriance.

Low retaining walls, whether they are made of rustic stone stacked without cement or of formal brick, can be softened with overhanging plants.

Drosanthemum hispidum. DEW FLOWERS. Flat, creeping succulent of Mesemb. family with tiny, gleaming purple flowers and icing-sugared leaves. Full sun, dry or shallow soil, will cover rocks or banks. Drought-resistant.

Erigeron karvinskianus (*E. mucronatus* or *Vittadinia*). SANTA BARBARA DAISY. Semi-trailing plant with tiny white daisies, blooming continuously. Spreads rapidly with strong roots. Excellent for covering large area or sandy banks, but very invasive in ordinary rockery. Drought-resistant.

Gazania uniflora. One of the best grey-leaved ground-covers, forming a spreading curtain on banks and walls. Brilliant yellow daisy flowers. Will grow in poor soil, excellent for sea-side. Water regularly, but must be well-drained. Other Gazanias which form cushions are good for dry places on slopes or level ground.

Geranium incanum. CARPET GERANIUM. Cushions of ferny foliage and mauve flowers throughout summer. Seeds and spreads freely, covering rocks, shallow soil and slightly sloping banks. Cut back at end of winter if frosted. Ivy Geraniums spread over a large area, but must be cut back occasionally and need tending to keep tidy.

Helichrysum argyrophyllum. GOLDEN GUINEA EVER-LASTING. Flat carpet of silvery leaves with yellow flowers in autumn. Will cover rocks and shallow soil, excellent for dry places. Likes moisture, but needs good drainage. Full sun.

Iberis sempervirens. EVERGREEN CANDYTUFT. Dark green leaves, snow-white flowers in spring. Mounds spread to 2 feet, best for small areas among rocks. Cut back after flowering for neatness. Prefers full sun, but will grow in partial shade.

Lampranthus (*Mesembryanthemum* family). MESEMBS. VYGIES. Dozens of species with dazzling, colourful flowers. Make cushions on ground. Ideal for poor, dry soil, rockeries and slopes. Drought-resistant.

Lippia repens. LIPPIA GRASS OR DAISY GRASS. The best lawn substitute for large areas of poor shallow soil on slopes or level ground. Makes dense mat, spreads vigorously by runners and smothers weeds. Hardy to cold, endures heat. Prefers full sun. Drought-resistant, but use lawn-sprinkler at regular intervals during dry season. Remove tiny mauve flowers in spring with the lawn-mower, as they attract bees which may be troublesome.

Lysimachia nummularia. CREEPING JENNY. Flat creep-ing stems with round leaves, yellow flowers. Prefers filtered sun and waterside with rich, light soil. Needs plenty of moisture.

Nepeta mussini. CATMINT. Fluffy blanket of grey leaves with mauve flowers in summer. Spreading perennial for level areas or slopes. Full sun and good drainage.

Sedum. STONE CROP. Many types with tiny, beadlike foliage or fleshy leaves that turn red in winter. Drought-resistant succulents for poor shallow soil in hot, sunny posi-tions. Will grow on the tiniest layer of soil on flat rocks.

Sempervivum. HOUSELEEK. Rosettes of succulent leaves, mainly grey. Must be massed for effect. Good for sunny places with little moisture and shallow soil.

Stachys lanata. LAMB'S EARS. Low perennial to 12 inches with soft grey leaves and spikes of lilac flowers, spreading easily. Becomes a little shabby in winter.

Thymus. THYME. Creeping mats of aromatic leaves adapted to any kind of well-drained soil. Best for small areas between paving, edging paths, etc.

CHAPTER ELEVEN

THE VALUE OF PERMANENT PLANTS

In the effort to maintain a well-filled garden without too much work and the constant twice-yearly replacement of annuals, one should endeavour to use as many permanent plants as possible. Besides the use of flowering shrubs and other woody plants there are many leafy bulbous plants, perennials and groundcovers which add luxuriance to the garden and these can be moved around from place to place, if necessary, without detriment.

It is wise to plan the garden in such a way that the shrubs and trees form the permanent bone-structure and background to the lay-out of the garden and the colourful annuals and perennials are grouped in several prominent places so that they are shown off to best advantage to the visitor. Somewhere between these two, there is a portion of the garden that is not always in the public eye or along the main thoroughfare. There is a need for cool green areas which will offset the highly-coloured portions and make the garden a place of rest and seclusion. A tuft of graceful Watsonia leaves at the foot of a small tree like *Dais cotinifolia*, for example, will give a wooded feeling and do much to create an informal appearance in the garden.

The use of permanent plants enables us to make a successful shrub border along a boundary hedge. When our trees and shrubs are young and small, we can plant annuals or even lawn between them, but as they grow, their encroaching shade and spreading roots dictate the need for stronger plants which will cover the ground with green. This is where one can introduce permanent plants, like Agapanthus, which will hug the skirts of the trees and shrubs, as well as many shade-tolerant groundcovers like Wild Strawberry or Ground Ivy.

One should always endeavour to group one's permanent plants in large areas of one kind of plant. Each type should blend informally into the other like perennials in a herbaceous border. Small creeping plants like violets can act as a border group to the taller ones and there are many that can combine to give the garden a luxuriant appearance.

Do not look upon permanent plants merely as patches or tufts of green leaves. Many of them have lovely flowers which bloom for a few weeks each year and add to the variety of the garden picture as well as provide material for the vase. They give the busy gardener a

respite from constant change in the garden, for some may be left in place for as long as five years or even longer, before being divided up, or they may be divided once in two years if necessary.

Some, like Agapanthus, have very strong root systems, which can be used to hold the soil on sloping ground; some, like Asparagus fern, will not mind competition from tree roots, while many, like Acanthus or Grecian leaf, will grow very successfully in the shade.

Permanent plants cannot be tabulated on a botanical basis. Their main characteristic is that they should be evergreen or semi-evergreen, so that there is always a patch of green where they are growing and one does not have the desire to rip them out and try and fill in spaces during a dormant season. Some of them have bulbs or corms, such as Watsonias, but it is only the evergreen Watsonias that could be regarded as permanent plants, for the deciduous Watsonias must be grouped under the heading of summer-flowering bulbs. A list of permanent plants will follow at the end of this chapter.

Some of these permanent plants, such as Bearded Iris, need better or more carefully prepared soil than others, such as Red Hot Pokers. It will always be best to prepare the soil well for any of them before planting, as they will be left in place for a very long period.

One should dig the soil well and incorporate as much well-made compost as one can spare. This will make it easy for the plants to become established and grow luxuriantly during their long stay in one position. In addition, one can give the plants a yearly application of compost, liquid manure or fertilizer before flowering in order to keep them growing luxuriantly. It will be necessary to water them, but this need be done only about once a week when rain does not fall. It is best to leave a garden spray to soak the ground thoroughly. Naturally, watering can be more frequent before the flowering period and it can be less frequent when the plants are resting. The plants should never be allowed to dry out for weeks at a time, however, as evergreen plants always require some moisture. Always try to divide evergreen plants after the flowering period, so that they have the longest possible time in which to become re-established before the next flowering period. It sometimes happens that such plants will not flower in the first season after being

THE VALUE OF PERMANENT PLANTS

divided, but if they are given good treatment they will often do so.

GOOD PERMANENT PLANTS

The following evergreen plants may be planted in groups to form long-lasting groundcovers. Many other suitable plants will be found in the lists following the chapters entitled "Groundcovers", "Gardening in the Shade", "The Beauty of Foliage", "Shrubs and Trees", "Bulbs for your Garden" and "Cultivation of Perennials".

Evergreen Bulbous Plants

Agapanthus orientalis.
Anigozanthos (Kangaroo's Paw).
Aristea, all species.
Billbergia, all species.
Chlorophytum (Hen-and-Chickens).
Clivia, all species.
Crinum moorei (semi-evergreen).
Cyrtanthus (Ifafa Lilies).
Dietes (Wild Iris).
Dierama (Harebells).
Hedychium (Ginger-Lily). Cut back.
Hemerocallis (Day-Lily). Evergreen types.
Hesperaloe.
Iris, Bearded.
Iris ochroleuca.
Iris unguicularis.
Kniphofia (Red Hot Poker).
Marica gracilis.
Nerine filifolia (Grass-leaved Nerine).
Pancratium (Spider Lily).
Phormium tenax (New Zealand Flax).
Tulbaghia fragrans (Sweet Garlic).
Yucca filamentosa (Yucca Lily).
Watsonias, Evergreen.

Evergreen Perennials and Soft-wooded Shrubs

Acanthus (Grecian Leaf).
Arctotis, many kinds (Gousblom).
Asparagus Ferns (Smilax and others).
Aubrieta deltoides (Aubrietia).
Begonia semperflorens and others.
Bergenia (*Megasea* or *Saxifraga*).
Centaurea cineraria (Dusty Miller).
Ceratostigma.
Chrysanthemum sp. (Marguerites, Daisy Bushes).
Dimorphotheca, many kinds.
Geranium incanum and others.
Helichrysum argyrophyllum (Everlasting).
Hypoestes (Ribbon Bush).
Nautochilus (Shell Bush).
Nepeta (Catmint).
Nephrolepis (Sword Fern).
Osteospermum ecklonis (Blue-and-White Daisy Bush).
Phlox subulata (Alpine or Moss Phlox).
Plectranthus (Spur Flower).
Salvias, in variety.
Senecio cineraria (Dusty Miller).
Senecio leucostachys (Finely-cut Dusty Miller).
Strelitzia reginae (Crane Flower).
Tradescantia virginiana (Moses-in-the-Bulrushes).
Violets.

Grasses and Rushes

Bambusa (Bamboo).
Briza (Quaking Grass).
Coix (Quaking Grass).
Cortaderia (Pampas Grass).
Cyperus papyrus (Papyrus Grass).
Cyperus alternifolius (Umbrella Plant).
Pennisetum ruppelii (Fountain Grass).

Succulents

Aloes, many species.
Bulbine caulescens (Cat's Tail).
Cotyledons.
Crassulas.
Euphorbias.
Mesembryanthemum family.
Sedums.

CHAPTER TWELVE

THE BEAUTY OF FOLIAGE

The discerning gardener will soon develop a keen eye for a good leaf and discover that plants can make a tapestry of green, grey or purple that creates pattern and interest long after fleeting flowers have passed. Foliage makes a garden mellow and can create many effects. One can obtain a tropical, luxuriant effect by using plants with large leaves, like Fatsia and Acanthus, or one can create a restful, cool atmosphere by using grey foliage, especially as a background for white flowers. Feathery foliage adds softness to the base of steps, walls or tall, erect plants. Spiky foliage sets off the rounded clumps of flowers in the herbaceous border.

The architectural value of plants is of great importance where striking shape is needed for accent and although such plants may also have notable foliage, they will be listed elsewhere. (See Chapter 4 on "House and Garden.") The Japanese have special cutting gardens, keeping only foliage in the landscape, evergreens being especially important. Evergreen foliage is of special value in preventing a bleak effect and in providing privacy in winter, but is not of chief consideration here. Interesting foliage is indispensable for flower arrangements. The subject of foliage is almost without end, for so much depends on one's own appreciation of its beauty and one could go to the ends of the earth in search of new material. For the sake of brevity, some suggested plant materials which are obtainable in this country are listed below as a guide.

Plants with Large Leaves

Acanthus. Grecian Leaf. Shiny green.
Alpinia speciosa. Shell Ginger. Flesh flowers. Perennial to 8 feet.
Aralia. Evergreen shrubs with glossy palmate leaves.
Artichoke, Globe. Grey, dull.
Arum Lilies (*Zantedeschia*). Arrow-shaped. Green or speckled.
Bergenia (*Megasea* or *Saxifraga*). Low, round leathery leaves, pink flowers.
Bocconia cordata. Plume Poppy. Tall perennial. Bold, bluish-green leaves.
Cannas. Green or brown leaves.
Colocasia. Elephant's Ear. Arrow-shaped huge, green leaves.
Crinum moorei and other species. Make bold clumps.
Cussonia. Cabbage Tree. Grey leaves at top of tall stem.
Ensete ventricosum. Wild Banana. Huge long leaves like bananas, ribbed red.

Eupatorium. Large heads of mauve flowers.
Fatsia (*Tetrapanax*). Tall plant, suckering.
Gunnera. Immense leaves for waterside. Not common here.
Hedychium. Ginger-Lily. 6 feet, white or yellow flowers.
Melianthus major. Kruitjie-roer-my-nie. Tall, ruffled leaves.
Monstera. Huge, split leaves. Shade outdoors in mild climates or house plant.
Musa. Banana. Bold long leaves.
Ricinus communis. Castorbean. Greenish bronzy leaves. Red burrs. Mahogany-leaved variety.
Salvia turkestanica. Broad, hairy, toothed leaves. Pinkish bracts and flowers.
Senecio petasitis. Velvety green leaves. Yellow flowerheads like Canary Creeper.
Sparmannia africana. Large rounded shrub. White flowers.
Statice latifolia. Low tufts of ripply leaves. Purple flowers.
Strelitzia. Crane Flower. All species. Bold leaves. Striking flowers.
Verbascum thapsus. Common Mullein. Toothed soft leaves and tall spike of yellow flowers.
Wigandia. Rough leaves. Blue flowers.

Plants with Feathery Leaves

Achillea. Yarrow. Green or grey foliage. Yellow, white or pink flowers.
Asparagus Ferns. Basket Asparagus. Green ferns.
Astilbe. Short, shade and moisture-loving. Plume-like flowers.
Athanasia parviflora. Soft shrub to 8 feet. Heads of yellow flowers.
Centaurea cineraria. Dusty Miller. Silvery leaves. Purple flowers.
Coleonema pulchrum. Confetti Bush. Medium shrub. Small pink flowers.
Erica. Heath. Several kinds like *E. vestita* and *E. atropurpurea.*
Euryops athanasiae. Clanwilliam Daisy. Shrub, yellow daisy flowers.
Fennel. Herb with edible roots. Full sun, poor soil.
Geranium incanum. Low, spreading plant. Mauve flowers.
Paranomus. Rounded shrub to 3 or 4 feet. Protea family.
Parkinsonia aculeata. Small tree. Yellow flowers.
Protea nana. Mountain Rose. Dark red flowers. Small shrub.
Senecio leucostachys. Finely cut, whitish leaves, creamy flowers. Also called Dusty Miller.
Serruria. All species, including Blushing Bride.
Spiraea arguta. Garland May. Small shrub, white flowers.

Tamarisk. Small trees. Pink flowers.

Tree-Ferns. Moisture, shelter and semi-shade.

Plants with Sword-shaped, Upright Leaves

Anigozanthos. Kangaroo's Paw. Curious green and red flowers.

Chasmanthe floribunda. Broad leaves. Yellow or orange flowers.

Curtonus paniculatus. Pleated leaves. Turn brown in winter.

Dierama. Harebell. Pink, red or white flowers.

Iris. Many different species.

Phormium tenax. New Zealand Flax. Large bold plant.

Wachendorfia. Red-root. Pleated leaves, yellow flowers, waterside.

Watsonia. Many species, tall and short.

Yucca filamentosa. Adam's Needle or Yucca Lily. White flowers.

Plants with graceful or grassy leaves

Agapanthus. All kinds. Blue or white flowers.

Bamboo in variety.

Chives. Herb with mauve flowers.

Clivia miniata. Strap-shaped leaves in tufts. Shade. Orange flowers.

Cortaderia selloana. Pampas Grass. For large gardens. Silvery or pinkish plumes.

Hemerocallis. Day-Lily. Large tufts. Yellow or orange flowers.

Job's Tears (*Coix Lacryma-jobi*). Annual grass with bead-like berry.

Kniphofia. Red Hot Poker. Orange or yellow flowers.

Liriope muscari. Lily-Turf. Low, tufted groundcover. Also variegated leaves. Small flower-spike.

Moraea spathulata. Yellow flowers. Long leaves in tufts.

Oplismenus (Basket Grass). Trailing, white and green stripes. Tender.

Pennisetum ruppelii. Fountain Grass. Tufted grass with mauve flower-spikes.

Phalaris arundinacea picta. Ribbon grass. Creeping. Striped white and green. Hardy.

Quaking Grass (*Briza*). Pendant sprays.

Plants with Grey or Silvery Foliage

Acacia cultriformis. Knife-Leaf Wattle. Large shrub. Yellow flowers.

Acacia podalyriaefolia. Pearl Acacia. Small tree. Yellow flowers.

Alyssum saxatile. Low grey mat of leaves. Yellow flowers.

Arctotis. All kinds. Colourful daisy flowers.

Centaurea cineraria. (*C. candidissima*). Finely cut oblong whitish leaves. Mauve or purple flowers.

Centaurea ragusina. (Sold in trade as *C. candidissima*.) Oblong, silvery-hairy leaves. Bright yellow flowers.

Cerastium tomentosum. Snow-in-Summer. Low ground-cover. White flowers.

Chrysanthemum ptarmiciflorum. Fern-like leaves, white flowers. Shrubby.

Cussonia paniculata. Cabbage Tree. Bluish-grey leaves on tall stem.

Dianthus. Pinks. Low plant for edge of border. Pink flowers.

Eryngium. Sea Holly. Blue, thistle-like flowers.

Eucalyptus cinerea. Florist Gum. Narrow tree. Rounded leaves.

Euryops pectinatus. Small shrub. Finely cut foliage. Yellow daisies.

Feijoa. Pineapple-Guava. Silvery green leaves. Pink flowers. Shrub.

Gazania uniflora. Low, spreading plant, yellow flowers.

Helichrysum argyrophyllum. Golden Guinea Everlasting. Flat, rock cover, yellow flowers.

Lavandula officinalis. True Lavender. Mauve flowers. Small shrub.

Leucadendron argenteum. Silver Tree. Small tree with silvery-green leaves.

Leucospermum reflexum. Pincushion Flower. Very large shrub. Red flowers.

Lychnis coronaria (*Agrostemma coronaria*). Rose Campion. White, woolly leaves, inch-wide, crimson flowers.

Nepeta mussini. Catmint. Low, spreading. Mauve flowers.

Podalyria sericea. Small shrub, tiny white flowers.

Romneya coulteri. Matilija Poppy. Blue-grey leaves. Large white flowers.

Salvia leucantha (Purple Salvia) and *S. farinacea*, blue flowers.

Santolina chamaecyparissus. Lavender-Cotton. Low shrub. Tiny, silvery-grey leaves, yellow flowers.

Senecio cineraria. Dusty Miller. Thick, green, white-woolly serrated leaves. Yellow or cream flowers.

Senecio leucostachys. Very finely cut, white-hairy leaves. Heads of creamy yellow flowers like *S. cineraria*. Also known as *S. cineraria* var. *candidissima*.

Stachys lanata. Lamb's Ears. Low, spreading plant, pink or mauve flowers.

Venidium fastuosum. Double Namaqualand Daisy. Tall, spring annual, orange flowers.

Verbascum. Lamb's Tail. Tall woolly spike with yellow flowers.

Plants with Reddish-Purple or Bronze Leaves

Acer palmatum atropurpureum. Japanese Maple. Small tree with finely cut foliage.

Ajuga reptans atropurpurea. Bronze-leaved Bugle. Groundcover. Blue flowers. Full sun for intense colour.

Begonia Rex. Outdoors in mild areas or house plant.

Berberis thunbergii atropurpurea. Purple Barberry. Prickly, deciduous shrub.

Corylus avellana purpurea. Copper Hazelnut. Deciduous shrub.

Dahlia. Bishop of Llandaff. Bronze leaves, scarlet, single flowers.

Fagus sylvatica atropunicea. Copper Beech. Slow tree.

Lobelia cardinalis. Bronze-leaved perennial. Scarlet flowers.

Prunus cerasifera. Brown-leaved Plums. Small deciduous trees. Also with pink variegation.

Ricinus communis purpureus. Mahogany Castorbean. Shrub to 10 feet, gleaming purplish leaves.

Zebrina pendula. Wandering Jew. Groundcover. Purplish flowers and underside of leaves.

Plants with Variegated or Coloured Foliage

Those with gold and green leaves need sunshine, while those with white and green leaves will grow in semi-shade.

Abutilon. Chinese Lantern. Hybrids with green and gold foliage.

Acalypha. All colours. Full sun in humid, frost-free localities.

Acer negundo variegata. Tree with green and white leaves.

Codiaeum (*Croton*). All colours. Full sun in humid, frost-free localities.

Coleus. Coloured variegations. Low plants for shade under trees.

Elaeagnus pungens variegata. Shrub with gold and green leaves.

Euonymus japonicus. Spindle tree. Large shrub. One variety with gold-margined leaves and one with central gold patch.

Geraniums. White and green leaves or with brilliant variegations. Sun.

Golden Cypress (*Chamaecyparis*). Gold and green. Likes moisture.

Hedera canariensis variegata. Canary Islands Ivy. Green and white foliage. Semi-shade.

Lamium. Dead-Nettle. Leaves marbled white. Yellow or pink flowers.

Ligustrum ovalifolium variegatum. Golden Privet. Shrub with gold and green leaves.

Plectranthus hirtus variegatus. Silver and green leaves. Low spreading plant. Give shade and shelter from frost.

Polygonum capitatum. Pink and green leaves, tiny pink flowers. Groundcover.

Sambucus nigra aurea. Golden Elder. Small tree with gold leaves. Also a green and white variety.

Symphoricarpus orbiculatus variegatus. Coral-berry. Yellow-margined leaves.

Vinca major (Periwinkle). Groundcover with plain green or gold variegated leaves. Blue flowers.

Shrubs and trees with Autumn Foliage

Acer buergerianum. Chinese or Trident Maple. Red leaves before dropping.

Acer negundo. Box Elder Maple. Yellow leaves before dropping.

Alnus americana. American Ash. Yellow leaves before dropping.

Berberis julianae. Wintergreen Barberry. Evergreen. Scattered scarlet leaves.

Citharexylum sp. Apricot-coloured winter foliage. Tender.

Greyia sutherlandii. Mountain Bottlebrush. Leaves tinged red before dropping.

Koelreuteria paniculata (Goldenrain tree). Yellow-orange leaves before falling.

Lagerstroemia indica. Pride-of-India. Leaves orange or red before falling.

Liquidambar styraciflua. Sweet Gum. Bronze, yellow and red shades before dropping.

Liriodendron tulipifera. Tulip Tree. Yellow leaves before falling.

Photinia serrulata. Evergreen. Leaves tinged red.

Platanus acerifolia. London Plane. Yellow leaves in autumn.

Rhus succedanea. Wax tree. Scarlet leaves before falling.

Smodingium argutum. Rainbow-Leaf. Multi-coloured foliage before dropping.

Spiraea prunifolia plena. Bridal-Wreath May. Orange leaves before falling.

Viburnum opulus sterile. Snowball Bush. Orange-red leaves before falling.

Shrubs and Trees with Coloured Spring Foliage

(Indigenous to Southern Africa.)

Lucky Bean Tree (*Afzelia cuanensis*). Red young leaves.

Msasa Tree (*Brachystegia spiciformis*). Red, pink, fawn young foliage.

Red-leaved Fig (*Ficus ingens*). Red young foliage.

Carnival Bush (*Ochna atropurpurea*). Bronze young foliage.

CHAPTER THIRTEEN

COLOUR IN THE GARDEN FOR SPECIAL OCCASIONS

The gardener's chief ambition is probably to have colour throughout the year. One of the best ways to ensure some note of colour in each calendar month is to plant a wide selection of flowering shrubs and trees, roses and numerous permanent leafy plants which produce flowers at different times. Their regular display forms the general background of the garden, but one requires, in addition, a blaze of annuals and colourful perennials to really put life into the garden picture.

A well-furnished garden always looks attractive, yet there are occasions when one wants the garden to look its very best for a special event. There may be a family wedding or the garden may be the venue of some meeting. The owner may simply want to enter the garden for a competition and devote his efforts to producing the best effect at a required time. It will be no consolation to offer the usual regrets saying, "You should have seen the garden last month".

If one has from four to five months' notice in which to plan the event that is to take place in the garden, the problem can be solved easily. Most people, however, suddenly realise in desperation that there are only two months or even six weeks left before the occasion and then try to find something to plant that will liven up the garden.

Special events at short notice can be decorated in an expensive way by buying dozens of potted flowering plants from nurseries and sinking these into the soil to create a mass of colour. Parks and gardens overseas do this constantly for bedding out in public places, removing the pots when the flowers are over and replacing them with others. Plants which flower while small are suitable and one may use Hydrangeas for midsummer and Hyacinths for midwinter. This, however, is an artificial, contrived effect which is not the true essence of gardening or of growing things for oneself. The same may be said for the woman who went to the flower market to buy wholesale quantities of gladioli and stuck them into the soil in masses on the day of her daughter's wedding or another who tied carnations to all the bare rose bushes in the garden. This is stunt floristry and certainly not gardening.

The average honest-to-goodness gardener who simply wants his garden to look its best must realise a few basic things. One cannot do the impossible and provide colour at any time or at too short notice.

Very few annuals will bloom properly in under two months. Sturdy seedlings which are already flowering in tins in nurseries may be purchased, but these should be planted very closely if a quick effect is required. In ordinary circumstances they will take about six to eight weeks to come into full bloom. Plants which can be depended on to provide a colourful carpet if they are bought when they are flowering are:

Violas—mainly in blue and yellow.
Tagetes (Lulu)—orange.
Dwarf Marigolds—yellow, orange and rusty red.
Alyssum—white and purple.
Ageratum—bluish-mauve.
Lobelia—light blue, dark blue and mauve.
Nierembergia—mauve.
Portulaca—mixed colours.
Verbena—mixed colours.
Begonia semperflorens—reds, pinks, whites. (Perennial often used as an annual).

All these annuals are dwarf in size and suitable for planting out in spring and summer for quick effects. Normally, one plants out Violas in March and has them flowering sturdily in the garden by July and August, continuing throughout summer, but the "special occasion" gardener has no time for normal methods and wants a display even if the plants are not so well grown individually.

The fact that they may not last so long in the garden is also no deterrent, provided that they make a splash for the specified time.

The gardener who wants a display during winter has a more difficult task if he has not thought about it early enough. Annuals grow more slowly during cold weather and most of our winter and spring annuals, like stocks and poppies, have a very long period of growth before flowering, taking from five to six months to bloom from the time of germination. Seedlings take about a month to six weeks less to come into full flower.

Quick effects in winter and spring, therefore, will be obtained by growing showy South African wild flowers which have a short growing period of from three to four months from seed. Seed of the following annuals planted in March will bloom in June:

Namaqualand Daisies (*Dimorphotheca sinuata*)—orange and mixed soft shades of yellow and buff.
The Double Namaqualand Daisy (*Venidium fastuosum*) —tall, hardy plants up to 3 feet with brilliant orange "double" flowers.
Nemesia (Cape Jewels)—brilliant mixed colours, excellent for window-boxes.
Heliophila (Blue Flax)—a dainty blue annual up to 12 inches which must be broadcast in quantities for a good show.

Blooming in four months from seed planted in March are the following:

Kingfisher Daisy (*Felicia bergeriana*)—blue daisy with yellow centre, 3 inches high, good edging plant.
Cotula barbata—Button Flowers—tiny yellow buttons, very showy in mass, good edging plant beside Felicia.
Anchusa capensis—Cape Forget-me-not—tall, 2 feet, with deep blue flowers, an excellent foil to Ursinia.
Ursinia (Little Sunshine)—12 to 15 inches, brilliant orange daisy flowers, often with mahogany ring.
Senecio elegans—purple daisies, yellow centre, massed effect, 15 to 18 inches.
Senecio arenarius—similar to above, but about 9 to 12 inches in height.
Silene coeli-rosa (*Agrostemma*) is a tall, hardy Mediterranean annual which can also be grown from seed broadcast in the open ground in March. It has dainty mauve trumpet flowers, showy in the mass. (Also see Chapter 25 on "Growing Annuals for Display".)

Although people in Southern Africa speak of having a winter garden, it is only in the milder parts of the country that the annuals will bloom in mid-winter, that is, in June and July. In the colder parts, some of the hardier flowers will commence blooming in July and continue into the spring, while others will only start blooming properly in August and September. One must rely mainly on winter-flowering shrubs for colour. (See Chapter 29 on "Shrubs and Trees".)

The gardener who can arrange for any function to take place in September is fortunate, for this is the time when all autumn-planted seedlings will be in full bloom and numerous flowering shrubs will form a colourful background. Many gardens will continue to be colourful in October as well. Irises and Roses are in full bloom at this time.

November is an in-between month in most gardens when the spring annuals are over and the summer annuals have not yet reached their peak of flowering. The gardener who has thought well ahead and planted biennials in the previous summer, however, will have a colourful display of Foxgloves, Canterbury Bells, Penstemon, Columbines and Delphiniums. Perennial plants like Evergreen Watsonias will commence blooming at this time, as well as pink Arums (*Zantedeschia rehmannii*) and many flowering shrubs. Floribunda roses are generally colourful in this month as they flower after the Hybrid Teas.

During December, the early August or September-planted annuals will commence blooming, as well as the autumn or winter-planted perennials like Cannas. Lilies come into their own during this time and Hybrid Tea Roses begin their second display of flowers. The properly-planned garden which has not depended only on annuals, will benefit from the colour provided by other plants.

January is probably the best month for gardens in the summer rainfall area. Lawns are green, deciduous shrubs are in full leaf and annuals planted out in spring will be in full bloom. The herbaceous border is at its peak of perfection. Gardens in the winter-rainfall area of the Cape are better in February or March, due to the later warming-up period in spring, but rely on flowering shrubs like Hydrangeas and trees like Flowering Gums to provide colour in January.

Plants like Red Salvias, which take a long time to bloom, will be dramatic in February and March, lasting until the frost, but seedlings should have been planted out in early summer from seed sown in August in tins. If one wants the main display of annuals by February and March, one should delay the planting of annuals to the end of October rather than at the end of August.

Brilliant effect in March can be provided by sowing seed of quick-flowering Zinnias directly into the open ground during November or December. It is not wise to plant out annuals later than the end of December in places with cold winters, or they will be destroyed by frost when they are in full bloom. Gardeners in areas with mild winters, such as on the south coast of Natal, northern Rhodesia and in the Congo may plant summer annuals as late as January, but it is best to keep to the calendar months in sowing annuals for good results. (See Chapter 14, "The Gardener's Calendar".)

Gardens in April must rely for colour on late-flowering shrubs, for few annuals will linger until this time. In any case, they should have been pulled out by April in order to make way for spring flowering plants.

May marks the beginning of cold weather in Southern Africa, except in sub-tropical places where colourful shrubs make a display. The spectacular golden Pigs' Ears (*Solanum mammosum*) make their appearance at this time and the fortunate grower of Proteas and Heath will be able to pick the first flowers of winter during this month. Only very early gardening birds will be picking stocks and sweet-peas in June, probably the bleakest month in the garden except where Namaqualand Daisies give a glorious sunshine glow on sunny days.

Poinsettias will bloom for those with warm gardens during July and the majority of spring annuals will commence flowering at this time only if they were planted early enough. Winter-flowering shrubs will be the chief attraction of the mid-winter garden. August is a pretty month if one concentrates on the bright colours of Ranunculus, Anemones and Daffodils, planted in clumps with annuals like Poppies and Primula. Early Prunus and Almond Blossom will detract from brown lawns and indicate that winter is over.

It can be seen, therefore, that one cannot simply rely on quick-growing annuals to provide colour all through the year, but must be prepared to plant all types of plants in order to have an attractive garden. The Chapter entitled "The Gardener's Calendar" will give one a planting scheme so that one does not forget to plant the right things at the right time.

COLOUR THROUGHOUT THE YEAR

Although colour is provided by established flowering shrubs and trees, the following bulbs, perennials and annuals may be relied on to furnish added colour and garden interest throughout the year in Southern Africa. These lists are by no means comprehensive, but are offered as a guide.

The months given below apply mainly to the highveld. Gardens in the south-western Cape may be from two to four weeks later as they take longer to warm up in the spring. In places with hot summers and mild winters, however, these plants flower from two to four weeks earlier than on the highveld. Such areas include the east coast from Port Elizabeth to Durban, inland to the Lowveld and northwards to the northern Transvaal, Rhodesia and the Congo.

JANUARY

Bulbous Plants
African Gladiolus (*G. psittacinus*).
Agapanthus (*A. orientalis*).
Arums, yellow and pink (*Zantedeschia*).
Begonia, tuberous.
Berg Lily (*Galtonia*).
Dahlias.
Flame Lily (*Gloriosa superba*).
Gayfeather (*Liatris*).
Gladiolus hybrids.
Harebells (*Dierama*).
Lilies (*Lilium* hybrids).

Pineapple Flowers (*Eucomis*).
Red Hot Pokers, Summer (*Kniphofia*).
Watsonia Stanford's Scarlet.

Perennials
Achillea (Yarrow).
Bergamot (*Monarda*).
Campanula carpatica.
Carnations.
Dragon's teeth (*Physostegia*).
Goldenrod (*Solidago*).
Helianthus.
Michaelmas daisies (*Aster* hybrids).
Pelargoniums.
Perennial Phlox (*Phlox paniculata.* Syn. *decussata*).
Rudbeckia (Cone Flowers).
Salvia turkestanica.
Shasta Daisy (*Chrysanthemum maximum*).

Annuals
Butterfly Delphiniums, Phlox, Marigolds, Zinnias and most summer annuals as in December.

FEBRUARY

Bulbous Plants
African Gladiolus (*G. psittacinus*).
Belladonna Lily (*Amaryllis belladonna*).
Crinum moorei.
Dahlias.
Gladiolus hybrids, summer.
Garden Montbretia (Tritonia hybrids).
Pineapple Flowers (*Eucomis*).

Perennials
Begonia semperflorens.
Cannas.
Echinacea purpurea (Pink Rudbeckia).
Monarda.
Pink Salvia.
Purple Salvia.
Salvia patens (Navy-blue Salvia).
Wild Phlox (*Sutera grandiflora*).

Annuals (especially if planted late)

Ageratum.	Marigolds.
Alyssum.	Petunias.
Browallia.	Red Salvia.
Candytuft.	Tagetes.
Celosia.	Zinnias, Giant.
Cleome.	*Zinnia linearis.*
Impatiens.	

MARCH

Bulbs
Belladonna Lily (*Amaryllis belladonna*).
Crinum moorei.
Dahlias.
Day-Lilies (*Hemerocallis*).
Pineapple Flowers (*Eucomis*).
Nerine bowdenii.

Perennials
   Anemone.
   Cannas.
   Carnations.
   Barberton Daisy (*Gerbera*).
   Gazania.
   Lion's Ear (*Leonotis leonurus*).
   Pelargoniums.
   Pink Salvia.
   Pycnostachys stuhlmannii.
   Ribbon Bush (*Hypoestes*).
   Verbena.
   Wild Phlox.

Annuals (if planted late)
   Ageratum.
   Celosia.
   Cosmos.
   Marigolds.
   Petunias.
   Red Salvia.
   Zinnias, Giant (if planted late).
   Zinnia linearis.

APRIL

Bulbs
   Dahlias.
   Day-Lilies (Hemerocallis).
   Nerine bowdenii.
   Nerine filifolia.

Perennials
   Begonia semperflorens.
   Cannas.
   Canary Creeper.
   Ceratostigma.
   Chrysanthemums.
   Lion's Ear (*Leonotis*).
   Ornamental Peppers (*Capsicum*).
   Verbena.
   Wild Phlox (*Sutera*).

Annuals
   Marigolds (if planted in November or December).
   Tagetes (if planted in November or December).
   Zinnias (if planted in November or December).
   Mimulus (Monkey Flower) (if sown in December).
   Browallia major.
   Impatiens.

MAY

Bulbs
   Anemones, starting.
   Narcissus, early-flowering types.
   Tulbaghia fragrans (Sweet Garlic).
   Red Hot Pokers, winter (*Kniphofia*).

Perennials
   Fuchsia fulgens.

   Lion's Ear (*Leonotis leonurus*).
   Ornamental Peppers (*Capsicum*).
   Pig's Ears (*Solanum mammosum*).
   Ribbon Bush (*Hypoestes*).
   Tuberous Begonias (if planted in December).
   Wild Phlox (*Sutera*).

Annuals
   Browallia (in sheltered places).
   Impatiens (in sheltered places).
   Poppies, Iceland (if sown in January).
   Primula malacoides.
   Sweet-peas (in sheltered positions).
   Virginian Stock (broadcast in March).

JUNE

Bulbs
   Narcissus.
   Nerine undulata.
   Tulbaghia fragrans.

Perennials
   Bergenia.
   Billbergia.
   Gazanias.
   Wild Phlox (*Sutera*).

Annuals
   Namaqualand Daisy, early planted.
   Poppies, Iceland.
   Sweet-peas, planted in March.
   Primula malacoides.
   Violas, starting.
   Virginian Stock.

JULY

Bulbs
   Bulbinella setosa (Cat's Tail).
   Daffodil, "Flower Carpet".
   Lachenalia rubida (window-boxes and pots).
   Nerine undulata.
   Tulbaghia fragrans.
   Red Hot Pokers, Winter Torch (*Kniphofia*).

Perennials
   Barberton Daisy (*Gerbera*) in warm places.
   Bergenia.
   Pelargonium mooreanum (More's Pelargonium).
   Pink Marguerite (*Chrysanthemum wardii*).

Annuals
   Namaqualand Daisy (*Dimorphotheca sinuata*).
   Poppies, Iceland.
   Primula malacoides.
   Schizanthus (Poor Man's Orchid).
   Stocks.
   Sweet-peas.
   Violas.
   Virginian Stock.

AUGUST

Bulbs

Bulbinella setosa (Cat's Tail).
Daffodils (*Narcissus*).
Grape Hyacinths (*Muscari*).
Hyacinths.
Homeria elegans.
Ifafa Lilies (*Cyrtanthus*).

Perennials

Bergenia.
Gazania.

Annuals

Dorotheanthus and *Dimorphotheca.*
Heliophila.
Poppies, Iceland.
Primula malacoides.
Venidium.
Violas.
Stocks.
Sweet-peas.

SEPTEMBER

Bulbs

Anemone coronaria.
Arums, White (*Zantedeschia*).
Babiana.
Bulbinella setosa (at Cape).
Freesia.
Gladiolus (wild species).
Homeria.
Hyacinths.
Ifafa Lily (*Cyrtanthus*).
Ixia (Wand Flowers).
Ranunculus.
Sparaxis.
Tulips.
Watsonias.

Perennials

Barberton Daisy (*Gerbera*).
Bellis perennis (English Daisy).
Cinerarias.
Dimorphotheca, Bloem Erf Beauty.
Pelargoniums.
Polyanthus Primroses.
Mesembs, early varieties.
Verbena.

Annuals

Calendula.
Cotula (Button Flowers).
Dorotheanthus and *Dimorphotheca.*
Felicia (Kingfisher Daisy).
Larkspur.
Linaria.
Lupins.
Nemesia.
Pansies.

Senecio elegans.
Silene coeli-rosa (*Agrostemma*).
Snapdragons (*Antirrhinum*).
Stocks.
Sweet-peas, late.
Ursinia.

OCTOBER

Bulbs

Agapanthus, early flowering.
Arum, White (*Zantedeschia*).
Chinkerinchee (*Ornithogalum thrysoides*).
Clivia miniata.
Daffodils, Late (Semper Avanti, Geranium, Mercato, Aranjuez, Actaea).
Diascia integerrima.
Dutch Iris.
Pinks (*Dianthus*).
Scilla natalensis.
Scilla peruviana.
Tritonia, Mossel Bay Kalkoentjies.
Watsonia angusta.

Perennials

Alyssum saxatile.
Barberton Daisies (*Gerbera*).
Begonia semperflorens.
Bellis perennis (English Daisy).
Delphinium.
Iris, Bearded and others.
Mesembs (*Drosanthemum* and others).
Pelargoniums.
Penstemon, Blue.
Polyanthus Primroses.
Poppies, Oriental.
Rehmannia.
Russell Lupins.
Verbena.

Annuals

Cotula (Button Flowers).
Dorotheanthus.
Felicia (Kingfisher Daisy).
Forget-me-nots.
Larkspur.
Lobelia.
Namaqualand Daisy (*Dimorphotheca*).
Pansies.
Poppies, Iceland.
Silene coeli-rosa.
Snapdragons.
Sweet William.
Ursinia.
Violas.

NOVEMBER

Bulbous Plants

Agapanthus, early flowering.
Alstroemeria, Ligtu hybrids and dwarf pink.
Arums, white (*Zantedeschia*).

Chinkerinchee (*Ornithogalum thyrsoides*).
Chlidanthus (Peruvian Daffodil).
Crinum bulbispermum (Orange River Lily).
Cyrtanthus parviflorus.
Day-Lilies (*Hemerocallis*).
Haemanthus magnificus (Royal Paint-Brush).
Hippeastrum (Amaryllis).
Red-root (*Wachendorfia thyrsiflora*).
Watsonia marginata (Mauve).
Watsonia pyramidata (Pink).
Watsonia stanfordiae (Cerise).
Watsonia, Stanford's Scarlet.
Wild Garlic (*Tulbaghia violacea*).
Wild Iris (*Dietes*).
Yellow Arums, starting.

Perennials
Arctotis stoechadifolia.
Barberton Daisy (*Gerbera*).
Begonia semperflorens.
Canterbury Bells.
Columbines.
Delphiniums.
Diascia integerrima.
Foxgloves.
Gaura.
Gazania uniflora.
Heuchera (Coral Bells).
Lobelia cardinalis.
Nepeta mussini (Catmint).
Nierembergia.
Pelargoniums, Ivy-leaved and hybrids.
Rehmannia.
Verbena, Red.

Annuals
Anchusa.
Calliopsis.
Eschscholtzia.
Larkspur.
Lobelia.
Pansies.
Sweet William.
Violas.

DECEMBER
Bulbous Plants
Agapanthus (*A. orientalis*).
Arums, yellow and pink (*Zantedeschia*).
Cannas.
Day-Lilies (*Hemerocallis*).
Lilies (*Lilium* hybrids).
Sprekelia (Maltese Lily).
Watsonia, Stanford's Scarlet.

Perennials
Achillea (Yarrow) all colours.
Barberton Daisies (*Gerbera*).
Begonia semperflorens.
Begonia, tuberous (if planted in September).
Centaureas, grey-leaved.
Chrysanthemums, Baby.
Coreopsis.
Diascia.
Dicentra (Bleeding Heart).
Gaura.
Gazania uniflora.
Geum.
Heliotrope (*Cherry Pie*).
Heuchera (Coral Bells).
Hollyhocks.
Limonium (Statice)—several.
Nierembergia.
Pelargoniums.
Penstemon, mixed.
Platycodon.
Shasta daisy (*Chrysanthemum maximum*).
Stokesia.
Verbascum.
Veronica.

Annuals
Ageratum.
Butterfly Delphiniums.
Candytuft.
Celosia.
Centaurea (Cornflowers).
Cuphea, Firefly.
Cynoglossum.
Gaillardia.
Godetia.
Gomphrena.
Lace Flowers, white and blue.
Lavatera (Mallow).
Lobelia.
Marigolds.
Nasturtium.
Nicotiana (Tobacco Flower).
Pansies.
Phlox.
Poppies, Shirley.
Portulaca.
Salpiglossis.
Sanvitalia.
Scabious.
Sunflowers (*Helianthus*).
Violas.
Zinnias, Giant.

CHAPTER FOURTEEN

THE GARDENER'S CALENDAR

One of the charms of gardening is that one can generally potter about doing the things one feels like doing without necessarily keeping to a tight schedule. If one is a little later in planting out annuals than one's neighbour, then there is always the consolation that your own will still be flowering when his are finished. If you have forgotten to sow seed, the nurseryman will come to your rescue with seedlings. If you've missed the opportunity to plant out roses and shrubs from the open ground in winter, you can buy them in tins and plant them at any time of the year. The growth of one's own seedlings is probably the only taskmaster, for when they are at the right size to be transplanted it must be done within a few days or their future growth may be affected.

There are definite cycles of growth in the garden and, although there is some latitude, one should try to plant things at the right time. Late planting may result in plants being cut back by frost before their flowering has ceased of its own accord. Planting too early can also be a fault in that the foliage of spring-flowering annuals which grows too luxuriantly before cold weather sets in is more likely to be affected by frost than if they were planted when the weather has started turning cooler. Autumn-flowering plants like Chrysanthemums and Dahlias will not give such good results if they are planted so early that they will mature during midsummer heat. Pruning too early will expose new shoots to late frosts, while pruning too late will delay both flowers or fruit.

It is possible, therefore, to recommend special periods for doing certain tasks in the garden, which vary slightly according to one's own climatic area. Gardens in the Cape warm up more slowly than highveld gardens and are generally a week or two behind in their planting times. Sub-tropical gardens in Natal do not have the problems caused by frost so that autumn planting can also be started a fortnight or month later than it is done on the highveld and this has the advantage that the weather will be cooler.

Only the more important tasks that depend on timely attention will be suggested here, month by month. It would be foolish to stipulate things like removing faded flowers or staking plants, for the intelligent gardener will do these automatically when plants need individual attention. The monthly calendar below will aid the amateur to cope with his work and plan in advance for a better garden. There are certain daily tasks which must be done to keep one's garden tidy, but these are not necessarily part of a monthly schedule, though most tidying up is done during the winter months, when there is less general activity in the garden.

How to Groom your Garden with Daily Tasks

Keeping the garden well-groomed and tidy not only makes for a pleasant appearance, but keeps down pests and even disease. Try to devote at least half-an-hour each day, preferably in the early morning, to routine removal of dead leaves from evergreen plants like Bearded Iris, evergreen Watsonias, Agapanthus, Red Hot Pokers and Day-Lilies. Remove dead twigs that may appear on roses, shrubs and trees at any time of the year. Remove faded flowers from annuals, perennials, bulbs, roses and some shrubs. Trim the edges of the lawn all through summer.

Pull out weeds while these are young and do not allow them to multiply so that they become overwhelmingly troublesome and time-consuming. Use a weedkiller, if necessary, over large outcrops of weeds, preferably while they are young.

Take time to walk around the garden each day noting whether plants are drooping for lack of water or whether they are troubled by pests. Spray as soon as foliage appears to be eaten by beetles in midsummer or at the first sign of invasion by other pests.

WHAT TO DO EACH MONTH OF THE YEAR

The Gardener's year starts in spring when everyone feels full of energy and enthusiasm for the new growing season. Presuming that one's garden is full of spring flowers which will not finish blooming until September, one must make plans for summer, so that one can whisk plants into the bare spaces as soon as these appear. The chief planting months in the garden are March for spring flowers, August to September for summer flowers and November for perennials and biennials which flower in the following summer. (See Chapters on growing Annuals, Perennials and Bulbs. See also the lists in "Preparing the Garden for that special occasion".)

SECOND HALF OF AUGUST

Watering. Keep watering spring-flowering bulbs and annuals and pay attention to watering evergreen shrubs. Start watering roses and shrubs that are showing signs of growth. Water evergreen lawns.

Fertilizing. Give dressings of manure or compost to roses, shrubs and new beds for summer annuals.

Seed. If one has a sheltered seedbox (see Chapter 20), start sowing seed in mid-August of warm-weather vegetables which have a long period of growth like eggplants, peppers and tomatoes, as well as late-blooming flowers like Red Salvia which can be transplanted as soon as the weather is warm enough. Otherwise, sow the seed in September and hope for a long, warm autumn. Sow seed of ordinary summer annuals towards the end of August for midsummer blooming or as late as December for autumn flowering. Aim to transplant seedlings into the garden by the end of September or the first week in October. Seed of some quick-flowering annuals (see Chapter 25), can also be broadcast into the open ground in September or as late as December.

Perennials. Divide and replant perennials into the border early in August, but not later than the end of September.

Bulbs. Plant *Hippeastrum* (Amaryllis) in pots or in the open ground so as not to miss the flowering period. Do this also with *Chlidanthus, Scilla natalensis, Haemanthus magnificus* and other bulbs which produce flowers in spring before the leaves appear.

Lawns. Scarify lawns which turn brown in winter. Continue to water evergreen lawns.

SEPTEMBER

Watering. Continue watering the foliage of spring-flowering bulbs which have flowered but still have green foliage. Do not cut it back or lift the bulbs. This may be a dry month so pay attention to watering shrubs, roses, irises and evergreen lawns.

Fertilizing. Continue to fertilize plants and beds if this was not done in September. Make compost with spent annuals and continue to do this each month of the year. Feed Camellias, Azaleas and other shiny-leaved shrubs as soon as they have finished blooming.

Seed. Continue planting seed of summer annuals and vegetables. Broadcast seed into the open ground.

Plants. Plant Chrysanthemums at the end of the month or at the beginning of October. Plant summer and autumn-flowering bulbs like Eucomis, Nerines, Montbretias, etc. Divide Water Lilies and fill pond.

Lawns. Aerate brown lawns with hollow-tined fork and apply compost if liked. Plan to give the first application of fertilizer as soon as the first summer rains fall.

Cuttings. Take cuttings of Fuchsias and soft-wooded or tender shrubs in particular.

Pests and Disease. Start spray programmes for Codling Moth on Apples. Keep snail bait handy.

OCTOBER

Watering. Water spring-flowering bulbs which may still have green foliage, but decrease gradually if foliage begins to turn yellow. Water garden regularly.

Seed. Sow seed of salad vegetables and maize in the open ground.

Fertilizing. Feed Roses at the end of the month as soon as the main flowering is over. Feed Irises as the first buds form. Feed Lawns. (See next page.)

Plants. Divide and replant Dahlias that are shooting or delay until the first week in November. Irises can be transplanted while in bloom according to their colours, otherwise it is best to wait until November.

Pruning. Prune rambler roses and spring-flowering shrubs like Weigela as soon as they have finished flowering.

Lawns. Fertilize brown lawns as soon as the first summer rains fall. Start mowing regularly as soon as growth starts. Fertilize and continue watering evergreen lawns.

Weeding. Pull out weeds while young and before they can seed themselves. Continue throughout summer. Use weed killer on gravel paths and drives especially when weeds are young.

Pests and Disease. Start spraying with fungicides on roses, fruit trees and tomatoes as soon as first rains fall or in areas of high humidity. Spray in advance for special pests—(Gladiolus for Thrip and Fly; Carnations for Bud Fly; Cucurbits for Melon Fly) and continue throughout season. Start spray programme for Fruit-fly on peaches, nectarines and guavas. (See Chapter on Insect Control.)

NOVEMBER

Watering. Water garden thoroughly if good rains do not fall after five days. Water annuals and perennials two or three times a week.

Seed. Sow seed in tins or seedbox of biennials like Delphinium, Columbine, Foxgloves, etc., for flowering in early summer of the following year. Sow successive plantings of warm-weather and salad vegetables. Sow early Cauliflowers.

Plants. Pinch back Chrysanthemums. Divide overcrowded Irises and replant in well prepared beds in another position if possible. Lift spring-flowering bulbs when foliage has ripened, dry and store. (See Chapter on Bulbs.) Transplant evergreen shrubs during rainy weather.

Lawns. Mow regularly. Water if good rains do not fall for a week.

Pests and Disease. Continue to spray susceptible plants with fungicides. Watch for Amaryllis Caterpillar on Nerines, etc. and spray immediately and regularly every week or fortnight until the end of February. Continue spray programmes for special pests as in October.

DECEMBER

Watering. Water all plants well during heat of mid-summer. Mulch with compost.

Seed. Sow seed of biennials if this was not done in November. Sow seed of Ranunculus and Anemone and keep shaded. Sow seed of quick-flowering summer annuals if these are needed for autumn display.

Fertilizing. Apply fetilizer as the buds form on flowers to promote large blooms and strong stems.

Plants. Divide evergreen Watsonias that have finished flowering, if necessary, and replant them.

Lawn. Keep mowing regularly and water deeply if rain does not fall for a week. Give second application of fertilizer about six weeks after first application.

Pests and Disease. Spray with fungicides. Continue with special spray programmes as described under October. Keep a watch for other pests and spray at the first sign.

JANUARY

Watering. Pay special attention to watering during hot dry weather.

Seed. Sow seed of winter flowering annuals like Poppies, Stocks, Violas, etc. that have a long growing period and should be transplanted by the end of February or beginning of March. Sow seed of Ranunculus and Anemone. This is the last month in which to sow seed of biennials which should flower satisfactorily in the following summer. Sow salad vegetables, cabbage and cauliflower.

Fertilizing. Feed roses at the beginning of the month while flowering for the second time or immediately afterwards, about six weeks later than the first application of fertilizer. Top dress with manure or compost.

Plant autumn-flowering bulbs that flower before the leaves like Belladonna Lily or Red Nerine.

Shrubs. Cut Hydrangeas that have finished flowering with a good length of stem.

Lawn. Mow regularly and water if rain does not fall for a week. Trim edges. Give third application of fertilizer towards the end of the month, about six to eight weeks after the second application.

Pests and disease. It is usually possible to stop spray programme for Codling Moth. Continue other spray programmes for special pests. Spray with fungicides at regular intervals throughout the month.

FEBRUARY

Watering. Continue as in January.

Seed. Sow seed of hardy winter-flowering annuals like Poppies, Stocks, Violas, but do not delay this after the middle of the month or they will flower late. Sow seed of Sweet-peas for early winter flowering and Snapdragons, Wallflowers and Calendulas for spring flowering. Sow salad vegetables and cool weather vegetables.

Soil. Prepare soil for winter annuals and vegetables, adding dressings of compost or manure, and remove spent summer annuals to make compost.

Lawn. Continue to mow and water regularly if rain has not fallen for a week. Do not fertilize later than the end of the month as growth begins to slow down in March.

Pests and Disease. Continue spraying with fungicides on roses or susceptible plants. Discontinue spray programmes as soon as fruit or members of the cucumber family are harvested. Continue to spray Carnations and for ordinary pests like aphis.

MARCH

Watering. Water winter seedlings, shrubs and evergreens regularly. Gradually withhold water if summer-flowering bulbs show signs of yellowing foliage.

Seed. Sow seed of quick-flowering winter annuals like Nemesia in seedbox or broadcast seed of Linaria, Cotula, Dorotheanthus in open ground not later than the middle of the month. Plant Sweet-peas until end of month. Sow onions and hardy winter vegetables.

Transplant seedlings of Violas into ground so that they can start flowering by the end of June. Aim to transplant all winter-flowering annuals and vegetables into the garden by the end of the month so as to give them time to get established before winter.

Plant spring-flowering bulbs of all kinds, preferably at the beginning of the month, but for a few exceptions. Plant Daffodils from mid-March to mid-April; Hyacinths at the end of March or early April, mid-way between Daffodils and Tulips. Prepare soil well before planting. Plant Lily bulbs which will flower in summer.

Cuttings. Take cuttings of Carnations and hardy shrubs.

Lawn. Mow less frequently as growth slows down. Do not water lawns which are dormant in winter after the end of the month, but continue watering evergreen lawns. Trim edges of all lawns.

Compost. Use summer annuals to make compost.

Tidy. Pay attention to general tidying up. Cut back perennials that have turned brown. Trim hedges.

Pests and Disease. Apply dieldrin to ant-infested soil once in three years or chlordane annually.

APRIL

Watering. Water spring-flowering bulbs and annuals regularly and well. Water evergreens regularly. Water roses and deciduous shrubs about once a fortnight or more frequently if the weather is hot and dry.

Seed. Sow quick-flowering annuals like Namaqualand Daisies during the first week, but not later, or it may be too cool for germination. In sub-tropical places seed can be sown until the end of April, but not later or it will flower when the weather is too warm in the spring.

Bulbs. Plant Tulips during second half of April and as late as the first week in May at the Cape, but not later or they will bloom during hot weather. Hyacinths should not be planted later than the first week in April. All other bulb planting should have been completed by the end of March. Pre-cooled bulbs can be planted later.*

Lawn. If lawns begin to turn brown, do not mow any more. Trim edges to give a neat winter appearance. Where lawns remain green, mow regularly. Water and mow evergreen lawns.

Compost. Continue as before.

Leaves. Stack fallen leaves in wire netting enclosure with layers of manure so that they can rot down on their own. Moisten occasionally.

MAY

Watering. Water spring-flowering bulbs and annuals regularly and well. Plant pre-cooled Hyacinths, Daffodils and Tulips.* Reduce water given to roses and deciduous shrubs, but water evergreen shrubs regularly.

Lawn. Keep mowing lawns if mild weather allows grass to grow. Water evergreen lawns in frost-free areas if liked. Treat lawns with 2,4–D if necessary.

Erect shelters for tender plants.

Tidy. Keep hedges trim. Pay attention to grooming the garden. Cut back yellowed foliage of Dahlias and perennials.

Plan. Order new roses and fruit trees and make holes ready for them.

JUNE

This can be a quiet time in the garden where one has to water and care for spring-flowering annuals and bulbs, winter vegetables, evergreen lawns and evergreen trees. One need only water roses and deciduous trees once in

*See *Bulbs for the Gardener* by Sima Eliovson.

three weeks. Make holes for new roses or fruit trees.

Tidy. Time should be spent in tidying the garden, weeding, removing dead leaves and growth or burning branches that are too hard for compost making.

Soil. Dig over any bare ground so as to aerate it, eliminate weeds and expose it to the beneficial action of winter weather. Give a dressing of lime to any soil or plants that may need it. (See Chapter 17.)

Construction. This is the best time for constructing paved areas, walls, steps, paths, rockeries or seedboxes.

Pests and Disease. Many pests such as aphids and Fruit-fly spend winter on evergreen foliage. Examine iris leaves for aphids and spray. Spray evergreen trees like guavas, loquats and avocadoes, especially near orchards, in case adults of Fruit-fly are sheltering in them.

JULY

Watering. Continue to water all growing plants, evergreen lawns and evergreen shrubs. Deciduous trees can go for a month or more without water and need not be watered during this month. They need to be planted in well-drained soil in the winter-rainfall area of the south-western Cape.

Plant. Be ready to plant roses or new trees that may be delivered at any time from the open ground.

Transplant any deciduous trees or shrubs that have not been doing well or require another position. Transplant *Magnolia soulangeana* in full flower.

Construction. Finish construction work started in June while the weather remains cool. Repair tools. Repaint garden furniture.

Plan changes in garden design at this time.

Lawns. Prepare ground for new lawns. Continue to water evergreen lawns. Weeds in lawns like *Poa annua* show up bright green against brown lawns and can be removed easily in winter. Also one has so little time to do this during summer. Remove all other weeds continuously.

Pruning. Start pruning roses, fruit trees or deciduous shrubs during the last week in July in areas with cold winters or a week earlier where there is no danger of frost spoiling new growth.

Mulch all trees and shrubs with well-rotted manure, especially Roses, Hydrangeas and young specimens, towards the end of the month. Use compost on Proteas and Heath.

Pests and Disease. Spray roses and fruit trees immediately after pruning with lime sulphur to kill overwintering pests like scale and their eggs. This is a general cleaning up spray. Repeat 10 days later. Use winter oils where necessary. (See Insect Control.)

Pools to add interest can be built in large or small gardens in many ways. The small rocky pool on the left has simple charm. The small-scale waterfall effect on the right is obtained by mounding soil against a boundary wall; water enters from a plastic hose laid a few inches under the surface of the soil and trickles over a rocky basin carpeted with moisture-loving, green *Helxine* (Baby's Tears). The flow is controlled by closing the tap when the pond is full.

This formal pool fits into the paved area with architectural elegance. Fresh green ground cover *Dichondra* relieves the paving. The brickwork of the double retaining wall may be softened later by creeping Fig (*Ficus pumila*) and miniature Ivies.

An excellent annual for window-boxes is the gay *Nemesia strumosa*, at its best in the spring. A warm, sunny position is essential in cold-winter areas.

Rocky hillside gardens, where the soil is shallow and dries out rapidly, are ideally planted with creeping or bushy Mesembs of many types and brilliant colours. Here *Lampranthus zeyheri* makes sparkling purple clumps in spring.

Plant a few bright annuals, like these dwarf Marigolds "Yellow Pygmy" and "Tangerine", at the edge of a group of leafy shrubs to light up a quiet corner when the shrubs are not in bloom.

An ideal mixed border with a graceful curve and tranquil background to offset the colourful annuals, perennials and shrubs within its generous dimensions. It is backed by a 3-foot dry wall, topped by a narrow, grassy walk and a clipped rosemary hedge, which gives it height and separates it from the garden behind.

A double border may flank a driveway, making a colourful impression when entering. One side only need be backed by shrubs. At the end of summer, plant spring-flowering annuals to maintain colour and fresh interest.

FIRST HALF OF AUGUST

Pruning. Finish all pruning during the first week and spray with lime-sulphur immediately afterwards.

Seed. Start sowing early-needed summer vegetables and annuals and keep in sheltered seedbox. Seed of Red Salvia can be planted at the beginning of August or even in mid-July if one has a warm sheltered place in which to keep the seedlings, which must be transplanted into the open only when the weather warms up in September.

Soil. Prepare soil and give dressings of manure and compost.

Plant new shrubs, roses, fruit trees from the open ground at the beginning of the month.

Divide Perennials and replant into the border.

Lawns. Scarify lawns preferably towards the end of the month. Continue to water evergreen lawns.

Pests and Disease. Keep watch for early pests like aphids and spray immediately. Apply dieldrin once in three years or chlordane annually to ant-infested soil if this was not done in March.

CHAPTER FIFTEEN

HOW TO MAKE CUT FLOWERS LAST

The pleasure of picking flowers as and when one likes far outweighs any extra trouble in growing them. Flowers grown in a garden will not drop their petals as easily as those bought and carried home.

Pick flowers for their lasting qualities, selecting those with strong stems, good colour and adaptability. Pick them at the right stage of development. Roses should be picked when the buds have loosened but are not fully open. Flowers of the daisy family, such as Chrysanthemums and Barberton Daisies, should be picked when fully open. Carnations should be picked when three-quarters open. Poppies should be picked in bud. Gladioli and Irises are best picked in bud with the lowest flower open. Remove the faded flowers in the vase. When cutting stems, make a cut at an angle so that the stem does not rest squarely on the vase and prevent water from entering.

The best time to cut flowers is in the late afternoon when it is cool, after 4 o'clock. The sugar content of the plant has built up during the day and the flowers will last longer than if picked in the morning. They may be picked in the early morning but never in the heat of the day. It is best to place the picked flowers in a bucket of cool water overnight, preferably out of doors in summer where they can be kept cool, and to arrange them the following morning. If they must be arranged immediately, give them fairly deep water and add more water to the vases in the morning. Flowers absorb more water in the first few hours after picking than at any other time. When picking flowers it is a good idea to carry a small can of water and place the stems in it instead of into a basket. One should immerse roses in water immediately after picking and snip off ¼ inch under water in order to get rid of air-bubbles.

Flowers last longer if their leaves are removed so as to reduce transpiration and other foliage can be used with them. Leaves should never be immersed in the water as they decay and pollute the water, shortening the life of the cut flower. Use a rose stripper to remove the thorns and skin at the same time from the lowest inch of rose stems.

Flowers with stems that ooze sap like Poppies, Barberton Daisies and Dahlias or that have milky latex like Poinsettia should have their stems burned or boiled in order to prevent the escaping juices from clogging the stem openings. The easiest way is to bunch the stems together and singe the ends in the bare flame of a gas fire or candle. Take care not to allow the heat to play on the flowers. Otherwise pour an inch or two of boiling water into a jug and stand the stems in it, leaving them until the water cools. Do not allow steam to reach the petals.

Flowers with woody stems like Hydrangeas, Chrysanthemums and many flowering shrubs absorb water better if the bark on the base of the stem is peeled off or the base is crushed or the end split upwards with the cutters.

Do not place the vase of flowers in a draught, in a hot sunny window or near a fire. Flowers last best in the coolest part of the room. Spraying with an atomiser during hot dry weather will help to keep them fresh. Wilting flowers can be soaked in tepid water and the ends of the stems cut off under water.

One can put things into the water in order to prolong the life of the flower. A little sugar in the water prevents the loose petals of Larkspur and Delphinium from falling and is also recommended for Asters and Chrysanthemums. Alum is said to make Hydrangeas last longer. A copper coin in the water is thought to prolong the life of some flowers. A little antiseptic like Dettol or Nomisol prevents contamination of the water so that decay is delayed.

No attempt is made here to instruct the gardener on flower arrangements. A lovely flower or graceful branch will inspire an arrangement and one should study the methods of those skilled at arranging flowers.

CHAPTER SIXTEEN

POISONOUS PLANTS IN THE GARDEN

Dramatic headlines in the Press, such as "Killer Shrub", referring to the Moonflower (*Datura candida*) or "Danger is blooming in the plant pot", referring to *Primula obconica*, sometimes startle people and make them pull out these plants, never to plant them again. If one pulled out every plant with poisonous properties, however, one would find many favourites disappearing from the garden scene. Whole books* have been devoted to the subject and it is as well to know of the dangers of chewing leaves and stems which may cause illness if not death. Children should be taught never to put parts of plants in their mouths and never to eat unknown berries or seeds. Bitterness is often a warning that many things are unfit for consumption and people have been warned against eating ordinary cucumbers or marrows which may develop bitterness at times.

Irritations of the skin can be caused by handling otherwise harmless plants. Some people will be affected by or allergic to a plant which has no effect on another person. Many saps are injurious if they enter the blood through cuts in the skin. Allergic people should be especially careful when picking flowers and should cut stems instead or breaking them and allowing sticky, milky or highly-coloured saps to run on to the skin. Skin irritations can be caused by picking otherwise harmless plants like Ivy, Sunflower, Chrysanthemum, Strawberry and Narcissus. Allergies like Hay-fever are caused by trees laden with pollen, like Acacias or Plane trees when the fruiting balls burst.

Facts exist about plants which have caused severe skin irritations to some people and illness or death to grazing animals. Those plants which are poisonous to stock should never be fed to pets and, although illness may not have occurred in humans, one should avoid chewing or biting the foliage or berries. Some examples of plants grown or found wild in Southern Africa are given here.

Annuals and Perennials. *Primula obconica*—irritating hairs. Scarlet Pimpernel (*Anagallis*)—sickness in dogs and horses. *Aster filifolius*—poisonous to sheep. *Senecio* —different species poisonous to animals and have killed

people when accidentally included with wheat. Blue-and-White Daisy Bush (*Osteospermum ecklonis*)—poisonous to cattle. *Dieffenbachia*—swallowing sap causes temporary loss of speech.

Bulbs. Arum Lily (*Zantedeschia*)—irritating sap causes swelling of throat. Tulp (*Homeria* species)—foliage poisonous to cattle and corm to humans. *Moraea* and *Bulbine* species— leaves poisonous to stock. Flame Lily (*Gloriosa*)—poisonous tubers if eaten. Bulbs of the following species are poisonous to stock and some to humans who might eat them— Blood Lily and Paint-Brush (*Haemanthus* species), Red Posy (*Boophane*), *Nerine*, Belladonna Lily (*Amaryllis belladonna*), George Lily (*Vallota*), Chinkerinchee (*Ornithogalum* species). The seeds of *Clivia miniata* are poisonous.

Shrubs and Trees. Plants with poisonous berries and seeds are Castorbean (*Ricinus communis*), Poison Bush (*Acokanthera*), many species of *Solanum* (Deadly Nightshade, Apple of Sodom, Winter Cherry, etc.), various species of *Cestrum* (Poisonberry, Ink Berry), *Jatropha*, the kernel of the Wild Almond (*Brabeium*), unless soaked to remove the bitterness, and the kernel of the ordinary Almond before it has ripened. The berries of the Syringa (*Melia azedarach*) are poisonous to pigs and fowls. The seeds and the leaves of the Stinkblaar or Devil's Apple (*Datura stramonium*) are poisonous and the leaf of the Moonflower (*Datura candida*) has a similar effect. The stem and leaves of the Oleander are poisonous to humans Wild Tobacco (*Nicotiana glauca*), Kruitjie-roer-my-nie (*Melianthus*) and some species of *Crotolaria* are poisonous to stock.

Shrubs with sap that can cause severe skin irritations are Poinsettia, Rainbow-Leaf (*Smodingium argutum*) and the Wax-Tree (*Rhus succedanea*). The last two belong to the same family as Poison-Ivy, which does not occur in this country. No indigenous species of Rhus is toxic. The oil in the skin surrounding the Cashew Nut (*Anacardium*) before it is peeled, is poisonous and irritating.

Succulents. The milky sap of the Naboom (*Euphorbia ingens*) and some other Euphorbias is blistering and irritating to the skin, while *E. caput-medusae* is poisonous to stock. *Cotyledon orbiculata* is fatal to fowls and stock.

The Medicinal & Poisonous Plants of Southern Africa by Watt and Breyer-Brandwijk.

CHAPTER SEVENTEEN

THE FERTILE SOIL

COMPOST; TYPES OF SOIL; ACIDITY AND ALKALINITY; FERTILIZERS; TRACE ELEMENTS

The soil is the basis of growing plants, yet little is done to improve it in the average garden. Garden soil is continuously being impoverished by removing plants that have taken up nourishment and by watering, which leaches the elements out of the soil. The aim of the gardener should be to put back into the soil what is being taken out and to add a little more besides. It is really quite simple to improve the soil in the average garden and the experienced gardener will soon see a theme running through his soil preparation, much as a cook who has a basic recipe for sauces. There is no need to worry about how much of this or that to mix into the soil—a dozen experts will provide a dozen formulas—for most plants will grow equally successfully in good fertile soil. Some plants may want it richer and some sandier than others; some will tolerate lime while others prefer acid soils; but apart from a few additions and omissions soil improvement boils down to a few necessities.

The greatest mistake made in gardens is the failure to dress the soil with bulky organic manures that improve the texture as well as enrich it with the chemical elements that promote different kinds of growth in plants. Reams can be written about the soil and its chemistry and there is a great deal to know about the different chemical values of organic materials that are added to soils as well as the merits of mineral fertilizers. All one's problems will be solved miraculously, however, if one realises that the soil texture must be improved first with a balanced organic material. All other knowledge of stimulating growth with special fertilizers, both organic and inorganic, will follow later.

Compost is the magical substance that should be added to the soil in unlimited quantities. This is a mixture of organic materials put together by man which decomposes to form humus. Humus is the fertile soil which accumulates naturally on forest floors where leaves and animal droppings have decomposed for many years. Leaf-mould describes humus which is derived from leaves alone. Compost and farmyard manure are the best organic materials to add to one's soil as they have more bulk than any other organic materials. Ideally they should be mixed together while making compost and can be safely applied to any soil.

WHAT ORGANIC MATTER DOES FOR THE SOIL

Organic matter in the form of compost improves the soil in many ways at the same time. Primarily, it improves the texture of soil, making clay soil lighter and adding body to sandy soils. By softening the texture of soil, it enables plant roots to spread more easily with subsequent more vigorous growth. Compost retains moisture so that it is possible to water less frequently. Earthworms and micro-organisms that make the soil more fertile can only exist where there is organic material in the soil and these will flourish if one puts compost into the garden.

Earthworms aerate the soil by their tunnelling, several feet deep, and enrich the soil by passing it through their bodies. Soil bacteria or micro-organisms live in the top six or eight inches of soil, called the top-soil, and break down both major elements and trace elements, making them available as food to plants. Soil fungi live at the roots of trees and break down complex substances, thus stimulating growth. The tree root together with its thread-like fungi or mycelium are known as mycorrhiza. Some plants, like Heath (Erica) and Orchids, are thought to benefit from specific soil fungi and this is known as mycorrhizal association. Interesting experiments on vegetables growing more vigorously side by side than on their own are taking place, and there are many secrets that may be discovered in the future, but all depend upon the existence of organic material in the soil.

Plants grown in soil containing compost are said to be more disease-resistant and can even withstand more easily the ravages of frost.* When there is organic matter in the soil, it is an insurance against anything going wrong. It acts as a buffer and slows down detrimental conditions that may arise, preventing diseases occurring through trace element deficiencies and poor growth through compacted soil and other causes.

THE USE OF CHEMICAL FERTILIZERS

These are derived from minerals or may be artificially

---

*See *The Living Soil*, by E. B. Balfour.

manufactured. They contain the elements which stimulate growth and which are also present in many organic materials. One hears a great deal of condemnation about using chemical fertilizers, but one should keep a sense of proportion about using them in the garden. There is no harm in using them provided that it is fully understood that they are not to be used as a substitute for organic materials. Chemical fertilizers do not improve the texture of the soil or add to its humus content, so that they should not be used exclusively as fertilizers. They do, however, provide nutrients to the plant quickly and in larger quantities than one can provide at one time in other ways. They should be used to give an added stimulus to certain aspects of horticulture—to improve the flowers of special prize plants; to feed lawns; to revive neglected trees and shrubs (see Care of Trees); to feed pot-plants that are growing poorly because of the limited amount of soil in the pots; to strengthen long-flowering crops like Carnations in rotation with organic feeding or for growing vegetables where sufficient manure is not available. Chemical fertilizers feed plants in hydroponics and ring culture of tomatoes.

Chemical fertilizers can be valuable if they are used in moderation and at the right time or one may do more harm than good. Being concentrated and easily soluble an overdose can easily be given and this might prove fatal. Excess nitrogen in soils can cause overproduction of foliage at the expense of flowers. In the case of fruit trees, this may lead to late harvests which expose the fruit to damage by bad weather. Stored fruit may suffer in quality. Plants suffering from an excess of nitrogen are more easily attacked by fungi or bacteria and are more easily damaged by hormone weedkillers. Continuous use of sulphate of ammonia will exhaust the lime in the soil and make the soil more acid. Nitrate of soda given in autumn will stimulate soft growth that is easily damaged by frost. Probably the only plants that can be treated exclusively with chemical fertilizers are lawn grasses, for grass itself adds organic material to the soil. (See Lawns, Chapter 24.)

Always remember that chemical fertilizers do not improve the quality of the soil, but feed the plant directly. The only way to improve the soil is by adding organic material to it—preferably in the form of farmyard manure and compost.

HOW TO MAKE COMPOST

The principle of making compost is to stack layers of plant material in a pile or heap so that it decomposes to make humus. Any heap of plant material will rot down after a year, but modern methods have been devised to hasten this process. The best compost is made with fresh manure, as animal residues are necessary to feed soil micro-organisms and fungi. The addition of manure assists decomposition, but other materials will also do so. These are known as starters or activators and include dried blood, sewage sludge, crushed papaw pips mixed with water, untreated tobacco dust and leaves as well as the inorganic sulphate of ammonia, used at the rate of a handful to the square yard. Ready-made organic activators can be purchased. It always helps to use a little material from an old heap to start decomposing new material.

Plant Materials Used in Compost Making include annuals and perennials that have finished flowering, vegetable peelings and fruit waste from the kitchen and weeds. The weeds are thrown into the centre of the compost where the greatest heat is generated and this destroys the seeds. It is wiser, however, to remove the seed-heads and certainly the bulbs of most weeds before adding them to the compost. Vegetable waste must not be left lying about on uncompleted compost heaps or it will attract rats. Newspapers and rags will also rot down, but should not be used to excess. Do not use diseased plant material or weeds which have been killed by hormone weed-killers.

It is best not to add layers of autumn leaves, grass cuttings or sawdust to the compost as these materials take a long time to decompose and tend to pack down and prevent the circulation of air. They are best left to decompose in heaps by themselves and may be added to the compost when half-rotted or used directly in the garden when well-rotted. It is a good idea to stack autumn leaves in a small enclosure made of wire-netting with layers of manure to assist rotting. Grass cuttings may be sprinkled in small quantities over more bulky material in the compost, but not placed in layers.

Use fresh green material in the compost or leave it overnight to become limp. Always moisten plant material before using it to make compost. Break it into shortish lengths, and cut up the thick stems of cannas and dahlias. Very hard materials like branches, dahlia tubers and prunings should be burnt and the resulting woodash used as a top-dressing anywhere in the garden.

METHODS OF MAKING COMPOST

One must establish a simple routine for making compost so that one can always have a supply on hand. It will take from 9 to 12 weeks to produce well-rotted compost and one should make it about once in three weeks to maintain the supply.

Compost can be made in heaps or bins above ground or in shallow pits, but it must be assembled in the same way in all cases. It is best to make it above ground in humid areas such as at the coast or in places with high rainfall where the atmosphere is moist, but it is best to make it in pits in dry inland areas in order to prevent excessive drying out. Compost should not dry out completely or decomposition will slow down, so that it helps to make compost in a partially shaded place.

How to Make Compost in a Bin or Heap

Bins. One should have two bins, in the form of slatted wooden boxes placed side by side, so that the compost can be thrown from one to the other after a month, in order to turn it. Instead of boxes one can make 3-foot high walls of wire mesh, bricks or concrete blocks with air spaces at the sides, all with removable wooden fronts. There should be no floor so that drainage is good and soil organisms can enter the compost. The boxes can vary from 2 feet to 6 feet square according to the size of the garden.

Heaps. The compost may also be built up in the shape of a pyramid-like heap which is about 4 feet square at the base and 3 or 4 feet high. New heaps can be added to one end every two or three weeks and the old portions can be used as soon as they are ready. The heaps can be enclosed by low wire fences to keep their appearance neat.

Method. Place the twiggy pieces of plant material at the base in order to assist aeration. Stack the moistened pieces of green material over it in a layer about 6 inches thick. Do not tread it down as air is necessary for the bacteria which cause decomposition, but chop downwards with a spade in order to eliminate large air pockets caused by rough materials. Place a 2-inch layer of fresh manure on top of this. If the manure is fresh an activator need not be used at all, but it can be sprinkled over the compost in addition to the manure or used entirely alone. Water this and top with a layer of soil which does not contain stones. Apply a dusting of lime after watering so that it is not washed down to come in contact with the manure. Do not add lime if you intend to use the compost as a mulch on acid-loving shrubs. Repeat the layers until the required height is reached. If there is not enough green material available, try to finish the heap within a month. After that time, the process is well advanced and it is advisable to start a fresh heap.

As soon as the heap is finished, cover the whole thing with an inch of soil all around so as to keep in the heat. If the compost is made in a bin, simply place the soil in a layer on top. Sacks can be placed over the compost instead of or in addition to the soil. A slanting piece of corrugated iron can be placed on top to carry off rainwater which might exclude air by saturation.

While preparing the heap, one can drive about three long stakes into the centre and withdraw them when it is finished. One can then pour ready-prepared activator down the holes if one has not used them while building the heap. They also act as air vents. The finished heap should be watered to keep it moist if it shows signs of drying out.

In theory, compost heaps should be turned twice, at monthly intervals, so that every part of the compost has a chance of being at the centre. If this is not possible, one can use the well-rotted compost at the centre and keep the half-decayed material to add to the next heap. The finished compost should have a pleasant earthy smell and be transformed into a rich, crumbly humus.

The Three-Pit System for Making Compost

The mention of a pit conjures up a picture of a huge hole filled with evil-smelling rubbish, but good compost can be made successfully and easily in a series of three shallow pits placed side by side. This is the practical method advocated by one of the exponents of compost making in the dry inland areas of Southern Africa, the late C. J. J. van Rensburg. Dig three pits, 3 to 4 feet square and no deeper than 15 to 18 inches. Leave a wall of soil about a foot thick between them. Fill the first pit with layers of moistened plant material, manure and soil, plus activators as when building a heap. Add a dusting of lime or omit this until later. Repeat the layers until the top projects slightly above the surface, as it will sink down when decomposed. Water and cover it with soil or sacks as before. If liked, pour the activators down vents left by withdrawn stakes. Water the compost if it shows signs of drying out in hot weather, but the earth walls should keep in the heat and moisture. If the pits are shallow and lightly filled there will be sufficient aeration.

After three or four weeks, dig out the compost and throw it into the second pit. At this stage one can add the sprinkling of lime which will hasten decomposition. At the same time start the whole process again with fresh plant material in the first pit. Leave behind some of the rougher pieces of half-decayed compost to start decomposition more quickly.

After a further three or four weeks, transfer the mixture from the second to the third pit and the material from the first pit into the second. After another three weeks, the compost in the third pit can be used in the garden or stacked in a shady place. If there is no room for three pits, dig two pits only and throw the compost from the second pit into a pile beside it, above ground, until it can be used. It is best to use all compost as soon as possible. The Three-Pit System is a neat and easy way of keeping a constant supply of compost on hand.

HOW TO PREPARE THE SOIL

Digging to make the soil soft in order to receive one's plants is one of the chief labours in the garden. This can be lessened if one keeps adding organic matter to the soil. Remembering that the top soil is that part of the soil which supports biological activity, we endeavour to keep it intact in one layer and simply to improve it from the top. Procedure varies slightly according to what one intends to plant.

If one is preparing the soil for shallow-rooted plants like annuals, it is not necessary to do more than dig to soften the top six inches and break up the lumps to a fine consistency. Do not sift the soil or it will be robbed of its fibrous content. Gardeners call this working the soil to a fine tilth. Spread a thick layer of well-rotted compost on top of this and lightly fork it into the top 2 inches so that it acts as a mulch which protects the lower layer. Do not dig it in more deeply than 6 inches or it will be lost to the bacteria that exist in the top soil. Where plants are already growing, one can spread compost on the surface without forking it in. The more one works the top soil, adding organic materials to improve its texture before planting each season, the less it will be necessary to dig. Eventually one will need to do no more than fork compost into the top two inches each season.

When planting bulbs that need to be placed from 4 to 6 inches below the surface, one should prepare the soil as for annuals. When planting the individual bulbs allow a little of the compost and topsoil to fall to the bottom of the hole so that the roots will have a good medium in which to develop. If one wishes to plant bulbs over a large area where the soil is hard and drainage is not particularly good, remove the topsoil altogether to a depth of six inches and set it aside. Loosen the subsoil to a further 6 inches and mix in as much fibrous material as one can gather. Use decayed grass cuttings, twigs or rough compost. Add coarse river sand and even small stones if the soil is heavy. Then replace the topsoil and spread a layer of compost on top as before.

This can also be done in rows over a large area, taking the topsoil out of a foot-wide trench, loosening the subsoil and covering it with the topsoil taken out of the next row. This is known as double-digging. Some bulbs must be planted in individual holes. (See Dahlias, Lilies, etc., Chapter 27.)

When planting trees, shrubs or roses which have deeper root systems, one can plant them in good garden soil without deep digging and aim to feed them from the top with dressings of manure. Where soil is poor, hard or clayey, however, it is essential to remove the topsoil and improve the subsoil so as to give the plant a good start. One can dig individual holes about 3 feet across and set aside the topsoil. Loosen the subsoil to a depth of about a foot and remove some of it if it is very poor and gravelly. Add a bucket or spadeful of manure to it so that the plant can benefit as the roots grow down during the following season, but spread a layer of plain soil, from 1 to 2 inches thick, over it so that the young roots will not touch it at first. If one can spare it, place good topsoil into the hole around the roots and fill in the top with plenty of compost mixed with topsoil.

CULTIVATING THE SURFACE

Digging or cultivating the soil between plants in order to keep down weeds can damage plant roots and must be done with great care and only when really necessary. Remove weeds when they are really tiny by turning over or scratching the top ½-inch of soil between seedlings without going too near them. Do not allow the weeds to grow large so that one has to dig deeply between plants. Some surface-rooting plants like Azaleas and Hydrangeas should never be cultivated with a fork, but weeds should be handpulled. Mulches laid on the surface will prevent growth of weeds. Eliminating weeds with a hoe can be done to some extent between rows of vegetables, but is never really necessary in flower beds.

Cultivating to make a dust-mulch in the belief that this conserves moisture should not be done except where it is necessary to break a crust which may form on the surface. Crusts prevent oxygen from entering the soil and should be broken, but one can prevent crusts from forming continuously by laying a mulch of compost on the surface.

AERATION OF THE SOIL

Well-drained soil is needed by nearly all plants. This simply means that it should be of a porous texture so that water can drain away easily and not collect at the roots. Few plants like having "wet feet", even though they may like a heavy soil which retains moisture for some time. Dry soil absorbs oxygen from the surface and this is displaced when the soil is wet. If aeration is bad, the plant roots produce carbon dioxide which cannot escape and this encourages fungus diseases. Heavy rains compact soil with their force and one should protect the surface with mulches of soft, absorbent compost. Overwatering also prevents aeration of the soil. (See Chapter 18.)

One can improve drainage in a number of ways. The best way is to build a terrace over a thick layer of stones, tins or builder's rubble. Mix sand or gravel with the filling soil, especially if this is heavy in texture. Take care to remove the topsoil before filling in the terrace and replace this on the surface. It will be found that most plants will thrive on this terrace. On a smaller scale, one can prepare individual holes for shrubs in the same way.

It is best to place shrubs that require good drainage on sloping ground where water runs off after rain. Rockeries, double walls and window-boxes all have good drainage where one can place special plants.

WHAT TO DO IF ONE HAS CLAY SOIL

Give the soil a top-dressing of agricultural lime (calcium carbonate) which helps to separate the particles. A month later, preferably in the spring, top-dress the soil with superphosphates, which lighten sticky soil. Mix in plenty of coarse river sand into the topsoil and fork in thick layers of compost and other organic fertilizers. Manufactured soil conditioners like Krillium will aid for a while, but the long-term policy of adding organic matter must be continued.

If desired, remove the topsoil and try to improve the drainage of the subsoil by adding quantities of rubble, half-decayed fibrous material and twigs. In extreme cases one should place pipes below ground to catch and drain away excess moisture.

WHAT TO DO IF ONE HAS SANDY SOIL

Sandy soils are easier to manage than clay soils, but they are usually poor and dry out rapidly, needing frequent watering. Introduce fibrous matter by top-dressing with plenty of compost and incorporate peat if possible. Lightly fork in organic fertilizers like bone meal and hoof and horn meal in equal quantities. Be careful not to overlime sandy soils as lime decomposes organic manures and makes the soil poorer. Apply lime if necessary a month before manuring the soil.

WHAT TO DO IF SOIL IS SALTY OR BRACKISH

Salty soils are generally poor and are common at the coast and in certain inland areas. Add gypsum (calcium sulphate), but be careful not to overdo this or the soil will become too alkaline and very poor. Top-dress with plenty of compost, manure and other organic fertilizers. Incorporate washed seaweed into the compost if one lives near the sea. Build up terraces so that the salt can be washed downwards.

Salt in the soil will cause stunted growth and death of roots. Excess salt in the air after gales at the coast will cause browning or death of leaves and can blacken annuals as if they had been burned by frost. Endeavour to plant salt-resistant plants on the outskirts of the garden

in order to protect tender plants in the interior. (See Chapter 1.)

ACIDITY OF THE SOIL

An acid or sour soil may be harmful to plants because it deprives them of essential plant foods like calcium (lime) and phosphates and may cause trace element deficiencies. Lime is an alkaline material that neutralises acidity, making soil sweeter, but it must be added to the soil with caution or it may do more harm than good.

Modern research has made it possible to measure the degree of acidity or alkalinity of the soil and this is expressed by a figure called the pH factor of the soil. A neutral soil has a pH 7. Acid soils are indicated by pH's below 7 and alkaline soils by numbers greater than 7. Indicators and soil testing kits are obtainable and enable the gardener to test his own soil if plants do not appear to be thriving.

One need not measure the soil accurately in order to grow plants successfully, however. Most plants thrive at a pH just below neutral and most garden soils are slightly acid or below neutral. Soils with a pH of 8 are known as alkaline, chalky or calceolareous soils. Few plants will survive at a pH higher than 8. Some plants are lime-tolerant, but most plants will succeed in lime-free soil. Other plants are lime-haters, while some, like Rhododendron, need very acid soils as low as pH 4. Degrees of acidity vary with different types of plants. Blue Hydrangeas need a very acid soil of pH 4.5 while Pink Hydrangeas need a much less acid soil of pH 6.

HOW TO CHANGE THE pH OF YOUR SOIL

HOW TO SWEETEN SOIL

By adding agricultural lime to acid or sour soil one can render it alkaline or sweet. One must first be sure that plants will tolerate it and then add it as a top-dressing to the soil. It will be washed downwards with watering. Too much lime in the soil can cause trace element deficiencies and even the death of plants as it "locks up" the elements and prevents them from becoming available to plants. It is usually necessary to add lime only once in every three years as a soil dressing, and only if the soil is deficient in it.

Lime hastens the decomposition of organic matter so that it eventually makes the soil poorer. One must keep adding quantities of organic fertilizers to the soil in order to restore fertility. Never add lime to the soil at the same time as manure, as it liberates the nitrogen in the manure and reduces its value as a fertilizer.

How to Make the Soil More Acid

Methods of making the soil more acid should be repeated twice or three times a year as conditions change through the action of rain and earthworms. The easiest and quickest way of making the soil more acid is by sprinkling aluminium sulphate around the surface of acid-loving shrubs and watering it in well. Use about two handfuls to the square yard. Sulphate of ammonia or iron sulphate will also make the soil acid. Other acid-reacting materials are soil sulphur (flowers of sulphur) and ammonium phosphate. In addition, organic mulches should be added to improve the humus content of the soil as well as make the soil acid. Replace them continuously throughout the year, especially on plants like Rhododendron, including Azalea. Leaves of Wattles, Oaks, Gums and Chestnuts, as well as Pine Needles, are suitable. Spent tea leaves and commercial tannic acid extracted from wattle bark, which is processed in Natal for the tanning industry, may also be used as mulches. Use compost which has not been made with lime as a mulch.

SOME LIME-HATING PLANTS

Vegetables and Fruit
Beans.
Citrus fruits.
Gooseberry.
Grapes.
Parsnips.
Plums.
Potatoes.
Pumpkin.
Tomatoes.
Squash.

Flowers
Arum Lily.
Orchids.
.Ferns.
Japanese Iris.

Lily.
Lupin.
Phlox.
Delphinium.
Begonia.
Cyclamen.

Shrubs and Trees
Azalea.
Camellia.
Erica (Heath).
Gardenia.
Grevillea.
Hydrangea.
Holly.
Magnolia.
Protea.
Rhododendron.

SOME PLANTS WHICH PREFER LIME IN THE SOIL

Vegetables and Fruit
Asparagus.
Cabbage.
Carrots.
Cauliflower.
Celery.
Lettuce.
Parsley.

Flowers
Calendula.
Cineraria.
Petunia.

Myosotis.
Poppies.
Stocks.
Sweet-peas.

Shrubs and Trees
Berberis.
Clematis.
Deutzia.
Lavender.
Lilac.
Ivy.
Spanish Broom.

SOME LIME-TOLERANT PLANTS

Vegetables and Fruit
Apples.
Cucumber.
Eggplant.
Melons.
Onions.
Peaches.
Peas.
Radish.
Rhubarb.
Spinach.

Flowers
Carnation.
Chrysanthemum.
Dahlia.
Marigold.
Narcissus.

Pansy.
Gladiolus.
Bearded Iris.
Snapdragon.
Zinnia.

Shrubs and Trees
Acacia.
Acer (Maples).
Buddleia.
Fuchsia.
Poinsettia.
Peony.
Hawthorn.
Rose.
Lonicera.
Genista.

USES OF LIME IN THE GARDEN

Calcium, the major constituent of lime, is one of the elements plants need for growth, but it is not a plant fertilizer. Lime improves the soil, provided that it is used with discretion. Judicious use improves the texture and fertility of the soil, but excessive use can impoverish it.

Agricultural Lime is the best form of lime for garden use. It neutralises the acid in soil and makes sour soil sweet. Such action liberates compounds like potash and makes them available to plants, so that it enables other elements to stimulate plant growth. Lime also assists drainage as it physically improves the texture of clay soils. On the other hand, an excess of lime prevents plants from using the nutrients present in the soil by reacting with some of the trace elements. Few plants can survive if there is too much lime in the soil. (See lists of plants which tolerate lime and lime-haters above.)

One should test the pH of the soil to see whether lime is required or not. Garden soils should be slightly acid in order to satisfy most plants and it is usually not necessary to apply lime as a top dressing more than once in three years.

When to Apply Lime. Lime should never be applied together with manure as it destroys its value as a fertilizer by liberating the ammonia (which contains nitrogen) quickly. It may be given as a top-dressing a month before manure or compost are added to the soil and will be washed downwards by watering. Lime decomposes organic matter and is added to the compost for that reason, but must not come in contact with manure in the heap. It will impoverish soil if organic fertilizers are not applied regularly.

Gypsum is a form of calcium used to rectify salty or brack soil, but cannot be added constantly for fear of increasing the alkalinity too much. It is better to improve such soil by adding large quantities of compost to it. (See page 89.)

NUTRITION FOR GARDEN PLANTS

Certain major elements are necessary for plant growth. Plants obtain carbon, oxygen and hydrogen from the air and phosphorus (phosphates), nitrogen, potassium (potash), calcium (lime), magnesium and sulphur from the soil. Minute quantities of other elements called trace elements are also needed for healthy growth. (See page 92.)

Phosphates, nitrogen and potash are of chief importance in the food value of fertilizers as they each play a definite part in the growth of plants. Phosphates stimulate the active growth of roots, stems and seeds and are used mainly on crops which are grown for their fruit and seeds. Phosphates are missing from most soils. Nitrogen, which is missing from many, stimulates leaf growth and is valued particularly for leafy crops. Potash is rarely deficient in soils, but is sometimes needed for plants that store starch and sugar such as apples, peaches, grapes and root crops. Potash frequently needs to be liberated by the action of lime in the soil.

The major elements are found both in organic and inorganic fertilizers. These can be given to plants together or separately according to what is required for horticultural purposes. All chemical compounds which contain the element carbon are classified as organic and those which to not contain carbon are inorganic. All natural fertilizers contain carbon. Urea is the only synthetically produced fertilizer which contains carbon. The following is a list of fertilizers in use today.

ORGANIC FERTILIZERS

ORGANIC FERTILIZERS CONTAINING NITROGEN

Nitrogen stimulates leaf growth and is important for crops that need to produce foliage and flowers. A shortage generally shows as a chlorosis or yellowing of the leaf, although this is also an indication of other troubles.

Farmyard Manure. This is a highly concentrated fertilizer which contains mainly nitrogen, some potash and a small amount of phosphates. It must be decomposed before it can benefit the plant and is a long-term fertilizer. It can be dug into the soil while fresh or well-rotted, but should not come in contact with bulbs or annual plants when fresh or it will rot the bulbs and burn seedlings. The safest way to apply it is to allow it to become well-

rotted in compost and this also makes it go much further. Perennials need more manure than annuals, while shrubs, trees and roses can be mulched heavily with it and be fed "from the top".

Old kraal or cattle manure is best for general garden purposes. Chicken manure is too strong to be used on its own unless it is well-rotted and old. It is best to sprinkle it lightly in compost or use it to rot down autumn leaves or grass cuttings. Horse manure is also strong and must be well-rotted before use.

Liquid Manure. This is made by hanging a bag of manure in a drum of water with the lid on until the water becomes tea-coloured. It can be diluted, about a pint to a gallon of water, for use as a stimulant to produce large flowers on annuals or to prolong the flowering season. Water it on to moist soil just as the buds form. Do not apply it to young plants or they will produce leaves at the expense of flowers.

Green Plants and Garden Refuse which are made into compost make one of the best organic fertilizers, for compost improves the texture of soil as well as supplying nitrogen and other elements. Compost-making enables one to use up garden refuse and fertilize the soil economically. It can be made according to a simple routine (see page 86) so that the owner of the smallest garden can have a constant supply of this essential organic fertilizer and soil conditioner. When it is impossible to make one's own compost, one may purchase it from many municipalities or buy used mushroom compost from commercial mushroom growers.

Green Manuring is done by farmers who plough a green crop into the ground and leave it to rot so that it adds humus to the soil, but the ground is generally left fallow until the material has decomposed thoroughly. This is not practical in a garden where one wishes to plant through all seasons. It is not advisable to plant before three months after green manuring as the decomposing green plant material takes nitrogen from the soil in order to aid decomposition. If there are growing plants in the area, they will suffer from a nitrogen deficiency, unless nitrogen fertilizer is added back in order to compensate. It is, however, difficult to guess how much to apply and one might easily overdo it with consequent ill effects. (See page 93.) It is much safer and easier to turn the green material into compost and dress the soil with it when well-rotted.

Fish, both fresh and dried, is rich in nitrogen and can be worked into the topsoil. Its fertilizing value should be balanced by applications of superphosphates and wood-ash or seaweed. Investigate whether lime is needed in the soil.

Dried Blood is a source of nitrogen, but does not become available to plants in acid soil. Mix it with soil and apply as a dressing.

Hoof and Horn Meal. This organic form of nitrogen is used both in the garden and for pot plants.

Waste Products like cottonseed husks, linseed meal and other vegetable wastes are organic materials with a low nitrogen content.

Urea. This is the nitrogenous solid content of urine, which is a valuable fertilizer. It is obtainable both in natural and synthetic forms. Natural urea is obtainable in the straw or manure gathered from stables. Pig urine has a greater percentage of urea in it than that of sheep, horses or cattle, in that order. Kraal manure has more urea in it than droppings collected from the field.

Synthetic urea is a highly concentrated form of nitrogen now being manufactured in this country in crystalline form. It should be dissolved in water according to the manufacturer's instructions. It was previously imported and used mainly in citrus and sugar farming, but will prove valuable to the gardener. Urea will, in time, replace the use of ammonium nitrate as it not only has a higher percentage of nitrogen, but is slower-acting and neutral in reaction so that it does not burn foliage. For this reason it can be used as a spray for foliar feeding of trees and other plants (see below) as well as applied to lawns and to the soil. Urea, being neutral, may be used on acid soil and will not increase the acidity of the soil as does ammonium sulphate, which is more useful on alkaline soils.

ORGANIC FERTILIZERS CONTAINING PHOSPHATES

Phosphates stimulate the active growth of roots, stems and seeds and are valued particularly for plants which are grown for their fruits.

Bone. Bones are crushed to form a meal and the more finely crushed the more readily available they are to the plant. Coarsely crushed bone meal is a slow-acting, long-term fertilizer which builds up soil fertility. It should be forked into the topsoil.

Guano. The excrement of sea-birds, guano is highly concentrated and rich in phosphates, but low in potash. If it has been collected from dry places it may also contain nitrogen, but this generally dissipates if gathered from places with a moist climate. Guano should be used in small amounts as a top-dressing, but may be applied freely if it has undergone the manufacturing process of being rectified or dissolved.

ORGANIC FERTILIZERS CONTAINING POTASH (POTASSIUM)

Potash promotes the formation of starches and sugars and aids plants to store these foods. It is useful for root crops, legumes and cabbages. Potash is present in all soils, but more so in heavy than in light soils. It is not readily leached out, but needs the presence of lime to make it available to plants. Its lack may be indicated by the browning of leaves and stunted growth.

Woodash (carbonate of potash) can be made by burning the hard parts of plants and can be added to most soils with safety. The ash should be sprinkled over the soil immediately or kept covered as it is very soluble when moist.

Seaweed is organic material that contains many elements including trace elements, but chiefly potash. Its fibrous character helps to aerate the soil.

INORGANIC FERTILIZERS

Inorganic, chemical or mineral fertilizers are made with varying amounts of nitrogen, phosphorus and potassium. Their formulas have numbers which refer to these elements in that particular order. A balanced formula like 6 : 3 : 2 is recommended for most herbaceous plants, but 2 : 1 : 2 is recommended for woody plants like shrubs and roses. Mineral fertilizers act quickly and supply nutrients directly to the plants, but do not improve the quality of the soil. They may be regarded as extra stimulants to plants, but should not be used exclusively without adding compost and manure to the soil. Lawn grasses are the only plants which may be treated exclusively with chemical fertilizers. (See special programme under Lawns.)

The best time to apply chemical fertilizers is just as the buds form on annuals like delphiniums and calendulas, so as to improve the size and quality of the flowers. Applied to annuals in bloom they prolong the flowering period. Concentrated chemical fertilizer may be dissolved in water and watered on to damp soil, while bulk fertilizer can be sprinkled on to moist soil and watered in. It may be raked into the surface of the soil before planting and watered in (at the manufacturer's rate per square yard), but should not be poured neat into a hole when planting a seedling. It may be applied a fortnight after transplanting seedlings when these are established, but do not allow them to touch damp foliage for fear of scorching. It is better to apply fertilizer in small doses than all at once. Concentrated chemical fertilizers may be used on pot plants and watered in or poured down holes to revive neglected trees. (See Care of Trees.)

INORGANIC FERTILIZERS CONTAINING NITROGEN

Sulphate of Ammonia. This nitrogenous, inorganic fertilizer is made synthetically. It loses its efficacy if mixed with woodash or lime. It acts quickly, turning lawns green and stimulating growth in about three weeks. It must be used with restraint or overproduction of green foliage will follow, sometimes at the expense of flowers, and this may also lead to fungus disease. Sulphate of ammonia eventually exhausts the lime in the soil and causes acidity, so that it should not be used constantly on crops except lawn grasses.

Nitrate of Soda is a soluble inorganic fertilizer which acts quickly, stimulating soft growth. It should not be used in autumn for fear of frost damage to this new growth. Constant use of nitrate of soda on heavy soil will make it sticky and difficult to work.

Nitrate of Ammonia, Nitrate of Potassium and Nitrate of Lime also contain Nitrogen and have a similar effect to Nitrate of Soda.

Limestone Ammonium Nitrate is now recommended in place of all the above nitrates. It is a quick-acting nitrogenous fertilizer, with lime added to offset any acidifying properties, and is safer to use.

Urea, synthetic. See page 90.

INORGANIC FERTILIZERS CONTAINING PHOSPHATES (PHOSPHORUS)

Mineral Phosphates. These are ground from rock deposits and called mineral or rock phosphates. They are slow-acting and can be added to any type of soil. They can be obtained mixed with superphosphates.

Superphosphates. This is a quick-acting dressing which is derived chemically from bones and rock phosphates. It is soluble in water. This valuable fertilizer is used on flowers as the buds begin to form and produces large blooms. It has long-lasting value in the soil and may be given as a dressing in the spring. Superphosphate causes an acid reaction in most soils and should not be used on acid soils unless they have been previously limed. It can be made less concentrated by mixing it with equal or double quantities of rock phosphate. Superphosphates lighten sticky clay soil.

Basic Slag. A waste product from steel production, this can be used in acid soils in place of superphosphate as it has a slightly alkaline reaction. It must always be applied separately.

INORGANIC FERTILIZERS CONTAINING POTASH

Mineral Potash. There are many forms of potash derived from mineral deposits. Sulphate of potash or potassium sulphate is considered to be the safest form of mineral potash to apply to most soils. Other manufactured potash salts are muriate of potash, potassium nitrate (also valued for its nitrogen content) and many less refined potash salts.

TRACE ELEMENT DEFICIENCIES IN SOIL

Trace elements in the soil which have been proved to be necessary for healthy growth are iron, boron, manganese, zinc, copper and molybdenum, while others may be added to the list in the future.

Most garden soils contain sufficient trace elements necessary for plant growth. Certain conditions may be created in the garden, however, which make it difficult or impossible for plants to take up these elements even if they are present in the soil. Such conditions then cause a trace element deficiency in plants. The chief causes for trace element deficiency are the wrong pH of the soil in relation to what each plant requires as well as poor soil structure and aeration.

Actively growing plants are able to absorb trace elements. If they do not appear to be thriving one should check whether they need an alkaline or an acid soil. Manganese and iron are most frequently lacking if the soil is too alkaline, while molybdenum is most frequently lacking where the soil is too acid for the individual plant. Sulphate of iron may be given as a soil application to acid-loving plants which suffer from chlorosis. Use it at the rate of 2 ozs. in 4 gallons of water. *Iron chelate* is a soluble organic iron complex, used at the rate of $\frac{1}{2}$ oz. in 4 gallons of water. It may be sprayed on to the leaves and is quickly absorbed. It may also be watered on to the soil around plants like Azaleas if the leaves are yellowing.

Plants need oxygen in the soil and this is missing if the ground is compacted through lack of fibrous matter. Compacted soil delays root growth and retards the absorption of trace elements. Poor aeration is aggravated by overwatering, for oxygen can only be absorbed when the surface of the soil becomes partially dry. (See The Art of Watering, Chapter 18.)

One can see, therefore, that good garden practice is the best way to prevent diseases caused by trace element deficiencies. One should always keep fibrous matter in the soil by adding compost or kraal manure to it, for this improves aeration and encourages the activity of microorganisms that make trace elements readily available to plants. The exclusive use of chemical fertilizers leads to trace element deficiency (except in the case of lawn grasses) as they do not build up the biological activity in the soil.

Aeration of the soil can be improved by keeping the top layer of soil soft and by breaking it up with a fork if a hard crust forms. Mulching with compost will prevent crusts from forming as well as keep plant roots cool. Good drainage is essential for the health of most plants and overwatering should be avoided.

It is no use adding a mixture of all the known trace elements to a sickly plant in the hope that it will recover, if growing conditions are not improved as described above. It has its dangers in that an overdose of any one trace element can kill a plant that requires only a limited amount of it. It is almost impossible for the layman to guess which trace element is necessary in a plant, for this can only be decided by laboratory tests. Some soils are known to be deficient in certain trace elements and one should obtain advice from one's local Department of Agriculture if one suspects that crop failures are due to mineral deficiencies. As an example, some soils in the south-western Cape are known to be deficient in zinc and manganese.

One can suspect mineral deficiencies by a chlorosis or yellowing of the leaves. Complete yellowing generally shows a deficiency in nitrogen, while yellowing with green veins indicates iron deficiency. Boron deficiencies cause pitting in apples, cracking of celery stems and browning of cauliflowers. The symptoms of mineral deficiency often resemble those of fungus diseases, wind injury and spray injury, so that only a trained expert will be able to tell whether a mineral deficiency is indicated. Indicator plants sometimes give the expert an idea of which elements are missing, but they can be misleading. Practical tests to spray plants with different solutions, or to inject them into the sap of woody plants may be carried out to see whether there is any improvement in growth, but this is not easy for the average gardener.

If trees and shrubs in the garden suffer from chlorosis, and all the practical steps in preventing trace element deficiencies described above have been taken, the gardener may experiment with weak solutions to see if the plant responds to any of them. One can ask the chemist to make a weak solution (from .1 to .5) of either zinc sulphate, magnesium sulphate or copper sulphate and try them separately as a spray on the leaves. (See foliar feeding below.)

PHYSIOLOGICAL DISEASES OF PLANTS CAUSED BY TRACE
    ELEMENT DEFICIENCIES

Manganese deficiency causes Mottle Leaf in Almonds, Apples and Beans in the south-western Cape and Mottle Leaf of Lemon, Naartjie, Fig, Pear, Peach, Plum, Potato and Rose. Zinc deficiency in the alkaline soil of the south-western Cape causes chlorosis in Apple, Apricot, Peach; Little-Leaf of Pear and Plum and Rosette of Pecan leaves. Spraying the foliage with a zinc or manganese spray might rectify these diseases in soil where these elements are known to be deficient.

Physiological diseases are also caused by too much or too little water, excess heat, wind and frost injury. Excess of nitrogen, lime or salt in the soil can lead to diseases and death of plants. (See under each heading above.)

FOLIAR FEEDING

This means spraying the foliage of trees so that they can be fed quickly through the leaves. This is done in order to revive a sickly tree or to feed an ordinary tree so as to produce better fruit or growth.

The older use of foliar feeding was only to supply trace elements to trees that showed signs of deficiency through chlorosis or yellowing of the leaves. In the past few years it has now become possible to apply the major elements through the leaves for the quick recovery of a tree, as well as to stimulate the growth of a healthy plant. This has been practised mainly in the citrus industry.

Foliar feeding is used chiefly to apply nitrogen in the form of urea to the leaves, as this is quickly absorbed and the results may be seen almost within a matter of days, instead of having to wait for weeks or even months. Foliar applications of phosphorus and potassium (potash) are not efficient as they are not so quickly absorbed and are likely to be washed off before they can be taken up by the leaves.

Foliar feeding does not replace the soil application of organic manures or inorganic fertilizers, as it is more troublesome to apply and possibly more expensive, but is especially useful in tree care when one wants a quick result for a tree or shrub that is not doing well. Urea can also be applied to the soil. (See under Fertilizers above.)

PLANT GROWTH REGULATORS

In recent years it has been found that hormones can be used on plants to stimulate or inhibit growth. These are not fertilizers. The action of growth-regulating substances is still a matter of experiment and the knowledge of how they act on plants still incomplete, so that they should be used with care and, possibly, restraint. They should be used strictly according to the manufacturer's instructions.

Root-forming hormone solutions have proved useful in rooting cuttings that normally prove difficult to strike and are useful in air-layering. Fruit-setting hormones can be used to make more certain the setting of fruit on tomatoes and fruit trees, especially if the petals have dropped through adverse climatic circumstances.

Gibberellin or Gibberellic acid (G.A.) is one of the newer plant growth stimulants that is still being subjected to experiment. It accelerates many types of plant growth. Its use, however, will not be merely to obtain tall plants, but to control many practical horticultural processes.

It assists seeds to germinate more quickly, especially useful for those which are difficult, slow or no longer fresh. Tree seedlings that are slow-growing in the early stages may be accelerated. G.A. has been used as a foliage spray on Pansies in order to lengthen the flower stems and to increase the number of flowers on Lady Slipper Orchids. It may shorten the growing period of biennials.

Experiments in America have produced grapes of better quality on longer bunches by spraying the bunches after fruit set. Treatment of the dormant twigs of deciduous trees breaks winter dormancy by inducing growth to begin where this might otherwise be delayed.

CHAPTER EIGHTEEN

THE ART OF WATERING

Watering is probably the most important task in the garden for, without sufficient water, the best fed plant would die. No amount of watering can make up for a good rain and one has only to see the growth put on after a rainy period to prove this to oneself. This gives an indication of how much water plants can absorb with benefit. Yet it is surprising that few people realise the importance of water and very seldom blame it on lack of water if their plants do not thrive. Whenever a shrub like a Camellia, for example, drops its buds, one should check whether it is receiving sufficient water, and whenever plants that are meant to thrive in the shade do not flower, it is usually because they receive insufficient water.

The problem of watering the garden is accentuated during periods of drought and heat. In the summer rainfall area of Southern Africa, there is usually a long dry period of intense heat in September and October before the summer rains begin in earnest. Early spring rains at the beginning of September force plants into luxuriant growth, which is even less able to withstand drought than if the early rains had not come. Hot winds deprive plants of even more moisture during this trying period, termed "suicide month" in parts of Rhodesia.

The enthusiastic gardener who has a large garden of precious plants despairs at such a time and cannot bear to walk around the garden at midday, noting drooping leaves. It is impossible to water the whole garden each day, which in any case is bad for the majority of plants, for this could only be a shallow watering. Sprinkling the surface of the soil does more harm than good, for it makes roots turn upwards in their search for moisture and makes it difficult for new plants to "take root" and become well established. Shallow watering also dries out rapidly and forces one to keep on watering frequently in an effort to keep the soil moist.

One must make a routine plan of how to water the garden in order to see that all types of plants, shrubs, annuals and perennials are watered adequately. One can divide an acre of garden into two or three areas for watering each type of plant so that no plant will miss its quota of water during dry periods.

Routine Plan for Watering. It may be suggested that all the shrubs on the one side of the garden are watered on Mondays and Thursdays while all the shrubs on the other side are watered on Tuesdays and Fridays. Wednesdays and Saturdays can be reserved for watering the roses. Besides watering the shrubs, the annual plants may be watered every day, especially while they are very young. Perennials can be watered two or three times a week if this is done properly. The rockery need only be watered twice a week, particularly if it is planted mainly with shrubby and perennial plants.

HOW TO WATER

Ground which is deeply soaked does not dry out as rapidly as soil which has been sprinkled only on the surface, so that if one waters properly one need not water the same plants continuously. Watering properly means to soak the soil to a depth of at least 6 inches in the case of annuals and perennials and even deeper in the case of shrubs and roses. One can test how deeply the water penetrates by inserting a trowel or spade into the soil to examine at what depth it is still wet.

It is extraordinary how long it takes someone with a hosepipe to soak the ground sufficiently, and few have the time or the patience to stand over the plants long enough. It really is essential to purchase a good sprinkler attachment for one's hosepipe, which will enable one to soak the ground scientifically and at the same time give one the freedom to attend to other tasks nearby, such as weeding and tidying up. Try to obtain a sprinkler that will cover a large area for this saves a great deal of time. The fine spray falling from a sprinkler allows water to fall gently like rain and does not compact the soil or cause poor aeration. It is less likely to knock plants over than the stream from a hosepipe, often turned on too strongly by an impatient garden "boy". If one must use a hosepipe, always adjust the nozzle so that the water sprays out without too much force and wave it about from side to side so that the water does not accumulate in puddles before soaking into the soil.

The sprinkler can be moved steadily along the herbaceous border or shrub border, leaving it longer in some parts than another if necessary. Beds which are in full sunshine will dry out more rapidly than shady ones and need to be watered longer or more often, but do not neglect the shady beds, for the small plants in these have competition from tree and shrub roots and need plenty of water.

For ordinary deep-rooted plants, one must aim to penetrate the soil deeply, then allow the surface to dry off partially so that oxygen can enter the spaces left by the evaporated water. One should try to give water which is equivalent to an inch or $1\frac{1}{2}$ inches of rain and this will penetrate to a depth of nearly 2 feet in the soil. To calculate the time it takes your own sprinkler to give water penetration of at least a foot, place an open shallow tin midway between the sprinkler and the outer edge of its spray and note how long it takes to fill the tin to the depth of an inch. Really deep watering does not dry out for a week. Commercial bulb growers allow their sprinklers to run for $2\frac{1}{2}$ hours in one position. The top 3 to 4 inches can be allowed to dry out without damage to shrubs or lawn while the top 2 inches can dry out in the case of mature annuals. Test with a trowel to see that the soil does not dry out more deeply before watering again. Annuals must be watered more frequently in the seedling stage as their roots are shallow and the surface should not dry out more deeply than half an inch. As a general rule, shallow-rooted plants require watering more often than deep-rooted plants. Sandy soils need watering more often than clay soils.

Specimen shrubs in the lawn and rose bushes in the rose garden need a different type of watering. In really hot weather the soaking which is adequate for perennials will not be deep enough for shrubs. Shrubs are better watered by removing the nozzle from the hosepipe and letting the water ooze out gently and sink down to the roots. Be careful not to allow the water to erode a hole and expose the roots. A water-breaker, which is a device fixed to the hosepipe, breaks the force of the water and enables a strong jet of water to be applied quickly without splashing or eroding the soil. Each shrub should be planted in a shallow "basin" of soil, at least 2 feet in diameter, or have a rim of soil around it. This basin should be completely filled to the brim before moving the hosepipe to the next bush. The shrub should receive at least 4 gallons of water at a time. If shrubs are to thrive properly they should be watered in this way twice a week during the summer months, except when there have been heavy rains. A good soaking may keep the soil moist for nearly a week. Watering can be commenced again when there has been no good rain for about five days. Light showers merely wet the leaves and do not reach the roots. Holes may be made over the root area of large trees so that they can be soaked more easily.

Roses should be irrigated in the same way as shrubs so that the water can sink down to the roots and also as a preventative against black spot. Penetration of this fungus disease takes place when the leaves are wet for a period of five or six hours, so that it is advisable not to wet the rose leaves when watering if possible. If a sprinkler must be used because of lack of time then it should be used before midday, so that the leaves have adequate time to dry off before the evening.

While watering the roses by moving the hosepipe from one rosebush to another, one can attend to essential tasks like keeping the soil free from weeds and fallen foliage as well as cutting off dead roses. In very dry areas, the rose beds can be sunk 3 or 4 inches below the surrounding paths and the whole surface can be irrigated. Sweet-peas are annuals with very deep root-systems and are best watered like roses by allowing the water to ooze out of the nozzle of the hosepipe and soak the bed every few days.

The Danger of Overwatering. People often hear that it is wrong to overwater, but this sometimes leads them to water insufficiently. The danger of overwatering does not lie in the fact that plants are given too much water, but that the soil is not allowed to dry out partially on the surface between waterings. Dry soil absorbs oxygen from the surface and this is displaced when the soil is wet. One must allow the surface to dry partially so that oxygen can enter the half-dry spaces, otherwise the carbon dioxide produced by the plant roots cannot be purified and plants may become stunted and attacked by fungus diseases. Overwatering also tends to leach nutrients and lime out of the soil, causing poor growth and acidity.

Do not, therefore, only water the surface and then stop for fear of overwatering. Do not be afraid to soak the soil deeply as described above, but only water again when the surface has dried to a depth of about 1 to 2 inches for mature annuals and bulbs or 3 inches for shrubs and lawns. Shallow-rooted seedlings should be watered as soon as the surface dries and should not be allowed to dry out deeper than about half an inch. It is a mistake to water soil if the surface is still wet.

Good drainage goes hand in hand with soil aeration, so that this will largely eliminate the problems of overwatering.

WHEN TO WATER

The question is often asked: At what time of the day should I water? Times of watering vary slightly in summer and in winter.

Summer watering. Shrubs and roses may be watered and irrigated at any time of the day in the manner described above. Annuals and perennials are best watered

Mass ordinary, easy-to-grow flowers in groups of separate colours for maximum effect. These make eye-catching combinations which may be varied with the seasons.

Orange *Ursinias* and yellow Button Flowers (*Cotula*) bloom together in early spring. Blue Kingfisher Daisy (*Felicia bergeriana*) acts as a foil to both.

Petunia "Fire Chief" and blue Lobelia "Crystal Palace" create an unforgettable colour combination in summer.

Achieve an artistic colour harmony for spring by planting the Gousblom (*Arctotis acaulis*) with its many glorious hues, beside cool-looking Bearded Irises.

Grouped in patches of red, white and pink, spring-flowering dwarf East Lothian Stocks are more effective than if the colours are mixed haphazardly.

Dwarf French Marigold "Spry" and purple Alyssum are trouble-free and striking companions, withstanding hot or dry weather during summer or autumn.

A bold planting of modern Bearded Irises creates a rainbow of colour which enhances all neighbouring plants. Although they bloom only in spring, their pleasant leafy clumps remain green throughout the year.

A lovely cascade for a low fence in warm, frost-free localities, is the spectacular Climbing Scarlet Clerodendron, *Clerodendrum splendens*.

Louisiana Irises are recent hybrids with showy, beardless flowers in many subtle hues.

with an overhead sprinkler before 10 o'clock in the morning, before the sun's heat becomes intense, or after 3.30 in the afternoon, when it becomes slightly cooler. There are two main reasons for this. In the first place, it is better for small annuals to be moist and fresh before the midday heat strikes them than to wait until they droop before reviving them with water. They will be better able to resist heat if their roots are not allowed to dry out, particularly before they have reached maturity. Young seedlings in sunny positions may have to be watered again at 4 o'clock in the afternoon in order to keep them moist and growing without any setbacks. This applies more to annuals than to newly-planted perennials which should be watered in the afternoons and only watered again in the morning if the soil is very dry and they seem unable to stand-up to the heat of the midday sun. As they get older, they should not require watering more than once a day and, if they are thoroughly soaked, they need be watered every other day or only every third day, depending on the temperature and the ability of the soil to hold water.

Another reason for not watering annuals and perennials with a sprinkler at midday during summer is an economical one. The water is evaporated by the sun while in the process of being sprayed, so that the full quota from the tap does not sink into the soil. It is then necessary to leave the sprinkler on for a longer period in order to obtain sufficient penetration of moisture.

Drops of water which remain on the delicate leaves of some plants act as lenses which allow the sun's rays to burn through them. Certain succulents like *Crassula falcata* will be damaged by such moisture at midday and tomato plants will wilt badly and be burned black if their foliage is wet during the sunny part of the day. Irrigating furrows may, however, be filled during the heat of the day, provided that the water does not splash on to the foliage.

As a routine for the day's watering in summer, therefore, one should start using a sprinkler as early as one likes in the morning, placing it on beds containing annuals and perennials and planning to cease by about 10 o'clock in the morning. At this time one should also water seedboxes and seedlings in tins.

After 10 o'clock one can use the sprinkler on beds of shrubs and sturdy perennials such as Agapanthus, Violets, Iris and other "permanent" plants. During the heat of the day one can irrigate shrubs, roses and trees. Watering need only be done at midday if there is no time to finish watering the garden in the cooler hours of the day, otherwise shrubs and roses may be watered earlier or later. It is better to water roses in the morning than in the

afternoon, even when irrigating, as a preventative against black spot. (See Chapter 38).

Winter Watering. The sun is not so hot during winter and does not dry the soil out as rapidly as in summer. It may not be necessary to water quite as often as during the summer months and it is not detrimental to water annuals during the warmest part of the day.

Seedlings and annuals that are wet at nightfall may have the moisture on their leaves turned to ice during cold nights, so that it is better not to water these towards evening. Annuals are best watered after 10 o'clock in the morning, when the sun has warmed them up slightly, and should not be watered after about 3 o'clock in the afternoon. The sprinkler can be used at midday on beds containing annuals and bulbs, for the weak winter sun will not evaporate the moisture as strongly as in summer.

The greater part of Southern Africa, which has a summer rainfall, often experiences six months with practically no rain from April to September. Plants which require a winter rainfall, therefore, must be watered copiously throughout the winter months. This applies particularly to spring-flowering bulbs like Tulips, Sparaxis and Daffodils, as well as spring-flowering annuals.

People often remain indoors during cold weather without a thought for the trees and shrubs on which they lavished care during summer. As a general rule, all evergreen trees and shrubs should be watered regularly throughout winter. They may be watered once or twice a week in the same way as they were watered during summer. Some spring-flowering evergreens like Azaleas and Camellias, as well as winter-flowering evergreens like Proteas, Pincushions and Ericas, require more water during winter than at any other time of the year and should not be neglected even in the coldest weather.

Deciduous trees, which show that they are dormant by the loss of their leaves, need not be watered much. They should not be left dry for longer than three or four weeks, however, and many can be watered as copiously as one chooses. Hardy deciduous trees like the Copper Beech, Crabapple and Prunus, as well as shrubs like Lilac, Weigela and Philadelphus, come from moist countries where rain often falls in winter and they should be watered regularly in dry areas. On the other hand, they will withstand dry periods of a month or more without harm.

Tender evergreen shrubs like Streptosolen, Hibiscus and Bouvardia should be watered in the mornings or at midday so that their foliage is dry by nightfall, for fear of frost damage. (See Chapter 19.) Frost damage is not so severe in moist places. Some tender shrubs and perennials like Fuchsias and *Begonia semperflorens* should not be watered much during the dormant period in winter in cold dry areas or they may suffer from the cold and even rot away completely. They should receive some moisture at least once in three weeks, however, in order to prevent complete drying out. These plants may be left out of doors quite safely in the winter rainfall area of the Cape, where the effect of cold is not felt in the same way as in dry, frosty areas.

Equipment for Watering. Sprinklers can be attached to one's hosepipe and range from inexpensive rotary sprays to very powerful mechanisms which distribute moisture like rain over a large area. Hardware stores and seedsmen offer a large range of sprinklers to suit individual requirements.

Sprinkler systems installed with underground pipes are expensive and usually far beyond the pocket of the average gardener. While labour still exists for gardens in Southern Africa, it is unlikely that sprinkler systems will be used much in this country. Movable struts and long pipes distributing water from holes at regular intervals are available in many shops, but the ordinary rotary sprinkler will serve the average gardener's needs if it is used correctly. A swinging spray which covers a large area is an efficient time-saver. The best sprinklers are those which fall softly over a wide area in imitation of rain. This prevents the ground from being compacted by the force of water and helps aeration. The labour of moving a heavy hosepipe from one tap to another in the garden is a very real burden to some people. This can be lightened by purchasing two hosepipes, each about 100 feet in length, to use in different parts of the garden.

Some parts of the garden require watering more often than others. Seedboxes require watering twice a day, as do tins of seedlings and shrubs awaiting planting out. It is an excellent labour-saving device to have a light plastic hosepipe, about 25 feet in length, attached permanently to a nearby tap, so that one can use it on seedlings whenever necessary without having to carry watering cans. The price of such a hosepipe is no more than that of a good seed-watering can and the nozzle can be adjusted to emit a very fine spray.

METHODS OF REDUCING THE NEED FOR WATERING

Soil which is shaded does not dry out as rapidly as soil which is fully exposed to the sun's rays. In order to shade the soil's surface without shading the plants themselves, the system of mulching was evolved. This simply means to cover the soil with a thick layer of material known as a mulch. The mulch keeps the roots cool and prevents moisture from drying out rapidly, so that one can reduce the number of times it is necessary to water plants. Mulches often prevent weeds from growing, prevent erosion and help to feed the plant. An organic mulch keeps soil

cooler in summer and warmer in winter. It attracts earthworms near the surface as well as beneficial micro-organisms. (See Chapter on "The Fertile Soil".)

MULCHING MATERIALS

Mulching has become extremely important in modern gardens which are plagued by droughts and lack of labour. Although the value of mulching has always been appreciated, research in mulching materials, particularly by leading Botanical Gardens in America, has opened new possibilities and techniques.

One could cover the surface of the soil with anything, even newspapers, but it is not practical to use anything as a mulch if it has to be lifted in order to water the plants. A mulch, therefore, must be permeable and remain in place while water is poured through it. Paper can be used in vegetable patches where it can be laid down between the rows and will eventually decay. The best mulches are those which are composed of organic material which will finally become part of the soil and do not have to be removed for any reason. This is particularly important when mulching small seedlings which will eventually cover the entire surface of the soil with their own foliage.

The secret of having a really effective mulch is to place it from 2 to 4 inches thick around one's shrubs or roses, so that the ground can be kept cool and moist for a long period and in order to keep down weeds. Well-mulched gardens, especially near the coast, can do without watering for a month or longer. It is important to weed the area before putting down a mulch of any kind and it is also important to soak the ground very well so that the maximum moisture can reach the roots and then be preserved by the mulch. Feeding should be done annually in spring before mulching, especially when the mulch is only partially decayed. The amount of fertilizer to be used has been established as 2 lbs. per 100 square feet of surface for every inch of mulch applied. Use a general fertilizer if desired. If plants become light in colour during summer growth, apply extra fertilizer watered through the mulch or as a side dressing. Mulches of many kinds are recommended in gardens, but it should always be remembered that appearance is important in the private garden. Newspapers and coal may make good mulches, but their use will not enhance the beauty of the garden. Living mulches, like groundcovers, have their value, but one must realise that they need water and cannot perform the same function as an organic or inorganic mulch.

Materials such as lawn clippings, chopped maize stalks or tobacco stems, ground mealie cobs, peanut hulls, spent hops, pine needles, wood shavings, sawdust, rough paper pulp, coarse straw, seaweed, partially rotted leaves, fibreglass, coal, cocoa bean husks, plastic film and wood chips may all be used as mulches. One must make use of mulches that are readily available, economical and easy to obtain or which are suitable for one's own climate. Good mulches should not pack down as the airspaces help in insulation. They should be light, airy and allow free air circulation and penetration of water. It is important to place the best-looking mulches near the house and, perhaps, use the less attractive ones at a distance. A variety of mulches may be used in one garden and this is often desirable.

Wood Chips. This is a favourite mulch in America as it does not disintegrate and may be used over and over again. Wood chips are a by-product of timber mills and are roughly about 2 inches long and an inch wide. They are useful only if one lives near timber mills, or the cost of cartage would be prohibitive. They would have to be chemically treated in areas which are plagued by wood-eating termites, or the termites would attack woody plants after making inroads into the wood chips.

All mulching materials with a woody base, like Castor-oil husks and cottonseed waste, which are obtainable from factories, should also be avoided in areas where wood-eating termites occur. Fully-grown Protea bushes have died within a month of placing such a mulch around them in the garden, the bark having been completely eaten through at ground level by the termites.

Cocoa Shells. These are the waste materials of chocolate manufacturing factories and make one of the finest mulches for a garden, if the cost of transport is not too high. The cocoa bean shells or husks are light and easy to spread, with a pleasant colour resembling rich soil, so that they blend into the garden unobtrusively and, in fact, attractively. They are particularly pleasant in a rose garden and, amusingly, give off a delicious smell of chocolate in the first week or two of use. They do not disintegrate rapidly and may be used successfully for at least a year.

Coffee Grounds are similar to cocoa bean husks in effect.

Compost. Always regarded as the very best mulch, this is only really effective if it is rough material. Very broken down, fine compost is like adding soil and, while excellent for improving texture and holding moisture, does not fulfil the requirements of a moisture-insulating mulch. If the compost is not fully decayed, as it seldom is when rough, one should add nitrogen fertilizer when applying the mulch. Spent mushroom compost is also suitable.

Leaves. Autumn leaves may be left under trees as they fall, so as to form a protection against cold, discourage weed growth and eventually become part of the soil. They make a better mulch if they are partially composted first, however, and do not mat or pack down. It takes about 3 years for oak leaves to break down properly, but one can keep 3 piles of leaves going so as to add a new leaf mulch each year. Keep the leaves in 3 ft. wire enclosures so as to keep them in bounds while decaying. When spreading a leaf mulch, which is inclined to blow about in the wind, enclose it with a low wire fence, from 4 to 6 inches high, or place a covering of chicken wire over the top of it. This is not attractive as a general rule. Leaves may be shredded so as to resist being lifted by the wind.

Peatmoss has a fine texture and colour, but has a tendency to dry out and then become impervious to water. It must be thoroughly moistened before use or it will cake on the surface and absorb water from the plant roots below it. It is expensive and should be kept for special shade-loving or acid-loving plants such as Azaleas and Begonias, which are kept moist.

Grass Cuttings are successful if they are used carefully and, as they accumulate rapidly in the garden, can be very useful. They should be piled up like leaves and not used for at least 2 to 3 years. They can be mixed with dried leaves or rough compost. Green grass cuttings should only be used if there is nothing else, as they pack down, generate heat while rotting, rob the soil of nitrogen and attract harvester termites (white ants). One must apply a good dressing of nitrogen before using green grass cuttings and treat them with dieldrin to repel the termites.

Sawdust is a good mulch if it is applied with nitrogen and a termite repellant. It is not toxic and does not make soils more acid. It is a good insulator. Coarse sawdust from a mill is better than fine sawdust from a carpenter's shop. Care must be taken so that sawdust is not a fire hazard.

Strawy Manure from stables is excellent, but must not be too fresh or it will burn plants.

Hay and Straw from farms and cattle feeds make good mulches, especially near the sea.

Seaweed or Kelp are good near the sea and add minerals to the soil. They should be finely chopped as their appearance is not attractive.

Pine Needles are very pleasant in places where they are readily obtainable. They are especially suitable for Rhododendrons. They are well-aerated and do not disintegrate easily or get blown about. They are light, neat and easy to move and re-use.

Stones and Gravel. These may be used where the effect is not too barren in appearance. Use small, rounded stones of good appearance or grey gravel chips. Stones sometimes heat up under hot sunshine and reflect heat on to the plants from their light surface. Stone mulches do not contribute nourishment to the soil and feeding must be done annually or more often. Organic material should be added to the soil to improve its texture before stone mulches are applied.

Plastic Film. Black polythene film is best used in strips so that moisture can find its way into the soil readily. It is not attractive and may be covered by a layer of gravel. It is inclined to build up heat and should be used carefully in summer. It does keep down weeds and keeps the soil loose and aerated, in a favourable condition for soil bacteria. It lasts for at least 3 to 4 years and is laid down in a single layer.

Its appearance makes it more suitable for the vegetable garden than the flower bed. It may be spread flat on the surface with small holes punched for seedlings. The holes will also let water through the plastic. The warm soil temperature beneath the plastic forces plants to make rapid growth and tender plants should be protected from frost if they grow too rapidly. The edges of the plastic must be anchored by soil to prevent wind lifting it and additional soil should be placed in the middle, at intervals.

Dust Mulch. This is not a true mulch, but only a term to describe the habit of gardeners of digging or hoeing the surface of the soil for about half an inch. The only real merit of this digging is to break a crust which may form on the surface and which prevents oxygen from entering the soil. Care must be taken not to injure plant roots and it is preferable to place an organic mulch on the surface to prevent crusts forming. Shallow-rooting shrubs like Azaleas or Hydrangeas should never be cultivated or the plants may die. It is best to place a thick mulch of leafmould on such plants.

CHAPTER NINETEEN

THE GARDENER AND THE WEATHER

Hot Weather. Very high temperatures, aggravated by low moisture, can cause premature ripening of fruit or shedding of leaves even on evergreens. Growth of flowers or fruit may be retarded and tissues may be permanently injured. Always try to water well during hot weather and do not let plants droop for want of water. Spray foliage of moisture-loving plants like Azaleas and Hydrangeas.

Do not cut away foliage on trees during hot dry weather or the branches may suffer from sunscald on being suddenly exposed to hot sunshine. Flowering cherries suffer from sunscald if their lower branches are removed. Train tomatoes on to single stems while young. If large side stems are cut away, the main stem will be exposed suddenly to too much heat and sunlight with possible injury to stems and flowers. Beans can be scalded in very hot, dry places.

Heat and moisture favour the growth of fungi which cause leaf diseases. Spray susceptible plants with fungicides from the beginning of the rainy period.

How to Protect Plants from Cold and Frost. Growth slows down during cold weather and many plants from cold countries become dormant during winter. At times the temperature drops below freezing point causing frosts. Hardy plants will grow normally again after the ice that has formed in the tissues thaws. A half-hardy plant continues growing after portions of it have been killed. A tender plant will be killed completely by frost. Frost accompanied by wind is more penetrating and destructive and is known as "Black Frost", for it blackens plants.

Ice forming in plant cells actually robs the plant of moisture as well as rupturing the cell. If a frozen plant is damaged badly it becomes incapable of absorbing moisture again and will not recover even if it is watered before the sun reaches it. Frost damage is not so severe in moist places as the plants are then not so severely deprived of moisture.

The home gardener can protect his plants from frost in a number of ways. Always plant tender or half-hardy plants in protected positions. A warm north wall or a north-west corner will provide protection from wind and cold. The overhanging branches of a tree and a windbreak of surrounding shrubs will also provide shelter. Dew which settles on plants during cold nights causes leaf injury to half-hardy plants if the sun shines on it before it has had a chance to evaporate. Tender bulbs and shrubs planted on a west wall are less likely to be injured by frost than if they are planted due north where the morning sun reaches them early. One can create a sheltered north-west situation for tender shrubs by massing shrubs or a hedge in a semi-circle or by planting them on the western aspect of large trees. Cold south winds may cause damage if the garden is very exposed, so that it helps to have a windbreak on the south side.

A south-west wall is fairly sheltered from frost, provided that plants do not mind partial shade. The east wall should be reserved for hardy plants which like cool conditions and shelter from hot afternoon sun.

Shelters can be erected around young plants which may be tender in the first two or three years. Ground temperatures in winter are colder than those a few feet higher, so that once plants grow up to about 3 or 4 feet they can resist the cold. Be careful not to smother the plant and deprive it of so much light and air that it will die of suffocation. Different types of shelters can be used according to the weather.

In most parts of Southern Africa, cold winter nights are followed by warm, sunny days. Small tender shrubs can be covered with upturned corrugated cardboard boxes towards evening which can be removed at about 9 or 10 o'clock the following morning. This must be done all through winter and is advisable for plants like Proteas which enjoy plenty of air circulation. It is not nearly as much trouble as it sounds. One can also throw calico sheeting or polythene film over tender plants on frosty nights, but do not let the latter touch the leaves when the sun shines for fear of scorching. Support it with sticks.

A more permanent structure of sticks covered with long dried grass or hessian can be made, but it should not cover the plant completely. Place sticks in a circle three-quarters around the plant with the north-west portion open. The sticks should be at least a foot higher than the plant. Stretch hessian over this fence or fix thatching grass to it to provide shelter from wind. Spread a roof of canvas, polythene film or grass over the top to prevent frost settling on the plant during cold nights. Sun and air will enter through the opening on the north-west side. One can also screen only the tops of some plants with hessian or polythene film nailed to four uprights.

What to Do During Periods of Drought. Shortage of water or an uneven water supply such as caused by drought following good rains can cause a disease called blossom-end rot which affects mainly tomatoes and chillies. A water-soaked spot appears near the blossom end and darkens, enlarging to cover a third of the fruit. Bacteria or fungi attack the area and cause rot. Water plants regularly and deeply to prevent the appearance of this disease. Keep down weeds as they compete with plants for water. Avoid stimulating new growth with excess use of nitrogenous fertilizers during periods of drought. Keep a mulch of compost on the surface.

Heavy and Continuous Rainfall can cause water-logging of the soil especially in the winter-rainfall area. Soil in the summer-rainfall area dries out more quickly because of the heat. As a result of waterlogging, oxygen is driven out, plants wilt suddenly and the roots emit a sour smell. Fruit will crack if the soil is flooded after being grown in dry conditions, so try to keep water supplies even.

Build up terraces in order to obtain good drainage in areas of heavy rainfall where soil becomes compacted and heavy. Pay special attention to drainage for plants which like dry conditions at a time when rain normally falls. Plants which come from a winter-rainfall area, for example, wilt and die suddenly as a result of heavy summer rains unless the soil is very well drained and vice versa.

CHAPTER TWENTY

PROPAGATION OF PLANTS

Growing plants from seed is the best method of raising annuals, perennials, bulbs, shrubs and trees. Certain plants must be raised from cuttings or by other vegetative methods as they have characteristics that do not appear or come true if they are grown from seed. This applies mainly to hybrids or varieties that have a particular shape or colour, such as weeping or variegated forms of plants or special fruit trees. Cuttings must be taken when propagating shrubs or perennials that do not set seed freely and is sometimes a quicker method than growing plants from seed.

GROWING PLANTS FROM SEED

Seed of some plants can be broadcast into the open ground (See Chapter 25, "Growing Annuals for Display"), but most seed is generally grown in tins or "flats" and the seedlings transplanted to the open ground when strong enough. One may use halved paraffin tins, wooden fruit-boxes, asbestos trays or clay pots. The owner of a garden which is half an acre or more should endeavour to build a seedbox or seed frame which will enable him to raise seeds with minimum trouble and maximum success.

How to Make a Seedbox (See illustration page 160). The ideal situation is against a hedge facing north. Mark an area 12 feet long from east to west and 3 feet wide. Either dig out the whole area (for a low seedbox) or dig a narrow trench all around, wide enough to hold a small concrete foundation for a brick wall which is to be 2½ feet high. Build the front wall up to this height and make the back wall one brick higher. Slope the top of the side walls from back to front. If liked, the seedbox can be a low one, with the front wall only a foot in height and sunk 18 inches below the earth. The higher seedbox, however, obviates tiring stooping.

The seedbox must have four glass lids which lift up independently. These may be hinged on to a wooden frame laid around the top of the brick walls or can be lifted out if necessary. The frames can be made of wood or iron. Each lid must have a notched stick (three notches at 6-inch intervals) to keep it open.

Preparation of Soil. Do not make a floor to the seedbox, but loosen the bottom soil and fill the box to at least a foot with stones, bricks, tins or rubble, which will provide ideal drainage. Fill the remainder of the seedbox with ordinary porous soil, mixed with sand if it is heavy in texture, to within 5 inches of the top of the front wall. The top 3 or 4 inches should consist of finely pulverised good garden soil, of which the top half inch may be finely sifted. Mix it with fine vermiculite in order to aid water retention or root formation. Peatmoss or sifted compost may also be added. The surface must be carefully levelled.

Preparation of Soil in Tins. Place a layer of stones at the base of the tins which must have holes for drainage. Rough material like pine-needles or dried grass can be used instead or in addition. Fill with good garden soil and sift the top half-inch as above. It is helpful to mix the soil with some fine vermiculite. Level off well.

How to Sow Seed. Use one tin for each type of seed. Use deep clay pots for seed of bulbs or shrubs that may have to grow for six months or more before transplanting. The large seedbox can be divided into portions according to how much room the seed will occupy. Start from the left hand wall of the seedbox, scattering the seed up and down until it is finished, then draw a line with a stick and insert the label at the side.

All seed should be scattered from side to side rather than sown in straight lines, as it will be spaced better and each seedling can grow unrestrictedly. If well spaced, seedlings seldom need to be pricked out before transplanting. Seed may be shaken up in a packet with sifted soil so as to distribute it evenly and avoid overcrowding. This is especially important when planting fine seed like that of poppy and primula.

Covering Seed. Very fine seed need not be covered, but simply pressed firmly on to the level surface with a smooth plank. A dusting of very fine sand can be applied through a fine sieve, but do not cover it thickly. Medium-sized and large seed can be scattered thinly, while very large seeds can be pressed individually into the soil, allowing half an inch or more between them. Cover seeds with finely sifted topsoil, shaken through a fine sieve or vegetable strainer, and not more thickly than the diameter of the seed. Press the surface with a smooth plank to consolidate seed and soil.

Watering. After covering all the seeds, soak the soil

with a fine spray on the hosepipe or with a fine-rosed, light, seed watering-can. Swing the spray from side to side so that the water becomes absorbed immediately and does not lie in one spot. If liked, the soil can be soaked before sowing the seed, but one must water the dry covering again. Close the glass lids and place a dark covering over them, such as canvas, rush matting or newspapers. Rest the lid fronts on a small piece of wood so that a little air can enter. Individual tins can be covered with hessian or wooden boards. They must be placed on bricks so as to allow water to drain away. For easy management, place them side by side on a low wooden trestle. They should be placed in a sunny, sheltered place.

Keep the soil moist until germination takes place. Lift the covers and water twice a day, about 10 o'clock in the morning and 4 o'clock in the afternoon. Do not water if the soil is very wet, but water before it dries completely or the growing seed will shrivel.

Care of Seedlings after Germination. As soon as the first seedlings break the surface, lift the lid to the first notch and to the second notch on the next day. On the third day, lift the lid altogether, but close it during the hot part of the day, from 10.30 a.m. to about 3.30 p.m. It is best to give the tiny seedlings full sun as soon as possible in order to prevent them from leaning towards the light or becoming spindly. Provided that one waters well before the sun is hot, they will not flag in the heat. Do not allow the soil to dry out and then water in the hottest part of the day or the seedlings may collapse. Some seedlings like shade at the beginning and should be planted together under one lid so that they can be kept shaded for a longer period than the others.

Pricking Out. Delicate seedlings like petunias or poppies may be pricked out before transplanting to the open ground. As soon as the seedlings have 4 leaves, plant them individually into tins of well-prepared dampened soil, spacing them about 3 inches apart. Use a tiny stick or dibber to make a hole for the delicate roots and press the soil firmly back into place. The smaller the seedlings, the less they seem to feel the shock of transplanting. Place the tins in a lightly shaded place and keep moist and protected from rain. After a few days, accustom them to full sunshine all day. This is called hardening off. Transplant after about three weeks when they will be strong and large enough. (See Transplanting of Annuals, Chapter 25.)

RAISING PLANTS BY VEGETATIVE MEANS

Division. This easy method of acquiring new plants is used on perennials (see Chapter 20) or on shrubs that form a thicket like Cestrum or Spiraea. Simply dig out one or more canes together with their roots and plant into tins or in their permanent position. Do this in autumn, winter or spring.

How to Grow Plants from Cuttings. Take cuttings during autumn or spring. Spring is better for tender plants. The easiest way is to break off a short side shoot with a portion of the main stem or "heel" attached to it. Another way is to remove a firm stalk from the top of the branch. Cut it from 4 to 9 inches in length, severing it cleanly below the junction of a leaf with the stem. Soft or greenwood cuttings may be removed in the same way. These are taken from the young shoots of fuchsias, geraniums, hothouse or perennial plants. The soft cutting should be short and mature enough to break when it is bent sharply.

Pull off all the leaves except the top ones and treat them with root-inducing hormones, especially if they are difficult to strike. Insert the cuttings two-thirds of their length into a tin of damp river sand, which has holes for drainage. Keep the cuttings shaded and the soil damp. Professional gardeners sometimes use a mist spray in a greenhouse which keeps the atmosphere continuously damp so as to facilitate rooting. Cover the pot of cuttings with an inverted bottle or with polythene film stretched over a wire frame to keep in the moisture. The polythene film must not touch the leaves. Polythene bags are most suitable. As soon as new leaves appear to be growing or the cuttings have been pulled out after about three weeks and seen to be growing roots, plant the cuttings into individual tins of good soil.

Some cuttings, like those of Poinsettia or Frangipani, grow so easily that they can be planted directly into the garden where they are to grow and simply watered. Some cuttings, like pieces of Ivy or leaf stalks of African Violets, will form roots if they are placed in a glass of water for about three weeks and may then be potted up. Lead the stems through slits of tinfoil stretched over the glass so that the leaves do not sink into the water.

Layers. This is a method of notching and pegging down branches of shrubs into soft soil containing compost, so that roots form at that point. Finally the branch can be severed from the parent plant to form a new plant. Some plants like creeping Cotoneasters or Rosemary will do this naturally in good garden soil. Slow growing plants like Magnolias must be layered for about two years before they will grow adequate roots. Layering requires patience and knowledge of which shrubs form layers readily.

Air-Layering. This method is used to propagate difficult-to-root or stiffly erect plants like roses or rubberplants. It enables one to root branches larger than the usual cuttings. It must be done in spring or summer when the temperature is high and the light is most intense. One should choose a stem of about ¼ inch in diameter and a year old.

Notch the stem just below a joint or node and wrap it with sphagnum moss which has been soaked in a root-forming hormone solution. Cover it with polythene film, which keeps in the moisture, and bind it top and bottom, preferably using insulation tape. In from six to ten weeks, when sufficient roots have formed and can be seen growing through the sphagnum moss, remove the shoot from the parent plant. Sever it below the notched area and make the top cut two joints above it. Remove half the leaves and plant the cuttings in clay pots. Keep the atmosphere moist and water well until the plants are established.

Grafting and Budding. These are practices best left to the nurseryman or enthusiast who wishes to make a study of these arts. They need attention, knowledge and experience.

CHAPTER TWENTY-ONE

WEED CONTROL

It is not essential for the gardener to know the names of weeds, for he will soon recognise them as having no garden value and realise that they multiply rapidly to the detriment of worthy plants, robbing them of light, water and nourishment. No gardener should have sleepless nights because there are a few weeds in the garden, provided that they are not unsightly or growing so aggressively that they prevent valued plants from thriving. The worst aspect of having weeds in the garden is that they shelter and provide food for pests like aphids, thrips, red spider and eelworm or act as hosts for bacteria and fungi so that diseases can be transferred to healthy plants. For this reason it is essential to remove weeds scrupulously from the vegetable garden and its surroundings or wherever one is growing prize flowers. The odd weed in the lawn or down the garden path must be removed more for aesthetic than for the above reasons.

The age old method of digging out weeds by hand is always best if it is done thoroughly and regularly. Sometimes weeds multiply so prolifically that the busy gardener cannot cope with them, especially when labour is scarce. Chemical weedkillers can help the modern gardener, but must be used with care or they may harm nearby plants or ruin a whole crop. Certain weeds cannot be controlled easily even with these chemicals, so that vigilance is needed to prevent them from becoming a curse. Such weeds are perennials which have numerous corms, bulbs or outlets deep underground, such as Sorrel (Oxalis), Wild Onion (Allium) or Nutgrass (Cyperus). One must simply dig deeply, especially when the plants are small, and wage constant war on them. Grasses like Quick-grass (*Cynodon dactylon*) or Kikuyu have underground runners and are difficult to eradicate as they store food and come up repeatedly after removal.

It is impossible to eradicate weeds completely as new infestations occur repeatedly. One can only attempt to control the growth of weeds so that they do not ruin one's efforts in gardening. It is essential to eradicate weeds when they are young, whether weeding by hand or when using chemicals. If one can remove weeds before they form seeds, one can reduce work in future years; as expressed in the old saying, "One year's seeding means seven years' weeding".

Weed Control by Hand. It is much easier to dig out weeds when they have just started growth than when they have grown large and there is less risk to nearby plant roots if they are pulled out before the mature weed has developed a strong root. Use a claw-like instrument or a fork to scratch at the surface of the soil, but do not chop at the ground between plants with a hoe for fear of destroying their roots, except in the vegetable garden, where one must leave enough space between rows to enter and eradicate weeds. Do not dig the soil while it is wet as this spreads disease and does not destroy the weeds so quickly. Loosening the surface of the soil in order to prevent a hard crust from forming not only allows oxygen to enter (see the Art of Watering), but checks weed growth. Avoid leaving large patches of soil bare as they are quickly over-run by weeds like Nutgrass which are difficult to eradicate. Weeds on lawns should be removed with a "daisy grubber" or two-tined fork that does not make large holes in the grass.

Mulches exclude light and prevent weed growth. (See under "Growing Vegetables" and "The Art of Watering", Chapters 33 and 18.)

In order to make weeding easier on a large bed set aside for annuals or on a bare piece of ground prepared for lawn, water it two or three weeks in advance of planting in order to start weed growth and then dig over the surface to remove most of the weeds before planting.

Weeds and Compost. Avoid adding weeds that have formed seeds to the compost. Many weed seeds are resistant even if compost is made by the best methods, while seeds on the outside of the heap seldom get hot enough to be destroyed. Young annual seedlings of weeds can be added safely. Never add weeds that have corms, nut-lets or bulbs attached to them, or they will be distributed all over the garden. The tiny spreading Spurge (*Euphorbia prostrata*) that sets seed so freely from under its creeping stems should also never be introduced into compost. Burn all such weeds or put them into the rubbish bin.

Never add weeds that have been killed by chemical weedkillers to the compost.

Weed Control by Chemical Weedkillers. These do not solve the weed problem completely and, as one must take precautions in using them, their use is not always convenient or advisable. They can be used mainly to control weeds on large areas of newly planted lawn or on pavements or gravel paths. Special weedkillers can be used to kill suckering trees.

There are several types of weedkillers, many of which are still in the development stage. Always follow the manufacturer's instructions implicitly when using them.

Precautions. All weedkillers should be used on calm days when there is not wind to blow the spray on to nearby plants or shrubs. It is best to water them directly on to the soil or weeds with a watering can, as fine sprays from a pump drift more easily. Keep separate equipment solely for applying weedkillers, in order to avoid injury to other plants. Wash utensils immediately after use with clean water. If one must use the equipment for other plants, wash thoroughly with washing soda and warm water. Do not allow weedkillers to come in contact with the eyes or skin and keep them away from open flames.

A recent development overseas is a wax bar containing 2,4–D, which is dragged over lawns to kill weeds and does not affect nearby plants.

How to Use Weedkillers

(a) To Destroy Garden Weeds. For ordinary annual weeds like Blackjack, Khakibos and many other broad-leaved weeds, as well as some annual grasses, use a selective weedkiller, like 2,4–D and its chemical derivatives. (Trade names are, Shell Weedkiller D. concentrate, Phordene 50, Kop 1, Kop 24, Hormotox 2,4,–D, Killrite 2,4–D, Horma-mine 2,4–D, Fernesta and Fernamine). 2,4–D may be applied to bare soil before the weeds appear (pre-emergence treatment) or soon after they appear (post-emergence treatment). It can be used on lawns after planting, leaving the grass unharmed, or on maize (mealies). Certain weed-killers can be used on strawberries, gladioli and other specified plants.

It is essential to apply 2,4–D to weeds when they are young and growing actively, from the time that they first appear until they are about three or four weeks old. The younger they are, the more easily they are destroyed. As soon as they have formed seeds or stopped growing, or even grow poorly during drought, the weedkiller will be much less effective. It is best to apply 2,4–D to bare ground before the weeds appear and then not to disturb the soil for two to three weeks. The soil or the weed foliage must be wetted thoroughly. When treating bare ground, it is best to water the weedkiller on to moist soil, or it can be watered on to dry soil if rain is imminent within a day or two. If growing weeds are treated, however, rain within 12 hours will wash off the weedkiller

before it has had time to be absorbed properly into the foliage. New lawns may be treated about 10 days after planting the grass. One can apply 2,4–D to mealies from five to seven days after sowing seed in order to prevent weeds from growing for several weeks, but once the mealies are up, do not apply until they are 3 inches high or on hot, sunny days or the plants may be injured. Strawberry beds should not be sprayed unless the plants have had 10 days in which to become established. One may have to repeat the spray at least once on lawns and three or four times on patches of weeds, at 10-day intervals.

Sesone. (Trade name Kop 1) is a selective weedkiller registered for use on Asparagus, Strawberries and Gladioli. It destroys germinating weeds and prevents their growth for four to six weeks.

(b) To Destroy Trees, Shrubs and Brambles. Woody plants that are difficult to eradicate such as Poplars or Gums, which send up new growth from stumps or pieces of root left in the ground, or prickly jointed Cactus and Brambles, or rampant shrubs that have become a pest in certain parts of the country such as *Lantana camara* in Natal and Port Jackson Wattle in the Cape, may be killed by means of a special brush-killer known as 2,4,5–T (Trade names are Shell Weedkiller LV concentrate, Kop 250, Low Volatile 2,4,5–T.) Do not use this on lawns or near any desirable plant. Keep the container sealed and store it away from any fertilizers, insecticides or other garden materials.

To kill a large tree, make cuts around the trunk with an axe, about 2 feet from the base, and paint them and the bark below with 2,4,5–T mixed with diesel oil or paraffin. If the tree is felled, apply this to the stump within 24 hours, soaking the cut surface and the bark to the point of run-off. Re-treat the stump if growth appears again. Small shrubs and saplings can be sprayed completely. Otherwise, cut down shrubs and treat the stems. Brambles must be sprayed when in full leaf and any new growth sprayed again in the following season.

(c) To Destroy all Plants, Grasses and Weeds on paths and tennis courts, one can use a non-selective or total weedkiller. As some are highly poisonous (such as arsenic compounds) or corrosive (such as sodium chlorate), their use by the ordinary gardener is not really advisable. Such chemicals are best confined to the experienced garden contractor or farmer. In any case, the treatment would have to be repeated after a few months or years to be really effective.

Sodium trichloro-acetate (Trade name Kop 3) is a non-selective weedkiller which may be used for perennial grasses on pavements and drives. It should be handled with care, but is not highly poisonous.

Simazone (Trade names Simazone 50 W and Kop 6) is a recent non-selective weedkiller which is safer to handle and can be used to clear weeds on pavements and paths where expense is no object. It is a wettable powder which can be sprayed on to the soil surface and is absorbed. It can also be used in weak dilutions as a selective weedkiller on Maize and Asparagus. Spray a few days after planting large areas, where it is not possible to weed by hand.

CHAPTER TWENTY-TWO

BASIC TOOLS AND LABOUR-SAVING EQUIPMENT

"THE RIGHT TOOLS FOR THE JOB"

The shops are full of tools for the garden, often bewilderingly so, yet some gardeners do not possess the basic essential tools with which to accomplish their work efficiently. A list of these has been compiled below, together with suggestions on how to use and care for them. This list may seem formidable, but it is not as extravagant as it appears, for many of these items will last for ten years or more if they are well looked after. They should be collected at the end of the day and stored under shelter. Implements should have mud cleaned off them so that they will be clean and ready for use.

The gardener will do well to check through this list to see that he has the necessary basic tools. Some gadgets will be mentioned later for those who like to find specialised tools for particular tasks. Few of us can resist those little articles that are such fun to use! Following on this list will be suggestions, together with accompanying constructional details, for labour-saving equipment that the author has used to keep the garden neat and efficient. They are especially useful for the gardener who wishes to make use of every inch of his ground.

SPADES

Large Spades. One large spade is necessary for digging and turning the ground. The handle, which is approximately the length of a walking stick, may be made of wood or iron. An iron handle is heavier than a wooden one, but has the advantage of not snapping when there is severe pressure on it. This large spade may be used for shovelling soil and manure, but it is best to have a special large shovel for this purpose as it saves time and effort. The blade holds twice as much as the spade and is especially curved up at the edges to prevent spilling.

Small Trowels are essential for digging holes when planting seedlings. These usually have a shaped wooden handle which fits into the palm of the hand. The basic one that is needed should have a wide, curved blade, roughly 4 inches wide. If possible, one should have a *Narrow Trowel* with a blade that is half this width. It will be found useful for transplanting small seedlings close together without disturbing the soil too much and also for lifting pricked-out plants from their boxes without damaging the roots. A *Miniature Trowel* will also be found extremely useful for handling seedlings or for potting up plantlets. This is less than half the size of the normal small trowel and is one such as a child would use.

FORKS

A Large Fork to match the large spade is essential for loosening soil, breaking up clods and for lifting and dividing plants like perennials. It may also be obtained with an iron or wooden handle.

A Medium-Sized Fork is extremely pleasant to handle when rough work is not necessary and is worth having even though it is not essential. This is light yet strong enough to dig out plants or bulbs and will be found especially useful when walking around the garden and digging out plants for one's friends.

A Small Hand-Fork to match the trowel is also necessary, mainly for digging and loosening the surface of the soil between seedlings. The small fork is also obtainable with a long wooden handle like that of a broomstick which enables the gardener to reach into the centre of a flower bed without trampling the soil. It also obviates unnecessary bending.

A Weeding Fork will be found useful for removing weeds from the lawn without removing too much turf. It has two pointed tines which grasp and lever the weed up in one easy movement.

A Hollow-Tined Fork is becoming an essential for those who take a pride in their lawns. (See Chapter 24.) This has hollow tines which pierce the ground and cut out a sausage-like sod which is automatically ejected from the top as soon as the fork is again inserted into the ground.

The Rake is essential for levelling the soil in flower beds before planting or sowing the new season's plants or vegetables. It has a handle like a broom and a cross-piece made up of a row of regular iron teeth.

A Broom Rake is not essential but saves labour in daily sweeping up of fallen leaves during autumn and winter. It is not as rough on the grass as an ordinary rake and does not remove additional soil like a broom.

The Hoe, with a long handle, is used to cultivate between rows of vegetables and cuts through weeds while tilling the soil. The hoe has a sharp blade which comes in two widths, broad and narrow. It is not essential and must be used carefully or it will damage plant roots.

Sieves. It will be necessary to have three sieves in order to cope with all types of garden work. A large builder's sieve is useful in a fairly large garden and is essential when laying out a new one. It will be used for sifting soil and screening all types of rubbish. Although it is not customary to sift compost, it may be necessary to sift this when there are numerous large twigs that have not decomposed or when large stones, wires or other unsuitable matter have crept into the compost.

A Round Garden Sieve, consisting of a circular, upstanding band of wood holding a finer stretch of wire mesh, is invaluable for preparing beds. Soil can be screened into a wheel-barrow through it and can also be sifted over large seeds in the open ground when sowing and covering it. It has a diameter of about 18 inches and can be manipulated quite easily.

The smallest sieve measures about 9 inches across and has a very fine wire mesh. An ordinary kitchen vegetable strainer with a handle can also be used in place of the regular garden type. This fine sieve is used for sifting the soil on the surface of the seed-bed before sowing fine seed and also for dusting an even layer of fine soil over the seed.

WATERING APPARATUS

A 2 or 4-gallon watering can is essential for watering small patches of plants, especially seedlings, or individual shrubs and trees, when it might be a waste of time to assemble the hosepipe. It may also be used for mixing or measuring sprays, although it is best to do this in a large bucket. A spray of water emerges from tiny holes punched in what is termed a "rose". The rose often becomes clogged with dirt or loosens with age. It is possible to purchase a separate steel rose with a rubber nozzle which fits on to all sizes of cans and does not slip off.

A Seed Watering Can is a helpful refinement which every enthusiastic gardener should have. It is small, holding about a gallon of water, and is very light and easy to lift. It is fitted with a very fine rose so that the water will not dislodge the seed before it germinates or harm the delicate young seedlings as they grow. The seed watering can should be stored when not in use so that it does not become clogged. It should not be used for other purposes as the rose will become loosened in time and cause disaster if it falls off into the carefully prepared seed-bed. Separate roses are not obtainable as yet.

The Hosepipe is an essential and may be obtained in rubber or plastic material. The diameter is normally ½ inch or ¾ inch, the latter size being more useful in the larger garden. Check which connections will fit the garden tap. The pipe may be purchased in different lengths, the most convenient being 100 feet. It is best not to have too heavy a hosepipe or this may knock over young plants, besides being very tiring to handle. The hosepipe should be kept in the shade when not in use and should be taken in each night. An iron reel may be obtained which makes it easy to roll up the pipe and keep it stored.

The number of hosepipes one owns depends on the size of the garden. It is desirable to have two long hosepipes for a garden of an acre in order to cope with the work, for the one pipe can be hand-held while the other is moved about with a spray attachment. It saves time and labour to have two hosepipes, for they can both be used for spraying the garden while handwork like digging, mowing or planting out seedlings is being performed. It is a good idea to obtain a short length of hosepipe, say 15 feet long, to be fitted permanently to a tap adjacent to the working area of the garden where there are seed-beds or potted plants. This saves the labour of carrying watering cans and, if a fine adjustment is made on the pipe, will make it unnecessary to buy a seed watering can. Care must be taken not to have too strong a jet when watering seedlings, no matter how fine the spray.

SPRINKLERS

Sprinklers are obtainable which fit on to the end of the hosepipe and make it possible to imitate rain by allowing the spray to remain on one spot. These water the garden ideally (see "The Art of Watering"), saving time and energy. There are many different sprinklers in the shops. Some rotate and send out a circular spray extending for a radius of 10 feet or more, while others cover a more oblong area. They are generally inexpensive and can be moved about with ease. Another type consists of a length of hosepipe, pierced with holes, which fits on to the ordinary hosepipe. This covers a larger area and does not have to be moved so frequently. It is especially useful for long beds like herbaceous borders. More expensive but powerful sprays may be purchased for large gardens. These swing from side to side and irrigate a large area without having to be moved often. An inexpensive gadget can be made to support the ordinary nozzle of the hosepipe so as to allow it to play on to a flower bed without attaching a spray. This is simply an iron stake which is formed into a 3-inch, inverted triangle at the top. The sharp end is plunged into the ground and the nozzle of the pipe rests firmly in the triangle.

SPRINKLER SYSTEMS

Underground pipes with built-in sprinklers for lawns and flower beds are obtainable. These are especially valuable for lawns in drier areas. Avoid placing plants which do not like to be watered or to have wet foliage together with plants which will benefit from overhead watering. For use in rose gardens it is best to obtain sprinkler-tops which spray the water sideways over the soil without wetting the foliage.

SPRAYING APPARATUS

It is essential to have some sort of spraying apparatus to apply poisons in order to control insect pests. A simple fly-spray, such as one used for the kitchen, is adequate, but the effort of spraying will be far less if a "continuous-spray" type of hand pump is used. As the handle is pumped in and out, a continuous spray is ejected and this lessens the work, also enabling one to move the spray in all directions without losing time. This type of spray is suitable for the very small garden, but as soon as one owns more than about three dozen roses, for example, then it becomes irksome to keep refilling the barrel of the hand pump.

A Stirrup Pump will be found convenient and quick. A steel tube is lowered into a bucket of ready mixed spray and this is connected by a rubber tube to a nozzle. The user holds the nozzle in one hand while pumping the handle of the spray slowly up and down with the other. A continuous fine spray will emerge until the liquid is finished. A knapsack spray allows for greater freedom of movement. All spraying apparatus should be rinsed out with clear water after use and before being stored away.

DUSTING BELLOWS

These are obtainable if dusting with powders is done. The poison is placed in a small can and shaken through a fine mesh onto the plants.

LAWN-MOWERS

Without wishing to extol one make of lawn-mower above another, it may be mentioned that many different types are obtainable, from simple hand-mowers to those driven by petrol or electricity. There are even new American mowers upon which the gardener can sit and steer while the lawn is being cut and there is a new radio-controlled mower which has been recently developed in England. These will indeed bring joy into the task of mowing the lawn when they are freely available to the average gardener in this country. Most gardens have an ordinary hand-mower which is quite adequate and most people manage to puzzle out the intricacies of keeping it

sharp and adjusted so that neither too much nor too little is cut off the lawn. The mower must be kept oiled and should be sharpened once at the beginning of spring and once again at the height of the growing season, if necessary. It should never be left out of doors when not in use. (See Chapter 24).

SECATEURS OR CUTTERS

Even if one engages a professional to do one's pruning, it is essential to have a sharp cutter for constant garden use. This will be used for cutting flowers and stakes, as well as for training back branches and performing many other useful tasks.

There are two main types of cutters which fit the hand. One has two sharp overlapping blades like a parrot's bill. The other has one thick flat blade and one sharp blade which snaps up against it. Both are suitable, provided that they make a clean cut and do not bruise the stems or they will leave an entry for disease into such plants as roses. The cutters must be kept sharp. An easy way of honing them is to obtain a piece of flint from any hardware store and draw it along the sharp edge of the cutter much in the same way as one sharpens a carving knife. When pruning, the blade may be sharpened several times during the day to keep it in good working order.

TREE AND ROSE PRUNERS

The same type of cutter described above may be obtained with long handles for pruning trees without having to climb on to ladders and may be used for reaching into the centre of rose bushes to prune off the stouter branches. This cutter has more leverage than the ordinary secateurs and takes much of the effort out of cutting thick branches. The wooden handles are about 18 inches long.

A tree pruner with broomstick-long handles is also obtainable, but this is not necessary for the average home gardener with a few fruit trees. It enables the owner of a large orchard to prune without too much climbing of ladders.

SAWS

The only saw that the gardener is likely to need is a pruning saw. All manner of saws are obtainable which must be sharpened once a year. The best type of pruning saw is the hacksaw type with a thin blade which can be turned in all directions. This enables one to reach between awkwardly situated branches and to saw them off from any direction. It is particularly valuable as it enables one to saw away from other branches and avoid damaging them. The blades are usually replaceable.

SHEARS

Hedge Shears. These are essential for keeping the hedge in trim. These generally have two stout wooden handles, about 18 inches long, which are held in both hands and manipulate two long, sharp blades. These must be kept sharp. Power tools are obtainable for this purpose.

Lawn Shears are necessary for keeping the edges of lawn neat.

WHEELBARROW

At least one wheelbarrow is necessary for carrying soil or plants in a garden. Wheels which have rubber tyres do not make marks on the grass and are easier to handle.

KNEE-PAD

A rubber knee-pad is a boon to those who plant out their own seedlings, for it both cushions the knees and keeps them clean. It is essential to kneel when working properly for no one can work deftly when assuming a hooped position. The rubber knee-pad is simply a small oblong or kidney-shaped piece of rubber with a honeycomb of rubber underneath which gives with one's weight. It is easily washed off and will last for years.

LABOUR-SAVING EQUIPMENT

Behind the facade of many a beautiful, well-cared-for garden, there is often a "horrible corner". Compost is usually made near here, leaving its inevitable residue of hard sticks and mounds of dry leaves or grass cuttings which are too much to cope with in making compost. The making of compost will be discussed in another chapter (Chapter 17), but, at the risk of repetition, it may be mentioned here that things such as grass cuttings may only be used in small quantities in the compost mixture as they do not break down quickly if they are used in thick layers. The correct procedure is to leave these to disintegrate in a heap by themselves and use them gradually in the making of compost. Somehow these heaps have a way of growing out of bounds and, coupled with the fact that one often fails to do the right thing at the right time, one frequently accumulates a heap of residue that is not suitable for adding to the compost. Leaves like pine needles and gum leaves also take so long to disintegrate that they also become a problem to store.

The best way to clear this up is to burn it and one may be comforted by the knowledge that the resulting woodash will also be beneficial to the garden. (See Chapter 17.)

A good way of storing leaves that can ultimately be turned into leafmould is to drive six 4-foot stakes into the ground and encircle this with ordinary chicken wire, leaving the top open. The fallen leaves which are raked up daily can be pitchforked into this wire cage and will pack down and weather in time. After about a year, they may be added to the compost in small quantities. The wire cage should be placed beneath a tree to prevent rapid drying out and will help to keep the garden neat and trim. One can add manure and activators to the leaves to hasten decay.

Ordinary burning of thorny hedge cuttings is messy and difficult if the material is not absolutely dry. As fire purifies, it will not matter if there are any diseases present on the wood. An INCINERATOR is a wonderful piece of labour-saving and efficient equipment which is simple to construct and easily accommodated in the smallest garden. It burns the rubbish rapidly and in small quantities. There is no danger of adjacent hedges and trees catching alight and the volume of smoke is reduced to a narrow column. The woodash can be taken out easily and may be used immediately in the garden or sprinkled over the compost heap.

How TO CONSTRUCT A DRUM INCINERATOR

If a brick incinerator is constructed it will be a permanent and long-lasting feature, but it will still burn on the principle of the type described below. For this it is necessary to purchase a 45-gallon steel drum with a loose lid fitting on to the top. A plumber will be needed to prepare the drum for those who do not have the facilities to do so.

Cut a semi-circular hole out of the side at the base of the drum. This should be about 10 inches wide at the bottom or wide enough to allow one's garden spade to enter the bottom of the hole. A circular piece of strong iron mesh must be cut to fit the drum and placed inside at a distance of about a foot from the base. This may be supported by resting on three iron brackets welded on to and projecting from the inside of the drum. An even simpler method of support is to weld three legs of its own on to the mesh and insert the whole platform into the drum. A hole should be cut on one side of the lid for the smoke to escape. Alternatively, one could ask the plumber to fit a small piece of chimney pipe to the side of the drum near the top. The lid must be left untouched. The whole drum should then be lifted off the ground and rested firmly on planks straddling two piles of bricks. If desired, legs may be welded on to the base of the drum, but these must be thick, level and sturdy or they might sink into the ground or become rickety. It is not absolutely essential to have the drum standing above the level of the ground, but this is advisable as it allows for easier handling and will prevent ash from

Leave space between brick paving and a boundary wall for plants that cling and spill over hard edges. This will create an inviting luxuriance that is refreshing on hot days.

Shade a hot verandah with the cool canopy of a tree that loses its leaves and will not deprive the house of sun in winter.

Ponds can be fitted into any garden. The large pond above provides scope for bold waterside plants, like the Swamp Cypress (*Taxodium distichum*) and New Zealand Flax (*Phormium tenax*) in the background. One can create a similar effect with small-scale plants, as in the pond below, less than three feet across. Graceful Flower-of-the-Incas (*Cantua buxifolia*) accents the left with Pineapple Flowers (*Eucomis undulata*) in the foreground. Cape Hawthorn (*Aponogeton distachyus*) emerges from a container sunk in the water.

accumulating at the aperture or rain water from entering and mixing with the ash.

How to Use the Incinerator

The loose lid is lifted off and the dry twigs and other materials are dropped in from the top and will rest on the mesh. Grass cuttings may be sprinkled amongst the twigs. Do not pack down the rubbish, but allow plenty of air to circulate around it so that it will burn more quickly. It is better to burn smaller quantities at frequent intervals than to try to burn it all at once. Replace the lid and set the rubbish alight. The concentrated space will cause the rubbish to burn very rapidly while the fine ash drops through the mesh on to the base of the drum. Before adding any fresh rubbish, poke down any ash that has not fallen through, for a clear mesh will allow a greater draught. Remove the woodash and use it immediately or store it in covered tins.

Liquid Manure Container

Liquid manure can be prepared simply by soaking a small amount of manure in a bucket of water for about a week and diluting the liquid to the colour of weak tea before use. Remove any scum that forms on the surface after a few days and keep the lid on the bucket. It is so much easier, however, merely to place a watering can on the ground, turn a tap and have liquid manure drip out, all ready to use whenever one wants it. The container is easy to construct and may be made to match the drum incinerator or can be half the size, according to one's needs.

If a 45-gallon steel drum is used, it must have a loose, closely fitting lid. A piece of iron mesh, sturdy and closely woven, should be inserted halfway across the inside of the drum. It may be supported by resting on iron brackets welded on to the sides and projecting inwards or may have three separate legs of its own to form a table. The mesh should not be welded into the sides of the drum as it should be removable for cleaning purposes. The plumber must fix a spigot 1 inch from the base of the drum to prevent any solid material clogging the outlet. The whole drum should stand above the ground, resting on planks straddling two piles of bricks. The height should allow for a watering can to stand beneath the tap while it is being filled. The drum may also have four iron legs welded on to it if these are broad and sturdy. Alternatively, it can be stood on bricks.

A small, closely-woven sack is filled with manure and placed on the iron mesh. It may be attached to the top by means of a picture hook which fits over the rim in order to keep the bag taut, or a hook may be welded on to the inside near the top, but this is not absolutely necessary. The drum is then filled with water and the lid replaced. The water will soon turn into liquid manure which is filtered through the mesh and will always be "on tap" when the spigot is turned. Dilute it with fresh water before use. Always apply liquid manure to damp soil and water it in.

CHAPTER TWENTY-THREE

SOME GARDENING TERMS EXPLAINED

DISBUDDING

This produces prize blooms on plants like Dahlias, Chrysanthemums, Carnations, Peonies, Roses or even Giant Zinnias or Marigolds. To disbud, pinch out the tiny secondary buds on either side of the main flower bud, using the thumbnail against the index finger. This is to avoid wasting the plant's energy in producing unnecessary extra flowers that detract from the beauty and quality of the single bloom. It can also be done on shrubs like Camellia and the Nodding Pincushion Flower (*Leucospermum nutans*.)

PINCHING BACK

This is the opposite of disbudding as it produces more flowers on a bushier plant. By pinching off the growing tip of the stem, energy is diverted to the sides and the secondary buds become stronger. Pinching back can be repeated on each side branch if quantity and bushiness are wanted instead of large blooms. This can be done to Chrysanthemums if a low, bushy effect is required or to produce a bushier plant on Petunias, Snapdragons or leggy shrubs like the Blushing Bride (*Serruria florida*). When the plant grows after being pinched or stopped, the point of growth is often called a "break". Plants often form natural breaks without being pinched back.

STAKING

This is a simple operation that often leads to plant injury if it is incorrectly done. Secure the stake in the ground before planting a bulb, perennial or shrub or you may injure the root or bulb when driving the stake in later. When staking perennials, use several light canes rather than a single stout, ugly stick. If liked, use short sticks at first and replace these with longer ones as the plants grow taller.

When staking standard roses or young trees, allow the plant to grow upright and never bend it towards a straight stake. Bind hessian around the trunk and leave a slack piece of string between the two so that the stake will not rub against the bark and cause injury.

CROWN

This is the point where the root and stem meet. Some perennials which die down during the rest period, such as Peony or Rhubarb, send out new buds from the crown.

POTTING ON

This term is used to describe transplanting of small potted plants into larger pots when they become too large for their pots. This is also called re-potting. This is done easily by placing one hand over the damp soil surface, with the plant emerging between the fingers. Turn the pot upside down and tap the edge of the pot sharply against a hard surface. The whole ball of earth will come out intact.

When several seedlings growing in one pot are each given a separate new pot, this is known as potting off.

SETTING

This describes the formation of the tiny fruit as soon as the flowers have faded on tomatoes or fruit trees.

STRIKE

This describes the growth of roots as on a cutting.

CHAPTER TWENTY-FOUR

THE LAWN

It is probably true to say that every garden in Southern Africa has a lawn, no matter how small, even if it does not have any other kind of plant in it. The lawn, therefore, is one of the most important features to every home owner, who realises that it enhances the value of his property, prevents dust from entering his house, provides a pleasant playground for his children and last, but not least, gives his ground a cool, green, cultivated look that implies peace.

From the economical point of view, a lawn is considered to be the cheapest and easiest means of covering the ground and the new home owner fondly imagines that if he plants his whole garden with grass he will eliminate all garden cares. For the first year or two these hopes may be justified, for the grass grows vigorously in the virgin soil without much attention and there are no tree shadows or strong roots to compete with the lawn for sunlight and moisture. After another season or two, however, the gardener will realise that, without care, the lawn will deteriorate and be a mockery of what it should be. The best gardener cannot make certain grasses grow in the shade of spreading trees if they need sunlight for healthy growth. One cannot expect grass to grow everywhere—on slopes, rocky soil or in competition with tree roots. Supplement the lawn with groundcovers. (See Chapter 10.)

It is a mistaken economy to plant a lawn over one's whole garden, aiming to cut out beds and add other features later. For one thing, it is not so easy to dig out grass roots once they have been growing strongly, and grass can prove to be worse than any weed in a flower bed. For another, it is better to plant out a smaller, clearly-defined area with grass and treat it well (that is by feeding, watering and cutting it adequately) than to plant a large area which is beyond one's scope and requires a large initial purchase of grass roots. The smaller, well-groomed lawn area near the house can act as a stock for multiplying your own grass. By cutting an inch or two off the edges one can have sufficient grass of the same kind to plant out elsewhere.

Some home-owners quail at the thought of spending any money on feeding and watering their lawns. If one plants grass, however, there are certain expenses that one must be prepared to incur, in the same way as one buys polish for one's floors. The requirements are moderate, but they should be given correctly and one should not waste time or money on unnecessary treatment.

WHAT GRASS TO PLANT

Aim to use only one kind of grass in planting the lawn. There is no doubt that the best lawn for the home garden is that which gives a smooth velvety surface and has a rich green colour. Grass which has fine or medium fine blades is best for this purpose. Coarse grasses may also be pleasantly green and have a good surface if they are cut well, but can never compare in appearance with the finer textured grasses.

One always hears a great deal about some grasses wearing better than others. The new gardener is often afraid to plant fine grasses in case they do not wear well, while he hopes that a coarse tough grass will stand up to all types of hard wear. The average family wear on the garden lawn, however, is unlikely to damage any but the finest lawn, which usually quickly recovers. It is better to choose coarse, tough, hard-wearing grasses like Kikuyu for school playing-fields, but these are not recommended in the home garden.

If one has a garden of about half an acre or more, one can compromise by planting a broad area of fine, ornamental lawn in front of the house, and planting a coarser grass like Swazi in the outer portions of the garden. The division between the two can be defined by shrubs, herbaceous borders and flower beds or rockeries.

Plant Grass to Suit your Climate

Southern Africa is divided into summer and winter rainfall areas and lawns behave differently in these two climatic zones. Lawns turn brown and remain dormant during winter in the larger part of Southern Africa, which usually has six months with very little rain from autumn to spring. In the south-western Cape, however, lawns are green during the rainy winter and spring months, going off and turning yellowish during the long, dry, midsummer months. Cape Royal, for example, will have its dormant period during winter on the highveld, but will remain green during winter in the Cape, and partly lose its colour in summer. Some lawns remain perennially green in places like the south coast of Natal, which does not have frost in winter.

Do not attempt to force a grass to remain evergreen by watering during the dry period, if it is the type of grass which becomes dormant in your area. By so doing, one will probably encourage fungus diseases to develop. This also encourages the growth of *Poa annua*, a bright green annual grass which thrives in moist or shady positions and becomes a weed on lawns which is difficult to eradicate because it seeds itself freely.

Some grasses naturally remain evergreen throughout the year, provided that they receive moisture, notably Kentucky Blue-grass and Bent grasses (*Agrostis tenius*). These require water all through the year and one must consider whether it is worth the trouble and expense of watering every week throughout the dry season. They will grow well in moist, humid climatic areas, such as around Knysna. They are valued particularly as they will grow under trees, and can be planted in small areas where extra feeding and watering will not be begrudged. They can also be used in small areas of the garden for special display purposes in combination with flowers or spring bulbs, where green grass is needed to enhance these.

On the whole, one should choose grasses that have been proved to do well in one's own area. If one were to move into an outlying suburb bordering on the veld, one could pick out the finer grasses growing in the veld and plant them as a lawn in the garden. Such grasses would probably prove to be vigorous and easy to maintain in spite of the vagaries of climate. As this is not always possible, one should purchase commonly grown grasses that have proved successful as a result of experience. It is not advisable to grow grasses that have proved successful in England, for example, unless your particular climatic area resembles that climate and has a similar rainfall.

Research stations in various parts of the country, notably the South African Turf Research Station at Frankenwald, near Johannesburg, carry out experiments which take the guesswork out of what grass to choose for one's garden. They usually concentrate on indigenous grasses which do well in this climate, working with various strains of grass found in different parts of the country. The following grasses have been proved to be satisfactory and the gardener will find one to suit his needs from amongst them. Most of them are easily obtainable, except where stated otherwise, but these are likely to become available shortly.

CYNODON GRASSES

Cynodons make the best lawn grasses. These are the most widely planted grasses in Africa, if not in all the warm regions of the world. Originally thought to have come from Asia, Europe and Australia, they have naturalised themselves in many countries. Over the years, local species and varieties, as well as strains, have been selected as lawn grasses, such as Florida, Magennis and Royal Cape. Some are fine grasses, while others are coarser in texture, but all multiply by means of creeping stolons or rhizomes, forming a densely matted surface in from 6 to 12 weeks. They are multiplied by planting out roots and portions of rhizomes.

Cynodon grasses become brown during the dry winter in the greater part of Southern Africa. Some, like Royal Cape, remain green during rainy winters in the south-western Cape and partly lose their colour during the long, dry summer. They also remain green where there is no frost in winter. All Cynodon grasses require sunshine and will not grow well in the shade under trees. Other shade-tolerant grasses, like Bents and Blue-grass, can be planted on the borders of the Cynodon. Cynodons prefer slightly acid soil, with a pH 6–6.5.

Cynodons such as Florida are widely used for golf courses in the summer rainfall area. It has been found that it is best to use grasses that turn brown and remain dormant during the dry winter, as it does not pay to keep the soil wet throughout the dry season. This practice also leads to fungus disease and the invasion of *Poa annua* grass. Bowling greens can be kept green until May, but watering should be discontinued after the first frost, which will turn the lawns brown. Royal Cape is the chief lawn used for golf and bowling greens in the south-western Cape.

Cynodon grasses should be mown closely to give a good surface. They can be clipped to the height of the thickness of a coin on golf greens and need daily mowing to keep it this height. In the home garden they can be mown to the height of one inch to create a thick, luxuriant carpet. Always cut frequently, a little at a time, to keep the lawn growing at the same height.

QUICK GRASS, KWEEK, COARSE KWEEK OR COUCH GRASS (*Cynodon dactylon*)

This is known as Bermuda grass in America. It is a coarse grass, thought to have originated in tropical Africa, which grows wild at the coast and elsewhere, being widely planted wherever a hardy and easy-to-grow lawn is needed. It will grow on clay or sandy soil, which is acid or neutral. (pH 5.3–7.)

ROYAL CAPE (*C. dactylon* var. Royal Cape)

This vigorous grass falls midway between the fine and coarse grasses. It is of a rich dark emerald green colour and retains its colour well into winter, turning green early in spring. Royal Cape remains green longer than any other indigenous grass. It makes an excellent lawn for the home garden where hardiness is important. It is recommended for sportsfields and is used on bowling greens and golf courses in the south-western Cape.

Royal Cape was originally selected from *Cynodon dactylon* (Kweek) growing on the Royal Cape Golf Course at Wynberg in the Cape. There are several strains, but none of these are as coarse as the original kweek grass. It makes a fairly fine lawn in the Cape, where growth is slower during the summer months due to dryness, but remains coarser in the summer rainfall area. It can be made to look very much finer, however, by frequent clipping.

Royal Cape is usually disease and termite free and grows well in a variety of climatic conditions. It should be given a regular fertilizing and cutting programme. Growth is fairly slow at first, taking from eight to ten weeks to become established, but it then forms a thick mat which cannot be damaged easily. Its vigorous growth may make it difficult to control, so that it should not be planted near rockeries which it may invade.

HALL's SELECTION (*C. dactylon* var. densus)

This medium-fine, dark green grass resembles Royal Cape, but produces an even thicker, denser mat. It is slower to become established than Royal Cape and is slightly tuftier in habit at first. Originally noticed on the Germiston Golf Course, it was established at the Frankenwald Turf Research Station.

FLORIDA GRASS (*Cynodon transvaalensis*)

This fine grass with a medium-green colour, is one of the best and most popular of the ornamental lawns. It is fairly hardy and is used on golf courses and bowling greens.

Florida grass turns brown early and is subject to termite attack, but remains a satisfactory lawn in the summer rainfall area. It grows quickly, becoming established in about six weeks. Regular attention in the way of feeding, watering and mowing should be given during the summer months. It forms a nap, growing in a north-easterly direction. It was found at Florida, Transvaal, in 1907.

MAGENNIS GRASS (*Cynodon magennisii*)

Magennis grass resembles Florida, but is darker and not quite as fine, although it remains one of the finer ornamental lawns. At one time it was most popular for cricket pitches, but is no longer recommended as it does not recover quickly from damage like scuffing. It will cover the ground in six or seven weeks. It requires regular maintenance during summer and is prone to red mite attack, causing brown patches. Magennis was originally selected from a Florida lawn planted at East London in 1920. It grows with a nap, like Florida.

ELLIOT GRASS (*Cynodon* species)

This fine, light green grass covers the ground quickly in about six to seven weeks. It turns brown at the first frost, taking on a reddish hue while dormant in winter, and becomes green in late spring.

Elliot grass should not be cut too low, especially during wet periods, and is best cut a fraction longer than Florida. It comes from the Cape and is less hardy than Florida. With careful attention to feeding, watering and mowing it can be made to look velvety. It has very little nap.

SKAAPPLAAS FINE (*Cynodon* sp.)

Also known as Velvet Grass, this very fine, medium-green grass is highly recommended as a lawn for the home garden. It is greener in colour than either Florida or Elliot and is more drought-resistant and hardy than either of these two grasses. If damaged by scuffing, it recovers more quickly than Florida and has been used on golf greens and fairways.

Skaapplaas Fine requires a regular fertilizing and cutting programme during summer and should be watered once a week during periods of drought. It grows rapidly and covers the ground closely in about six weeks. It turns brown during the dormant period in winter, from about April onwards, and is often tinged red in autumn.

It was originally found on a farm in the Orange Free State and used on golf courses at Vereeniging in 1935.

FRANKENWALD FINE (*Cynodon* strain)

This very fine grass can be made to look like the baize on a billiard table if it is regularly fed, mown and well-watered (twice a week during dry periods in summer). It has been planted on a tennis court at the South African Turf Research Station at Frankenwald and stands up to weekly play without showing signs of damage. It is likely to prove very popular as soon as it becomes freely available.

This very promising grass was found locally at Frankenwald in 1957 and is thought to be a hybrid.

BRADLEY GRASS (*Cynodon bradleyi*)

This is one of the finer grasses, although not as fine as Florida. It may be recognised by its hairy-edged leaves. It is a quick-growing, greyish-green grass which covers and spreads well, but has lost its popularity in recent years because of its susceptibility to Button disease. This is said to be caused by the activity of a nematode which forms galls on the stems and leaves. The grass then forms tufts resembling small buttons. Button disease becomes obvious from February onwards and the grass dies out in patches in autumn. Long cutting is said to help Bradley grass withstand Button disease, but there is no effective control known. As other types of Cynodon are resistant, Bradley is best uprooted and replaced by these in places where the disease proves troublesome. Bradley grass was discovered in the veld outside Johannesburg in 1910.

RIETONDALE (*Cynodon* strain)

Quick-growing, coarse grass that needs frequent cutting. It is similar to Bradley and also susceptible to Button disease.

CAMPBELL GRASS (*Cynodon* strain)

This is a coarse grass, grown mainly in Natal, where it remains green during winter.

UMGENI GRASS (*Cynodon* strain)

This fine grass is used for golf courses on the east coast.

MANDY GRASS (*Cynodon* strain)

A fine evergreen grass which is hardier in texture than Umgeni. It was found at the Durban Country Club.

FRANKLIN GRASS (*Cynodon* strain)

This fine strain was found at Mt. Edgecombe, Natal.

TIF GRASS

Tif Grasses come from the U.S.A. and their use is still in the experimental stages in southern Africa. They are fine grasses that are a darker green than Florida, but with a similar fine texture, and have a well-developed root system. They are known as Tif Lawn and Tif Green. Dwarf Tif has small, short leaves and grows slowly.

BUFFALO GRASS OR SEASIDE QUICK (*Stenotaphrum secundatum*)

A prostrate grass which forms a spongy mat, this is useful for sandy soils on the coast from Durban to the Cape, where it is indigenous. It remains evergreen at the coast and does not require frequent cutting. It may be recognised by its broad leaves with rounded tips.

BEREA GRASS OR COAST GRASS (*Dactyloctenium australe*)

A tufted grass which sends out short runners, this forms a soft groundcover which is easy to mow. It is well known in Durban, where it will grow in semi-shade as well as sun.

DIGITARIA

These are broad-bladed, coarse grasses that spread very quickly and are propagated by stolons forming on the surface. Swazi and Richmond grasses are the two species that are grown extensively in South Africa.

SWAZI GRASS (*Digitaria swazilandensis*)

This is a yellowish-green grass with broad, coarse blades. It is probably the best of the coarse grasses for the home garden, for it requires little maintenance. It will cover the soil in four to five weeks and grows well on poor soils. As it has no deep rhizomes, but spreads on the surface, it can grow in places where there is very little topsoil. It grows vigorously, eliminating weeds as well as seeming to resist termites. If there is a mixture of grasses on poor soil, Swazi will push out other strong grasses such as Royal Cape. Where the soil is well fertilized, Royal Cape will push out Swazi grass.

Swazi grass remains easy to cut in spite of its vigorous growth. Because of its surface-growing habit, it does not grow tall quickly and, therefore, does not need such frequent cutting as other lawns. If mowing has been delayed and it has been left to grow too long, it does not lose its colour when cut as do other lawn grasses. It should be cut once a week during the rainy period, but need only be cut once a fortnight during the remainder of summer.

The main disadvantage of Swazi is that it browns off quickly in dry summer weather, but greens up again when rain falls. It may be watered in order to prevent its losing colour and should be thoroughly soaked once a week if rain does not fall during summer. It is sensitive to frost, turning brown at the first frost and remaining dormant throughout winter.

If one has a large garden, it is a good idea to plant Swazi in the further portions of the garden, in order to simplify maintenance. Swazi grass was discovered in Swaziland and has been popular since 1934 on fairways and in large gardens on the Highveld.

RICHMOND OR WYNBERG GRASS (*Digitaria diversinervis*)

This grass is very similar to Swazi, but has shorter, darker green leaves. It spreads even more quickly than Swazi grass and is particularly valuable in warm climates where it grows well in the shade of trees.

MAURITIUS BLUE-GRASS (*Digitaria didactyla*)

This is called Macintosh grass around Hillcrest. It is an indigenous grass found and grown in parts of Natal.

KIKUYU (*Pennisetum clandestinum*)

This tough, vigorous, hardy grass was hailed with enthusiasm when it was first introduced from Kenya. It spreads rapidly by means of thick rhizomes and stolons, covering the ground with a thick mat of bright green grass in about five to six weeks. It eliminates weeds and stands up to rough wear, so that it is recommended for rugby fields, parks, paddocks and school playgrounds, but is too thick and uneven for polo or cricket fields.

Its very vigour is its downfall in the home garden. It invades flower beds and rockeries, dips down a foot or more and comes up on the other side of concrete paths, and competes with shrubs and trees for moisture. Because of its deep-rooting system, which may go down to 4 or 5 feet, it is almost impossible to eradicate without laborious digging. In the end, Kikuyu grass will prevent the expansion of most garden planting and limit the variety in the garden. One can prevent Kikuyu from invading flower beds by driving sheet iron vertically into the soil along the edges of the lawn to a depth of about 2 or 3 feet. This seems an unnecessary waste when other grasses will form a more satisfactory lawn with less trouble and maintenance in cutting.

Kikuyu must be cut very frequently during summer with a strong mower in order to keep it smooth. Cut it as low as possible, down to half-an-inch. It is hard work to scarify it at the end of winter and it is certainly unsatisfactory in a small garden. It will remain green nearly all winter if it is watered regularly, but otherwise loses its colour. Heavy frost will turn it brown. It needs feeding and moisture in the same way as other lawns.

Kikuyu grass is not quite so difficult to control in the winter rainfall area of the Cape, where it does not grow quite so vigorously during the dry summer months and retains its greenness during the rainy winter. It should, nevertheless, only be planted in very large gardens and be separated from flower beds, rockeries and shrubs by means of paths, thus, unfortunately, limiting its landscape value.

Some people are in favour and some against Kikuyu grass for all purposes, while some areas in America, for example, have actually quarantined it. It has its place on large areas with hard wear, but should not be planted thoughtlessly in the average garden.

EVERGREEN LAWNS

The two types of evergreen lawns grown in this country are Kentucky Blue-grass and Bent grass. Both are introduced from Europe and America. They are best grown in moist, cool climates where they receive rain at regular intervals such as at Knysna in the Cape. In places which have a long dry season they must be watered regularly throughout the year. They should be soaked thoroughly with a good lawn sprinkler once a week, if no rain has fallen.

These evergreen grasses are particularly useful in the summer rainfall area where it has been found that they will grow in shade under large trees, provided that they are well-fertilized and watered. They can also be planted in small areas of the garden to form an excellent spring picture with spring-flowering bulbs and blossom, where the green grass enhances the beauty of the flowers. These grasses may be watered together with the nearby flowers. If daffodils are planted in the grass, it will have to be grown to its full length of about 6 inches, as the lawn cannot be cut while the bulb foliage is growing and ripening. Otherwise these grasses should be clipped frequently to produce a fine-textured lawn. Bent grasses will grow on acid or alkaline soil, while Blue-grass prefers a more neutral soil.

BENT GRASS (*Agrostis tenuis*)

There are many species of Agrostis, the best known in this country being *Agrostis tenuis*. This has several common names in different parts of the world, namely Colonial Bent, Rhode Island Bent, Prince Edward Island Bent and New Zealand Bent. As a great deal of seed is exported from New Zealand, the *Agrostis tenuis* in this country is called New Zealand Bent. It is also known in South Africa as Hubbard's Bent and Brewsia grass. It originally came from Europe and was naturalised in America and other parts of the world.

Agrostis tenuis is a soft fine grass which makes a beautiful lawn in about six weeks, staying green in winter if it is watered once or twice a week. It is tufted in habit and spreads slowly by means of short runners. It will grow in the sun and under large shady trees, provided that it receives some sun for part of the day. Bent grass requires well-drained, moist soil and the ground must be well prepared and fertilized before planting. It will grow on mildly acid to neutral soils (pH 6.5–7). At one time it was widely planted on golf courses and bowling greens in the summer rainfall area, but was found to be too costly and troublesome to maintain over large areas during the long dry season and has been superseded by Cynodons.

Agrostis tenuis is usually propagated by seed sown in March or in October and may also be propagated vegetatively during the rainy season. If the grass has been left to grow long, tufts of stems and leaves may be severed and planted in small clumps in the soil. Roots will spring from the nodes on the stems. Keep moist until the lawn is established. The grass may be cut regularly thereafter. Close clipping makes an excellent surface and this grass is best cut low.

KENTUCKY BLUE-GRASS (*Poa pratensis*)

This forms a medium-fine, bluish-green lawn if it is clipped regularly to a length of about 1½ inches and should not be cut too low. It is valued as it remains green during winter, but needs plenty of moisture and good soil in order to grow successfully. It may be left uncut if it is planted as a cover for spring bulbs such as daffodils, and will grow up to 6 inches or more in length. It is propagated by means of seed and may be spread by planting plugs.

Kentucky Blue-grass will grow under trees in deep shade if it is fed and watered carefully. It may be planted on the borders of Cynodon lawns where these grasses have become thin through lack of sunlight. Although the colour will be different from the main lawn, the effect is luxurious and cultivated. If the Blue-grass borders shrubs and groundcovers, it will be watered regularly together with these plants. It should receive watering twice a week if rain does not fall. It must be fed regularly or it fades in colour. Fertilize the soil before planting. It prefers a neutral or alkaline soil (pH 6.8–7.5).

WHEN TO PLANT THE LAWN

Lawns should be planted at the beginning of the rainy season while the weather is warm enough for rapid growth. The best time to plant a lawn is in spring, when the weather and the soil have warmed up, but the time varies slightly according to the climate.

In the winter rainfall area, where the climate is moist and often rainy until October, a lawn is best planted at the beginning of September, or in mid-August if it is not too cold. Once the lawn is established, it should be watered once a week during the summer months. Lawns may also be planted in April at the commencement of the rainy season, but growth is very slow during winter and it is best to wait until the spring.

In the summer rainfall area, where rain seldom falls until October, it is best to delay planting until the end of September. There is no purpose in planting in August and watering artificially, for this is unnecessarily expensive and the grass covers more slowly than when good rains fall. Lawns may be planted all through summer, provided that the soil is not too wet to handle, but should not be planted later than February, as growth begins to slow down and young lawns may be damaged by frost in cold areas. Reserve the winter months for digging and raking the soil in preparation for planting. A temporary lawn of Italian rye grass can be sown during winter, but this may become a troublesome weed later and is not generally advisable. Water the soil and allow the weeds to grow and be eradicated a few weeks before planting the lawn, if possible.

HOW TO PREPARE THE SOIL

Dreadful visions of having so sift the soil of one's whole garden before planting a lawn discourage many new home owners. Elaborate deep digging is no longer practised, however. Provided that one's soil is reasonably light,

so ensuring good drainage, all that is necessary is to dig the soil to the depth of a spade, or one spit, as it is known. This is approximately 6 to 9 inches in depth. Large stones should be removed, but it is not necessary to sift the soil. Sifting is actually detrimental, for it removes the fibrous matter in the soil and makes it pack down and lose its porous quality. After digging, knock down all lumps and rake continuously until a fine surface is obtained. Where soil is of the clay type, place a thick layer of sharp river sand on the broken surface and mix it into the top 3 or 4 inches before raking the whole area to a fine tilth.

If one has any compost available, this can be spread on the top in large quantities and once again turned into the upper 2 inches to lighten the surface. Peat may also be used in this way. Manure will add organic matter and enrich the soil, but introduces many weed seeds. Spread some inorganic fertilizer like 6 : 3 : 2 on to the surface of the soil (at the recommended rate) before planting, even if one has added the above organic substances. Rake it into the top inch. If the topsoil is good, delay adding fertilizer until the lawn has covered the ground.

In places where the lawn is to be planted on a filled-in portion, such as on a terrace, over a hole where a tree has been removed or over a place where a trench was dug for pipes, soak the area in order to provide for settling. Then rake and eliminate lumps.

Levelling the Soil

First break up all lumps on the surface. One must then eliminate bumps and fill in small hollows before final raking of the soil. Fix a straight, thick piece of plank to a broom handle and use it over the surface like a rake. If desired, slip the rake over two bolts fixed on to a plank and use the rake as the pusher. This will enable you to push the soil about until the hollows are smoothed out.

One can also roll the surface of the soil with a garden roller in order to discover which are the high and low spots. Rolling is not advisable on any but a sandy soil, however, for fear of compacting the ground. It is quite easy to obtain a level surface without rolling. Always rake a rolled surface in order to break the crust.

Do not aim to make your lawn surface as level as a table, but allow for a slight run-off of water. Decide which is to be the higher and lower side of your lawn, according to the lie of your land and the position of your house. Do not allow the slope to run down into the front of your house, but away from the house or from one side to the other. If the soil slopes naturally down to your house, you will have to arrange a level area in the front, digging back and building a retaining wall or other feature to hold the remaining soil. This can often be turned into a pleasant feature. (See Garden Plans, Chapter 3.) The slope can be almost imperceptible to the naked eye and can drop 6 inches in 100 feet.

Mark the high side and low side by means of stakes and drag the soil with a heavy wooden block so that it slopes gradually in the required direction. Three heavy planks nailed together like steps will aid in grading the soil. Do not be nervous that you will not grade your slope correctly. A lawn forms a wonderful sponge-like surface and absorbs large quantities of storm water. Provided that there are no hollow portions in which the water can collect, the lawn will absorb most rainwater. If desired, water the soil for about three weeks before planting the lawn in order to allow weeds to grow. Then pull these up and re-smooth the surface. One can use a weed-killer after planting, however, in order to avoid doing this. One can, if liked, rake chlordane, dieldrin or 5 per cent DDT dust into the soil to repel ants and termites. (See Chapter 37.)

HOW TO PLANT THE LAWN

All lawns in Southern Africa, apart from the evergreen lawns, are planted by means of roots or stolons. These can be purchased by the bag, quite inexpensively. Purchase grass from reliable nurserymen and buy it only when you are ready to plant. Keep the bag in a shady place and take about a bucket full at a time from the bag. One can moisten the bag if the weather is very hot and dry. One bag goes a long way and may plant an area 50 feet by 50 feet. If possible, water the surface of the soil two or three days before you are ready to plant. This will make a slightly damp, firm surface which is good for the grass roots and is easy to handle.

In order not to disturb one's level surface, aim to plant the lawn in rows from one side to another. Use a string as a guide. Tie the string to two short sticks and peg these into the ground at either side of the lawn, working across the width. Dig out a shallow trench, about 1½ inches deep, with the aid of a trowel and lay the roots in this trench, about 2 to 3 inches apart. Separate the roots while working and if you have a long stolon with roots attached, stretch this along the bottom of the trench. Then cover the roots completely with soil and level off. Move the string a few inches towards you and plant another row in the same way.

The distance between the rows varies according to the purpose of the lawn. On bowling greens, rows are placed from 4 to 6 inches from each other. In the home garden the rows can be 6 inches apart, but where economy is practised, they can be up to 9 inches apart. Coarse grasses like Swazi can be planted in rows from 9 to 12 inches apart. The closer the rows, the quicker the grass will cover, but the grass needs some room in which to spread.

Do not allow the grass roots to stick up above the soil level, or they will spoil the level surface of the lawn. Do not plant in tufts for the same reason and take care to separate the roots. Work quickly to plant as large an area as possible. The work may take several days, but try to work exclusively at it.

As soon as the rows have been planted to a width of about 6 feet, water the surface gently with a fine spray so that the roots will not dry out. Do not flood the area for fear of creating an uneven surface. Once the whole lawn has been planted, the sprinkler can be allowed to soak the whole area thoroughly.

Keep the soil moist for five to six weeks, watering every day if it does not rain, until the grass shows signs of covering. Watering can then be reduced gradually.

PLANTING EVERGREEN LAWNS BY SEED

Prepare the top surface even more finely than when planting roots and level well by drawing a plank across the surface. Scatter the seed evenly, dividing the area into sections if necessary and spreading the seed uniformly in each marked portion. Then scatter a ¼-inch-thick mulch over the seed, using a mixture that will hold moisture better than plain soil. The topsoil may be mixed with vermiculite, sifted old kraal manure, compost or pre-soaked peat.

Keep the seeded area moist until the grass is well up, watering by hand each day to prevent washaways. This may take three or four weeks. As soon as the grass blades begin to bend over, when they are about 2 inches long, mow the lawn for the first time with a sharp mower. Dull blades may tear the seedlings out of the soil.

WEED CONTROL IN LAWNS

Weeds in lawns are mainly a problem while the lawn is growing. Once the lawn has formed a vigorous mat and is well fed and watered, it will crowd out weeds.

At the beginning one can spray the newly planted lawn with a weedkiller so that the weeds, on germinating, will be killed before they can grow large. Weedkillers must always be used with caution on calm days and with regard to plants growing nearby. A wax bar recently developed overseas may solve this problem as it is dragged over the lawn surface and there is no drift. Careless use of weedkillers can burn and destroy grass. Weeds, however, can also be controlled by mowing. As soon as the new grass covers, in about six or seven weeks, it may be mown. This will cut the tips off the weeds and the continual cutting that follows will weaken the annual weeds which will be crowded out eventually. Hand-weeding is probably the best method, but care must be taken while weeding not to tread down the moist soil while the new grass is growing. Place a plank across the surface and stand on this in order to prevent one's feet from forming hollows on the surface.

WEEDS ON MATURE LAWN

Large weeds on a mature lawn should be gouged out with a special narrow forked implement. They can also be removed individually by using a mechanical eradicator operated with a foot pedal. Always remove weeds before they have had time to grow large and form seeds. Weedkillers may be used on lawns, but are only really effective if the weeds are young. It should not be necessary to use weedkillers on well-fed lawns. Rather apply a nitrogenous fertilizer to stimulate growth and suppress most weeds.

Some weeds are best removed laboriously but thoroughly by hand. This applies particularly to the Oxalis weeds, which multiply by means of a deeply placed corm which must be dug out, and the spreading brown *Euphorbia prostrata* which is very difficult to eradicate due to its free seeding habit. The annual grass, *Poa annua*, which invades shady moist places in gardens, sets seeds freely when it is only an inch or two in height. Frequent mowing through one season, so as to prevent it from setting seed, may eradicate it. Otherwise, one must tolerate it as a groundcover under trees which, unfortunately, becomes a nuisance in flower beds. Hand weeding is the most effective means of eradication.

A weedkiller called Gramoxone (Paraquat) has been recommended for the control of *Poa annua* and other small annual grasses in the seedling stage. This does not affect the root systems of most other lawn grasses, but may turn ordinary lawns brown for about 10 days. It should not be used on shallow-rooted lawns like Swazi grass. One pint in 40 gallons of water is sufficient to control 1 acre of the annual grasses, so that it must be used with care over small areas. It is most effective on bright, sunny days.

For broad-leaved weeds on lawns, like Dandelions, some *Oxalis, Dichondra, Erigeron* and *Matricaria*, Fernamine 4 is recommended. It should be used in the proportion of 1 gallon in 20 gallons of water to cover one acre of weed. It does not kill *Euphorbia prostrata* or Watergrass.

WATERING THE LAWN

Lawns which suffer from lack of water first lose their resilience, which is shown by footprints remaining on the dry grass. The colour fades, then turns brown and the grass

dies. The roots may remain alive long after the top dies and the lawn can be revitalised when it receives moisture, but it will suffer if it is continually allowed to die back in dry weather. Some lawns are more drought-resistant than others, and lawns seldom die permanently through lack of water, but should be watered thoroughly during summer if rain does not fall for about a week.

Grasses which become dormant in winter need not be watered from May until the end of August or even September and will not suffer in any way. Evergreen lawns need moisture all through the year and must be watered regularly once or twice a week if rain does not fall. This will prove too costly when evergreen lawns are planted over large areas in places which receive no good rains for about six months, so that these should only be planted in special small areas for display or under shady trees where they will thrive and the extra trouble and expense of watering are justified.

One should give the lawn a deep thorough watering once a week in order to encourage deeper, cooler roots, which may go down to 12 inches or more. Daily sprinkling will cool the air, but will not supply enough water for the lawn's needs.

Water is lost by evaporation in dry areas. One aims to replace the lost water when watering the lawn each week. The lawn requires at least an inch of water replacement at the coast and about double that amount in the hotter, drier inland climates. This will sink down about 15 inches into the soil. It does not matter if the soil dries out partially, in fact it is beneficial, as the air then enters the spaces. It is only when the soil is allowed to dry out completely that the lawn will die.

A lawn sprinkler will have to remain in one spot for about two or even three hours in order to build up an inch of water. Test how long it will take your sprinkler to add an inch of water to the lawn by placing shallow tins near it and noting how long they take to fill to the depth of an inch. (See Chapter 18.) Sandy soils will be more quickly penetrated than clay soils, but also dry out more rapidly and will require more frequent watering than clay soil. It might not be necessary to water the clay soil more often than once a fortnight.

Do not leave the sprinkler in one position until pools of water collect on the surface, and turn off automatic sprinkler systems when this happens or the grass will become scalded. The water will not be absorbed by the roots because of lack of air in the water-logged soil, although transpiration continues to take place through the leaves, and a drying-out effect will result.

It is essential to purchase a good lawn sprinkler in order to care for your lawn easily. Try to obtain a sprinkler that will cover a large area so that you do not have to drag it about to too many spots. Allow a small amount of overlapping to take place when moving the sprinkler, as few sprinklers cover the whole area evenly. They usually water the area nearest the sprinkler most deeply. Sprinklers are best used in the early morning when the air is still and the spray is not blown about.

There may be hard spots on the lawn which are not penetrated by the sprinkler. Aerate the area with a hollowtined fork and allow the hose to run slowly on to the spot and penetrate it deeply.

Sprinkler systems can be sunk into the ground and will water the lawn evenly if they are scientifically worked out. These may be placed in the soil before planting or sunk into an existing lawn. The pipes may be made of iron piping, plastic tubing or other materials. Sprinkler systems which water the whole lawn at the turn of a tap are not really necessary if there is sufficient labour available.

FEEDING THE LAWN

The lawn is the only portion of the garden which can be fed exclusively by the use of mineral or inorganic fertilizers. One need not fear that the soil will be robbed of organic matter, for grass itself adds organic matter to the soil by means of its decaying roots and leaves. Grass, in fact, restores fertility to otherwise barren soil.

The fact that a lawn consists of thousands of plants crowded together makes it important to feed it regularly and adequately or it will not perform well. It needs vast quantities of nitrogen which cannot be supplied in sufficient quantities by the normal dressings of manure or compost we give our lawns. Mineral fertilizers are readily available and do not introduce weeds. A lawn at the Frankenwald Research Station has been fed exclusively with mineral fertilizers for 20 years and shows no detrimental effect.

Mineral fertilizers for lawns are based on grass growth requirements. Phosphorus (in the form of superphosphates) is needed for root growth and nitrogen (in the form of ammonium sulphate and ammonium nitrate) is needed particularly for green leaf-growth. Most soils in this country possess sufficient potash for lawn needs but some coastal places lack potash in the soil. The mixture 2 : 1 : 0 is used to feed lawns on average soils (indicating high nitrogen and phosphorus, but no potash) while 2 : 1 : 2 is used on sandy soils which are usually potash-deficient at the coast as well as inland.

Phosphates are generally applied at the beginning of the season, while ammonium sulphate is applied during summer in order to keep the lawn green. A general garden fertilizer, like 6 : 3 : 2, is applied when planting a new lawn, but 2 : 1 : 0 is used on established lawns to maintain green growth.

Apply fertilizer at the beginning of the growing season when it will do the most good and about twice again during the season at six-week intervals. Stop applying fertilizer about the end of February. This will enable growth to slow down in April, just before the dormant period and possible early frosts in May. In mild climates where lawns remain green during winter, fertilizer may be given in May, although soil activity slows down during winter.

Do not give a lawn more than the required amount of fertilizer each season and divide this into small applications two or three times a season. One can wait to make each application when the lawn appears to need it or apply it at regular calendar intervals. Lawns will generally show their need for feeding after six or eight weeks by loss of colour and vigour, requiring less mowing. If one wishes to green up a lawn for a special occasion, apply ammonium sulphate about a month ahead. Fertilizing may show an immediate effect in midsummer, but may take longer when growth is not so rapid.

Fertilizer must be applied evenly or growth will be uneven and tufty. It can be mixed with a little soil before broadcasting by hand. It can also be placed in a box on wheels (a hopper) containing a row of holes beneath, but one must not stop or make turns without shutting off the flow of fertilizer or too much may fall out and burn the lawn. Apply in straight lines and spread evenly with the back of a rake or a plank.

General garden fertilizer mixtures like 6 : 3 : 2 or 2 : 3 : 2 should be spread dry and then watered in. Ammonium sulphate and Limestone ammonium nitrate can be applied dry or dissolved and watered in to the surface with a watering can.

How to Fertilize a New Lawn

Apply 6 : 3 : 2 before or immediately after planting. Use at the recommended rate given by the manufacturer per sq. yd. and poundage per acre. As soon as the grass begins to cover, follow with applications of ammonium sulphate or urea every six weeks. Use at the rate of $\frac{1}{2}$ to 1 oz. of ammonium sulphate per square yard or urea at $\frac{1}{4}$ to $\frac{1}{2}$ oz. per square yard at each application. Do not use more than a total of 3 oz. per square yard for the season, divided into three or four applications.

How to Fertilize an Established Lawn

At the beginning of October, preferably after the first rain, apply 2 : 1 : 0 at the manufacturer's recommended rate per square yard and poundage per acre of lawn. In potash-deficient soil, use 2 : 1 : 2. Follow with applications of ammonium sulphate at approximately six-weekly intervals during summer. Use 3 oz. per square yard each season, divided into three applications of 1 oz. at a time (300 lb. per acre of lawn). If desired, give ½ oz. at a time, but not more often than once a month.

Urea, in granular form, is now considered the best way of applying nitrogen to average soil, as it does not alter the pH and is easy to handle. Use it every 6 or 8 weeks following the first balanced fertilizer. Dissolve 1 tablespoon (about ¼ oz.) in 2 gallons of water and apply this over 1 square yard of lawn. It can be applied through a mix-nozzle attached to the hosepipe. (Use 1 lb. dissolved in 4 gallons of water for 64 square yards.)

It may sometimes be advisable to give a little extra super-phosphate in midsummer, about January, which will act as a booster to the root system. This helps to obtain a better response from nitrogen applications. The super-phosphate should be used in powder form as it will then be washed in immediately and not be picked up by the lawn mower. Use ½ oz. per square yard.

THE USE OF TOP DRESSINGS

The practice of spreading a load of black soil on to one's lawn in order to feed it and make it turn green is outdated. The lawn will turn green quickly as a result of growing through the black soil after being watered, whether the topsoil is rich or poor. Most bought topsoils contain little food value in comparison to mineral fertilizers and often serve to compact the soil as well as introduce foreign weeds.

Topsoil should only be used in order to level up uneven portions of the lawn. It can be spread thinly over the hollows. It is better to apply the topsoil thinly every few weeks than to put down a thick layer all at once. The best top-dressing is composed of a mixture of half good soil, a quarter compost and a quarter of coarse sand. Avoid clay.

Pure well-rotted compost or finely pulverised manure may also be used as a top-dressing once or twice during summer. This must be done in addition to mineral fertilizers and not in place of these, as one could never obtain sufficient to give the lawn adequate stimulation. They are mainly added to improve the quality of the soil with their fibrous matter. The fact that they may introduce weeds is second-ary, as the vigorous lawn will crowd out weeds unless these are troublesome pests like *Euphorbia prostrata* and *Oxalis*, which seed freely or have corms deep underground. Manure and compost may be spread on the surface of the lawn and brushed well in, but are best applied after aerating with a hollow-tined fork. Such aeration will lessen compaction of the soil and can be done to small areas where the lawn does not grow well or as an annual or bi-annual treatment to the whole area.

AERATION WITH A HOLLOW-TINED FORK

The "fork" consists of two or three hollow tines with sharp edges which are joined by a cross-bar and have a sturdy handle. One steps on to the cross-bar in order to drive the tines two to five inches into the soil. Men have more strength and weight to do this than women, although it is a simple operation. It is best done after rain when the soil is soft, but the lawn can also be soaked the day before using.

Press the fork into the lawn and then pull it out. Then press it in about 3 or 4 inches away. The cylindrical sods which were in the fork are forced out when the fork is pressed into the ground for the second time. Walk slowly up and down the lawn in straight lines, pressing the fork in at regular intervals, until the whole surface has been punched. The sods or cores are then gathered up.

Spread the manure, compost or coarse sand over the surface and brush them across the lawn. These materials then sink down into the holes and add their value to the soil without compacting it.

Do not attempt to aerate your lawn by driving an ordinary fork into it or by rolling it with a spike roller. This simply makes matters worse by compacting the soil at the point where the spikes or tines enter.

MOWING THE LAWN

The more food and water the lawn receives, the more it will grow and the more it must be cut. If fertilizer stimulates long growth which is not cut off, the leaves will turn brown at the base where they do not receive sunshine and when the lawn is finally cut, it will show brown patches. These will green up after a few days if the lawn is watered. Sometimes the damage is so severe that the top dies and the grass receives a set-back until the roots put forth new growth. One must be prepared to mow frequently but lightly and aim to remove a little top growth at a time.

Set the lawn-mower at the required height at the beginning of the season and keep the mower at that height for the remainder of the growing period. The height of your lawn varies according to your requirements and the type of lawn. Coarse grasses, like Kikuyu or Kweek, should be cut as low as possible, about ½ an inch in height. They form such a thick mat that it becomes difficult to keep them closely cut. Although coarse, Swazi grass does not need frequent cutting because of its spreading rather than up-right growth. Finer grasses may be mown very low, so that a coin can be slipped between the cutting blades and the ground, or they may be mown at a height of an inch, which gives a thick velvety feeling to the lawn. It is better to mow higher on a home lawn and lower on a lawn like a bowling green. The more one mows, the finer and more velvety the lawn surface will be. Bent grasses may be mown low to make a fine lawn, while Kentucky Blue-grass should not be mown lower than 1½ inches in height.

LAWN-MOWERS

The area and type of lawn one has dictates the type of lawn-mower one should purchase. Hand-operated lawn-mowers cut the grass as well as power-driven mowers, but one requires a great deal of energy to cut a large lawn adequately by hand. When there is a great deal of garden work to be done, one cannot always spare the labour to attend to the lawn in addition. Few lawns over a quarter-acre can be efficiently maintained by a hand-operated mower in midsummer. One can reduce the size of the lawn by planting lawn substitutes that do not require mowing in some parts of the garden. One can also plant Swazi or Richmond grass, which do not require such frequent mowing, in the outer areas of the garden, if not over the whole area.

The ordinary hand-operated lawn-mower cuts on the principle of a turning cylinder composed of five or more blades which must be sharpened each season.

POWER MOWERS

These may be either electrical or petrol driven. They are quick and easy to manipulate, saving time and energy. On the whole they give a more even surface to the lawn than a hand-operated mower.

There are two main types of power mowers, based on the turning cylinder with five or more knives or on the rotary blade principle. Each has its followers. The former makes for a neater lawn surface and has a box to collect the grass clippings. The latter is valuable for cutting coarse and tall grasses, such as on pavements, and can cut close to walls, trees and paths. Rotary mowers usually cannot be adjusted as low as the many-bladed mower. They usually leave clippings on the lawn which may have to be swept away if they look untidy.

LEAVING CLIPPINGS ON THE LAWN

Where harvester termites are not troublesome, clippings may be left in place on the lawn, provided that they are kept very short so that they fall down between the grass blades and remain fairly inconspicuous. This means that the lawn must be mown very frequently so that one removes only a little top growth at a time. Too many clippings left on lawns may prevent evaporation and lead to fungus disease. The clippings will rot down eventually and add organic matter to the soil without introducing weed seeds. As the decaying process will rob the lawn of nitrogen, one must be careful to add sulphate of ammonia to the lawn

regularly during the mowing season, as recommended under Fertilizing.

USING LAWN-MOWERS WITH CARE

Always mow the lawn in one direction from one side to the other. For a very fine finish, mow the lawn for a second time going in the opposite direction or diagonally. Do not mow wet grass or you will not get a good finish and may spoil your mower. If the ground below is not soaked, one can drag a piece of sacking over the lawn to remove dew and drops of water. Be careful not to scrape the bark of trees with the mower for fear of causing crown gall to develop.

CUTTING LAWN EDGES

As grass spreads horizontally, one must cut it down at the edges in order to keep it well groomed and prevent it from invading flower beds. This may be done by clipping with a hand shears, or slicing downwards with a spade-like implement. Special power-driven tools are efficient but not generally obtainable.

One can lessen the work of trimming the edges of the lawn, as well as keep the shape of the bed exact, by placing a hard material around the border of the lawn where it meets flower beds. Simply sink a line of bricks level with the soil and allow the grass to creep over the edge. When trimming the edges, cut down on the far edge of the brick. This will hide the bricks which otherwise give a hard look to the garden. Never allow the bricks to point upwards in a jagged, overlapping design as this is hideous and does not make clipping easier, as the grass grows up into the crevices. A neat divider can be made by driving 6-inch wide corrugated aluminium vertically into the soil.

A line of paving stones like slate can be placed along the front edge of a herbaceous border in order to prevent the lawn from encroaching into the bed. This acts as a path on which to walk when looking at the bed if the lawn is wet.

Never allow grass to grow right up to the front rocks in a rockery or it will grow into the rock crevices. Curve the edge of the lawn to follow the line of the rockery and keep the soil free of lawn at least a foot away. One can grow many small plants in this area which help to soften the look of the rocks.

PROGRAMME OF LAWN CARE

When the weather warms up at the end of winter, generally towards the end of August, one should scarify a lawn which has been dormant through winter. This means removing the old dead grass which will clog the new season's growth and prevent the absorption of water. Rake the area thoroughly to loosen the long runners and brush the whole lawn with a stiff-bristled broom. Remove the piles of swept clippings. Do not worry if the earth shows through. Use the mower to cut off any thick growth that may remain. It will not hurt the lawn to be cut right down to the bottom of the stems. Fill in any hollow places with a mixture of topsoil, compost and sand. This treatment does not apply to evergreen lawns.

Aerate, with the hollow-tined fork, any hard spots in the ground where the lawn does not grow. Fill the plug-holes with the topsoil mixture or with pure coarse sand. Top-dress at any time during the summer in addition to the fertilizing programme.

Apply fertilizer in spring. Start mowing as soon as the lawn begins to grow. Water if rain has not fallen for a week. Apply nitrogenous fertilizer every six or eight weeks during the summer months. Give the final fertilizer application in February. Apply fertilizer once in May in mild winter areas where lawns remain green during winter. Mow the lawns that become dormant in winter for the last time about the end of April so that they will look trim during winter.

Insect Pests on Lawns

Few insect pests harm lawns other than harvester termites and wood-eating termites. To eradicate the harvester termite, apply a bait of sodium fluosilicate. To repel wood-eating termites, water the lawn with 5 per cent DDT. BHC or calcium arsenate. (See Chapter 37 on Insect pests and their control.)

To rid the lawn of ordinary ants, water with an insecticide containing dieldrin. To keep crickets off lawns, water with BHC.

For mite infestations, which do not often trouble lawns, spray with Malathion. Worms and caterpillars on lawns can be destroyed with DDT or BHC sprays.

Earthworms, which are beneficial creatures, sometimes form casts on bowling greens or golf courses. They can be destroyed on the lawn by applying dieldrin (5 oz. per 100 square yards) and watering it in. It is best applied after rain when the earthworms are active and near the surface. As a rule, earthworms should not be destroyed in the home garden.

Diseases Caused by Insects

Button Disease. This is caused by a nematode which kills small areas of lawn, causing them to dry out in button-like patches. It attacks Bradley and Rietondale grasses. This cannot be treated without killing off the lawn and the best way of overcoming it is to replant with resistant lawns.

If it is too much trouble to dig up and replant the whole area, one may plant tufts of new lawn into the Bradley grass, making small holes about 10 inches apart or gouging out rows in which to plant the new grass. The resistant grass will grow over the infected grass and eliminate the Button disease. This takes about two seasons. It is quicker to remove all the infected grass and plant new lawn, but this creates more initial trouble, if not expense.

Fungus Disease of Lawns

Fungus diseases sometimes attack lawns especially in warm, moist places where humidity is high. Well-drained soil will lessen the possibility of fungus diseases. Always check bad drainage or compacted soil and aerate the soil by means of a hollow-tined fork. Fungi attack weak-growing plants, so that one should feed one's lawn to restore vigorous growth. Do not overwater lawns, but allow them to dry out partially after a good soaking.

Brown patch and dollar spot are the diseases most spoken of with regard to lawns. Both come as a result of compacted soil with poor drainage. Brown patch is more common than dollar spot. Brown patches are not always caused by a fungus, but come as a result of uneven water supply. Good rains are often followed by a week or two of hot, dry weather and brown patches appear almost over-night on lawns. As soon as rain falls again, the brown or burnt areas become green once more. Regular deep watering of the lawn at such times will help to alleviate this condition. A lawn which is stimulated by fertilizers needs constant mowing so that a little of the top is removed at a time. If mowing is delayed, too much green growth is removed at once and the basal part of the grass appears as a brown patch.

Brown Patch disease is caused by compacted soil and by the development of a heavy mat of grass, also known as thatching. Apply a hollow tined fork to the patch to improve aeration, then give it a strengthening solution of superphosphate at the rate of $\frac{1}{2}$ oz. per square yard, followed by a fungicide treatment. Water the affected portions of lawn with fixed copper fungicides, captan or mercurial fungicides. The latter are extremely poisonous and should be handled with great care. The organic fungicide Thiram is also recommended for fungus treatment on lawns. As a preventative, copper fungicides can be used on the lawn once a week during summer at the commencement of the rainy season.

Malachite green is sometimes recommended for fungus diseases on lawns. This contains copper, but is chiefly a dye which stains the brown lawn a brilliant bluish-green. It can be used in addition to a fungicide if it is important that the lawn should look its best for an occasion.

Fairy Rings. These are caused by a fungus that sends out mycelium in a ring around it, often several feet from the centre. The grass turns darker green at the edge of the ring, as the nitrogen given off by the fungus living on the decaying matter of the lawn turns it darker green before finally destroying the lawn at that spot. Toadstools often appear on the edge of the ring, being the fruiting bodies of the fungus. The thickened mycelium actually prevents the penetration of water into the soil, so that aeration is part of the treatment when a "fairy ring" is seen. Treatment with fungicides, especially mercurial types, is recommended. An effective treatment has been evolved by making a hole, from 12 to 18 inches deep, in the centre of the ring and pouring a concentrated dose of fungicide into it. This then seems to find its way into the whole infected area.

LAWN SUBSTITUTES

One of the biggest parts of lawn maintenance is mowing. If one could retain a pleasant green cover on the ground without having to cut it, it would lessen the work in the garden. Groundcovers of many kinds can be planted to clothe the floor of the garden and to grow under trees where some lawns do not thrive. (See Chapter 10 on Groundcovers.)

The only groundcovers that can take the place of lawn are those which remain low and green and can be clipped once or twice a year if necessary. *Dichondra repens* (Lawn-leaf, also known in this country under the name of Wonder-Lawn) and Lippia grass (*Lippia repens*) are the two best lawn substitutes. Both require even more moisture than ordinary Cynodon or Digitaria grasses, but not more than Blue or Bent grasses. Both are evergreen and are particularly valuable for planting between paving stones on crazy paving or on slightly sloping banks. They are not suitable as large lawns as they do not stand up to traffic like ordinary lawns. Both require plenty of moisture and regular feeding. Lippia grass is more drought-resistant than Dichondra and can take a little more traffic. It is a much darker green, however, and attracts bees with its numerous tiny flowers in spring. These can be mown off to prevent the bees from being a nuisance. Dichondra is best planted in a small area enclosed by paths or paving or it might invade ordinary lawns and flower beds. Dichondra can also be mown two or three times a year in order to keep it trim, if desired, and to prevent seeding.

TREES IN LAWNS

Trees in lawns must be heavily fed and deeply watered or they become shallow-rooted and feed on the surface in competition with the grass. They can be fed annually or whenever the lawn does not appear to thrive beneath them. Mature trees can be fed by boring holes over the root area and applying fertilizer as described in Chapter 29 under "Feeding". Cut out plugs of lawn and re-set after feeding.

Trees which are not suitable for lawns are those which have troublesome root systems, like Belhambra or Poplar; drop too much leaf-litter, like Acacias, or cast too dense a shade, like the Camphor Tree. Large spreading trees are worse than smaller spreading trees or tall upright trees, as they cast a larger area of shade. The grass will become thin through lack of light and one will finally either have to pave the area or underplant it with shade-tolerant plants and groundcovers. (See Chapter 9 on "Gardening in the Shade".) By removing the lower branches of large trees one can enable the sun to reach the grass in the morning or afternoon, but the southern aspect may remain shady and have to be planted as a shade area. Some trees, like Deodar, grow with their branches touching the ground over their whole root area, and these will not deprive the lawn of too much sun. Many large trees can be allowed to develop without a trunk in this way. It is best to compromise by planting larger trees on the perimeter of the garden, where the underplanting has its correct place in the landscape and where it may be possible to plant evergreen grasses on the edge of the sun-loving main lawn. Lawns tolerate afternoon shade more than morning shade and this should be borne in mind when considering the position of a shade tree in the garden.

A good specimen or shade tree on a lawn should, therefore, be small and spreading or tall and upright. It should have a deep-rooting system which will cause no serious trouble. Deciduous trees which drop all their leaves at once create less mess than some evergreens which continuously drop their leaves, like the Silky Oak. Evergreens with large neat leaves, like Magnolia grandiflora, remain tidy. Trees which cast a dappled shade, like Melia (Syringa) allow the sun to reach the grass for part of the day. Trees in lawns must be able to withstand normal lawn watering.

Some Good Shade Trees for Lawns

Mexican Cherry (*Prunus capuli*). Deciduous, for short period, medium size, moderate growth.

Brown-leaved Plums (*Prunus cerasifera*, varieties). Deciduous, small and large, rapid growth.

Flowering Cherries (*Prunus serrulata*). Deciduous, small and large, slow growth.

Flowering Crabapples (*Malus floribunda* and *M. alden-hamensis*). Deciduous, small and large, slow growth.

Cherry-laurel (*Prunus laurocerasus*). Evergreen, small, moderate growth.

Photinia serrulata. Evergreen, medium, moderate growth.

Magnolia grandiflora (White Magnolia). Evergreen, medium, slow growth.

Magnolia soulangeana (Purple Magnolia). Deciduous, spreading, fairly slow growth.

Glossy Privet (*Ligustrum lucidum*). Evergreen, medium, rapid growth.

Loquat (*Eriobotrya japonica*). Evergreen, medium, slow growth. Remove lower branches.

Box-Elder Maple (*Acer negundo*). (Green and variegated.) Deciduous, medium, rapid growth.

Trident or Chinese Maple (*Acer buergerianum*). Deciduous, small, moderate growth.

Honey Locust (*Gleditchsia triacanthos*). Deciduous, fairly large, spiny, rapid growth.

Melia azedarach (China-berry). Deciduous, large, spreading, rapid growth.

Pin Oak (*Quercus palustris*). Deciduous, tall, large, rapid growth. Cut lower branches.

Holly Oak (*Quercus ilex*). Evergreen, tall, large, moderate growth.

Evergreen Oak (*Quercus incana*). Evergreen, tall, moderate growth.

Hymenosporum flavum. Evergreen, tall, upright, moderate growth, dislikes wind.

Kaffir Plum (*Harpephyllum caffrum*). Evergreen, medium, slow growth. Only for mild winters.

Sweet Gum (*Liquidambar*). Deciduous, tall, upright, moderate growth.

Celtis africana (Camdeboo Stinkwood). Deciduous, large, light shade, rapid growth.

Flame Tree (*Brachychiton acerifolium*). Evergreen, medium, upright, moderate growth.

Brush-Cherry (*Eugenia*). Evergreen, medium, upright, moderate growth.

Deodar. Evergreen, tall, pyramidal, slow. Allow branches to rest on ground.

Pompon Tree (*Dais cotinifolia*). Deciduous, small, upright, moderate growth.

Pride-of-India (*Lagerstroemia*). Deciduous, small, rapid growth. Dislikes winter watering.

Lavalle Hawthorn (*Crataegus lavallei*). Deciduous, small, slow growth.

Pagoda Tree (*Sophora japonica*). Deciduous, medium, rounded. Moderate growth.

Tulip Tree (*Liriodendron*). Deciduous, tall, moderate growth. Likes moisture.

Tung Nut (*Aleurites*). Deciduous, dense shade but medium-sized, half-hardy.

Silver Tree (*Leucadendron*). Evergreen, lovely tree, but may not stand up to lawn watering in summer. Half-hardy.

Yellow-wood (*Podocarpus*). Evergreen, tall, narrow. Likes moisture. Slow growth.

Trees that are not Suitable for Lawn

Ailanthus (Tree of Heaven). Throws up root suckers.

Acacias. Brittle, leaf litter.

Ash (*Fraxinus*). Gross feeder.

Belhambra (*Phytolacca*). Dense shade. Main roots rise up with growth and disturb soil.

Camphor Tree (*Cinnamomum*). Shade too dense, unless branching from ground level. Too large.

Carob (*Ceratonia siliqua*). Shade too dense. Flowers have unpleasant smell.

Chestnut (*Castanea*). Too large. Shade too dense. Flowers have unpleasant smell.

Cape Chestnut (*Calodendrum*). Needs deep, good soil and good rainfall. Half-hardy.

Catalpa bignonioides. Too large. Shade too dense.

Elm, small-leaved or Chinese (*Ulmus parvifolia*). Surface roots and suckers.

False Acacia or Black Locust (*Robinia pseudacacia*). Troublesome suckers.

Jacaranda. Too large and spreading. Leaf litter.

Mulberry (*Morus*). Messy fruit drop, brittle branches.

Pepper tree (*Schinus molle*). Leaf and berry litter.

Plane Tree (*Platanus*). Too large. Southern portion would need paving.

Poplar Trees. Root system troublesome. Suckers.

Silky Oak (*Grevillea robusta*). Too tall, too much leaf litter.

English Oak (*Quercus robur*). Too large. Southern area would need paving.

Tipuana tipu. Spreading shade. Southern portion would need paving.

Weeping Willow (*Salix babylonica*). Too large, invasive roots.

odern Lilies (*Lilium* hybrids) like this Olympic hybrid, are magnificent in midsummer.

Hybrid Day-lilies (*Hemerocallis*) are bright, gay and a useful standby in leaf and flower.

swimming pool can fit gracefully into the general garden design in a tranquil setting of green lawn and suitable summer-flowering plants. Here Hydrangeas bloom spectacularly under a large Syringa Tree (*Melia azedarach*).

Dew Flower (*Drosanthemum hispidum*) drapes a sparkling purple curtain over large rocks in dry situations, while the luxuriant leaves of Sweet Garlic (*Tulbaghia fragrans*) soften the base.

The empty lower bed and border in this rockery may be fi with showy low-growing annuals to offset the Heath and o small shrubs above.

Steps up the bank alongside a rockery should harmonize and tie in with the rocks.

Brilliantly coloured *Dorotheanthus bellidiformis* (Bokbaai Vygie Daisies) make ideal low-growing annuals for rockery b nestling between permanent plants.

CHAPTER TWENTY-FIVE

GROWING ANNUALS FOR DISPLAY

The wonderful flower displays that gardeners plan for spring and summer consist mainly of annuals, although colour is also provided by shrubs, perennials and bulbs. Annuals grow from seed and produce flowers within the season, expending all their energy on a brilliant show which will last from two to six months, depending on their individual habit. They must then be pulled out to make way for other plants and, while this gives the gardener extra work in the garden, it also provides novelty and an opportunity to try out new colour schemes against a background of permanent plants which make up the main structure of the garden.

Brilliant and showy as they are, annuals should not be planted everywhere, for they are transient and when they are pulled out the garden is bare. Do not swing to the other extreme and leave annuals right out of the garden, however, unless one lacks the time, energy, interest or money to devote to them. The herbaceous border would be dull without a few patches of annuals and it is amazing how a few inexpensive annuals like dwarf yellow marigolds or tall white tobacco plants can light up a group of dark-foliaged shrubs. Annuals will provide extra colour notes for the waterside, rockery or tubs on the terrace. Nurserymen always raise seedlings for those who cannot grow their own from seed. For those who cannot spare the labour to plant out seedlings, there are many annuals that can be grown from seed thrown or broadcast straight into the ground, needing little attention besides watering.

The artistic gardener will achieve outstanding effects by using even the most common and popular annuals with regard to their colours and heights. They should be used in broad deep patches here and there, rather than in a formal bed. A mixed bed consisting only of clumps of annuals in separate colours can be planted for spring or for summer.

Dwarf edging plants include mauve Ageratum, purple or white Alyssum, multi-coloured dwarf Phlox, Dorotheanthus, Virginian stocks, yellow or orange dwarf Marigolds, blue Nemesia and Lobelia. The really compact dwarfs can be used in the rockery where they look like alpine plants. Annuals of medium height and sometimes spreading habit include Petunias, Gaillardia and Celosia. Really tall annuals include Scabious, Cosmos, Cleome, Cornflowers, Sunflowers, Venidium, *Silene coeli-rosa* and Zinnias in all shades. Always buy annuals in separate colours, for the mixed colours look spotty and seldom create as rich an effect. Seedmen's catalogues are filled with scores of annuals and one should try growing a few new ones each season as a matter of interest.

Annuals are useful for quick effects. Climbing annuals like *Mina lobata* will decorate a fence until the more permanent creepers and shrubs are fully grown. Ordinary bedding annuals can be grown in pots ready to sink into the soil when there are sudden spaces such as those left by bulbs which have died down after flowering.

Times for Planting Annuals. Although there are definite times for planting annuals, one can extend the season by staggering plantings. Early spring planting will ensure early summer flowering, but a later planting will ensure an attractive display late into autumn. Annuals create colour and interest all through the year in Southern Africa, for there are annuals which bloom in mid-winter and spring as well as during the summer months. (See lists below and Chapter 14.)

HOW TO GROW ANNUALS

Most annuals need full sunshine while others are suited to shady conditions. (See "Gardening in the Shade", Chapter 9.)

Soil. Soil for annuals should generally be light and well-drained. Prepare soil by digging to a depth of about 6 inches, since annuals are generally shallow-rooted. Spread a thick layer of well-rotted compost on the surface and fork it lightly into the top 2 inches. Leafmould, peatmoss or even vermiculite will help to keep the soil soft and retain moisture. Avoid using pure manure unless it is very well-rotted, but be careful not to dig in more than a thin layer or it may burn the young seedlings. Soil which was manured in the previous season is excellent. Small amounts of liquid manure or chemical fertilizers can be given when the buds are forming so as to improve the flowers and later to prolong the flowering period.

Watering. Keep the shallow-rooted seedlings of annuals moist while young, watering every day in dry weather, and do not let the soil dry out until the plants are established. As soon as they are growing vigorously, allow the top inch of soil to dry out before watering it again, making certain that the soil is moist below that level. Test with a trowel. Do not overwater annuals by watering them if the soil is wet up to the surface, or oxygen will be prevented from entering the soil. On the other hand, do not wet the surface only, or the roots will turn upwards seeking moisture. Allow the sprinkler to run for half-an-hour to an hour before moving it and then it will only be necessary to water two or three times a week. As a general rule, annuals need more water than perennials.

Transplanting Seedlings. Choose a cool or cloudy afternoon and see that the soil in the tins is moist, but not too wet. Lift each seedling with a trowel, retaining as much earth as possible. Do not squash the roots into a small hole, but dig a hole deep enough so that the roots can hang straight down. Hold the seedling by its leaves and see that it is planted at the same level at which it was planted in the seedbox or tin. Deep planting will rot away the stems of most seedlings. Some long-stemmed seedlings, like marigolds, are better planted deeply, as deep as the first seed-leaf.

The distances between seedlings must vary according to the size of the mature plant. Most dwarf annuals for display can be spaced about 5 or 6 inches apart. Crowding of plants stunts development, but do not plant them too far apart, for the leaves should meet and keep the soil cool and shaded.

Shading. After transplanting seedlings during spring and summer shade them from the heat of the sun for a few days until they become established. Seedlings which are planted in autumn seldom need shading as the weather is cooler, except in the case of early-planted seedlings like poppies or stocks.

One can provide filtered shade in several ways, by placing slatted wooden frames over a whole bed of plants or by shading each seedling individually by placing branchlets of pine trees or jacaranda leaves on the north side of them or by covering them with ready-made plastic or paper "caps". Water the seedlings without moving these devices. After a few days, as soon as the plants appear to be fresh and strong, remove the shades permanently. Do this in the late afternoon so that they can benefit from the cool night air.

Further Care of Annuals. Remove the faded flowers of annuals or else the plant's energy will be diverted to producing seed and the flowering season will be shortened. Even if annuals produce masses of flowers, make an attempt to snip off the dead ones from time to time. If one wishes to save seed, wait until the end of the flowering period or mark selected plants with cotton before letting them all go to seed. Annuals make wonderful material for the compost once their flowering period is over.

Propagation. Annuals are always grown from seed and a seedbox is almost an essential in a garden where annuals are raised regularly in spring and autumn. (See Chapter 20.) Raising seedlings in advance will enable one to transplant them as soon as the ground is vacant. Sowing seed in tins or in a seedbox before transplanting is more economical than sowing it in the open ground, but one can broadcast the seed of many annuals in order to avoid the labour of transplanting and shading. Plants sown in the open do not suffer any check from transplanting. Seeds which germinate quickly are most suitable for broadcasting as are plants which do not transplant well. For a selection, see the lists below.

How to "Throw" Seed into the Open Ground. Prepare the soil as described above, being particularly careful to break down all the lumps at the surface and level off with a straight plank. If the surface is rough, it is a good idea to cover the top with a ½-inch layer of sifted topsoil, rubbed through a coarse round garden sieve. One can mix this with peatmoss or fine vermiculite, both of which absorb water, although this is not absolutely necessary. One can water the soil before planting, soaking it well with a fine spray, but be careful not to disturb the level surface.

Choose a quiet day for sowing seed in the open, for the slightest puff of wind will send it flying before it can be anchored with a cover of soil. Outline the area to be sown with a stick or mark patches for different annuals before sowing. If the seed is large, like that of Namaqualand Daisy, it can be scattered over the surface with the hand. If it is small or fine, like that of Linaria or Virginian Stock, it must first be mixed with sifted soil. Mix a teaspoonful of seed with about two cups of fine soil, shake it up well and scatter it over the surface. The seed must be well distributed or the seedlings will be overcrowded and probably restricted in growth. Some annuals do not mind being overcrowded, but the larger ones do best if they are well spaced. It is possibly better to plant closely than too far apart, as this makes for a more natural and showy effect. Featherlight seed, like that of Ursinia, should be sown in tiny patches and covered before it flies away.

Cover the seed with a thin layer of sifted soil which will hide it from sight and anchor it firmly. Use plain soil if vermiculite has been incorporated into the base as it helps to show that the entire surface has been covered with the topsoil. Using dry soil to cover damp soil will also differentiate between the two. Water the soil again, waving a fine spray from the hosepipe or watering can from side to side so that the water is absorbed immediately and does not lie on the surface. Water thoroughly to begin with and keep the surface damp until germination takes place. If it is very hot, one may cover the soil with newspapers or sacking which help to keep it damp and dark. Remove these promptly as soon as the first seedlings break the surface, or they will become lengthened and weakened. Keep the soil constantly moist even if it means watering twice or three times a day. Do not allow the tiny seedlings to dry out in the early stages of growth and do not be afraid of over-watering. Watering may be reduced gradually when the seedlings become strong and vigorous.

Weed a large area by spanning it with a plank resting on bricks at opposite sides of the bed. Otherwise, set a few flat rocks or pieces of slate into the bed to act as stepping stones. These will probably be half covered by the mature plants and look pleasantly natural.

ANNUALS WHICH ARE SUITED TO OPEN-GROUND SOWING

Some of these annuals do not transplant well and are best grown from seed thrown into the open ground. A few of them need rich soil and plenty of moisture or shade. Their special needs will be noted in individual descriptions later as well as in the lists below. Most of the following annuals can be grown in seedboxes and transplanted when large enough, but are well adapted to sowing in the open ground. They are particularly useful to the gardener who does not want to be bothered with raising seedlings or who is late with his seasonal planting.

The best time to sow summer flowering annuals in the open ground is in mid-September or early October, when the weather has warmed up thoroughly. They can be sown as late as December for late summer and autumn display. Spring-flowering annuals should be sown during March. Those which mature quickly, like Namaqualand daisies, can be sown as late as the first week in April. Do not sow too early or the luxuriant growth which develops may be injured by frost. It is not advisable to sow seed in the open ground later than the second week in April, or the tiny seedlings may suffer frost injury and not develop properly until spring, if at all.

OPEN GROUND—WINTER AND SPRING-FLOWERING ANNUALS
Sow during March, except where otherwise stated.

Candytuft (Iberis)—or in spring. Also in seedbox. Good, rich soil, sun, moisture. Hardy.
Carnations, annual—sun and good soil. Endure drought when mature. Hardy.
Centaurea cyanus (Cornflower) and C. imperialis (Sweet Sultan)—or spring or late summer. Thin to a foot apart. Also seedbox. Well-drained, good soil. Hardy.
Clarkia—February, March, April or spring. (See growing hints below.)
*Cotula—Warm, sunny situation, poor soil, moisture while young. Also in seedbox. Sow first week in April.

Dimorphotheca (Namaqualand Daisy)—end March or first week in April. Also seedbox. Grows easily. Moisture while young.
Dorotheanthus (Bokbaai Daisy). Also seedbox. Moisture while young. Full sun, good for edging, rockeries and warm slopes.
Eschscholzia (Californian Poppy)—or spring. Dislike transplanting. Stand heat and drought when mature.
*Felicia (Kingfisher Daisy)—Full sun, ordinary soil, moisture while young.
Gaillardia—or spring. Grows easily but prefers rich soil. Withstands drought. Hardy.
Godetia—or spring. (See growing hints below.)
Gypsophila—or spring. Like lime.
Helichrysum (Everlastings)—or spring. Good light soil. Pinch to bush out.
Heliophila (Blue Flax)—light soil, moisture while young. Warm, sunny situation.
Larkspur—or spring. (See growing hints below.)
*Linaria—or spring. Good light soil, full sun, moisture.
Lupin—February to March. Well-drained, good soil. Dislike lime.
Mignonette—January to March. Thin out to 9 inches apart. Rich soil. Flower through spring and summer.
*Nemesia—Transplants well. (See growing hints below.)
Senecio elegans—or spring. Light, good soil. Warm sunny position.
Silene coeli-rosa (Agrostemma)—Hardy. Grows easily in ordinary soil, moisture while young.
Sweet-peas (climbing and dwarf)—See growing hints below.
*Ursinia—or spring. Full sun, well-drained soil. Stands drought when mature.
*Venidium (Double Namaqualand Daisy)—Hardy to cold, full sun, moisture while young.
*Virginian Stock (Malcomia)—Sow thinly in ordinary soil, sun. Also seedbox if liked.

OPEN GROUND—SUMMER-FLOWERING ANNUALS
Sow during September except where otherwise stated. Most can be sown again in December for autumn-flowering.

Blue Lace Flower (Trachymene coerulea or Didiscus)—or autumn in mild districts.
Calliopsis—or in seedbox. Sun, good soil, moisture.
Candytuft (Iberis)—also in seedbox, or autumn. Good rich soil, sun, moisture.
Centaurea (Cornflower and Sweet Sultan)—or late summer or autumn. (See above list.)
Cleome—thin out to 2 feet apart. Full sun, good soil. Also transplant while small.
*Cosmos—mid-September to November. Full sun, poor soil, moisture while young.
*Cynoglossum (Chinese-Forget-Me-Not)—Full sun, ordinary soil, moisture.
Four-o-Clock (Mirabilis jalapa)—Full sun, poor soil.
Gypsophila—or autumn. Likes lime.
*Helianthus (Sunflower)—or seedbox. Full sun, ordinary soil.

*Very quick effect.

Helichrysum (Everlastings)—or autumn. Good light soil. Pinch to bush out.

**Ipomoea* (Convolvulus or Morning Glory)—Sun, ordinary soil.

Linum (Flax)—Full sun, light soil.

**Marigolds*—transplant easily, best in seedboxes.

**Matricaria*—or seedbox. Grows easily in ordinary soil, full sun, moisture.

Molucella (Bells of Ireland)—Sun or partial shade.

**Nasturtium*—well-drained soil, full sun or too much leaf growth. Do not plant too deep.

Nemophila (Baby-Blue-Eyes)—Also spring, full sun.

Nicotiana (Tobacco Flower). Light shade, moisture.

Nigella (Love-in-a-Mist)—or autumn.

Phacelia—also in March. Full sun, light loam.

**Phlox*—also in seedbox. (See growing hints below.)

Poppy (Shirley). Sun, good garden soil, moisture.

**Portulaca*—or seedbox as they transplant well. Full sun, ordinary soil.

Salpiglossis—or seedbox. Full sun, good loamy soil, moisture. Thin out to 9 inches apart.

**Tagetes signata pumila*—or seedbox. Grows easily. Bright edging.

Tithonia—tall annual which seeds itself in ordinary soil. Sun.

Viscaria—or seedbox. For rockery and edging. Sun, moisture.

**White Lace Flower*—Sun or partial shade, ordinary soil.

**Zinnia*—or seedbox. Full sun, good garden soil, moisture.

ANNUALS WHICH ARE BEST RAISED IN A SEEDBOX

SEEDBOX—WINTER AND SPRING-FLOWERING

Sow seed in March unless otherwise stated. Some will bloom in mid-winter if sown earlier, so that seedlings can be planted out in March.

Anchusa (Cape Forget-Me-Not)—Sow in January for early spring flowers, or in August for autumn display. Light soil, sun or light shade, moisture.

Antirrhinum (Snapdragon)—Also early spring. (See growing hints below.)

Arctotis acaulis—A perennial treated as an annual. Full sun, well-drained soil, moisture while young.

Bellis perennis (Double Daisy)—Full or partial shade, rich, light soil and moisture.

Calendula—January to March. (See growing hints below.)

Cheiranthus (Wallflowers)—Sow in February for early flowers or as late as May. Hardy, likes cool weather and moisture.

**Chrysanthemum*, Annual—Sow from February to July. Grows easily and quickly.

Dianthus (Pinks and Sweet William)—January to May. Rich, light soil, open sun and moisture.

Lavatera (Mallow)—or spring. Seeds itself in ordinary soil. Sun.

Lobelia—or spring in cool districts. (See growing hints below.)

Myosotis (Forget-me-Not)—also in spring and summer. Shade or sun with moisture. Rich light soil. Germinates slowly.

**Nemesia*—February to April. (See growing hints below.)

Poppy, Iceland—Sow in January for winter flowers. (See growing hints below.)

Primula malacoides—Sow in January for winter flowers. (See growing hints below.)

Schizanthus (Poor Man's Orchid)—See growing hints below.

Stocks—Sow in January for winter flowers. (See growing hints below.)

Viola—Sow in January or February for winter flowers. (See growing hints below.)

SEEDBOX—SUMMER-FLOWERING

These will bloom by midsummer if seed is sown in mid-August or September in sheltered seedboxes. Some may be planted as late as December for autumn display.

Ageratum—Full sun. Good for edging or groundcover for roses.

**Alyssum*—Sun, moisture. Can be planted in autumn in mild districts. Also sow in open.

**Amaranthus*—Brilliant foliage, quick effect. Can be sown in open if liked. Needs full sun. Good for hot dry places.

Anagallis (Pimpernel)—Sun or afternoon shade in hot places.

Anchusa (Cape Forget-me-Not)—Sow in August for autumn flowering. (See above list.)

Aster—(See growing hints below.)

Balsam—Humidity, moisture, rich soil and shelter from hot winds. Tender. Pots.

Boronia—Full sun, light peaty soil, moisture in summer. Dislikes wind.

Brachycome (Swan River Daisy)—Full sun, well-drained soil.

Browallia—Partial shade, moisture, rich light loamy soil. Pots.

Calendula—better in autumn. (See growing hints below.)

Candytuft (Iberis)—or autumn, in seedbox or open. Rich soil, sun, moisture.

**Celosia* (Cockscomb)—open ground if liked. Sun, rich soil, moisture.

Cladanthus (Palm Springs Daisy)—Full sun, good garden soil, moisture.

Cleome—Better in open ground.

**Cuphea* (Firefly)—Sun, moisture. Flower quickly.

Dahlia (Coltness or Unwin Hybrids)—Sun, good soil, moisture.

**Delphinium* (Blue butterfly)—Sun, rich soil and moisture.

Echium (Blue Bedder)—shade, ordinary soil.

Euphorbia marginata (Snow-on-the-Mountain)—Sun, ordinary soil.

Gaillardia, Annual—or autumn. Grows easily, but prefers rich soil. Withstands drought.

Gilia—sow early and transplant while small or sow in open. Takes several months before flowering. May be sown in autumn in mild districts.

**Gomphrena* (Globe Amaranth)—Grows easily in poor soil. Sow in open also.

*Very quick effect.

Helianthus (Sunflower)—Full sun, ordinary soil. Sow in open also.

Impatiens (Zanzibar Balsam)—Perennial best treated as annual in area with cold winters. Shade, moisture, rich light soil.

Kochia (Summer Cypress or Burning Bush)—Sun, good soil, moisture.

Lobelia—(See growing hints below.)

*Marigolds—Grow easily. Also in open ground if liked. Full sun, ordinary soil.

*Matricaria—Grows easily in ordinary soil. Full sun, can be clipped. Or open ground.

Mimulus (Musk and Monkey Flower)—Shade and moisture.

Petunia—(See growing hints below.)

Phlox—(See growing hints below.)

Portulaca—Full sun, ordinary soil, or open ground. Good for between paving or groundcover beneath roses.

Salpiglossis—or open ground. Full sun, good loamy soil, moisture.

Salvia splendens—Sow in July or August in sheltered seedbox or will not bloom till late summer.

Sanvitalia (Trailing Zinnia)—Full sun, light soil.

Scabiosa—Hardy, good soil, likes lime. Sow in autumn in hot climates.

Torenia (Wishbone Flower)—Shade or sun, with humidity. Moisture. Good for pots or edging.

Verbena—(See growing hints below.)

Xeranthemum (Everlastings)—Grow easily in ordinary soil. Sun.

*Zinnia—or open ground. Needs full sun, good soil, plenty of moisture while young.

CLIMBING ANNUALS FOR QUICK EFFECTS

Plant in September or October.

Ipomoea (Convolvulus, Morning Glory).
Dolichos (Hyacinth Bean).
Mina lobata.
Thunbergia alata (Black-eyed Susan) really perennial.
Cobaea scandens (Purple-Bell Climber) really perennial.

HINTS ON GROWING FAVOURITE ANNUALS

Antirrhinum (Snapdragon). These hardy annuals grow best during cool weather and should be sown early in March so that plants will bloom in spring. They may be sown in early spring, but are susceptible to rust where heavy rains fall in summer. Require full sun and well-drained soil with regular watering. Soil should be medium-rich, containing compost, although they will withstand poor soil and drought when mature.

Aster. Summer-flowering annuals that grow easily in light loamy soil, Asters dislike hot soil. They need plenty of sunshine, but afternoon shade is beneficial in places with hot summers. Water regularly. Plant out in September when all danger of frost is over.

*Very quick effect.

Calendula. Hardy annuals, these are best sown from January to March for winter or spring flowering, but may also be planted in spring for late blooming. Sow in the open and thin out to 8 inches apart or transplant while young. Need a rich but light loam. Apply fertilizer or liquid manure as the buds form.

Clarkia. Hardy annuals which do not transplant easily, these should be sown in the open ground in autumn and thinned out to 6 inches apart. They may also be sown in spring. Require a medium-rich soil and shelter from wind. Stake if necessary.

Godetia. Hardy annuals for spring or summer flowering, they prefer cool, moist conditions especially while flowering. Give rich soil and afternoon shade in hot places.

Larkspur. Hardy annuals which do best if sown in late summer or autumn for spring flowering, they may also be planted in spring. They dislike transplanting except when very small and should be thinned to about a foot apart. Need light good soil and regular watering during winter, but very little water during rainy summers. Need sunshine, but afternoon shade is beneficial in hot places. Give fertilizer or liquid manure when buds form.

Lobelia. Shade-loving annuals which are good for edging, window-boxes or groundcovers under trees, they like rich light soil containing compost and adequate moisture. Lobelia will grow in the sun, particularly at the coast where they endure drier soil. Sow seed thinly in seedbox in March or April and transplant into a shady position which is protected from frost or wait until August if it is too cold. Seed sown in August will not bloom till January. Lobelia will flower throughout summer and may be cut back after flowering to induce fresh crops.

Nemesia. Half-hardy, spring-flowering annuals, they should be given a sunny sheltered spot against a north or west wall in areas with cold winters. Quick to flower. Seed sown in March will flower in June. Need good well-drained soil and are suitable for window-boxes. Sow direct into ground or in seedboxes. Transplant well.

Pansy. Heartsease. Strictly perennials, these are best treated as annuals. Sow seed in January or early February so that seedlings can be planted out by March. Pansies require rich, light soil containing plenty of well-rotted manure. They need sunshine, but benefit from afternoon shade. Water regularly. Pinch back early flowers and give liquid manure as buds begin to form. Limit flowers to six to a plant if they are needed for exhibition.

Petunia. Useful summer-flowering annuals, Petunias grow easily in hot, sunny places. Need good garden soil containing well-rotted manure or compost containing lime. Shear back lightly after summer flowering is over to induce autumn bloom. Seed is very fine and should be mixed with fine sand before sowing in tins or seedbox covered with glass. (See Propagation in Chapter 20.) Keep moist and shaded while young. Sow thinly or prick out into tins to strengthen before transplanting. Shade seedlings at first. Guard against snails and slugs both in seedbox and garden.

Phlox. Quick to flower, Phlox brighten the summer garden or window-box. Choose separate colours and grow dwarf hybrids. Plant in a sunny place from spring to early summer. Fine seed should be thoroughly mixed with sand and scattered in open ground consisting of rich soft loam. Firm well and cover with newspapers until germination takes place. Keep moist while young. Seed may also be sown in boxes and planted out while small.

Poppy, Iceland. Hardy perennials which are treated as annuals, Iceland Poppies bloom during mid-winter and spring. For early blooming, sow the fine seed in December or at the beginning of January in the seedbox and transplant seedlings by the beginning of March. Choose a sunny position and space the plants about 9 inches apart. The soil should be light and rich, containing well-rotted compost or manure. Poppies dislike hot soil and should be watered regularly. Fertilizer can be given towards the end of winter.

Oriental Poppies are true perennials and must remain in their permanent position. They need similar treatment to Iceland Poppies with even more moisture and prefer afternoon shade in hot places.

Primula. *P. malacoides* (Fairy Primula) is a hardy winter and spring-flowering perennial that is treated as an annual. It grows so easily that it seeds itself in gardens. Seed should be sown in midsummer for early blooming. Seed sown in November will bloom from May throughout winter and spring. Space seedlings about 6 inches apart. Primula do best in partial shade, but also flourish in full shade or full sun provided that the soil is good and moisture adequate. Mix plenty of compost into the soil so that it is light and yet retains moisture.

P. obconica is used mainly as a spring-flowering pot plant but can be grown outdoors in the shade. It is a perennial which is treated as an annual. Some people are allergic to the foliage.

Schizanthus. Poor Man's Orchid. Spring-flowering annuals, they require shelter from frost. Choose a sunny situation with morning shade or grow in pots in a greenhouse or on a sheltered porch. Soil should be well-drained and mixed with compost or peatmoss. Stake while young as the flowering bushes fall over when mature. Turn pots so that they receive light all round. Sow seed in March or April in seedboxes.

Stocks. (*Mathiola.*) Hardy annuals which are prized for their fragrant flowers in early winter and spring, Stocks require care in the early stages. They dislike transplanting except while small, yet are not usually grown from seed sown in the open ground as the tiny seedlings damp off easily in rainy weather. They must be thinned to 9 inches apart. Stocks generally need several months of growth before flowering and seed should be sown early, preferably during January or February. It is not advisable to plant too early in the hope of having earlier flowers, as midsummer humidity and heavy rains cause losses to seedlings. Seed sown at the beginning of February produces vigorous plants that often "catch up" with earlier plantings. Ten-week Stocks bloom more quickly and can be planted as late as March. There are many types of Stocks including tall column Stocks, dwarf edging Stocks and medium branching Stocks which are most useful for picking. *Mathiola bicornis* is a low scented annual for informal planting. Stocks are grown during summer in places with cold climates.

Sow Stock seed thinly in a seedbox with a lid. Germination takes place in two days and seedlings must be given light immediately or they develop into lanky plants. Transplant carefully into well-prepared soil in the open ground as soon as the plants have four leaves, choosing a cool afternoon. Stocks could be grown individually in jiffy pots to aid transplanting. Shade the plants for at least a week and do not allow the young plants to dry out. Once established, Stocks should be watered regularly and deeply. Allow the top 2 inches to dry out before watering again, making sure that the soil is moist beneath, or the plants will suffer from overwatering. Stocks need a sunny situation but dislike hot soil so that they benefit from afternoon shade in hot places. Window-boxes are generally too hot for them. Drainage must be good and the soil should be mixed with plenty of well-rotted compost containing manure, but fresh manure should be avoided.

Sweet-peas. These fragrant winter and spring-flowering annuals are climbers which need support. Dwarf bushy types, known as Bijou or Knee-High Sweet-peas, grow to 18 inches with flowers suitable for cutting and make a fine show. Sweet-peas require sunshine and are best grown to face north or east. Winter-flowering types do best facing north and late spring-flowering types prefer an east facing position so that they are shaded from hot afternoon sun. Sow seed of winter-flowering Sweet-peas in March or in January or February for very early flowers. Spring-flowering varieties can be sown from the end of March to mid-June.

The soil must be well-prepared, but it is no longer considered necessary to dig deep trenches before planting. Remove the topsoil to a depth of about eight inches and loosen the subsoil to a spade's depth. Choose a situation where drainage is good or mix sand and rough compost into the subsoil. Mix the topsoil with plenty of well-rotted compost containing lime and decayed manure and replace it. Dig an area about 2 to 3 feet wide for one row of plants. As Sweet-peas do not transplant easily, the seeds are best sown in their permanent positions and thinned out to about 9 inches apart. Seed may be soaked overnight before planting. If liked, plant individual seeds in jiffy pots to be planted directly into the ground, or in small terracotta pots, to be tipped out carefully, or in empty eggshells, cracked at the base.

Support for Climbing Sweet-peas must be provided before planting. The easiest method is to erect a trellis a few inches from a wall. Lean bamboo canes against the wall or drive them erect into the ground, lacing them together with rows of string or raffia spaced about 6 inches apart. Ready-made string netting is available. Wire netting is not recommended as it becomes too hot. If there is no suitable wall, Sweet-peas can be grown on sturdy supports placed in a sunny, sheltered portion of the garden. Make a fence with a double row of 6-foot stakes tied at the top or tie six stakes together at the top to form a wigwam. In each case, tie rows of raffia or string around the stakes at 6-inch intervals to the top. (See illustration page 161.)

Water Sweet-peas by soaking the soil deeply about twice a week, as they have long roots. Allow the young shoots to grow up to about 4 inches in height, but as soon as the second shoot emerges from the base and grows up to about an inch in length, cut away the first shoot as it will never develop vigorously. Allow the secondary shoot to become the main stem. Sweet-peas should be trained to have a single main stem from the beginning so that they will produce exhibition type blooms on long, straight stems. If one allows them to develop many bushy stems and tendrils, they will flower in profusion, but the flowers deteriorate after a few weeks, producing fewer blooms

and shorter, twisted stems. Nip off any side shoots which develop from between the leaves and the main stem. Do this each week with a pair of small, sharp scissors. As the main stem grows, tie it to each row in turn with a piece of raffia. Cut off all tendrils, as these twist the stems and tangle the flowers. A few tendrils may be left if they catch the string and do not touch the plant, but are best removed. Once the main stem reaches the top of the trellis it can be cut off to keep it within reach. Remove faded flowers so as to prolong the flowering period.

Verbena. Hybrid plants which are strictly perennials, these are treated as summer annuals which flower for a long period. Their low, spreading habit makes them ideal for rockeries, window-boxes and informal planting. Verbenas need full sun and well-drained soil or they become mildewed. They flourish in good garden soil mixed with well-rotted compost containing lime. Water regularly during hot dry weather, but do not overwater. Seed should be sown in the seedbox at the beginning of August so that the seedlings can be transplanted into the garden in September.

Viola. Tufted Pansy. Among the most useful long-flowering plants for display, Violas form colourful ground-covers in beds on their own or planted with daffodils, tulips or around shrubs. Plant in patches of separate colours. Seed should be sown in January or early February so that the seedlings can be transplanted in the garden by mid-March. They start flowering in June and bloom profusely throughout spring, summer and autumn. Remove dead flowers periodically to prolong flowering and give liquid manure at the end of spring. Violas grow easily in good garden soil containing plenty of compost, needing regular watering and full sun.

CHAPTER TWENTY-SIX

CULTIVATION OF PERENNIALS

All plants except annuals are perennials, but gardeners usually reserve the word perennial to describe herbaceous plants that grow into vigorous clumps during summer and die down in winter. These are the herbaceous perennials of the herbaceous border, which form an important group in any garden. They are very easy to grow, requiring ordinary good garden soil that is, preferably, on the light side. Perennials will grow in ordinary soil, but respond magnificently to feeding. As they are generally left in the soil for more than a year, manure or rich, well-rotted compost can be forked liberally into the soil before planting. Compost or peatmoss will improve the texture. Perennials should be given plenty of water while growing and may be kept completely dry during winter, although it is beneficial to water them once a month during winter. Too much water without good drainage while they are dormant can lead to rotting and loss of the plants.

Although they have a dormant or rest period during winter, perennials are not lifted and stored dry like bulbs or their roots will dry out too much. After cutting back the dead stalks in autumn, however, the clumps of perennials can be dug up and temporarily replanted elsewhere in the garden. Simply dig a shallow hole, place all clumps of the same kind side by side, and just cover them with soil. This is known as "heeling in". One can water the plants to settle them and then leave them alone until spring. Label the clumps carefully and do not mix up the colours.

When to Divide Perennials. The safest time to divide herbaceous perennials is at the end of winter or in very early spring when growth begins and the green tips show. If one is to be away or too busy during this time, one can also divide and replant perennials in the autumn, but this should only be done for convenience and not as a matter of preference. There is always a danger of losing the tiny plants set out in autumn, through rotting or cold, whereas the old clumps generally remain unaffected. There is no purpose in dividing in autumn, even though one might think that the plants have a longer time in which to become established and may flower earlier, for plants set out during our warm spring simply race ahead and flower as soon as the others. In places like the south-western Cape where autumn is long and spring is cool, late flowering perennials, like Monarda, can be divided in autumn, if desired, so that the firmly established plants will bloom with a good display. In cool countries where snow insulates plants, autumn division is preferred.

It is easier to divide and replant perennials in the herbaceous border in spring, so that one can keep in mind what one is planting and leave spaces shortly to be filled by annuals. Some plants, like Lilies, must be planted in autumn in the border and their position marked with stakes, but these are bulbs.

How to Divide Perennials. Plants like perennial Phlox and Michaelmas Daisies form thick cushiony clumps which sprout into dozens of new plants in spring. Using a small fork, prise these shoots away from the outside edge, disentangling the roots as much as possible. If the soil is hard, it helps to dampen it beforehand and remove some of the soil. If there is any difficulty in separating the plants, cut down into the roots with a sharp penknife or spade. Select strong young plants and discard the old woody plants at the centre. Replant the young plants immediately without allowing them to dry out and water to settle them.

Some clumps like Echinacea (Pink Rudbeckia) may be difficult to separate into single plants. Do not struggle to do so, but simply cut the clump into halves or quarters, depending on its size, and plant the smaller clump. This can be done by chopping it across with a spade or, more gently, by inserting two garden forks back to back in the centre and levering them apart. Perennial roots seem to resist quite rough handling and grow vigorously as long as there is one live shoot left.

A few plants resent being chopped up too small like *Salvia patens*, pink Salvia and Monarda. Others, like Peony, should not be disturbed at all and simply left to grow into huge clumps.

How Often to Divide. It is only necessary to divide the really vigorous, spreading perennials that overrun others or that become so overcrowded that they flower poorly. These include Physostegia, Michaelmas Daisy, perennial Phlox, Achillea and Erigeron. For best results one should also divide Cannas each year. Otherwise, leave all plants undivided for at least two years. It is best to replant the border every three years, enriching the soil, altering the arrangement and introducing different plants.

Some plants, like Lilies, Day-Lilies and Pokers, should be left undivided for five years or until they cease flowering through being overcrowded. Others, like Peonies and flowering shrubs should never be disturbed and are best placed on the outer edges of the border so that they will not interfere with soil preparation.

Propagation. Perennials can also be grown from seed and from cuttings. Only a few plants, like Dianthus, are commonly grown from cuttings, while the vast majority can be grown from seed. Division is the easiest and quickest method of propagation.

SOME SPECIAL PERENNIALS

Some favourite garden perennials cannot be grown with as little care as the common herbaceous perennials. Although they grow easily enough, they each need special treatment in order to flower well and grow into healthy attractive plants. Many of them have large flowers that are valued for cutting besides their garden appearance, such as Carnation and Chrysanthemum. Others, like Bearded Iris, are important enough to form the major part of a garden. Most cultural advice given stresses the difficulties of growing these plants and makes people afraid to attempt growing them. Basically, they are simple to grow, but require specific treatment and will amaze the amateur gardener with the way in which they respond to correct cultivation.

Biennials are plants which are really perennials, but must be treated differently in the garden.

How to Grow Biennials in General. These are plants which are strictly perennials, but deteriorate so much after a season or two that gardeners discard them. They cannot be grouped with annuals, however, for they take longer than one season to grow and flower. Popular garden plants that fall into this category are Columbines (*Aquilegia*), Foxgloves (*Digitalis*), Canterbury bells (*Campanula medium*) and Delphiniums. Some of these will be described in detail later in this chapter.

All these plants are grown from seed which should be planted during summer to flower in early summer of the following year, around November. To give them the best opportunity to develop, the seed should be sown in November, December or January, the earlier the better. It is advisable to plant the seedlings into the open by January, so that they can grow vigorously before the time for winter's rest. Some may disappear completely during winter, like Delphiniums, while others, like Foxgloves, remain evergreen. Water the plants during winter if their leaves are green, but withhold water from those plants which die down naturally. They will commence growth

again in spring, when they should be well watered, and will bloom in early summer.

Pull out plants like Foxgloves and Canterbury bells after they have bloomed, as they do not flower well the following season. Shade-loving Columbines may bloom satisfactorily for one more year if they are grown in rich, light soil, given a dressing of compost and sufficient water.

CARNATION

Carnations produce an astounding number of lovely cut flowers, but are somewhat of a taskmaster. If one does not establish a routine for their care, they will soon grow out of hand and the flowers deteriorate. The amateur can be as successful with them as the commercial grower, however, for it is their very ease of growth which makes it necessary to control them and pay them attention. A small sunny patch, about 10 feet by 10 feet, can be filled with about fifty plants, which will be more than the average gardener will need or be able to cope with.

Carnations grow easily from seed, but one is never sure how good the plants will be until they have flowered. The easiest way to obtain new plants is by taking cuttings. These are only worth taking from really good plants with strong flowers in good colours. Ready-rooted cuttings may be purchased from specialist nurseries, to be planted immediately on arrival.

Taking One's Own Cuttings. This may be done in spring or autumn. Cuttings taken in March are best as they will commence flowering in early summer, whereas spring cuttings will only commence flowering in late summer. Choose cuttings from mature plants that have been blooming for some months and take them from the lower half of a flowering stem, but not so near the base that they are old and woody. A cutting is simply a new shoot that emerges as a tuft of leaves from between the stem and a leaf. Pull this tuft of leaves downwards and away from the stem. Trim the jagged edges of the tiny stem level with a sharp knife, but take care not to cut away too much or slit the stem. Bunch a few cutting together

 and stand them upright in a glass containing enough hormone root-growing solution to just cover the stems. Leave overnight and plant out the following day. Root the cuttings in a seedframe or tins or on a piece of well-drained ground bordered by bricks. Use a mixture of good garden soil and river sand rather than pure river sand in order to obtain stronger plants. Level and soak the soil about half an hour before planting. Plant the cutting about ¼ inch deep, but no deeper for fear of rotting. Firm the soil around it and plant the

next one $\frac{1}{2}$ inch away. Fifty cuttings can be planted in four rows in a single flat tin. Water them gently without knocking them over. Cover them closely with a polythene film to keep in moisture and place a wooden cover over this to keep out the light. Leave for 48 hours, then open the lid and polythene cover for an hour to admit light and air, but do not allow the sun to shine directly on the cuttings. Open the lid a little more each day. If preferred, replace the wooden cover with a slatted lid so that filtered light, but not hot, drying sunshine, can reach the cuttings. The cuttings will grow roots in three weeks and can then be pulled out and examined. They can be left in the soil and sand mixture to develop larger roots if necessary, but not in pure sand which has not sufficient nourishment.

If one can tend them carefully, the cuttings may be planted directly into the open ground. It is safer to grow them in the nursery for a while, however, so as to reduce possible risk of loss and in order to select only the strongest plants. Plant them at the same level into a seedframe or tins containing compost, pinch them back to induce bushiness once they start growing and transplant them into the garden when they are about 6 inches in height.

Planting Out Rooted Cuttings. Choose an open, sunny position as Carnations must not have "wet feet". Prepare the ground about a month before planting out. Contrary to popular belief, good Carnations require good feeding, so that one must dig in a liberal quantity of well-rotted manure or compost containing manure. The soil must be light and well-drained. Dig to a depth of about a foot, break up the lumps, then spread the compost on top, forking it into the top few inches. Level very well and break down the lumps as much as possible.

Carnations must be planted in rows in order to tend them, but the area they cover need not be square, so that they can be fitted more artistically into the landscape. Plant the rooted cuttings about 15 inches away from each other in the rows and at least 18 inches between each row so that one may walk between the mature plants. Plant them at the same depth as before, just enough to keep them upright, and firm the soil well. They will root themselves strongly even though they are planted $\frac{1}{4}$ inch deep.

The plants must be artificially supported from the beginning. Carnation plants are heavy and have a tendency to fall over during wind and rain. Once they have done so they cannot be righted successfully. The flower stems lie on the ground and the whole patch becomes out of hand. Individual basket supports composed of two or three widening circles of wire joined by wire uprights which are pressed into the ground, are the most satis-

factory. The wires are soon obliterated by the luxuriant foliage which develops. The lowest circle should be at least 6 inches across and inserted 3 inches above the surface, while the second circle should be at least a foot across. Where Carnations are grown commercially, lengths of wire fixed to stout stakes are run down the rows, on either side of each plant, but this is unsightly in the garden.

Feeding. Unless Carnations are fed properly they will develop small flowers and floppy stems. Feeding must be done regularly and gradually, for overfeeding will cause splitting of the calyx and subsequent early petal fall.

Feed the plants once in every three or four weeks throughout the growing season, alternating the following materials. Do not apply anything up against the woody stem, but sprinkle it around the plant where the roots can absorb it easily.

    (a) Compost containing manure—lay this as a mulch on top of the soil.

    (b) One teaspoonful of general fertilizer like 5 : 13 : 5 to each plant, sprinkled on to damp soil.

    (c) Superphosphates—one teaspoon to each plant, sprinkled on to damp soil.

Liquid manure, applied to damp soil, may be given as an alternative to any of the above feeds. During mid-season, one should apply a light dressing of agricultural lime. Woodash may be sprinkled on to the soil and watered in.

Watering. Carnations must receive adequate water, even though they have the reputation of enduring dry conditions. Soak the soil for two hours once a week during the growing season and water more often if conditions are very dry. One can irrigate the plants or use an overhead sprinkler. Do not wet the foliage after midday for fear of encouraging rust.

Spraying. To control Carnation Bud Fly, spray every week to ten days with DDT emulsion or spray weekly with Dipterex wettable powder and water. To control Rust, spray with a fungicide containing sulphur, from the beginning of the rainy season. (See Chapter 38.)

CANNA

Usually considered to be so easy to grow that they are frequently hideous through neglect, Cannas make an outstanding contribution to colour in the garden. They bloom from November, or earlier, until the frosts cut them down in May and even longer in sheltered positions. They create long-lasting appeal in the herbaceous border and can be used for striking bedding schemes and accents in the landscape. Their wide range of colours comes in subtle shades, while some have decorative bronze foliage. Different types vary in height from 18 inches to 7 feet. Choose the colours while the plants are in bloom, if possible, and plan harmonious combinations for the following season. One should only grow good varieties and these may be purchased from bulb nurseries.

Cannas have thick underground stems with pointed shoots that develop into new plants. They multiply so quickly in a season that they are best divided each year, but can be left untouched for two years. Divide them by breaking or cutting through the underground portion to leave only one or two shoots. This is best done at the end of winter, shortly before new growth starts, but can be done in autumn if one does not want to make a mistake about the colours or if it is otherwise convenient. Water after replanting and leave them dry for the remainder of winter. Water copiously as soon as growth starts in spring.

The plants should be spaced about 12 to 15 inches apart and planted just below the surface. Cannas need full sunshine and thrive in hot situations, even facing west, if they receive plenty of water at the root all through summer. Soak the ground thoroughly, about twice a week or more often if the weather is dry. They are greedy feeders and need a thick layer of well-rotted manure forked into the top three inches of soil before planting. One can add a further dressing of compost or manure as a mulch in February, if desired. The faded flower heads must be broken off continuously, together with seed-pods. As soon as the flowering stem is exhausted, remove it above a basal leaf. Cannas are singularly pest and disease free, but one might need to spray against the common green aphis.

CHRYSANTHEMUM

These plants are not very popular among gardeners as they seem to need plenty of care. They merely need one timely pinching back, however, and some regular disbudding to become the glorious aristocrats seen at the florists. Also, there are many bush types of "mums" which need no disbudding and which make valuable splashes of colour in the shrub border. Chrysanthemums are exceptionally valuable because they flower in autumn when the main summer display is over. One should not plant them early to obtain earlier flowers, as they bloom best when the days are shorter in autumn.

Rooted cuttings of Chrysanthemums should be planted out during September, into rich, light soil in full sunshine. They will also grow with some afternoon shade. Mix plenty of well-rotted compost or manure into the top

few inches of soil. Plant them at the same depth at which they were grown in the nursery, and about 12 to 15 inches apart. It is essential to pinch out the growing point when the plant is about 6 inches in height. No matter when they were planted out, one should endeavour to stop them or pinch them back during November. The flowering period depends on this stopping. Whether one is growing prize individual blooms or tiny flowers for display, it is essential to pinch back the stem in order to encourage bushing out. The bushy types need no further stopping, but the large-flowered types can be pinched back again if desired. Allow four or five branches to develop from the first stopping point and pinch each one back again, if desired, when it is a few inches in length. Each of these branches can be left to produce one flower only and need not be pinched back. The fewer blooms that are allowed to develop on the plant, the larger and better will be their quality. (Illus. p. 208.) Constant pinching and training over a bamboo frame is the secret of the Japanese Cascade Chrysanthemums. Give fertilizer as the buds form. Stake the plants while young with the aid of one to three thin bamboo stakes. It is useful to have more than one stake for the large-flowered types, so as to support the individual flowers.

Chrysanthemums like plenty of air circulating about them, but can be grown in the mixed border where other plants can be used to hide their legginess. Well-grown plants, however, will have healthy foliage and not be unsightly at the base. Water deeply and regularly about two or three times a week. Control black aphids strictly.

Old plants can be left in the soil during winter or lifted and heeled in elsewhere like other perennials. They should be divided each spring by replanting the young individual shoots and discarding the old centre of each clump.

DELPHINIUM

Butterfly Delphiniums are annuals which must be grown in spring and summer, but there are many species and hybrids, notably Pacific hybrids, which are prized in the garden. They bloom during spring and early summer, but it is essential to plant them during the previous summer in order to obtain the best results. Delphinium seed must be sown while it is very fresh or it may not germinate. A fortnight in the refrigerator is said to stimulate germination, but the main requirement is that one should plant the seed almost as soon as it ripens, which is generally around November. It takes about three weeks to germinate and should be kept moist and shaded in the early stages. Plant out the seedlings in their permanent position as soon as they are sturdy enough.

Delphiniums require full sunshine, but will not mind a

little afternoon shade. The soil should be well-drained and contain large quantities of humus or well-rotted compost and manure. It should be light and fertile. Plant the seedlings at the same depth in which they were growing in the nursery and about a foot or more apart, depending on their size when mature. Keep them well-watered and growing vigorously during summer, but decrease water gradually as soon as they show signs of dying down. They can be kept dry during winter, but an occasional watering will not harm them if the soil is well-drained. Give plenty of water at the first sign of growth during spring and mulch with a layer of well-rotted compost. Apply a balanced fertilizer as soon as the buds begin to swell and show colour and again after the flower stalks have been cut back. This can be done during the first season as well. Delphiniums seldom bloom again as successfully as in the second season, so that the old plants are generally discarded and new ones should be grown again from seed for the following spring.

DAY-LILY (HEMEROCALLIS)

These herbaceous plants with tuberous roots form leafy clumps and are so easy to grow that they require little special care. They may be evergreen or die down completely in winter, but do not need to be moved from their permanent position for several years. There are many modern hybrids in gold, orange, bronze, deep mahogany, red and even shades of pink and peach, so that one could almost fill a garden with their leafy, permanent forms. They come in large, medium or small sizes. Their lily-like trumpet flowers turn to face the light, so that they are best planted with a background of shrubs or a wall so that they are seen to advantage. They need several hours of sunshine, but will thrive on the outskirts of the shrub border, provided that they receive sufficient water. They prefer soil which contains humus.

Day-Lilies bloom at intervals during spring and summer and should be watered most at this time. The evergreen types should receive water regularly throughout the year, but less during winter. They may be multiplied by division of the root and grow easily from seed sown in spring. Seed germinates in a few weeks and the seedlings can be transplanted as soon as they become fairly large and sturdy. Keep them moist in the early stages.

IRIS

(With rhizomes). For Irises with bulbs see under Bulbs.

I. BEARDED IRIS. There are many kinds, both tall and short. The modern hybrids bloom for about six to eight weeks in spring, during September and October, making a rainbow of breathtaking colours. They make showy cut flowers, with new buds opening each day. Their evergreen swordlike foliage is useful as a permanent groundcover. Bearded Iris may be grown in a bed on their own, but are best used as accents in clumps of one colour in the shrub border or amongst herbaceous perennials.

Bearded Iris are best left undisturbed for at least three years, but need to be divided after five years. This can be done while the plants are in bloom, so that one can see the colours, or soon after the flowering period, during November and December. It does not matter if they are divided later, but are best not disturbed later than the end of January, as they need a long period of growth before the next flowering period. Lift the clumps carefully, preferably on a cloudy day, and shake the roots free of soil. Break the rhizomes apart, keeping the healthy young ones and discarding the woody or puckered old stems at the centre. Snip the foliage fan back to form a pointed arrow-head about 8 inches long before planting. Cut back any excessively long roots if necessary. Keep the roots shaded until one is ready to plant and try to replant on the same day. Plant immediately on arrival from the nursery, although the plants can remain out of the soil for up to ten days.

Plant Irises in groups of at least three of one colour together, placing each rhizome about 10 to 15 inches apart at the points of a triangle. Aim eventually to plant groups of 20 of one colour, spaced 8 inches apart for concentrated effect. Start another colour group 2 feet away. To plant each rhizome, dig two 4-inch deep holes side by side, leaving an inch-wide ridge between them. Place the rhizome on top of the ridge with half the roots spread into one hole and the other half in the other, rather like a man on a horse. Cover the roots with soil,

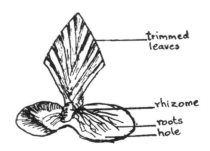

pressing them firmly down with the fists. Allow the top of the rhizome to protrude about $\frac{1}{2}$ inch above the surface of the soil. Do not worry if the fan of leaves seems to tilt at an angle, for the new foliage will emerge upright. Soak the plants well and then water about once a week or more often if the weather is hot and dry. Water Irises regularly once a week throughout the year if rain does not fall. Be careful not to let them dry out in winter, when watering can be reduced to once a fortnight if it is cold. Irises need more water than is generally supposed in hot, dry inland areas where the soil is well-drained.

The soil should be prepared in advance of planting.

Good drainage is the most important consideration and the beds may need to be raised above the level of the paths in areas of heavy rainfall or where soils are heavy. Incorporate sand into clay soils. Where soils are naturally gravelly, one need only improve the topsoil. Irises need good, fertile soil and do not flourish in poor soil. Dig a thick layer of well-rotted compost into the top few inches of soil and avoid crude manure. Add a dressing of bone-meal, which is a slow-acting fertilizer. Superphosphates may be added in addition. A light dressing of lime should be given in autumn or winter. A little superphosphates may be given as a dressing when the flower spikes appear in early spring, so as to increase the size and quality of the blooms.

Remove old flower stems close to the rhizome soon after flowering. Always pull off leaves which have turned brown. This will help to control pests and disease. Keep the soil clean and free of other plants or weeds, but do not cultivate deeply for fear of breaking the shallow roots. From time to time, scrape off any soil that has washed over the top of the rhizomes so that sunlight can always reach them and water does not settle on them. This will prevent rhizome rot, which is the chief trouble of Irises. It is generally caused by poor drainage, acid soil and can be aggravated by overfeeding. Dig up affected rhizomes, cut away the soft parts and dry them out in the sun. Dip them into a dark solution of Permanganate of Potash and dry again before replanting. It is best to replant in fresh soil.

Green aphids must be sprayed as soon as they are noticed. (See Chapter 37.) They frequently spend winter on Iris foliage which should be carefully watched. Leaf Spot is a common fungus disease on Irises, which is prevalent during rainy periods. Cut back any heavily spotted leaves and spray with a fungicide like Bordeaux mixture or Copper oxychloride. It is best to do this as a routine during March or April, when Irises are usually at their lowest ebb, and again at the beginning of the rainy season.

Some serious Iris growers use a combination spray to protect their plants from fungus disease, aphids, thrips, Iris borer or any other pest that may attack buds and leaves, even though some of these may never attack new plants, but it is easier to treat each separately.

II. JAPANESE IRIS (*Iris kaempferi*). These have beardless, flat-topped flowers in early summer and there are many cultivated forms in glorious colours. *I. kaempferi* must not be confused with other less spectacular species from Japan, *I. japonica* and *I. tectorum*, which do not have the same variety of colours. *I kaempferi* must be grown in quite the opposite way from Bearded Iris, for they require plenty of water at the root and an acid soil. Their roots can be covered with a few inches of water during summer, which dries out in winter, so that they flourish in shallow ponds or in boggy soil where a pond overflows or in a hollow beside a dripping tap. They can also be grown in ordinary garden beds, provided that they are watered generously during spring and summer.

They die down during winter, but should not be lifted and stored or the roots will dry out. It is best to leave them undisturbed for several years to form thick clumps. They may be divided and transplanted in autumn, winter or very early spring. Be particularly careful not to let the new plants dry out as the roots develop slowly, not really being fully grown until midsummer. Plant the woody rhizomes just below the level of the soil, about a foot apart. Water well and keep them moist. *Iris kaempferi* need full sunshine, but light or afternoon shade is beneficial in hot climates. They need good garden soil mixed with plenty of well-rotted compost that does not contain lime.

III. LOUISIANA IRIS. These are hybrids of fairly recent origin. (See illustration on page 97.) They may be treated like Japanese Iris, but will tolerate more shade. They will grow in full sun or partial shade under deciduous trees. The soil must be moist and preferably acid, the best situations being near the waterside or in well-watered "basins". Dig well-rotted manure from 12 to 18 inches below the surface and mix compost into the top layer. Plant the rhizomes an inch or two below the surface, about 18 inches apart, and mulch with leafmould or peat. Renew the mulch periodically. Water regularly and especially in August before spring flowering. Divide every two or three years after flowering if necessary. Evergreen types may require protection from heavy frost by planting near hedges or buildings.

OTHER IRIS. There are numerous types of Irises which are valuable for different effects in the garden and have interesting or beautiful flowers. The Iris lover should join an Iris Society or study special books devoted to the Iris and its culture. Among the better known are the tall, leafy *I. ochroleuca* with white and yellow flowers and *I. unguicularis* (*I. stylosa*) with evergreen foliage, that produces its short lavender flowers in mid-winter. The leaves can be sheared off in autumn to expose the flowers if desired. Other interesting Irises like *I. sibirica*, Spuria Iris, and *I. douglasiana* are also becoming popular. These are lime-haters.

LUPIN, RUSSELL

Most annual Lupins grow easily from seed broadcast in the open ground and will tolerate poor soil, but Russell Lupins require a little more attention. These magnificent hybrids bloom in spring and bear tall spikes of regular flowers in magnificent colours. Seed should be sown in midsummer so as to produce flowering plants in the following spring. The seedlings should be transplanted as soon as possible into their permanent positions as they do not survive moving easily. They can be sown in jiffy pots to facilitate transplanting.

Russell Lupins like full sun, but will also grow in lightly shaded positions where the soil is good, as they do not flourish in poor soil. The soil should be light and well-drained, especially where winters are wet. Fork in well-rotted compost which does not contain lime. Give a dressing of general fertilizer or superphosphates when the flower spikes form. Water deeply and regularly throughout the growing period. Russell Lupins can be divided after two years, but are usually discarded in favour of new plants grown from seed. They can be grown from 3-inch cuttings taken from the base of the plant. These damp off if they are not given sufficient air circulation. Cuttings taken in spring will bloom in the autumn.

PEONY

Herbaceous Peonies with their huge, aristocratic flowers in October are comparatively new to Southern Africa, but have been found to grow successfully and easily, once their requirements are understood. They improve with the years, producing better flowers and becoming large bushes which should be left undisturbed and treated more like shrubs than perennials. It is important to find the right position as they will remain there for many years and will not bloom successfully in the wrong situation. There are several different flower shapes and the harmonious colours vary from white to pink and red and even yellow in the newest varieties. There are also early and later-blooming types.

Peonies do better in full sunshine than in shade and should only be given a little light afternoon shade. They like an open position which is cold during winter, for they are hardy and enjoy a cold season. Peonies can be grown in groups of three to five at the side of a herbaceous border or in a bed by themselves. They should be spaced about 3 feet apart.

Plant them where no peonies have grown before. Heavy yet well-drained fertile soil containing humus is best.

Prepare the holes at least a week in advance of planting so that the soil can settle down to the right level and one can plant the new peonies on arrival. Dig to a depth of 1 or 2 feet and mix some well-rotted manure into the bottom of the hole. Work in some superphosphate or bone-meal. Mix as much well-rotted compost into the top 6 inches as one can spare. Pack the soil down well. Water the soil and allow it to settle for a week.

The chief reason for failure with Peonies is that the crown is planted too deep. There should be two or three eyes or buds on each crown and these should be no deeper than 2 inches below the surface. They must be firmly planted so that they do not sink down any deeper in the future. The fleshy roots may be shortened to 6 inches and spread outwards. Work good soil mixed with peatmoss around the roots, pressing it down firmly but gently. Water thoroughly and keep moist until the shoots emerge or, if the shoots are already present, shade them with twigs for about a week. The plants seldom produce flowers in the first season.

Peonies are greedy feeders and should be given a mulch of well-rotted manure or compost containing manure, immediately after flowering. Do not give manure before new growth starts in spring, as this may cause a fungus disease called bud blast which turns the foliage black. Cut off any such leaves and spray with a fungicide, but be careful not to overwater or overfeed at this time. Too much feeding in early spring will also cause leaves to grow instead of flowers. When the flower buds form, the plants may be given a sprinkling of general fertilizer or superphosphates.

When the foliage turns brown naturally in autumn, it should be cut off completely. Be careful not to dig up the roots during winter. Remove a little of the topsoil each year when adding the annual mulch of manure so that the crowns will not be buried too deeply as the years go by. Do not attempt to divide peonies before five years, but the clumps can be broken up after that time if absolutely necessary. Peonies may be grown from seed and bloom in three or four years.

PRIMULA

The perennial primulas like *P. pulverulenta* and *P. cockburniana* are seldom seen in this country. They need shade, moisture and cool, woodland conditions. Seed should be sown in autumn and takes any time up to two or three months to germinate, while the seedlings grow slowly, so that these are plants for the specialist. They do not survive for long and new plants must be grown again from seed. *P. obconica* is a perennial pot-plant which is best treated as an annual.

POLYANTHUS PRIMROSES (*Primula polyantha*). Polyanthus Primroses are modern hybrids with "bunches" of colour-ful flowers at the top of tall strong stems. They are very decorative and bloom during spring. The older type of cowslip, with smaller, bright yellow flowers, and the old-fashioned single primrose with its pale yellow flowers on short thin stalks, have a charm of their own and, while not as popular as the polyanthus primrose, can be cultivated in the same way.

Polyanthus Primroses are plants for partial shade and will make a good groundcover in between Azaleas or under small evergreen or deciduous trees. They like light, rich, soil containing plenty of humus mixed with well-rotted manure. They must be well-watered during winter and kept moist in spring. Water them in summer if the leaves are still green, but they generally die down for a while in midsummer. New plants are best raised from seed sown in early or midsummer, pricked out into boxes and transplanted into their permanent position in March or April. Seedlings may be purchased and good plants can be recognised by their rich green, wrinkled foliage. Plants with light green, straight leaves generally give poor flowers. Superphosphates can be given just before the flowering period to increase the size of the flowers. Old clumps of Polyanthus can be divided and replanted in autumn, but generally lose in vigour and quality. Spray against aphids as soon as these are seen.

OTHER PERENNIALS AND BIENNIALS FOR DIFFERENT PURPOSES

Anemone japonica (Japanese Anemone). Autumn-flowering, dormant in winter, 2 to 3 feet. Need good soil, moisture, afternoon shade.

Arabis (Rock Cress). Spring-flowering, hardy perennial for carpeting hot, dry places. Rockery. Edging.

Aubretia. Evergreen, hardy, spring-flowering. Suited to light shade, needs moisture. Rockery.

Begonia semperflorens (Bedding Begonia). Groundcover for shady places with rich soil, moisture. Flower through-out year, but tender. Take cuttings in spring or grow from seed.

Dahlia imperialis (Tree Dahlia). Tall accent plant, grows without attention in poor soil. Flowers often spoilt by frost. Cut down in winter.

Dianthus (Pinks) Sweet William (*D. barbatus*) is a biennial which should be planted in midsummer to flower in the following spring. Open sun, rich, well-drained soil and moisture in dry weather.

Perennial Pinks make spreading mats with sheets of flowers in spring. Divide or grow from cuttings every third year.

Chinese Pinks (*D chinensis* var. *laciniatus* and *heddewiggii*, etc.). Although biennial, these may be treated as annuals and sown in autumn or spring.

Gazania. Sow seed in March for spring flowering. Sunny, well-drained soil as in rockery. Likes hot, dry summer.

Gerbera. (Barberton Daisy). Spring-flowering. Sunny, well-drained soil, excellent for rockery, keep dry in winter. Will grow in light shade in hot places.

Heuchera (Coral Bells). Summer-flowering. Likes partial shade, rich soil, moisture.

Hollyhock (*Althea* hybrids). Sow seed in November to flower in following spring. Pull out plants after flowering as they are susceptible to rust.

Hunnemannia (Mexican Tulip-Poppy). Like *Eschscholzia*. Warm, sunny position in rockery. Grow from seed.

Lathyrus latifolium (Perennial Sweet-pea). Rambling screen for fences or terrace walls. Easily grown and hardy. Sow seed in late summer or autumn.

Limoneum latifolium (*Statice latifolia*). Sunny, well-drained soil, dry situations. Sow seed in spring.

Limoneum roseum (Pink Statice). As above, but needs water in hot, dry inland places and morning shade in cold areas. Likes salt in soil. Leave undisturbed.

Nierembergia (Cup Flower). Compact plants for rockery or informal situations. Sun, well-drained soil. Sow seed in autumn or spring. Replace after a while.

Phlox subulata (Alpine Phlox or Moss-Pink). Low-spreading, evergreen plants for rockeries and walls in dry, sunny situations.

Pyrethrum (Painted daisy). Plant seed in autumn to flower in following summer.

Violet. Evergreen perennials which like rich soil, partial shade and moisture. Hardy, but Parma Violets require shelter from morning sun. Divide in autumn every two or three years.

CHAPTER TWENTY-SEVEN

BULBS FOR YOUR GARDEN

Bulbs are among the most rewarding plants in the garden and so easy to grow that even the inexperienced amateur can be successful with them. They are really the nearest thing to packaged gardening that one can imagine, for many bulbs have their flowers fully formed inside them, merely awaiting the stimulus of moist soil to make them grow and bloom.

Some people complain that bulbs have only one flower a year and take up too much space. This is only true for some bulbs, however, and many are so exquisite that they are remembered long after their flowering period has passed. In addition, bulbs can be planted closely together and provide a large number of blooms for the amount of space they occupy. The majority of garden bulbs bloom in the spring and help to fill the winter garden, while they can easily be lifted and stored to make room for summer flowers. Bulbs by the score can be grown in terracotta pots out of doors, brought on to the terrace while in bloom and whisked away to an inconspicuous corner afterwards, or grown in pots for indoor decoration.

The term "bulb" is loosely used by gardeners to describe any plant that has the ability to store its life force in an underground, thickened portion which can be lifted out while the plant is dormant, kept loose out of the soil for several months and replanted when growth starts once more. True bulbs, corms and tubers are all called "bulbs" by gardeners, probably due to the fact that commercial bulb growers cultivate and sell many such plants and also because it is not always easy for the novice to see the botanical difference between them. The best-known examples of true bulbs are Daffodils, Tulips, Hyacinths, Dutch Iris and Lilies. Corms include Gladioli, Freesias and Watsonias. Tubers include Arum Lilies, Anemones and Tuberous Begonias, while Ranunculus and Alstroemeria have tuberous roots.

Many bulbous-rooted plants like Agapanthus, Cannas and Bearded Iris, which have swollen underground stems and fleshy roots, are also often grouped with bulbs, but these are treated more like herbaceous perennials in the garden and will be found under the Chapters 11 and 26 on "Permanent Plants" and "Perennials".

HOW TO GROW BULBS

Soil. Bulbs need light, fertile soil containing plenty of well-rotted compost. Crude manure must not come in contact with bulbs, but may be incorporated in the compost. Drainage should always be good and clay soils must be lightened by the addition of sand, compost or peatmoss. Prepare the soil well to a depth of 6 to 9 inches or more, according to the size of the bulbs to be planted, and no further feeding will be necessary.

Depth of Planting. The majority of bulbs may be planted with their tops as deep as their own height below the surface. Some will pull themselves downwards as they grow and can be planted several times deeper than their height. Babianas* should be planted 6 to 8 inches below the surface for best results and Lilies should have 4 to 6 inches of soil above them.

Some bulbs need planting with their necks at or above the surface of the soil, like Red Nerine, Hippeastrum, Pineapple Flower (*Eucomis*) and Belladonna Lily (*Amaryllis belladonna*), while others should have part of the bulb itself exposed to the air, like Blue Squill (*Scilla natalensis*).

Time to Plant Bulbs. More bulbs are spoilt by planting at the wrong time than for any other reason. Bulbs which are planted and watered heavily when they should be dormant will frequently rot. Bulbs which remain for too long out of the ground will generally wither and die. It is best to keep them in the soil for as long as possible and not to delay planting dormant bulbs later than the correct recommended time.

The majority of bulbs bloom in the spring and must be planted in autumn so that they have about six months in which to develop. March is chosen as the best month in which to plant spring bulbs in Southern Africa, with a few exceptions, noted below. Special pre-cooled bulbs can be planted later, yet will bloom sooner.*

Many lovely bulbs bloom during summer and should be planted during September. Lilies bloom during summer, yet they are true perennials and should be planted in

*See *South African Wild Flowers for the Garden* and *Bulbs for the Gardener* by Sima Eliovson.

Treasures for a shady bed with rich soil are Impatiens, luxuriant Begonias, Strawberry Saxifrage. The variegated Canary Islands Ivy on the tree trunk is kept within arm's reach by constant picking.

A shady area is paved between rock-rimmed beds spilling graceful plants. (See Chapter 9.)

Conceal one part of the garden from another with shrubs, creating a vista through an opening which is an invitation to explore.

Groundcovers form a rich carpet instead of grass. (See Chapter 10.) Striped green and silver *Zebrina pendula*, purple-backed, likes a sheltered place in the shade of a shrub, while *Ajuga reptans* is hardier and can be more exposed.

Undulating beds bordering boundary trees and shrubs can be filled with showy perennials.

Strong permanent plants (see Chapter 11) cover the area between trees and shrubs where grass would not thrive. Red Hot Pokers (*Kniphofia*) and *Iris ochroleuca* form a leafy background to spring-flowering Pinks (*Dianthus*) and Yellow Arums emerging into the sunshine beside the Nodding Pincushion (*Leucospermum nutans*), in bloom on the right.

March, even though they only appear above ground at the end of winter.

Choosing a Situation. Do not plant spring and summer-flowering bulbs side by side as the treatment of each type will interfere with the other.

Most bulbs prefer sun to shade, but light shade will not spoil them, particularly in hot climates where shade prevents delicate flowers from shrivelling in the spring. Spring-flowering bulbs which are tender to frost, like Freesias, indigenous Gladioli and Sparaxis, should be given a position shaded from the morning sun or the leaves may be browned and flowering spoilt. They do well on a west-facing wall or a south-west aspect. Shade will produce longer flower stems. These bulbs will also do well in the sun facing north, provided that they have some shelter from the overhanging branches of a tree.

Bulbs do not seem to mind tree roots and spring-flowering bulbs are ideal for planting under deciduous trees which provide cool shade during autumn and plenty of sunshine during winter and spring. Lovely spring garden pictures can be created by planting grape-hyacinths or daffodils beneath flowering plum or peach trees. Summer-flowering bulbs like *Eucomis* (Pineapple Flowers) and *Haemanthus* are good for partially shaded positions under large trees.

How to Plant Bulbs. It is best to plant bulbs in clumps of at least one dozen of the same kind. After preparing the soil, place the bulbs on top of the ground in the position in which they are to be planted. Do not place them in stiff lines even though they can be placed at more or less equal distances from one another. If a "natural" look is required, the bulbs can be scattered on to the soil and planted where they fall, but some rearrangement will usually be necessary. Dig each hole with a trowel and place the bulb in it, filling in and levelling the soil before planting the next bulb. Do not allow air pockets. If the soil is moist and one is afraid of rotting, throw a handful of coarse river sand at the bottom of the hole on which to place the bulb.

Care of Bulbs. After planting, water bulbs very well so that they will commence growing. Do not be impatient to see signs of growth above ground, for many bulbs like daffodils and hyacinths will take 10 weeks before their leaves break through the surface. Many bulbs lie under a blanket of snow in their native haunts and only appear above ground in the spring. All this time they will be producing strong roots and shoots and should not lack water even if they cannot be seen. Aim to keep the soil damp but not waterlogged. Good drainage will protect the bulbs from rotting through overwatering. Test the soil with a trowel and if it is damp, do not water. If the top 2 inches are dry, water deeply with a sprinkler in order

to replace evaporation. It is better to soak the ground for two hours with a sprinkler once a week than to water the surface lightly and frequently.

Continue to water freely once bulbs have emerged and do not allow them to dry out while growing or flowering. Water deeply and regularly with the aid of a sprinkler. Drops of water falling like rain do not compact the soil and fall gently on to delicate plants which are often flattened by strong jets of water from an impatiently held hosepipe.

Do not cease watering bulbs after they have flowered, for the plant continues to grow for five or six weeks afterwards, generally forming a new bulb underground or even perfecting the flower for the following year, as in the case of Narcissus. Care after flowering will prevent disappointment in the flowering for the following year.

Do not cut back or destroy the foliage until it dies down naturally, for the leaves make the food which is stored in the bulb. Premature lifting of the bulb will interrupt this process. Reduce water gradually when the leaves start to ripen or turn yellow. As soon as all the completely yellow leaves come away easily when pulled, the bulb is ready to be lifted and stored if necessary.

Puzzling Behaviour of Some Bulbs. A few bulbs behave strangely in that their flowers are produced before the leaves and gardeners find it difficult to understand how to care for them. The chief difficulty is to plant them in the ground at the right time or the flowers may be spoilt. One must know when the flowers are due to appear and plant the bulbs at least two to three weeks before they are expected, so that one does not miss the flowering period. Many bulbs belonging to the Amaryllis family have this peculiarity. The flowers of the Red Nerine may shoot out while the bulb is in storage while others, like those of Hippeastrum and Amaryllis, may never develop for the remainder of the season. One must continue to water these plants while the leaves are green, so that they can develop the flower for the following season. See details under individual bulbs.

These plants can be grown in large terracotta pots and kept there during the dormant period, but should be watered at the first sign of growth at flowering time. They can also remain in the soil in the garden, but should be kept as dry as possible while dormant. Plant them on sloping soil or on a raised terrace or rockery which will ensure drain-off of rainwater and prevent rotting while dormant.

Lifting and Storing Bulbs. It is not necessary to lift and store bulbs if one has a climate where the rainy season does not occur when the bulbs are meant to be dormant. Spring flowering bulbs should be lifted in the summer-rainfall area, while summer-flowering bulbs (except Lilies) should be lifted in the winter-rainfall area of the south-western Cape. It is possible to avoid lifting the bulbs if they are planted in very well-drained, raised soil, but there is always a risk of rotting and losing one's bulbs, so that it is best to lift and store them. Even if they do not rot, some bulbs do not flower well if they have not been allowed to dry out thoroughly and will commence growing before the ideal time. If dormant bulbs of tulips and daffodils remain in the soil during summer, the warmth of the soil may destroy the flower for the following season.

Dig the bulbs up carefully on a dry, sunny day when the ground is not too wet. Allow them to dry off thoroughly in a shady place for a day or two and do not cook them in the hot sun. Remove lumps of soil which may adhere to the bulbs and place large bulbs in a layer in open wooden boxes like tomato boxes. Double layers are permissible, if the bulbs are dry, but bulk storage often induces mildew and serious loss. Small bulbs may be stored loose in clean, dry jam tins. All bulbs are best kept on the cool floor of a garage or shed, and should not be placed high up near the roof where the temperature is high.

Tubers shrivel more than bulbs and corms and should be placed in boxes with layers of dry sand or vermiculite between them in order to keep them plump.

Naturalising Bulbs. If one has the right climate for leaving spring or summer bulbs in the ground, they can be left in place for several seasons so as to develop luxuriantly in a "natural" manner and eliminate storage problems. As the years pass, however, the flowers will become crowded and smaller, so that it will be necessary to lift and divide the bulbs in order to increase the quantity and quality. Most bulbs benefit through being lifted each year while some can be left in the ground for three years or more before showing signs of deteriorating. Plants with corms like Gladioli should be dug up and replanted each year in order to produce good flowers as the old corm may affect the growth of the new one to some extent. In any case, Gladioli should be replanted each year in fresh ground in order to avoid disease.

Increasing Stocks of Bulbs. Most bulbs multiply rapidly by developing daughter bulbs or offsets which may be separated from the parent bulb and produce flowers when they have grown to full size. Small bulbs multiply more rapidly than larger bulbs.

Some bulbs may be grown very easily from seed and this is the best method of increasing stocks. Seed of Anemones and Ranunculi sown in midsummer will bloom at the same time as corms planted in autumn and frequently flower better. Freesias grow easily from seed and bloom in

the second season, although modern hybridists make them bloom within eight months. Most bulbs bloom in the third season of growth, with exceptions. Some species of Gladioli, like the scented *Gladiolus venustus*, and the Fairy Lachenalia (*L. mutabilis*) bloom in their second season, while others take longer.

In general, plant the seed of bulbs in terracotta or asbestos pots at the same time as the bulbs. They usually take a full month before germinating and should be kept moist and shaded for this period. Do not give up watering bulb seed, for some, like Lilies and a few others, take about six months before the first leaf shows above ground. Allow the seedlings to remain in their containers for the first season without transplanting them, unless the plants become too large, as is the case with Day-Lilies (*Hemerocallis*). They can be planted out in the following year or replanted in larger pots if they are still small. The young seedlings frequently grow for 18 months without becoming dormant, so that one should continue to keep them moist if the leaves are green, drying them off only if the foliage turns yellow.

Other methods of increasing bulbs, like growing Lilies from scales, require a little more care. The scales are stripped off the bulb and each one is planted at an angle of 45 degrees in tins containing a mixture of sharp sand and compost. Each will grow into a new plant and develop a new bulb. The black bulbils which form on the stems of Tiger Lilies can be detached and grown in seed boxes until they mature.

Commercial growers increase stocks of Hyacinths in an interesting fashion. When the bulb is dormant they cut out a large, cone-shaped section from the base of the bulb. While the bulb lies in storage, numerous tiny offsets grow around the crater formed at the base of the leaf scales and these can be planted out at the beginning of autumn to form new plants.

Growing Bulbs in Pots for Indoor Decoration. Bulbs may be planted in pots, grown out of doors in the shade of a tree and then brought into the house for the few weeks that they are in flower. This is the ideal way to grow Lachenalias, valuable for winter decoration, and other small bulbs like species of Gladioli as well as many rarities and curiosities.

It is preferable for the pots to have holes for drainage, but the bulbs can also be planted in ornamental bowls without holes, provided that care is taken not to overwater them. It is advisable to place a few pieces of charcoal at the bottom of such a bowl, for this not only helps drainage, but absorbs gases and moisture. It is always necessary to place a layer of stones at the bottom of the pot for drainage, whether it has holes or not.

Bulbs contain enough food in themselves to produce and maintain their flowers for a season, provided that they receive moisture. That is why Narcissi can be grown supported on stones standing in a bowl of water, Hyacinths will grow in a specially-shaped glass containing only water, and many bulbs will bloom even if they are planted in moist fibre or moss, even though these materials have no food value. Such bulbs will have spent all their energy in flowering and will have absorbed no new nourishment in order to produce the following year's flowers, so that they would not bloom again. They would bloom again, however, if they were planted in soil in the pot. A mixture of good soil and compost, plus a little peat-moss or vermiculite which retains moisture, is ideal for bulbs in pots.

Always plant one bulb in the middle of the pot and place the others in a circle around it, leaving about an inch of space between each bulb. One generally needs six bulbs in order to create a good effect, depending on the size of the bulb and its flowers. Hyacinths have thick flower stems and can be planted in threes in 5-inch pots. Choose only one type of bulb or one colour variety so that one can be sure to have them flowering at the same time.

Small bulbs may be planted in shallow bowls as they need not be planted deeply. Lachenalias should be planted just below the surface. Daffodils and Hyacinths should be planted in pots which are at least 5 inches deep so as to provide room for the long roots that develop freely. Although they are usually planted 3 inches below the surface in the garden, they should be planted with their necks level with the surface of the soil in pots, but need special treatment in the early stages if they are to flower successfully.

Special Treatment for Daffodils and Hyacinths in Pots. In order to prevent these bulbs from producing long green leaves with short flower stems, so that the flower nestles down among the leaves instead of growing above them, one must resort to trickery. One must simulate what happens to the Daffodils and Narcissi which are planted 3 inches below the surface in the garden. There are two ways of doing this, but both are based on the idea of depriving the growing bulb of light for at least 10 weeks. This retards the growth of foliage until the flower stem has had a chance to grow out of the bulb properly.

The easiest method is to sink the whole pot up to the rim in soil in the garden and then to cover it with a 3-inch layer of clean river sand, sawdust or vermiculite. If one wishes to keep an ornamental pot clean, it can be sunk into a trench or box filled with one of these materials, which are cleaner than garden soil. Keep the bulbs moist until the foliage breaks through the 3-inch layer, then lift the pot out into the light and care for it either indoors or outside. The plant will be blanched when it is lifted, but the leaves will turn green rapidly in the light.

The second method is to place the pot of bulbs in a dark, cool cupboard and keep it there for about 10 weeks before bringing it into the light. If one takes the pot out too soon, the leaves will grow up rapidly at the expense of the flowers, which will remain short-stemmed. The secret is to wait until the flower has left the bulb. In the case of the Daffodil, the flower stem must be at least 2 inches long, no matter what size the leaves are. In the case of Hyacinths, the flower stem should be 2½ to 3 inches long with the base of the stem distinctly thinner than the rounded top. The soil must be kept damp and the cupboard can be opened in order to water the bulbs about once a week, but the pots should be replaced in the cupboard immediately.

Become a Bulb Collector. There are literally hundreds of bulbs to choose for the garden and one should always try at least one new one each season. A dozen bulbs of a new species will give interest and variety to any garden. Apart from the numerous hybrids being produced overseas, one should grow the fascinating bulbs which grow wild in this country. Many of these were the parents of modern hybrids like Gladioli and Freesias. There are many beautiful treasures which are rare and still little known to the world which gardeners in this country should endeavour to obtain and multiply. If one has only a few rare bulbs one can grow them in pots out of doors under a tree until they multiply. They can be re-potted each year or simply topped with a layer of compost.

Space does not allow any descriptions of bulbs here, but they can be found in catalogues, special bulb books and garden dictionaries. All the indigenous bulbs will be found in *South African Wild Flowers for the Garden* by the author. The most important cultural hints are given below for those bulbs of major interest to gardeners. A suggested list of other bulbs worth planting will be given at the end of this chapter.

TIPS ON GROWING POPULAR OUTDOOR BULBS

Alstroemeria. Peruvian Lily. Bloom in spring and summer. Tuberous roots may be planted in autumn or early spring, requiring plenty of water while growing in summer. They should not be dried out completely while dormant and are best not lifted once established.

Amaryllis belladonna. Belladonna Lily. Blooms in autumn before leaves appear. Plant in February with neck at soil level in partial shade or full sun. Keep dry in well-drained soil when dormant during summer.

Anemone coronaria. St. Brigid (Double) and De Caen (Single) hybrids flower in spring. Plant during the second half of February for early winter flowers or as late as the end of April. Press the small, irregularly-shaped tubers into soft soil, about 2 inches deep and 4 to 6 inches apart, with the points up if possible. If in doubt, plant them on their sides. They are hardy plants and do best in semi-shade, especially afternoon shade, with plenty of moisture. Tubers may be stored for two to three years without deteriorating, but are best planted out each year. Anemones seem to exhaust themselves with flowering and the tubers should be discarded after two years. They grow very easily from seed sown in December or January in order to bloom in winter or early spring. Transplant the seedlings under a deciduous tree which will shade them until the weather becomes cooler.

Anemones, Japanese. (*A. japonica.*) Bloom in autumn and die down in winter. Plant tuberous roots in spring in moist, shaded position. Leave undisturbed.

Arum Lily. See *Zantedeschia*.

Arum palaestinum. Black Arum. Flowers in spring. Plant tubers in shaded, sheltered position in autumn.

Babiana. Flower in spring. Plant corms in March, about 6 inches deep and 2 to 3 inches apart. Water during winter and give early morning shade in cold areas. Dormant in summer, but need not be lifted during summer if planted deeply and soil is well drained.

Begonia, Tuberous. Flower in midsummer. Plant tubers in rich, light loam in September. Imported tubers planted in December will not bloom until April or May when it may be too cold. Best grown in partial shade or full shade with plenty of moisture. Lift and store where winters are rainy.

Bulbinella. Cats-tail. Bright yellow "pokers" in midwinter, hardy to cold. Plant clumps of fibrous roots in autumn with necks at soil level. Give full sun and plenty of water in winter, but keep dry in summer when dormant. Plant in well-drained rockery in summer-rainfall area to avoid rotting. Do not lift and store or roots will dry out. Plants should be left undivided for several years.

Chlidanthus. Flowers appear in spring before foliage. Plant in August in full sun and keep moist during summer. Need not be lifted while dormant in winter, if they can be kept fairly dry.

Crinum moorei. Blooms in late summer. Foliage is more or less evergreen, dying down for a short time after flowering. Cut leaves back at flowering time for a spectacular effect. Easy to grow and enjoys partial shade. Need not be divided for five years or more. Protect from Amaryllis caterpillar during midsummer. Other species of Crinum flower in early summer and need plenty of moisture during summer.

Cyrtanthus. (*C. mackenii* and *C. o'brienii*.) Ifafa Lilies. Bloom in early spring before new leaves appear. Plant in early August. Need sandy, well-drained soil, shade and moisture in summer, but keep dry in winter. Need shelter in cold areas.

Daffodil. See *Narcissus*.

Dahlia. Summer and autumn-flowering. Dahlias are tuberous rooted plants, but are so distinctive in the garden that they are usually treated as a class on their own. They are valuable for adding bright colour in the herbaceous border as well as for growing in formal beds for cut-flowers and for exhibition. They come in a wide range of colours and vary in size from tiny pompons to large decorative types, as wide as a dinner plate. The most popular types today are the cactus and semi-cactus dahlias in small or medium sizes, which have graceful, narrow petals and last well both in the vase and on the bush. There are dozens of different cactus dahlias and of the many other distinctive classes such as collarettes, singles, decoratives and peony-flowered dahlias. The dahlia lover should visit autumn flower shows which feature dahlias more than any other flower and see the displays provided by specialist nurseries. The intricacies of studying dahlia forms can be learned by joining special dahlia societies.

Dahlias grow so freely and easily that they are frequently despised by some gardeners who may have tired of their flamboyance. Grow them with restraint in the garden, however, and they will once more become a valued standby. Choose colours which blend well together for the vase or plant them in clumps of one colour in the border. Grow different dahlias every other season and they will never become boring. Cultivation of dahlias is simple, but certain rules should be followed for the greatest success. Plant the tubers at any time from August to the beginning of November, but later planting is preferred as this ensures late summer and autumn flowers which bloom better than during the intense heat of midsummer. Dahlias need full sun, but enjoy afternoon shade in hot climates.

The whole bed should be dug over before planting dahlias if the area is not too large. Otherwise, each hole can be dug separately for each plant, provided that the surrounding soil is in reasonably good condition. It is not necessary to dig very deep holes. Remove the top soil to a depth of 6 inches and a foot in diameter. Loosen the soil to a further 6 inches and replace it with some good garden soil if it is very poor or of a clay texture. Soil for dahlias should be on the light side and clay soil must be mixed with compost and sand. A spadeful of well-rotted manure or compost can be mixed into this bottom soil, but must not come in contact with the tuber. This common fault leads to rot and failure to grow. Place a 1-inch layer of plain soil over this mixture and then throw on a handful of clean river sand. Drive a 3 to 4 foot stake into the side of the hole and secure it firmly. Place the dahlia tuber horizontally on the river sand with the bud or shoot pointing upwards and next to the stake. The bud should be 3 or 4 inches below the surface. Fill in around the tuber with pulverised top-soil, being especially careful not to damage the shoot. Give each tuber 4 gallons of water. Protect the young plants as they emerge by encircling the whole area with a line of snail bait and keep watch for cutworms. (See Chapter 37.)

Water deeply and regularly once or twice a week and do not allow dahlias to lack moisture. As soon as the stem develops a joint, pinch back the growing points so as to encourage the plant to form a strong bush. Tie the stems to the stakes as they grow, using raffia at intervals of a foot. Dahlias are greedy feeders and should be fed from the top as soon as the first buds form. It is possible to feed them from the top only without having placed any manure in the original hole. The best way to feed is to place a mulch of manure around the plant. This not only supplies nutriments, but keeps the soil cool and moist. Liquid manure can also be applied at intervals to prolong the flowering period. A handful of super-phosphates can be given to strengthen the stem. Dahlias like a little lime, but this must not be applied together with manure.

Disbudding dahlias can be done in several ways according to the purpose of the plants. The average person should select stems which will be long enough for cutting and take off all buds above this point except the central one. Always allow only the central bud to develop on any cluster, pinching off the others as soon as they have formed. By limiting the buds on a stem one can improve the quality. Exhibitors of prize blooms only allow one flower at a time to develop on a whole bush and probably only obtain five flowers during the season. Otherwise, dahlias bloom prolifically and can be kept in bloom for a long time by constant picking. Always remove faded flowers and cut them with a good length of stem.

Storing and Dividing Dahlia Tubers. Dahlias must not be disturbed until the foliage has turned yellow naturally. Cut back the bush, leaving the woody stems showing a few inches above ground. The clumps of tubers can be levered up carefully with the aid of two sharp spades and stored in boxes of dry, sandy soil during winter, under cover of a roof. This is essential in the winter-rainfall area. In areas with dry winters, how-

ever, the tubers may be left in the soil and dug up and divided before replanting in October, or they may be taken out if the ground is needed for other plants and buried in warm, dry soil in the back garden, awaiting division in the spring.

When dividing dahlia tubers, remove all soil with a pointed knife or by washing with a hosepipe. Gently separate tubers or cut them apart with a sharp penknife. A portion of the "neck" or "collar" of the old stem must be attached to the tuber and this can be cut out in a V-shape. No tuber will grow into a plant without this piece of stem attached, for it is from this point that a bud or "eye" will develop into a shoot. It is best to delay dividing tubers until they have started growth so that one can see the bud beginning to develop into a shoot. The experienced worker can tell if a swelling will develop into a bud, but it is safest not to plant a tuber which has no obvious "eye". If in doubt, place the tuber in a box of damp soil for a week. The eye will swell and indicate whether one should plant it or not. Small tubers produce the best plants and should not be discarded in favour of large tubers. (See illustration on page 208.)

Green Cuttings. These generally produce the best plants and multiply dahlias most freely. Allow the tubers to shoot in the ground or in storage before dividing. Sever the green shoots as soon as they have developed two joints. They should be pencil thick and about 3 inches long. Plant them singly in small pots of sharp river sand and keep moist and shaded, preferably under glass, for about two to three weeks in order to grow roots. As soon as the leaves start growing, transplant the cuttings to the open ground and keep them moist.

Seed. Hybrid Dahlias do not come true from seed, but fascinating seedlings may result for the hobbyist, to be reproduced vegetatively later. Seed is sown in spring and grows easily. Colourful, low bedding dahlias, like single Coltness hybrids, are sown annually and the tubers are generally discarded.

Eucomis. Pineapple Flower. Bloom in midsummer. Plant large bulbs in September with neck at soil level, about 15 to 18 inches apart. Divide clumps after three years. Will grow in full sun or partial shade under trees. Need moisture in summer and dry conditions while dormant in winter.

Freesia. Bloom in spring. Plant corms in March, 2 inches deep and 2 inches apart. Shelter from frost with morning shade or grow in pots in cold climates. Prefer semi-shade, but must have some sun. Do not flatten plants with strong watering. If necessary, support with twigs or grow through wire mesh stretched about 8 inches above ground. Freesias can be attractively grown through low, supporting annual plants like Lobelia.

Gladiolus.

(I) Modern Hybrids. These are the well-known florist's flowers, blooming in summer and autumn. The corms may be planted at any time from spring to midsummer, coming into flower in about 90 days. Plant the corms at three times their depth so that the plant will stand erect and good root growth will be made before the leaves emerge. Gladioli should be planted in full sun in light, well-drained soil, with plenty of moisture while growing. The flower stem should be picked when the lowest bud shows colour and all the remaining buds will open in the vase. As soon as the foliage ripens, lift the corms and store them over winter. Pull off the old stem, but do not remove the protective fibre.

Always replant Gladioli in fresh soil to reduce possible spread of disease. Common pests are thrip and the Gladiolus Fly which can be controlled by regular spraying with DDT emulsion. (See Chapter 37.) Cormlets forming at the base of the stem can be planted like seed and will develop into big corms in two years. Gladioli increase easily by division and by seed.

(II) Indigenous species from the Cape bloom in spring. Plant the corms in March, 2 inches deep, in pots or in the open ground. Provide semi-shade in the summer-rainfall area with shelter from morning sun in cold places. Lift during the dormant period in summer and replant in fresh soil each year. *G. cardinalis*, the New Year Lily, has a long growing period and is only dormant for two months in January and February.

Gladioli which grow wild in the summer-rainfall area should be planted in September and dried off during winter.

Gloriosa. Flame Lily. Flowers in midsummer. Plant in early September, placing long brittle tubers horizontally 3 inches deep in rich, light soil in partial shade. Can be planted beside small deciduous shrubs which act as a support. Do not lift, but keep dry while dormant in winter. Grow in well-drained soil or in tubs in winter-rainfall area. If it is necessary to store, dig up carefully and keep in boxes of sand so as to prevent shrivelling. Excellent in pots.

Hippeastrum (formerly *Amaryllis*) hybrids. Flowers appear in spring and leaves shoot up soon afterwards, often appearing with the flowers. Need moist, well-drained soil in summer and should be kept dry in winter. Dry off the plants in May even if they still have green leaves. Recommence watering in August. These plants are ideal for growing in large, individual pots. Plant large bulbs with necks just above soil level. When the flower bud emerges, give the plant a teaspoon of concentrated liquid fertilizer

and repeat when the flower opens. Feed once during summer with balanced fertilizer.

Hyacinths. Flower in spring. Plant at the end of March or in early April, midway between planting Daffodils and Tulips. Plant top of bulb 3 to 4 inches below the surface. Keep moist so that the bulbs can make strong root growth before the foliage appears above ground after about 10 weeks. Plant in a position where the flowers will receive afternoon shade in spring, as they prefer cool conditions. Hyacinths can be planted in pots for indoor decoration and require special treatment for successful flowering. (See page 145.)

Iris. Bearded Iris, Japanese Iris and new Iris hybrids. (See Chapter 26 on Perennials.)

Dutch Iris (*Iris xiphium* hybrids). Also English and Spanish Iris. These bloom in spring and the bulbs should be planted in March, about 2 to 3 inches deep and 3 inches apart, in groups of at least one dozen. They will grow in full sun, but prefer light shade while flowering in hot, dry climates. Provide well-drained, light soil with plenty of moisture while growing. Dutch Iris dislike lime. Lift and store bulbs where summers are rainy.

Ixia. Wand Flowers. Spring flowering. Plant corms in early March, close together and about 2 inches deep, in light, well-drained soil such as in a rockery. Need morning shade in cold places, but must have sun at midday. A warm, north-facing position is best in cold areas. Keep dry while dormant in summer, or lift and store.

Lachenalia. Cape Cowslip. Flower in mid-winter or spring according to the different species. Plant bulbs at the beginning of March, close together and just below soil level in light, well-drained soil. Ideal for shallow bowls with holes, to be brought indoors when in bloom. Will grow in full sun or light shade. Fairly hardy. Lift and store immediately after foliage dies down as the soft bulbs rot easily.

Lilium. Lilies. Different types bloom from spring until February. There are many lovely lilies for gardens, varying from dwarfs like *L. pumilum* and chalice-shaped modern hybrids to tall, stately plants about 7 feet in height, like *L. Henryi* and the modern Aurelian hybrids. Modern trumpet lilies are now obtainable in yellows, lime and bright pink shades where formerly they were only white or pale shades. The cup-shaped hybrids vary from pale yellows to strong reds. Consult a reliable grower for a selection and choose lilies that have proved to grow well in your area.

Lilies are most attractively planted in groups of one type in the herbaceous border or in front of the shrub border. It is best to plant them where the ground will not be disturbed in winter, for lilies are true perennials and must remain in the ground during winter, even though the growth above ground has disappeared. All lily bulbs should be planted in autumn, with the exception of *L. candidum* (Madonna Lily) which is planted at the end of January. Bulbs are sent out from the nursery from March to early June, depending on when the different types become dormant. Plant them immediately in well-prepared soil, as they should not be stored for long. Choose a position where the soil is well-drained and mix in as much well-rotted compost as possible. Lilies dislike crude manure and lime. Lilies must have plenty of sunshine, but do well with light afternoon shade in hot climates.

Dig a hole with a trowel for each large, fleshy-scaled bulb and plant it with its top from 4 to 6 inches below the surface. Smaller varieties have smaller bulbs which should be planted 2 inches below the surface. Space the bulbs about 1 to 2 feet apart depending on the ultimate size of the plant. Secure a 3 to 4 foot wooden stake in the hole and place the bulb alongside it. Fill in carefully with good topsoil mixed with compost. Soak the soil deeply. Water deeply about once a month to promote root growth until the shoots emerge in the spring.

It is most important to place a mulch of compost or peatmoss over the surface after planting in order to keep the soil temperature cool. Lilies need cool soil always and like to emerge from a low groundcover into the sun. Plants can be grown over the lilies in order to act as a means of keeping the roots cool and moist. The taller bulbs look attractive growing up through blue-flowered perennials like *Salvia patens* and Ceratostigma, while the shorter ones can be grown in association with shallow-rooted annuals like ageratum or violas. Periwinkle (*Vinca major*) makes a permanent living mulch for Lilies.

Commercial growers soak the ground with sprinklers for two hours every 10 days during summer, and it is best to water deeply once or twice a week in the garden. Do not sprinkle the top frequently or the water will not penetrate deeply enough. Continue watering lilies regularly after flowering until the foliage turns yellow naturally. Then water monthly during winter to keep the plants alive. Do not disturb lilies for three or four years and only divide when they seem overcrowded. Remove faded flowers in order to conserve the strength of the bulb.

To ensure that you plant disease-free lily bulbs, always purchase them from a reliable nursery which specialises in growing lilies. Virus diseases and botrytis fungus disease wreak havoc with lilies and are almost impossible to control if they enter a garden. Fortunately, neither are common in this country. Growers avoid planting the well-known orange Tiger Lily (*L. tigrinum*) beside the resistant varieties as it is prone to virus disease, so that it is advisable to grow them apart in gardens. It is important to spray against aphids as these are the chief agents in spreading disease to healthy plants.

Lilies may be propagated by taking the scales off the bulbs during midsummer and planting them separately into sand at an angle. The easiest and least expensive way to multiply lilies is to grow them from seed, which also assures virus-free plants, since virus diseases are not transmitted by seed. Sow the seed in flats or in the open ground, spacing it about ½ inch apart if possible. Lily seedlings should be given light dressings of compost during the growing period. They should be left in the beds until the bulblets are at least half an inch in diameter. They can then be transplanted in autumn to larger beds or to their permanent position.

Some lilies germinate quickly and seedlings may reach flowering size in the second year. If the seed is sown in late autumn, the seedlings appear above ground in spring. If seed is sown in spring, growth appears above ground in a short time. Such lilies include *L. candidum* (Madonna Lily), *L. Davidii*, *L. Henryi*, *L. longiflorum* (St. Joseph Lily), *L. pumilum*, *L. regale* (Regal Lily) and *L. umbellatum*. The slower lilies are called the two-year type, as the autumn-sown seed normally does not appear above ground until the second spring. These include beauties like *L. auratum* (Golden Ray Lily), *L. martagon* (Turks Cap Lily) and the Pink Tiger Lily (*L. speciosum*). The slow lilies can be hastened by refrigeration at special temperatures. The amateur can gain a few months by sowing the seed in spring or early summer in flats and keeping these moist in a cool cellar until winter. They must be mulched in winter and the seedlings will appear above ground in spring.

Montbretia. (See *Tritonia*.)

Muscari. Grape Hyacinths. These bloom towards the end of winter and during spring. Plant in March about 1 inch deep and 2 to 3 inches apart. Prefer full sun but will grow in shade and require moist soil. Plant in a broad patch rather than an edging line. Ideal for planting under spring-flowering trees like flowering Peach. Divide annually or every second year. Lift and store immediately foliage ripens or growth will start again within a month and flowers may lose in quality.

Narcissus. This is the correct botanical name for all Daffodils, Jonquils and Narcissus known to gardeners. Those called Daffodils generally have large single flowers which are mainly yellow, the best of the early-flowering types being "Flower Carpet". There are also miniature Daffodils like the Hoop-Petticoat Daffodil (*Narcissus bulbocodium*) and the Triandrus group as well as many little-known Jonquils. A Jonquil has grassy leaves and clusters of small, scented flowers. The improved giant jonquil "Trevithian", with scented yellow flowers, is grown mainly today. Plants called Narcissus by gardeners have clusters of small flowers in many colour variations. So many named hybrids exist today that it is best to ask for them by name and see illustrations when purchasing bulbs. (See colour illustration and "Bulbs for the Gardener.")

Different varieties of Narcissus bloom over a period of two or three months from late winter to spring and one should not plant too few of one kind, but group clumps of at least 25 in one large bed. Try interplanting them with blue Violas as an effective groundcover. Do not plant them in lawn which turns brown in winter, but in an evergreen type such as Kentucky Blue-grass or Bent grass which has the advantage that it need not be cut while the foliage ripens.

Plant Daffodil bulbs from mid-March to mid-April, but not later or the flowers will be short-stemmed. The top of the bulb should be 3 or 4 inches below the surface. It can be deeper, but not shallower. Space them from 3 to 4 inches apart. They grow best in full sunshine, but can be given partial shade in hot climates. Do not plant them in full shade or the stems will become too long and the flowers small. It is best to plant them beneath a small deciduous tree like Flowering Peach as the leaves will have dropped by the time the foliage emerges after about 10 weeks. Water regularly and well during the growing period. Pre-cooled bulbs can be planted later.

Care after flowering is particularly important for Daffodils or one will not obtain good flowers in the following season. The following year's flowers are formed in the bulb after the present flowers have faded, and the plant must be tended carefully. Remove the faded flower together with the ovary, but do not remove the stem unless the flowers are being cut for the vase. It is essential to keep watering the plant until the leaves turn yellow and die down or ripen naturally. It is an added incentive to water if plants like Violas are still flowering between them. Never cut back the leaves or move the bulbs until they are fully dormant. Some people tie the foliage in a knot, thinking that this improves the following season's flowers, but this is not necessary and one may injure the leaves and so introduce disease by doing this. A porous mulch may be laid on the soil to keep the plants cool in hot weather. Always plant the bulbs in good soil from the beginning and only give them liquid manure or artificial fertilizer, if desired, when the foliage is a few inches high, but no further feeding is recommended by commercial bulb growers.

Best results are obtained if the bulbs are lifted each year and stored in a cool airy place on the cement floor of a garage. They will not rot if they are left in the ground during the dormant period, but unless the ground is shaded and cool in summer, the heat of the soil may destroy the future season's flowers. Summer rains may also force premature growth when the weather is still too warm. If the bulbs are left in the ground, they should not remain in once place for longer than two or three years, but must then be lifted and divided in order to increase both the quality and quantity of the plants.

Nerine. Bloom in late summer and autumn. The Red Nerine (*N. sarniensis*) flowers in March before the leaves appear and should be planted towards the end of February. Groups of five or six are best grown in large pots so that they can be dried off easily in the summer-rainfall area. They seem to enjoy cramped root-growth. Plant five or six bulbs close together with their necks at soil level. Every bulb will not flower each year, but one or two may flower spectacularly in the pot and can be brought indoors while flowering.

Pink Nerines grow mainly during summer and become dormant in winter, but some remain evergreen. Plant them in well-drained soil and keep them dry when the foliage dies down. Dust the foliage with 10 per cent DDT dust at weekly intervals from November onwards in order to control the Amaryllis Caterpillar.

Ornithogalum. Chinkerinchee. Bloom in late spring and early summer. The cut flowers last for six weeks and may still be in bloom around Christmas time. Plant the bulbs in March, just below soil level and about 3 or 4 inches apart. Plant them in full sun and keep moist during winter and spring. "Chinks" are very easy to grow in any garden and seem to be quite hardy to the frosts experienced in this country. As they multiply rapidly, it is best to lift and divide them annually as soon as the foliage has ripened, as the dormant period is fairly short. They may be left in the ground in the summer-rainfall area, provided that the soil is well-drained, as the soft bulbs do not rot easily.

O. saundersiae. Giant Chinkerinchee. Summer-flowering. Plant the bulbs in spring in full sun, just below the surface and a foot apart. Dormant in winter.

Polianthes. Tuberose. Bloom in summer. Plant tuberous roots in September, just below the surface and 6 inches apart, in full sun. The old plant may not bloom again, so break off young shoots at the beginning of spring and discard the old crown. They remain dormant in winter and are suitable for planting in the herbaceous border.

Ranunculus. Bloom in early spring. Plant tuberous roots with "claws" pointing downward, about 2 inches deep and 5 inches apart. They may be planted at the beginning of March in mild districts with no frost, but are best planted at the end of April or beginning of May in cold areas, so that they will not produce too much foliage that may be affected by frost. Ranunculus should be planted in full sun in rich, light, well-drained soil mixed with plenty of compost. Lift and store roots while dormant during summer, but discard after two seasons' growth. The roots will keep in storage for two to three years, but it is best not to skip a season before planting them.

Ranunculi grow easily from seed sown in midsummer to bloom in winter or spring. Shade seedlings at first by planting them under a deciduous tree like Syringa (*Melia*).

Scilla hispanica (*S. campanulata.*) Bluebell. Bloom in spring. Plant bulbs in March about 3 inches deep and 5 inches apart. Will grow in full sun at the Cape, but need afternoon shade in hot or inland districts. They need moisture in winter and are hardy to frost.

S. natalensis. Blue Squill. Blooms in spring before the leaves appear. Plant large bulbs three-quarters out of the soil on sloping ground or amongst rocks, leaning forward at an angle. Allow these to multiply into colonies. Give moisture in summer, but keep dry in winter. Need well-drained soil in winter-rainfall area or should be grown in pots.

Sparaxis. Velvet Flowers. Bloom in spring and make an excellent colour combination with Grape Hyacinths. Plant corms in mid-March, about 2 inches deep and 3 inches apart. They need rich, light, well-drained soil with plenty of compost and moisture in winter. Give full sun in mild areas or shelter from morning sun in cold places. Lift and store in places with heavy summer rains.

Sprekelia. Maltese or Jacobean Lily. Blooms in early summer just before the leaves appear. Grows easily in light, sunny soil. Needs winter rest.

Streptanthera. Spring-flowering. Grow like Sparaxis.

Tigridia. One-Day Lily or Tiger Flower. Bloom during midsummer. Plant bulbs in spring, about 2 inches deep and 3 inches apart, in groups in the herbaceous border. They need good, light soil and full sun, but will also bloom in semi-shade. Dormant in winter, but need not be lifted if the soil is well-drained. They grow so easily that they will come up even if other plants grow over them and receive water in winter.

Tritonia. Garden Montbretia. Bloom in summer. Corms should be planted in spring. Will grow in full sun or semi-shade under trees. Lift and divide each winter or they multiply too rapidly and commence growth too early.

T. crocata and other spring-flowering species, known as Mossel Bay Kalkoentjies or Blazing Stars. Plant corms in March to flower in October. These grow easily in sun or semi-shade, but require morning shade in cold areas.

Tuberose. See Polianthes.

Tulbaghia fragrans. Sweet Garlic. Blooms during mid-winter or early spring while foliage dies back slightly. Plants need moisture all year, but less during winter, and

will grow in full sun or semi-shade. Allow clumps to thicken without disturbance for several years. Divide bulbs after flowering or in early spring, planting them just below ground level.

Tulip. Bloom in spring. The main fault in planting tulips in this country is to plant too early before the soil is cool. Tulips should not be planted before the second half of April and may be planted as late as the first week in May at the Cape. The bulbs should be planted about 5 inches apart and the tops should be 3 inches below the surface of the soil, but not deeper. If planted deeper, the autumn soil remains too warm and does not cool off at night. It is only in spring that deep soil is cool. Warm conditions will delay the flowering period and the blooms will appear in late spring when it is too hot.

Tulips prefer full sun, but may also be grown in light shade in hot climates. Growth will not be so sturdy in very shady positions. Afternoon shade is preferable to morning shade in places where the spring is hot. Tulips enjoy frost. Prepare the soil well by mixing plenty of compost and sand together. A light texture with good drainage is ideal. The foliage will not appear above ground for at least two months, but the soil must be kept moist or root-growth and all subsequent growth will be retarded. Soak it well after planting and allow the sprinkler to run for two hours every 10 days or for half-an-hour every three days. Mulch with grass, if liked, in order to keep the soil moist. A better idea is to plant a groundcover of Forget-me-nots or Lobelia which make a perfect foil for tulips in the spring. Tulips look attractive in groups of six of one kind in a bed of Grape Hyacinths.

Tulips must not be picked with long stems for the vase or the leaves will be removed automatically and the bulb will not flower in the following season. Cut the stem only above the topmost leaf. If the flowers have not been picked, and this is best for the bulb, break the faded flower off so as to prevent seed forming. Be sure to keep watering until the foliage dies down naturally.

Storing Tulips. Tulips must be lifted when the foliage ripens and stored while dormant. The parent bulb will split into two or three daughter bulbs which will flower in the following season if the plant has been well grown as described above. Otherwise, the daughter bulbs will be small and have to be grown for another season or two before flowering again.

Commercial growers are very scientific about temperatures for storing tulip bulbs, for the flower develops while the bulb is in storage. The gardener can store the bulbs quite easily and have success in flowering, however, by placing them in a wooden box on the cement floor of a garage. The floor is cooler than a shelf near the roof. Do not pile them in the box so thickly that they develop mildew, but it is not necessary to spread them in a single layer.

Watsonia. These fall into three horticultural classes:

(I) Spring-flowering Watsonias which grow in winter and die down in summer. Plant corms of these in March, about 2 inches deep and about 6 inches apart. These should be lifted annually and divided where rains fall during summer. Otherwise, divide every third year. Water well during winter.

(II) Summer-flowering Watsonias which grow during summer and die down in winter. Plant corms in September, 2 inches deep and 6 to 12 inches apart, depending on the size of the plant. Give plenty of moisture in summer and dry off in winter.

(III) Evergreen Watsonias which bloom during spring, summer or autumn. These retain their foliage throughout the year and should be watered regularly, especially during summer and for the few months before flowering time. Plant the corms 2 inches deep and 15 inches apart as they form large clumps which should be left undisturbed for about five years. Remove dead leaves periodically. Divide for replanting while in flower or immediately after flowering.

All Watsonias require well-drained soil containing compost and need plenty of water during the growing period. The flower of the deciduous Watsonia is formed when the corm commences growth, so that it must be watered especially well in the early stages. Watsonias generally prefer full sun, but will grow in shade for half the day. Give morning shade to tender spring-flowering types that may be spoilt by cold frosts in winter.

Zantedeschia. Arum Lily. Calla Lily. There are two main sections which need different cultivation:

(I) *Z. aethiopica*. White Arum. Pig Lily. Bloom in spring. Plant the tubers in February about 2 inches deep and 1 foot apart in rich, light soil which can be kept moist all through winter and spring. The plants die down for three months during midsummer and may be dried off, but will not rot if they are watered. The plants will flower in full sun, provided that their feet are wet and can be grown along a small stream. They prefer shade in hot climates and need protection from frost in dry places with cold winters, which can be provided by overhanging tree branches. A form of this species grows wild in the summer-rainfall area and flowers during midsummer, dying down in winter.

(II) *Summer Arums*, such as the Pink Arum (*Z. rehmannii*) and Yellow Arums (*Z. pentlandii* and *Z. tropicalis* and varieties). Plant the tubers in mid-August, about 2 inches below the surface and six inches apart. These plants must be grown in full sun or they will not bloom properly. They must have plenty of water in summer. The soil should be rich and well-drained, but they grow easily in most soils. The tubers can be left in the ground while dormant in areas with dry winters, but should be lifted and stored in the winter-rainfall area or they will rot. They make good pot plants. The tubers should be divided annually or every second year for better flowering.

OTHER BULBS WORTH GROWING

PLANT IN SPRING

Acidanthera.
Allium neapolitanum, A. cowani.
Ammocharis—Ground Lily.
*Anoiganthus—Mock Fire-Lily.
*Boophane—Red Posy.
Bravoa geminiflora.
Brodiaea uniflora (Triteleia).
Crocosmia aurea—Falling Stars.
Curtonus paniculatus—Pleated Leaves.
Dierama species—Harebell.
Eucharis—Amazon Lily.
Galtonia candicans—Berg Lily.
Haemanthus katherinae—Blood Flower.
*H. magnificus, H. natalensis—Paint-Brush.
Liatris—Gay-Feather.
Littonia—Climbing Bells.
Schizostylis coccinea—River Lily.
Vallota speciosa—George Lily.
Zephyranthes—Rain Lily.

PLANT IN AUTUMN

Calochortus—Mariposa Lily.
Camassia—Quamash.
Chasmanthe—Pennants, Suurknol.
Chionodoxa—Glory-of-the-Snow.
Cyanella capensis.
Dipidax—Star-of-the-Marsh.
Ferraria—Spider Flower.
*Haemanthus coccineus—April-Fool.
Hesperantha—Evening Flower.
Homeria—Cape Tulip, Tulp.
Leucojum—Snowflake.
Moraea villosa—Peacock Flower.
Romulea—Satin Flower.
*Sternbergia lutea—Autumn Daffodil.
Veltheimia viridifolia—Forest Lily.
Wachendorfia thyrsiflora—Rooiknol, Red-root.

*Flowers appear before the leaves.

CHAPTER TWENTY-EIGHT

GROWING SUCCULENTS AND CACTI

Succulents and cacti may be grown indoors or out and generally need so little attention that they are almost trouble-free. In gardens where labour is lacking, succulents are a joy, for they seldom need watering if rainfall is adequate. Most of their troubles, such as rotting, occur through over-watering at the wrong time or through heavy rains falling at the wrong season. Most of the succulents grown in gardens come from South Africa and most of the cacti from Central and South America. The greater portion of these countries receive summer rainfall, but many of the plants come from places with as little rainfall as 5 inches a year or where the only moisture is supplied by the morning dew. Many grow near the coast where sea mists give the plants needed moisture, which they store in their fleshy leaves.

Over-watering of succulents and cacti in gardens can be controlled by supplying excellent drainage, such as that found in rockeries. Succulents and cacti can be grown on sloping ground and are excellent subjects for hillsides. They should only be grown on level ground if the soil is porous and water does not stand about after rain. When watering the succulents, try to supply water to the roots and do not let it fall on the leaves, for the hot sun shining through drops of water on the leaves may burn them.

Most succulents need an airy, sunny position, although a few will tolerate shade, such as Crassulas, Kalanchoes, Haworthias, Gasterias, Senecios and Sedums.

The soil for succulents should not be too poor, but should contain well-rotted compost or peat. Do not enrich it heavily with fresh manure. The soil should be light rather than heavy. Water heavy soils even less frequently than light or sandy soil. Depth of soil is not essential, for many will grow in crevices in rocks. Some, like Sedums and Stapelias, will grow on an inch of soil provided that drainage is good. These, as well as annual succulents like Portulaca and Dorotheanthus, can be planted to fill the cracks between crazy paving or soften the appearance of rocky steps, needing less maintenance than any other type of plant.

Most succulents dislike frost and should be given a warm, sheltered position in areas with cold winters. A great many winter-flowering Aloes will have their flowers spoilt by frost and should be planted on a north-facing rockery with shelter from the morning sun provided by a rock or shrub growing nearby. In cold places, succulents must be grown in pots and brought indoors during winter.

Succulents suffer from very few pests and diseases if they have suitable conditions for growth. White scale may infest Aloes, but can be removed with Malathion dust or spray. Fungus infections may occur in places with high rainfall. One should note whether the plants are receiving enough sunshine and pay attention to drainage. They may have to be grown in pots where rainfall is high.

Many succulents make ideal pot plants and can be given just enough water to keep them alive. The pots can be grouped in clusters and placed decoratively on a sunny terrace or a flight of garden steps, where they provide luxuriant growth without worry about drought. Certain succulents and cacti that need very little moisture must be grown in pots placed on a sunny porch with a roof that will protect them from too much rain, or they will damp off. These are mainly small specimen plants which are grown for their curious shape, like the Stone Plants (Lithops) and Anacampseros. These are generally beloved by collectors, but do not belong to the ordinary garden. Succulent and cacti specialists usually become fascinated by forms and highly scientific about naming the plants in their collections. This is a study in itself and there are specialised books to interest such people.

Most gardeners are more interested in leafy succulents that grow luxuriantly and make a decorative impact in the landscape. Do not dot them about haphazardly, but group them so that they are most effective. Small plants like Echevarias and Sempervivums can be planted in thick wavy bands alongside paths or driveways, so that their rosettes make a decoration in themselves. Plant Aloes of one kind in a rockery bed, like *Aloe striata* or *Aloe variegata*, instead of an assortment in different sizes which flower at different times. Many people dislike succulents because they have always seen them planted inartistically with the collector's angle uppermost. The clever landscape gardener can use them to striking effect, however, and they may solve many problems of maintenance where lack of labour is a difficulty.

Many succulents make good groundcovers for banks in situations where it would be too dry for any other plant.

Nothing could be more brillliant in spring than a bank of Lampranthus, which are the most colourful members of the vast Mesembryanthemum family. They form large cushions which spread and hold the soil. The sour Fig (Carprobrotus) does not have such masses of flowers, but forms a thick strong curtain on a rocky or sandy bank, needing very little moisture. Drosanthemum makes a showy, mauve-flowered curtain. The bright annual Dorotheanthus is a valued edging or rockery plant which likes moisture during winter, and is one of the loveliest Mesembs in the spring garden, even though it does not bind the soil on a bank. Sedums and some Crassulas spread and make a useful permanent groundcover on a dry bank, even though their flowers may not be of special interest.

It is not quite as easy to fit cacti into the general garden scheme as they have a stark "desert" appearance. Some, however, make good accent plants for Spanish-American style homes or contemporary architecture. Those who dislike the spines which are always present on cacti, making them troublesome to handle, are advised to grow the more amenable spineless succulents. It may be of interest to note that all cacti are included under the term succulents, but not every succulent is a cactus.

The following lists may be helpful in selecting succulents for different purposes.

"LEAFY" SUCCULENTS SUITABLE FOR GROWING IN POTS

This list does not include specimen plants mainly grown by collectors.

Aloes, smaller kinds like *A. aristata, A. variegata, A. brevifolia, A. chabaudii.*
Aeonium. Foliage like green rosettes, yellow flowers, shrublet.
Cotyledon orbiculata. Pig's Ear. Round fleshy leaves, pinkish flowers.
Crassula arborescens. White flowers. Bushy plants with fleshy leaves.
C. portulacea. Pink Joy. Pink flowers. Bush as above.
Echevaria. Low plants with foliage like flat grey roses.
Echinopsis. Prickly ball sends out large, mauve, delicate blooms.
Epiphyllum. Fuchsia Cactus. Flattened stems develop brilliant, drooping flowers. *Zygocactus* is similar.
Euphorbias. Smaller kinds with bold, branching forms.
Gasteria. Low plants with variegated, thick, tongue-shaped leaves and pinkish flowers.
Haworthia. Pointed rosettes of speckled leaves.
Kalanchoe blossfeldiana. Small upright stems with scarlet flowers.
Opuntia. Prickly Pear. Smaller kinds. Dramatic shapes.

Rat's Tail Cactus (Aporocactus). Prickly, thin drooping stems; bright flowers.
Rochea coccinea. Red Crassula, Klipblom. Bushy plant, crimson posies of flowers.
Senecio (Kleinia) galpinii. Low plant; fluffy, orange flowers.
Stapelia. Carrion Flower. Spreading, upright stem; curious star-shaped flowers.

SUCCULENTS SUITABLE FOR THE ROCKERY

Include any of the above list, plus the following:

Aloes, large and small, notably *A. striata, A. cooperi, A. cryptopoda, A. wickensii* and *A. arborescens* (for large rockeries).
Bulbine. Katstert. Fleshy leaves. Smaller "poker" of yellow flowers.
Crassulas, all kinds, notably *C. falcata, C. perfoliata, C. multicava.*
Dorotheanthus. Low, annual plant with brilliant Mesemb, flowers in spring.
Euphorbia splendens and others. Christ-Thorn. Prickly branches, scarlet flowers.
Kalanchoe tubiflora (Bryophyllum). Stiff stems to 2 feet; mainly pinkish flowers. Several other species.
Mesembryanthemum family (Vygies). All members suited to the rockery, particularly *Lampranthus* and *Drosanthemum.* Brilliant flowers in spring.
Portulaca. Low annual plant with bright flowers in summer.
Portulacaria afra. Elephant's Food. Large shrub with small round leaves. Pink flowers when mature.
Sedum. Some are creeping with foliage like small beads. *S. spectabile* has large greyish leaves and flattened heads of mauve flowers.
Sempervivum. Low plants with foliage like rosettes; sprays of pink flowers.

LARGE SUCCULENTS WITH ACCENT VALUE

Aloes, many large species, notably *A. candelabrum, A. ferox, A. marlothii, A. thraskii* and others.
Agave americana. Century Plant. Very large rosettes of bluish, tough leaves, often spiny at tip or variegated with yellow stripes. Tall stem with flowers only appears after about ten years.
Cereus. Upright or climbing, prickly. Several such as "Queen-of-the-Night", with large white flowers opening at night.
Cissus juttae. Wild Grape, Tree Cissus. Thick trunk. Fleshy leaves and reddish, grape-like fruits.
Cotyledon paniculata. Botterboom. Thick trunk. Thin waving branches at the top.
Euphorbia ingens. Naboom. Tree-like, with many branches forming rounded head. Yellow flowers, pink fruits in warm areas.
Kalanchoe prolifera (Bryophyllum proliferum). Shrub to 10 feet. Large, fleshy, divided leaves. Green and red flowers.
Opuntia. Prickly pear. Decorative, prickly rounded stems. Must be controlled or it spreads. Edible fruit.

CHAPTER TWENTY-NINE

TREES AND SHRUBS IN THE GARDEN

The uses of trees and shrubs in a garden are endless and no garden is worthy of the name without them. Shrubs and trees have been mentioned in the lists throughout this book, belonging to every aspect of gardening. Their flowers and foliage lend variety and they are comparatively easy to tend. Shrubs and trees are generally permanent acquisitions and should be planted in carefully considered positions, both for the sake of their climatic needs and their appearance in the landscape. The subject has been fully treated in the author's book *Flowering Shrubs, Trees and Climbers for Southern Africa*, where numerous shrubs have been described and instructions given on how to grow them. A few essential hints are given here, nevertheless, as well as some suggested lists to assist in choosing shrubs and trees for the average garden.

CHOOSING A TREE FOR THE AVERAGE GARDEN

Plant deciduous trees near the house, so that one is not deprived of winter sun and plant evergreens on the boundary for privacy. Do not plant too many trees on the boundary with the intention of pulling out the alternate ones later, as one never does and the trees will not develop to their fullest extent. They should just touch when fully grown or have a little space between them. The spaces can be masked by planting other trees in front of them. While the trees grow, use the area between them as a flower bed containing geraniums or other quick-growing plants. One can use large quick-growing shrubs or bamboos as a temporary screen if liked.

Do not plant large forest trees in a small garden of less than half an acre, but concentrate on smaller trees with light foliage that will not overpower the garden when they are mature. An occasional tall tree that does not become too massive or dense, such as scented Yellow Blossom Tree (*Hymenosporum flavum*) or the Flame Tree (*Brachychiton acerifolium*) makes for interest and can act as a shade tree in a small garden. One can choose a shade tree from one of the larger trees listed below, but it is best not to plant more than one large forest tree in the average garden, as one can obtain shade from many smaller spreading trees.

A shade tree should be quick-growing, but not so vigorous that it will interfere with the growth of other plants or spoil the lawn with its raised roots, like Belhambra. One must realise that one might have to pave the area under a shade tree when it is mature and the lawn can no longer compete for light under the tree's shade.

The area beneath the tree can then be treated so as to provide shelter for shade-loving plants and groundcovers. (See illustration in Chapter 9.) Visualise whether one will want such a feature near the house or near other beds before choosing the site for your shade tree. A shade tree is best placed within easy reach of the house, a tennis court or swimming pool, where refreshments can be carried with ease. (See lists of suggested shade trees below.)

Every tree has its own beauty, but can be out of place or even a hazard in a small garden. There is no such thing as a bad tree, but some trees have troublesome roots or absorb so much moisture from the soil that they can ruin a small garden. Roots of trees like Lombardy Poplars seek moisture for a considerable distance and may cause cracking of buildings, while others lift up paving or block drains. Even in large gardens it becomes difficult to grow other plants within a considerable distance of such trees. In some new towns the municipal regulations prohibit the planting of certain aggressive trees in suburban gardens. Yet in the right setting in a very large garden of over 5 acres or on a farm garden, there is nothing more magnificent in autumn than an avenue of golden Lombardy poplars or a group of these stately trees on the banks of a stream or dam. (See lists of unsuitable trees for average gardens on page 160.)

PLANTING TREES AND SHRUBS

Deciduous trees are best planted in spring or when they are dormant, so that the roots are established before the leaves appear. Evergreens are best planted out when the air is moist, at the beginning of summer in the summer-rainfall area or in autumn in the winter-rainfall area of the south-western Cape. In places with cold winters, it is best to plant in spring, while in hot places with mild winters, it may be better to plant in autumn. Most trees and shrubs are purchased established in tins and may be transplanted at any time of the year, provided that this is done carefully.

Always prepare the soil well for trees and shrubs as

they will remain in position for many years and thrive if they are given a good start. Make a hole 2 feet deep in good garden soil, but as deep as 6 feet in poor soil when planting large trees. The diameter of the hole should be at least 3 feet or 2 feet wider than the spread of the roots. If the soil is badly drained, make the hole deeper than usual and fill the base with stones or build up a terrace. Add as much compost to the topsoil as possible and mix well-rotted manure and bonemeal into the bottom of the hole. Do not allow the manure to come into direct contact with the roots of the young tree or shrub.

Water the soil in the tin the day before planting so that it is damp. Make three cuts down the sides of the tin with a sharp tin snips and bend back the pieces without disturbing the roots. Lift the whole ball of the soil carefully and place it in the prepared hole, planting it level with the surface. When planting dormant deciduous trees with bare roots, which are sent out from nurseries at the end of winter like roses and fruit trees, place the tree on a slight mound and spread the roots outwards and downwards. Pack the soil firmly around the roots, so that no air pockets will form. Place a stick across the hole so that one can judge the depth at which it should be planted, no deeper than it was growing before, as shown by the earth mark on the stem. This is best done if one person holds the tree and the other fills in the soil. Water the tree as soon as it has been planted, giving it at least 4 gallons of water. Large trees will require more water. Place a heaped rim of soil around the tree or shrub, so as to make an irrigation basin.

Established trees may be transplanted when quite large, but deciduous trees should not be more than 20 feet high or have a trunk thicker than 6 inches in diameter if possible. It is best not to attempt to move a tree more than 12 inches in diameter or the tree may die. Evergreens must be transplanted when much smaller and seldom survive if they are taller than 6 feet. Transplant deciduous trees at the end of winter while they are still dormant, but evergreens should be moved on a cloudy, rainy day at the beginning of the rainy period, preferably in spring or early summer. The soil may be removed from the roots of deciduous trees, but evergreens must be lifted with a ball of earth intact around their roots. Dig a deep trench around the tree and wrap the soil in hessian secured with string. Then dig beneath the tree and slide it onto the hessian which is tied around the earth above like a Christmas pudding. One may plant the tree with the hessian around it as it will rot away in time. Spray the foliage frequently after transplanting and cover the tree with polythene film for a while to prevent excessive evaporation.

Staking. Stake young trees and remove the stakes as soon as the trunk becomes sturdy enough. Never bend the tree towards a straight stake, but allow it to grow upright. Wrap a band of hessian or cloth around the trunk before tying the string around it in order to avoid injury to the bark, then tie the other end of the string to the stake. Leave a short piece of string between the two, but be careful that the stake will not rub against the bark. Remove the band each year and re-tie it in a different place so as to allow for growth and for light to reach the bark.

Watering. Water newly planted shrubs and trees regularly about twice a week, giving at least 4 gallons of water. When they are established it may be necessary to water only once a week, provided that they receive a deep slow soaking. Mulching with compost and other materials conserves moisture. (See page 98.) Do not flood or overwater trees growing in badly drained soil. Water evergreen shrubs and trees regularly throughout the year, especially during dry winters, such as Proteas, Azaleas, Camellias. Deciduous shrubs and trees may be watered once a month or even less often during winter.

Do not allow grass to grow right up to the trunk, but keep it away for at least 2 feet all around. If the bare look is disliked, enrich the soil and plant shallow rooted annuals like Lobelia and Viola around the tree. These flower for a long time and require moisture which will benefit the tree. Permanent groundcovers like Wild Strawberry (*Duchesnea*) are also suitable. Otherwise, mulch the surface with stones, peat or compost. In areas where wood-eating Termites are troublesome, dig 5 per cent DDT dust into the soil. (See Chapter 37 on Insect Control.)

Feeding. Feed young trees and shrubs each spring by spreading half a wheel-barrow of well-rotted manure on top of the soil around the roots. Repeat in midsummer if possible. Compost may be used at any time if it is available. Be careful not to pile these materials against the base of the stem or they may cause rot and death by raising the level of the soil around the tree.

Do not feed mature trees that are growing vigorously in a well-tended garden. When a mature tree grows poorly or shows signs of losing vigour, however, a special feeding may resuscitate it. Lawns growing poorly near mature trees must be given special feeding as the tree robs the lawn of food and moisture. This is best done in spring and may be repeated in midsummer if desired, but never later.

The tree's feeding roots extend slightly beyond the rim of the outer branches and one must apply fertilizer to the whole root area. It is not sufficient to spread manure only around the trunk of a mature tree. One must drill holes over the area, pour plant food into the holes and water liberally.

First soak the whole root area the day before feeding by leaving the sprinkler running for about two hours.

Make holes by driving a pointed stick or iron bar into the moist soil to a depth of 18 inches, making each hole about 2 inches in diameter. Start in a circle around the outer rim of the tree's branches and make concentric circles to within about 2 feet of the trunk, spacing the holes from 1 to 3 feet apart. Use a balanced fertilizer like 2 : 1 : 2 at the rate of 1 lb. for each inch of the trunk's diameter, but not more than 3 lb. per tree. Divide the total into as many holes as have been made. Pour the fertilizer into the holes and fill them with water. Then fill the holes with good soil or compost.

Pruning Trees and Shrubs. For pruning of special shrubs, see under Chapter on Pruning. Few trees need pruning in the same way as roses or fruit trees.

Pruning of trees should be limited to removing broken branches or those crossing through or below the head of the tree. Remove branches at a fork and paint the cuts immediately with tree-sealing compound, but do not allow it to run on to the bark and cause injury. Do not shorten main branches if possible as this spoils the grace of the tree. Do not cut into the old wood of evergreens like conifers as it seldom sends out new growth. Trim evergreens regularly as they grow, in order to shape them or keep them in check if necessary. Pinch or shear back the young soft growth when it is about 3 inches long and repeat this a few weeks later. Avoid doing this at the end of summer when growth has slowed down.

Do not cut away the lower branches of evergreen trees like Deodars. Many deciduous trees like Pin Oaks, Maples, Eugenia and Virgilia do best with their lower branches touching the ground, but the space is often required beneath them for shade or for planting in a small garden. If they are allowed to grow naturally with their branches on the ground, however, one is not faced with the problem of what to grow beneath them.

Tree Surgery. This means re-shaping an old, mature or decrepit tree which may be suffering from drought, lack of fertility or from having been checked so much by transplanting that it must be severely cut back, its branches being reduced to stubs. Tree surgery must be applied to trees which have had their branches broken off by wind or have developed decaying cavities through bad pruning.

It is better to plant a new tree than to patch an old one, but this may be worth doing if the tree is important as a shade tree or as part of an avenue or if it is a slow-growing specimen. Only repair small cavities as a rule. Gouge out the rotten heartwood to beyond the decay. Paint the surface with a fungicide and coat it with tree-sealing compound. Fill it with concrete containing double the amount of sand to cement and pack it in well so that decay will not start again beyond the filling. Finish off just inside the cambium layer so that the bark will grow over the edge of the filling.

One can brace large branches with an iron rod and a V-shaped crotch to prevent them from rubbing against one another. Large branches which begin to split at a crotch can be bolted together. Drill a hole through the branches and bolt a rod into place. Do not wrap a chain or wires around the branches as this will injure the bark. Decay may start where a tree splits. All limbs must be sawn off without leaving stumps or cutting away too much bark. Avoid injury to bark with lawn-mowers or by using trees as a support for fences. (See Cankers under Bacterial Diseases in Chapter 38.)

If one must remove roots in transplanting, it might be necessary to thin out or cut off a corresponding amount off the top of the tree. Roots are often injured when filling soil is placed 2 or 3 feet over them when changing the level of the soil in an old garden. Cover the ground with loose stones and bring these as near to the surface as possible in order to ensure aeration. Avoid covering the root area completely with paving material, using porous brick in preference to other materials and leaving parts of the area open for planting.

Do not allow vines to grow freely all over trees or the trees may die. If growing miniature Ivy or Canary Islands Ivy up the trunk, keep it to one side and do not let it climb above reach into all the branches. Do not burn leaves close to trees or paint sticky substances directly on to the bark. Do not allow motor oil to seep over the root surface or use too many insecticides or weedkillers in the soil near the tree.

Keep a watch for insect pests and destroy them before they do too much damage. (See Chapter 37 on Insect Control.) Vigorous growth in good soil will prevent attack to a large extent. Always purchase healthy plants. Burn diseased leaves. Spray with fungicides if the tree is not too large or eradicate diseased trees.

For treatment of the area under shade trees, see Chapter on "Gardening in the Shade".

CHOOSING A TREE FOR THE GARDEN

SHADE TREES FOR A SMALL GARDEN

1. Evergreen

Brush Cherry (*Eugenia paniculata australis*) 25 to 40 feet. Slow. Remove lower branches.
Carob (*Ceratonia siliqua*) 30 feet. Remove lower branches.
Cotoneaster glaucophyllus serotinus. 12 feet. Prune off lower branches.
Flowering Gum (*Eucalyptus ficifolia*), 30 feet.
Hymenosporum flavum. 25 feet. Upright.
Kaffir Plum (*Harpephyllum caffrum*), 20 to 40 feet. Tender.
Loquat (*Eriobotrya japonica*) 20 feet.
New Zealand Christmas Tree (*Metrosideros tomentosa*), 25 feet. Slow. Sea-tolerant.
Ngaio (*Myoporum laetum*), 15 to 25 feet. Quick.
Oleander (*Nerium oleander*), 12 to 15 feet. Rounded.
Pearl Acacia (*Acacia podalyriaefolia*), 15 to 20 feet. Quick.
Photinia serrulata. 12 to 25 feet. Upright, dense.
Pittosporum. All species. 10 to 20 feet. Upright.

2. Deciduous

American Ash (*Fraxinus americana*). Large when mature, but grows slowly.
Box-Elder Maple (*Acer negundo*) 25 to 30 feet.
Brown-leaved Plums (*Prunus cerasifera*), 20 feet.
Chinese or Trident Maple (*Acer buergerianum*), 20 feet.
Flame Tree (*Brachychiton acerifolium*), 30 to 50 feet.
Flowering Peach (*Prunus persica florepleno*), 20 feet.
Frangipani (*Plumeria*), 15 to 30 feet. Sub-tropical areas.
Mexican Cherry (*Prunus capuli*), 25 feet.
Orchid Tree (*Bauhinia variegata*), 20 feet.
Pagoda Tree (*Sophora japonica*), 20 to 30 feet.
Pride-of-India (*Lagerstroemia indica*), 12 to 15 feet.
Purple Magnolia (*Magnolia soulangeana*), 15 feet, slow.
Pussy Willow (*Salix caprea*), 20 feet.
Queensland Lacebark (*Brachychiton discolor*), 30 feet. Slow.
Snowdrop Tree (*Halesia carolina*), 20 to 40 feet.
Tung nut (*Aleurites fordii*), 25 feet. Spreading. Shelter in cold areas.

OTHER SMALL TREES FOR SMALL GARDENS

Some are large shrubs. Evergreens can be used on the boundary for screening.

1. Evergreen

Bixa orellana. 10 feet. Rounded, rapid, sub-tropical.
Bottlebrush, Tree or Weeping (*Callistemon*), 15 to 20 feet.
Brazilian Glory Bush (*Tibouchina semidecandra*), 10 to 20 feet. Loses leaves in cold areas.

Cotoneaster pannosus. 12 feet. Rounded.
English Holly (*Ilex aquifolium*), 10 to 30 feet. Slow.
Florist Gum (*Eucalyptus cinerea*), 20 feet. Narrow.
Forget-me-not Tree (*Duranta repens*), 8 to 15 feet. Taller in hot climates.
Kurrajong (*Brachychiton populneum*), 25 to 40 feet. Slow.
Laurestinus (*Viburnum tinus*), 10 feet. Slow.
Long-leaved Yellow-wood (*Podocarpus henkelii*). Tall tree but slow.
Orange Firethorn (*Pyracantha angustifolia*). 10 feet. Prune lower branches.
Pyramid Tree (*Lagunaria patersonii*), 20 to 40 feet.
Rocket Pincushion (*Leucospermum reflexum*), 10 feet. Rounded. Not for very small gardens.
Scarlet Grevillea (*Grevillea banksii*), 15 feet. Shelter.
Shuttlecock Flower (*Calliandra* sp.). 9 feet. Spreading.
Silver Tree (*Leucadendron argenteum*), 15 to 52 feet. Upright. Shelter from frost.
Single Camellia. 15 feet. Dense. Fairly quick.
Spanish Broom (*Spartium junceum*), 10 feet. Narrow.
Spindle Tree (*Euonymus japonicus*). 10 feet. Slow. Hardy.
Strawberry Tree (*Arbutus unedo*), 20 feet. Slow.
Tea Myrtle (*Melalauca nesophila*), 10 to 30 feet.
Tecoma stans. 15 feet. Fast. Shelter.

2. Deciduous

Almond (*Prunus communis*), 15 to 20 feet. Rapid.
Cabbage Tree (*Cussonia paniculata*), 10 feet. Slow.
Chinese Hat (*Holmskioldia speciosa*), 10 feet or more. Warm climates.
Coral Tree (*Erythrina crista-gallii*), 12 feet. Young growth tender. Spreading.
Daubentonia punicea (Sesbania), 6 to 9 feet.
Flowering Cherries (*Prunus serrulata*), 15 feet, slow.
Flowering Crabapples (*Malus floribunda*), 20 feet, slow.
Golden Tassels (*Calpurnia aurea*), 15 feet.
Judas Tree (*Cercis siliquastrum*), 10 to 40 feet. Slow, needs warmth.
Kaffirboom (*Erythrina caffra* and *E. lysistemon*), 15 to 40 feet. Tender.
Lavalle Hawthorn (*Crataegus lavallei*), 15 feet, slow.
Lilac (*Syringa* sp.), 9 feet. Best in cold places.
Pompon Tree (*Dais cotinifolia*), 12 feet, upright.
Pudding-Pipe Tree (*Cassia fistula*), 25 feet. Half-hardy.
Red-bud (*Cercis canadensis*), 10 to 40 feet. Slow, needs warmth.
Poinciana gilliesii. Bird-of-Paradise. 8 feet.
Tamarisk, all kinds. 9 to 12 feet.
Tree Convolvulus (*Ipomoea arborescens*). 15 to 20 feet. Tender.
Wax Tree (*Rhus succedanea*), 10 feet.
Wistaria Tree (*Bolusanthus speciosus*). 15 to 20 feet. Needs warmth.

LARGE SHADE TREES FOR LARGE GARDENS

1. Evergreen

Acacia elata (Cedar Wattle), 60 feet. Quick.
Acacia baileyana (Bailey's Wattle), 25 feet, spreading.

These two seed-boxes of varying height, are constructed on the same principle. (See Chapter 20.) They enable one to grow seedlings with minimum trouble and maximum success.

Some methods of Shading. (See Chapter 25.) Seed sown in the open may be shaded by means of newspapers held down by sticks (left). On the lower bed, young seedlings are shaded individually with shady caps or Jacaranda leaves, while they are shaded *en masse* by means of a slatted frame (right).

Divide a clump of perennials with the help of two forks. (See Chapter 26.)

←—Rooting cuttings is made easier by using a polythene bag supported by sticks. (See Chapter 20.)

A Carnation cutting when it is first taken from the plant (left), then stripped for planting (centre) and after having grown roots (right). (See Chapter 26.)

A series of wigwam supports for growing Sweet-peas may be erected when a wall or fence is not available.

These supports become pillars of fragrant bloom in winter and spring. (See Chapter 25.)

Camphor Tree (*Cinnamomum camphora*), 30 to 40 feet. Rounded, spreading. Likes warmth.

Cape Chestnut (*Calodendrum capense*), 20 to 25 feet. Tender. Semi-evergreen.

Cedar of Lebanon (*Cedrus libani*), 70 to 100 feet. Magnificent park tree. Slow.

Cork Oak (*Quercus suber*). 60 feet. Slow. Corky bark.

Deodar Cedar. 40 to 80 feet. Pointed, spreading at base. Slow.

Himalayan Evergreen Oak (*Quercus incana*). 80 feet. Long, toothed leaves. Medium-fast.

Holm or Holly Oak (*Quercus ilex*), 60 feet. Toothed, small dark green leaves. Slow.

Keurboom (*Virgilia oroboides*), 25 feet. Rounded. Quick. Replace after 15 years.

Magnolia grandiflora (White Laurel Magnolia). 50 feet. Slow.

Mexican Evergreen Oak (*Quercus reticulata*), 50 to 80 feet.

Moreton Bay Chestnut (*Castanospermum australe*), 30 to 60 feet. Coastal areas.

Nandi Flame (*Spathodea campanulata*), 60 feet. Hot climate.

Pepper Tree (*Schinus molle*), 25 to 50 feet. Strong root system. Hot, dry and cold areas.

Sausage Tree (*Kigelia pinnata*), 30 feet. Semi-evergreen. Frost-free lowveld.

Silky Oak (*Grevillea robusta*), 50 to 100 feet. Hardy.

Tabebuia pallida. 40 feet. Spreading. Sub-tropical seaside.

Tree Hibiscus (*Hibiscus tiliacus*), 18 feet, spreading. Frost-free warm coast.

Thunder-Tree (*Trichelia emetica*), 40 feet. Tender.

2. Deciduous

African Elm or Camdeboo Stinkwood (*Celtis africana*). 25 feet. Spreading.

Belhambra (*Phytolacca dioica*). Dense shade but roots rise above ground.

Catalpa bignonioides. 60 feet. Spreading.

Chestnut, Spanish (*Castanea sativa*). 50 feet. Spreading. Cool districts.

China-Berry or "Syringa" (*Melia azedarach*). 30 to 60 feet. Spreading. Quick.

Chinese Oak (*Quercus serrata*). 50 feet. Shining, light green, toothed leaves.

Chinese Parasol Tree (*Firmiana simplex*). 50 feet. Palmate leaves. Warm districts.

English Oak (*Quercus robur*). 80 to 100 feet. Spreading, slow.

Flamboyant (*Delonix regia*). 30 to 40 feet. Flat-topped, spreading. Sub-tropical.

Floss-Silk Tree (*Chorisia speciosa*). Large thorny, flowering. Needs warmth.

Honey Locust (*Gleditschia triacanthos*). 30 to 80 feet. Quick, poor soil, hardy.

Jacaranda acutifolia. 40 feet. Spreading. Evergreen in hot, moist areas. Medium-fast.

London Plane (*Platanus acerifolia*). 50 feet. Hardy. Strong root system. Medium-fast.

Paulownia tomentosa. 40 feet. Spreading, quick.

Pin Oak (*Quercus palustris*). 60 feet. Pyramidal. Fairly quick.

Pink Cassia (*Cassia javanica*), 30 feet. Half-hardy. Loses leaves for short period.

Potato Tree (*Solanum macranthum*). 20 feet, spreading. Sub-tropical areas.

Tipuana tipu. 30 feet. Spreading. Quick.

Trembling Poplar (*Populus wislizenii*). 90 feet. For huge gardens or parks. Suckers if roots are injured. Rapid.

Weeping Willow (*Salix babylonica*). 50 feet. Best near water. Penetrating roots may invade pipes. Quick.

OTHER LARGE TREES FOR LARGE GARDENS

1. Evergreen

Monkey-Puzzle Tree or Chile Pine (*Araucaria araucana*). 50 to 100 feet. Hardy. Conifer with sharp-pointed leaves. Slow.

Norfolk-Island-Pine (*Araucaria excelsa*). 100 to 200 feet. Columnar, tiered. Warm coastal districts. Slow.

Pines: Medium-fast, grow 3 to 5 feet a year.

Italian Stone Pine or Umbrella Pine (*Pinus pinea*). 80 to 90 feet. Effective landscape pine with flattish crown. Good in S.W. Cape.

Monterey Pine (*Pinus radiata*). 80 to 140 feet. Commonly planted, fast-growing. Pointed tip. *Pinus elliottii* is now recommended in its place, especially in the summer-rainfall area, as it is more hail resistant. It is not as tall or spire-like as *P. radiata*, but grows as quickly. 80 to 100 feet.

Pinus patula. 80 to 90 feet. Distinctive tree with light green, long needles to 12 inches, hanging down like fringes. Rounded when mature. Comparatively slow.

Pinus roxburghii (*P. longifolia*). 80 to 120 feet. Long light green leaves arranged in stiff radiating clusters, not as long or drooping as *P. patula*. Neat-looking, symmetrical tree, comparatively slow-growing.

P. pinaster (Cluster Pine). 80 to 100 feet. Not recommended in the Cape where it seeds freely and overwhelms indigenous flora. Upright, stiff glossy needles in clusters at tips of branches.

2. Deciduous

American Sweet Gum (*Liquidambar styraciflua*). 60 feet. Upright, slow, moisture.

Baobab (*Adansonia digitata*). 100 feet. Fascinating elephantine tree for very large gardens in hot, dry areas from Zoutpansburg northwards. A curiosity.

Copper Beech (*Fagus sylvatica atropunicea*). Slow. Cool districts, moisture. 30 to 50 feet.

Maidenhair Tree (*Gingko biloba*). 30 to 100 feet. Erratic at first, graceful when mature. Hardy but likes warmth and moisture.

Tulip tree (*Liriodendron tulipifera*). 50 to 100 feet. Slow, moisture.

Swamp Cypress (*Taxodium distichum*). 100 feet. Slow. Hardy. Likes moisture in soil or deep acid soil near water.

Wych Elm or Scotch Elm (*Ulmus glabra*). 50 to 100 feet. Does not sucker from root. Hardy, fairly slow. Rich soil.

UNSUITABLE TREES FOR AVERAGE GARDENS

Belhambra (*Phytolacca dioica*.) Dense shade but too large and spreading for average gardens. Buttressed roots rise up and prevent paving or growing plants beneath tree.

Black Locust (*Robinia pseudocacia*). 40 feet. Suckers and seeds freely. Quick and good for large gardens in dry, hot places.

Blue Gum (*Eucalyptus globulus*) is one of the fastest-growing trees but becomes a giant and absorbs vast quantities of water from the soil. It is suitable for a farm garden. Liable to be broken by wind.

Hakea in the S.W. Cape. Seeds freely and overwhelms indigenous flora. Several species except *H. saligna*, which has broad leaves.

Pines. These are generally too large for the average garden, but form a pleasant background tree in very large gardens. Never plant them close together in a row. Avoid planting the Cluster Pine (*Pinus pinaster*) in the S.W. Cape as it seeds too freely and overwhelms the indigenous flora.

Poplars. All Poplars have powerful root systems and sucker easily, preventing other plants from doing well near them. Some are so aggressive that they lift concrete, crack walls and interfere with underground pipes. They are beautiful, hardy and grow rapidly, but should only be planted in a very large garden or on a farm. The worst offenders are the Lombardy Poplar (*Populus nigra italica*), Carolina Poplar (*Populus canadensis*) and Grey Poplar (*P. canescens*). The cottonwood (*P. deltoides*) is less aggressive, but will also sucker if the roots are injured and its white "cotton" is a nuisance in spring.

Tree of Heaven (*Ailanthus*). Root suckers.

Wattles (*Acacia*). Many Wattles are ornamental and suited to the garden, but some seed so freely that they become troublesome. They tend to die back and take a great deal out of the soil. Avoid planting the feathery-leaved Wattles like the Silver Wattle, *Acacia dealbata*, which suckers, and the fast growing Black Wattles, *A. decurrens* and *A. mollissima*. Cape gardeners should eradicate the Port Jackson Willow (*A. cyanophylla*), Rooikrantz (*A. cyclops*), Blackwood (*A. melanoxylon*) and others which spread too easily and overwhelm indigenous flora.

Willows. These take too much out of the soil in the average garden, but are more satisfactory if they receive plenty of water. They are really best for very large gardens and do well in swampy ground or near water.

SOME USEFUL CLIMBERS (T=Tender)

For Shady Places. Many will grow in full sun, others in semi-shade.

Asparagus Ferns.
Canary Creeper (*Senecio tamoides*).
Clematis montana and hybrids.
Clerodendron, Bleeding Heart (*Clerodendrum thompsoniae*). T.
Clerodendron, Scarlet (*Clerodendrum splendens*). T.
Cascade Creeper (*Polygonum aubertii*).
Creeping Fig (*Ficus pumila*).
Golden Vine (*Stigmaphyllon ciliatum*). T.
Honeysuckles (*Lonicera*), all kinds.
Ivy (*Hedera*), all kinds.
Japanese or Boston Ivy (*Parthenocissus tricuspidata*).
Jasmines, all kinds.
Lilac Vine (*Hardenbergia comptoniana*).
Mandevilla (Chilean-Jasmine). T.
Maurandia barclaiana.
Mauve Bignonia (*Clytostoma callistegioides*).
Monstera deliciosa. T.
Philodendron sp. T.
Potato Creeper (*Solanum jasminoides*).
Snail Vine (*Phaseolus caracalla*). T.
Star-Jasmine (*Trachelospermum*).
Stephanotis (Madagascar-Jasmine). T.
True Virginian Creeper (*Parthenocissus quinquefolia*).
Wax Plant (*Hoya carnosa*). T.
Wistaria (*W. sinensis*).
Zimbabwe Creeper (*Podranea brycei*).

For Sunny Places. Some of the above will do even better in full sun, such as Potato Creeper, Mauve Bignonia and Wistaria.

Bluebell Creeper (*Sollya heterophylla*).
Bougainvillea, all kinds. T.
Cat's Claw Creeper (*Doxantha unguis-cati*).
Coral Vine (*Antigonon leptopus*). T.
Crimson Wax Trumpet (*Ipomoea horsfalliae*). T.
Cross-Vine (*Bignonia capreolata*).
Cup-of-Gold (*Solandra nitida*). T.
Distictis riversii.
Dutchman's Pipe (*Aristolochia elegans*).
Giant Trumpet Climber (*Beaumontia*). T.
Golden Shower (*Pyrostegia ignea*). T.
Mexican Blood Trumpet (*Phaedranthus buccinatorius*).
Passion Flower, Red (*Passiflora manicata*).
Purple-Bell (*Cobaea scandens*).
Purple-Wreath (*Petrea volubilis*).
Rubber Vine (*Cryptostegia grandiflora*). T.
Snake Vine (*Hibbertia volubilis*).
Trumpet-Vine (*Campsis radicans*).
Wonga Vine (*Pandorea pandorana*).
Wood-rose (*Ipomoea tuberosa*).

SOME USEFUL FLOWERING SHRUBS

These are grouped according to sizes and according to whether they need sun or shade. Small shrubs help to furnish the garden more than any other plants and can be numerous even in the small garden. Use them to fill up flower beds, for foundation planting under windows, in rockeries, under trees, on banks and in many places where they supply permanent colour with little labour. Group the smaller ones in threes or fives for best effect.

SOME MEDIUM-SIZED SHRUBS (5 feet to 7 feet)

For Shady Places. Many will also grow in full sunshine.

Azaleas, Purple and White.
Bridal-Wreath May (*Spiraea prunifolia plena*).
Camellias, single and double.
Globe Flower (*Kerria japonica*).
Glossy Abelia (*Abelia grandiflora*).
Gold Flower (*Hypericum sinense*).
Golden-Bells (*Forsythia*).
Holly Mahonia (*Mahonia aquifolium*).
Hydrangea macrophylla.
Japanese Flowering Quince (*Chaenomeles lagenaria*).
Jasmines.
Lemon-Verbena (*Lippia citriodora*).
Pineapple-Guava (*Feijoa sellowiana*).
Port Wine Magnolia (*Michelia fuscata*).
Snowball Bush (*Viburnum opulus sterile*).
Yesterday, Today and Tomorrow (*Brunfelsia calycina eximea*).

For Sunny Places

Autumn Cassia (*Cassia corymbosa*).
Cancer Bush (*Sutherlandia frutescens*).
Carnival Bush (*Ochna atropurpurea*).
Cestrums, Red, Pink, Yellow.
Chile-Heath (*Fabiana imbricata*).
Daisy Bushes or Marguerites (*Chrysanthemum sp.*).
Daubentonia punicea (*Sesbania*).
Fire-Dart Bush (*Malvaviscus mollis*).
Flower-of-the-Incas (*Cantua buxifolia*).
Heaths (*Erica cerinthoides, E. bauera, E. vestita, E. mammosa*, etc.).
Oxford and Cambridge Bush (*Clerodendrum ugandense*).
Proteas, many species.
Rosemary Grevillea (*Grevillea rosmarinifolia*).

SOME SMALL SHRUBS (4 feet or under, or slender)

For Shady Places. Most of these will also grow in full sun.

Abutilon megapotamicum (climbing or drooping).
Azaleas, pink and red.
Bouvardia.
Coral-berry (*Symphoricarpus orbiculatus*).
Cotoneaster microphyllus and *C. horizontalis*.
Dwarf Yesterday, Today and Tomorrow (*Brunfelsia calycina floribunda*).
Fuchsia hybrids.
Garland May (*Spiraea arguta*).
Hebe speciosa (*Veronica*).
Hypericum calycinum.
Juniper horizontalis, low, spreading branches.
Mackaya bella.
Plectranthus behrii and *P. saccatus*.
Red May (*Spiraea bumalda* Anthony Waterer).

Scarlet Clerodendron (*C. speciosissimum*).
Snow-berry (*Symphoricarpus albus*).

For Sunny Places

Beauty-Berry (*Callicarpa*).
Blushing Bride (*Serruria florida*).
Ceratostigma wilmottianum and *C. plumbaginoides*.
Christ-thorn (*Euphorbia splendens*).
Confetti Bush (*Coleonema pulchrum*).
Coral-Bell Bush (*Russelia*).
Crane Flower (*Strelitzia reginae*).
Dwarf Pomegranate (*Punica granatum nana*).
Euphorbia fulgens (*E. jacquiniflora*).
Flame Pea (*Chorizema cordatum*).
Heaths (*Erica regia, E. patersonia, E. peziza, E. viridipurpurea*, etc.).
Lavender (*Lavandula* sp.).
Marmalade Bush (*Streptosolen jamesonii*).
Mountain Rose (*Protea nana*).
Nodding Pincushion (*Leucospermum nutans*).
Pig's Ears (*Solanum mammosum*).
Purple Barberry (*Berberis thunbergii atropurpurea*).
Purple Lantana (*L. montevidensis*).
Podalyria sericea.
Potentilla fruticosa.
Red Cardinal (*Erythrina zeyheri*).
Rock-Rose (*Cistus crispus*).
Rosemary (*Rosmarinus*).
Shrimp Flower (*Beloperone*).
Tambookie Thorn (*Erythrina acanthocarpa*).
Yellow Flax (*Reinwardtia indica*).

WINTER-FLOWERING SHRUBS AND TREES

May, June and July are bleak garden periods when spring bulbs and annuals have not yet come into full bloom, so that flowering shrubs are of great value during this time. The highveld with its cold winter is particularly barren during these months, for many winter-flowering shrubs which brighten warm, frost-free areas are too tender for high altitudes. Nevertheless, many hardy shrubs flower during winter and one can place more tender specimens in warm, sheltered positions in order to protect them from frost and preserve their flowers.

Winter-flowering Shrubs and Trees for Cold Areas

Balloon-Pea (*Sutherlandia frutescens*).
Bauhinia galpinii (till frost).
*Blushing Bride (*Serruria florida*) (May to July).
*Bouvardia (till June or frost).
Bridal-Wreath May (*Spiraea prunifolia plena*) (from June).
Camellias, especially single and double red.
*Cape Honeysuckle (*Tecomaria capensis*) (till frost).
Chimonanthus praecox (Winter-Sweet).
Cotoneaster glaucophyllus (till mid-June).
Cotoneaster pannosus (till June).
Chinese Lanterns (*Abutilon*).

*Give a warm sheltered position for best results.

*Crane Flower (*Strelitzia reginae*).
Confetti Bush (*Coleonema pulchrum*) (May to September).
Crataegus lavallei (till end May).
Coral-berry (*Symphoricarpos orbiculatus*).
Daphne (from July).
Erica baccans (Berry Heath).
Erica bauera (Bridal Heath).
E. cerinthoides (Red Hairy Erica) (July to November).
E. diaphana (Translucent Heath).
E. discolor (Ever-flowering Heath).
E. glandulosa (Sticky-leaved Heath).
E. patersonia (Mealie Heath).
E. plukenetii (Tassel Heath).
E. vestita (Wide-mouthed Heath).
Forsythia sp. (from mid-June).
Fuchsia, all kinds (till June).
*Golden Shower (*Pyrostegia ignea*).
Hebe speciosa (*Veronica*).
Hemizygia obermeyerae (till frost).
Holly (*Ilex aquifolium*) Berries.
Iboza riparia (till frost).
Japanese Flowering Quince (*Chaenomeles*) (from June).
Jasminum polyanthum.
Lantana montevidensis (ever-blooming).
Lion's Ear (*Leonotis leonurus*) (till June or July).
Mexican Blood Trumpet (*Phaedranthus* or *Bignonia cherere*) (ever-blooming).
*Nodding Pincushion (*Leucospermum nutans*) (May to September).
Pearl Acacia (*A. podalyriaefolia*) (from mid-June).
Podalyria sericea (Silver Sweet-pea Bush) (May and June).
*Poinsettia (*Euphorbia pulcherrima*) (from June).
Polygala virgata (Bloukappies).
Protea barbigera. (Giant Woolly-beard). (June to November).
Protea compacta. (Bot River Protea.) (From May).
Protea cynaroides (King Protea) (from May).
P. repens (True Sugarbush) (from May).
P. neriifolia (Oleander-leaved Protea) (from June).

P. nana (Mountain Rose) (from June).
Purple Magnolia (*M. soulangeana*) (till July).
Pycnostachys stuhlmannii (till mid-June).
Pyracantha angustifolia (Orange Pyracantha).
Reinwardtia indica (Yellow Flax).
Ribbon Bush (*Hypoestes aristata*) (till mid-June).
*Shrimp Flower (*Beloperone*) (ever-blooming).
Tea Tree (*Leptospermum scoparium nichollsii*).
Wigandia macrophylla (from mid-June).
*Wild Phlox (*Sutera grandiflora*) (almost ever-blooming).

Winter-flowering trees and shrubs in warm, frost-free areas

Brunfelsia (Yesterday, Today and Tomorrow) (from July).
Christ-thorn (*Euphorbia splendens*) (ever-blooming).
Daisy Bushes (*Chrysanthemum* species).
Frangipani (*Plumeria*) (till July).
Golden Shower (*Pyrostegia ignea*) (till July).
Grevillea banksii (ever-blooming).
Hibiscus rosa-sinensis (blooms nearly all year).
Impala Lily (*Adenium obesum multiflorum*) (from July).
Jasmines.
Kaffirboom (*Erythrina lysistemon*) (from July).
Nandi Flame (*Spathodea campanulata*).
Oleander (*Nerium oleander*).
Orchid Tree (*Bauhinia variegata*) (from mid-June).
Plectranthus myrianthus.
Poinsettia (*Euphorbia pulcherrima*).
Petrea volubilis (Purple Wreath) (from July).
Pig's Ears (*Solanum mammosum*) (from May).
Solandra nitida (Cup-of-Gold) (from July).
Solanum macranthum (Giant Yesterday, Today and Tomorrow).
Tecoma stans (Yellow Bush Tecoma).
Tibouchina semidecandra (Brazilian Glory Bush) (nearly all year).
Zimbabwe Creeper (*Podranea brycei*) (nearly all year).

---

*Give a warm sheltered position for best results.

CHAPTER THIRTY

CULTIVATION OF ROSES

No garden is complete without the rose in one of its forms, even if one has but a single specimen. Roses are so easy to grow and produce so many blooms even without much attention that anyone can grow them. They have certain easily-supplied requirements and will survive an astonishing amount of neglect. One should endeavour to give them all they require so that one can get the best results from these accommodating plants, for the finest florist's blooms cannot be compared to the fresh and perfect roses that one can pick from one's own garden.

CHOOSING ROSES

It is important to plant good roses and not buy a cheap selection without knowing their names. One should also purchase roses from well-known growers who specialise in producing strong, healthy plants and good, tested varieties. Always buy the best plants, for it is better to pay a little extra for each plant and have fewer bushes, if necessary, than to economise at the expense of quality. Roses will last for 20 years or more if they are well cared for, so that the initial expense is soon forgotten. Some roses have been known to bear flowers for over 50 years, but the chances are that the gardener will have pulled them out in favour of new hybrids long before they reach that age.

Roses grow in different shapes such as bush, standard or climbing roses, and serve different purposes in the garden. There are also different rose groups which are suitable for different effects and one should know something of their attributes in order to decide where to plant the different types and to know how to prune them. (See "Pruning of Roses", Chapter 31, Section I.)

ROSE GROUPS

Most modern roses are hybrids which are constantly being selected and improved by nurserymen. Hundreds of special names are given to new roses, such as "First Love" and "Independence", but these all belong to a few large groups, based on the parentage of the hybrids. It is not necessary for the gardener to know the parents of his roses, but only the group to which they belong. This information is usually given when roses are purchased.

It is a consolation to the gardener, who may be bewildered by the numerous types of roses listed in horticultural dictionaries, to know that there are only three or four groups of roses grown today, of which only two are really popular, namely the Hybrid Teas and the Polyanthas, which include Floribundas. These are specially bred to stand up to the rigours of cold winters and to provide all the needs of the modern gardener—roses for cut flowers as well as for colourful, massed effects in the landscape. Other roses include novel miniature roses and large shrub roses, which are usually species that are grown on their own roots.

The three best known groups of roses grown today are called Hybrid Teas, Hybrid Perpetuals and Polyantha or Floribunda roses. Floribunda roses are similar to Polyanthas and are treated in the same way. Hybrid Perpetuals are older roses than Hybrid Teas and are seldom seen in modern gardens, but will be dealt with for the benefit of those who grow them. Both Hybrid Teas and Polyanthas or Floribundas are available in bush, standard and climbing forms.

BUSH ROSES

Hybrid Perpetuals (*HP*). These originated in 1837 and were very popular at one time, but have retired into the background in favour of the Hybrid Teas. There are very few grown in Southern Africa, probably only Frau Karl Druschki (white), Druschki rubra (red), Sachsengruss (pink) and Hugh Dickson (red). They have large, fragrant flowers in red or white but never yellow, on large free-flowering bushes. They do not flower perpetually, however, as the name indicates. They do not suit the formal rose garden, but may be grown on their own as hedges in the garden, in the border, or as isolated specimens.

Hybrid Teas (*HT*). These originated in 1867, with a Hybrid Perpetual as one parent and a Tea rose (*Rosa odorata*) as the other. The strong yellow colours of modern roses were introduced with another yellow-flowered parent, the Austrian Briar. Hybrid Teas form the largest group of present day roses and new hybrids are constantly being added each year. They flower more freely than the older Hybrid Perpetuals and have the well-formed roses most frequently seen at exhibitions and florists, e.g. Comtesse Vandal. They bloom mainly in October and have a second flush of blooms in January, as well as producing occasional flowers throughout summer and autumn. Hybrid Teas are the best roses for the formal rose garden and for cut flowers. They make neat bushes and require more careful pruning than any other type of rose.

Polyantha Roses (*Pol*). These may be recognised easily as they bear large clusters of small flowers at the top of each stem. The individual flowers are not so perfectly formed individually as the Hybrid Teas, but create a colourful massed effect in the garden, e.g. Orange Triumph. Polyantha roses are especially valuable for bedding, for they bloom almost continuously throughout summer and autumn. They are used for grouping in beds beneath standards or on their own, mixed with other flowers in the border or used as low hedges edging paths. They also last well in the vase and are useful for hot as well as cold climates. The flowers may be single or double, have wavy petals or small flat petals packed into tiny rosettes, but are seldom fragrant. There are both taller and shorter forms of the bushes and they are also available in climbing form.

Modern Polyantha roses are hybrids springing from the Japanese or Polyantha rose, *Rosa multiflora*. Hybrids from another Japanese rose, *Rosa wichuraiana*, also bear flowers in clusters and are treated in the same way.

Floribunda roses (*Fl.*) are hybrid Polyantha roses which have been further crossed with Hybrid Teas. They also have flowers in clusters, but usually have larger, better formed flowers in smaller clusters, e.g. Fashion. As they are treated in the same way as Polyanthas it does not matter whether one can distinguish between them or not. They are very popular nowadays as they are showy in massed groups in the garden. They extend the rose season as they generally bloom after the Hybrid Teas, being at their best in November.

Grandiflora is a new name given by the American Rose Society to describe roses which have something of both Polyanthas and Hybrid Teas in their make-up. They are still called Floribundas in England. This is a new race of tall and vigorous plants with flowers that are large and high-centred like the Hybrid Teas, but are produced either singly or in clusters like the Floribundas. They may be grown in the formal rose garden or on their own. Grandifloras are pruned like Hybrid Teas, as they resemble these in shape, but should be pruned more lightly.

This new class was formed in 1955 with the advent of the rose Queen Elizabeth and since then the reclassification of certain older roses, which grow in similar fashion, has been accepted. For example, the deep yellow Buccaneer, formerly classed as a Hybrid Tea, and dark red Carrousel,

formerly classed as a Floribunda, are both now reclassified as Grandifloras. As time goes by there is no doubt that others will be added to the list. At the present time there are about eight, including Montezuma, Roundelay, Dean Collins and June Bride.

At flower shows, single specimens of Grandiflora are judged with Hybrid Teas. If the rose is disbudded, as when there are two or three blooms on a single cane, it should be placed in a special class.

Garnette Roses. These are recent developments of Floribunda Roses that are especially valuable as cut flowers and are popular with florists. The miniature-sized buds open wide to reveal many petals and they last for a long while in the vase. They grow in clusters on ordinary bushes or smaller than average bushes.

Miniature or **Fairy Roses.** These are tiny novelties which grow to less than a foot in height, e.g. Tom Thumb. They are suitable for window-boxes or rockeries and may be used as edging plants. Also grow them in groups in large tubs. They must be pruned back after flowering. They grow on their own roots and are derived from the Chinese rose, *Rosa chinensis minima*.

STANDARD ROSES

These are simply bushes which are grafted on to 3–4 foot long canes, mainly Hybrid Teas, but can also be Floribundas. They create a more formal effect in the garden and are often used to line pathways. They form a good background to a bed of bush roses, giving a two-tiered effect. They require pruning in winter and should be more severely trimmed than bush roses.

SHRUB ROSES

These are usually wild roses or species that grow on their own roots and can be grown as shrubs or hedges. They can be planted and almost forgotten as they require very little attention, except for removing some very old wood each year, e.g. Banksia Rose (*Rosa banksiae*) and Dog Rose (*Rosa canina*). They are suitable for climates with mild winters and grow easily in poor soil. They form large bushes and some ramble freely. There are many other old-fashioned roses such as the Briar Rose, the Moss Rose, the French Rose and the Damask Rose which would be suitable for gardens in Southern Africa, but these are not obtainable locally.

CLIMBING ROSES

Roses are not true climbers like shrubby climbers, for they need to be trained and tied to their supports. They are used to cover walls, trellises and pergolas. There are two main types of climbing roses, which are differentiated because they must be pruned differently. These are given various names, but are usually known as Ramblers and Climbing Hybrid Teas.

(1) Ramblers

Early Rose hybridists gradually developed climbers for the garden by selecting the taller growing Tea roses, Noisette roses and Multiflora roses. Hybrids of the Japanese *Rosa wichuraiana* proved to be superior to the older types and many of these are still popular today, such as Dorothy Perkins. These roses were called Ramblers, for they ramble attractively over rustic archways and fences. They have large clusters of small flowers which are usually red, pink or white. They make a good display in spring or early summer, but seldom bloom again in the season.

The term "Rambler" is loosely applied today to many other improved varieties of climbers which evolved with the years and need a similar method of pruning. These are also sometimes called Large-flowered Climbers (LC) or climbing Polyanthas. They are grouped together because they bear their flowers in clusters, although the individual flowers vary in size, shape and colour, including yellows, oranges and many new shades. They usually bloom only in spring or early summer, but may occasionally produce more flowers later in the season. The "cluster" roses that belong to this group include the improved climbing Wichuraianas such as Paul's Scarlet Climber, the Hybrid Noisettes such as Lemon Pillar and the Climbing Polyantha and Floribunda Hybrids, such as Gloria Mundi and Climbing Goldilocks. The climbing Polyanthas do not bloom as continuously as their bush counterparts.

(2) Climbing Hybrid Teas

These form the second important group of climbers which are grown today. They are merely strong-growing varieties of Hybrid Teas and have the same names as their bush counterparts, for example, Talisman and Climbing Talisman. They have the same well-formed flowers in many different shades. They bloom profusely in late spring and continue to produce flowers at intervals throughout summer. They are sometimes called ever-blooming climbers, but this is an exaggerated term. If these roses are treated badly, they may revert to bush form. Climbing Hybrid Teas are suitable for training on to trellises and have a slightly more formal appearance than the roses which bear their flowers in clusters. Their flowers are generally superior in shape and they bloom for a far longer period in the year.

A CHOICE OF GOOD ROSES

It is a difficult task to recommend a list of roses since the choice is so wide, while new and improved varieties are constantly being developed. The author feels, however, that whereas the experienced gardener can judge the merits of a new rose, it is not easy for the beginner to make a preliminary choice. In an effort to help the beginner, therefore, the following lists have been prepared.

Most of these recommended roses are well known and have been successful in gardens in Southern Africa. A few are very new, but seem to be champions in every way. Many good roses had to be omitted as it seemed wise to restrict the list for the beginner in order not to bewilder him at the outset. As it is, there are far too many roses here for the average garden, since one should endeavour to grow at least three bushes of each variety in order to create a garden picture or have sufficient of one kind of rose to fill a vase.

Choosing roses is so much a matter of personal taste that the gardener should try to see roses in bloom at flower shows and rose nurseries before making a final decision. The beginner should not try every new rose enthusiastically, but start with well-known roses that have proved successful in his area. Give a new rose a fair trial and if it does not please you by the third season, pull it out and try a new one. Do not be afraid to eliminate a rose that you do not like or that has not proved itself a good grower in your garden. Be ready to buy a few new roses from time to time to replace these or add to your collection. This helps to rejuvenate your interest in your rose-garden, should this ever wane.

BEGINNER'S SELECTION OF ROSES

I. Hybrid Teas (HT), Hybrid Perpetuals (HP) and Grandifloras (Gr)

Rich Red or Crimson
Avon. HT.
Christian Dior. HT.
Chrysler Imperial. HT.
Crimson Glory. HT.
Happiness (Voortrekker). HT.
Josephine Bruce. HT.
New Yorker. HT.
Nocturne. HT.
Papa Meilland. HT.
Roundelay. Gr.

Red Shades
Charlotte Armstong. HT.
Peter Frankenfeld. HT.
Rubaiyat. HT.

Coral
Cherry Brandy. HT.
Hawaii. HT.
Montezuma. HT.

Polynesian Sunset. HT.
Super Star (Tropicana in America). HT.

Rich Pink
Eden Rose. HT.
Queen Elizabeth. Gr.
Show Girl. HT.
Sterling. HT.
The Doctor. HT.

Light Pink
Confidence. HT.
First Love. HT.
Lady Luck. HT.
Michelle Meilland. HT.
Picture. HT.
Sachsengruss. HP.

Pink Blends
Bonne Nouvelle (Good News). HT.
Comtesse Vandal. HT.

Pink Blends—contd.
Dainty Bess. HT.
Helen Traubel. HT.
Tiffany. HT.

Yellow
Buccanneer. Gr.
Cecile. HT.
Eclipse. HT.
Golden Masterpiece. HT.
Golden Sun. HT.
Grandpa Dickson. HT.
Kings Ransome. HT.
Madame Pierre du Pont. HT.

White
Frau Karl Druschki. HP.
June Bride. Gr.
Pascali. HT.

Virgo. HT.
White Christmas. HT.

Mauve
Blue Moon. HT.
Cologne Carnival. HT.
Heure Mauve. HT.
Silver Star. HT.
Sterling Silver. HT.

Yellow and Orange Blends
Beauté. HT.
Chicago Peace. HT.
Golden Dawn. HT.
Lucky Peace. HT.
Mojave. HT.
Peace. HT.
Rose Gaujaard. HT.
Suspense. HT.
Sutter's Gold. HT.

II. Floribunda Roses (Fl.) and Hybrid Polyanthas (Pol)

As these are different heights (dwarf, 18 inches, medium, 2½ to 3 feet and tall, 4½ feet) it is best to plant several bushes of one type only if a uniform appearance is desired. Plant three to five of one kind in groups in a mixed border with other plants or in a rose bed.

Deep Red
Europeana. Fl.
Frensham. Fl.

Red Shades
Cocorico. Fl.
Independence. Fl.
Permanent Wave. Fl.

Orange-Red
Fire Fly. Fl.
Floradora. Fl.
Geranium Red. Fl.
Korona. Fl.
Salmon Perfection. Pol.
Sarabande. Fl.

Coral Shades
Bobby Lucas. Fl.
Coup de Foudre. Fl.
Espoir. Fl.
Irish Mist. Fl.
Jiminy Cricket. Fl.
Niquette. Fl.
Spartan. Fl.
Vogue. Fl.

Pink
Elsie Poulsen. Fl.
Frolic. Fl.
Lilibet. Fl.
Pinkie. Pol.
Pink Parfait. Fl.
Pink Rosette. Fl.

Pale Coral and Pink Blends
Fashion. Fl.
Ma Perkins. Fl.
Pinnochio. Fl.
Rosemary Eddie. Fl.

Blends and Unusual Shades
Café. Fl.
Circus. Fl.
Masquerade. Fl.
Rumba. Fl.
Samba. Fl.
Yellow Pinnochio. Fl.

Yellow
All Gold. Fl.
Golden Delight. Fl.
Gold Gleam. Fl.
Goldilocks. Fl.
Green Fire. Fl.
Jan Spek. Fl.

White
Iceberg. Fl.
Ice White. Fl.
Irene of Denmark. Fl.
Summer Snow. Pol.

Lavender Shades
Jacaranda. Fl.
Lavandula. Fl.
Lavender Pinnochio. Fl.
Lavender Princess. Fl.

IIa. Garnette Roses

Garnette—red
Coral Garnette—pink.
Gold Garnette—deep yellow.
Yellow Garnette—yellow.

Red Verona—red, but a larger flower than that of Garnet.
Zorina—coral-red.

III. Standard Roses

Most standard roses are mainly Hybrid Teas or other types of bush roses grafted on to tall canes for special effects, so that they may be obtained in the same varieties as bush roses.

IV. Shrub Roses and Miniature Roses for the Landscape

As there are comparatively few of these roses available, the grower will be able to make a selection quite easily from nurserymen's catalogues.

Shrub Roses include *Sparries Hoop*, with trusses of large pale pink flowers, growing to 5 feet and spreading to about 6 feet; *White Wings*, with prolific white single flowers, and *Golden Wings*, which has single yellow flowers.

The Hybrid Polyantha rose Cecile Brunner (Sweetheart Rose) is best planted as a shrub as it grows too vigorously for the ordinary rose garden in this country. For shrubby climbers, see below.

V. Climbing Roses

Section A. Climbing Hybrid Teas (CHT)

Numerous Hybrid Teas are available as climbers, so that only a few are mentioned below for the sake of brevity. High Noon is available only as a climber.

Red
Climbing Chrysler Imperial.
Climbing Crimson Glory.
Climbing Etoile de Holland.

Red Shades
Climbing Charlotte Armstrong.
Climbing Texas Centennial.

Pink
Climbing Doctor.
Climbing Lady Sylvia.
Climbing Queen Elizabeth.
Climbing Picture.
Climbing Show Girl.

Pink Blend
Climbing Comtesse Vandal.
Climbing Tiffany.

Yellow
High Noon.
Climbing Madame du Pont.

Yellow and Orange Blends
Climbing Peace.
Climbing Talisman.
Climbing Sutter's Gold.
Climbing Mrs. Sam McGredy.

White
Climbing White Christmas.

Section B. Climbers with Flowers in Clusters

These include Climbing Floribundas (CFl), Climbing Polyanthas (CPol) and Large-flowered Climbers (LC) which are hybrids. They all bloom profusely in clusters and must be pruned after flowering.

Red
    Blaze. LC.
    New Blaze. LC.
    Paul's Scarlet Climber. LC.

Pink
    Climbing Fashion. CFl.
    New Dawn. LC.

Lavender
    Climbing Lavandula. CFl.

Blends
    Climbing Circus. CFl.

Orange-Red
    Climbing Floradora. CFl.
    Gloria Mundi. CPol.
    Orange Triumph. CPol.

White
    Climbing Iceberg. CFl.
    Summer snow. CPol.

Yellow
    Lemon Pillar. LC.
    Climbing Goldilocks. CFl.

Section C. Shrubby Climbers for Landscape Planting

Several large vigorous climbers which are best planted on their own to ramble freely over fences and walls, include the Banksia Rose (*Rosa banksiae*) in white or creamy yellow, and Mermaid (Hybrid of *Rosa bracteata* or McCartney Rose) with large single lemon flowers. Berlin is a semi-climbing or shrub rose with single scarlet flowers; Bonn has orange-scarlet flowers and Climbing Meg has salmon-peach flowers.

WHERE TO PLANT BUSH ROSES IN THE GARDEN

Before ordering one's roses, one must decide on where they are to be planted. There are many places in a garden for roses besides the area set aside especially for them, known as a rose-garden.

Rose-gardens are useful and can be very attractive. They are often concealed so that the roses are not visible during winter when they are bare and they make a delightful place to visit during summer. Having all one's roses together makes it easier for pruning and spraying purposes and they can never be overlooked for any reason. The garden, however, should be one of at least a quarter of an acre if it is to have a separate section devoted exclusively to roses. Rose-gardens are particularly useful when growing Hybrid Teas, which need more severe pruning than other roses and which are used mainly for cutting for the vase.

Another race of roses, the Polyantha and Floribunda roses, have also become popular in recent years and are used in beds for display rather than for cut flowers, although they also last well in the vase. Polyanthas may be grown in the rose-garden and are even attractive when used as a low hedge marking the boundary of the rose-garden. They may also be used in beds in any part of the garden or in groups in the mixed border.

Standard roses are seen, all too often, marching up the side of the driveway, spaced about 6 feet apart. They are far more attractive when planted as a background to bush roses, creating a two-tiered effect, or when planted in a bed and underplanted with dwarf Polyanthas or showy annuals.

Climbers are, of course, suitable for growing against the house and on trellises inside the garden. They are not very good on wire fences on the boundary as they do not provide privacy during winter. Trellises may be erected to enclose the formal rose-garden, to line a pathway or to back the mixed flower border. A very attractive rose "border" can be arranged with climbers on a trellis in the background, standards in front of these and a bed of bush roses in the foreground. This should be placed in a prominent position so that it can be seen when all the roses are in full bloom.

The rose lover will learn to tuck roses into many odd corners of the garden and to grow shrub roses and large climbers as single specimens. Familiarity with roses will teach you how to combine some colours with other plants and to underplant tall varieties of roses with contrasting annuals like violas and ageratum. Plant annuals around roses during summer, but not during winter if possible.

THE ROSE-GARDEN

The rose-garden is generally composed of regular beds which are set into a formal pattern. The beds may be any shape, but they should be at least 5 feet wide so that two rows of roses can be planted in them and the gardener can attend to them while standing on the path between the beds. There should be at least 12 roses to a bed. It is not advisable to set each rose into a circle cut out of the lawn as this interferes with feeding and hampers root growth. A rose-garden on a slightly lower level enables one to look down on the roses.

Pathways between rose beds may be composed of slate, brick, gravel or lawn. It is advisable to use a lawn substitute like Lippia grass, which requires no mowing, rather than ordinary lawn, as this requires so much labour in the way of mowing, cutting the edges and feeding. Even crazy paving with lawn between requires a lot of labour in clipping. It is better to plant annuals like Alyssum, Nierembergia and Portulaca in the joints between the slate or a groundcover like Wonder-Lawn (*Dichondra*) or Carpet Bugle (*Ajuga reptans*).

Depending on the size of the rose-garden and the number of beds in it, one can group roses according to

(1) FORMAL CIRCULAR GARDEN — Will hold about 80 roses in a diameter of 35 feet

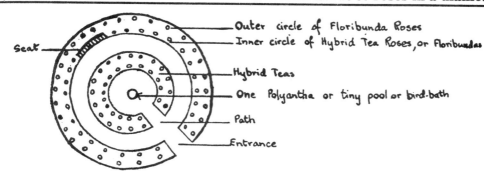

(2) ANOTHER CIRCULAR PLAN

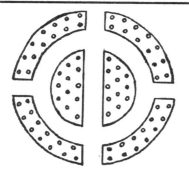

(3) SIMPLE OBLONG ROSE GARDEN

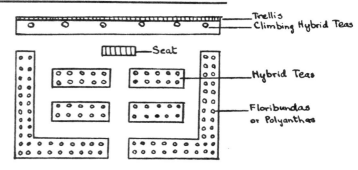

(4) ASYMMETRICAL DESIGN FOR A ROSE GARDEN

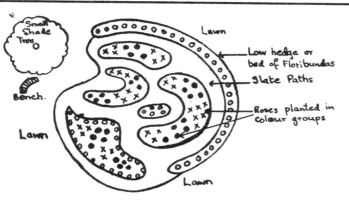

(5) FORMAL, SIMPLE, CLASSIC DESIGN

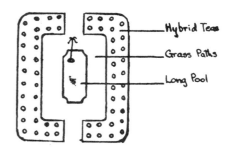

(6) A BORDER OF ROSES — Place so that it can be seen from the front

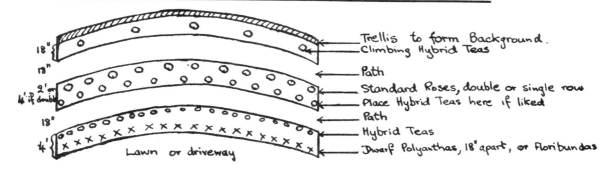

colour and type. It is always advisable to have at least three of one kind of rose. This enables one to have a good splash of colour when they are in bloom and also to be able to pick a bowl of roses all of one colour. If one has too little room, then one can group all the red roses in one bed, pinks in another and yellow in another. These will not be as uniform as they would be if they were of one type, as different roses grow to different heights and there are many different variations to a colour.

Some people like to mix their colours together and the effect may be very pleasant. In doing this, however, one must know the colours of one's roses in order to prevent violent clashes. Separate bright colours with whites or roses with paler, blended colours like Peace. Mixing roses in beds is said to aid the prevention of diseases which attack one type more than another.

When planning the shape of the rose-garden it is pleasant to incorporate a special feature like a tiny pool or a garden seat into the plan. A rose-garden can be made to contain as few as four dozen roses or as many as two or three hundred. The basic designs shown on the opposite page can be increased in size.

Where to Plant a Climbing Rose

A. Against a Wall

(*a*) Provide a trellis made of wood.

Use thin slats of wood nailed together to form an attractive asymmetrical shape against the house, at least 6 inches from the wall to allow for air circulation.

(*b*) Drive nails into the wall and tie the climbing canes to these with pieces of string, 15 to 18 inches long. The string is concealed by summer growth and the plant does not rest on the wall. This allows it plenty of air circulation and enables the blooms to grow out freely in graceful curves. Re-tie the strings each year after pruning.

B. Against a Trellis

Split pole trellises or wooden fences may be erected anywhere in the open garden to form a background to a bed lining a path, to enclose a rose-garden or patio or to separate one part of the garden from another. A simple open construction is best and the roses can be tied to these with raffia each year after pruning. In areas where white ants destroy wood, it is best to fix the supporting poles in the ground with a small concrete block or metal base. In some areas it is sufficient to paint the supports with wood preservatives.

RUSTIC DESIGN. Use twisted and gnarled branches of odd lengths and shapes, placed diagonally on a basic square frame. Plant the climbing rose to one side so as to allow part of the trellis to show.

HOW TO GROW ROSES

Where to Place One's Roses

Roses need as much sunshine as possible in order to thrive and should not be planted near shady trees whose roots will enter into competition with their own or rob them of moisture. An open position with sun all day is ideal, but a minimum of six hours of sunshine is necessary if roses are to thrive. If shade is unavoidable, then afternoon shade is preferable to morning shade.

Type of Soil

Roses grow in nearly every kind of soil, but have a preference for heavy soils that hold them firmly in place. They are one of the few types of plants that seem to thrive on a clay type of soil. No one should avoid growing roses, however, with the assumption that their soil is unsuitable. The addition of sufficient humus will lighten a very clay soil yet give more body to a sandy soil. Sandy soils will require more dressings of compost and should have peatmoss forked into them in large quantities.

SIMPLEST CONSTRUCTION

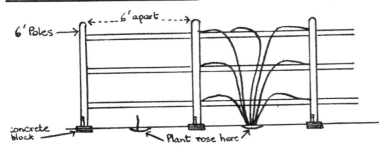

SIMPLE OPEN TRELLIS — Allows view of garden beyond

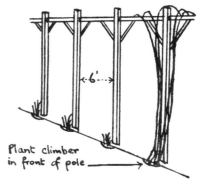

Roses like a slightly acid soil such as is found in most parts of Southern Africa, with a pH of 6 or 6.5. Very acid soils can be treated with lime and very alkaline soils with powdered sulphur or aluminium sulphate to bring them into the correct condition. If the roses seem to thrive anyway, it is unnecessary to worry about changing the alkalinity or acidity of the soil.

Drainage. "Roses must never have wet feet" is the old gardening adage and it is true that drainage for roses must be excellent. To test the drainage in your future rose-garden, dig a hole to two spades' depth and fill it with water. If the water seeps away within a few hours the drainage is satisfactory, otherwise one should either locate the roses elsewhere or improve the drainage.

At one time gardeners thought that it was sufficient to place a pile of stones at the bottom of the hole to take care of the drainage, but where the soil was impervious this served only to collect the water in one spot. The ideal way to improve drainage is to construct terraces on sloping ground on a foundation of plenty of rubble, so that the water drains away perfectly. In areas of heavy summer rains, such as in parts of Rhodesia and the mountain areas of the Transvaal and Natal, this method is strongly recommended. Where the garden is absolutely flat, the beds may be raised above the level of the surrounding paths. This should be done in places where there is a high water table as in parts of the Orange Free State.

In ordinary porous garden soils, the level of the bed should be about an inch below the surrounding paths and in very hot dry climates the level of the bed should be sunk to a depth of 3 or 4 inches below the paths so that irrigating water can collect on the surface.

PREPARATION OF THE SOIL FOR NEW ROSES

If there is a large area to be planted, the soil should be prepared two or three months in advance to allow it to settle properly and be well levelled. If one needs to plant only a few roses in an established rose-garden, the holes may either be prepared well in advance or they may be made only two or three weeks before the roses are expected.

One should dig over and loosen the top 6 inches of soil on a large area for a new garden, then level the ground and mark out the shapes of the beds and paths with the aid of sticks and string. Allow the beds to be 5 feet wide to hold a double row of plants. It is best to place only two rows of roses in a bed so that one does not have to step into the bed when picking roses, but can reach them comfortably from the surrounding paths. The paths between the beds should be about 3 feet across, depending on the design of the garden and the amount of space available.

Each Hybrid Tea or Grandiflora rose should be spaced about 2½ to 3 feet apart and the roses staggered in a double row so that each one will have a maximum of space and soil. Polyanthas and Floribundas can be planted as close as 18 inches apart, while climbing roses should be planted from 6 to 8 feet apart. The position of each rose should be marked by pushing a stick into the soil and the holes can then be prepared for the planting period.

If the rose bed is small it will be better to prepare the whole area of the bed, but it is easier and more economical to dig and prepare individual holes when the rose-garden is large. Dig each hole 24 inches in diameter, first removing the top soil to a depth of 6 inches and setting this aside on the path. Dig out some of the soil below this, removing every stone to a depth of 18 inches from the surface. One bucketful of this subsoil can be removed and replaced with a full bucket of well-rotted manure or manure mixed with compost. The manure must be well mixed with the subsoil and then the mixture can be levelled. The plain topsoil can be put back on top of this, or it can be mixed first with some well-rotted compost or some peatmoss before replacing it. Water the hole in areas where there is no rain for months in winter, so that the soil will settle. Replace the stick in the centre of the hole so as to indicate where to plant the rose when it arrives.

WHEN TO ORDER ROSES

Roses may be ordered at any time from nurserymen, but should not be ordered too soon before planting-out time. It is best to order at least a month before the roses are due to be sent out from the open ground in order to ensure obtaining the required varieties and to get the best plants. One might otherwise have to put up with leftovers or accept other varieties.

WHEN TO PLANT A NEW ROSE

New roses may be bought established in tins like shrubs and planted out into the garden at any time. The more widely accepted and economical practice, however, is to order them from the open ground during the dormant period. Any gaps may be filled in later in the year by paying a little more and buying plants growing in tins.

The chief period for planting roses from the open ground is at the end of winter just before they are about to commence new growth, usually during July and August in Southern Africa. They are shaken free of soil at the nursery, packed in bundles of dampened soil and despatched without delay, ready to be planted immediately on arrival.

A second semi-dormant period in roses occurs after the first midsummer flush of bloom. During this brief two or three-week period in January, roses may also be purchased from the open ground and planted with as little delay as possible. Some nurserymen in the summer rain-fall area prefer planting out at this time because of all the rain and moisture in the air, which helps the roses to become established more quickly than during the hot dry spring months. Gardeners in Rhodesia, who import dormant roses from England at the time of the northern hemisphere's winter, are accustomed to plant out in January with good results. Spring planting, however, gives the roses a longer period in which to become established before the winter and is more generally recommended.

Whichever time of the year is chosen, it may be seen that it is always necessary to plant bare-root roses from the open ground with the greatest haste, so as to give them the best chance to be transplanted successfully. Unnecessary delay and drying out may set them back so that they take longer to begin growth or may even die back altogether. It follows that the ground must be prepared well in advance, for the nurseries have to send out hundreds of orders and roses always seem to arrive at the most inopportune moments. Everything should be set aside and the roses planted as soon as possible after arrival.

If one is forced to delay planting, keep the unopened bundle in a cool shady place for a day or two. If they must be kept for a longer period, up to two weeks, it is best to unpack the bundle and bury the roses completely in a trench of soft soil, keeping the soil moist. This treatment will make the buds plump. Rose plants that appear dry and shrivelled on arrival may also be buried in this way for a few days to swell them.

Roses may also be "heeled in" while awaiting planting. This means stacking them half-upright in the ground and covering the roots and half the stem with soft soil before watering. They should be "heeled in" in a cool place where they cannot dry out in the sun.

How to Plant a New Rose

If one receives roses in a good healthy condition one can plant them straight from the bundle. If it is a hot day, it is advisable to wait until the cool of the afternoon before unpacking and planting. Keep the moistened bundle in the shade of a nearby tree and open it only to remove a few roses at a time for immediate planting. Keep these in a pail or small bath of water in the shade whilst awaiting their turn. During very cold spells it is perhaps best not to soak the roses, but merely to wrap them in moistened sacking. Always keep the dry air from the roots except for the few moments that it takes to remove them from the bundle to the waiting hole.

Preparation Immediately Before Planting

The hole that was prepared for the new rose in advance of its arrival must be opened just before planting, by removing the topsoil to a depth of about 5 inches. If desired, this topsoil could have been left standing at the side of the hole when it was originally dug, but it is apt to look untidy and be dispersed if left too long. The hole should now be large enough to allow the roots to spread naturally.

If there are any broken roots or stems on the new rose, these should be cut off neatly and quickly. Roses from a reliable nursery usually arrive properly pruned and are invariably healthy. If they require shortening or shaping, this should be done rapidly before planting. Always cut above an outward facing bud and seal the new cut with tree-sealing compound after the rose is planted. Any rose that appears to be diseased should be discarded immediately. Rough swellings at the crown, which may indicate crown gall, or swellings on the roots should not simply be cut off, hoping for the best. Such a rose will die later and be a source of infection to other roses. The nursery would prefer to be notified of the disease and probably be glad to replace the plant. Luckily, such an occurrence is rare, but it is as well to be prepared for it.

Judging the Depth to Plant the New Rose

Arrange a small mound or cone of the fine topsoil at the base of the hole and place the new rose tree on top of this. If the new plant consists of one shoot growing out at an angle from the stock, hold the stock at an angle so that the shoot is upright. Rest a stick horizontally over the open hole to act as a guide. The bud union, which is the lump at the base of the stem from which new growth springs, should be just below the level of the stick. Heap a little more soil up on the mound beneath the rose or remove some in order to attain the correct height. When the rose is planted, this bud union should be just below the surface of the soil and not more than an inch below ground level.

If one places the bud union two or more inches below the surface this may lead to decay and failure. If one places it a couple of inches above the ground, however, this leads to drying out and new shoots will not be encouraged to grow freely from the union. Consequently, the life of the rose may be shortened as it does not replenish itself sufficiently with new wood. In places where roses are killed back to the ground by frost, the soil covering over the bud union will protect any dormant buds which will put forth new growth in spring.

PLANTING THE NEW ROSE

Holding the rose upright in the hole while it rests on the soil mound, press the ends of the roots down gently into the soil. The roots must not curl upwards or be bunched together, neither must they be folded under. Then sprinkle fine soil into all the spaces between and beneath the roots until they are covered. Press this soil down firmly with the palms of the hands. Next, add a few spadefuls of topsoil, spreading it evenly around the plant. It helps to have an assistant holding the rose firmly while adding the soil. When the hole is about three-quarters full, place one's feet on either side of the plant and tread around it gently, allowing the weight of the body to pack down the soil and give the rose firm anchorage. Press the soil firmly around the stem of the rose so that it will not wobble about when touched. Never jerk the rose upwards to test its firmness, for fear of tugging at the delicate feeding roots.

The hole may now be filled with two gallons of water which is allowed to soak down completely. Next, fill the remaining loose soil into the hole, mixing some fine compost into it if possible, and level off the surface with the hand. Each rose should be planted in a "basin" with a 2–3 inch rim of soil around the edge to hold water. Another two gallons of water may now be poured gently around the edges of the "basin" and allowed to sink down. If desired, all the watering can be done after the hole is filled, but the top layer of soil must be kept loose.

The rose must now be kept moist by watering regularly in this way for at least a month. It should be given about 4 gallons every third or fourth day, depending on the porous quality of the soil and whether the weather is warm or cold. In places which have a hot, dry spring, it helps to place straw or hessian loosely around the stems to prevent drying out. This straw also protects the plants from frost damage. Some people mound up their plants with a few inches of loose soil, but one must be very careful when removing this in spring in case one damages new growth.

Standard Roses must be staked and the stakes should be driven into the holes before the rose is planted in order to avoid damaging the roots. The stakes should be sharpened and buried a foot below ground, with the top reaching the base of the bushy head. Place the stake on the north side to shade the stem and wrap it with hessian for the first year to prevent scorch. A piece of hessian should be tied around the stem of the rose and secured with string. This string should then be tied around the stake without allowing the stem to rub up against it. The hessian should be tied in a different position each year, in order to prevent damaging the stem. Rub off any growth that may appear on the stem.

CARE OF ESTABLISHED ROSES

Feeding Established Roses. It is not necessary, or even advisable, to feed new roses for the first year. After the first winter pruning, these, as well as older established roses, should be given a heaped spadeful of old kraal manure, laid on the surface as a mulch and watered in. This supplies nitrogen and organic material to the soil. Woodash, which provides extra potash, may be sprinkled around the roses and watered in.

One should fertilize roses about two or three times a year, using a general garden fertilizer like 6 : 3 : 2 or a rose fertilizer like 2 : 1 : 2. Give each rose a heaped tablespoon at each application, spreading it in a circle on the soil about 6 or 8 inches from the base of the plant. Work it in lightly and water it in immediately. Never allow fertilizer to touch the stems or leaves, especially when these are wet or they may be burned.

The first application may be given early in the spring, about mid-August. Fertilizer should always be given after the first flush of bloom in October, at any time in November. Follow this with another application one month later. A mulch of well-rotted manure or compost may be given during summer. Do not feed roses in any way after February or this may stimulate tender new growth that will be injured in winter. One may suspect trace element deficiencies if the leaves show signs of chlorosis, but trace elements should not be added indiscriminately or they may do more harm than good. (See Trace Element Deficiencies in Chapter 17 on "The Fertile Soil".)

Watering Established Roses. Roses should be watered at least twice a week throughout the summer months when there has been no rain. It is best to do this on regular days each week so as to make certain that the plants are not watered erratically. It is best to water at soil level by allowing the hosepipe to fill the "basin" around each rose with about 4 gallons of water. The water should trickle slowly into the hole without washing the soil away from the roots, soaking the soil to a depth of at least a foot. Light sprinklings dry out quickly and cause shallow rooting so that the rose cannot survive hot weather. The use of a water-breaker enables one to water quickly without eroding the soil. (See Chapter 18.)

Watering by means of an overhead sprinkler is permissible only if done before midday, so that the leaves can have at least five or six hours in which to dry off before the evening. Black spot penetrates leaves that are allowed to be wet for too long. Overhead sprinkling also washes off protective fungicides on the leaves. Special nozzles can be fitted to irrigation pipes, spraying the water sideways so that the ground is soaked without wetting the foliage.

Try to water regularly without overwatering at odd times or the plants will not be able to withstand periods of drought. Be careful not to overwater as autumn approaches, for it is not wise to encourage too much succulent growth that will be tender to frost. Towards the end of autumn, in April, one can reduce watering to once a week, unless there is a hot spell. During May one can lengthen the intervals between waterings, until, in June and July, once in two or three weeks is sufficient. In the winter rainfall area of the Cape, it is particularly important to have excellent drainage so that water runs off quickly.

Mulching Roses. Thick mulches around roses conserve moisture and keep down weeds as they do with other plants. (See Chapter 18). Cocoa bean husks make an excellent mulch for roses. Good mulches are layers of compost, old leaves or peatmoss laid down each spring. Peatmoss must be well-moistened or it will absorb water from the soil and cake on the surface. These mulches will be incorporated into the soil by the end of the season. Pine needles may be used in some places.

Mulches like grass clippings, sawdust and cottonseed husks, unless the soil is treated with termite-repelling insecticides, are to be avoided in most parts of the summer rainfall area of Southern Africa, as they attract white ants (termites) which will make short work of the woody rose stems. Mulches must not make the roses too wet or encourage too much sappy growth which may be damaged by sudden cold.

Dwarf annuals like portulaca and pansies, which are grown around rose-bushes in summer, act indirectly as a mulch. The extra water that they require is beneficial to the roses and their foliage helps to shade the soil. Annuals should not be grown around roses during winter, however, as this prevents the roses from having a rest period and also hinders winter cleaning up against disease.

Spraying Roses. Immediately after winter pruning, roses should be sprayed thoroughly with lime-sulphur as a general cleansing spray, as it is a combined insecticide and fungicide. This will help to prevent scale insect infestation and fungus diseases.

Green aphids trouble roses from the time the first shoots appear and must be controlled by hand or by spraying with one of the many insecticides available. (See Chapter 37 on Insect Control.) Keep a weekly check on these and other common insect pests like red spider, thrips or mealybugs which may appear.

Keep down ants in rose-gardens, for these disturb ladybirds which are the natural enemies of aphids and so increase insect infestation. (See under Ants, Chapter 37.) Rose or chafer beetles can be controlled by dusting the leaves with DDT from November until such time as they disappear naturally. Do this only if absolutely necessary as ladybirds may be killed by the same insecticides. Anything that causes the leaves to be injured or to drop off must be watched and checked as this weakens the rose bush and may lead to die-back.

Black Spot and Powdery Mildew are the most serious fungus diseases of roses and are difficult to control. Mulching roses prevents spores from rising up to infect the leaves and one must sweep up and burn infected foliage. Avoid wetting the leaves by watering after midday. Dust the foliage with one of several recommended fungicides as a preventative, commencing at the start of the rainy season and continuing every week or fortnight during summer and autumn. (See Chapter 38 on Fungus Diseases.) Check the ventilation of plants that suffer from Powdery Mildew and move them if necessary.

CHAPTER THIRTY-ONE

PRUNING

Roses, Fruit Trees, Shrubs and Trees

INTRODUCTION

Pruning—Is it a Worry or a Pleasure?

To prune means to trim or cut away superfluous branches. This is a simple statement for what usually turns out to be a complicated garden operation. The fact that complicates the process is that it is performed by different individuals on different plants, no two of which are alike. To the novice who is trying to pin down an old hand to showing him exactly what to do, pruning always seems to be a puzzle. There are certainly some general rules to guide one, but the details of carrying them out will always vary with the individual. As one gains more and more experience, one also gains tolerance and realises that is is not necessary to have hard and fast rules when dealing with plants.

Pruning is really a fascinating operation, as anyone who has attended a pruning demonstration by an expert will tell you. To watch a rose bush or fruit tree being systematically shaped before your eyes has almost the same fascination as watching a hole being dug out by earth-movers for a new building. A "pruner-watcher" has an advantage over the "hole-watcher" in that he can anticipate the pruner's next move in his own mind and, if he is wrong, no one need know about it. If he is right, then there is a glow of satisfaction as a reward. The satisfaction may not come very often, let me hasten to say, as very few people will do the same thing in the same circumstances. Pruning calls for the individual assessment of each plant, owing to the fact that each plant has a different shape to begin with.

When you are finally confronted with your very own rose or fruit tree, which seems to have a diabolically different shape from any other that has ever been seen, then the feelings of inadequacy rise up and make you wish to hand over the pruning tasks to the nearest willing worker. But wait a while before doing this, or you will be depriving yourself of interest and your plants of the special care that cannot be bought. This is the individual thought and attention that is not limited by the amount of time that can be spent on each specimen. It is hoped that the following guidance will help you to attempt your own pruning in a relaxed and confident way that wil bring good results and turn anxiety into pleasure.

THE REASONS FOR PRUNING

Roses and Fruit Trees. We prune in order to obtain better fruit or better blooms. At the same time we wish to strengthen a healthy plant that will bear for many years to come. We do not prune in order to enter our roses or fruit trees in a contest for shapeliness, yet a well-pruned bush will have a trim and attractive appearance without our consciously striving for it.

Flowering Shrubs and Trees. We prune these in order to obtain better flowers in some cases and also to improve the general shape of the plant, for example, by checking uneven growth and developing standards on some shrubs and trees.

Pruning when doing Other Tasks. Pruning also takes place when attending to the following tasks:

Trimming. This is essentially for shaping plants like hedges. No thinning out is practised. (See Hedges, Chapter 6.)

Training. When training grapes or roses on to trellises and walls, the plants must first be pruned and then trained on to supports. Creepers can be trained in a pattern and superfluous growth removed.

Transplanting. When transplanting deciduous woody plants, the roots will be cut and the top should be reduced accordingly. Evergreens may only require slight trimming or stripping of leaves.

Repairing. This is known as Tree Surgery. It involves reshaping old, mature or decrepit trees and repairing broken, badly pruned or decayed trees. (See Chapter 29 on Trees and Shrubs.)

Cutting Flowers. When cutting roses for the vase, we cut above an outward-facing bud and follow the principles of pruning. When cutting flowering shrubs for the vase, we do not destroy the shape of the bush.

THE PRINCIPLES OF PRUNING

The idea of pruning is based on nature's example of dropping twigs and flowers and retaining only the best branches of trees. Knots on trees indicate the healed

Late-flowering Daffodils (*Narcissus*) to extend the daffodil season: *Top row:* Pink Select, Tonda, La Rianta, Actea. *Centre row:* Mt. Hood, Mrs. R. O. Backhouse, Mary Copeland, Mercato, Yellow Cheerfulness. *Bottom row:* Cheerfulness, Aranjuez, Semper Avanti, Daphne, Geranium.

Like all dahlias, these Cactus Dahlias are prolific bloomers, easy to grow and multiply freely. They last well in the vase.

Hippeastrum (*Amaryllis*) may be planted singly in pots and grouped on steps near the entrance when in bloom.

Purple Wreath (*Petrea volubilis*) is a spectacular climber enhanced by the nearby red Flowering Peach in spring.

In this Johannesburg garden the Hydrangeas (*H. macrophylla*) are thriving in the half shade of a Jacaranda tree.

The double Poinsettia (*Euphorbia pulcherrima*), which is all the more showy when it loses its leaves during dry winters inland, must be given a warm, sheltered position in cold localities.

Climbers soften the walls of a house. The glorious Bougainvillea "Killie Campbell" spreads a dramatic curtain at this entrance.

Every garden should find space for the Nodding Pincushion (*Leucospermum nutans*), a spreading, free-flowering, indigenous shrub particularly suited to rocky slopes.

Erect a wire arbour which will be transformed by the pendant sprays of Wistaria each spring. Orange Clivia (*C. miniata*) grows in its shade and blooms at the same time. Spring flowers *Venidium*, Anemones, Ranunculus and Violas enhance the foreground.

wounds left by nature's pruning, but knot-holes indicate decay. We improve on nature's pruning by removing old, broken or diseased wood on trees before decay can set in and by severing these with a clean cut, which we seal until the wound heals. Regular annual pruning of small branches prevents decay, for if we wait until a branch is very large before severing it, we leave a large wound instead of a small one. Large wounds invite decay more than small ones, which heal more quickly.

For this reason, we hesitate to cut into the old wood of roses or fruit trees. The large area of the cut exposes the plant to disease. It is also unlikely that old woody branches will put forth new shoots. The only time we are forced to cut into old wood is when we have to reshape an old, badly-pruned plant which has no new growth to take its place. Normally, we simply cut the old wood right out and allow vigorous new wood to replace it.

In the case of roses and fruit trees, where we want good quality of flowers and fruit, we also thin out healthy wood in order to reduce the competition of too many branches bearing blooms or fruit. The energy of the plant is diverted into stronger parts which can produce fewer and better fruit or flowers. This reduction in quantity of fruit also prevents the tree from being overloaded. The thinning out process removes weak or badly formed branches as well as branches which interfere with one another's growth by touching each other and crossing over one another. While removing such branches, we admit sunshine and air and keep the tops of the fruit trees or rose bushes open.

Pruning stimulates growth and a slow plant may grow better after cutting back. But pruning is not the only remedy that will ensure the vigour of the tree. Nutrition and adequate moisture are most important. The enthusiastic novice must not wield the shears indiscriminately or he may do more harm than good. Plants should be pruned only when necessary and allowed to develop their natural shapes. The whole character of a flowering shrub can be destroyed by clipping, for pruning not only corrects faults but develops the plant's desirable attributes. It is better to prune too little than to overprune.

The danger of overpruning fruit trees is that by removing too much top growth, the root energy is diverted into producing more wood at the top which does not bear fruit. If heavy pruning continues, the tree produces shoots at the expense of fruit. This leads to a vicious circle of having to prune more to clear the inside of the tree and a possible reduction in the crop. Light annual pruning keeps the tree bearing without developing too much wood. Hard pruning is only done when a neglected tree must be re-shaped and brought back into bearing

condition. Root pruning is sometimes practised to lessen the amount of nutrition taken up by the roots so that there is less growth at the top, but this should only be performed when all other pruning fails.

In hot dry places, where too much sunshine may scald the bark of trees, one should thin out less than in cool humid areas.

On the whole, therefore, fruit trees should be allowed to retain their natural form and one should simply remove superfluous wood and keep them within manageable size. Training on to walls, trellises and cordons should only be practised where space is very limited. These methods require attention, labour and specialised knowledge.

By following the golden rules of pruning, listed below, we indirectly improve the shape of the bush, maintain its healthy growth and limit its branches to strong-growing stems that produce the best roses or fruit.

GOLDEN RULES OF PRUNING ROSES OR FRUIT TREES

A. We remove dead wood.

This is now useless and will only deprive the plant of sunlight and room for growth as well as harbour pests. It often causes the healthy wood below it to die back.

B. We remove old wood.

Nature starves and discards old wood. We hasten its removal so that growth can be directed into the production of new, vigorous flowering wood.

C. We remove weak twigs.

These only clutter the plant and use some of the nutrition which should be conserved for the strong stems that produce good flowers or fruit.

D. We remove superfluous wood.

This includes branches that cross over or rub up against one another or branches that fill up the centre of the tree and exclude light. We thin out some good growths in order to space remaining branches into a strong framework.

E. We shorten the remaining stems.

Shortening the main stems keeps the fruit tree low for harvesting. Shortening leaders and side branches by half strengthens the remaining portion and stimulates new growth from the top bud below the cut.

A FEW "DON'TS"

Do not:
1. Overprune.
2. Cut into old wood unless absolutely essential.
3. Remove old wood if there is no new wood to take its place.

SECTION I

PRUNING OF ROSES

Roses must be pruned regularly or their flowers will deteriorate and the bush will gradually die back. Whether one has half-a-dozen roses or a hundred, one must understand how to prune them or one will not enjoy beautiful blooms on healthy bushes that will bear for 20 years or more.

Try your best to prune your own roses rather than allow a stranger to do your pruning for you. You will remember how your roses have behaved in the previous season—whether they grew vigorously and had good flowers or not. The real expert will, of course, be able to prune roses successfully without having seen them beforehand, but pruning does not only occur once in a season. All cuts to a rose bush may be regarded as part of the pruning operation and the owner of the garden will have to know something of pruning in order to treat his roses correctly all through the year, even when cutting roses for the vase or removing faded flowers. The advantage of doing your own pruning is that you can see how the roses grow as a result of your cutting and so gain further experience. Also pruning should be done carefully, and, unless one is very confident, slowly. A cut which is carefully done takes time and will not lead to die-back. The gardener who is not so pressed for time will prune more satisfactorily than someone who must, of necessity, finish all the bushes on the same day.

Pruning is not an exact science, but a practical operation based on reasoning. Everyone's ideas are slightly different and there are always new trends to follow, but the general principles are what count in pruning, plus some common-sense. Remember that you are dealing with a living plant that will continue to grow and produce flowers even if it has not been given the best shape in the world. Treat it with consideration, without either lopping off branches too enthusiastically or letting it be smothered with twiggy growth, and it will reward you with choice blooms for your garden and for your vase.

It is not difficult to prune roses once the simple basic principles are understood. Apart from the fact that bush roses, standard roses and climbing roses are pruned differently because of their shapes, one must also realise that they belong to different groups of roses that must be pruned by different methods. It is essential to know a little about these groups of roses so as to understand why their pruning differs. (See Chapter 30 on "Cultivation of Roses".)

WHEN TO PRUNE ROSES

The time to prune most roses is when the leaves have fallen in winter and the plant is in a dormant state. Some roses must be pruned after flowering when they are in leaf, while corrective pruning may be done at intervals throughout the year.

Winter pruning varies with the climate. It must be realised that pruning stimulates new growth about three weeks after it has taken place. In cold areas, tender new shoots emerging too soon from their winter dormancy may be nipped off and destroyed by late frosts. Secondary shoots sent out later will not be as well placed as the original ones and there may also be further frost damage leading to die-back. One must time one's pruning so that new growth will take place when all danger of severe frost has passed and when the sap is ready to rise and produce new shoots. In the cooler parts of Southern Africa, therefore, pruning should take place towards the end of winter and not in early or mid-winter. The best calendar time to prune is during the last week in July. A week earlier or later will not make much difference, but no matter how cold the weather, roses should not be pruned later than mid-August or the flower crop will be delayed too long.

In places with mild winters, roses may be pruned at any time in July for convenience, but the last week in July is the best as it marks the end of the dormant period and the start of new growth. Roses may never lose all their leaves in mild climates and go on producing blooms throughout winter. Disregard the appearance of the bush and prune the roses just as if they were bare. Remove all old leaves that remain on the bush after pruning in order to ensure that they will not carry any disease present over to the next season.

If one is a serious exhibitor at flower shows, one can delay or advance the time of blooming according to the time when the roses are pruned. Make a note of the date when the roses were pruned and then take note of when the different varieties bloom. If they bloom too late or too early for the show, prune some varieties earlier or later as required.

Spring-flowering roses like climbing Polyanthas should be pruned in summer immediately after they have flowered, in the same way as spring-flowering shrubs. They do not need any further pruning in winter. Bush Polyanthas that bloom twice in summer may be pruned after the first flowering period and once more during winter.

Corrective pruning may take place at intervals throughout the year. Dead wood can be removed at any time and flowers must be cut correctly whether they are to be used for the vase or removed in order to prevent seed formation. One may correct pruning errors during spring.

If certain dormant buds have not developed, a further cut may be necessary. Young growths which are developing inwards may be rubbed off with discretion and very weak straggly growths may be cut out.

Keep a watch for fresh basal shoots and do not imagine that they are all unwanted suckers coming up from the wild roots. Scrape away the soil to see whether they come from below the bud union or not. If they do, they are suckers and should be removed immediately. If they spring from the bud union or from above it, then they are the valuable new shoots that will eventually replace the old flowering wood of the bush. Pinch back the tips of these when they are about 12 inches long, in order to encourage branching and hardening. Long growths which have shot up rapidly can be shortened to about 2 feet in length during summer.

Tools Required for Pruning Roses

Pruning shears or secateurs, of medium weight, which fit comfortably into the hand, are essential. These are inexpensive and can be purchased from seedsmen or hardware stores. There are numerous makes, any of which is suitable, provided that it has good strong blades that will cut through a branch cleanly, without tearing at it and leaving rough edges that provide an entry for disease. Extra blades may be purchased for some makes. Hand-pruning shears will remain in use for the remainder of the year while cutting flowers for the vase.

Pruning Saw. This is essential when dealing with climbers which have stout stems or with bushes that are more than two years old. The best type of saw is a light one that has a narrow, $\frac{1}{2}$-inch blade that can be turned in any direction with the aid of a screw or other device. This enables one to insert the saw into the base of the bush and saw off any branch easily at any awkward angle without damaging other branches nearby or changing one's position frequently. The blades should be replaceable and kept sharp.

Gloves will protect the hands from thorns and abrasions, enabling one to proceed more quickly.

Other Materials to Assemble

A tin for depositing small pieces of infected wood, if any.

A rag dipped in disinfectant for wiping the blades of tools in case one cuts into infected wood.

A tin of bituminous tree-sealing compound and several short sticks with which to dab it on.

HOW TO MAKE A CUT

The golden rule for cutting the stem of a rose, whether pruning or whether cutting blooms for the vase, is to cut above a bud. When making a cut, one should always cut on the slant.

How to Recognise a Bud

Everyone can recognise an unopened flower-bud that will unfurl into a full-blown bloom. The buds on the stem of a rose, however, are neither as large nor as obvious. When examining the bare branches in winter, one can see tiny bumps at intervals up the stems. These are the buds, which are also sometimes called "eyes". The buds are dormant shoots which will develop into stems bearing flowers and foliage. During summer, one cannot see the buds so clearly, but they are always present just above the joint where the leaf springs from the main stem. When cutting flowers during summer, therefore, cut just above a leaf.

Why We Cut Above a Bud

Every portion of a branch must be put to use and the smallest piece of branch that has no work to do will wither and die. Dead wood seems to make the healthy stem beneath it die and this causes what is known as "die-back" and the subsequent deterioration of the whole bush.

The sap rises to the top of a stem and puts forth new growth at a bud. There are many buds along the stem, but the fresh sap always rises right to the top bud and the flow stimulates new growth at that point. If there is no passage-way above it, the sap will be diverted into the bud and strongly stimulate its growth as soon as winter is over. When cutting the stem above a bud, one must cut as close to the bud as possible without damaging it with the pruning shears, otherwise the small portion of stem above it, being useless, will die and so threaten the whole healthy stem with the danger of die-back.

For the same reason, when cutting weak, twiggy growths off the main stems, cut as close to the main stem as possible, so that no tiny useless stumps are allowed to remain. Also, when cutting side growths off climbing Hybrid Teas, do not leave short stumps, but be careful not to damage the bud close to the stem, the basal bud, that will send out the new season's flowering shoot.

The Direction of the Bud

By cutting off the stem above a bud, we can encourage the sap to travel in the direction that we wish it to go and so control the shape of our bush. By choosing a bud which is situated on the outside of the stem and severing the stem above this outward-facing bud, we stimulate the bud to grow and so force the new stem to grow outwards. By cutting above a bud pointing sideways or inwards, we force a new stem to grow in these directions.

When pruning, it is always customary to choose an outward-facing bud so that the bush will remain open in the centre and receive air and sunshine. There is an exception to this rule in the case of the rose Crimson Glory, which is cut above an upward or inward-facing bud in order to prevent it from sprawling on the ground. (See page 181.)

Cutting Correctly on the Slant

When cutting above an outward-facing bud, one should point the secateur in the direction that the new stem is expected to take and cut at an angle of about 45 degrees to the ground. The new shoot grows out at this angle and one aims to make the cut parallel to the direction in which the new branch is expected to grow. Hold the secateur with the tip of the blade pointing upwards and, starting from the opposite side of the bud and level with it, aim to finish the cut just above it. Allow just under $\frac{1}{4}$ of an inch of stem to remain above the bud. Do not cut closer to the bud than $\frac{1}{8}$ of an inch or it might be damaged by the compression of the main stem. A sharp secateur will sever the stem quickly without squeezing it and consequently damaging the bud. It is in order to prevent squeezing the stem that some people use a pruning knife, but this might result in one's fingers being cut instead of the stem, as it is not easy to handle a pruning knife. When commencing the cut with the secateur, do not start the slanting cut lower than the level at which the bud is situated on the stem, or this will weaken the junction of the new branch.

The angle of the cut enables moisture to run off easily and so avoid stem rot. The cut should never be made straight across. This angle cut is made whether one removes a long piece or a short one and whether one shortens a main stem or a short leader. (See illustrations, page 224.)

Picking Roses for the Vase

Whenever one cuts roses for the vase during summer, one must remember to cut above the bud which is situated at the base of a leaf growing outwards and at an angle, as described above. It is advisable to pick one's own roses always and not allow anyone to help themselves to the flowers unless they understand how to cut correctly. When picking roses, one is practising summer pruning which will affect the welfare of the plant.

The length of stem one should remove varies according to the time of the year. Cut roses with short stems in spring or early summer and with longer stems from mid-summer onwards. It is important to leave as much foliage on the plants as possible during the first half of summer as this is needed for the manufacture of food for flowers and new growth. When cutting blooms with short stems, leave from five to seven healthy leaves on each shoot and even when removing roses with long stems, leave two or three healthy leaves at the base. Do not retain too many leaves in late summer or too many shoots will grow out from the axils of the leaves and the more numerous flowers produced on these will be short-stemmed and inferior.

One must not allow roses to set seed and faded flowers should be removed before all the petals have dropped. They must not be twisted off at the tips, but cut off in the same way as fresh blooms or this will also lead to the production of numerous inferior flowers. Blooms should not be removed with any length of stem from new roses. Faded flowers should be cut off above the first leaf and the length of stem can be increased towards the end of the first summer.

When cutting clusters of flowers from hybrid Polyanthas and Floribundas, remove at least 4 or 5 inches from the main stem and do not cut immediately below the base of the cluster. The whole head should be cut for the vase when the centre buds have opened. Very much longer stems can be cut from climbing Polyanthas and Floribundas, which must be pruned after flowering in any case.

Roses last best if they are picked in the late afternoon or evening and stood in deep water overnight before arranging. Scrape the bark off the bottom inch of the stem to assist water absorption.

STEP BY STEP DETAILS OF HOW TO PRUNE ROSES

One must first remove dead or diseased wood, then shape the rose according to its group. Different groups of Roses must be pruned by different methods. (See details below.) Hybrid Teas form the most desirable and popular group of modern roses, although they require more careful pruning than any other type of rose. They will be dealt with first. The following types will be detailed separately in this section:

Bush Roses—Hybrid Teas, Hybrid Perpetuals, Polyantha and Floribunda Roses, Shrub Roses, Miniature Roses.

Standards—Mainly Hybrid Teas, also Polyanthas.

Climbers—Climbing Hybrid Teas and Ramblers (including large-flowered climbers and climbing Polyanthas and Floribundas).

PRUNING BUSH ROSES

Theories on Pruning Hybrid Teas

Ideas on pruning Hybrid Teas have changed in recent years. There have been many theories about the merits of hard or low pruning and light or high pruning.

In cold climates with plenty of rain where growth was very prolific, it was customary to prune the bushes hard back to within a foot of the ground, so as to check growth and keep the bushes low in order to cover them in winter as a protection against frost. In recent years, however, the theory developed that the more foliage a plant has on it the healthier it becomes. Constant removal of too much wood exhausts roses as they are robbed of their leaves which manufacture the food for good blooms and growth. The practice known as light, high or long pruning then evolved, in which case the main stems were allowed to grow to a height of 3 to 4 feet. Light pruning could only be practised in mild climates, however, for severe frost cut the tops back severely. Medium or moderate pruning remains the best method for all varieties and is the course most people prefer to take. This represents the happy medium between the two methods and means shortening the main stems by about half of their length and training the bush to a height of about 2 or 3 feet from the ground.

The fact that made gardeners first cut back their bushes severely was that they noticed that the harder they cut back their bushes, the more growth these put on in the following season. The saying evolved, "the harder the pruning the stronger the growth". They did not realise that the plant would eventually exhaust itself in trying to replace the lost growth each year. One can make use of this tendency, however, in order to influence the growth of different varieties of roses in the season following pruning. If one wishes a weak rose bush to grow vigorously one should prune it hard back. If one wishes a vigorous rose bush to grow more moderately, then one must prune it more lightly.

The fact that was not realised in hard pruning was that by continually cutting back the same stems, new growth was only taking place at the top of old stems, which became woody with age and incapable of putting forth tender new shoots lower down. If the top wood failed to put on new growth the rose might die back or, at any rate, never develop new stems and a better shape. By eliminating some old wood at the base each year, it means that every new main stem that emerges from the grafted Hybrid Tea Rose will remain present, for about three to four years and finally take its turn in being removed. There is, therefore, a constant succession of new wood and the bush is continuously being replenished. A rose can be expected to keep on flowering for 20 years or more if it is well cared for.

Shaping and Re-shaping. In spite of whether you believe in light pruning or not, do not hesitate to cut an old bush hard back if it has had a bad start or needs re-shaping through faulty pruning. Drastic action is permissible occasionally. For example, a new bush might have developed only one long stem, shooting out at an angle from the base with a tuft of branches at the top. It is best to cut such a bush right down to within 8 inches from the ground and wait for it to develop a new bushy shape from that point. In other words, one can cut into old wood only if it is necessary to reshape the plant and encourage branching.

It might be necessary to be more ruthless with young plants at the end of the first year than in later years. That is the best time to cut it back and try to develop a shapely, well balanced framework. Some people believe that the hard cutting back of a rose after the first year gives the roots a chance to develop with the upper growth, but this may only retard top growth. Development will be ensured by good feeding rather than by removal of the top growth.

PRUNING HYBRID TEA ROSES

Hybrid Teas bloom on young wood that is developed in the current year of growth. The new shoots are all-important. These may arise from the base above the budded union with the roots and produce flowers in the same season. This young vigorous wood will produce good flowers for about three years, but should then be removed in favour of fresh young wood coming up annually to take its place.

To begin with, one must study each plant as an individual. The general idea is to open up the centre of the bush so that sunlight may enter and to clear space for the development of flowers, to encourage the growth of new flowering wood, to cut out old or dead wood and to remove small insignificant twigs.

Cutting out Old Wood and Dead Wood

Do not gaze at the tangled mass of branches and make a worry of each one. Before trying to decide where to cut, squat down and look into the heart of the bush. There, at ground level, you will be able to distinguish between the old gnarled branches and thick young vigorous stems. Cut out the old wood that is at least three years old at ground level or a little higher, at the point above a joint where a vigorous young main stem has grown outwards at a good outward-facing angle. Remember to make the cut on a slant, parallel to the direction of the new main stem. This one cut will often rid you of a forest of small twigs with one stroke.

If there is not sufficient new wood to take the place of the old wood, then it is better to delay the removal of the old wood for another season, in the hope that the rose will develop plenty of new wood if it is well fed, watered and sprayed. If the rose is younger than three years, there will be no old wood to remove at the base. Dead branches should also be removed at the base or just above an outward-facing bud on healthy wood beneath it.

If one is not sure about which old wood to remove, proceed with opening up the centre of the bush so that one has a better idea of the framework of the plant.

Opening the Centre of the Bush

One must remove the inward-facing branches that fill the centre of the bush. By cutting these as close to the main stems as possible, the bulk of the twigs at the centre of the bush will be cleared quickly. Continue cutting off all short twiggy growths which are pointing into the centre of the bush, without leaving any short stumps. When all this preliminary trimming has been done on the inside, it is much easier to turn one's attention to the main stems and decide what to remove on the outside of these.

Pruning the Main Stems

The thick main stems, each with numerous twigs and branches, must be pruned separately before deciding which of these to retain. Some may have to be removed, for the aim is to retain from three to five stems, depending on the vigour of the bush. Strong-growing roses should be allowed to retain more main stems than weak ones. (See Theories, above.) One should prune these main stems first before deciding which to remove, if any. It is easier to space them evenly after they have been pruned.

First remove the thin twigs which spring from the sides of the main stem. One then remains with vigorous main stems bearing numerous strong side branches. One must remove some of these in order to have a clean main stem with perhaps a fork midway or near the base.

If there are two branches crossing over one another, remove one, always retaining the healthier, stronger-growing one if possible. If there are three stems near the top, all equally strong and scarcely differing in size, cut out the central stem first, as this is generally the oldest. Remove a second branch if the remaining branches are too close.

If there are two outwardly-facing side branches from the same main stem, one above the other, growing at the same angle, it is a matter of choice which to remove. One should note the height of the other main stems and leave either the higher or lower branch if this matches the other heights. One should keep the younger and healthier growth if it is vigorous enough and not thinner than a pencil. If one of the branches dips into a loop

before ascending, discard it in favour of the straighter one, even though the straighter may be older and not in such good condition. Moisture can settle on the loop and the branch may break at that point.

While examining your bush in order to decide which branches to remove, keep a look-out for insect holes and cut below them. If you cut across a stem and find it hollow, make cuts further down at short intervals until you come to healthy wood. A wasp enters the stem through the freshly cut end which has not been sealed with bituminous compound and hollows it out to act as a nest for its eggs. This injury causes die-back on the rose.

Shortening Main Stems

When all the superfluous growth has been removed from the main stems, one must then decide where to cut the top of each main stem. It must be cut above a good outward-facing bud so as to encourage the growth of a new outward-facing stem at that point. Always cut the main stem across at an angle so as to allow the moisture to run off it. This outward-facing bud will grow into a strong stem which is then called a "leader". (See illustrations on page 224.) At the end of the season, this leader must be shortened by approximately two-thirds of its length, again above a suitable outward-facing bud. In this way, the rose bush grows taller with the years, until each whole main stem becomes old and takes its turn at being cut right out at its base.

There may be two leaders close together at the top of the main stem and one may be tempted to leave a fork at the top. One of these should be removed without leaving a stump. Do not allow weak forks to remain at the top of a main stem, or they will produce a mass of twigs that will lead to short-stemmed flowers.

Do not strive to make all the main stems grow to the same height. Be guided by the general height of each bush and the position of the healthy, outward-facing buds on each main stem. Try to keep them more or less the same height, or the sap will rise higher in the longer branches and stimulate their growth unevenly, but the bushes should not look as if they have been razed level with a giant scythe. Some bushes must be taller than others when pruned, according to whether they are tall, vigorous roses that must be lightly pruned or weak ones that should be harder pruned.

Spacing the Framework of a Hybrid Tea

If one has too many main stems at this stage, one or more may be removed at the base. Always remember to cut out the oldest wood first. A weak rose should be left with three stems and a stronger growing rose with five stems. One stem more or less will not matter if it helps to maintain the balance and general shape of the bush. It sometimes happens that there is a large gap between two of the main stems. It would be advisable to allow a strong side branch to remain and grow in that direction to fill that area. Be careful of removing main stems too freely. It is better to leave an extra one rather than remove vigorous flowering wood and its foliage.

The tip of every side branch or strong fork or leader that remains on the pruned bush, must be slightly shortened in order to stimulate new growth. A cut should be made carefully at an angle to the stem and just above an outward-facing bud. A rose like Crimson Glory has a tendency to grow with its branches spreading sideways, rather close to the ground. In this case, one should cut to an upward-facing, inward bud, so as to force the stems to grow upwards and so form a shape that holds the flowers well above the ground and is more uniform with the other types of roses in the garden. Roses that form a wide-spreading framework, like Charles Mallerin, can also be pruned to inward-facing buds in order to make them grow more upright.

Finally, while pruning one rose bush after the other, do not bend down carelessly and sit on the rose you have just finished or damage the stems in any other way. This may seem to be a very elementary point, but the newly trimmed rose bush can be broken very easily by allowing its thorns to catch on to clothing.

PRUNING HYBRID PERPETUALS

These roses need very light pruning. They bloom on old wood which can be retained for several years. They are very strong growers and must be trimmed correctly, however, or they become large and difficult to handle. They are not suitable for planting between Hybrid Teas in the formal rose-garden as their form is so different, and are best used as hedges or as single specimens. They may be pruned in several different ways according to taste.

Hybrid Perpetuals respond well to ballooning or pegging down. They send out long, whip-like branches which should be caught at the tip and bent in a circle towards the base of the plant, where they can be tied to the plant's own stem or to short pegs driven into the ground. These stems may also be spread sideways and pegged down to the ground at a distance from the centre. These long growths will flower freely all along their length and are very showy. If the faded flowers are removed and the rose well fed, one might receive a second display in the same season.

Each winter, one must simply cut off the side shoots that have flowered, leaving the old framework of the balconed or pegged bush. All the basal buds remaining on this wood will develop into flowering wood in the following spring. It is important to leave the framework of old wood on the bush, as the new flowering growth always arises from the previous year's wood.

As new long shoots arise from the base, they should be trained to follow the shape of the older ballooned or pegged wood. Eventually, after about three or four years, the older branches can be cut right out at the base if the bush becomes too crowded, but only if there is sufficient mature wood to take its place.

If one does not like the rather formal appearance of the ballooned or pegged down bush, then one can leave Hybrid Perpetuals to develop into large specimen bushes like shrubs. They will form good hedges. They will produce masses of short-stemmed flowers which make a good display and may bear as many as 200 at a time. One should not prune such a bush except for the removal of dead flowers. These may be cut after blooming or during winter, as far back as the old wood.

If one tries to cut back a Hybrid Perpetual like a Hybrid Tea and prune it into a fairly low bush, it will send out extremely long growths, up to 5 or 6 feet long, with about one flower at the tip. It will prove a disappointment and be rooted out from the rose garden very quickly. This is probably one of the reasons why so few Hybrid Perpetuals are grown nowadays.

PRUNING POLYANTHA BUSH OR BEDDING ROSES

Polyantha roses, whether tall or dwarf, bloom on old wood and require very little pruning. They are planted in beds for display. The faded flower heads should be cut off near the top of the stem immediately after blooming in spring. Remove about 4 or 5 inches of the main stem, cutting just above a leaf. If these roses are well fed and watered they will produce a second crop of roses in late summer. During winter, the old flower head can be removed again with longer stems. This amounts to the bush being more or less lightly trimmed by about 8 inches all around. Always cut above a bud.

If the old flower head is borne on an old stem, then this may be cut at the base during winter, provided that there is enough new wood to replace it. The new shoots constantly coming up from the base will form the next year's plant. Do not thin the bush out too much, but leave sufficient stems so that the bush will form a rounded mass of colour when in bloom. As a general rule, one can remove old wood when it is about three years old.

Climbing Polyantha roses require different pruning. (See "Pruning Climbers" page 184.)

FLORIBUNDA ROSES

Floribunda roses are similar to Polyanthas and also keep sending up new stems from the base. They may be pruned in the same way. Do not cut them back severely in order to make them provide a massed effect, but allow each stem to grow naturally, simply cutting off old flower heads with a 6 or 8-inch length of stem. Remove flower heads after flowering and again in winter. Remove old canes at the base after a few years.

GRANDIFLORA ROSES

Although these bear their flowers in clusters as well as singly, they are not pruned like Floribundas but more like Hybrid Teas. They must be lightly pruned, however, as they are tall, vigorous roses which must not be cut down severely, e.g. Queen Elizabeth. Remove the whole cluster of flowers a few inches below the head, cutting just above a bud. This should be done after the flowers have faded and again in winter. Remove weak twigs, but do not reduce the number of main stems as much as when pruning Hybrid Teas.

PRUNING TALL SHRUB ROSES

Species roses and large roses grown as shrubs in the garden require very little pruning. One should only remove dead or diseased wood and cut back very weak or straggling branches. Always remove spent flowers.

MINIATURE OR FAIRY ROSES

These should be sheared back after the first flush of blooms is over. They will then produce a new crop of flowers and may be cut back again after the second blooming period.

PRUNING STANDARD ROSES

These must be pruned in the same way as their bush counterparts, for they are simply bushes grafted on to the top of long briar canes. They are mainly Hybrid Teas, but may also be Polyanthas. On the whole, they should be pruned more severely than the bushes in order to prevent top-heaviness. Cut off long growths from midsummer onwards to maintain a neat and balanced shape.

PRUNING CLIMBERS

PRUNING CLIMBING HYBRID TEAS

These roses produce long canes that must be tied to a support. They can be bundled around the pillar of a pergola, but are best placed against a trellis or wall where their canes may be spread out like a fan and their roses displayed to advantage.

Climbing Hybrid Teas put on a great deal of growth in a season, producing long waving branches at the top of the canes. In view of all this seasonal growth, the pruner must limit the number of main stems, so that there will be sufficient room for the flowers to develop, as well as to improve the quality of the blooms.

It is the accepted rule to allow seven main stems to remain each year, three of which are curved and spaced out evenly on each side and tied to their support with raffia. The central one is allowed to grow straight up with its top curved to left or right. (See illustration page 227.) If one is hard put to it to find seven good main stems, then five will be sufficient until new canes develop in future seasons. New shoots will develop from every bud along the main stems and produce a massed display of flowers in the spring. If the faded flowers are removed and the rose is well cared for, it will bloom profusely again in January and produce odd flowers at intervals throughout the season.

When one regards the tangle of branches at the end of winter, one must, in the same way as when pruning a Bush Hybrid Tea, examine the plant at ground level. Here it is easy to see which of the long canes is old, thick and gnarled. Any wood that is over four years old should be removed if there is sufficient wood to take its place.

Always bearing in mind that one must leave seven canes, if possible, remove the oldest canes at ground level, with the aid of the thin-bladed saw. Before cutting, examine the old stem and note whether a new vigorous one springs from it at any point from a stump up to about 2 feet from the ground. If this is the case, remove the old cane above the point from which the new cane springs from the old wood. Cut slantways in the direction of the new branch.

If the plant has been badly pruned in the past and nearly all the main stems are old, do not cut them all out at once. Remove a few and leave some to be removed in the following year, or the plant will be too weakened by the removal of nearly all its wood and foliage. Ideally, one should remove some old wood annually so that the wood on the climber is never older than three or four years and it produces vigorous new flowering wood each year. In this way the plant can be kept healthy and flower production will continue for many years.

Once having chosen the main stems and removed the superfluous canes, one must remove all side growths. These have borne flowers in the previous summer. All the lateral growths, both long and short, should be cut off as close to the main stem as possible, without leaving any stumps, but without damaging the basal bud which will send up a new flowering shoot in the spring. If in doubt about whether there is a basal bud, leave a short stump of about an inch, cutting just above the first bud.

The seven bare canes should now be spread out and tied against their support in one or two places. It is best to secure them with raffia, which is soft and will not cut into the stems. Wind this firmly around the support and then loop it around the main stem without forcing it too firmly against the support. Bend the stems gently without forcing them into position or they may snap. Even if they are not ideally shaped, they should be spaced out as evenly as possible. (See illustration page 225.)

After tying the main stems back into position, shorten the end of the main stem, if necessary, cutting just beyond an upward facing bud. The length of the stems should suit the size of the support and be in proportion to the general shape of the climber.

Climbing Hybrid Teas which are tied to pillars must be untied and allowed to wave about freely while cutting out old wood and trimming the laterals off the main branches in the same way as described above. One must then tie the canes back against the pillar and shorten their height, level with the top of the support.

PRUNING RAMBLERS

(These include climbing Polyantha and Floribunda hybrids and climbing Wichuraianas.)

Ramblers are easy to prune and are very useful for covering arches, picket or wire fences or banks where they can grow freely and easily without necessarily being trained into a formal shape. They must also be tied against their support each year and should be spread out to obtain the best result.

Ramblers flower in spring or early summer on the wood which develops during the previous summer. The wood which has borne flowers in spring should be cut out immediately after the flowers have faded, in the same way as that of a spring-flowering shrub like Weigela. The whole stem should be removed at the base of the plant. This should be done not later than about January, so that the energy of the plant can be directed into producing new flowering wood during summer. As the new wood develops from the base during summer, it can be tied back and trained against the support. It will produce flowers in the following spring. These ramblers require no further pruning during winter.

If the wood which has flowered was not removed after the flowers faded, it can be removed during winter, but it stands to reason that the plant will not be at its best in the spring as the new growth has not had the full benefit of all the available nutrition from the root. Some of this food has been wasted on the old flowering stem that should have been removed after blooming in early summer. Climbing Polyanthas seldom bloom again in the season like their bush counterparts. It is easy to distinguish between new growth and old wood during winter, for the old wood will still be tied to the support, while the new growth waves about freely. It may not be so easy to bend back the new canes into position once they have been allowed to grow freely all summer, so that one must make the effort to prune these roses correctly after flowering and not leave all one's pruning to winter.

Shrubby Climbers, like the Banksian Rose, flower on old wood and should be allowed to ramble freely over a large support. Remove wood that is over four years old periodically, if necessary.

TASKS WHICH MUST FOLLOW IMMEDIATELY AFTER PRUNING

Sealing. Immediately after the bushes have been pruned, all the newly cut edges, large or small, must be sealed. Sealing prevents decay taking place while the wound heals and prevents insects or moisture from penetrating the vulnerable core of the stem. It is done by dabbing the cut with a tree-sealing compound containing bitumen, using a small stick. It hardens almost immediately. The compound must not be applied too freely or it will run over the top of the stem and congeal on the all-important top bud that is preparing to grow into a new leading branch.

It is important to paint the cuts almost immediately and not leave this task to the next day as it is easier to see the cuts while they are fresh. Once they have dried up overnight, they may be overlooked. At one time it was thought that one should only paint the larger cuts of over a $\frac{1}{4}$ inch in diameter, but it is best to seal all the cuts, large or small, as they are all avenues for the entry of insects or disease.

Pruning a large collection of roses can be tiring and it is both time and labour saving to have someone following one's progress, removing the shorn branches from the ground and painting the cuts. Children may be inspanned to do this work, but care must be taken to see that they do not allow the tree-sealing compound to run over on to the buds.

Cleaning Up. Every tidy person will clean up a mess after finishing a task, but it is important to clean up quickly and thoroughly after pruning. Every leaf, petal or twig that has fallen to the ground should be picked up or swept away without damaging the pruned bushes.

On these may lurk the rudiments of disease and pests that will attack the roses in the new season to come. Spores of mildew and insect pests may shelter under them during winter. All the clippings and leaves left from pruning should be burnt as soon as possible, so as to prevent any disease spreading in the garden.

Spraying. Immediately after pruning, while the weather is still cold, one should spray the bushes with Lime Sulphur and repeat this about 10 days later. (See Chapters on Fungicides and Insecticides.) Watch for early infestations of green aphis which will attack the newly opening buds and spray the bushes immediately with nicotine sulphate, Malathion or other sprays. (See Insect Control, Chapters 37 and 39.)

Revise your Work. When all the roses have been pruned and all the cuts sealed, it is quite a good idea to examine them again the following day, when you will see them through different eyes, and make some further cuts. But do not be too drastic. It is better to leave some of the removals for the next year in case you denude the tree too much. On the other hand, it is easy to see where you have been too timid and have left too many forks on a main stem. This applies particularly to pruning Hybrid Tea bushes.

Everyone, even a child, can appreciate the look of a bed of roses that has had "a good haircut". It does give one a feeling when looking at these brave new shapes, that there is a fresh start ahead for the coming season, a chance to remedy one's mistakes of the past and to give one's roses a good start in becoming healthy bushes bursting with excellent roses fit for a flower show.

SECTION II

PRUNING OF FRUIT TREES

The subject of pruning fruit trees can lead one into the most intricate theories and be one of the most skilled operations in horticulture if one is a commercial grower, but the average gardener who owns a small orchard need not be troubled with the finer points of methods of pruning, mainly developed overseas. Training trees to grow on walls or trellises (called espaliers) or on strands on the ground (known as cordons) are methods developed because of lack of space. The training must begin in the nursery and needs skilled knowledge and labour to maintain the correct shape and bearing ability of the tree. This artificial shaping of fruit trees is not practised in Southern Africa to any extent, for the climate is such that growth is generally too vigorous for dwarfing and space is not usually a problem.

This section on pruning fruit trees applies only to certain deciduous trees bearing large fruits like peaches, plums, apricots, apples and pears. These are most commonly grown in areas with cool winters. Other deciduous fruits and nuts like cherries, figs and almonds are also grown, but do not need much pruning. These will be dealt with at the end of this chapter. Large areas of Southern Africa enjoy winters that are often too mild for the success of deciduous fruits, and evergreen fruit trees such as citrus, as well as tropical fruits like mangoes, avocado pears and papaws, are grown in large numbers. None of these require pruning in the same way as deciduous fruits. (See Chapter 32 on "Growing Fruit".)

WHY WE PRUNE FRUIT TREES

The object of growing fruit trees is to obtain as much fruit as possible. An unpruned tree will yield large quantities of fruit which is usually small and may be of inferior quality. Most people prefer to have less fruit, provided that it is larger and of better quality. By pruning, we reduce or thin out the number of branches on the tree and so limit the amount of fruit that the tree will bear. This remaining fruit derives more nourishment from the tree and will, therefore, grow larger and be of better quality. By pruning or shortening the side branches, one also ensures that they do not break with the weight of too much fruit.

During pruning, one must not lose sight of the fact that we mainly want to obtain a good yield of fruit and are not performing an exercise that is an end in itself. Pruning is merely a means of improving the fruit crop and keeping the tree healthy for that purpose. It must not be overdone or exactly the opposite effect will be obtained.

THE PRINCIPLES OF PRUNING FRUIT TREES

The general principles of pruning, as described in the introduction to pruning, should be read before proceeding with this portion. Pruning a fruit tree is very much like pruning a rose bush on a larger scale, with some major differences. One does not cut all the side twigs off the main stems of a fruit tree as is done on a rose bush, for to remove them would be to deprive oneself of all the fruit. Also, one cannot expect to cut away old branches at the base, as this would spoil the framework of the tree. It is only in the way in which we open up the centre of the tree so as to allow sunlight to penetrate and ripen the fruit; the way in which we remove superfluous wood and the way in which we make the actual cut, that the pruning of fruit trees and roses is alike.

The tree is shaped carefully when pruning so that it forms a balanced *framework* that will both bear the weight of the fruit and distribute it evenly, so that it will receive sufficient sunlight for growth and ripening. This framework must be built up when the tree is young, by cutting drastically if necessary, even though this delays the formation of fruit. A mature tree that is badly shaped should not be re-shaped drastically or the fruit will be lost. It is better not to aim to perfect the shape of an old tree, but merely to encourage fruiting by promoting healthy growth and cutting out superfluous wood. If a badly shaped tree is more than 20 years old it is better to replace it altogether. One can, however, reduce the size of a tall, young, well-shaped tree by cutting back or "de-horning" the main stems in winter. One aims to keep trees fairly low-growing in order to facilitate spraying, harvesting and further pruning.

Superfluous branches that shade the fruit and prevent it from ripening should be removed regularly from fruit trees. Such superfluous branches are those that cross over one another, fill the centre of the tree or grow parallel to one another. Other unwanted branches, such as those that rub against one another, so damaging their bark and providing an entry for disease, must also be removed. Dead wood must always be removed and old fruiting wood should be removed periodically so that new wood can take its place.

By encouraging new fruiting wood to take the place of old wood, we keep the tree bearing for many years. In this way we may describe pruning as a stimulating process which increases fruit-production and prolongs the life of the tree. By shortening or cutting back the side branches of a tree, as well as the main branches, we encourage new shoots to grow from all buds on the tree. The same amount of nutrition from the root finds an outlet into these new shoots.

The Danger of Overpruning

Constant hard cutting back of the main branches will lead to the production of too much wood and the tree will tend to produce shoots instead of fruit. The forest of long branches which tends to develop at the top will then have to be cut back again and so the behaviour pattern is set for a vigorous tree constantly struggling to produce leaves for sustenance, without bearing fruit. The remedy for bringing back such a tree into bearing is to prune very little until the balance of growth is restored. One should remove only one long shoot from the top of each main branch each year. If this does not help, then root-pruning may be tried. *The danger of over-pruning, therefore, is that it reduces the fruit crop.*

The art of pruning sufficiently is based on observation of the behaviour of the tree in the previous season. If it has produced a satisfactory crop of fruit and put on

a good proportion of new wood growth, then one should prune reasonably. If the crop has been extremely large and no new wood has appeared, then one can prune severely to encourage new growth. If the side branches are already very short, they can be nipped at the top to stimulate growth and the fruit buds can be thinned by rubbing off with the fingers.

It is essential to distinguish between a *fruit-bud* and a *leaf-bud*, that will only produce leaves and new shoots, when pruning. It is also important to realise that *different types of fruit trees bear their fruit in different ways*. If one has no knowledge of this, the fruit-buds can be destroyed even by removing very little wood. Peach, plum and apricot trees bear their fruit along the sides of the long young branches which grew the previous summer, while apples and pears bear fruit at the tips of the old branches and short old twigs known as spurs. It follows, therefore, that the tips of the small branches of apple or pear trees must not be cut off or the fruit will be removed. Some long, thin branches that could not bear the weight of any fruit may be shortened, however, which means that some of the coming season's fruit will be sacrificed, but the branch will thicken and strengthen sufficiently to hold fruit in the future. Tip-bearers must, therefore, be pruned differently from the other stone fruits.

In general, therefore, one aims to keep the natural form of the individual fruit tree, simply removing superfluous wood and keeping it within manageable size. One must not overprune, but one must use judgment in the amount of pruning necessary so as to thin the crop and encourage the growth of new fruiting wood. Remember that no two trees are exactly alike and must be pruned differently. The more practice one has, the better one will be able to improve by experience.

WHEN TO PRUNE FRUIT TREES

Winter Pruning

The best time to prune fruit trees in Southern Africa is during the last week in July or the first week in August. This marks the end of winter when the weather warms up rapidly and growth begins. In areas which experience very cold winters, the pruning of peaches and apricots can be delayed in case late frosts might damage the expanding fruit buds. The pruning can even be done after the blossom has fallen, so as to note frost-damage, but this may lead to the loss of fruit. The tiny fruits which are forming must be allowed to set and will drop easily if the branches are knocked about during pruning, unless one prunes extremely carefully and lightly. Fruit trees require a winter spray after pruning, which should not be applied when the weather is too warm. Late pruning may cause the tree to be burnt by the winter spray, so that it is best to try and prune the trees during the first week in August at the latest. Grape vines should be pruned in winter, not later than the end of July, for fear that the cuts may "bleed" once the sap has risen.

Pruning after Frost

Any wood that has been damaged by frost will have to be cut away when pruning at the end of winter. Ever green fruit trees like citrus may be damaged by frost occasionally. One should allow these trees to put on a few inches of new growth in spring before cutting off the injured wood.

Summer Pruning

Sometimes green shoots and leaves are removed during summer so as to allow the fruit to ripen in the sunlight. This is done about a month before the fruit matures. The removal of foliage from the tree, however, checks the food supply to the roots and lessens their growth. Less root growth leads in turn to less growth of new shoots on the tree. Summer pruning, therefore, checks the growth of the tree and should not be practised generally. It is useful in checking growth on artificially shaped trees (also see Bonsai) and may be used with discretion when a mature tree is putting on too much wood growth at the expense of fruit.

Tools Required for Pruning Fruit Trees

Secateurs. The same sharp secateur that is used for pruning one's roses may be used for cutting the small branches of the fruit trees. Replaceable parts should be purchased so as to keep one's cuts clean and without ragged edges that provide an entry for disease.

In addition, a *tree secateur* may also be used if desired. This is a larger, stronger secateur with long handles that enables one to cut above one's head without climbing a ladder and which has stout blades that can cut through fairly thick branches. The handles are usually about 18 inches in length. Secateurs with handles several feet long are used in large orchards by commercial growers.

Saw. The same thin-bladed saw (with replaceable blades) that was used on the rose bushes may be used on the fruit trees, particularly if it is of good quality. This saw should be sufficient for the gardener who has pruned regularly and lightly each year and who owns a few trees. Where branches are very old and thick or the orchard is large, it is advisable to have *an additional saw* with a broader, stronger blade, which need not be adjustable.

A step-ladder. A ladder should be used in order to reach the higher branches of mature trees. The best type is one that opens with its own support and does not rest against the branches.

How to Make a Cut

When cutting off the branches of a fruit tree or rose bush, the same principles must be followed. *When shortening a side or lateral branch* one must always cut above a bud and cut at a slant. *When removing a lateral branch*, one must always cut as close to the main stem as possible without leaving a stump.

(a) When shortening a side or lateral growth. This includes ordinary growths (called feathers) or the top growth (called a leader). The sap always rises to the topmost bud and stimulates new growth at that point. When shortening a branch, we cut directly above a bud and expect new growth to spring from that point. We do not leave a short stump above the bud, for that piece of stem does no work and will die back. Dead wood is to be avoided as it often causes healthy wood below it to die back. It also harbours pests which may bring disease to the tree. When removing part of a leafy shoot during summer, always cut above a joint between stem and leaf where a bud will be hidden. The cut will stimulate this to grow into a new stem.

When cutting above the bud, we make the cut at a slant of 45 degrees so that water will not collect at the top of the twig. The cut should be started on the opposite side of the bud, at the same level, and made with the secateur pointing upwards, finishing the cut about ⅛th of an inch above the bud. Care must be taken not to damage the bud while making a cut with the secateur.

The direction of a new branch can be controlled when cutting above a bud. Always choose an outward-facing bud so that the new shoot will grow out in the right direction. If there is a large space between two main branches, due to previous pruning errors or to misshapen growth, one can then sever a "leader" above a bud facing the direction in which one would like a new branch to grow, in order to fill the gap and extend the framework of the tree.

(b) Removing a lateral Branch. A stump does not heal as rapidly as a clean cut made as close to the main stem as possible. The smaller the wound the more quickly it will heal and the less likely that decay will enter the tree. Although we seal the wound in order to protect it while it is healing, we try to make it as small as possible. A slanting cut on a stump is larger than a cut made straight up against the side of the trunk. When removing small branches regularly each winter, one does not need to make large wounds and it is easy to remove them without leaving stumps that will wither and die back. When removing a large branch, however, the wound will be larger and one must take more care in severing it. Use a sharp light saw. Start by making a cut upwards from underneath the branch and then saw down from above to meet this point. This will prevent the heavy branch from falling and tearing a strip of bark off the trunk below it. Such bark damage will provide an additional entry for disease and may prevent nutrition from reaching the branches above it. Particular care must be taken not to leave a stump and yet not cut so closely that one removes a larger circle of bark than necessary, so making the wound even larger. The surface can be trimmed with a sharp knife to make it perfectly smooth.

Treatment of Wounds

All wounds which are ¾ of an inch in diameter or larger, should be painted with a bituminous tree-sealing compound as soon as pruning is completed and while the cuts are still fresh. Care must be taken not to let the compound run over the tip of a stem on to the top bud.

How to Distinguish Between Fruit Buds and Leaf Buds

Buds are situated at intervals all along the length of the wood of fruit trees. They develop in the joint between leaf and stem. They usually develop after a period of rest. When the tree has had a dormant or rest period and is bare of leaves, one can see the buds all along the length of the stem. Some look like tiny notches and others like tiny swellings. As the sap rises at the end of winter, the buds swell and become slightly larger. By the time one commences pruning at the end of July or during the first week in August, they protrude clearly. Some buds or "eyes" always remain dormant, but most buds develop into fruit or shoots bearing foliage.

Some buds contain only leaves and are called **Leaf buds,** while some contain only flowers and may be called flower buds, blossom buds or **fruit buds.** The term fruit buds will be used throughout this chapter. A third type of bud contains both flowers and leaves and is known as a mixed bud, but is usually also called a fruit bud so as to distinguish it from a bud bearing only foliage.

On examining the buds closely, especially on peach trees, one can see that the buds are usually grouped together in twos or threes, but may also be single. Where there are triple buds, one can always be sure that they contain fruit as well as shoots, but fruit will also develop from other buds. In general, one may say that fruit buds are always plumper than leaf buds. These remarks apply to peach, apricot and partly to plum trees.

Apples and pears bear their fruit in a different way from peaches or apricots and their fruit buds are different in appearance. The fruit is borne at the tips of long branches as well as on spurs and, in some varieties, only on spurs. Some plums, especially prunes, also bear fruit on spurs. **Spurs** are short branches, often less than an inch in length, with their nodes or growth areas compressed together. These form a thickened layer, often woolly in appearance, which ends in a slight point and may be easily recognised. Both fruit and leaves spring from this layer on the spurs. The spurs appear as short thickened branches and spring from any place on the main stems. Some varieties of apples and pears, known as tip-bearers, also bear fruit at the tips of the longer branches and the thickened tips resemble those of the spurs. Ordinary leaf buds are also present in apples and pears and form slight swellings along the bare branches in winter.

It is important for the pruner to recognise the different fruit buds or he may remove all the fruit buds from a twig and leave only foliage. Some people may feel that it would be easier to wait until the tree is in blossom before pruning, so that one could be sure to retain fruit buds, but this is not advisable for it might endanger the fruit crop. In the first place, the blossom should not be knocked about or it will drop easily and may drop before it has had the opportunity of being fertilized by insects. Secondly, one must spray after pruning to rid one's tree of last summer's pests and enable it to have a healthy start. Spraying should be done before new growth has started and not after the tree has blossomed.

HOW TO PRUNE A NEWLY-PLANTED YOUNG TREE

For the first two or three years of a fruit tree's life, one aims to prune it into a good shape, so that it will be easy to prune for the remaining 15 to 20 years of its life. One does not aim to reap fruit during this time, although some trees may produce a small crop. The shape that one aims to develop is a cup or vase-shaped framework of branches that allows sunlight to penetrate the centre of the tree and benefit all growth evenly, as well as aid in the formation and ripening of the fruit.

Primary Framework

At one time, the gardener received a young fruit tree that was no more than a fairly straight stick of about 2 or 3 feet in length. This was called a maiden tree and represented one year's growth. After planting this stick, the gardener would be forced to cut it back severely to 1½ or 2 feet from the ground, leaving about four blind buds at the base and another three or four good buds above them. These would be expected to develop into the future main branches of the tree. If the tree were not cut back, growth would spring from these buds anyway and the central portion would also grow longer, so that the tree would become a dense bush and not a vase-shaped structure. Once the central stem had thickened, it would be almost impossible to prune the mature tree into the required shape and certainly not without a setback in its development, for it would mean removing a tremendous amount of growth all at once.

Nowadays, this preliminary work is often done in the nursery and the gardener is able to save a year's growth by purchasing a second-year tree that is already shaped. This sapling should have three or four evenly-spaced shoots springing from the main trunk, which is about "knee-high" or less from the ground. At this stage one should not cut the branches back severely, or this will restrict root growth and subsequently delay top growth and fruiting. Only cut back about one third of any branch which needs shortening and thin out any superfluous shoots that appear to be spoiling the balanced cup-shape of the young tree.

If one cannot purchase a second-year tree, then one must cut the straight stick back as described above and wait a year for the buds to develop into young branches. In order to make sure that these buds will grow, it is advisable to notch the top four or five buds which are left on the sapling after cutting it back "knee-high".

Notching. Notching is done to induce growth on bare stems. Select buds facing the direction in which you require the branches to grow. Remove a tiny wedge of wood just above each bud by means of a sharp knife. This wedge must not be wider than one-eighth of an inch. Its removal simply checks the flow of sap which is now directed into the bud and stimulates it into activity. Notching may be done in order to encourage any bud to grow in a desired direction. When notching buds that are required to form main branches for the framework of a young tree, one should space the notches about 3 or 4 inches above one another, as this space will be entirely filled by the fully grown branches of the mature tree.

During the first summer after the tree has been shaped, one should rub off any new shoots that appear on the trunk below the three or four main shoots, in case they outgrow them and spoil the shape. These main shoots should grow out at a wide angle to the trunk. By placing them at different levels, the framework of the tree will be strengthened.

When the tree is fully two years old and is about to be pruned during its third winter, then one may select leaders to increase the size of the framework.

Selecting a Leader

Each young main branch will have produced several lateral or side branches during its first summer's growth. One must select one of these to be the leader. This will extend each main branch so that it grows outwards at an angle of about 45 degrees, thereby enlarging the cup-shaped framework of the tree.

Select a strong shoot that is growing in an outward-facing direction. It usually curves upwards at an angle to the main stem. Holding the secateur parallel to the direction in which this shoot is growing, cut the main stem off at an angle so that the portion growing above the leader is removed. If there are any other strong shoots immediately below the leader, remove these as close to the main stem as possible, so that they will not compete with the leader during the coming season of growth.

Shortening the Leader

The leader can then be lightly shortened by cutting off the tip at a point *directly above a bud*, in the same manner as in the rose bush. The amount to be shortened varies with the type of growth. If the shoot is long and thin, it may be reduced by half to two-thirds of its length. If it is short and stocky, reduce it by one third or less. Shortening the leader will stimulate a new shoot from the topmost bud and this in turn will become the leader of the following year. In this way the tree increases in size from year to year.

Side shoots which have developed lower down on the main stems should not be removed. These are the "feathers" which will clothe the main branches and bear the fruit. Strong shoots which develop lower down on the framework may be retained so that they can develop into strong lateral branches, but none should be so strong as to compete with the main branches or the leaders. They should be well spaced and not grow into the centre or too near the ground. The lateral branch will have to be shortened slightly just above an outward-facing bud. This will develop into a leader in the following year and the leaders will continue to be selected and shortened each year in the same way as those on the main branches. Any long, thin, side branches should be cut back by two-thirds of their length. Other shorter side shoots should be left alone or very lightly tipped above a bud.

If the young tree has been correctly shaped in the first three winters, it will be easy to see how to continue to prune it in future years.

Fruit Bearing

The young tree will bear light crops of fruit from about the third year onwards, bearing heavier crops as it matures. By the fifth or sixth year it will be fully mature and bearing its full crop. If it starts bearing a very large crop very early, as is the case with certain plums and peaches, then one should prune to reduce the crop in order to prevent the tree from becoming exhausted and even stunted in growth. Here one should thin out the branches without spoiling the shape and size of the tree and also shorten the side branches, but not remove them entirely. It is best to remove most of the young fruit by hand after it has formed.

On the other hand, if one's trees are very slow to bear, then one should prune very lightly and not reduce any of the main branches from the top.

PRUNING A MATURE FRUIT TREE

First remove any dead wood that may be present on the tree, whether it is a whole branch or a short stump, and saw it off neatly. Before starting to prune, stand back and look at the tree as a whole. One will see a mass of twiggy branches, all of different shapes and sizes. One will notice readily that several thicker branches grow from near the base of the tree to the top. These are the main branches of the framework. There should be from three to five of these main branches, spaced more or less evenly around the tree. Other thick lateral branches fork out at intervals from these main branches, while the whole tree is covered with numerous twiggy branches and short shoots.

The first aim is to open up the centre of the tree in order to admit sunlight. One must look into the centre of the tree and cut off all large branches which grow into the centre of the tree. These should be sawn off close to the main stems. The whole inside of the tree must not be "cleaned out", however. All short sturdy growths up to a foot in length should be left untouched. Any very thin, long growths that point directly inward should be cut out altogether or shortened by two-thirds of their length. Wherever two or more shoots grow out together from the one point, only one should be retained, while the others should be removed entirely. The best situated shoots on the inside surfaces of the main branches will grow at an angle towards the sides and not point directly inwards if possible.

Next, one must extend the framework of the tree. The main stems will be curved upwards in a rough cup-shape, allowing the sun to penetrate the centre. The main stems are stout and become thicker with age. One aims to keep them covered with vigorous young twigs and branches called "feathers", which bear the fruit and foliage. At the same time, the main stems continue to grow at the top and so the tree develops in size.

The main stems always tend to develop a fork at the top, at the point where they were cut back the previous winter. The gardener must control the way in which the tree grows, so that all the forks develop evenly and hold the main branches away from one another, leaving plenty of room for fruit and foliage. Trees, however, do not grow in a geometrical pattern. There are often groups of three or five branches which have developed from the cut made the previous season and the gardener must decide which of them to retain. One must always aim to retain the most vigorous, sturdy young branches that will be well able to support the crop of fruit. If there are three branches growing out at the top of the main stem, then one should remove all but one, choosing the most vigorous and suitably placed which is growing in the right direction. The other young branches or leaders should be cut off as close to the main stem as possible, without leaving useless stumps.

After the leader has been selected, it should be shortened by cutting directly above a bud, in the same way as the leader on a rose bush. The amount of wood to cut off varies according to its length. The general rule is to remove two-thirds of its length. If it is short and sturdy, as little as one-third may be removed, but the longer and thinner it is, the more can be removed. By continuously making one's leaders fairly short, from the time that the tree is first planted, one can keep a tree growing fairly low so that one need not stand on a ladder either to pick the fruit or prune. It is much more convenient to keep one's trees on the short side in a garden.

The danger of topping fruit trees without selecting a leader. One sometimes sees older trees with a forest of long, fruitless twigs springing from the tops of the branches. This wood growth has been brought about by levelling off the top of the tree without thinning the groups of leaders near the tops of the main stems. It is also the result of overpruning in that the harder one cuts back the branch, the more the tree produces wood in order to replenish itself, at the expense of fruit. (See also page 187.) One cannot remedy the condition by severing all these growths at once, for a new crop of wood will appear in the following season. The only way to restore the balance of growth is to remove a few of these long growths each winter, or even to leave them severely alone for one season. If this fails to remedy the situation, root-pruning can be done as a last resort. (See page 194.)

Superfluous wood, as well as dead wood, should be removed from all fruit trees. Wherever two branches cross over one another and one is deprived of sunshine, they should either be removed or they should be pulled apart and held there artificially until they have grown in that position. This can be done by tying a rope around the crossing branches and securing this to a stake in the ground or even by placing a long wedge between them for a season. Branches which rub together and so damage their bark should either be cut out altogether or shortened sufficiently so that they do not interfere with each other's growth. Parallel branches that shade one another must be thinned either by removing one of these or by shortening it to form a short side branch. Every branch that is shortened must be cut directly above an outward-facing bud.

The final aim of pruning is to reduce the fruit crop so that the tree should not be overloaded and to shorten the branches so that they can bear the fruit. The different types of fruit trees, however, bear their fruit differently and must, therefore, be pruned differently at this stage.

PRUNING OF DIFFERENT TYPES OF FRUIT TREES

Peach trees, nectarines, apricots and some plums bear their fruit differently from apples, pears and other plums, like prunes. The first group bears fruit all along the young branches, while the second group bears fruit at the tips of the branches and on spurs. (See "How to distinguish between Fruit Buds and Leaf Buds" above.) The methods of pruning different types of fruit trees continue on different lines after the preliminaries described above.

SECTION A. PEACHES, APRICOTS AND PLUMS

PRUNING OF PEACH TREES (ALSO NECTARINES)

The peach tree bears fruit heavily and we prune primarily to thin the crop every year. Having cleared the centre of the tree and shortened the leaders, one must then turn one's attention to the numerous smaller branches springing from the main stems. One aims to retain as many of these "feathers" as possible, for they will bear the fruit as well as the foliage. Peaches bear on one-year-old wood, so that it is always important to retain young wood and advisable to thin in such a way that only the old wood is removed. It will be noticed that three shoots frequently spring from one point on the main stem. The central twig should be removed at the base. This is usually the oldest and its removal leaves room for the others to develop. If the twigs are so crowded that there may not be enough room for the large fruit or even the foliage to develop, then remove all

except one, which should be the sturdiest of the one-year-old wood.

Some of the "feathers" along the main stems will be long and others short. Any branches which are about 12 inches in length should be left untouched. Those which are 18 inches or more in length, should be shortened to about 12 inches in length, cutting above a bud. In other words, they may be shortened by about one-third to half of their length.

Before shortening, examine the branch to see whether there are any fruit buds present. If there is only one, shorten the branch so that the fruit bud is retained on the tree unless it is situated near the end of a long thin branch that would be too weak to bear the weight of the ripe fruit. If there are several fruit buds on the young shoot, estimate how heavy the fruit crop might be and remove some of the fruit buds when shortening it.

It is best not to be too drastic in removing fruit buds, for not every blossom will develop into fruit. There are natural hazards such as violent storms, hail, wind and lack of fertilization that sometimes prevent the fruit from setting. It is always possible to reduce some of these young branches in length in later weeks, when the fruit is set and one can see the tiny embryos swelling after the blossom has fallen. Do not leave all the decisions to later weeks, however, or the fruit may be endangered by the shaking of the tree when cutting branches. Any cuts over three-quarters of an inch in size will have to be sealed once more.

If one has the time, one can shorten every single small branch on the tree, be it ever so slightly, so as to stimulate new growth from the tip, but this is not necessary and one can leave the naturally shorter branches untouched, provided that the tree is bearing satisfactorily. One should shorten any obviously old twigs in order to stimulate them to send out new fruit-bearing wood. If they have no buds on them, they can be removed entirely. Be cautious about removing "feathers" from the main stem which may become gnarled with age and not put out new growth freely. Avoid bare patches on the main stem in case it becomes scalded by the sun and leave any type of shoot that will shade it, even if the shoot does not bear fruit or is a watershoot.

When pruning a peach tree one will find it necessary to thin out some of the "feathers" completely. They should be spaced evenly along the main branches, starting as close to the base as possible. From about one-third to two-thirds of the fruit-bearing shoots may be removed entirely in the process, but this will not be detrimental if the tree is growing well.

A formal circular rose garden, slightly sunken, is partly ringed with climbing roses. *Robinia hispida* adds its lilac flowers to the spectacle.

A group of popular Floribunda roses showing Vogue and Ma Perkins at the top and, below, Espoir, Independence and Fashion.

Some Hybrid Tea roses: *Top centre:* Etoile de Holland. *Centre row:* Sutter's Gold, Virgo, Ophelia, Comtesse Vandal, First Love. *Bottom row:* Crimson Glory, Charles Mallerin, Peace, Charlotte Armstrong, Eclipse.

Vigorous Grandiflora roses—pink Queen Elizabeth and vibrant Montezuma.

Paul's Scarlet Climber has showy clusters of flowers in early summer. It should be pruned immediately after flowering.

The sparkling yellow blooms of High Noon, a Climbing Hybrid Tea, enliven a brown, split-pole fence.

PRUNING AN APRICOT TREE

The apricot is pruned in the same way as the peach, but it has a more spreading and sweeping growth that must be checked more severely.

All the "feathers" on the main stems, except the very short ones, should be shortened to outward or upward-facing buds. If the tree becomes very open in the centre it should be allowed to develop inside-facing branches to shade the bark. Avoid bare patches on the main stems and retain watershoots if necessary. These must, of course, also be shortened. Short twiggy spurs which develop on the apricot will bear the best fruit and should not be cut away.

PRUNING PLUM TREES

Most plum trees bear their fruit in the same way as peaches and apricots. The prune bears fruit on spurs like apples and pears and can be pruned in a similar fashion.

Plum trees develop a vase shape very easily and bear heavy crops of fruit. All the long thin "feathers" should be shortened by half and only the very short ones left untouched. Half of the "feathers" can be removed altogether in order to thin the fruit. Short fruit-bearing spurs will develop and these should be left untouched for a few years. They can also be thinned out occasionally in order to prevent exhaustion from overbearing.

The prune tree requires very little pruning once it has been well shaped. Leaders should be selected and shortened each year and other strong branches near the top should be removed. Only very long side branches need be shortened as the tree bears mainly on spurs. Rubbing or crossing branches must be removed as usual and weak wood can be shortened.

SECTION B. APPLES AND PEARS

It is most important to shape these trees well from the beginning. They grow more slowly than most other fruit trees and usually live longer, so that they should be pruned to establish a well-spaced framework which will bear the fruit evenly and allow foliage to develop freely. Both apple and pear trees usually develop a neat structure quite naturally and need very little shaping or pruning after about five years.

Some apples and pears bear their fruit only on spurs while others bear their fruit at the tips of their branches when young (called tip-bearers) and develop spurs as they grow older. It follows that the tips of the branches should not be cut off as freely as they are on peach and apricot trees. Spurs should not be touched while pruning or the fruit will be removed.

When shaping the tree at the beginning as well as in later years, some of the fruit will have to be sacrificed. One should never allow fruit to develop at the tips of the leaders at the top of the main branches or on the leaders at the top of the strong lateral branches which spring from the main branches. The leaders may be shortened by half of their length.

The mass of side shoots that clothe the main branches and the strong lateral branches must be thinned in order to allow sunlight to penetrate what would otherwise become a dense tree. Some of these side shoots will have to be removed altogether and the remainder spaced evenly along the branches. Aim to retain the shorter, thicker twigs, which will be sturdy enough to bear the weight of the heavy apples or pears and to remove the long, thin shoots. The shorter twigs should not be topped or the fruit will be cut off and, even if there is no fruit present that season, any cutting will retard the formation of fruit-bearing spurs at the tip. If many of the side shoots are long and thin, it might be necessary to shorten them in order to develop sturdiness and to sacrifice any fruit for a while. The long thin twigs can be shortened to 4 or 5 inches in length and they will thicken considerably in the coming summer, possibly developing a new fruit bud at the tip in the following spring.

After five or six years the short branches and fruit-bearing spurs will be well established and very little further pruning will be necessary. Annual thinning of side shoots will still be necessary to prevent the trees from becoming too closely knit, but this depends on the vigour and general growth of the tree. Where growth is very vigorous one should thin out, but not shorten, the lateral shoots. Where growth is slow, slight shortening of lateral shoots, from about one-third to half of their length, will induce the tree to put on new growth. After several years, the old fruit spurs can be thinned if they are too crowded or the tree seems to be losing vigour with age. This will rejuvenate an older tree and may be done every three or four years. On the whole, however, one does not prune to thin the crop when pruning apples and pears, which are not produced as freely as peaches and apricots.

PRUNING ALMONDS AND CHERRIES

These trees do not need to be pruned like other deciduous fruit trees. Crossing or rubbing branches should be removed and the branches may be thinned if desired. This can be done every 3 or 4 years. Badly shaped trees can be re-shaped by pruning and dead wood must be removed. Young shoots of cherries may be shortened in order to encourage the formation of fruiting spurs, but if the tree is bearing well, it should not be cut.

PRUNING FIGS

Figs need never be pruned in the home garden and often do best when they are left alone. There are two crops of figs which are both suitable for consumption. The spring crop is produced at the tips of the branches and if these are removed during winter the fruit will be lost. The second crop is produced on current wood during summer.

In commercial orchards, the first crop is generally used as green fruit for preserving, while the second crop is used for jam. A heavy first crop makes the second crop undesirable commercially, except for jam production. It has been found that the removal of the first crop, which is not desirable for commercial purposes as the fruit is too big and too light, will improve the quality of the second crop for sale as fresh fruit. The removal of the first crop takes place by pruning in winter, generally in the 4th year when the tree comes into bearing. The tips are removed and the tree is thinned and shaped. Lateral branches will form during summer, bearing a later crop on current wood.

PROCEDURE AFTER PRUNING FRUIT TREES

This is the same as the procedure after pruning roses, but the essentials will be enumerated here.

All cuts of three-quarters of an inch and larger must be **sealed** with bituminous tree-sealing compound as soon as pruning is completed and while the cuts are still fresh. Care must be taken not to let the compound run over the tip of the stem and damage the top bud. Sealing or painting the wound protects it from decay while it heals underneath. If decay sets in it will penetrate the heart of the tree and may cause the death of the tree. Stubs must not be left on the tree as these prevent healing.

Burn all twigs and branches removed by the pruner, so that no diseases or pests will remain on the ground and so re-infect the tree in the coming season. Sweep the ground well.

The trees must be **sprayed** with lime sulphur as soon as possible, while the weather is still cold. (See Chapters on Insecticides and Fungicides.)

Feeding. Each tree should be given a wheelbarrow of old kraal manure each spring. (See Chapter 32 on "Growing Fruit".)

ROOT PRUNING OF FRUIT TREES

This is a drastic method of encouraging better fruit which should only be done if ordinary pruning fails. By reducing the size of the roots, one limits wood growth at the top and the root energy may be directed instead into the formation of fruit. Root-pruning may also be used to check the top wood growth of a mature tree that has been badly pruned and where the pruner finds it difficult to restore the balance of growth only by not topping for a year and thereafter removing one or two forks at a time.

Root-pruning is performed by digging a circular trench about 3 feet from the base of the tree and trimming the roots cleanly with the help of the secateur and a saw. In the case of an older tree, one should dig the trench at a greater distance from the base of the tree, and only dig half the circular trench during one winter and the other half during the next.

How to Prune Grape Vines. See Chapter 32 under "Growing Berries and Vines".

SECTION III

PRUNING OF FLOWERING SHRUBS AND TREES

Most shrubs do not require pruning and are best left to grow naturally, developing their characteristic shapes. Dead wood must be removed and long growths may be cut back almost at any time of the year to balance the shape of the bush. Some shrubs may have to be cut back in order to keep them compact or be reduced in size because they are too tall for their position, such as when they may project above a window sill. Some shrubs take kindly to clipping and can be used for hedges, while others, like Magnolias, resent trimming and will replace branch removals slowly.

Certain shrubs, however, must be pruned regularly in order to improve the size of their flowers. As a general rule, deciduous shrubs require pruning more than evergreens. It is essential to know the time of flowering so that one does not remove the flower crop by pruning at the wrong time. Pruning of flowering shrubs can be done in winter or summer, according to the needs of each shrub.

PRUNING OF TENDER SHRUBS

Tender shrubs, which do not necessarily need pruning, may have the tops of their branches browned by frost in cold areas. This dead wood will have to be cut away, but this should only be done in the spring, when all danger of frost has passed, in order to prevent later frost damage. The dead wood will protect the part below it until the spring. The more old wood left on the bush the less likely it is that it will be affected by frost in the following winter.

PRUNING OF EVERGREENS

On the whole, evergreens require light pruning. The best time to prune evergreens is immediately after the flowers have faded. If it is essential to reduce the size of the plant, this should be done two or three times at intervals during summer rather than a drastic pruning given at one time. One should always avoid removing too many leaves at once, as they nourish the plant. Uneven growths must be pruned carefully. Azaleas sometimes produce long canes that rise above the bush and create a two-tiered effect. The tips of these shoots should be pinched back several times during spring and summer, just before they reach the top of the bush. If they have already risen above it, they must be clipped back.

In general, quick-growing evergreens may be trimmed back more readily than slow-growing evergreens. One should consider carefully before cutting back a slow-growing evergreen, for it may receive a set-back and take years to resume its natural shape. Semi-evergreen, vigorous bushes like Purple *Cestrum* and *Jochroma tubulosum* may be cut back severely at the end of winter and will replace nearly all the wood during the following summer. This treatment will improve the general tidiness of an old bush. Quick-growing Chinese Hibiscus (*H. rosa-sinensis*) is an evergreen that is best grown as a single specimen. It takes to clipping, however, and is used as a hedge in mild climates, where it may be sheared in autumn and in spring. In areas with cold winters, it should be trimmed only at the end of winter, but is best left untouched and grown as a single specimen in a sheltered position. The evergreen Brazilian Glory Bush (*Tibouchina semidecandra*, formerly *Lasiandra*) is often broken by wind. The long brittle branches can be pruned back severely at the end of winter and new growth will spring up rapidly from all places on the woody stems.

Some evergreen bushes which grow with medium rapidity may become thinned out if neglected and do not receive enough moisture. These can be rejuvenated by pruning severely at the end of winter. Plants like *Mahonia aquifolium* and some species of *Hypericum* respond to this treatment. The main branches can be shortened severely or even removed altogether to make way for fresh basal growth, but an effort must be made to feed the plant with manure or well-made compost and to water it regularly thereafter.

REMOVING DEAD FLOWERS FROM EVERGREENS

Cutting off dead flowers is a form of pruning. These should be removed as soon as the flowers have faded. This is not always necessary and often involves too much labour for general practice. One must be guided by the behaviour of one's shrubs before deciding whether it is necessary to remove the flowers or not.

It is easier to remove large flowers than numerous small flowers. This, too, depends on the individual habits of different shrubs. Proteas, for example, should have their dead flowerheads removed in spring, or these will remain on the bush for years. Their presence does not affect production of the following season's blooms, but they are unsightly. Pincushion Flowers (*Leucospermum*) which also belong to the Protea family, need not have their dead flowers removed, for they disintegrate after flowering. Occasional shortening of leggy branches is desirable as this encourages bushing out. Heaths or *Erica*, like *Protea*, also retain their dead flowers and the stems should be pruned back after blooming. This has the advantage of keeping the bush compact and tidy.

It would be tedious to pick off the myriad flowers of Azaleas, Gardenias or Camellias and these need not be removed except when cutting for the vase. If one wishes to remove them all, each short cluster of twigs should be removed individually rather than shearing the bush indiscriminately. In moist parts of the country near the mountains, where growth is very rapid, the bushes can be trimmed more severely. They should not be trimmed after midsummer, however, or the following season's flower buds may be sacrificed. Camellias may be disbudded to one terminal bud if liked.

The presence of seed-pods sometimes prevents free flowering. The Tea Tree (*Leptospermum*), in common with other Australian evergreens like *Eucalyptus*, *Callistemon* and *Melaleuca*, retains woody seed-pods on its branches for years, which only release the fine seed when they are picked. If the Tea Tree or Bottle-brush has not flowered well, or if one wishes to reduce the size of the bush, it can be pruned back severely in the spring. Otherwise it is best to allow it to develop without interference.

PRINCIPLES OF PRUNING DECIDUOUS SHRUBS

Deciduous shrubs that replenish themselves with fresh growth can be pruned more drastically than evergreens or slow-growing deciduous specimens. Deciduous shrubs must be divided into those which bloom in the spring and those which bear flowers during summer.

The normal time to prune deciduous shrubs is in winter when the branches are bare and the sap is low in the dormant period. If one cuts back certain spring-flowering shrubs like *Weigela*, Mock Orange (*Philadelphus*) and Lilac, at this time, however, then one will remove the branches that bear the spring flowers and these will be lost. The correct time to prune such shrubs is in the spring, immediately after they have bloomed, and in spite of the fact that they are in leaf. This means that one can pick the flowers freely for the vase, for they must be removed as soon as they have faded. During the remainder of the summer, these plants will produce wood that will bear flowers in the following spring. Correct pruning of spring-flowering shrubs will ensure a neat and pleasing appearance during their dormant period in winter.

Deciduous shrubs that bear flowers in summer or autumn can safely be pruned during winter. These put on new growth during spring that will bear flowers in the summer. This is described as bearing flowers on the current year's growth. Roses belong to this category, as well as shrubs like Red May, Tamarisk and Hydrangea. They may be pruned heavily so as to encourage plenty of strong growth.

(a) DETAILS OF HOW TO PRUNE SPRING-FLOWERING DECIDUOUS SHRUBS

EXAMPLES: *Deutzia*, Pearl Bush (*Exochorda*), *Forsythia*, spring-flowering Honeysuckle (*Lonicera*), Lilac, Mock-Orange (*Philadelphus*), May (*Spiraea cantoniensis*), Snowball Bush (*Viburnum opulus*), *Weigela*, *Wistaria*.

It is important to prune as soon after the flowers have faded as possible, in order to give the bush a long period in which to produce new flowering wood for the following spring. At this time it is also easiest to see exactly which branches have flowered and to remove these completely. If one is familiar with the method of pruning this type of shrub, one may attempt to prune later in summer or even in autumn, but the following spring's flowers will not be so successful as the flowering wood has had a shorter period in which to develop.

Begin by examining a flowering stem. This may have borne short sprays of flowers all along its length, which may be as long as 8 feet in the case of *Weigela* or *Philadelphus*. It may be cut back to ground level or to a point on an old stem from which a new vigorous stem springs. The new stem should grow in an outward direction and be situated at a height of anything up to 2 feet from the ground. It should be below the portion that has borne flowers and must not be weak or drooping. Continue the removal of long flowering stems even though one appears to be cutting out a tremendous amount. Provided that one leaves about a dozen strong, tall stems of new wood, one will have a good spring display as the bush puts on plenty of fresh growth during summer. Remove all old, weak, thin shoots that have not flowered. One can tell their age by the hardness of the stem. (See illustrations of pruning *Weigela*, page 240.)

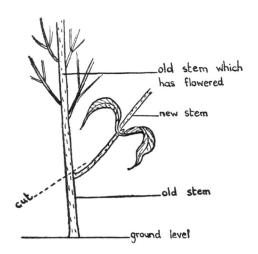

If the bush has not been pruned correctly in previous years, one will find tangled twigs and some very thick trunks. Saw off these very thick growths at ground level, so as to make room for young basal shoots. It is best to remove half of these trunks in the first spring after the flowering period and the other half in the following spring.

If one is a few weeks late in pruning and has forgotten which stems have flowered, it is quite easy to distinguish between the different types of wood. Wood that has flowered usually has short hard twigs protruding from it. These have borne the flowers and this may be noticed particularly in *Weigela* and *Philadelphus*. The main stem is rather hard and greyish, while the younger wood has a coppery tinge and is much more pliable. The young wood bears only leaves, without a vestige of flowers.

One should not prune spring-flowering shrubs later than autumn. One can remove old wood as was done in early summer, but as much young wood as possible should be left on even if the growths are short. One can recognise older wood in autumn as it has become even greyer and more brittle than before, while the leaves might have become a darker green. The young leaves are large, vigorous and a fresher green. At this late stage in the season, the bush should not be pruned so drastically that there is hardly any wood left or it will affect the spring flowering. Plan to remedy the major errors in the coming spring.

Forsythia. Forsythia bears its flowers right up against the stem, but one can recognise wood which has flowered as the vestiges of the flowers will be found right against the stem. *F. intermedia* does not branch as freely from the ground as *F. suspensa*, so that the flowering stems need only be cut back to about 2 or 3 feet from the ground. They will branch out again from this point.

Lilacs (*Syringa*). Lilacs sucker at ground level and soon develop into a tangle of twigs with poor flowers if they are not pruned. Each spring, after flowering, remove three-quarters of the number of suckers at ground level, always removing the oldest first. One should encourage well-branched stems with evenly spread shoots at the top, which will produce twin flower buds each summer.

An old lilac bush should never be simply severed at the top. This only results in thin stems and inferior flowers, if any. Always prune it near the ground and try and give it a balanced shape. Allow new growth to spring from old stumps, which must be limited in number. Each bush should have two or three healthy, low-branching sucker stems in addition to new strong shoots from old stumps, which can be removed in rotation in future years.

(b) DETAILS OF HOW TO PRUNE SUMMER-FLOWERING DECIDUOUS SHRUBS

EXAMPLES: Hydrangea, Tamarisk, Pride-of-India, (*Lagerstroemia*), Red May (*Spiraea bumalda* var. Anthony Waterer), Pink May (*Spiraea menziesii* var. *triumphans*), Pomegranate (*Punica granatum*), Ceratostigma, Ceanothus, Hibiscus syriacus, Clematis jackmannii, Buddleia davidii.

Some summer-flowering deciduous shrubs must be pruned while others do not necessarily require pruning, although they will not suffer if they are cut back. It is necessary to prune Hydrangea, Buddleia and Late Tamarisk (*Tamarix pentandra*), for example, or their flowers will become too small and their branches tangled, and it is advisable to prune Pomegranates, so as to prevent the branches from breaking because of the weight of the fruit as well as to keep the heavy fruit off the ground. It is not strictly necessary to prune shrubs like Pride-of-India, *Hibiscus syriacus* or *Ceanothus*, however, unless they have grown too large for convenience. It is best to deal separately with those that require pruning.

The best time to prune hardy summer-flowering shrubs is at the end of winter. Where specimens might be damaged by frost, one can delay pruning until the weather warms up slightly.

Red May and Pink May. The dead flowers should be removed from these bushes during summer as this prolongs the flowering period. During winter, all dead blooms can be removed and the bush should be trimmed neatly into a rounded shape. No further pruning should be done.

Ceratostigma, which is a small straggling shrub, should be trimmed back into a low rounded shape each winter. The seed heads should be removed at the end of summer if one wishes to prevent the plant from spreading all over the garden.

Shrubby perennials like *Leonotis leonurus* and *Sutera grandiflora* may be pruned back at the end of winter when all danger of frost has passed. The old woody stems may be cut out at the base and new flowering stems will spring up to take their place.

Clematis

Clematis jackmanii. This hybrid climber flowers in summer and autumn on new wood and can be cut back almost to within a foot of the ground in August. Early flowering *Clematis montana*, however, flowers on the previous season's wood and its main stems should not be pruned back. Dead wood or weak, thin wood may be removed after flowering.

Clematis brachiata, Traveller's Joy, can be cut right back at the end of winter if it becomes too rampant. Otherwise, it can be left to ramble freely up a tree or on a support.

Pomegranate (*Punica granatum*). During winter, the fruiting Pomegranate should be pruned to five or six sturdy main stems. Cut out all twiggy growth and clean the main stems to a height of about 2 feet from the ground. Allow the stems to branch naturally from that point, removing weak or crossing branches. This treatment will keep the fruit off the ground and limit the amount of fruit so that its weight does not break the branches.

Tamarisk. The spring-flowering Tamarisk (*T. gallica*) can be pruned in winter to keep it tidy and within bounds, but its natural feathery shape should not be spoilt. It is best to prune it at ground level, removing all suckers and allowing one or two main trunks to develop. These should be cleaned of all twigs to a height of 3 feet and then allowed to branch naturally. Crossing or twisted branches may be removed. The remaining long thin branches will produce flowers all along their length, arching into a cloud of pink.

Late Tamarisk (*T. pentandra*) needs a more severe pruning. It should be allowed to develop five or six main stems, each branching and developing forks to the top. All tiny twigs should be removed, for new foliage and flower sprays spring from the old wood in the coming spring. Each main stem has a tendency to form a tuft of branches at the tip. Do not shorten all of these to the same length, but remove several completely, leaving only two which are evenly spaced. This will encourage an evenly branched tree of good shape. The whole tree can be sheared back almost to the ground every four years if desired.

Pride-of-India (*Lagerstroemia*). If Pride-of-India is not pruned, it will form a large, rounded, free-flowering tree which is effective in the landscape.

In warm, frost-free climates, where growth is very rapid, Pride-of-India may grow too large and bushy. In order to reduce its size, choose five or six main branches and shorten these by at least half of their length, so that they are about 3 or 4 feet from the ground. They can be allowed to branch at the base and then re-branch higher up. During the following summer, they will put forth long, waving branches bearing a large plume of flowers near the top. These new growths may be shortened by two-thirds in the following winter. Although the flowers are larger, the appearance of the whole tree is not quite as showy as when it is left unpruned. Pride-of-India is sometimes used as a deciduous hedge inside the garden and will flower well if it is cut back only at the end of winter.

Hydrangea (Christmas Flower). Few plants in South Africa have aroused as much controversy in their pruning as *Hydrangea macrophylla*, which is the most popularly grown species. Hydrangeas grow so easily in most parts of the country that gardeners have been able to prune them by almost any method and yet obtain flowers, although not always to their liking. The fact is that the Hydrangea can be pruned in several different ways according to whether one wants early or late flowers, a massed display or fewer, larger flowerheads. The ideal requirement is to obtain large, rounded bushes displaying an even mass of medium-sized blooms in midsummer. (See illustration on page 177.) The beautiful displays usually seen around Christmas time in the southern hemisphere have given rise to the popular name.

Hydrangeas must not be pruned according to a strict routine and one must use one's judgment in deciding how to treat them. They may have to be treated differently each year, depending on the way in which they have grown or flowered during the season and on the amount of old wood present. They cannot be left entirely unpruned or the flowers will become very numerous and much too small. Ultimately, the bush would become choked with old, gnarled trunks, leaving no room for the new shoots to come up from the base and replenish the bush with young wood. In this way, the life of the bush would be shortened. Well-pruned and well-fed Hydrangeas can be expected to bloom regularly for about 15 years, when they should be replaced.

Light Pruning to obtain a Massed Display in Midsummer

Plants which have flowered well and produced a massed display of flowers should be lightly pruned in summer and given a second light pruning at the end of winter.

In January or early February, immediately after the main midsummer display of flowers, the old flowerheads should be removed, cutting back about 8 inches to just above a strong bud. This stem will produce good flowers again in the following summer if it is young and healthy. It will become woody after the second year and should be cut down, leaving only two or three buds at the base of the stem and cutting just above a strong green bud. One or two strong canes will develop from this point, bearing flowers early in the following summer.

Old gnarled wood which develops at the base of a mature bush must be sawn off at ground level, even if it means sacrificing good flowering wood at the top. This need not be done each year, but only when the stem becomes very thick or crosses and rubs against other stems. The space cleared by an old cane will be filled by young shoots pushing up through the ground in spring. This old wood may be removed in February or in July, when it may be easier to see the stems while they are leafless. When sawing off the old wood at the end of winter, be careful not to damage the tips of the new shoots coming through the ground.

At the second light pruning period in July, one should not remove any new wood that has grown up during summer, but simply trim the bush slightly. This means removing about 8 inches off all the stems, cutting above a good strong bud. At the same time, one should remove dead wood or any weak, thin or withered growths from the base that give no indication of strengthening in the future. If the bush has a trim shape, then it is not necessary to shorten the stems at all and the top shoots will produce blooms in early summer in mild climates.

Hydrangeas remain evergreen in mild climates, only losing their leaves where winters are cold and dry. Pruning should be done in July even in areas where the plants remain evergreen, as this is the rest period before new growth commences in spring.

Heavy Pruning to obtain Flowers in late Summer or Autumn

It must be remembered that the growth put on during one summer will bear flowers during the following summer. If one prunes Hydrangeas severely during winter, by cutting the bushes hard back, the new growth will produce autumn flowers, which is often too late for most gardeners' requirements. In addition, the flowers may not be as evenly massed for display as when the bushes are lightly pruned. In places where growth is very rapid, such as in the luxuriant climate of the Natal coast, it is customary to cut the plants back almost to within a foot of the ground and still obtain a summer show of flowers, but the display of blooms is not always evenly massed and the plants may not bloom until very late if they are too severely pruned.

Severe pruning produces fewer stems and larger flowers, often up to 14 inches across. For general garden purposes, it is better to have a massed display of heads which are 8 or 9 inches across.

Tall Hydrangeas of 8 feet or more may be reduced in size by occasional hard cutting back in winter, even if it means sacrificing early summer flowers. They should be cut back to about 2 feet from ground level, leaving three or four buds on each stem.

Frost Damage. In cold places where Hydrangeas are frosted back, the dead wood will have to be removed in August, when all danger of frost has passed. If the amount of wood removed impairs flowering year after year, the bushes should be transplanted to a more sheltered position or protected by a covering. (See Chapter 19 on "The Gardener and the Weather".)

Cutting Flowers for the Vase

When cutting Hydrangeas for the vase, one must bear in mind the method of light pruning. Unless the bush is tall, it is not advisable to cut the flowers with very long stems. Some people like to retain the flowerheads on the bush until they turn russet or greenish in autumn, as these make interesting flower arrangements. Their late removal, however, may delay the following season's blooms as it will reduce the chance of obtaining strong new flowering canes that would produce early flowers. The canes would normally have sprung up from the buds stimulated by cutting off the flowers immediately after they have faded.

How to Rejuvenate an Old Hydrangea

An old bush that has developed a thicket of woody canes can be rejuvenated and encouraged to produce new flowering canes from the base. All the old stems may be removed by cutting them back to ground level in July, but this means cutting back the whole bush. A full season will be needed for the new shoots to mature and the summer flowers will be sacrificed. If the new growth prospers, it will produce flowers late in the season.

A slower, but less drastic method of eliminating old canes without sacrificing summer flowers, is to saw off two or three of the woody stems at ground level each winter. This will create space for new shoots to come up from the base and gradually allow the bush to replenish itself with young wood.

CHAPTER THIRTY-TWO

GROWING FRUIT

Growing one's own fruit is seldom economical, yet is compensated by the pleasure of picking fruit off one's own trees at the right moment of ripeness. Few gardens are large enough to contain an orchard, but one or more fruit trees can be fitted into almost any garden, while berries and vines can be included in the tiniest garden.

Choice. One must be guided in the choice of fruit trees according to one's climate. Advice on the varieties of fruit recommended for each area must be obtained from one's local nurseryman or local Department of Agriculture. The winter-rainfall area of the south-western Cape is ideal for growing deciduous fruits like Apples, Pears, Peaches, Nectarines, Plums and Apricots, as well as nuts like Almonds or Walnuts and many evergreen fruit trees. Cherries do well in the eastern Orange Free State near the mountains, where winters are extremely cold and rainfall is good. Most deciduous fruits do well on the highveld with its cold dry winters and summer rains, although some varieties do better than others. Deciduous fruits do not thrive in places with very hot summers and mild winters, as on the Natal coast, the Lowveld, low altitudes in the northern Transvaal, Rhodesia and most areas further north. In such places one can grow sub-tropical fruits like Papaw, Banana, Citrus and Mango instead. At higher altitudes in hot countries one can grow many deciduous fruits successfully.

In places with mild winters, where deciduous fruit trees are not sufficiently cooled during the dormant season, they suffer from "delayed foliation". The trees do not easily break their winter dormancy and both flowers and leaves are delayed in opening or open irregularly. This results in a poor set of fruit and insufficient foliage on the tree to shade the growing fruitlets or protect them from cooling dews at night, so that they often crack as a result of sudden changes in temperature. The trees can be assisted to break their dormancy by spraying with winter oils, made more efficient by adding D.N.O.C. compounds to them. This is generally done in the latter half of August and especially to Apples and Pears.

Recent experiments have shown that the treatment of the dormant twigs of deciduous trees with Gibberellic Acid has induced growth to begin and this may be used to break winter dormancy in the future.

When choosing fruit trees, buy only the best varieties from a reliable nursery, and those which are popular with the family. Remember that many trees need another variety planted nearby in order to assist cross-pollination. It is usually necessary to purchase two varieties of Apple, Pear, Cherry or Almond, whereas Peaches, Apricots, Prunes, Guavas, Figs and Quinces can generally be planted singly. Dwarf fruit trees are being developed in some countries and both these and espaliered trees are grown where space is limited. The latter must be especially shaped from the commencement of growth. Neither type is freely obtainable in southern Africa.

The Site for fruit trees should be sunny, so do not plant them where they will be shaded by large trees or buildings. They need an open situation and should not be planted on low-lying ground where water will collect or where lack of circulation may aggravate leaf diseases. Do not plant them on the lawn if fallen fruit may be a nuisance when mowing or where one might have to feed with extra nitrogen.

Planning the Orchard. Most deciduous fruit trees should be spaced at least 15 feet away from one another. Large, spreading evergreen trees should be planted 25 feet from any other. Huge trees like Pecan Nuts are ideally planted 60 feet from one another, so that they can only be planted in a very large garden.

One can grow crops of shallow-rooted vegetables or strawberries between young trees, but not within 4 feet of the stems, so as to avoid competition with the tree roots for nourishment. One can plant grass between mature trees, but this must be mown short and both trees and grass must be given extra nitrogen (sulphate of ammonia) and extra water or the grass will rob the trees of both. If liked, one can lay narrow slate paths around the trees and edge them with neat herbs like parsley or chives.

The soil should be deep, fertile and well-drained. Plant fruit trees on a raised terrace if rainfall is excessive and the soil is heavy.

Care and Feeding. Give each tree a generous annual dressing of old kraal manure at the end of winter and mulch them with well-rotted compost during the hot summer months. A general fertilizer containing potash can be given when the first fruits form. Apply lime only if the soil needs it, not more often than once in three years and a full month before dressing with manure. It is not necessary to dig the soil around the trees. Weeds must be removed while young. Give each tree at least 4 gallons of water once a week if good rains have not fallen. Young trees can be watered twice a week until they are established.

Most fruit trees require regular care in the form of pruning and spraying.

Pruning. Deciduous fruits require more pruning than sub-tropical fruits, and of these, Prunes, Cherries, Apples, Pears and Almonds require comparatively little pruning, except perhaps in the early stages. (See Chapter 31 on Pruning and individual trees listed below.)

Pests. Some trees require more spraying than others. Do not grow Apples if you are not prepared to spray regularly against Codling Moth, which may also attack Pears, Walnuts and Quinces. Peaches, Nectarines or Guavas should not be grown if you do not wish to carry out a spray programme against Fruit-Fly. (See Chapter 37 on "Common Insect Pests and Their Control".) Most other pests can be combated when seen. Spray at the first sign of aphids or scale. Scale is particularly troublesome on Citrus trees. All deciduous fruit trees must be sprayed when dormant each winter with Lime Sulphur as a cleansing spray. (See "Chemicals used in Plant Protection", Chapter 39.)

Disease. Spray regularly with fungicides from the beginning of the rainy season if one is troubled with leaf disease like Mildew or Peach Leaf Curl (See Chapter 38 on "Fungus Diseases".) In areas where large trees like Mangoes and Mulberries are affected and it is unpractical to spray them, it is best to avoid growing them.

Planting New Fruit Trees. Deciduous fruit trees are generally sent out from the nursery towards the end of winter. As they have bare roots, the holes should be prepared a few weeks in advance so that they can be planted on arrival without delay.

Dig the holes at least 3 feet in diameter and about 2 feet deep, keeping the top soil on one side. Half fill with the bottom soil mixed with old kraal manure, but replace the bottom soil with good garden soil if it is poor. Cover the manured soil with a 2-inch layer of good plain soil and add an extra spadeful to make a mound in the centre. Place the roots on top of this mound and fill in with topsoil, mixed with well-rotted compost if possible. Be careful not to plant the tree deeper than it was planted previously. Pack the soil firmly around the roots, treading it down. Place an encircling rim of soil around the tree to form a basin, which will prevent

water from running away, and give each tree 4 gallons of water immediately.

Evergreen fruits such as citrus are generally planted as above. Many sub-tropical fruits are obtainable established in tins and can be planted out with the earth intact around the roots. (See below under each tree.)

HINTS ON GROWING DIFFERENT FRUITS

Only the most popular fruits will be listed below. Many shrubs and trees with edible fruits like Amatungulu (*Carissa grandiflora*), Brush-Cherry (*Eugenia*) and Pineapple-Guava (*Feijoa*) are grown more for ornament than for their fruits and will not be listed here as they do not belong to the orchard.

GROWING DECIDUOUS FRUITS

Almond. An excellent tree for all except sub-tropical gardens, Almonds need little care. Plant in a sheltered place in cold areas as they flower early in August and late frosts may damage the crop. Plant two varieties. Prune only to remove crossing branches. Strong shoots can be shortened. Bears fruit in 4th year.

Apple. Hardy and needs a cold winter. Prune for shape in the first five years. Bears fruit in from three to five years. Plant early and late varieties. Spray Apples in advance for Codling Moth. Plant two varieties.

Apricot. Hardy, but blooms early and dislikes spring frost. Prefers dry atmosphere with irrigation to humidity. Prolific. Do not overprune. Spray for leaf diseases.

Cherry. Needs cold winter and plenty of water, particularly in spring, but a well-drained soil. Do not prune except to shorten some shoots when the tree is young. Heavy winter pruning causes gumming. Shoots are best shortened in summer after fruiting. Plant two.

Fig. Thrives in warm, sub-tropical regions in the winter-rainfall area, where there is plenty of rain when the young fruits swell during spring and dryness in summer when the figs are ripening. Lack of moisture in the soil in spring will make the young fruits drop. Figs dislike intense cold. They require rich, well-drained soil and no pruning except to keep growing uniformly when young. Plant 25 feet apart. Protect from Fig Borer where troublesome. (See "Insect Control" Chapter 37.) Purchase self-fertilizing varieties or plant more than one.

Mulberry. A large, prolific tree, the Mulberry grows easily and needs no pruning, but long branches can be shortened. The Weeping Mulberry is smaller. The Mulberry needs moisture in spring and summer, but will endure drought in winter. May suffer from leaf diseases in humid areas and from White Peach Scale.

Nectarine. Grow and prune like Peach. Spray in advance against Fruit-Fly.

Peach. Hardy, but dislikes late frosts. Needs careful annual pruning. Needs fertile, very well-drained soil and should be watered regularly from early spring to late autumn. There are dozens of varieties of free-stone and clingstone peaches, suitable for canning or eating. Watch for aphids or scale and spray in advance against Fruit-Fly and with fungicides for Peach Leaf-Curl.

Pear. Long-lived trees with ornamental blossom, Pears need cool winters, but dislike heavy frosts. Grow easily and need little pruning, especially after the first three to five years. Need regular watering by irrigation, but soil must be well-drained. Will grow in heavier soil than Peach. Space 25 feet apart. May be necessary to spray against Codling Moth. Plant two varieties.

Persimmon. An unusual fruit grown mainly for ornament, it must be eaten when ripe and soft. Needs regular watering, but no pruning. Japanese dwarf forms are best.

Plum. Long-lived, easily grown and adaptable trees, there are plums to please every palate. The Japanese Plums include the best known commercial varieties like Santa Rosa, Satsuma, Gaviota, Kelsey and Methley, while the European Plums include the Sugar Prune and Prune d'Agen. Fertilize Plums well as they bear prolifically and water particularly during spring and early summer. They are fairly disease-resistant. Prune carefully and do not overprune. (See under Pruning, Chapter 31.)

Pomegranate. A hardy shrub, this grows easily with little attention. Remove lower branches to a height of 3 feet as they are weighted to the ground with the heavy, ornamental fruit in late summer.

Quince. Small, hardy trees that grow easily, Quinces will grow in heavy or wet soils although they prefer well-drained soil. Fruit should be stewed or made into jelly. No pruning needed except occasional thinning. Sometimes troubled by Codling Moth and Apple-and-Quince Borer.

Walnut. Needs deep rich soil and a cool, moist winter, with regular irrigation at other times. Slow-growing at first, it is a large spreading tree which needs a 10 foot radius. No pruning necessary. May need to spray against Codling Moth or fungus diseases, but it is not practical for the home gardener to spray large trees.

GROWING EVERGREEN AND SUB-TROPICAL FRUITS

Avocado (Alligator Pear). Does best in warm, frost-free, humid places like the Natal coast and low altitudes in Swaziland, the eastern and northern Transvaal and north of the Limpopo. Some varieties are hardier than others and will bear fruit in warm gardens on the highveld, north of Johannesburg and in Pretoria. Different hybrids and varieties mature all through the year, but the fruits must be picked and kept in a warm place to soften and ripen. Fuerte is the most popular self-pollinated hybrid, ripening from autumn to spring.

Avocadoes can be grown from seed, but better results are obtained by planting grafted plants established in tins. Plant in spring and summer, spaced 30 feet apart. Stake and shade the young plants which will bear in three or four years. Avocadoes need shelter from strong winds. Water once a month during winter, giving a deep irrigation, and only water during spring and summer if good rains have not fallen for three or four weeks. Water every two weeks during the flowering period. Acid soils of pH 5.5 to 6.5 suit Avocadoes. Deep, well-drained soil will eliminate root rots. If the soil is light or shallow, mulch at regular intervals with well-rotted compost. Fertilize in spring or autumn with manure and superphosphates and add small amounts of nitrogen fertilizer three or four times a year. In commercial orchards, Avocadoes are sprayed annually with zinc sulphate to correct zinc deficiencies, while magnesite is worked into the topsoil every three years to supply magnesium requirements.

Banana (*Musa*). Easily grown in the right climate, Bananas have special requirements. They must be grown in warm, completely frost-free climates, for they will not set fruit well if the weather is cold. They need full sunshine with shelter from strong winds. The fruit sets better in a humid atmosphere, although plenty of water can be given where the climate is dry. Thick grass mulches will conserve moisture as well as keep down weeds and the plants can be deeply irrigated every week when grown away from the humid coastal belt. At the coast, young plants should be irrigated weekly and mature plants once a fortnight during the dry season. Ideal climates are the eastern coastal belt and low altitudes in the eastern and northern Transvaal and Rhodesia.

The soil should be rich and heavy, but good drainage on sloping ground prevents root rots. It should be acid, but not below pH 5.5. Dig holes 3 feet wide for each plant, but no deeper than 2 feet as they are shallow-rooted. Dig in plenty of manure and compost and add 2 lb. of rock phosphate to each hole. Superphosphates can be added, but not on a very acid soil. Repeat the manure and phosphate feeds annually as well as adding $\frac{1}{2}$ lb. of potash. The dwarf Cavendish or Chinese Bananas, growing to 8 feet, are hardier and more disease-resistant than the taller common Banana. Space the plants 6–8 feet apart in rows from 10 to 12 feet apart. Bananas are sensitive to eelworm infestation and should not be planted where

Tomatoes have been grown. Dust with copper fungicides at the beginning of the rainy season if fungus diseases occur in warm, moist areas.

Banana plants should have one tall thick stem which will bear fruit, with one or two shorter suckers coming up to replace it. All other suckers must be removed at ground level and may be used to form new plants. The ripening fruit may be covered with a large leaf to protect it from sunscald, while plastic covers may be used only during winter. As soon as the first bananas turn yellow, cut the whole bunch from the plant and cut back the entire stem to ground level. Allow one sucker to grow up and bear fruit each year, but the parent plant should be discarded after six to eight years. In order to propagate new plants, remove suckers from spring to late summer when they are from 2 to 3 feet high. Pieces of the parent root can also be divided to form new plants and bear even earlier than suckers.

Cashew Nut (*Anacardium*). A spreading evergreen tree, suited only to hot, frost-free areas at the coast, the Cashew Nut will tolerate poor soil and very little water. The nut is borne at the tip of a swollen portion of the stalk known as the Cashew Apple, which is edible. The nuts are roasted before being removed carefully from the shell. Broken shells should not be handled as the nut is encased in a skin containing a poisonous, irritating oil. The trees are grown from seed planted directly in the soil, 25 feet apart.

Citrus Fruits. The most important Citrus fruits are the Orange, Lemon, Naartjie (Tangerine and Mandarin) and Grapefruit. Some lesser known or grown species and hybrids are the Lime, Citron, Tangelo, Kumquat and Calamondin. All Citrus fruits are evergreen and may be grown in a similar way, although they have slightly varying climatic requirements. Growing Citrus is a specialised major industry in this country, but the gardener can grow Citrus trees with ease, provided that the climate is suitable and the soil well-drained. The trees are ornamental even if they do not produce a commercial crop and are worth growing for their perfumed blossom alone. As they generally live for 30 years or more, choose the site carefully and pay attention to planting, watering and feeding. The trees bear in from five to seven years.

Climate. Citrus grows best in frost-free areas. The trees can endure light frosts, but will be killed by heavy frost and cold in the region of 15 to 20 degrees F. Some Citrus fruits tolerate cold more than others. Naartjies and Bitter Oranges are slightly more hardy than Sweet Orange, Grapefruit or Lemon, in that order. Limes and Citron are most sensitive to frost. The gardener in cold, winter areas can plant the trees in a warm, sheltered position, where surrounding hedges and trees form a windbreak, and there are few places too cold for a Lemon tree in this country. Citrus trees dislike wind which dries the fruit and leaves, causing them to drop, or may break branches.

One should obtain advice on the best varieties to plant from one's local nurseryman or the Citrus Research Station in Nelspruit. Washington Navel is recommended for areas above 3,000 feet where there is a fairly even temperature, as they dislike hot, dry winds following cool weather. In sub-tropical places where summers are very hot, therefore, it is best to plant Valencia and mid-season Oranges, Lemons and Grapefruit, which are better able to withstand sudden high temperatures. Citrus fruits can be grown at any altitude from the coast to 6,000 feet, provided that the climate is suitable. One should plant recommended varieties in humid areas, where humidity aggravates certain fungus diseases.

Soil. Unless drainage is good, Citrus Trees may die of fungus attack like Dry Root Rot. Heavy clay soils are unsuitable and the soil should be light and well-aerated, even though it may be poor, as one can always fertilize it. Light medium loam soil is best and should be good to a depth of at least 3 to 5 feet. Citrus will grow in acid soil as low as pH 4 or in slightly alkaline soil, but dislike brak soil and high alkalinity beyond pH 8.

Planting. Citrus trees are planted from July to January in sub-tropical places and from September to March in places with cool winters. The saplings are sent out from the nursery with bare roots or balled, and the holes should be prepared well in advance to receive them. Space them about 20 feet apart or at half this distance provided that one removes the alternate trees after about ten years. Dig each hole about 3 feet across and 2½ feet deep. Fill the bottom half of the hole with topsoil mixed with a large bucket of manure and 6 lb. of rock phosphate or superphosphate. Fill the top half of the hole with good topsoil, mixed with some well-rotted compost, and use the remaining sub-soil to make a rim around the tree making an irrigation basin 3 feet across. Water to settle the soil before the trees arrive.

Open the soil and plant the tree on arrival. The bud-union must be higher than the level of the soil when planted. Water immediately, soaking the soil well. Repeat a few days later and gradually increase watering to once in 10 days until the new growth has matured.

Watering. Young trees must be watered more often than mature trees, but trees laden with fruit require large amounts of water at each irrigation. Citrus trees should be watered once a fortnight for the first three months, but mature trees need not be watered more than once a month, provided that they are given a deep irrigation. This means leaving the hosepipe to flood the basin for from half an hour to two hours, depending on the size of the tree, giving the equivalent of at least half an inch of rain. It is especially important to irrigate the trees during flowering and fruit-setting time, from July and August to the end of March. As the tree grows, enlarge the irrigation basin to the outer edges of the branches. Most of the tree's roots are in the top 3 feet of soil, mainly in the top foot. Mulching with compost or grass will conserve moisture and keep down weeds.

Allow the top 2 or 3 inches of soil to dry out before watering again, or the soil will be deprived of oxygen and the trees will suffer from overwatering. For this reason it is best not to plant shallow-rooted plants, which require frequent watering, within 3 or 4 feet of the tree. Be careful not to allow the trees to wilt before watering again.

Feeding. After the second year give each tree 3 lb. of superphosphate annually. Spread kraal manure thickly over the irrigation basin each spring after the third year. In addition, ammonium sulphate may be given twice during summer, but not more than 1 lb. annually for each year of the tree's age. If Citrus trees are grown on lawns, this should be increased to 6 lb. annually for each year of the tree's age, given in three or four applications.

Care. Protect the stems of young trees from sunburn by white-washing them or by wrapping them with brown paper, but keep it at least an inch above soil level. Remove weeds while young and do not dig deeply as this injures roots and may cause fungus disease.

Pruning. Remove suckers and new shoots developing on the main stem. In the second year, remove weak or crossing limbs only if necessary to establish a balanced shape. Paint over all cuts with tree-sealing compound. The only annual pruning that may be done is to remove dead, frosted or broken shoots and trim the lower branches so that they do not touch the soil. Heavy pruning or removal of foliage will dwarf the tree and reduce the crop. Remove some of the young fruit in the first three years.

Pests. The chief pests which trouble Citrus are aphids and scale insects of several kinds. (See Chapter 37 on Insect Control.) These can be kept down by controlling ants and by using sprays like Malathion which kill these as well as Citrus psylla. False Codling Moth is sometimes troublesome. Scale insects may also be suffocated by oil sprays, but one must use them correctly or they may cause leaf injury or fruit drop. (See "Chemicals used in Plant Protection" Chapter 39 and under Insect Control.)

Disease. Sooty Mould can be prevented by controlling aphids. (See Chapter 37.) Fungus diseases of commercial importance, like Fruit or Black Spot, are controlled by spraying with fixed coppers from the beginning of the rainy season. Zinc or magnesium deficiencies, indicated by yellow mottling of the leaves, can be corrected as for Avocado.

Types of Citrus Trees
Orange. The Sweet Orange (*Citrus sinensis*) is the most important type of orange for eating and there are several early, mid-season and late varieties. Washington Navel is the best early variety and stands a fair amount of cold. Valencia oranges are the last to mature and may be grown in sub-tropical as well as colder regions. The Sour Orange (*C. aurantium*) can only be used for making marmalade. It is also called Seville or Bitter Orange.

Lemon. There are many varieties of Smooth and Rough Lemon. The Meyer Lemon is more frost-resistant than the Eureka Lemon. Lemons can be picked green to ripen indoors. Lemon trees are not as long-lived as Orange and may need replacing after 10 or 15 years.

Grapefruit (Pomelo). These trees thrive in hot, low-lying places. While tolerant of cool weather, they develop thick-skinned, acid fruits with little juice in cold areas.

Naartjie (Tangerine and Mandarin). The Naartjie can stand slightly colder climates than the Orange. It is recommended that they be grown from seed, for budded varieties generally succumb to virus disease after about seven years.

Lime. Tender and only suited to frost-free localities.

Tangelo. A hybrid between the Tangerine and the Grapefruit (Pomelo). The better crosses resemble the Tangerine in flavour, while the less desirable crosses are more bitter, like Grapefruit. They should be propagated from seed, like Naartjies.

Kumquat. A large, fairly hardy shrub, the Kumquat is closely related to Citrus and may be grown in the same way. It has small, pungent orange fruits of which the Meiwa variety bears the sweetest.

Guava. The large Guava of commerce (*Psidium guajava*) is a spreading evergreen tree, reaching a height of 15 feet or more. It grows easily in frost-free or sub-tropical places and can stand slight frost. Guavas need plenty of water, especially when the fruit is setting, and thrive in the winter rainfall area. The soil must be well-drained and should be fertile for best results. Prune the trees regularly after bearing in order to keep them low. Severe pruning in October will encourage bearing in winter. Guavas grow easily from seed, but good varieties are propagated by layers, cuttings and suckers. Plant from autumn to spring, spaced 18 feet apart. Guavas are seldom troubled by pests except for Fruit-fly. Use a baited spray. (See Chapter 37.) The Fruit-fly not only attacks the fruit, but also shelters on the trees during winter.

The **Strawberry Guava** (*Psidium cattleianum*) has small, round, purplish-red fruits with a piquant flavour, mainly ornamental. It grows to about 8 feet. It can be grown on the Highveld, preferring a sheltered position. No pruning is necessary.

Litchi. A small, spreading, sub-tropical, evergreen tree, the Litchi thrives on the frost-free, humid Natal coast and Transvaal lowveld. Young trees are tender, but established trees can stand some frost. The weather should be fine and dry when the trees flower in July and August. The fruit matures in December and January and must be picked when ripe. The tree is self-fertile and pollinated by bees.

Litchis require deep, rich soil with plenty of water. Mulch the shallow roots with fallen leaves. The tree should be sheltered from wind and the brittle branches can be supported inside the tree by stout poles. Litchi-trees may be planted and fed like Citrus, but are spaced 30 to 40 feet apart. No pruning is necessary. Propagation is by air-layering.

Loquat (*Eriobotrya japonica*). The Loquat Tree is grown for its ornamental evergreen foliage as much as for its small yellow fruits, which ripen during spring. The flowers appear in late summer. The Loquat thrives in most gardens and on any soil, being fairly hardy, but does best where winters are mild, especially near the coast. It needs no pruning except to shape it in the early stages. Water regularly for best results. Spray Loquats during winter if they are planted near Peach or Nectarine trees, as they provide a home for the over-wintering Fruit-fly.

Macadamia Nut (Queensland Nut). Tall evergreen tree with delicious nuts. Needs fertile soil, good rainfall, mild winters. Plant 30 feet apart.

Mango. A large, spreading evergreen tree, the Mango is easy to grow, but particular about climate. It is suited only to sub-tropical, frost-free areas with heavy summer rains, but with a long dry period of at least four months during winter and early spring, when the flowers bloom and the fruit is setting. The lightest frost will kill the flowers, while rain and hot winds will prevent the fruit from setting. Moist weather while flowering causes fungus diseases. Mango trees do not need irrigating in the right climate, as they have very deep roots. If desired, one or two very deep irrigations can be given during the flowering period and immediately afterwards, but the trees should not be watered before the flowers appear or during summer. The Mango needs no pruning and will grow on most types of soil, preferring a medium-heavy soil, but cannot tolerate bad drainage.

Mango trees can be planted out in the same way as Citrus, but with soil around the roots and not with bare roots. They are propagated by budding and there are several improved varieties. Budded trees are generally smaller and more satisfactory than seedlings. The trees are spaced from 25 to 40 feet apart. Young trees should be given plenty of old kraal manure, but nitrogenous feeding should be given with restraint so as not to over-stimulate growth.

Olive. A slow-growing evergreen tree, mainly of commercial importance, the Olive does best in the winter rainfall area at the Cape. It needs well-drained soil and dislikes frost. It is drought-resistant in summer. Prune for the first five years for a uniform shape. The Olive bears in the sixth year.

Papaw (*Carica papaya*). Papaw trees are sensitive to frost, but grow easily in a hot climate. They are drought-resistant and thrive in almost any type of soil, provided that it is well-drained and not very heavy. Papaw trees are prone to fungus disease in damp soil and areas of high humidity. Fertile soil is suitable, but one should not dig manure into the holes for young trees, in case of fungus infection. Dig 1½ lb. of rock or superphosphates into each hole. Top dress with old kraal manure after two months, but do not place it too near the stem. The trees may be given a combined dressing of kraal manure and superphosphates six months later and annually thereafter.

Male and female flowers are borne on separate trees and these cannot be identified until they start flowering, which is generally when they are about six months old and three feet in height. It is necessary, therefore, to grow several plants and thin them out after six months, leaving one male to every 25 female trees. The female flower is five-petalled and borne singly on short stalks, while the male flowers are joined to form a short tube and borne on long stalks. Some trees have both male and female flowers.

Papaws are grown from seed which should be sown in September and October or December and January. The seed-bed must be well drained and consist of plain soil topped with a layer of river sand to reduce the risk of root-rot. Transplant carefully when 6 to 9 inches high. Remove large leaves a few days before moving and choose a cloudy day for transplanting. Keep the moistened soil around the roots and do not plant deeply. Water immediately and shade lightly for a few days. Young plants need water every five or seven days for the first few weeks, but established trees need only be watered every three weeks in the dry season, preferably by irrigation. Space the plants three feet apart in rows ten feet apart. They can be planted in the rows between long-lived Citrus, Mango or Litchi trees, for they bear well only for three or four years, and should then be replaced. They start bearing in 12 to 15 months after transplanting. The fruits generally ripen from spring to late summer and are best picked when ripe

Pecan Nut. A long-lived deciduous tree which grows to more than 100 feet in height and spread, the Pecan is suitable only for a very large garden. Commercial growers space the trees 60 feet apart. The tree is self-pollinated by wind. It is a deep-rooted, moisture-loving tree and should be grown in fertile, deep soil which is well-drained. It is suited to growing in low fertile valleys of large rivers and in sub-tropical areas, although it will stand light frost.

Irrigation is preferable to rainfall at flowering time around October, but otherwise good rains are necessary, especially in summer and autumn. The trees must be deeply irrigated from early in August, a month before shooting starts, until the leaves drop in autumn. Hot, dry winds at flowering time will limit the crop. The soil should be top-dressed with kraal manure each spring, while mature trees can also be given nitrogenous fertilizer and potash. Zinc sulphate sprays are recommended every third year if mottled leaves appear. The trees are transplanted while dormant. Gardeners can plant seedlings, but budded varieties are grown commercially. They take four to seven years to bear. Pecan nuts ripen in late summer and should be gathered when they begin to fall from the tree.

Pineapple (*Ananas comosus*). A tropical herbaceous plant, the Pineapple needs a frost-free hot climate at low altitudes up to 3,000 feet, preferably in the summer rainfall area. The plant has a small root and a short stem, almost hidden by a rosette of stiff, spiny leaves. The fruit stem grows up from the centre and bears a pineapple at the tip. The plant needs full sunshine. Very drought-resistant, it need not be watered except during the dry season. Water by irrigation, but do not allow the water to settle around the plants. Well-drained loamy soil is best, while clay soil is unsuitable. Pineapples like acid soil between pH 5.5 and 6.2. Rake the soil finely before planting and destroy all weeds, but do not use chemical weedkillers. Do not dig deeply when weeding around plants because of their weak roots. Manure is

not recommended in the soil, especially for the Queen variety, but a little well-rotted compost may be added. The best fertilizer to apply in the eastern Cape coastal area is mixture 8-6-8, while that recommended for Natal and the Transvaal is mixture 6-10-3. When the leaves turn yellowish or summer rains have been heavy, nitrogenous fertilizer may be given in April. Place fertilizer near the roots, but do not let it fall into the heart.

The Queen variety is smaller than the Smooth Cayenne variety, but is sweeter, more yellow, firmer and less juicy. These are the two most popular varieties. Planting takes place during the rainy season from October to February. Propagation is done in several ways. Suckers can be removed at ground level or from between the leaves at the base of the fruit stem; offsets or "slips", which are swellings formed below the fruit, can be planted to form new plants; crowns, being the leafy top of the fruit, can be cut off and replanted, but the cut surface should be dried for a week before planting. The Smooth Cayenne is grown mainly from crowns. The Queen Pineapple can also be grown from stumps or pieces of the old fruit stem cut off after harvesting. Plant the Smooth Cayenne variety in double rows 18 inches apart, spaced from 12 to 18 inches apart in the rows, but staggered diagonally opposite one another. Leave 4 feet and plant another double row. The smaller Queen variety is planted 15 inches apart in single rows spaced 4 feet apart.

The new plants will bear fruit in from $1\frac{1}{2}$ to $2\frac{1}{2}$ years, depending on their growth. Pineapples ripen in late summer in the eastern Cape, but earlier in the lowveld and more tropical places. A second crop is planted to ripen towards the end of winter. After harvesting, all the fruit-stems and suckers of the Queen Pine should be removed and may be replanted if desired. The Smooth Cayenne has fewer suckers, so that one should remove only the offsets or slips from the old fruit stem for replanting. Each plant bears for about four to eight years and should be discarded when it begins to deteriorate.

Tree Tomato (*Cyphomandra betacea*). A short-lived plant growing from 6 to 10 feet, the Tree Tomato bears ornamental fruits in 18 months from seed. These should be stewed or made into jam. Give the plant a sheltered position in cold areas.

GROWING BERRIES AND VINES

Cane Fruits. Youngberry, Booysenberry, Loganberry, Blackberry. The thornless Youngberry grows best and yields more heavily than any other berry in this country, followed closely by the Booysenberry, which is largest and bears later. They do very well in the winter-rainfall area, but can also grow elsewhere. Young plants are set out at the end of winter and must be kept moist. Plant them 3 to 4 feet apart in full sun. If space allows for two rows, leave 6 feet between them. Mulch around the roots to reduce the need for watering. An annual dressing of manure can be given each spring, as well as a little balanced fertilizer.

Most varieties of berries bear fruit during midsummer. As soon as the berries have been picked, cut out the old canes at ground level. Young canes sprouting from the base will now be about 4 feet long. They can be tied on to supports when they lose their leaves in winter. Allow four to six to remain to a plant and remove the weakest. The canes can be wound around fencing wires in loose spirals or they can be wound around 6-foot poles near each plant and tied with three rows of raffia. Shorten canes above the poles. Remove suckers that emerge between the rows in order to prevent a thicket forming and to facilitate weeding. In case of leaf diseases, spray with a fungicide at the beginning of the rainy season. Control aphids.

Cape Gooseberry (*Physalis peruviana*). A perennial which is grown as an annual, this grows easily in all parts of Southern Africa. It is tender to frost and seed must be sown early in cold winter areas. A member of the Tomato family, it should not be planted following any other member of the family. Cape Gooseberry needs a well-drained but not over-fertile soil. Sow seed in seed-boxes in July or August, transplanting the seedlings as soon as the weather is warm enough. These will bear fruit in midsummer. In places with a mild autumn, they can also be planted as late as November. Water young plants well, but mature plants need only be irrigated every two or three weeks during dry weather.

Granadilla or Passion Fruit (*Passiflora edulis*). A luxuriant vine, the Granadilla grows almost anywhere, but prefers a warm, frost-free climate. Plant it in a sheltered position in cold areas and provide shelter from wind. Granadillas are grown from seed which must be rubbed in sand, washed and dried. Grow in tins and transplant when a few inches high. The vine must be trained on to a strong fence and the home gardener can drape it over a split pole fence. Granadillas can be pruned to a single stem, however, which divides into two branches at the top and is allowed to grow on either side, supported by wires. After gathering the fruit in late summer or in spring, the long shoots can be shortened to near the main stem.

The soil should be well-drained, light and fertile. Add kraal manure and rock phosphates or superphosphates to the hole for the young plant and repeat annually each spring or in autumn in the winter rainfall area. Water the plants regularly when the weather is dry, especially during August to October when flowering. The fruit ripens mainly in midsummer. The vines last only about five to eight years. Granadillas are sensitive to Eelworm and may be stung by the Pumpkin Fly. Control Mealybug.

Grapes (*Vitis*). Ideal for the home garden where space is limited, a Grape Vine can be trained to shade porches or grown on fences and pergolas. Grapes thrive in the winter rainfall area of the south-western Cape, which is hot and dry when the fruit ripens in February and March. Some varieties can be grown in the summer rainfall area, both on the highveld and lowveld, especially those which ripen early.

Soil. Grapes require a sunny position and should have morning sun to lessen the risk of fungus infection. Well-drained, aerated soil, to a depth of at least $2\frac{1}{2}$ feet, is essential. It may be either sandy or heavy, but not compacted or over-fertile. Grapes like an acid soil of pH 5 or 6. A mulch of well-rotted compost or manure should be placed around the roots each year. If manure is insufficient, nitrogen fertilizers may be given. Rock or superphosphates should be mixed into the soil before planting and given as an annual dressing. In manganese-deficient soils of the Cape it is necessary to spray with manganese, while sulphur sprays may also be necessary.

Care. Water by irrigation. Keep down weeds and control ants which encourage Mealybug. After pruning, spray with freshly made Bordeaux mixture to control Powdery Mildew. Spray with fungicides from the beginning of the rains in areas of heavy summer rainfall.

Planting. Grow only the best plants as they will bear for a life-time. The famous Grape Vine at Graaff-Reinet is about 80 years old and still bearing. Purchase grafted, rooted cuttings from a recognised nurseryman, who will recommend the best varieties for your area. The rooted cutting will be about 18 inches long. Trim long roots back to 6 inches. Plant the whole rooted cutting deeply, covering it with soil, and allow only a tiny, 1-inch knob to show above the ground. Mound this knob with soil. Water well. Space the vines from 3 to 6 feet apart, depending on the vigour of the variety.

Training and Pruning. Allow the stem to grow up freely during the first summer. At the end of winter, during the first week in August, cut back the stem to from three to six buds from the base, cutting above the bud. It should then be about 15 inches in length. The top bud will send up a 3-foot growth during the following summer. Remove any side shoots that develop from between the leaves and stake this main stem to a stout stick. Lead the main stem from its wooden stake on to

Perold Trellis

Stake → | 20" space |
| 10" |
| 36" |
Soil

Overhead Trellis

3'6" Cross-bar →

Stout fencing pole, 3'6". →

← 15' space →

Young Vine

H. System on Pergola

Two pairs of side shoots forming an H

Top of leader lying horizontally over pergola

the trellis which should be erected at this stage. (See below.) Cut off the top when it reaches the wire, so that 2 short leaders will branch out from this point. Train these to grow to the left and to the right. The leaders are allowed to grow to a length of 18 inches. The masses of shoots that grow from this point each spring will bear grapes in the following summer and must be cut back to this point again each winter. The old wood of a vine does not bear fruit, but when pruned, produces new growth that bears fruit. Pruning also limits growth and produces better quality fruit. It is best done in July or the first week in August.

Types of Trellis. Table Grapes can be trained in several ways. (See illustrations above.)

The Perold System is simplest, consisting of three wires strung above one another, but does not produce sufficient space for the vine to develop. **The Overhead System,** which enables the vine to form a horizontal canopy, is best. It consists of a series of stout T-pieces, holding five wires spaced at regular intervals above the ground. The height is generally 3 feet 6 inches and the cross-bar is the same length, but both can be increased to 5 feet and the cross-bar should be slanted so that the vine will face the east. Vines growing over this large area, as well as on a pergola, should be allowed to grow a longer main stem from the beginning and the leader may be trained by the **H system,** also known as the **Verandah Trellis.** The leader is allowed to grow over the top of the pergola which is roofed in with wires. Two pairs of side shoots are allowed to develop from this leader so that they form an H with the leader joining them. The fruit-bearing shoots are cut back to these main stems each year.

Strawberry (*Fragaria*). The strawberry may be grown in all parts of the country, but does best where humidity is high in summer as in the winter-rainfall area of the south-western Cape, especially near the coast. The Ever-bearing varieties are the most popular, being the most vigorous, prolific and virus-resistant. The Koeël is also

recommended, though not quite so prolific. There are many varieties of Strawberries which grow easily and form thick groundcovers, including the tiny, pointed alpine or French Strawberries. New hybrid commercial Strawberries are constantly being developed overseas.

Soil and Feeding. Good drainage is essential and the soil should be loamy, but neither too light nor too heavy. Strawberries like a slightly acid to neutral soil (pH 5.9) and it is seldom necessary to add lime. When preparing the soil for a bed, add plenty of well-rotted compost which will help to conserve moisture. Dig to a depth of 6 to 8 inches and pulverise the lumps. Level carefully. A general fertilizer and superphosphates may be added when planting. Potash is important and can be given separately in early spring. The plants can be fed with a balanced liquid plant food at intervals from the beginning of the flowering period until the fruits ripen. If a powdered plant food is used, water after fertilizing so that none remains on the leaves or it will burn them.

Planting. Strawberries planted from June to August generally bear in December or January. Plant them in a warm, sunny place in areas with cold winters and mulch with grass if it is very cold. If one is not able to plant immediately on arrival, heel the plants into the soil in order to prevent drying out. Keep the roots moist with damp sacks before planting. Dig a hole from 4 to 6 inches deep so that the roots will spread downwards. Set the crown just above ground level and no deeper. Firm the roots very well and water immediately. Spacing depends on the method of culture described below.

Watering. Water regularly and evenly throughout the year, especially at fruiting time and if good rain does not fall. Allow the sprinkler to run for a long time at each irrigation, so that the ground is soaked to a depth of about 5 inches. Allow the top inch or two to dry out before watering again, or the plants will suffer from over-watering, but the shallow roots must not be allowed to dry out or the plants wilt for lack of water. Good watering

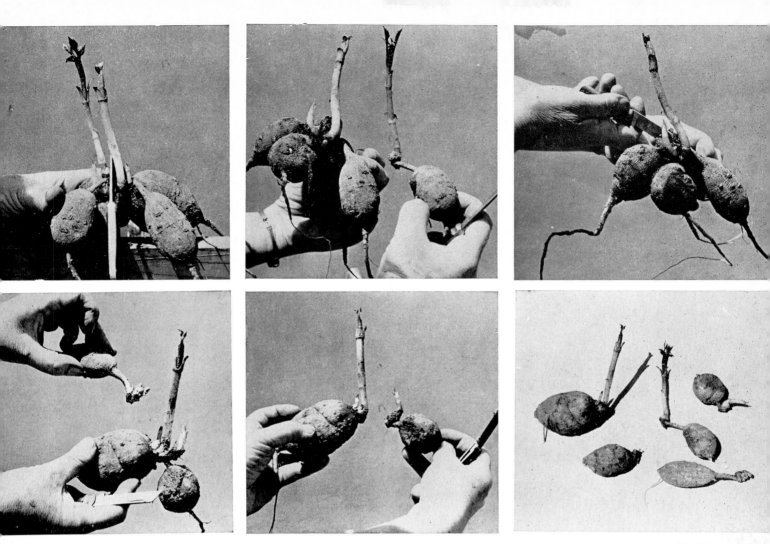

Careful division of a clump of Dahlia tubers will give one several new plants of the same kind. This small clump has yielded five good tubers, some with long shoots and others with swelling buds. In the bottom right-hand picture, they are shown in the position in which they should be planted. (See Chapter 26.)

A prize-winning Daffodil should have its trumpet at right angles to the flower stalk, as shown on the right. (See Chapter 27.)

Good double Chrysanthemums should be disbudded to produce the beautiful bloom on the right instead of the poor flowers on the left-hand stalk. (See Chapters 23 and 26.)

Until one's trees grow in a new garden, one can cover the ground between them with showy annuals and perennials.

When trees are fully grown, however, one can replace the delicate annuals with strong permanent plants and shade-loving plants that will resist root competition. (See Chapters 9, 10 and 11.)

once or twice a week should be sufficient, watering more often when bearing begins. Sandy soils must be watered more often than heavier soil.

Care. Keep weeds down, especially during summer. Pick fruit every two to four days. One can keep the fruit off the ground by mulching with straw or pine-needles, but a mulch sometimes keeps the soil too cool and delays fruiting or attracts insects. The straw can be sprayed with 10 per cent DDT before spreading it to repel wood-eating Termites. Aphids and mites must be controlled. In case of Leaf-spot or Mildew, spray with fungicides before or after flowering.

Propagation. After fruiting, Strawberry plants send out runners which bear young plants at their tips. These can be severed and lifted in autumn or early spring to start new plantings. They can be trimmed and heeled in to await replanting when convenient. The parent plant bears well for one to three years and should then be discarded. A new patch should be planted every year or at least once every second year. The formation of runners poses a problem to gardeners who must keep them in check in order to improve the quality of the fruit. Several methods of culture are used, according to the time and labour at one's disposal or to the type of fruit wanted, as follows:—

Matted Row System. This is the easiest system, requiring the least maintenance, and used by most commercial growers. Mark out a long bed 18 to 20 inches wide and plant a row of Strawberry plants down the centre, spacing them 4 to 6 inches apart. Allow the runners to spread over the whole bed, re-arranging them judiciously to fill all the spaces. As soon as the plants grow over the edge of the bed, trim them back. Remove excess plants here and there in the second season. If liked, extend the runners according to a definite pattern, allowing them to form three rows of plants in all, one on either side of the original row. Cut off all other runners. This will improve the size and quality of the fruit, but requires more attention.

In order to make even more use of available space, make a wider bed, 42 inches across, and plant two rows of Strawberries down the centre, spacing them 4 inches apart. Allow this double row to spread and fill the bed as before.

Hill System. This can be used in the home garden to obtain larger fruit, but requires more attention. All the runners are cut off as they appear in midsummer, leaving only the parent plant. Grow each plant on a small hill, placed diagonally opposite each other in double rows, spacing the plants about 6 to 9 inches apart and the double rows about 2 feet apart. Allow the plants to bear for two years before discarding.

Pots. Plants may be grown in individual pots and the runners cut off as they appear. Pin the runner to moist soil in a nearby pot to obtain a new plant. This method can be used in greenhouses or on verandahs.

Terrace. Plant Strawberries on the edge of a terrace or double wall so as to facilitate tending, but cut off all runners.

Barrel Method. Use where space is limited or as a garden ornament. Remove the top and bottom of a heavy barrel. Bore 1-inch holes in the sides, spacing them a foot apart. Fill the barrel with fertile soil. Insert the plants through the holes from the outside. Water the soil from the top. A pipe with holes in it may be placed down the centre to facilitate watering if desired.

CHAPTER THIRTY-THREE

HOW TO GROW VEGETABLES

The best way to enjoy growing vegetables is to grow only those which are family favourites or those which are highly priced in the shops. Growing vegetables in the home garden enables one to have unusual vegetables that are not often obtainable, like Broccoli, or that taste better when freshly picked like Globe Artichokes, green Beans or Sweet Corn. Young vegetables like baby Carrots can seldom be bought and do not take as long to grow as the giant Carrots that can be purchased inexpensively. Salad vegetables interest everyone, but must be sown with restraint, a little at a time, or the supply so quickly exceeds the demand. Herbs are of interest to the enthusiast, although Parsley and Chives are a must for picking fresh daily. Grow a few favourite vegetables each season so that one can give them adequate space and attention as well as rotate one's crops.

As a rule, vegetables need a sunny position, fertile, well-drained soil and regular watering.

Soil and Fertilizers. It is most important to add compost and well-rotted manure to the soil for vegetable growing. This improves the texture of the soil and conserves moisture as well as feeding the plants.

When preparing beds for vegetables, dig over the top 6 to 8 inches of soil and fork a 3-inch layer of compost containing well-rotted manure into the top few inches. If the soil is heavy, add sand or peat. If the subsoil is poor, or the plants have deep roots, remove the top 6 inches of soil and loosen the bottom soil, incorporating manure or twiggy material, and then replace the topsoil. If the soil is enriched with organic material each season, it will be unnecessary to double dig every year. If one is short of manure one can make the most of it by digging it into the vicinity of the rows where the roots can benefit most from it, rather than spread it all over the vegetable patch. This is one of the advantages of growing vegetables in regular rows.

Farmyard manure is one of the best materials for the vegetable garden and should be dug into the ground during winter. If used in the spring it must be well-rotted and is best incorporated with compost. Root vegetables must not be given fresh manure, but grow well in soil containing well-rotted compost. Lime should only be applied if the crop needs it and must be added a month before the manure is applied.

Inorganic chemical fertilizers can be given to augment organic manures, particularly if the latter are in short supply. They can be dug into the soil before planting, in which case they should be placed a few inches down where the roots can find them, for they should not come into contact with the seed or roots of young seedlings, but do not put fertilizer down too deeply for shallow rooted vegetables. These fertilizers can also be sprinkled on to moist soil and watered into the soil around the plants from two to four weeks after transplanting. As a second application a nitrogen fertilizer or a balanced fertilizer can be given when the first flowers or fruits form. They are usually used at the rate of 1 to 2 oz. to the square yard. A balanced fertilizer like 6 : 3 : 2 is recommended for most vegetables. Special formulas were used previously for certain vegetables such as Potatoes, but now it is recommended that extra phosphate, in the form of superphosphate, is added at planting time.

Superphosphates are valuable for most vegetables and can be dug in at planting time, as they are long-lasting in the soil and not readily leached out like nitrogen fertilizers, but rock phosphates are best used in acid soils unless these are limed.

All leafy plants, like Lettuce, Cabbage and Spinach need nitrogenous fertilizers particularly; those which are grown for their fruits like Tomatoes, Peas, Beans or Maize need phosphates, while root vegetables like Parsnips, Carrots, Turnips or Potatoes need potash.

Watering. Some vegetables need more water than others. Shallow-rooted vegetables which like cool soil, like Lettuce, need more frequent watering than deep-rooting Tomatoes. Young vegetables should be watered more frequently than mature vegetables, as their roots are shallower, but as soon as they are established they should be watered deeply about once or twice a week rather than sprinkled each day. One should aim to give at least an inch of water which sinks down to about 18 inches. (See the Art of Watering, Chapter 18.) Water mature plants again when the top 2 or 3 inches of soil are dry, depending on their size.

Mulches play an important part in conserving moisture and keeping down weeds. Compost acts as a mulch, but one can also lay down mulches which would not be attractive in the flower garden such as straw, newspapers or plastic film.

Weed Control. This is especially important when growing vegetables. If weeds are not eradicated while small they will soon smother the plants or injure their roots if pulled out when large. Weeds harbour pests like eelworm and aphids as well as spores of disease, so that it is vital to control weeds in the vegetable garden. Even if the ground is left bare for a season, weeds must be removed continuously. In order to avoid repetition, this will not be mentioned while discussing each vegetable below, but it is an essential task in tending the vegetable garden.

Planning the Vegetable Garden. It is most important to draw a plan on squared paper in order to see how much one can include in the vegetable garden before buying seed or seedlings. One can put a neat edging of Parsley in the front, dwarf vegetables like Beans towards the front and taller ones like Mealies or Tomatoes at the back, trained on to fences if necessary. In order to give vegetables the maximum of sunshine, rows are generally planted from north to south, but one must be careful not to shade short vegetables with taller ones, grouping these in the back half of the rows. Perennial vegetables like Asparagus or Rhubarb should be placed on one side so as not to interfere with annual vegetables. Artichokes are so decorative that they can be grown in the flower garden.

Make the most of available space by sowing quick-growing vegetables like Radishes together with slower maturing Carrots, so that the Radishes will be eaten long before the carrots are fully grown. Small, quick-maturing plants, like Lettuces, can be planted between large, later-maturing plants like Cabbages. Train Cucumbers, Squash and Tomatoes on to fences if space is limited.

As soon as one crop is finished, one can replace it with another, but this should always be of an entirely different type. Varying one's crops, called crop rotation, helps to control insect pests and plant diseases. Try to leave one-third of the vegetable garden free for at least a month during winter so that one can dig, lime and manure the soil. It is no use letting the ground lie fallow or it becomes infested with weeds. It is better to plant it with a grass like Italian rye, a legume crop or with ordinary flowers for cutting.

Crop Rotation. Never plant the same vegetable twice consecutively on the same spot. One tries to avoid planting vegetables that belong to the same family to follow each other on the same spot as they are affected by the same diseases. Members of the Cabbage family and the Potato family are particularly susceptible to diseases common to each family. Tomatoes and Potatoes

are so sensitive that they should not even be planted side by side for fear of transmitting Blight from one to the other.

Provided that one adds sufficient manure to the ground each time one plants a crop, it is unlikely that the home gardener will have many crop failures, but it is wise to avoid planting root crops or leaf crops one after the other even though they do not necessarily belong to the same family, as they take the same type of nourishment out of the soil. Root crops like Carrots and Parsnips should not follow one another as they do belong to the same family, whereas Beets and Radishes do not. Radishes often suffer from the same diseases as the Cabbage family and should not follow its members in the home garden. Leaf crops like Lettuce, Spinach, Swiss Chard, New Zealand Spinach and Celery do not belong to the same family, but one should avoid planting them one after the other if possible.

Peas, Beans and Broad Beans belong to the Legume family and improve the fertility of the soil as they form nitrogen nodules on their roots. They should not be planted to follow each other or on the same spot for three years. They should always be followed by a leaf crop which can make use of the nitrogen which they put into the soil. Onions, which occupy the soil for a long period, should always be followed by a soil-improving crop like Peas or Beans. One can grow Sweet-peas in the vegetable garden during winter as an alternative to Peas or Beans.

In order to make the most of crop rotation, one should manure the soil heavily during winter, then plant a leaf crop that will benefit from the nitrogen in the manure. Follow this with a root crop that does not need heavy fertilizing. Thirdly, plant a legume crop that will restore nitrogen to the soil. Naturally, one can add dressings of compost and inorganic fertilizers if necessary for each crop.

The following related plants are placed in groups so that the gardener can choose one from each group in order to practise crop rotation.

(1) Potato family (*Solanum*): Potato, Tomato, Egg-plant (Brinjal), Peppers or Cape Gooseberry.
(2) Cabbage family (*Brassica*): Cabbage, Cauliflower, Kale, Broccoli, Brussels Sprouts, Turnip, Swede, Kohlrabi.
(3) Cucumber family (*Cucurbits*): Cucumber, Squash, Marrow, Pumpkin, Melon.
(4) Legumes: Beans, Broad Beans, Peas, Sweet-peas.
(5) Onion (*Allium*): Leek, Chives, Shallot, Garlic.
(6) Carrot family (*Umbelliferae*): Carrot, Parsnip, Parsley, Celery, Celeriac, Fennel.
(7) Mealies, Sweet Corn, Pop Corn.
(8) Lettuce, Endive, Chicory (*Compositae*).

When to Plant Vegetables

Most mistakes in growing vegetables are made by planting them at the wrong time. One cannot stipulate the exact month in which to plant as climate varies according to locality. Plants can be divided into those which grow best during cool or cold weather and those which must have warm weather and cannot survive frost. Planting seasons, especially of quick-maturing crops, can be extended over several months so that one can have a constant supply of vegetables in the home garden. Times vary according to whether the different vegetables are planted on the cold Highveld and midlands, the frost-free Lowveld and coastal regions or the winter-rainfall area.

Warm-Weather Vegetables. Seed will not germinate unless the soil is warm, although some can be grown in sheltered seedboxes and transplanted as soon as the weather warms up, usually around September. This is particularly important for plants which need a long season for maturing, like Egg-plant, Peppers, Sweet Potatoes, Okra and Gooseberries. Those which require a shorter season of growth can be planted at intervals from September onwards, but do not plant too late or they will be killed by the first cold weather of winter. These are Beans, Sweet Corn, Tomatoes, Potatoes, Cucumber, Squash, Marrow, Pumpkin, Watermelon and Sweetmelon. Warm-weather vegetables which are normally planted during summer can be grown in winter in frost-free regions like the Lowveld, the Natal coast and many areas north of the Limpopo.

Cool-Weather Vegetables. These vegetables enjoy cool temperatures and cannot tolerate excessive summer heat. They are generally sown from midsummer to autumn, from January to April. Some may be tender to frost in the seedling stage and should be planted out early so that they can grow quite large before the cold weather sets in. Cauliflower can be sown as early as November or December for this reason, while cabbages are sown soon afterwards. Those which can tolerate light frosts, but should be well established before cold weather sets in, and which will mature in winter or early spring are Cauliflower, Peas, Broad Beans, Lettuce, Swiss Chard, Celery, Beetroot, Carrot and Parsnip. Some cool-weather vegetables can stand a fair amount of frost, including Cabbage, Kale, Kohlrabi, Turnip, Spinach and Onion.

Harvest Vegetables Early

The home gardener should not worry if his vegetables are not large. The flavour is more important than the size. Young vegetables are tastier than mature ones, Carrots being sweeter, Cucumbers crisper and Marrows and Beans more tender. Once Beans are sliced and cooked no one will worry about whether they were long or short, straight or curled. Do not wait too long before picking mature vegetables like Egg-plant or they will become bitter. Try to cook vegetables like Sweet Corn or Peas as soon as possible after picking. Asparagus should be eaten within a few hours of cutting.

HOW TO GROW FAVOURITE VEGETABLES

Artichoke (Globe). A perennial which dies down each winter. Plant rooted shoots 6 feet apart in late winter or early spring, July to September. Fertile, well-drained soil. Add manure and feed with ammonium sulphate as buds form.

Artichoke (Jerusalem). Plant tubers in spring, 6 inches deep and 2 to 3 feet apart. Will grow in poor soil, but do better in good soil. Grow to 6 feet. Harvest in autumn, leaving some tubers in the soil.

Asparagus. A perennial which dies down each winter, it will last for 15 years without disturbance. Plant roots or crowns in August, at least 2 feet apart in rows about 3 to 4 feet apart. Do not plant less than 15 plants and do not expect a full crop for two years, depending on the vigour of the crowns. Seed grows easily, but one should not harvest the spears before the fourth year. Select the strongest seedlings and transplant into rows after a year.

Asparagus needs sandy, well-drained, neutral soil (pH 6.5 to 7). Mix plenty of kraal manure and compost into the top foot of soil during winter and add fertilizer 6 : 3 : 2. Plant the crowns firmly in a trench so that they are 8 inches below the surface and cover with 3 inches of soil. Keep the soil moist while growing and water deeply each week during summer if good rain does not fall. Give nitrate of ammonia in midsummer, applied to moist soil at the rate of 1 oz. to the square yard. Cease watering from April to mid-July. Do not cut back the brown tops until winter. Then fill in the trench and let the soil protrude in a ridge an inch or two above the ground. Each winter apply manure and balanced fertilizer to the soil on either side of the ridge and apply nitrates in midsummer. Water regularly and deeply so that the soil is moistened to 18 inches. (See Watering, Chapter 18.)

Harvesting Asparagus spears must be done with a special rod, sharpened and flattened at one end like a chisel, which is inserted below the soil to sever the stalks as soon as the tips break the surface in spring. In the first season, cut the spears for two or three weeks and then allow the tips to grow into greenery. Mature plants can be harvested for six to eight weeks each spring.

Beans. Plant dwarf or runner beans from spring to late summer in places with cold winters or during winter in the frost-free Lowveld. Broad beans are a cool-weather crop to be planted in autumn.

Beans can be grown on almost any soil provided that it contains compost or kraal manure and sufficient moisture. They dislike brak soil or acid soil below pH 5.5. On poor soil, top-dress with limestone ammonium nitrate when the plants are about three weeks old and repeat three weeks later or when the flowers form. On sandy, manganese-deficient soil as on the Cape Flats or on alkaline coastal soils of the S.W. Cape, spray with manganese sulphate. (Dissolve 2 oz. in 4 gallons of water and spray after germination and again when buds open.)

Water soil well before planting seed, but not afterwards, for fear of causing a hard surface crust to form and prevent emergence of the seedling. Plant seed 2 inches deep in sandy soil, but much shallower in heavy soil. Water young plants about twice a week on sandy soil or once a fortnight on clay soil and preferably not in the heat of the day. Remove pods continuously.

Dwarf Beans. Plant seed 3 inches apart in rows about 2 to 3 feet apart. There are many kinds of dwarf or French Beans including stringless wax or green Beans or non-stringless varieties, some more resistant to bacterial wilt than others. It is important to plant resistant varieties in hot places with heavy summer rains, such as "Florida Belle", "Streamliner" ("Granda"), "Logan" and "Top-crop". Lima Beans include both dwarf and runner types and must be planted in early summer.

Runner Beans. Erect a double row of 6-foot stakes joined at the top and linked by strands, placing them 3 feet apart. Plant six seeds together at the foot of each stake, thinning to three or four to a hole. There are several varieties of runner beans, many of which are good bearers and rust-resistant. "Green Savage" and "Can Freezer" are early, stringless varieties; "Lazy Housewife" is stringless and rust-resistant; "Kentucky Wonder" and "Italian Runner" are late, non-stringless varieties. "Scarlet Runner" is a late variety with ornamental flowers and stringy pods which is suitable for cool climates.

Broad Beans. Plant seed in early April or May where heavy frosts fall in winter. Place seeds 6 to 9 inches apart in rows 2½ to 3 feet apart. Plant two seeds together and remove the weakest when the plants are 3 inches high. Broad beans need deep fertile soil, heavily manured with compost or kraal manure. Top-dress with super-phosphates and balanced or nitrogenous fertilizer if necessary. Poor soil and drought make plants more subject to aphis attack and disease. Nipping out the top shoot does not discourage aphids, but encourages more shoots to develop. Harvest the pods while young and

about 4 inches long. Later only the shelled beans can be eaten.

Beetroot. A cool-weather crop which may be planted in autumn or spring. Beetroot grows best in spring with regular watering. Light, well-drained soil which has been heavily fertilized for a previous crop is best, but one can add well-rotted compost. Beetroot requires a neutral soil (pH 5.8 to 7) and will tolerate brak soil. Sow the seed sparsely where it is to remain, in rows a foot apart, and thin the seedlings to 2 or 3 inches apart. Use when 2 or 3 inches in diameter as young Beets are more tender.

Broccoli. This cool-weather vegetable is like a delicately flavoured Cauliflower. Sow seed from midsummer to late summer and transplant early so that growth is well established before winter. Plant seedlings 2 or 3 feet apart each way. Broccoli requires fertile soil and plenty of water like Cabbage. Aim to harvest about June before the heads open, cutting the heads with a portion of the stalk. Sprouting Broccoli has loose green heads which can be cut continuously as they mature, while Heading Broccoli has a larger, paler head similar to Cauliflower.

Brussels Sprouts. A cool-weather vegetable which is cultivated like Broccoli, Brussels Sprouts should be planted 2 feet apart in rows 3 feet apart. Sow seed from December to March or until April in the Lowveld and transplant when 6 inches high. Cold weather makes the heads firm. Harvest the little heads from the bottom as soon as they are firm. Break the top bud of the plant as soon as all the heads are well formed in order to hasten maturing, which takes four months from sowing time. Aphids attack Brussels Sprouts and should be controlled at the first sign. Healthy, well-grown plants resist attack more easily. Brussels Sprouts require rich soil and plenty of water like Cabbage.

Cabbage. This grows best during cool weather but can be grown all through the year. In the winter rainfall area seed is sown mainly from February to April or from June to July. Cabbage can be grown during summer in cool soil with plenty of water. In the Eastern Province seed is sown from July to August, but can also be planted from November to March. On the Highveld, cabbages are grown as a winter crop when sown from November to January or as a summer and autumn crop when sown from July to November. In the Lowveld, cabbages are grown mainly during winter and spring and sown from January to May. When planting cabbages for winter, one aims to sow early and transplant the 6-inch seedlings so that they can be well-advanced before winter sets in.

Soil for Cabbages should be deep and fertile and not more acid than pH 5.5. The ideal pH is a little over 6. Add heavy dressings of well-rotted manure or rich compost to the soil, which can be placed in rows if supplies are limited. One can top-dress with nitrogen fertilizer on moist soil during the growing period. Cabbages must be watered regularly and well. The heads of mature cabbages may crack if water is applied after periods of drought. Lack of water may cause cabbages to "bolt" or run to seed. Bolting can also be caused by changes in weather from cold to hot or poor growth as a result of poor soil. Some varieties like "Cape Spitz" bolt when exposed to cold. Harvest cabbages as soon as the heads are big and firm, for once they are solid they will not grow larger.

Late varieties of cabbages are spaced almost two feet apart in rows which are 2½ feet apart, while earlier varieties can be spaced a little closer together. There are several of each kind. Early varieties include "Glory of Enkhuizen" and "Main Crop" with rounded heads; moderately early "Cape Spitz" with a pointed head, and "Late Flat Dutch" with a flattened head as well as many others. Savoy Cabbage does well in cold, frosty places and Red Cabbage can be grown like other types of cabbage.

Capsicum (Peppers). Perennial, warm-weather plants, peppers are grown as annuals in places with cold, frosty winters. They can be grown during autumn and winter in the Lowveld. As peppers need a long period of growth before harvesting in autumn, one should sow the seed early in a sheltered seedbox, about July or August. Peppers may be harvested when green or allowed to turn red. Large sweet peppers are generally eaten green, while thin peppers or Chillies are left to redden. Some ornamental types are grown for decoration only.

Soil should be light and enriched with compost or manure, with a pH from 5.5 to 6.7. The soil must be well-drained, although the plants need plenty of moisture. Superphosphates are beneficial, but only apply ammonium sulphate if plants show a nitrogen deficiency with yellowed leaves. Practise crop rotation.

Carrot. Carrots are grown mainly in early spring for harvesting in summer. They can also be sown in February and March for harvesting in winter. They are grown during winter in the Lowveld as they do not like the heat and humidity during summer. Prepare the soil well as carrots are not transplanted. Soil which was well-fertilized for a previous crop is best, as carrots develop forks if they come in contact with fresh manure or if the soil is hard. The soil should be light and fertile with a pH 6.5. Mix well-rotted compost into the top six inches before planting. Top-dress with nitrogenous fertilizer in two small applications if growth is poor.

Water the soil well before sowing the seed thinly in

rows a foot apart. Cover with newspaper until germination takes place. Thin to two inches apart or harvest as baby carrots. Carrots must not lack water and will mature in two or three months after sowing. There are several varieties. "Oxheart" is a short, thick, early variety suitable for shallow or heavier soil. "Cape Market" is thought to be a hybrid between "Chantenay" and "Nantes".

Cauliflower. Not as easy to grow as cabbages, cauliflowers require cool, moist growing conditions, yet are affected by frost if the head is not protected by leaves. Seed should be sown from November to February, varying from early to late varieties, so that the plants can be well-established before winter. Early varieties do best on the Highveld and Lowveld, while early or late varieties are recommended for the winter rainfall area.

Soil should be rich and not more acid than pH 5.5. Apply well-rotted kraal manure in the rows if supplies are limited. Seedlings should be transplanted when they are about 6 inches high and spaced about 2 feet apart in rows 3 feet apart. If sufficient manure is not available, apply three or four small top-dressings of nitrogenous fertilizer, sprinkling it on to moist soil. Cauliflowers need plentiful and regular watering so that their development is regular. Harvest as soon as the heads are firm and white. One can prevent yellowing by the sun and protect the heads from rain by tying the outer leaves above the head a short while before harvesting, or breaking off a big leaf and placing it on top of the head. The closely-folded leaves on improved strains naturally protect the head so that it is unnecessary to do this. If harvesting is delayed it may cause loose heads or uneven or "ricey" surfaces, but this may also be caused by poor seed.

Celeriac (Root Celery). Plant at the same time as Celery, generally in early spring to be harvested in autumn. The turnip-like root can be boiled and used in salads, but the tops are discarded or used as "soup celery". The tops can be used continuously if one does not dig out the root and the old leaves should be removed continuously to keep the top of the root smooth. Celeriac requires deep, well-manured, moist soil and is grown like Celery except that the leaves are not blanched and it is always planted on the surface. Cover the root with soil to whiten it.

Celery. Celery needs rich soil, plenty of water and special attention in blanching the leaves. The soil must be well drained and loamy, for celery cannot thrive in clay soil, and should not be brak or very acid, the ideal reaction being pH 6. Apply plenty of well-rotted manure or compost before planting. One can plant the seedlings on the surface or in a trench to make it easier for blanching. The trench should be 10 inches in depth and width and the base of the trench enriched with compost and manure.

Seed is sown from September to midsummer for a succession and may also be sown in autumn in the S.W. Cape, Natal and the Lowveld. It germinates slowly and unevenly and should be sown ¼-inch deep in a seedbox, keeping it moist and shaded until it germinates. Transplant seedlings carefully when about 4 inches high, spacing them 9 inches apart in rows at least 18 inches apart. Shade them in hot weather, but accustom them to full sun as soon as possible. Water liberally and regularly, keeping the soil moist but not waterlogged. Topdress with nitrogen fertilizer a month after transplanting. Give a second application three weeks later and a third when blanching commences. Celery can be harvested in from four to six months.

Blanching must be started after about three months when the plants are half-grown and should not take longer than two or three weeks or the plants may rot or lose flavour. There are several methods, of which earthing-up is the most common. Do this in one operation or gradually if one has the time. Lift the leaf stems and tie them loosely together with raffia at the top beneath the leaves. Mound up the earth on either side, leaving the green leaves exposed. Do not allow soil to fall into the centre of growth or the plant will rot. The home gardener will find it cleaner and easier to blanch with paper or boards. Place 9-inch-wide strips of heavy brown paper upright on both sides of the rows against the plants and keep them in place with hoops of wire pressed into the soil. One can also wrap the individual plants with paper or slip large envelopes or straw bottle covers over the tops, open at both ends. Long planks, a foot wide, can be placed upright on either side of the rows and kept in place with pegs, ridging the soil up outside.

Chives. A perennial which belongs to the Onion family, Chives can be grown in a permanent position so that the leaves can be plucked and used like spring-onions in salads, having a more delicate flavour. The clumps need not be divided for three or four years and this is best done in spring. Otherwise sow seed at any time of the year. Flat-dwellers can grow Chives in pots.

Cucumber. A warm-season plant which cannot stand frost, cucumber is sown in spring, but may be grown in the Lowveld in mid-winter. Heavy rains and humidity cause leaf diseases common in Cucurbits so that it is preferable to grow them in the dry season and irrigate them. The soil should be light and contain well-rotted manure or compost. Superphosphates may be worked

into the region of the root area before planting. Cucumbers do well after a legume crop. Nitrogen fertilizer may be sprinkled on to moist soil while growing if the plants become light green.

Cucumbers may be trained on to a fence if there is little space and this keeps the fruit off the ground. Seed is sown where the plants are to remain, in furrows or hills. If one makes a furrow, place the seed near the top in order to avoid flooding when watering. To make a slight "hill", scrape the soil into a mound 2 feet in diameter so that it is a few inches above the surface and will enable irrigation water to run off. Level the top, leaving a slight ridge around the rim and plant four or five seeds on the top. Never water Cucumbers with a sprinkler for fear of encouraging mildew. Keep the stems and leaves out of the irrigating water. Water deeply at least once a week and moisten the soil from time to time if it is hot and dry. Cucumbers must not suffer from drought. Pick the fruit while it is young and tender and do not injure the vine when picking. Spray Cucumbers at the first sign of mildew with sulphur or Karathane and control aphids. Spray in advance for Pumpkin and Melon Fly where this pest is troublesome. (See Insect Control, Chapter 37.)

Egg-plant (Egg-fruit, Brinjal). A warm-weather vegetable for summer, this may be grown during winter in the Lowveld. It needs a long growing period before harvesting and should be sown in sheltered seed-boxes in August or September, so that the seedlings can be planted out as soon as it is warm enough. Transplant when about 3 inches high, spacing the plants about 2 feet apart in rows 3 feet apart. Water well and shade if necessary. Egg-plants need regular, deep watering. The soil must contain manure or compost and have a pH between 5.5 and 6.7. A balanced fertilizer can be given while growing. Otherwise, grow like peppers and tomatoes. One can pick some of the fruits while small, cooking them whole in stews and leaving others to grow to full size. This makes it unnecessary to thin the fruit. Practise rotation of crops and do not plant on eelworm infested soil.

Endive. Cultivate like Lettuce, giving well-manured, well-drained, sandy soil. Water regularly or the leaves become bitter and blanch the inner leaves as the green leaves become bitter. Do not blanch for longer than about three weeks or when the plants are wet or they may rot. When they are about three months old and well-developed, tie the leaves around the top with raffia. Otherwise cover with straw, paper or two boards meeting at the top. Remove the covers if the plants appear to rot at the top.

Horse Radish. A perennial plant which is grown for its pungent root, Horse Radish grows easily in soil which was well-fertilized for a previous crop or it produces hairy, forked roots. It should be planted from July to September from 6-inch cuttings taken from side roots trimmed from the main roots when harvesting. Plant the cuttings upright about a foot apart and cover with 2 inches of soil. Irrigate regularly throughout summer. The plants may be dug up and the roots used in autumn, about March or April.

Kale. A curly-leaved vegetable, this is cultivated in the same way as Cabbage. Being cold-resistant, it is planted from midsummer onwards to mature in autumn, winter or early spring.

Kohlrabi. Kohlrabi likes cool weather for growth and should be sown in late summer or autumn. The rounded stem, which thickens just above the ground, should be eaten when 2 or 3 inches across or it becomes hard and pungent. Sow thinly in rows 18 inches apart and thin out to about 8 inches apart or transplant seedlings carefully. A member of the Cabbage family, Kohlrabi is cultivated like Cabbage and requires fertile soil and plenty of water. It takes up to three months to mature.

Leeks. Leeks take about 5 or 6 months to mature and are suitable for the larger vegetable garden. They grow easily provided that they have very fertile, well-drained soil and plenty of water. Too much water in the top soil induces heart rot. They like cool weather and are best sown from January to March, but may be sown in spring where it is not too hot and dry. Sow in seed-boxes and transplant when about 6 inches high, spacing 6 inches apart. Be careful not to plant too deeply and firm the roots well. Otherwise, sow thinly in rows 9 inches apart and thin out. Leeks can be blanched by ridging up the soil when they are well developed. They can be planted in a trench to make blanching easier. Dig it one foot wide and deep, enriching the soil with well-rotted manure or compost and mix in a balanced fertilizer.

Garlic. Plant cloves in late autumn, about April. Needs light, loamy soil.

Lettuce. A quick-growing salad vegetable. Lettuce is frequently bitter when grown in the home garden. This happens when the weather becomes hot or because water supplies are uneven. Lettuce should be grown during the cooler months when the days are short in autumn, winter and spring, from March to September. In places with cool summers it can be grown up to November. Lettuce is generally frost-hardy except while young. Mature Lettuces should be picked if frosted and used immediately.

Soil for Lettuces should be light, fertile and slightly acid (pH 5.8 to 6.5). It need not be deep as Lettuce has a shallow root system. Lettuce does well following legumes like Peas or Beans. Fork liberal quantities of compost or well-rotted manure into the top few inches. Add superphosphates to most soils and mixture 6–10–3 to soils in the S.W. Cape.

Sow seed directly into the ground, sowing small amounts at three-week intervals for a continuous supply. Sow thinly in rows 18 inches apart and thin out to 9 inches apart, transplanting seedlings into empty spaces a fortnight after germination. One can sow seeds in seed-boxes and transplant if liked, but this is not usually necessary. After the first deep soaking of the soil, moisten it each day as soon as the surface is dry, for Lettuce must not wilt for lack of water. As soon as the heads begin to form, apply ammonium nitrate to moist soil to stimulate rapid growth. Pick as soon as the heads are firm in from two and a half to three months.

There are several types of Curly Leaf or Butter Lettuce which have different forms with solid heads or loose-leaved growth. Cos Lettuce is a third type with long, upright leaves. Some Lettuces, like "Great Lakes", are more tolerant of heat and may be grown during the warmer months.

Maize (Mealies), Sweet Corn. A summer crop, Maize is easy to grow on most soils, but must be well-fertilized for best results. The soil should be neutral to slightly acid, for maize tolerates acidity more than alkalinity. Manure is essential and should be applied liberally before planting. Superphosphates are beneficial and can be added with the manure, but not to sour soils. Acid soils should be limed a month before adding the manure, otherwise use rock phosphates instead.

As soon as the soil is warm enough, generally during September, sow the seed where the plants are to remain, planting them about 2 or 3 inches deep. Plant two seeds close together and thin to one plant when they are a few inches high. Aim to space the plants at least 18 inches from one another in rows 3 feet apart. Plants spaced too closely with the mistaken impression that this aids pollination frequently do not produce ears. One can also plant two or three seeds in "hills" spaced at least 3 feet apart each way in order to facilitate weed control. Practise weed control scrupulously in the early stages, particularly before the plants form tassels. Sow at least a dozen fresh seeds every fortnight until December so that one can have a few plants coming into bearing throughout summer.

Water regularly once a week or every ten days, giving the equivalent of 1 to $1\frac{1}{2}$ inches of rain if good rains have not fallen. Some people hill up the soil around the stalks when cultivating to keep down weeds, but if one scrapes away more than 2 inches of soil one is liable to injure the roots. Keep the roots covered with soil. Suckers which form in the early stages should be removed, as they dissipate the plant's vigour, have different periods when mature and hamper the control of Maize Stalk Borer. Examine the young plant when it is about 18 inches high for speckled leaf markings, which indicate that the worm may be boring into the stalk. Pour a teaspoon of DDT powder, Endrin or Dipterex into the crown or leaf funnels. Never leave old Mealie-stalks in the ground during winter as they harbour the pests. Dust the silk and cobs before ripening with 5 per cent DDT dust in order to protect them from infestation. Weed control aids in keeping down pests.

Maize should not be interplanted with any other vegetables, but should be followed by legumes to restore fertility to the soil. One can give an application of liquid manure or sodium nitrate as the flowers form if growth seems weak. The silk turns brown during ripening and the ears should be plump and firm when ready for use, with the kernels full of milky juice. Maize is sweet and tender when fresh and becomes tough if picked too late. It should be cooked as soon as possible after picking.

Some varieties mature more quickly than others, Sweet Corn maturing more quickly than ordinary Maize, in from two and a half to three months. It can be obtained with yellow or white kernels and seedsmen offer old favourites as well as improved varieties. Pop-Corn may be grown in the same way and stored for use when the kernels are dry.

Melon. Sweetmelon (Honeydew), Muskmelon or Spanspek (Cantaloupe) and Watermelon all belong to the Cucumber family (Cucurbits) and are cultivated in a similar way. Frost-tender, they can only be planted when the weather has warmed up in September, but may be planted as early as July in the lowveld. Melons grow best in places with hot summers where rainfall and humidity are low. Cool or humid weather spoils the quality of the fruit and encourages leaf diseases. They grow best in the long dry summers of the south-western Cape, arid regions of the northern Cape and the dry, sub-tropical northern Transvaal.

Soil should be light, loamy and well-drained to a depth of three feet. Prepare soil at least a month before planting, adding lime if necessary. Melons need a slightly acid soil. Add large quantities of manure to poor soils and less to fertile soil, placing it near the root area. Work in superphosphates fairly deeply as well as a general mixture like 6 : 3 : 2 if manure is insufficient. Melons grow

well after a legume crop and one must practise crop rotation in growing them. They require plenty of growing space, especially Watermelons, and seed is sown directly in the ground as seedlings do not transplant well. Grow them in "hills" like Cucumbers, sowing five seeds to a hill and thinning to two plants. They can also be sown in furrows, spacing Muskmelons 6 feet apart and Watermelons 8 feet apart. Sow two seeds to a hole and thin to one plant. Cover the seeds with straw if planted early. Keep the foliage growing to one side to avoid trampling the plants. Water by irrigation and do not allow the plants to wilt for lack of water, but do not overwater or wet the foliage if possible. Reduce water as the fruits begin to mature. Spray with fungicides at the first sign of Mildew (see Fungus diseases) and start a spraying programme for Melon Fly in advance if it is troublesome in the area. (See Insect Control, Chapter 37.)

Mushroom. See "Specialised Gardening", Chapter 35.

Okra or Gumbo. A warm-weather crop which needs a long, hot summer for growth, Okra will be killed by frost. Sow seed in early spring and transplant 18 inches apart in rows 2 feet apart. Gather the pods while tender and about 3 inches long, from midsummer onwards. Pick continuously or the plants will stop bearing.

Onion. Onions grow easily, but require patience, for they take several months to mature. There is a great deal to the commercial growing of Onions, but the home gardener need not worry about too many detailed requirements. Onions are hardy, cool-weather plants which are generally planted in autumn, but can endure drought and heat when ripening in summer. They thrive at the Cape where the climate is ideal. Seed should be sown in the seedbox during February or March, but can be sown as late as May in the Cape. The seedlings transplant well when they are about eight or nine weeks old, when they should be about 6 inches high and almost as thick as a pencil. Nitrate or sulphate of ammonia can be given in the seedbox to promote vigorous growth from the beginning.

It is important to prepare the soil well in order to grow Onions successfully. The surface should be raked very level and be as fine as possible without sifting. The soil must be well-drained, of a light sandy texture, and fertile. Dress with well-rotted manure or compost which willl prevent compacted soil which retards the development of the bulb. Artificial fertilizer 6 : 3 : 2 can be worked into the top 3 inches before planting. Onions dislike very acid soil and lime may have to be applied a month before the manure in order to bring the pH above 5 on heavy soils and above pH 5.5 on sandy soils. Pale green or yellowish leaves indicate lack of nitrogen, which may be given as a top-dressing a month after transplanting.

This must be done with restraint on varieties like "Texas Grano" which grow large easily.

Seedlings must not be planted deeply or they will not form bulbs. Cover only the roots and about $\frac{1}{4}$ inch of the stem and do not plant more deeply than they were growing in the seedbox. The transplants may fall over but will grow upright later. Water regularly from the beginning, but reduce water towards ripening time especially in the last month when they prefer drought. Onions may be used green or ripened thoroughly if they are needed for storing. The leaves will turn brown when fully ripened. Do not try to hasten ripening by trampling or bending over the leaves as this encourages neck rot and may spoil the keeping quality. Ripe onions must be dried. This can be done under cover and the foliage plaited and hung up to store. Some onions keep longer than others.

Early ripening or short-day varieties of onions like "Texas Grano" and "Early Cape Flat" are best grown in the summer rainfall area where the summer days are shorter than in the Cape. Late varieties bolt and do not form proper bulbs in these areas. Most varieties do well at the Cape, including the above as well as late varieties like "Cape Straw", "Australian or Spanish Brown", "Copper King" and "Caledon Basterui", which keep best in storage.

Parsley. A biennial herb, this can be grown for two seasons, cutting back the foliage in the second year in order to prevent seeding. Parsley grows easily in neutral, light soil containing compost or manure. Sow seed in spring or autumn in the open or in the seedbox, for seedlings transplant readily when they have three or four leaves. Water regularly.

Parsnip. A root vegetable, grow Parsnip in the same way as Carrot. Sow seed in early spring from August to October and again in February and March. It should be sown on the open ground and thinned out. Cover with newspapers or grass as it germinates poorly. Parsnips take from four to six months to mature.

Pea. Valuable legumes which put nitrogen into the soil, Peas like cool weather and are sown in autumn. As the flowers may be affected by severe frost in cold areas, one should sow the seed in April or May so that they will flower towards the end of winter when the worst cold is over. In warmer areas like the lowveld, seed may be sown as early as March or in January in Natal. It may also be sown all through the winter months, but not later than August. Peas can be sown until September in the Free State and northern Cape.

Soil for Peas should be neutral with a pH of 6 to 7.2. It can be sandy or heavy but must be well drained, for Peas do not like water at the roots which can go down to 3 feet. One should build up a terrace in places with brak soil or a high water table. Apply lime to acid soil and fork in plenty of manure or compost a month later. Keep this in the rows if it is not plentiful. Superphosphates can be added when planting, but must not come in contact with the seed. A top-dressing of balanced fertilizer 6 : 3 : 2 can be added while growing if manure is insufficient. A nitrogen fertilizer can be given when the buds form. Peas should follow a root crop and be followed by a leaf crop. Do not plant Peas on the same spot for three years.

Water the soil well and then sow the seed directly into the ground from 1 to 3 inches deep. It germinates in from one to three weeks according to the depth of planting. Do not water again unless the soil shows signs of drying near the seed. Space Peas about 3 inches apart, leaving 2 feet between each row. If liked, plant a double row about 3 inches apart and leave $2\frac{1}{2}$ feet between the rows. Water regularly as soon as the top 2 inches of soil is dry and water especially carefully when the flowers form. Pick Peas regularly as soon as the seeds are fully formed in the pods, which is generally from three to three and a half months from sowing.

There are several varieties of dwarf Bush Peas, growing from 2 to 3 feet in height, of which "Greenfeast" is the most popular, being adaptable and disease-resistant. There are also a few runner varieties growing to $3\frac{1}{2}$ feet, which give best results if trellised.

Potato. Potatoes require space and attention for good results. The soil should be well drained, light and fertile, containing organic material so that the plants can develop freely. Shallow or clay soils give poor results. As Potatoes are heavy feeders, add plenty of well-rotted manure and compost to the soil before planting as well as a balanced fertilizer like 6 : 3 : 2. Superphosphates should be given before planting as they are valuable for Potatoes. Place inorganic fertilizers about 3 inches away from the seed when planting. The soil should be neutral to slightly acid. Potatoes are sensitive to eelworm infestation and should be planted in clean soil. Do not plant Potatoes near Tomatoes and pay attention to crop rotation.

Potatoes are tender to frost and are planted from August to January. They are grown from pieces of tubers known as Seed Potatoes. Always purchase clean Seed Potatoes from a reliable source in order to avoid diseases like Scab. Seed potatoes should be planted when they start sprouting and can be placed in a warm spot under sacking for a few days to encourage sprouting. They can be cut so as to allow two or three eyes or buds to each piece. The cuts dry quickly and the pieces should be planted within a few hours. Space them from 12 to 18 inches apart in rows 3 feet apart and make furrows, covering them with 3 or 4 inches of soil. Water the soil well before planting the Potatoes and then delay watering again until the plants are up and the surface soil becomes dry. Do not allow a hard crust to form on the surface and break it up if necessary. Irrigate potatoes once a week, applying the water in furrows on either side of the plants. Do not water during the hottest part of the day or wet the foliage if possible. Regular spraying with fungicides from the beginning of the rainy season will help to control Blight. (See Fungus Diseases, Chapter 38.)

Gradually hill the soil up around the growing plants in order to keep the soil loose and weed-free. This will also protect the tubers from the larvae of the Potato Tuber Moth. Close up all cracks in the soil as soon as the first flowers form and especially if Potatoes are left in the soil late in the season. Potatoes can be dug up when "new" or half-grown. Mature potatoes will be ready for use when the plants begin to wither after about three or four months. The plants can be pulled up and the potatoes lifted or they can remain in the soil for several weeks, but should not be watered. The potatoes are ready to be eaten if the skins do not come off easily, otherwise they can be left in the soil for a week longer. The most popular late-maturing variety is "Up-to-Date", while there are several early varieties like "King George". (For Sweet Potatoes, see page 220.)

Pumpkin. This is a member of the Cucurbit family and is grown in much the same way as Melon or Cucumber, needing the same care in control of pests and disease. A warm-weather plant, the pumpkin will grow in cooler conditions than Melons, but it is best to plant early varieties in places where frost comes early, as it needs a long growing season. Plant in September in the colder parts of the summer rainfall area or in August in warmer places. Protect young plants with caps at night if planting early. Pumpkins can be planted from autumn to spring in the Lowveld. Early planting reduces infestation by pests and diseases which are common in midsummer. Spray in advance against Pumpkin Fly where this is common and spray with fungicides at the first sign of mildew when the rains begin.

Soil should be light, neutral and fertile. Fork in compost and manure before planting and add inorganic nitrogen fertilizer later if plants become light green in colour. Plant in hills as for Cucumber, sowing about eight seeds and thinning to three plants to a hill, which should be 5 feet in diameter. If sowing in furrows, sow three or four seeds together and thin to one or two plants. Moisten the soil before planting and do not water again until germination takes place or the seeds may rot. Cover with newspapers or straw to prevent drying out.

Pick Pumpkins with a piece of stem attached before the skins harden. One should be able to penetrate the skin with the thumb nail. If they are to be stored during autumn and winter, they should be left on the vine until mature. They are then cured by leaving out of doors for a month, covered at night, in order to develop a hard skin. They can also be hardened by keeping them indoors for a fortnight. Pumpkins must be stored side by side in a cool, airy shed. "Plat Wit Boer" is the most commonly grown variety.

Radish. Radishes grow quickly in light, fertile soil and mature in about a month. Mix well-rotted manure or compost into the top 3 inches and add fertilizer if necessary. The soil should have a pH of 5.2 to 6.7. Sow the seed directly on to well-prepared, fine soil, sowing it thinly in rows six inches apart or scattering it over a small square. Keep the soil moist until germination takes place and then water whenever the surface dries. Pull radishes while young and crisp. Sow every two or three weeks for a succession, from early spring throughout summer and autumn. Radish seed can be mixed with Carrot seed in order to save space, as carrots take longer to mature.

Rhubarb. Rhubarb grows best in climates with contrasting seasons like warm and rainy summers and cool, dry winters or wet winters and dry summers. There are both summer and winter varieties. Those which grow during summer and die down during winter include "Early Paragon" and "Royal Albert", while those which grow during winter and spring are "Ever-bearing" or "Topps Crimson Winter". Purchase crowns of summer varieties to be planted in early winter or spring, while winter varieties can be planted in autumn.

Rhubarb will grow in any soil, provided that it is well-drained and slightly acid. As it is a gross feeder, mix plenty of manure or compost in a hole made for each plant, digging it down a foot deep over an area of 18 inches in diameter. Space the crowns 3 feet apart each way or leave 4 feet between the rows. Plant the crowns at soil level and mound up 3 inches of soil over them. Water regularly while growing, but only at the sides of the mound. One can give further dressings of manure while growing or sprinkle a general fertilizer on to moist soil and water it in. Remove flower stems as soon as they appear. Pull only the thickest and longest stalks from mature plants, but do not allow them to grow too tough. Do not pick too many stalks at a time or the plant may die. One can encourage long stalks to grow up to the light by placing a box or tin, without a top or bottom, over each plant.

Salsify or **Oyster Plant.** Cultivated for its edible, fleshy roots, Salsify is grown like Carrot. Sow in autumn or spring in rows 15 inches apart and thin to 2 inches apart in the rows. The roots are ready to use after about four months.

Shallot. Grow like Chives and use green stems or use mature bulbs like Onions. Divide and plant cloves in autumn.

Sou-Sou or **Chayote** (Climbing Squash). A warm-weather perennial which dies down in winter, Sou-sou belongs to the Cucumber family and is eaten like Marrow. It is a vigorous vine which must be trellised and needs an area of at least 10 feet square in which to spread. As it is a heavy feeder, the soil should be well fertilized with manure. The whole fruit is planted into the soil in early spring with the stem end projecting slightly and a new plant grows from the seed inside it. The vine starts bearing in four or five months, but bears well only in the second year.

Spinach. A cool-weather, leafy annual, spinach runs to seed if grown during long hot summers. It is generally planted in autumn, but can be planted in spring where winters are severe. The soil should be light and fertile, containing compost. Keep it cool and moist, but it must be well-drained. Sow the seed directly into the ground in rows 15 inches apart and thin out if necessary. The leaves can be harvested in one and a half to two months.

Spinach, New Zealand, or **New Zealand Ice Plant.** Not a true spinach, this spreading plant is more heat-resistant than ordinary spinach and grows more easily. The leaves near the tips of the stems are gathered continuously and old shoots can be cut back every fortnight to stimulate new growth throughout summer. Sow seed of New Zealand Spinach in spring in rows spaced 3 feet apart and thin the seedlings to 18 inches apart. Soak seed for 24 hours to aid germination.

Swiss Chard (Spinach Beet). This cool-weather vegetable is cultivated for its leaves, which can be cooked like spinach, while the long stalks can be cooked separately. It is thought to be healthier than ordinary Spinach and grows more easily. It is best sown in late summer or autumn as it is not successfully grown during midsummer. Where summers are hot and winters mild it can be sown in autumn or mid-winter. There are several varieties including "Lucullus" and "Fordhoek Giant". "Green-cutting" can be grown in warm places while "Dark-leaved, broad-ribbed" is very hardy to cold. The soil must be rich, containing manure and compost and a dressing of superphosphates. Accelerate growth later with a top-dressing of nitrogenous fertilizer. Sow thinly in rows about 18 inches apart and thin seedlings to about a foot apart. Harvest after about three months.

Squash. All squashes are closely related to Pumpkin and are grown in the same way. They can be stored during winter, but do not keep as well as Pumpkins. Those which store well are called winter squashes and include "Butternut", "Little Gem" and "Table Queen". Golden or green "Hubbard Squashes" belong here, but are regarded as a type of Pumpkin. Those varieties which are eaten while young are called summer squashes or vegetable marrows and include "Golden" or "White Custard Squash", "Caserta Summer Squash", "Long Green Bush" and "Long White Bush". The last two can be picked while only 3 or 4 inches long and cooked as pale green baby marrows.

Swede. This resembles a Turnip and also belongs to the Cabbage family. It should be grown in the same way as Turnip, but takes longer to mature. It likes cool weather and should be sown in autumn, winter or early spring.

Sweet Corn. See Maize (Mealies).

Sweet Potato. The Sweet Potato (*Ipomoea batatas*) does not belong to the Potato family (*Solanum*). It is very frost-sensitive and requires four to six months of warm weather for growth. The tuberous roots are harvested and stored during winter when the plant dies down, but it can be grown as an ornamental vine even if the Sweet Potatoes are not dug up. It can be grown indoors as a trailing pot plant.

Sweet Potatoes are easily grown in good soil which is well drained and contains organic matter, but should not be over-fertilized. They may be fertilized only with superphosphates and muriate of potash, if necessary. Soil reactions can be variable, but soil below pH 5 should be limed, particularly if superphosphate is applied. Sweet Potatoes are greedy feeders and can be planted following a legume crop. They are sensitive to eelworm and should not follow or be followed by other sensitive crops like members of the Potato family.

Sweet Potatoes are generally planted on top of six-inch ridges to aid drainage, but this method is better suited to moist climates than dry areas. They are planted by means of rooted cuttings about 9 inches long, obtained from the tips of healthy vigorous plants. Pieces of Sweet Potato will sprout and grow if placed in a dish of water and cuttings can be taken from these plants. The cuttings must be transplanted to moist soil, spacing them 18 inches apart in rows about 3 feet apart. Do not allow a hard crust to form on the soil and do not overwater the plants or the roots will become rough, too large or cracked. Water at regular intervals during dry winters. There are both early and late varieties and many new ones are being developed.

Tomato. These belong to the Potato family (*Solanum*) and should not be planted alongside Potatoes as they are particularly susceptible to diseases of Potato like Blight. They should not be planted where any other members of the Potato family were planted in the previous season or be planted twice in the same spot in succession. They do well following a legume crop and can be planted following winter Sweet-peas grown for cutting. As they are sensitive to eelworm infestation, one should keep the soil weed-free and treat infested soil with a soil fumigant. They can be grown by the ring-culture method as a protection against eelworm. (See below.) Tomatoes are frost-tender and are grown during summer, but may be grown during winter in mild frost-free places. Warm, humid summer weather aggravates fungus diseases and special wilt-resistant varieties must be grown in places like the Lowveld, such as the universally popular "Marvel" or "Hortus 5". There are many varieties of large tomatoes like "Marglobe", "Pearson", "Potentate", "Rutgers" and others. Decorative Cherry Tomatoes and pear-shaped "King Humbert" Tomatoes are excellent for salads or jam-making. Yellow Tomatoes are obtainable as well as red.

Soil. Prepare the soil well in advance, if possible, and mix in large quantities of well-rotted manure, particularly in sandy soils. Superphosphates are valuable in sandy soils, especially at the coast. A balanced fertilizer like 6 : 3 : 2 can be mixed into the soil before planting, to supplement the manure, particularly if this is in short supply. Otherwise, give it as a top-dressing a few weeks after transplanting and again as the first fruits form.

Planting. As Tomatoes take four or five months to begin bearing, sow the seed as early as possible. Where winters are cold, sow the seed in sheltered seedboxes in July or August for midsummer harvesting or in September or October for late summer. In frost-free areas, sow seed in late summer or autumn. The seedlings take about six weeks to grow to 6 inches, when they can be transplanted as soon as all danger of frost has passed. Select the strongest seedlings and plant during the cool of the afternoon. Space them about 18 inches apart in rows at least 4 feet apart so that one can walk between the plants without bruising them. If liked, plant a double row, with the plants 18 inches apart. Plant the long stems quite deeply, except in areas of high rainfall, where they might rot. Water immediately and shade the seedlings for a few days.

Watering. Tomatoes should not be overwatered, but an irregular water supply will cause Blossom-end Rot to develop. It is best to irrigate Tomatoes, without wetting the foliage, regularly and deeply once a week, so that the water will sink down to 2 feet. As they develop a large root system, the whole area can be soaked. If it is necessary to use a sprinkler, it must be used very early in the morning before the sun becomes hot, and the foliage should be dusted with a fungicide like Zineb to prevent fungus diseases from developing. Start dusting tomatoes regularly with fungicides at the start of the rainy season to prevent Blight. Start in the seedling stage in areas of high humidity.

Supporting Tomatoes. If the plants are not supported, they will lie on the ground and be damaged by trampling, while much of the fruit will rot. Each plant can be tied to a single 6-foot stake or a tripod of three stakes. It saves space to erect a fence made of 6-foot stakes linked by rows of string at 9-inch intervals. Plant the tomatoes between the stakes and tie them individually as they grow to the string. In order to save labour and unnecessary handling of the plant which may spread disease, tie a row of string on either side of the stakes, looping them around each stake so that the plants will be held upright between the parallel strands. Use stakes at least 2 inches in diameter so as to separate the strings. Start at the bottom row, adding extra rows at 9-inch intervals as the plants grow higher, but do not pull the upper rows as tightly as the lowest row, so as to allow the plants to develop.

Pruning. Many people nip out the side shoots of tomato plants as they grow out from between the main stem and the leaves, in order to improve the quality of the fruit. This is not absolutely necessary. In some cases the yield may be lower and the fruit more sunburnt. The side shoots must only be removed when they are tiny. Large branches must never be removed for fear of sunburn or damage to the plant.

Ring Culture of Tomatoes

This method was discovered accidentally in 1946, during experiments which took place at the Tilgate Research Station, Sussex, England. It was found that Tomatoes produced a massive secondary root system when growing in bottomless containers standing on moist ash and that the plants were healthier and produced more fruit than those growing in similar containers, but standing on a tiled floor. Ring culture aids the plants to resist fungus diseases and can be used when the soil is infested with eelworm. The ring-culture method of growing tomatoes is used in England both in greenhouses and out-of-doors and may be adapted to growing other plants like Chrysanthemums, Runner Beans or Lettuce.

Preparation of Soil. Dig a trench 5 inches deep and 12 inches wide. In cold areas, site the trench in front of a north-facing wooden fence to hasten growth. Fill the trench with rooting material or an aggregate, allowing this to project an inch above the surface so that no surrounding soil can wash on to it. Edge it with bricks if necessary. Weathered cinder ash is recommended as the best aggregate. It is first passed through a one-inch sieve, then through a fine sieve to get rid of the fine dust before being left to weather out-of-doors through one winter. It must then be watered heavily each day for a week to rid it of any injurious chemicals before use. Another suitable rooting material is a mixture of three parts of building sand and gravel mixed with one part of coarse vermiculite. Peat can also be used, but should then be placed in a layer on top of the soil and held in place by bricks. If placed in the trench it may become too wet.

The rooting material or aggregate should be laid directly on to the soil so that the water can drain away easily, but if the soil is infested with Eelworm or Wilt diseases, it can be separated from the rooting material with a layer of cement, polythene film or any other impervious sheeting. If this is done, drainage pipes will have to be inserted into the rooting material.

The pots or "rings" which will contain the Tomato plants must be bottomless and measure 6 to 9 inches in diameter and about 12 inches deep. They can be made of metal, plastic, wood, clay pipes or asbestos. They are stood on the rooting material at intervals of 18 inches. Half fill with a mixture of fertile light soil containing compost, a little peat and sharp sand. Tamp this well down so that it rests firmly on the rooting material below. Push a thin bamboo stake into the back of each pot. As soon as the weather is warm enough, transplant the tomato seedlings, one to a pot, so that the final soil surface is 1½ inches below the rim of the pot or "ring".

Treatment. Water the plants in the usual way for the first three or four weeks until the roots grow down into the rooting material or the first fruit forms. From this stage onwards, the plants are watered with a liquid fertilizer given through the "rings" every seven days and not watered otherwise. The rooting material, however, is

given a daily drenching of plain water. The "rings" can sometimes be watered on very hot summer days. Do not apply the fertilizer to the rooting material or aggregate, or it will be flushed away when watering.

One should use a concentrated balanced fertilizer which is readily dissolved in water, as coarse fertilizers which have to be watered in are not suitable. Try to obtain a feed which is nearest to the recommended proportion 6–6–7 with magnesium added. Make a 1 to 100 solution by dissolving 6 oz. of fertilizer in 4 gallons of water and add 1 teaspoon of Epsom salts (magnesium). Give each plant 2½ pints of this mixture every seven days. This will be enough for about 12 plants. Instead of the recommended 6–6–7, one may use one of the concentrated soluble fertilizers available on the market. These should be used at a third of the above dilution, namely 2 oz. to 4 gallons of water.

Turnip. A cool-weather root vegetable, Turnip belongs to the Cabbage family. It needs heavily-manured, light soil where drainage is good and benefits from superphosphates. Inorganic fertilizers can be given as a top-dressing to promote rapid growth. The best time to sow seed is in autumn or winter, but it can be sown in spring at the Cape. Seed should be sown thinly in rows spaced about a foot apart. Turnips need regular watering and should be harvested in about two and a half months when they are 2 or 3 inches in diameter. There are several varieties.

Vegetable Marrow. See Squash.

GROWING HERBS

Collecting herbs can become a fascinating hobby and one can grow them in the vegetable garden or in an enclosed space planned with formal, old fashioned charm or as path-edgings that give out scent at every footfall. Creeping Thyme, Chamomile and Peppermint are valuable in this respect, while Chives make a pretty edging to a shrub border. Rosemary and Lavender make trim hedges delineating paths; prostrate Rosemary is excellent for overhanging walls or rocks; the Bay Leaf is a neat evergreen shrub, while Anchusa, Bergamot and Borage have long found their way into the flower border. Their flowers can be added to fruit salads to improve the taste as well as the appearance. Ordinary flowers can also be eaten, such as crystallized Violets, Rose-petal jam and Marigold petals in pea soup.

Some people use herbs in food and drink more than others, but it might prove interesting to grow a few new ones each season in order to become familiar with them. About three bushes of a kind will be enough for average home use. Some can be grown in window-boxes or even in pots on the kitchen window-sill. When growing herbs in window-boxes it is best to grow each herb in a pot to itself to prevent vigorous herbs overgrowing others. Annual and perennial herbs should be planted separately. If space is limited, fence in the roots of aggressive perennials like Mint with corrugated metal, 6 inches deep. Weed out seedlings of Fennel or it will seed itself everywhere.

Most herbs grow easily in well-drained fertile soil which is not too rich. An ideal soil mixture should contain equal parts of sandy topsoil, well-rotted compost and peat. A dressing of lime can be given before planting especially for plants like Thyme, Marjoram, Sage and Lavender. Wood-ash may be given as an annual dressing. Herbs generally like a place in the sun, although some will thrive in partial shade. Herbs should be watered about once a week or more often during drought, some needing more water than others, particularly until they are established. Herbs can generally be grown from seed sown in spring in the open or in seedboxes. The sweet variety of Tarragon must be grown from divisions, for the variety that can be grown from seed is almost flavourless and bitter. Vigorous creeping herbs like Mint or Thyme can be grown from roots begged from a friend, while Mint can also be grown from cuttings made from pieces of stem stripped of leaves.

Herbs can be used while the leaves are fresh or can be dried and stored in jars with screw tops. They should be cut on a dry day as they come into flower and hung up in a cool, airy place to dry. The leaves are dry enough to store when they crumble in the hand.

The shortest list of herbs should include Parsley, Mint and Chives. For cultivation of Chives and Parsley, see under their separate headings amongst vegetables. Other basic cooking herbs include the perennials Sage, Thyme, Tarragon, Origanum (Crete Dittany), Sweet Marjoram (*Origanum vulgare*) and the annuals Dill and Basil.

LIST OF CULINARY HERBS

Annuals: Anise, Basil, Borage, Coriander, Chervil, Dill, Summer Savory.

Biennials: Caraway, Parsley.

Perennials: Bay Leaf (a tree), Chives, Fennel, Lovage, Marjoram, Origanum, Peppermint, Rosemary, Sage, Spearmint, Tarragon, Thyme, Winter Savory.

CHAPTER THIRTY-FOUR

HOUSE PLANTS

Growing plants in pots for indoor decoration need not be confined to flat-dwellers without gardens. Many gardeners find it necessary to have at least one flowering pot-plant in a house, not only for variety, but to save the time and labour of picking and arranging flowers for several vases every few days. Flowering pot-plants can be cared for in the garden when they are not in bloom. Many outdoor subjects can be grown in pots, especially those which tolerate shade. Several small shrubs are ideal for tubs on the sunny verandah, like The Shrimp Flower (*Beloperone*), Dwarf *Leptospermum* and small Heaths (*Erica regia* and others), while *Fuchsia* and *Azalea* need some shade. Large shrubs like *Greyia*, *Sparmannia* or trees like *Grevillea* may be grown in pots for their decorative foliage. Plants which grow in the shade out-of-doors in summer, like *Torenia*, make excellent annual pot plants, while perennials like *Impatiens* and *Browallia* go on flowering all through winter indoors. Numerous bulbs are ideal for growing in pots to bring into a room when they are in bloom, such as *Hyacinth*, *Lachenalia*, *Hippeastrum* (*Amaryllis*), Blood Lily (*Haemanthus katherinae*), *Clivia* and many others. *Geranium* and many succulents (see Chapter 28) as well as numerous annuals can be grown in pots and placed on verandahs or window-boxes.

The plants generally grown as house plants are chosen because of their decorative foliage as well as flowers, and are expected to have a long life. Growth is usually slow and they should be able to grow with ease in the generally dry atmosphere of the home. Most difficulties in growing pot plants stem from incorrect watering or lack of light.

Light. Most house plants are able to tolerate shade, but do not dislike sunshine. Foliage plants generally survive with less light than flowering house plants. The best place for plants that require bright light is a table near a north-facing window, where direct sun seldom falls on the plants during summer, but it is sunny and warm in winter. Slow-growing, leafy plants will tolerate duller light, but can be brought into bright light occasionally if they are not thriving. Individual light requirements for each plant are listed below.

Watering. Growth generally slows down when the temperature falls and most house plants should be kept on the dry side in winter. Overwatering at any time will cause rot and the lower leaves of large plants may drop. The roots must have oxygen and this is excluded if the soil is watered constantly when wet. As soon as the top soil becomes dry, one should water sufficiently to moisten the roots and not merely wet the surface. Wilting during warm dry weather denotes lack of moisture and the plant may die if it is not revived immediately. Clay pots absorb moisture from the ball of roots so that it is best to soak the whole pot in a basin of tepid water so that both pot and soil are thoroughly moistened. Allow the water to come up half-way so that the leaves do not dip into the water and do not leave the pot in the water for longer than half an hour. Soak pots about once a week or once a fortnight. If the soil dries out between soakings, water in a trickle at the inside rim of the pot, using a can with a slim spout. A wick can lead from the saucer up into the soil for plants that need moist soil. Large pots which cannot be soaked must be watered from the top. Fill the pot to the brim and allow the water to sink down. Repeat this several times in order to dampen all the soil.

All pots have a drainage hole at the bottom and usually have their own saucers. Ivy can be grown in a container without a hole if the bottom third is filled with coarse pebbles. Add a few pieces of charcoal if possible and water sparingly. Ceramic pots dry out more slowly than clay pots. Clay pots without saucers can be stood inside metal or pottery containers or wicker baskets.

Humidity. Dryness of the atmosphere can cause failure in some plants which need humidity, while overwatering will lead to death. Grow them in the bathroom or kitchen if these rooms are not too cold or create a humid atmosphere in several ways. Place the pot inside a larger pot and pack the space between with moist peat or moss, or cover the pot for most of the day with a clear plastic cake cover. Syringe the leaves occasionally. Place the pot, wrapped in moss, in a clear glass bowl covered with a lid or piece of glass which must be removed occasionally to admit air. A glass garden or terrarium can be made by this method. Using a glass fishbowl or large decorative cookie bowl, line the base with moss, layer it with gravel and half fill it with fibrous soil. Plant small, humidity-loving species in it like *Saintpaulia*, *Begonia*

ow to cut above a bud on the slant. (See Chapter 31, Section I.)

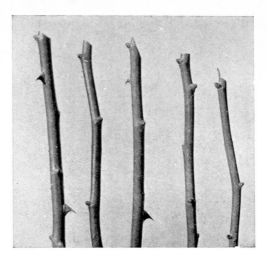

Only the left-hand stem is cut at the correct angle. The others (from left to right) are either too high, too slanting, too straight or too ragged.

Close-up showing a new shoot growing out from the bud after pruning. This will form a leader.

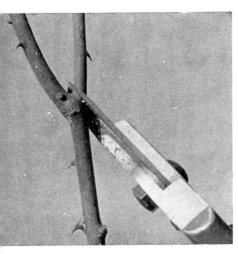

ow to prune a fork near the top of a main stem of a rose bush.

PRUNING

An apple tree branch showing thickened fruit spurs. (See Chapter 31, Section II.)

A well-shaped young peach tree before being pruned. (See Chapter 31, Section II.)

After pruning, the peach tree remains with adequate "feathers" which will produce abundant fruit of good quality.

Stages in pruning a Hybrid Tea rose (Crimson Glory), from the untouched dormant bush to the final stage. (See Chapter 31, Section I.)

Stages in pruning a Climbing Hybrid Tea rose showing (i) the old growth; (ii) how to remove old canes at the base; (iii) how to clean the remaining young stems of superfluous twigs and (iv) how to re-tie them into place against the trellis.

semperflorens, Fittonia, Peperomia, Coleus, Maranta, Ferns and miniature Ivies. Replace them when they grow too large. Do not overwater them. Cuttings grow easily in this medium.

Soil and Feeding. Rich, light, open soil, which is not rammed hard to exclude air, will ensure health and success for the plant. Mix together equal quantities of good garden soil with well-rotted compost or peat. Add sharp sand or rotted pine-needles to assist drainage. A little vermiculite can be added to the mixture, especially for small pots which may dry out quickly. Place a layer of gravel or broken crocks at the base for drainage and half fill with soil. Fill in the soil around the plant and water immediately. The surface should be about half an inch below the rim in order to allow for watering.

Pests and Care. Pests most likely to trouble house plants are scale, mealybug and red spider, while aphids may attack verandah plants. These can be controlled with the same chemicals that are used for outdoors. (See Insect Control, Chapter 37.) Mealybugs may be removed with alcohol and cottonwool in order to avoid spraying hairy leaves. Examine the underside of leaves occasionally to check pests at their first appearance. Wipe shiny leaves with a soft damp cloth or dip trailing vines like Ivy in a dish of soapy water once or twice a year in order to control mites.

TIPS ON GROWING POPULAR HOUSE PLANTS

Although most house plants can be grown in a greenhouse or hot-house, the following can all be grown in ordinary rooms where the climate is suitable. The lists have been grouped in two sections, comprising those which are grown for their flowers and those which are grown chiefly for their decorative foliage.

I. Growing Flowering Pot-Plants

African Violet. See *Saintpaulia.*

Anthurium. Flamingo-Flower. *A. scherzerianum* is medium-sized and has a flower which lasts for three months, while the tall *A. andreanum* has a flower which remains fresh for five months. Both come in pink and red varieties. As the plants grow larger, the flowers increase in size. Remove the flower as it fades. Another generally comes up to take its place. Purchase potted plants that have been brought into flower in a hot-house as propagation is difficult and slow.

Anthuriums grow indoors in places with cold winters, but can be grown out-of-doors at the coast and at low altitudes. They like moisture and humidity in summer. Place them in bright shade, but they dislike strong sun.

They must have good drainage and light fibrous soil containing leaf-mould. The aerial roots can be allowed to grow out of the pot, but place a piece of rotting bark and broken crocks on top in order to keep them firm and to supply additional moisture. Syringe the leaves during summer.

Ardisia crispa (*A. crenata*). Small, stiff, evergreen shrublet with bright red berries, this can be grown indoors or on a shady verandah, as well as out-of-doors in mild areas. Needs moisture. Grow from seed in spring or cuttings of half-ripe wood.

Begonia. There are hundreds of Begonias, some grown for their foliage and others for their flowers. Spectacular tuberous Begonias are treated as bulbs. (See Chapter 27.) Most herbaceous Begonias (such as *B. semperflorens*) can be grown out-of-doors in the shade in summer, dying down during cold winters, but remain evergreen indoors and flower into winter. They generally go off slightly in winter and should not be overwatered, but give them warmth and shade at this time. They need light, open soil containing compost. Do not allow water to settle on the leaves or the crown, which should be planted just above soil level. Keep them away from gas fumes. Grow from seed or cuttings of stem and leaves.

Calceolaria. Perennials best treated as annuals, these are not easy to grow in places with warm summers as they like a cool, moist climate with an average temperature of about 60 degrees F. They are easily damaged by rain or frost and are best grown in a cool, moist shade house or on a cool, shady verandah. Seed should be sown in November or December to bloom in the following October. As it is very fine, sow it in pots and soak these from below. Keep the plant moist.

Cineraria. Perennial usually treated as an annual. Colourful, daisy-like flowers are showy and can be grown out-of-doors under a tree where winters are mild. Grow well in pots if given moisture, light shade and cool, airy conditions of growth. Sow seed in late summer, about February, to bloom in spring. If sown in May they will flower in December, but must be kept shaded.

Columnea. Several evergreen species which are particularly suitable for hanging baskets. Give light shade without direct sunshine. The soil should be light, containing compost, sand and peat. *C. splendens* is fairly hardy, but requires moisture and a draught-free position in winter. Columneas do well in greenhouses and hot-houses.

Cyclamen. Showy gift plants, these can be kept growing and flowering for several years if watered properly. Place the pot in a draught-free position with reflected light, as it does not like strong sunlight. Keep the soil moist during the growing and flowering period, soaking the pot about once a week and adding water only at the outer rim of the pot. Never allow water to fall on the tuber or crown or it will settle and cause stem rot. Gradually lessen water as the foliage begins to die off in summer after flowering. When the plant is leafless, keep the pot on a cool window-sill in the bathroom or kitchen and add a little water from time to time in order to keep the tuber plump and prevent shrivelling. Re-pot the tuber in February, planting it half out of the soil, or keep it in the same pot and give it a liquid feed when the first buds form. Seed may be sown in midsummer and the little plants will not die down until after they have bloomed properly in 18 months. Nip out flower buds that form before this time. Miniature hardy Cyclamen (*C. neapolitanum*) thrives out-of-doors in the shade where winters are cold.

Episcia. Flame-Violet. An evergreen perennial, this has velvety leaves with silver or pink markings and coral-coloured flowers during summer. It will spread in a bowl or moss-lined basket and hang over the edges.

Gloxinia. See *Sinningia*.

Hoya carnosa. Wax Plant. Dainty, twining evergreen creeper with fleshy leaves and pink flowers. Can be trained along a support or wound around a mossy pole or wicker cage. Give shade and moisture in summer, but keep on the dry side in winter. Likes to become cramped in a large pot. Grown from cuttings in spring or air-layering.

Impatiens holstii. Zanzibar Balsam, Snapweed. Grow as a brilliant, shade-loving annual under trees during summer, but will flower through winter indoors or in mild climates. Give full shade and moisture at all times. Pinch back to make young plants bushy. Sow seed in spring or take cuttings when plants get shabby.

Primula obconica. See under Perennials. Grow in pots, giving semi-shade, as strong flowers develop in sunlight. They flower in winter and spring, dying back a little in summer. Give sufficient water to keep foliage alive and increase water when growth starts in autumn. Discard the plant after about three years. Sow seed in autumn to flower in the following autumn. The hairy leaves may be irritating to some people.

Saintpaulia. African Violet. Favourite of all house plants, these flower most of the year, but more prolifically in spring and summer. They are obtainable in many shades of purple, pink and white. They grow easily if watered correctly and given enough light. Place near an east or north-facing window where they receive direct sunlight for part of the day. Hot west sun should be diffused through a screen. They will not flower well in the dull light of a south window. Turn the pot a quarter round each week to keep them growing and flowering evenly.

Soak the pot about once a week and add water if necessary by inserting a slim spout under the leaves at the side of the pot. Do not water on to the crown of the plant as this causes Crown Rot or wilt. Water with tepid water as soon as the top soil dries. Cold water falling on the leaves stains them. African Violets enjoy humidity and can be grown in a terrarium, but survive well in a dry room. Brush dust off the leaves with a pipe cleaner or an old leaf. Feed once a month during the growing season with a soluble plant food. Remove Mealybugs.

Keep a single shoot growing and remove side shoots with a pencil point. Root these in sand to form new plants in a month. Leaves will grow roots in a glass of water. Cover the glass with tinfoil and lead the stem through a slit. Otherwise root in damp soil or vermiculite. Plant in a small pot and re-pot annually into a slightly larger pot.

Sinningia (*Gloxinia*). Colourful bell-shaped flowers make these striking room plants. They grow during summer and bloom in late summer and autumn, dying down in winter. Store the tubers dry during winter, but plant out and water as soon as they show signs of growth in spring. Give bright light, but not direct sunlight. The plants enjoy warmth and humidity while growing. Water like *Saintpaulia* and propagate by leaves in the same way or by seed. Take stem cuttings when the old tubers sprout in spring.

Stephanotis. A large climber with fragrant, waxy flowers, this will grow out-of-doors in a warm position, but also indoors or in greenhouses. Will tolerate light shade or sunshine, but does not like a cold position. Give rich, light soil, plenty of moisture and provide a support.

Streptocarpus. Cape Primrose. Although many species can be grown, the hybrids are mainly seen. These are generally evergreen and produce several crops of flowers a year if fertilized with liquid manure after flowering. Give light soil containing leaf-mould and light shade. Fine seed is sown in late summer to flower in the following summer. Also propagate by division or leaf cuttings, which develop roots from slit veins.

II. GROWING LEAFY POT-PLANTS

Most of these are evergreen and have attractive foliage so that they are decorative all through the year. They may be small, large or climbing. The vigorous climbers must be given support, allowing them to twine on a mossy stick. Make a cylinder of chicken wire, pack it with moss and place it in the pot. Small trailing Ivies can be trained to cling to pieces of driftwood placed in the pot.

Aphelandra squarrosa. Small plant with large glossy leaves boldly veined with white, this also has yellow flower-spikes. Cut whole stem back to a good pair of leaves after flowering. Re-pot each year in spring. Needs bright shade and humidity. Keep soil moist, even to the extent of being wet.

Aspidistra. Old-fashioned, but probably the easiest of all indoor plants, this will grow in poor soil or dim light without much attention. Divide in spring. It has numerous glossy stiff leaves coming up in a "fountain".

Begonia. The Rex group with its numerous varieties are the best known. They have beautiful plum-coloured or bluish foliage with a silvery sheen. See growing hints under flowering pot-plants above.

Bromeliads. A large group of striking plants which belong to the Pineapple family, these have showy flowers in winter, spring and summer. Most of them are epiphytes on trees (such as *Tillandsia*, the Airplant), using their roots simply as an anchor, while some, notably *Billbergia*, grow in rocky soil. They grow almost as easily as succulents in dry rooms, provided that the centre cup made by the leaves is filled with water. Water freely during summer, filling the leaf funnels, but spray very lightly in winter. Bromeliads can be tied to driftwood with their roots packed with damp fibre or they can be planted in pots containing fibrous soil and compost. Well-drained soil will prevent rotting at the base of the plant. Bromeliads need shade in summer, but should be given warm sunshine in winter. Propagate by large side shoots which start growing after the parent plant has flowered.

Among the most desirable Bromeliads are *Vriesia splendens* with flame flowers and banded leaves, and *Aechmea fulgens* with violet flowers and red berries.

Caladium. Fancy leaf Caladium. Large, spear-shaped leaves, shaded with silver, rose and green make a striking show all summer. The plant dies down in winter and the tubers should be kept dry. Plant these in early spring, about three to a pot. Place them in semi-shade, out-of-doors if liked, and give plenty of water during summer. Do not confuse with *Coleus*.

Chlorophytum. Hen-and-Chickens. Common, easily-grown house plants with green or striped leaves, these thrive under trees in the garden. They are attractive in pots placed on a shelf so that new plants forming at the tip of the flowering stem hang downwards. Give shade and moisture.

Cissus. Grape Ivy. Several species of which the Kangaroo Vine (*C. antarctica*) is the best known. A tendril-climber with large, light green leaves, sometimes toothed, this grows quickly and easily. It can be nipped back frequently in spring and summer to make it bushy. Cissus likes semi-shade and will tolerate low light and humidity, but should not be overwatered, especially in winter. Propagate by cuttings of ripe wood.

Codiaeum. (Croton). Large shrubs with colourful leathery foliage of all shapes and sizes, these can be grown as pot-plants only where the atmosphere is humid and make good greenhouse subjects. They need sunshine in order to preserve the leaf variegations.

Coleus. Medium-sized plants with brilliant leaf variegations in rose, green, tan and other colours, these must have some sunshine or they lose their intensity. Increase sunshine if they do so. Too much water also makes them pale, but they must not be allowed to wilt for lack of water, especially in summer. Coleus becomes shabby in winter and it is best to cut it back and let it send out new shoots which can be cut off and re-potted. Pinch back the young plants when they have about six leaves in order to make them bushy. Do not allow them to flower. If the stem grows too long, nip off the tip and root it.

Although seed may be sown in spring and provides new variegations, new plants grown each year from cuttings give the best results. They can be grown out of doors under trees as a summer annual, dying down during cold winters, but may come up in spring if the roots are strong and part of the stem remains.

Colocasia. Elephant's-Ears. Huge, arrow-shaped green leaves, these will grow in semi-shade or sun, but need rich soil, warmth and moisture in summer. They die down in winter and the tubers should be kept on the dry side in the pot. Can be planted near a pond. Propagate by division.

Croton. See *Codiaeum*.

Dieffenbachia. Dumb-Cane. Large, graceful plants with long stems and broad leaves, many marked with white or greenish-yellow, there are 20 varieties. Do not chew any part of the plant as the sap numbs the throat for a while. Dieffenbachias need rich, light soil and bright or filtered light, becoming leggy in poor light. They like humidity and should be placed out of draughts. Propagate by air-layering.

Dracaena. Ribbon-Plant. Large or small plants, these resemble a young Maize plant and generally have leaves striped or spotted with white and yellow. Give moist soil with good drainage. They dislike cold night temperatures, but are long-lived when established.

Fatshedera lizei. A hybrid between English Ivy (*Hedera*) and *Fatsia*, this is a tall, upright plant with green lobed leaves like Ivy. There is also a variegated form. Fatshedera can be trained to climb a little. It is easy to grow in poor light, but prefers bright light.

Ferns. Ferns need fibrous soil which should not dry out, although some hardy ferns will tolerate dryness, especially in winter. These can be grown in a hanging basket. Give ferns filtered sunshine. They have decorative foliage of many kinds.

Asparagus Fern (*Asparagus plumosus*). This and the Basket Asparagus (*A. sprengeri*) and Smilax (*A. asparagoides*) grow easily indoors or in the garden in shade or filtered sunlight. They withstand winter drought as they have moisture-storing tubers.

Bird's Nest Fern (*Asplenium*). A rosette of broad, ripply large leaves with thin black veins and stems. Needs moist soil.

Maidenhair Fern (*Adiantum*). Delicate fronds must receive only indirect light. Requires plenty of moisture.

Staghorn Fern (*Platycerium*). Flattened, divided greyish-green leaves. Needs soil with compost or peat as some are epiphytic in nature. Likes moisture and humidity, but do not overwater in winter.

Sword Fern or Boston Fern (*Nephrolepis*). Easy to grow indoors or out, it withstands drought. Various types of fronds, some finely divided and called Ostrich Plume or Crested Fern.

Ficus elastica. Rubber Plant. A striking tall plant to 10 feet or more, this has bold, glossy drooping leaves. There is also a variety with creamy variegations.

F. elastica decora has broader, more erect leaves and a reddish tip. It grows more quickly. The Fiddleleaf Fig (*F. lyrata*, formerly *F. pandurata*) has wavy-edged leaves which broaden at the top.

These plants grow fairly slowly and seldom need re-potting. They should be kept on the dry side in winter and watered freely in spring and summer, but not over-watered. Dim light and overwatering can cause leaf drop. Bring the plants into the light occasionally if they are placed in a poorly lit position, for they prefer bright shade, but do not want full sun. Feed only in summer and avoid re-potting during the semi-dormant stage in winter. Wipe the leaves occasionally with a damp, soft cloth. Propagate by air-layering.

Fittonia. Small, trailing plants with white or red-veined leaves, Fittonias need deep shade, moist soil and humidity. Shower the leaves with a fine rose when watering and keep a clear plastic cover over the plant most of the time in places with a dry atmosphere.

Hedera. Ivy. Favourite indoor trailing plants, these are best allowed to hang downwards, but can be trained to cling to driftwood. Ivy needs bright light, preferably with some direct sun, and rich, well-drained soil. Do not dry out completely, but do not overwater. Pieces of Ivy grow roots in water, damp soil or vermiculite. Propagate in spring and summer.

English Ivy (*Hedera helix*) is the large, dark green garden climber which has many dainty varieties suitable for growing indoors. Those with variegated leaves need more light than plain green types. If they lose variegation, cut them back in spring to a good variegated leaf.

Variegated Canary Islands Ivy (*H. canariensis* var. *variegata*) has large green leaves edged with cream. It keeps its variegation in the shade, provided that the light is bright. It grows slowly at first, but will cover a large screen. It grows well in hot, dry areas, but needs moisture at the root.

Maranta. Prayer Plant. A medium-sized plant with light green leaves, geometrically spotted with dark green, that become erect at night. It likes moisture, humidity and deep shade.

Monstera. *M. deliciosa* is a tall climber with enormous slit leaves, growing up to 2 feet or more in length. It has an arum-like, edible flower which generally appears when it is grown out-of-doors in hot places with mild winters, ascending tall trees by means of aerial roots. It is a dramatic plant for a large room. *M. pertusa* (*Philodendron pertusum*) is a climber which is more suitable for ordinary rooms as it has smaller leaves, growing up to about 15 inches. It is sometimes called Cut-leaf Philodendron.

Monsteras need rich, porous, moist soil and warm winter temperatures. Keep it rather dry in cold weather. Give bright light and a large container. Cut the top back if a climber is not wanted.

Palms. The Kentia Palm (*Howea*) is the most easily obtainable and a dainty palm suited to growing in rooms. It has numerous slim stems topped with graceful arching leaves. It is slow-growing and need not be re-potted for years. Give it bright light, warmth and moist soil.

Peperomia. Small to medium-sized plants with masses of rounded, decorative leaves, there are both variegated and green forms. Those with crinkled leaves are most decorative and need more humidity than the others. They have fascinating spikes of tiny green or whitish flowers. Peperomias should be given medium light and porous soil. Keep them dry rather than wet, as the leaves are thick and fleshy. Propagate by stem cuttings. Leaf cuttings taken from variegated types may revert to green.

Philodendron scandens. Heartleaf Philodendron. The most popular and long cultivated of a large number of species, this is a tall climber with heart-shaped, pointed green leaves. There is also a variegated form which is not easy to grow and tends to revert to green. Do not confuse this with *Scindapsus*. Heartleaf Philodendron must be given a support on which to cling. It will grow vigorously if given light, well-drained soil, bright shade and plenty of moisture, especially in summer. Syringe the leaves in dry places. It likes warmth, but will stand chills. It can be cut back in spring to induce new growth. Propagate by stem cuttings of several joints with a leaf attached.

Several other Philodendrons are grown. Fiddleleaf Philodendron (*P. panduriforme*) is suitable for large interiors and has three-lobed, pointed leaves. *P. ilsemannii* has huge, green, spear-shaped leaves growing to 2 feet or more and marbled with white or tinged with rose. *P. imbe* has a reddish underleaf. *P. bipinnatifidum* is not a climbing plant, but has a short stem and large, lobed leaves. The plant often referred to as Cutleaf Philodendron is *Monstera pertusa*.

Pilea cadieri. Aluminium Plant. A compact bushy plant with silvery leaf markings, this grows easily if given plenty of moisture and kept out of draughts in winter. Feed and re-pot as it grows. Propagate by cuttings.

Sansevieria. Bowstring Hemp. Spiky, tough, tongue-shaped leaves which are generally variegated, these may be tall or short. Grow easily in dim light and poor or heavy soil. Propagate by division or leaf cuttings.

Schefflera actinophylla. Tall luxuriant plant with large hand-shaped leaves divided into five glossy leaflets, hardy and suitable for a hall. Give strong light, but not full sun. Fairly slow growing. Do not overwater.

Scindapsus. Devil's Ivy or Ivy-Arum. A climbing plant with heart-shaped leaves similar to *Philodendron scandens*, this is variegated and needs more light. It can be distinguished from variegated Philodendron as the leaf is not so deeply cleft at the top of the "heart". *S. aureus* is blotched and streaked irregularly with pale gold. "Golden Queen" is a deeper gold, while "Marble Queen" is green and silver.

Syngonium. Small climbing plants that are suitable for average rooms, these are upright at first but can be trained to climb up a stick to 5 feet or trail downwards. They generally have glossy, dark green divided leaves, although one is shaped like an arrowhead. They are hardy and grow quickly and easily, tolerating even duller light than Philodendron. Give rich light soil containing compost.

Tradescantia. Wandering Jew. Several with shining or hairy green leaves and prostrate, rooting stems. They will grow indoors or out in shade or sunshine. Need moist soil and shelter from frost.

Zebrina pendula (*Tradescantia zebrina*). Wandering Jew. Striped green and silver leaves, purple beneath and with reddish-purple flowers, this grows like Tradescantia. Grow in a pot or hanging basket. Makes a good groundcover in the shade out-of-doors. *Z. purpusii* is a bright purple species from Mexico that can be grown in full sun in warm places.

CHAPTER THIRTY-FIVE

SPECIALISED GARDENING

GROWING MUSHROOMS: THE GREENHOUSE: GROWING ORCHIDS: SOIL-LESS CULTIVATION: BONSAI

There are several types of gardening which require the attention and knowledge of a specialist or hobbyist, as well as some equipment. Ordinary gardening consists essentially of growing plants in suitable fertile soil, watering them regularly and feeding occasionally. People who want to grow orchids or mushrooms, however, cannot simply put them into the garden in the usual way, but must be prepared to spend some money on equipment and devote time to their cultivation.

Other interesting hobbies which take people's fancy, such as growing miniature trees, known in Japan as Bonsai, or growing plants by means of soil-less cultivation, also require special methods, detailed below. Ownership of a greenhouse enables one to grow many plants besides orchids that are too tender for one's own climate or may be grown out of season and an idea of what this involves will be described below.

I. GROWING MUSHROOMS

Mushroom growing generally appeals to everyone, but can only be undertaken if one is prepared to devote time and attention to it, as successful methods of cultivation are most exacting. Commercial mushroom growing is a highly scientific and all-absorbing venture which requires a great deal of labour and expense. The hobbyist can grow mushrooms on a small scale for his own table, however, provided that the necessary steps are executed promptly and correctly.

Mushrooms do not need light in the same way as green plants which cannot grow without it. For this reason they can be grown in a dark cellar, provided that it is well aired. Unless one lives close to a stable or can obtain fresh manure easily, it is not practical to cultivate mushrooms. They are best cultivated in a room under a roof, but may also be grown under a tree in suitable climates. (See below.)

The Growing Room. This may be any size, as small as 6 by 3 feet or very much larger. An ordinary room attached to the house would be suitable for growing mushrooms, but it must have outside access in order to be practical. It is best to construct a special little house

of concrete blocks or to convert an outhouse. A cellar with an outside entrance is suitable.

The room must be cross-ventilated but not draughty. Two windows are best, but one window and a 6-inch fan on the opposite wall will be satisfactory. An ideal window should be situated about 12 inches above ground level and screened to keep out rats. The windows are generally covered by wood to exclude the light, not because the light is detrimental, but because it generates heat.

The growing room must be kept cool in summer by opening the ventilators and circulating the air by means of a fan. It would be necessary to insulate the room well in sub-tropical places in order to keep the temperature cool in summer. An outdoor house should have a ceiling insulated with fibreglass or vermiculite, while a cellar might probably be the coolest place.

No heating would be necessary in sub-tropical areas, but it is necessary during winter in cold areas such as on the highveld. The room can be heated by a hot water pipe or by any other means and the temperature kept at 60 degrees F. If one does not wish to heat the growing room one should grow mushrooms only during the warmer months, whereas they could be grown throughout the year if the room is heated. The easiest months for mushroom cultivation are during spring and early summer when the humidity rises and it is warm, but has not yet become too hot.

It is not necessary to have any tables or benches in the growing room as the mushrooms are grown in movable trays which are stacked upon each other in a honeycomb or open-brick formation. (See sketch.) The lowest trays should stand on blocks so that air can circulate freely around them. The higher tiers generally produce better

Sketch showing spacing for sixteen trays

than the lower. Each tray should measure about 2 feet by 2 feet by 6 inches deep and be made of wood. One should have at least 15 trays in order to grow sufficient mushrooms for one's own use.

Preparation of Medium for Growing Mushrooms. The medium or compost, as it is known, consists solely of manure and straw which must be broken down so that it becomes suitable food for the growing mushroom. Horse manure is best and should be reasonably fresh, about two to three months old. Cow manure is not as good while pig manure is satisfactory, but more difficult to work. The manure should contain 40 per cent of wheat or rye straw. Some hays break down too soon and become compacted, while sawdust takes too long to decompose and compacts too much.

The compost may be prepared out-of-doors or under a shed. The manure and straw must be piled into a long heap, preferably 5 feet high and not less than 4 feet 6 inches wide. A smaller heap will not heat up sufficiently. About 3 inches of the large heap acts as an insulating barrier. Water the heap and turn and water it three or four times during a period of three weeks. It is unnecessary to cover it with hessian or straw as it must have air. It must be neither too compacted nor too loose, or it will dry out.

After the second turning add lime in the form of gypsum (Calcium sulphate) to the heap. Use about 40 lb. to a ton of manure. The manure must not be acid and the addition of lime during the decaying process assists in breaking it down. The pH of the resulting compost should be pH 8 to 8.5. Spray the heap and the surrounding area with BHC or some other insecticide to eliminate flies. The compost must be pasteurised at the end of the three week period in order to avoid possible trouble with pests or moulds.

Pasteurising the Compost. To do this, pack the compost into the wooden trays and stack them in tiers in an oven. Place a one-inch piece of wood underneath each box so that the air can circulate between the boxes. A simple clay or Dutch oven is best for this purpose, or it may be built of brick. One must be able to keep the heat constant between 120 degrees F. to 140 degrees F. for a period of 24 hours. It would be ideal to have a thermostat. The oven may be heated by electricity, gas or by hot water pipes circulating from a slow combustion stove. One can use the same means for heating the growing room. The compost creates its own heat, but needs a supplementary heat. If the heat goes above 140 degrees F. there is a danger of other fungi growing.

After 24 hours, take the trays out of the oven and stack them in the growing room. They should be cooled as quickly as possible, but the cooling process could take a week. Place a thermometer in the compost. As soon as it registers 80 degrees F. it will be ready for planting the spawn. The compost should be moist at this stage. When it is placed in the oven it should be wet from being watered in the turning process and when it comes out it should still contain about 70 per cent of moisture. To determine this in a simple way, weigh a pound of the pasteurised compost in a tin, then dry it out in an oven and re-weigh it. It should now weigh about 4 oz.

Planting the Mushroom Spawn. Mushrooms grow from spawn which consists of mushroom spores and their thread-like roots (mycelium) growing on a medium. One can purchase dry spawn, which looks like fibrous compost, in one pound cartons, one being enough to plant about nine trays. Fresh spawn looks like grain covered with moist wool and can be obtained from some commercial growers. Mushrooms grown from fresh spawn grow about a fortnight earlier.

When planting dry spawn, cut it up into pieces the size of walnuts and plant them about 9 inches apart each way, staggering the rows. Push them down about 2 or 3 inches deep, the deeper the better. When planting fresh spawn, push back the top few inches of compost, sprinkle the spawn over the surface and cover it again.

The compost must be kept moist, but should need no further watering. If it is too dry one can spray lightly with tepid water, but it is not advisable unless absolutely necessary. About two to four weeks after planting, thread-like mycelium begins to appear on the surface, looking like whitish cottony film. At this stage it must be cased.

Casing. This means covering the compost with an insulating layer of moistened soil, from $1\frac{1}{4}$ to $1\frac{1}{2}$ inches thick. The casing provides protection for the compost, preventing evaporation and supplying moisture while acting as a support for the growing mushroom. It is also beneficial in many other ways which are not fully understood, forming a subject for scientific research.

Contrary to expectations, the soil used for casing should be a stiff clay subsoil which has been dug from a deep hole in the ground, the deeper the more sterile. Do not use topsoil or loam. The clay should be gravelly in texture and not too fine or it packs down. Very fine clay can be mixed with ash to lighten it. Mix the soil with lime, using about 1 lb. to a wheelbarrow of soil, so that the pH will be about 8. The mushroom itself produces oxalic acid as it grows, which eventually stops its growth.

Moisten the casing thoroughly before placing it on the compost. Water it again with a fine rose after four to seven days in order to keep it completely moist, but do not wet the compost below. Keep it in this moist condition until the first pinheads of mushrooms appear, about two weeks after casing. Water every two or three days for another seven to ten days, when the mushrooms will be large enough to pick.

Picking. The larger the mushrooms are allowed to grow, the better. Do not pull the mushrooms out of the soil, but twist them off. They do not all develop together. After the first flush there may be an interval of a week to ten days when another flush will appear. One can expect about four or five flushes from the tray, the strongest coming at the beginning. There is a certain amount of overlapping in growth.

As soon as the mushrooms have stopped growing, one must empty the trays and begin the whole process again. Spawn must be purchased anew each time. The spent mushroom compost can then be used in the garden to add organic matter to the soil.

Cultivating Mushrooms out of doors. Although one can cultivate mushrooms out of doors, the results are not as reliable as indoor cultivation, but the amateur without a growing room may like to try this. This method will be more successful in a temperate climate with humidity in the atmosphere.

Choose a protected, shady position under a tree and prepare a long mound beneath it. Use the same compost of manure and straw that is prepared for the trays and pile it into a heap from 18 inches to 2 feet in height and about 2 feet wide. It can be made as long as desired.

Plant the dry or fresh spawn as described above about 3 inches or more down towards the middle of the heap. Keep the compost moist. The heap must be cased completely with soil in the same way as the tray is cased for indoor cultivation. One need not fear that poisonous mushrooms will find their way into the mound, as they will not grow in the same conditions as the cultivated mushroom. In any case the cultivated mushroom will prove too great a competitor for any other mushroom.

II. THE GREENHOUSE

A greenhouse or glass-house is a luxury that every enthusiastic gardener would like to own in time, whether it be for the purpose of growing orchids, ferns and tender house-plants or simply for the pleasure of pottering around in its peaceful seclusion.

Greenhouses do not necessarily have to be heated by artificial means, depending on what types of plants one wishes to grow. An ordinary unheated glass-house will give sufficient protection to enable one to grow many plants that require more warmth and humidity than can be obtained out-of-doors. True greenhouse plants and many house-plants do not really require high temperatures. Plants like Calceolarias that require cool, moist conditions yet protection from rain storms and frost, can be grown in an unheated greenhouse, where the problem would be to keep it cool enough in summer.

It is not necessary to have a heated house at all in many parts of southern Africa, such as at low altitudes in Natal, especially near the coast, the Transvaal Lowveld and in many parts of Rhodesia. A hot-house is necessary in cold, dry areas inland, such as on the Highveld and in parts of the Cape, so that it is possible to create humid conditions all through the year and give the plants sufficient warmth in winter. Amateur gardeners use hot-houses mainly for the cultivation of orchids (see below), but they can be used also for growing many pot plants which need humidity and warmth.

Construction of the Greenhouse or Glass-house. It is possible to buy pre-fabricated glass-houses which can be erected easily. The minimum size for a glass-house should be 8 feet wide by 12 feet long and about 8 to 10 feet high at the ridge. Anything smaller will not be worth the expense of construction as it is more difficult to control the temperature in a smaller house. Serious orchid growers should not construct a house less than 15 feet by 10 feet with a height of 9 feet at the ridge.

A glass-house is seldom ornamental and is best placed independently in an out-of-the-way corner of the garden. Lean-to glass-houses can be placed against the north wall of a house or out-house, which must then be waterproofed to prevent the dampness from affecting the wall. A greenhouse may be sunk about 3 feet below ground level so that

Side view of Sunken Greenhouse

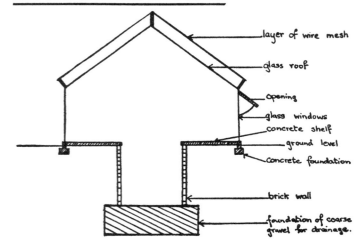

layer of wire mesh
glass roof
opening
glass windows
concrete shelf
ground level
concrete foundation
brick wall
foundation of coarse gravel for drainage.

the shelves are flush with the surface outside. This helps to keep the temperature warm and more humid in winter, but has the disadvantage that rainwater collects at the entrance which takes the form of a flight of steps. One must dig a square, a few inches deep, below the entrance to the door so that rainwater can drain into it. The sunken greenhouse may be slightly more economical to construct and less prominent in an ordinary garden.

The ridge of the glass-house should run from north to south if possible, so that all the plants can benefit from the maximum amount of light as the sun passes over from east to west. The light should come in from the top, so that the roof must be made of glass. The glass should be protected from hail or breakage by stretching wire mesh over it, at least 6 inches above the surface. New plastic materials, such as fibreglass and Rigid P.V.C., can now be substituted for glass. They do not break like glass and are more economical to construct.

A lean-to roof construction is often cheaper than a gabled roof and one may build a greenhouse or hot-house facing in the direction of the sun so that the plants have the maximum amount of light. Place the back wall of the greenhouse running from east to west and have the pitch of the lean-to roof sloping down towards the sunny side. In the southern hemisphere this will mean facing north and, in the northern, facing south. The slope should be at an angle of 40 degrees in order to allow the condensation that forms underneath to run off and not drop on the foliage. Large drops mark the leaves and flowers.

Glass-houses must have ventilation and shading. One must be able to open fanlights or windows so that one can reduce the temperature inside the house, yet the greenhouse must not be draughty. It is best not to have openings in the roof as rainwater might drip through, but place the fanlights under the eaves.

Shading is essential during the hot summer months. One can place bamboo or reed mats or palm leaves on the roof of the house, but these must be removed on dull days. As this involves too much labour for the amateur, it is best to paint the glass thinly with a white proprietary paint or rubber paint in order to diffuse the light. The few dull days experienced in this country will not be sufficient to harm the plants. A new method of shading is the use of a plastic cloth called saran cloth. Although this is comparatively expensive, it has the advantage that it is light and easy to remove during winter if necessary. It can be obtained in various meshes, so as to allow different densities of shade for the needs of special plants. Some plants need more shade than others. It is no use trying to beautify the glass-house by growing a creeper over it as it will cast too dense a shade. One can scatter a little thatching straw over the wire mesh to break the sun's rays.

Staging of plants inside the greenhouse should be simple and formal. The usual method is to have a central doorway at one end with a central pathway and a 3-foot shelf on either side. One could also build a central pyramid of steps in the centre, in which case the lower plants would receive more shade than those near the top. One could combine both these methods in a large, wide greenhouse.

Slatted hard-wood shelves are best, since they allow for drainage and free circulation of air and warmth, especially important when cultivating orchids like Cattleyas. To preserve the wood, paint with two coats of white lead paint every second year, removing plants while this is done. Never paint the wood with creosote which gives off fumes fatal to the plants. Concrete shelves are long-lasting, but should be covered with a layer of fine gravel chips in order to hold moisture and aid drainage of the pots. In the case of orchids, which require excellent drainage, one must stand each pot on an upturned empty clay pot or place a slatted wooden rack on the concrete shelf, at least 4 inches above it.

One can build one shelf in the form of a window-box for displaying or growing plants. Build it in the form of a brick trough at least 12 inches deep. Makes holes for drainage below and fill the base with a 3-inch layer of gravel, ashes and crocks for drainage, then fill it with good soil. The front could be edged with ornamental rocks and one could display many plants like *Impatiens* and *Browallia* in it, so that it resembles a miniature rockery. One could also use such a box for growing plants that like cool, moist conditions like *Cineraria*, *Calceolaria* and *Cyclamen*. If one wanted to grow large shrubs in it the box could be extended down to the floor.

The floor of the hot-house should be made of earth so that all the moisture which is sprayed about can drain away. If the drainage is not good, one should raise the whole floor above the outside level. Scatter fine gravel over the surface in order to keep one's shoes clean or place a few pieces of slate down the centre for walking, but do not cement the whole floor. Before erecting the greenhouse, it is best to excavate the floor area to a depth of 18 inches and fill this with coarse gravel and clinkers so that water will not collect and stagnate on the floor of the house. Cleanliness is essential in a greenhouse, otherwise insect pests collect under unnecessary objects. If space is limited, however, one can place pots of special plants which like dim light on the floor under the shelves, such as *Fittonia* and Ferns. In a greenhouse which is not sunken and where there is more light beneath the shelves, one could grow *Impatiens*, *Saintpaulia* and other plants which require more light.

How to Create Humidity in the Glass-house.
Humidity is created by spraying water on to the floor, the walls of the greenhouse and on to the shelves between the pots, without necessarily watering the plants. This is known as "damping down" and should be done every morning throughout the year in dry places, but must be increased to three or four times a day during summer if the atmosphere is very hot and dry. The more one opens the ventilators to cool the house, the more frequently one must damp down to prevent drying the atmosphere. There should be about 70 to 80 per cent of humidity in the greenhouse or orchid house and one can read this on an instrument known as a hygrometer. If the weather is cold in winter one must decrease the humidity and not damp down more than once a day, limiting this to the early morning.

In order to increase humidity, one should build brick cemented troughs, about 6 to 9 inches deep, on the floor under the shelves and fill these with clean water. One can dip a syringe or watering can into this water, which will have the advantage of being at the same temperature as the house, in order to water the plants. Plastic basins can be used instead of fixed troughs. It is helpful to have a tap inside the house so that one does not have to open the door more than necessary.

Automatic devices can be used in order to save labour in damping down. This can be done in several ways and the humidity can be controlled by a humidistat. The use of charcoal boxes and fans is very successful. A wire basket filled with charcoal is hung outside the wall of the hot-house, showing through an aperture in the wall. Water drops from a spray on to the charcoal and moist, fresh air is drawn into the hot-house by means of a fan placed inside the hot-house and in front of the wire cage. The air circulates around the house and prevents the spread of fungus diseases. Fans to circulate air are always advisable, especially when growing orchids. Mist sprays are also useful in creating humidity. They are best placed under the benches and should be controlled with humidistats.

Any electrical work done in a hot-house must be done by a qualified electrician because of the danger attached to moisture with electricity.

Watering the Plants. Greenhouse plants require varying amounts of water, but most plants should be watered once a day, sprinkling them from the top with tepid water and soaking the pots and their contents well. During hot summer days the foliage of many plants, including most orchids, should be syringed in the afternoon, in addition to watering the pots in the morning. Overwatering of the plants in the greenhouse is prevented by preparing the pots properly with excellent drainage.

Potting Greenhouse Plants. Ordinary greenhouse plants should be planted in pots containing equal parts of sand, peat and good rich topsoil. One can add a fertilizing mixture to this, using $\frac{1}{4}$ lb. to a bushel of soil. This consists of two parts of hoof and horn meal, two parts of superphosphate and one part of sulphate of potash. The bottom of the pots should have a layer of small pieces of gravel or broken crocks to allow for drainage. Orchids need more drainage and different potting. (See below under "Orchid Growing".)

How to Create Warmth. A small hot-house can be heated most easily by means of a thermostatically controlled electric tubular heater in order to maintain a steady temperature. The tubes are placed against the walls near the floor and the hot air rises to warm the house. A convection heater may also be used. Heating can also be done by means of a combustion stove feeding hot water pipes and this is usually done in a larger hot-house.

The amount of heating can be regulated according to the type of plants one wishes to grow. Heating is not used during the summer months, but will be necessary during winter if one is growing orchids in dry inland districts. Although it is unnecessary to heat the house in the hotter parts of the country, it would be wise to have a heater available in case of unseasonable weather or even a few days of unusually cold weather. It is possible to grow ordinary house-plants in an unheated glass-house even on the highveld during winter, but then one must be prepared to cover the roof at night with mats in order to prevent the penetration of frost during cold spells. Plants like *Primula obconica* and *Calceolaria* will be killed by severe frost, even though they like cool conditions of growth.

Regulating the Temperature. The temperature of the hot-house must be controlled to suit the requirements of the plants one wishes to grow and it is essential to have one or two thermometers fixed to the walls or hanging from the roof in order to check whether the temperature is kept constant. Hot-houses are named according to the ideal temperatures required for certain plants, particularly orchids. They are called the Cool house, the Intermediate or Cattleya House and the Stove or warm house. Most house-plants, as described in Chapter 34, can be grown in any of these temperatures, although some must have a cooler atmosphere. (See list of companion plants given below.)

Although the temperatures given for each house are sharply defined, it will be found impossible to keep strictly to them, but they should serve as a guide.

COOL HOUSE
Winter. Minimum night temperature = 45°–55°F.
          Minimum day temperature = 55°–65°F.
Summer. Night temperature = 65°F.
          Day temperature = 75°F.

INTERMEDIATE HOUSE
Winter. Minimum night temperature = 55°F.
Minimum day temperature = 65°–70°F.
Summer. Night temperature = 75°F.
Day temperature = 85°F. (But more likely to go up to 100°F.)

STOVE HOUSE
Winter. Night temperature = 65°F.
Day temperature = 75°F.
Summer. Night temperature = 75°F.
Day temperature = 85°–100°F. with high humidity.

The amateur in the S. hemisphere will find it easier to keep the house warm in winter than cool enough in summer. The more one opens the fanlights and windows in order to cool the air, the more frequently one must damp down the house in order not to lose the necessary humidity, particularly in places with dry atmospheres. This is especially important when growing orchids which will shrivel if the atmosphere is not humid enough.

This is why it is so difficult to grow Cool House orchids like Odontoglossum and Miltonias in this country of warm summers, even in places where winters are cold. If one wishes to grow these, one would have to erect a sprinkler system for cooling the roof with a continuous spray of running water. Shade the house adequately in order to keep the temperature both cool and humid in summer.

The most practical temperature to aim at is that of the Intermediate or Cattleya House, which is suited to the culture of the most popular orchids, Cattleyas, as well as many other orchids and the majority of companion plants. Tropical orchids, like *Phalaenopsis* and some Dendrobiums, need to be grown in the stove house, which will be found more difficult to heat in winter and uncomfortably warm to work in in summer. It is hardly worth it for the amateur to bring the temperature up to that of the Stove House as there are comparatively few tropical orchids available for growing in it, while most of the decorative companion plants to grow with these will grow equally well in the Intermediate House. If one is keen to grow tropical orchids like *Dendrobium nobile* or *Phalaenopsis*, one can place them in the warmer part of the Intermediate House. They can be enclosed with a partition of glass or polythene in order to create a warmer atmosphere.

Choosing Plants for the Greenhouse. The plants which may be grown in the ordinary unheated greenhouse are those described in Chapter 34 on House Plants, as well as many other shade and humidity-loving, tender plants. Many of the following can be grown in the hot-house, but also enjoy a cooler atmosphere, provided that they have humidity.

Achimenes.
Anthurium.
Ardisia.
Begonia.
Bouvardia.
Browallia.
Caladium.
Calceolaria.
Chlorophytum.
Cineraria.
Cyclamen.
Ferns.
Fuchsias.
Hippeastrum (Amaryllis).
Impatiens.
Kentia Palm.
Mimulus.
Philodendron scandens.
Plectranthus.
Primula obconica.
Saintpaulia.
Sansevieria.
Schizanthus.
Sinningia (Gloxinia).
Streptocarpus.

III. ORCHID GROWING FOR THE AMATEUR

Orchids are fascinating mainly because of the construction of their flowers, both large or small. There are numerous interesting species, although the amateur usually thinks mainly of the large-flowered hybrid Cattleyas most frequently seen in florists' windows.

Orchids are divided into terrestrial and epiphytic orchids, which are cultivated differently. Terrestrial orchids may be grown in loamy soil in the garden, provided that the temperature is not too cold in winter, or they may be grown in pots containing leaf-mould and soil. The tubers must not be watered while dormant and are best lifted and stored like ordinary bulbs. Terrestrial orchids which may be grown out of doors, provided that they are sheltered from frost, include the indigenous *Ferraria* (Spider Flower), *Satyrium* (Ewa-Trewa), *Eulophia*, *Habenaria* and many others.

Epiphytic orchids grow in trees in nature, using their roots to anchor themselves to a fork in the tree, but draw nourishment from the leaf-mould that collects in the bark and from the air. Many orchids have swollen stems or pseudobulbs for storing food. Some species can be fixed to deciduous trees out of doors, provided that the atmosphere is warm and humid enough, while others can be grown on a barky log and kept on a sheltered verandah. They must be kept on the dry side in winter. The best known species in this country is *Ansellia gigantea* and its variety *nilotica*, which grows wild from Natal to Rhodesia.

Hot-House Orchids. Some orchids like *Ansellia* can be grown in hot-houses as well as out-of-doors. *Epidendrum radicans* will grow in the Intermediate House, but is drought-resistant and will grow in a sunny, protected place in the ordinary garden. It will grow in fibrous loam or pure fibre in pots. Cut back the flowering stems after blooming. Keep the plant dry in winter, but spray it with water in summer. *Cypripedium insigne* (Lady's Slipper Orchid) and some Cymbidiums can be grown in pots in a shade house or on a shady verandah in summer and kept in a hot-house during winter in cold areas.

How to Grow Cattleyas. These are evergreen orchids which bloom at different times according to the variety. Amongst the easiest to grow are *Cattleya maxima*, which is most suitable for hanging baskets, and *C. mossiae*, but there are many other desirable varieties. Do not pick the flower for the first three days after opening or it will collapse, but after that it will last in water for up to three weeks. The flowers keep better if the plant is moved into a cool greenhouse or room.

Cattleyas are Intermediate House orchids which need plenty of light and high humidity. They are strong and will not die easily, but will not flower if they receive set-backs during cultivation.

The ideal **temperature** for Cattleyas should vary between 50°F. and 90°F. In practice this varies from 45°F. to 100°F. and over. During summer the temperature will vary from 75°F. at night to 85°F. during the day, but is more likely to rise to 90°F. or 100°F. on hot days. The atmosphere must be kept humid or the orchids will shrivel in hot, dry weather, and it may be necessary to damp down three or four times a day to maintain at least 80 per cent of humidity. The more ventilation one gives to cool the house, the more frequently one must damp down, and one can scarcely err on the side of making the atmosphere too moist. When damping down, water the stage between the plants as well as the floor. Damp down the house even if one grows orchids in a shade house in a hot, moist climate like Durban's, as the wind can be drying.

Always **water** the plants from the top, soaking the pot and spraying the leaves. During summer the foliage can be given an additional light spray each afternoon. Only water the pots themselves when they are dry, or the orchid roots may decay as a result of overwatering.

Cattleyas need a resting period in winter and should not be watered frequently, although the house itself must be dampened in order to maintain the humidity. The ideal temperature on winter nights should be 60°F., and 80°F. to 85°F. during the day. If the temperature drops as low as 45°F. on winter nights, one should not make the house too wet or moulds may form on the plants. Damp the house down once a day in the mornings, but water the pots about once a week or less often during the resting period. If there is any sign of shrivelling, give the plants more water.

Rainwater is excellent for watering orchids and it would be ideal to have a tank inside the house to collect the water that drains off the roof. One can use tap water, but this should be allowed to stand in troughs before

using so that it warms up to the same temperature as that of the house. If the water is too alkaline and white deposits appear on the plants, one can add hydrochloric or dilute phosphoric acid (a few drops to 25 gallons of water), to bring the pH to 5.5 or 6, but one must test the water to prevent overdoing the acidity. All orchids like acid conditions.

Potting. Cattleyas must have excellent drainage so that the pots can dry rapidly in spite of being watered frequently. If the shelves are not made of slatted wood, each pot should stand on another upturned pot or on a slatted wooden rack raised 4 inches above the concrete shelf. Cattleyas are best grown in pure Osmunda fibre in order to develop a healthy root system. This is freely obtainable. It should be soaked and cleaned, if necessary, before using. Sphagnum Moss (Bog Moss) is sometimes mixed with the fibre, but this rots easily if the pot is wet and may also cause the Cattleya roots to rot. One can place a few tiny pieces of sphagnum moss on top of the fibre to indicate when water is needed, as it holds water for a long time.

One can obtain special clay orchid pots with enlarged openings. Otherwise one should enlarge the drainage hole in an ordinary pot. Fill the bottom third of the pot with crocks (broken pot pieces), placed vertically, and pack it firmly with damp Osmunda fibre, ramming it in with a stick. The rhizome must rest on top of the fibre, but the roots must be pushed into it, packing the air spaces in firmly. Soak the new pot thoroughly. One can also prepare hanging baskets for Cattleyas and other orchids. These may be made in the form of boxes made entirely of slatted wood. Always line the basket or box with woodland moss and then pack it with Osmunda fibre and plant the orchid in the usual way. Douglas Fir Bark is now proving a popular medium for potting as it is easier to work with than with moss. It is chipped into different sizes for small or large plants. It is inert material which does not provide nourishment and plants which grow in it must be fed with artificial fertilizers.

Cattleyas need to be re-potted about once in three years when they have grown too large for their pots, but should not be disturbed otherwise. Divide the rhizome, leaving four pseudobulbs to a piece. Once a stem has flowered it will never flower again, but it must not be removed as it remains as a source of food. Only discard a very shrivelled stem if necessary when re-potting. Old roots which cling to the basket or pot may be severed. The best time to re-pot is in spring when the plants start shooting and the new roots are not longer than an inch, as they are brittle and can be injured easily.

Orchids can be grown from seed only by special means,

and the amateur should purchase mature plants which are ready to flower.

There is no need to feed Cattleyas or most other orchids, as they obtain their nourishment from the air and water and rely on the trace elements they absorb from the Osmunda fibre. Feeding is a matter of personal preference and can give good results. One can feed orchids with mineral fertilizers provided that this is not overdone, as there is a danger of feeding solutions settling on the fibre as it dries out rapidly and toxicity may develop. Feeds must be soluble and applied in solution at half the strength given to ordinary pot plants. One should not feed more frequently than once a month, and then only during the period of active growth from spring to late summer. Feeding must be given when growing orchids on inert materials like bark or stones. It will have to be more frequent and will depend on experience. The normal procedure is to feed with fish emulsion and a solution of 30 : 10 : 10 once a week.

Pests and Diseases. The worst pests in greenhouses are slugs and snails, which can be baited with metaldehyde. Tie cottonwool around the lower stems bearing flowers to prevent slugs from crawling up and damaging the flower. Thrips, scale and red spider are also troublesome, and one can prevent infestation by sponging the leaves every three months with cottonwool dipped in soapy water. Remove scale and mealybugs on Cattleyas and other orchids with a camelhair brush dipped into a solution of one part of methylated spirits to three parts of water. Spraying with ordinary insecticides in the enclosed space of a glass-house increases their toxicity and one should take precautions when using them.

Diseases like fungus rotting of plants can be prevented by air movement and fans should be used to circulate the air.

Tips on Growing other Orchids

All orchids require moisture throughout the year, given less often in winter, especially those that require a resting period. Deciduous orchids like some Coelogynes drop their foliage, leaving only the pseudobulb, and they must be given just enough water to prevent shrivelling.

Cypripedium hybrids and *C. insigne* are not grown in Osmunda fibre, but in a compost of equal parts of rough soil and peat with ¼ part of chopped sphagnum moss mixed with small broken crocks.

Cool House orchids need a winter temperature of 45°F. to 55°F. and a summer temperature of 55°F. to 60°F., but it is difficult to keep the temperature lower than 75°F. Damp down frequently as soon as the temperature rises above 50°F. and increase ventilation. One cannot grow them easily in ordinary rooms as they need humidity. Cool House orchids are difficult to grow in southern Africa

and include *Odontoglossum, Oncidium, Miltonia* and *Cypripedium insigne*, the last named being easiest.

Tropical orchids like tropical Cypripediums, Dendrobiums and Phalaenopsis need higher temperatures than Cattleyas, 65°F. to 75°F. during winter and 75°F. to 85°F. and more during summer. They may be grown in the warmer part of the Intermediate or Cattleya House.

Light. Intensity of light is important for orchids. This may be measured by a light-meter which can be obtained graduated in foot candles. Cattleyas require about 2,000 foot candles; Cymbidiums about 5,000 foot candles; Phalaenopsis from 800 to 1,000 foot candles and Cypripediums from 800 to 1,000 foot candles.

Other Orchids to Grow with Cattleyas in the Intermediate House

Angraecum sesquipedale. Tall plant with large white flowers.

Ansellia gigantea var. *nilotica.* Long sprays of yellow flowers spotted brown. Also grows out of doors in trees in warmer parts of the country and in the stove house.

Bulbophyllum. Best in hanging baskets or on pieces of bark. Dormant in winter.

Coelogyne cristata. Sprays of yellow and white flowers. Dormant in winter.

Cymbidium. Many-flowered spikes. Likes less heat and light than Cattleyas. Water throughout year, especially while growing in spring and summer, less in winter.

Cypripedium. Lady's Slipper Orchids. Many varieties. *C. insigne* has sprays of smaller flowers and is the most easily grown. It flowers in winter in the hot-house and may be taken out-of-doors in summer and placed in a shade-house. Keep moist and humid all year.

Dendrobium nobile and *D. phalaenopsis.* Sprays of large rosy, purple or white flowers. These are tropical orchids that may be grown in the warmer part of the Cattleya House. They like plenty of light, preferably morning sun, but need to be raised in this way.

Epidendrum radicans. Grows even better in full sun out-of-doors in a sheltered place. Heads of small red or orange flowers at the tips of long stems.

Laelia and *Laeliocattleya* hybrids. Culture as for Cattleyas.

Phalaenopsis. Moth Orchid. A tropical orchid which can be grown in the warmer and duller part of the Cattleya House. Shade from direct sunlight especially in spring or summer.

Stanhopea wardii. Sprays of fragrant golden flowers, spotted red. Best in hanging baskets as flowers emerge underneath.

Vanda. Erect plants. *V. coerulea* with sprays of blue flowers, *V. sanderiana* with large rose and white flowers.

Keep moist throughout year, slightly less in winter. *V. teres*, with variable flowers, needs a more decided rest in winter.

Companion Plants for Cattleyas

Commercial growers will devote the whole house to growing orchids, but the amateur will find it practical and desirable to grow other plants to fill and decorate the hot-house. One should not devote less than one quarter of the space to orchids or they might be neglected. The orchids should dominate and the other plants must fit in with their treatment. Many will also grow in the Stove House, Cool House or out-of-doors.

Flowering Plants

Anthuriums.
Aphelandra.
Begonia.
Billbergia.
Bromeliads.
Clivia.
Episcea.
Gesneria.
Impatiens.
Ixora.
Kalanchoe.
Pavonia rosea.
Primula obconica (in winter).
Saintpaulia.
Streptocarpus.

Foliage Plants

Breynia nivosa (or Stove).
Caladium.
Crotons (Codiaeum).
Dieffenbachia (or Stove).
Eranthemum.
Fittonia (or Stove).
Peperomia.
Pilea.
Maranta.
Nidularium tricolor.
Plectranthus (or outside).
Sansevieria (or outside).

Plants for Hanging Baskets in Cattleya House

Asparagus sprengeri.
Begonia sutherlandii.
Columnea gloriosa.
Columnea microphylla.
Chlorophytum.
Epiphyllum.
Episcea.
Ferns.
Oplismenus (Basket Grass).
Orchids like Cattleya, Coelogyne.
Plectranthus.
Tradescantia.
Zebrina.

Climbing Plants for Cattleya House

Allamanda.
Begonia coccinea.
Cissus discolor.
Clerodendrum thompsoniae.
Clerodendrum splendens.
Fatshedera lizei.
Hoya carnosa.
Mandevilla.
Monstera deliciosa.
Philodendron in variety.
Stephanotis.

IV. SOIL-LESS CULTIVATION

Experiments on growing plants without soil started as early as 1699, but it was not until 1936 that these methods were adapted to growing crops by Dr. F. Gericke of California under the name "Hydroponics", meaning "water-growing". Plants were suspended with their roots immersed in a waterproofed tank of water, and a balanced formula of chemicals was fed to them daily. The difficulty of supporting the plants and the lack of aeration proved this to be a generally unsatisfactory practice.

Sand-Culture. An easier way of practising hydroponics was to fill the tank with washed river sand. This supported the plants, which were fed chemically by passing a nutrient solution through the sand. In place of sand, one can use other growing media such as wood shavings, sawdust, washed cinders or washed gravel of uniform size, from $\frac{1}{4}$ to $\frac{1}{2}$ inch in diameter. Vermiculite is now used to a large extent, especially in South Africa, where it is produced. The vermiculite absorbs and retains moisture and keeps cooler than other materials on hot summer days. Vermiculite is an excellent sterile material which has many uses in the garden, apart from its use as a supporting medium for plants in soil-less cultivation.

When to Use Soil-less Cultivation. Soil-less cultivation is a highly scientific method of growing plants where conditions are not favourable for growing them by normal horticultural or agricultural methods. In arid places where rainfall is low, or in places where the soil is rocky and shallow or infested with pests or disease, it will produce crops which are clean and free from soil-borne disease. The controlled nutrition, if properly done, produces excellent results. In the average garden which is meant to beautify the home, however, the growing tank would have to be situated in a secluded position somewhere in the background. Its only purpose would be to raise vegetables, as flowers should fit into the garden lay-out unless they are only wanted for cutting. Commercial growers may find it practical to force flowers by using soil-less cultivation, but would have to assess its advantages very carefully before investing any capital in it. Flat-dwellers or people with tiny gardens may find it a satisfying hobby.

One of the disadvantages of taking up soil-less gardening as a hobby is that it requires continuous attention. One is likely to become a slave to the tank, for as the plants must be fed each day and there is no nourishment in the sand or vermiculite, it becomes impossible to go on holiday without leaving someone in charge who understands what is to be done.

Requirements

Growing plants without soil does not mean that they can be grown without sunshine, warmth or ordinary care. The situation for the growing tank should be open, sunny and well-ventilated. Although the plants may be placed a little closer than in the open garden, they must be given sufficient space for their aerial parts to develop. The average person who decides to practise soil-less cultivation would be advised to purchase a ready-made nutrient powder, to be used according to the manufacturer's instructions. It would be far too complicated for the ordinary person to work out the chemical feeding required for each type of plant.

A certain amount of equipment is needed. On a small scale, the plants may be grown in pots or window-boxes. A small home unit consists of a water-proofed box or trough of timber or asbestos, mounted on 18-inch legs. A convenient size is 4 feet long by 8 inches wide and 6 inches deep. Tilt the box slightly to one end or construct it with a slope at the base for drainage. Attach a piece of hose from the base of the trough to the base of a 4-gallon bucket. This will hold the nutrient solution and should be lifted to feed the plants and lowered to act as a drainage utensil. A pulley system is optional but labour-saving. Feed the plants about three times a week or more often and keep the medium damp.

A standard bed for large-scale use consists of a water-proofed brick or concrete growing tank, approximately 4 feet wide and up to 20 or 30 feet long. It should be from 9 to 12 inches deep. The floor is made of concrete, and drainage holes must be made at the sides of the bed, preferably at intervals so that excess liquid can drain out. Water mixed with the nutrients is percolated into the vermiculite from a 45-gallon drum placed at a height over one end. The solution is generally given once a day, but may have to be given twice a day.

Before planting seedlings, always rinse off any materials or soil that may cling to the roots. After spraying with insecticides, wash the vermiculite or sand with fresh water before applying the next feeding solution.

Those who wish to practise soil-less gardening should study specialised books devoted to the subject.

V. BONSAI

The Chinese and Japanese perfected Bonsai, which name means the art of growing miniature trees in shallow bowls. This is a horticultural craft which requires skill, artistic appreciation and a great deal of patience. It is based on limiting both root and top growth of a tree so that it grows to perfection in miniature. Bonsai is meant to express the beauty of nature and the trees should not be made to look grotesque, but they may be trained to "weep" or assume a wind-swept appearance, provided that this approaches, as far as possible, the natural growth of the tree.

Many kinds of trees and shrubs may be dwarfed, both evergreen and deciduous, the latter having the appeal of the changing of the seasons, frequently with accompanying autumn-tinted foliage. The best trees should have small leaves and dense twigs as large-leaved trees like Magnolias appear out of proportion. The most popular pines in Japan are the Japanese Red Pine (*Pinus densiflora*) and the Five-needled Pine (*P. parviflora*). The Japanese are fond of flowering Cherries, which are not so easy to cultivate, as well as flowering Crab-apples and Peaches, flowering Quince, fruiting Pomegranate, Persimmon and Orange; evergreens such as Oriental Arborvitae (*Thuja orientalis*), Juniper, Spruce and Cedar; deciduous trees like Wax Tree (*Rhus succedanea*), Trident Maple (*Acer buergerianum*) and Willows; Bamboos and shrubs like Wistaria, Forsythia, Holly (*Ilex serrata sieboldii*) and Azaleas. The Azalea (*Rhododendron obtusum*) is probably the easiest plant to cultivate as Bonsai. Many other trees may also be cultivated, notably Bailey's Wattle (*Acacia baileyana*), the indigenous Camdeboo Stinkwood (*Celtis africana*) and *Schotia brachypetala*. Bonsai can also be created with large landscape stones, field grasses and tiny wild flowers. These are all cultivated and not to be confused with Japanese gardens containing ornaments that are not living.

True masters of the art in Japan explore the mountains and rock fissures to find ancient trees stunted by the elements. They must have a graceful shape. These are dug up and planted in pots containing sandy loam and tended carefully until they take root. They erect shelters to keep off the sun and wind, removing these at night so that the trees are exposed to the evening dew. During the day the foliage is sprayed with water until the trees take root. Periodic pruning of the top and root keep the tree growing in miniature for many years.

Modern Bonsai growers generally select and start with interesting-looking young plants in tins at nurseries, so saving a year or two of growth and avoiding the difficulty of germination.

Bonsai can also be grown from cuttings which take root, using Willow, Ivy, Gingko, Sophora and Holly. When growing subjects from seed, discard seedlings that do not have a good appearance while young.

How to Create a Bonsai from Seed. Seed which comes from a cold climate should first be chilled, while seed of Acacias should have boiling water poured over it. In order to aid germination, plant the seeds in individual thumb pots filled with fine vermiculite or peat. One can add a few grains of fertilizer as a starter. One can make tiny pots of paper or composition that will disintegrate so that the whole thing can be transplanted without set-back. Place two seeds in each pot and remove one if they both germinate. Keep them moist in a warm dark place until they germinate after about a month. Give the seedlings light and air as soon as they appear, but keep them moist and warm. They may be transplanted when they have four leaves. The seedlings may also be grown in clusters if liked and separated when large enough.

Transplanting. Plant each seedling into a small temporary container such as a dried, scooped-out orange skin or an ice-cream carton. Make a few holes for drainage through which the roots can grow, but place tiny stones or wire mesh over these to prevent the soil from falling through. Fill with good soil containing peat and transplant the tree into it. Water and keep it shaded for a week, then bring the tree into the light.

The tree will remain in this container for a year, during which time one must prune off any roots as they appear, cutting them off at a slant with scissors. Check the branch growth in proportion by nipping off the tips of the branches as they grow. Water the soil as soon as it dries out and spray the foliage from time to time. Keep the seedlings in a sheltered place so that they are not affected by rain or cold. After one year, when the small tree will be about 3 or 4 inches high, it should be transplanted into the permanent container.

Some growers do not use temporary containers like an orange skin, but tiny clay thumb pots. They tip out the plants every three months and trim any roots that begin to spiral around the pot.

The Pots. These should be attractive and made of earthenware or wood. They should harmonize with the tree and have muted colours. The container must be shallow, from 1 to 5 inches deep and from 6 to 12 inches across, in proportion, depending on the tree to be grown. The shape may be oblong or round. Confining the roots to a shallow container helps to dwarf the tree. The container must have drainage holes at the bottom and should be stood on a tray to catch any drips.

Place a layer of fine gravel and sand in the bottom quarter of the bowl. Sprinkle a little crushed charcoal on top of the base. Fill the bowl with a soil mixture composed of equal parts of sifted topsoil, well-decayed sifted leaf-mould, black peat and river sand. The river sand should be mixed with equal parts of finely crushed brick. Azaleas should have more leaf-mould and more peat. One can add a sprinkling of slow-acting fertilizer like hoof and horn meal if desired. Various soil mixtures may be used, but they must be able to retain moisture yet be well aerated and contain grit.

Cut away the temporary container and scrape away about a third of the old soil from the ball of roots. Place it in the container, arranging it at one side of the oblong container for best effect, but in the centre of a round bowl. Do not plant it deeper than the level at which it was

growing before or it may rot and die. It is better to err on the side of planting too shallow. Shallow planting enables one to see the network of roots above the ground, resembling those of an ancient tree, and gives the plant a sense of stability. Press the soil in firmly around the roots, a little at a time, so that there are no air pockets. Water gently with tepid water. Keep the pot partially shaded and moist for about three weeks. A suitable stone can be embedded into the surface for effect, if liked, and natural mosses can be used as well.

Pruning. As soon as the little trees have formed branches that are about 2 inches long, they must be pruned as they grow in order to stimulate a dense growth of small twigs and to prevent the crown from growing too large. One should pinch off the tips of the branches with the fingers while they are growing vigorously, so as to stimulate further shooting. Keep pinching the new growth so that the twigs ramify, and do not wait till it toughens so that it must be cut off with scissors. The trunk should taper gradually towards the top. Do not cut back a thick trunk to reduce the height of the tree as this spoils its natural symmetry. Trees may be grown with a single trunk or as many as five trunks.

One can train the trunk and branches to grow in any direction once the tree has been in the pot for at least six months. This is done by spiralling soft copper wire around the trunk or branch, after placing one end in the pot. Gently bend the wire at the desired angle, being careful not to split the branches by holding them together at a fork. Cut the wire away after a year, by which time it should have hardened into shape. Avoid grotesque or twisted shapes. Training enables one to create the artistic outlines frequently seen in trees growing in their natural state.

An ordinary Bonsai grows to about 2 feet in height and breadth. Miniature or baby Bonsai are as small as 3 inches in height, being planted in tiny pots about an inch in width.

Root-Pruning and Transplanting. Transplanting must be done regularly in order to renew the soil in the pot so that the tree can be kept alive for many years. Root-pruning is done at the same time and this balances the top pruning so that the tree can be kept growing in miniature. Flowering plants like Azalea are re-potted each year; broad-leaved, quick-growing, deciduous trees like Maple need to be re-potted every two years, while slow-growing evergreens like Red Pine and Thuja need only be re-potted once in three, four or even five years. Most trees are re-potted in spring.

Root-pruning should be done quickly in a place which is sheltered from sun and wind, preferably in a damp

Weigela is a spring-flowering shrub which is dense with foliage after flowering (left). All the long flowering stems are pruned out immediately after blooming (right), but the bush will produce luxuriant growth again during summer. (See Chapter 31, Section III.)

Cannas are bold and vigorous perennials, invaluable for summer-long colour effects in the large garden.

Three Bonsai of different types. (See Chapter 35.) The pine on the left is a popular choice, but the others are indigenous trees which form unusual subjects. The boerboon (*Schotia brachypetala*) is in the central bowl and three Camdeboo Stinkwood (*Celtis africana*) are planted in a little group.

House plants are popular and decorative. (See Chapter 34.) The back three include the Flamingo Flower (*Anthurium scherzerianum*), brilliant-foliaged *Coleus* and *Peperomia caperata*, with quaint white "candles". Front row, left to right: *Purple Tradescantia*; Strawberry Saxifrage (*Saxifraga sarmentosa tricolor*, Chapter 10); Aluminium Plant (*Pilea cadieri*); fleshy *Peperomia obtusifolia variegata* and the ever-popular African Violet (*Saintpaulia*).

room. When the tree is tipped out of the pot it will be a mass of roots. One should separate these gently with a pointed stick, without breaking off root hairs, and remove about two-thirds of the old soil. One must cut off the root tips, leaving as many fibrous roots as possible. Root-prune young plants more freely than old plants. Do this as quickly as possible. Wash the pot well and replace the plant carefully at the right height. Water immediately and shelter from sun and wind until the roots become active again.

General Care

The trees should be kept outside, bearing in mind the requirements of each plant. Pines and Pomegranates need sunshine, while Azaleas and Alpine plants need shade. It is best to provide morning sun, using bamboo screens. Do not keep them under shady trees or their growth will not be robust. Protect the Bonsai from frost, wind and dryness. They should not be placed in a glass-house during winter, as they need to experience the elements.

One should try to give the trees a rest in winter, watering less often, but do not allow them to dry out completely. Water freely about once a day, saturating the pot and moistening the foliage. Allow the top inch of soil to dry out completely before watering again or the plants will suffer from overwatering. Too much water in summer will stimulate too rapid growth. The foliage may be sprinkled in the late afternoons in order to keep it clean and healthy. Pests can be avoided by cleanliness and healthy growing conditions. Insecticides can be used if necessary, but only if the soil is damp.

Feeding is essential but must be done in moderation. Overfeeding spoils the appearance of a Bonsai and can lead to adversity. Fertilizers can be given two or three times a year during summer and autumn, but it is best to delay this until two or three months after re-potting. One should use bone meal, hoof and horn meal, soya bean meal, cotton seed meal or any other slow-acting organic fertilizer, but not inorganic fertilizers. One can sprinkle small quantities of the above-mentioned fertilizers on top of the soil and water them in, or one can allow them to soak in water and dilute the liquid to be used as weak liquid manure. Fruit trees can be given daily feeds of this weak liquid from spring to midsummer. Azaleas need acid soil and can be watered with a weak tea solution or mulched with rotted pine-needles.

CHAPTER THIRTY-SIX

PESTS AND DISEASE IN THE GARDEN

INTRODUCTION

Pests and disease are the gardener's enemies and although they both damage or even kill one's plants, one must understand the essential differences between a pest and a disease in order to combat them successfully. Insect pests can be seen with the naked eye, except for tiny mites like red spider, which can only be seen under a magnifying glass. Each insect has a life cycle of its own and hatches from an egg through various stages into an adult. This makes it possible for us to destroy it in several ways. Although insects are a hardy race, we have the means to keep them at bay, and, with luck, we might never suffer any serious damage from their attacks.

Diseases, however, are caused by fungi, bacteria and viruses. Fungi causing disease can usually only be seen when they have grown sufficiently to damage the plant, while bacteria and viruses cannot be seen, being known only by the damage they do. It is necessary, therefore, to spray in order to prevent disease, rather than to wait until it has taken hold, when it will usually be too late to control it for that particular season, if not for all time.

The essential difference between combating pests and disease, therefore, is that we only spray against pests when we see them in the garden, but we are forced to spray in anticipation to prevent disease, planning a programme throughout the year. Some serious pests like fruit-fly, which fly into the garden at any time and lay their eggs in young fruit, must also be combated by anticipating their arrival and spraying according to a planned programme. One cannot, therefore, lay down general rules, but must simply deal with each common problem in turn.

HOW TO PREVENT DISEASE AND INSECT ATTACK INDIRECTLY

Healthy vigorous plants seem to resist insect infestation more than weak plants, which often succumb or become stunted. A healthy, well-cared-for garden is an indirect insurance against insect pests as well as disease. Healthy plants growing in good, well-drained soil with adequate water are more disease-resistant than weak, ill-nourished plants. Good cultivation and feeding, which keeps one's plants vigorous, therefore, will do more to prevent disease than many a spraying.

Keeping the garden scrupulously clean is not only an aesthetic measure, but also an economic proposition, for it eliminates hiding and breeding places for insects and lessens the expense entailed in spraying against them. Rubbish in corners and under hedges, dead twigs and leaves left lying about, heaps of grass cuttings and leaves which have not been treated with an activator to help break them down into compost, all make a home for insects. Disease-infected leaves and twigs from previous years, which have not been burnt, harbour the spores which will reinfect your plants in the new growing season. Continual sweeping away of shed rose petals and leaves will prevent spores from lodging under them and rising up to infect the new growth. Removal of dead branches on trees and shrubs not only prevents die-back on the plant, but eliminates insect hide-outs.

Weeds are often the hosts of plant viruses and also provide a home for insects, so that keeping one's ground free of weeds helps to combat both insects and disease. One should not weaken one's plants by allowing them to be choked by weeds, which steal their food and sunlight, nor should the ground go untilled, for many insects or their eggs lie beneath the protective stones and sods awaiting their time to emerge. Continual working of the soil in flower or vegetable beds keeps down weeds and keeps soil pests on the move.

Many insects are carriers of disease and by destroying eggs as well as the adults, one can help to prevent disease. Although ordinary ants (not termites) do no harm to plants, they encourage aphids and mealybug infestation. (See under "Ants," Chapter 37). Ants should, therefore, be kept away from rose gardens, vineyards and orchards, where these pests do most damage.

One should encourage the natural enemies of insect pests, or at any rate, learn to recognise them so that they are not killed in ignorance. The quaint praying mantis feeds on grasshoppers and mosquitoes, amongst other insects. The daddy-long-legs does no harm to plants, but eats aphids and mosquitoes, although its larva may do some damage. Spiders usually make their home in trees and rolled-up leaves, but do no harm to the plants, while they do consume possibly harmful insects. The tiny

242

Vedalia ladybird, which comes from Australia, consumes scale and aphids and has been known to save crops in the past. One would have to obtain large numbers of these to keep the rose-garden free of aphids, and there is no guarantee that they would not fly over to one's neighbour's garden instead! Nevertheless, one should place them on one's roses whenever possible.

Birds are possibly the gardener's greatest friend in keeping down insect pests, so that they should be encouraged and forgiven if they sometimes eat one's fruit and berries. Earthworms merely till the soil and the gardener will soon learn to distinguish between them and the voracious millipedes which eat the roots of plants. The presence of earthworms denotes a fertile soil and they will soon transform a hard soil into a workable one.

Is it Worth Spraying in the Garden?

In spite of keeping your plants growing well with adequate food, water and care, one cannot altogether escape pests and disease in a garden.

One does not have to reach for the spray-pump as soon as one sees a green-fly or two. Removing these by hand is best if there are only a few. As soon as pests show signs of multiplying, however, they must be controlled before they become an epidemic and do irreparable harm to one's plants. In general, spray as little as possible.

Certain plants attract pests more than others and it is entirely a matter for the individual grower to decide whether it is worth growing them or to eliminate them in order to reduce the need for spraying. Apple trees usually attract codling moth, so that it is essential to spray them regularly and correctly. If one cannot be bothered, it is best to leave apples out of the home orchard. Peaches and nectarines are prone to attack by fruit-fly and, as it is essential to spray against this serious pest, these fruits should also be eliminated if one does not care to spray. If one has room only for two or three fruit trees, it might be easier to restrict the selection to comparatively trouble-free plums, prunes and figs or to easily-grown nuts like almonds. To take the risk of not spraying one's trees will endanger one's neighbour's fruit, for the pests fly over the fence and make it more difficult for everyone in the long run. Gardeners near commercial fruit-growing areas should pay scrupulous attention to keeping their trees free of pests, in order to prevent endangering the country's crops indirectly. Laws should really be enforced to prevent people growing fruit trees if they are not prepared to spray them in order to control the more serious pests.

Green aphids will always be attracted to the tender young shoots of roses and the juicy leaves of the bearded iris. Few gardeners, however, could envisage omitting these plants from the garden in order to avoid spraying. If the aphids are not allowed to gain control at the beginning of spring, however, it is unlikely that they will prove to be serious pests for the remainder of summer and autumn.

A few diseased leaves on a tree might clear up on their own, after paying attention to feeding and watering, while insects might also disappear naturally before they do irreparable harm. Do not be unnecessarily alarmed, therefore, providing that the disease is not fatal or that the insect infestation does not reach epidemic proportions. Do not be lulled into security, however, for if one does not keep one's eyes open in the garden one can allow an unnecessary epidemic to occur. Whenever one takes a walk around the garden, look at the leaves and branches of the trees and other plants and be on the watch for the odd white woolly Australian bug, aphids, or the ugly shell-like incrustations of scale.

It may be seen, therefore, that one cannot have a garden and never have to spray sometime or another. One can reduce the necessity to spray by restricting the choice of plants one grows, but that is rather a negative outlook and few gardeners will be prepared to do without their roses or other flowers, although many might more cheerfully omit fruit trees.

It is extraordinary how little spraying is really necessary in a garden in the long run. If the correct remedy is used at the right time it will eliminate the worry and expense of combating a later epidemic and reduce the likelihood of loss of plants and trees through disease.

Overspraying without knowledge, in excess of what is really required, will not necessarily keep the garden free from harm and has been known to have adverse effects. Sprays containing arsenic and mercury build up residues which are dangerous to life and must be used with restraint and only if really necessary. One must realise that many chemicals damage plant tissues and cause burning, distortion of leaves or leaf injury, with consequent stunted growth and even dropping fruit. Never use more than the manufacturer advises on the label. If only a few insect pests are present, remove them by hand if possible, rather than use chemicals.

Knowledge of when to spray will avoid plant injury. During very hot weather, for example, one should refrain from using certain chemicals like sulphur or Karathane, while members of the cucurbit family should be sprayed with Malathion only when the plants are dry. Knowledge of when to spray will also save beneficial insects. DDT sprayed on to apple blossom in order to combat codling moth will also kill pollinating bees, so that it is best to delay the first spray until the petals have almost dropped— the correct time is described as "three-quarter petal drop". DDT should not be sprayed on to open garden flowers if possible, for the same reason. Chemicals cannot always differentiate between good and bad insects, unfortunately, so that many beneficial insects like ladybirds are killed by using insecticides. In some cases, the gardener cannot avoid this and simply has to take the chance of killing them because of the greater evil. As a comforting thought, it is possible that the beneficial insects are not present. The eradication of one pest may lead to the infestation of another. DDT, which controls codling moth on apple trees, also kills the natural predator on woolly aphids, so that this may become a new menace and the trees must be sprayed with Lindane as a result.

SPRAY AT THE RIGHT TIME

(I) When to Spray Against Insect Pests

Certain insect pests need only be controlled when they are seen to damage the garden. Holes chewed in the leaves of shrubs and roses during midsummer indicate that beetles are about at night and the foliage can be sprayed during the day in order to poison the night marauders. It would have been a waste of time and materials to have sprayed this foliage in the spring as a preventative measure, for the adults would not then have been present.

Some serious insect pests, like codling moth and fruit-fly, must, however, be guarded against by spraying in anticipation, for early spraying will prevent the adult from laying eggs inside the young fruit. Once the egg hatches inside the fruit, which provides the larva with food and shelter while it develops, it is too late to destroy it by spraying and the damage is already done.

One cannot, therefore, lay down hard and fast rules in the control of insect pests. In general, one should spray against insect pests only at the first signs of infestation. There are a few exceptions and one can learn these only by studying each insect individually.

The main thing to know is not to embark on a costly spraying programme without some knowledge of the insect's behaviour. It is essential to attack the insect at the correct period. If one sprays citrus trees when the raised pimples caused by the citrus psylla are noticed on the leaves, it is generally too late, as the tiny insect has already left its saucer-like home in order to blister new leaves, so that one must control the pest in advance by spraying the young foliage.

Frequently, when spraying insects in the pupal stage, it has as little effect as a shower of rain on the roof of a well-built house, so that one must endeavour to attack the insect in its more vulnerable larval stage, as soon as one sees the caterpillars crawling around. Insects are most easily destroyed in the beginning of the larval stage or during the moulting period. The adults fly about and are comparatively tough.

One cannot follow a time-table of spraying according to the calendar, but according to when plants begin their growth. Plants flower and set fruit at different times in the different climatic areas of any large country.

One spray seldom gives complete results. The smallest percentage of insects remaining alive will multiply and must be sprayed once again. Also, eggs, which remain unharmed during spraying, will hatch and the same spray should be repeated from ten days to a fortnight later. One spray destroys the good as well as the bad insects and allows the pests to breed again, usually a little ahead of the good ones. One should encourage the natural enemies of insects such as birds, ladybirds, fish, toads and even harmless snakes.

(II) When to Spray Against Disease

To know everything about plant disease and to be able to diagnose what is ailing a plant or a tree calls for as much experience and knowledge as a doctor possesses. Only a trained specialist could attempt to diagnose the variety of diseases that attack plants.

The home gardener, however, can learn the common diseases that are likely to attack his roses, fruit trees, ornamental shrubs and other plants in order to take precautions against them. Prevention is the best cure for disease, since once a disease has taken hold it is almost impossible to cope with it. By using sprays that cover plants with a protective film at the right time, one can prevent many diseases from entering the leaves and taking hold. These must obviously be used early in spring while the leaves on deciduous trees are new and healthy, so as to prevent the spores from entering and infecting the leaves with fungi or bacteria. It is best to spray just as the leaves reach their full stage of growth. The spray should be repeated as soon as the protective film on the leaves wears off or when new young foliage appears. As a rule, disease occurs during moist weather and spraying should commence at the start of the rainy season.

If one has failed to control diseases like black spot and mildew during one season, one is usually given a reprieve during winter, provided that the damage has not gone too far. By cleaning up thoroughly during winter and starting a new spraying programme at the right time, one is usually able to improve matters in the following season.

What Sprays to Use Against Insect Pests

When the subject of insect pests is broached, the gardener sighs dejectedly and wishes fervently that someone would invent a general garden spray that would kill all pests at the same time.

The spray has not yet been invented, however, that will destroy the multiplicity of insect pests that ravage crops and gardens. Owing to the fact that there are so many different types of insects, it is impossible to design an insecticide that will kill all of these at once. Most insecticides attack one or more groups of insects, and the scope of the newest insecticides is very much widened, but the gardener will still have to know something about the insect and its habit before understanding when to combat it and what insecticide to use against it.

Even when an insecticide that gives perfect results for certain pests is finally discovered, there is no guarantee that it will always be in use, for insects frequently build up an immunity towards it. In every group of insects there are resistant and non-resistant strains. The latter are always killed off and as it is almost impossible to achieve total destruction, the resistant strains live on and multiply, breeding more and more resistant strains as the years go by. After a decade of spraying, one might find that a well-tried remedy is no longer effective, so that continuous investigations into sprays must take place, as what is used today might be superseded in a year or two. The codling moth, that affects nearly all apple trees, was, for example, kept well under control by arsenate of lead for many years, but could only be controlled by DDT during the last decade. Should the insects build up a further immunity to this, and they are showing signs of doing so in parts of the Western Province, other chemicals may be needed to supplement or replace DDT. New information from experiments with new materials used by scientists change the position from season to season.

All this change makes things even more confusing to the everyday home gardener, who wants to simplify rather than complicate his activities. To add further to his difficulties, there are some 700 proprietary products registered in South Africa alone, many using parallel chemicals. It is now a law that all proprietary sprays and powders must have their contents printed on their labels, so that the gardener who has a basic knowledge of what is wanted will be able to purchase that particular chemical from whichever firm he prefers. Some firms specialise in making only one or two types of chemicals, so that it does not always follow that any one firm produces a complete range of items needed. Most of the seedsmen and hardware stores carry very representative stocks of proprietary brands. These should be used strictly according to the manufacturer's instructions on the label.

As man discovers more potent ingredients to destroy insects, a very serious danger arises, for many of these chemicals are toxic to human beings. Certain powerful chemicals like Parathion must not be used without wearing protective clothing and gas masks, for they can be inhaled or absorbed through the skin. Such a chemical will be useful only to the commercial grower who has the facilities for the necessary precautions and to whom it is worthwhile going to all the trouble involved. Phosphorous sprays like Parathion have caused several deaths to farm labourers in South Africa through insufficient regard for the precautions necessary when using them. Arsenical sprays applied in fine mists by fruit farmers have been known to drift into the farmer's water supplies and build up residues that later caused arsenical poisoning in the family. Powerful mercurial sprays, used for fungus diseases, are extremely poisonous and must be handled with extreme caution.

These highly poisonous sprays should never be used by the home gardener. Less poisonous but highly effective materials can be used instead, but even these must be used only with the strictest regard for the manufacturer's instructions.

There is a very big difference between the methods of pest control as applied by farmers and by gardeners. The farmer must make every effort to eradicate pests with the most powerful and rapid means that modern research can offer, but the home gardener should refrain from using the same methods, except where the pest has not responded to less potent control and where it has become a menace to his whole garden and that of his neighbours. But in all cases, the danger of some chemical sprays cannot be over-looked, and unless one is prepared to take the same trouble that the commercial grower takes, in the way of wearing protective clothing and respirators, it is best not to use them. The old saying "familiarity breeds contempt" should be borne in mind, for carelessness may lead to serious illness, if not death. It would be a great benefit to gardeners if a progressive horticultural firm would train a spraying team which would provide a service to apply certain highly poisonous sprays on demand.

It is not always necessary to use the latest and most potent sprays in the garden, however. Many insects can be controlled quite easily with old-fashioned and nonpoisonous sprays like derris powder, which can be used freely for caterpillars in the vegetable garden. These may not be so effective as the more potent chemicals, but if they kill the pests then they will be satisfactory. If one can eliminate insects like aphis with nicotine sulphate (also poisonous, but easily handled) with one spray at the beginning of the season and another spray 10 days later to catch the second generation of insects hatching from the eggs, it is possible that one will have no further infestation during the season. It would not be necessary, therefore, to use a potent spray with longer lasting effects. Where constant infestations take place, however, Malathion, which lasts for two or three days, or a systemic insecticide like Metasystox, which has a residual effect of up to three weeks, will save the gardener time and energy.

Recipes for making up basic sprays seem redundant in these modern times. Few people can find the time to spray their gardens with ready-made, cheap and effective mixtures, so that it seems superfluous to advise people to spend time and energy weighing materials and brewing up mixtures before even commencing to spray. These may be more economical, but the extra cost is negligible when purchasing the ready-made article which is balanced perfectly in a modern factory and one's time is often more precious than money.

A list follows in the next chapter of the most common insect pests in the garden, together with details of the various materials available today that can be used to destroy them.

What Sprays to use Against Disease

Owing to the fact that the gardener can deal with only a few of the more common diseases in the garden, it is almost easier to learn how to combat disease than it is to destroy insects. That one will be wholly successful depends on the weather and on many other conditions, but one can aid matters by applying fungicides regularly. The sprays must all be used as a preventative measure. The difficulty in combating disease comes from the fact that once it takes hold it is almost impossible to cure. One can remove the branches of diseased trees and repair and clean out cavities in some cases, but here again it is necessary to know how to combat each disease in turn.

A list of the more common diseases of plants and their control will be found in Chapter 38.

The Technique of Spraying and Equipment

Although one uses the term "spray" for convenience, one can also apply poisons by means of dusting powders. Sprays are mixed in liquid form and are less wasteful than dusts, while dusts involve less trouble as there is no previous preparation necessary before using.

Simple bellows are obtainable in which to place dusts, which can be shaken in a fine layer over leaf surfaces. It is best to apply dusts in the early morning or the late evening. At these times the air is cool and the dust will settle on the leaves. During the hotter part of the day, thermal currents cause the dust to rise and one does not obtain the maximum benefit from the material deposited.

Spraying can be done at any time, although it is best not to leave it too late so that the leaves can dry off before nightfall. Liquid mixtures must be forced out of a spray by pressure and can be ejected in the form of a stream or a fine mist. The solution should be agitated while spraying so as to keep it thoroughly mixed. Sprays can be made up by diluting liquids or adding water to wettable powders.

Spraying equipment varies from small fly-spray pumps to power sprayers. Very small cheap pumps are not really worth buying as they have to be filled continually and soon become clogged. A good type of pump for the home gardener is the stirrup-pump which sends out a continuous stream of liquid in a fine spray, so that one can cover the plants with ease. Small tanks or "knapsacks" carried over the shoulder, with a continuous jet, give the gardener the greatest amount of freedom of movement in the garden. Power sprays mounted like wheelbarrows are suitable for golf courses and large estates as well as small commercial orchards. Large models with hoses like fire-engines are suitable for municipalities and farmers, but certainly not for the home gardener.

The chief requirement in spraying is to obtain good coverage. All parts of the plant should be wetted thoroughly —both the top and underneath surfaces of the leaves, the trunks of trees and even the soil around the tree in some cases. The spray must no run off and saturate the ground wastefully, but one should stop as soon as all parts are uniformly wet.

Spreaders are substances used to enable the spraying material to cling to the leaf surfaces. Some products are already mixed with spreaders. One can purchase ready-made and harmless spreaders to mix with one's sprays. Common household materials, like soft soap or soap flakes, can also be used.

Precautions. Even when using fairly safe sprays, certain precautions should be taken. Do not spray on a windy day in case some of the spray drifts into one's face. Do not spray upwards for the same reason and use a small step-ladder when spraying trees or large shrubs. Use eye-shields whenever spraying if possible. Do not allow inexperienced garden "boys" to measure out or apply sprays without supervision.

Rinse out spraying equipment with fresh water after use in order to prevent clogging or contamination when using other materials later. If possible a separate spray-pump should be reserved for weedkillers. It is best to throw away small amounts of spray solution left over. If one is sure that they will keep, they can be stored and labelled carefully and placed out of reach. Keep all poisons on a high shelf out of reach of children and preferably in a locked cupboard. Use special spoons and basins for measuring and stirring poisons and do not use kitchen equipment for preparing spray materials.

Wash the hands and even the face with soap and water after spraying operations. Hose away spray which has collected on concrete or paving in the garden.

Some Old-Fashioned Practices, Useful and Useless

Banding—A band of material such as hessian, is sometimes wrapped around apple-tree trunks in order to capture the larvae of the codling moth. They crawl down the tree and pupate in its warm protection and they may be destroyed when the sacking is removed periodically. This is certainly an aid to combating codling moth, but should be done in addition to spraying, not as a substitute.

A band of sticky material is sometimes painted around tree trunks to kill ants, which encourage aphids and mealybugs. It is advisable to wrap a six-inch band of paper or sacking around the trunk of the tree and spread the substance on to this, for young trees may be killed if it is smeared directly on to their bark. Renew the band periodically as the bodies of insects accumulate on it, much as flies stick to fly-paper. This banding may be used for insects which crawl up the trunk, but will not control flying insects. The sticky material is sold under proprietary names.

Banding with wire netting is the only practical method of controlling the Fig Borer. (See Chapter 37.)

White-Washing Trees—White-washing the trunks of fruit trees in orchards is an old-time remedy used to discourage climbing and boring insects. It does not kill them and is a useless panacea for insect control, although it may be useful as a protection against trunk sunburn in hot places.

CHAPTER THIRTY-SEVEN

COMMON INSECTS AND PESTS AND THEIR CONTROL

Insects are divided into those which chew the foliage of plants and those which pierce the stem and suck out the plant juices. Methods of control have been based on the fact that chewing insects should be killed by spraying the leaves with stomach poisons, while sucking insects should be killed by the use of contact sprays, which hit the insect's body and destroy it. With the discovery of new insecticides, however, many double-purpose sprays have evolved. It is now possible to kill both sucking and chewing insects with one type of chemical, and these may, in time, supplant many of the older, more widely used insecticides by simplifying the gardener's choice of poisons. There are also chemicals called systemic insecticides, which are absorbed into the sap of plants and kill the sucking insect pests that prey on them without affecting the beneficial insects that eat other insects or the bees that pollinate the flowers.

The great disadvantage to the gardener, however, is that most of these materials are very poisonous to human beings and they cannot be used unintelligently or without displaying extreme caution. At the risk of repetition, it must be said that the basic poisons used in insect control are sold under numerous registered trade names, which, however, specify the chemical contents on the label. It is most important to use these brands strictly according to the manufacturer's instructions, noting the amount of dilution, the use and non-use of spreaders, the compatibility of the spray material with other ingredients and the precautions which must be taken. Some chemicals cause plant injury if they are mixed together, while a few enhance each other and can be mixed together. As a rule, one should not mix chemicals. (See Chapter 39.)

Chewing insects consist of thousands of different kinds, some quite large in size, the most common being beetles, grasshoppers, cutworms and caterpillars. They are usually killed when the insects are attacking or just before they do their maximum damage. The chief poisons used to control them today are DDT, BHC, Chlordane and dieldrin. Derris powders and lead arsenate were formerly the chief poisons used.

Sucking insects are generally very tiny, but exist in such numbers that they do even more damage than the chewing insects, causing wilting, discoloration and stunting of the plant. The most common sucking insects are aphids (plant lice), scale insects, mealybugs, thrips, mites and some insects like the Stinkbug or Bagrada bug. The best known poison for killing sucking insects for many years has been nicotine sulphate, followed closely by lime-sulphur, sulphur dusts and mineral oil sprays. Some of the new stomach and contact poisons which are used mainly for sucking insects, but will also kill chewing insects, are DDT, Toxaphene, BHC, Lindane, Kelthane and Malathion. Systemic insecticides like Metasystox kill sucking insects and others like Ovotran kill the eggs of mites. These chemicals vary in their poisonous qualities and the even more toxic materials like Parathion, HETP and TEPP are recommended only to the farmer and not to the gardener, who seldom has the facilities to apply them in safety.

It is not easy to recognise which is a chewing and which is a sucking insect, so that it is best to deal with each insect individually and give the chief methods of control which are recommended for use in the home garden.

It is important to distinguish between the harmful insect and the beneficial insect, so that one does not destroy one's friends instead of one's enemies. The best-known beneficial insects are ladybirds, which devour aphids and mealybugs; wasps, which are parasitic on some insects; the praying-mantis, which eats grasshoppers and mosquitoes, and the spider, which catches possibly-harmful insects. Pollinating insects like bees must be protected, while earthworms, which till the soil, must be distinguished from millipedes, which gnaw plant roots. Ants do not harm plants directly, but should be controlled in places like rose-gardens and orchards, for they increase aphis and scale infestation.

INSECT BEHAVIOUR

Most insects have a life cycle, hatching from an egg into a larva which changes into a pupa and finally emerges as an adult. The larva, which is usually in the form of a caterpillar, is usually the most destructive stage, when it chews foliage and flowers voraciously in order to grow. The adults of some insects, like grasshoppers, are equally destructive, but some merely perform their function of laying eggs. This cycle is known as the metamorphosis.

Insects are most easily destroyed in the larval stage, for it is not easy to detect eggs and destroy them before they hatch. The pupa is usually impervious to poisons, secure in a tiny, barricaded casing. The adult is not easy to control, but many insects can be attacked in this stage.

Some insects have an incomplete metamorphosis, without having true larvae. The young of aphids, scale insects and thrips, for example, resemble the adults and do as much damage as the adults. Insects which have a complete metamorphosis are mainly moths and butterfies, beetles, weevils and flies.

There are many classes of insects, fascinating in their differences, but their characteristics will only be noted here with reference to the way in which they damage our plants. The order *Hemiptera* is the most important one for the horticulturist, for it consists of insects like aphids, scale, mealybugs and stinkbugs, all of which have piercing mouth-parts and suck the juices from plants. It is obvious that only the most common insects of importance to gardeners can be described here. Identification of other insects and methods of control can be obtained from one's local Department of Agriculture.

APHIDS (PLANT-LICE)

There are numerous types of aphids, belonging to the family *Aphidae*, of which several are well-known in gardens. These are the green aphis (Green-fly) which is common on Roses, Iris and most garden flowers; the black aphis, seen on Chrysanthemums and Broad Beans; greyish aphis, mainly seen on members of the Cabbage family, and yellow aphis, seen on Oleanders and Asclepias. Aphids of many kinds occur on fruit trees, oaks, ornamental shrubs, grasses and Strawberries. Aphids are very small insects, normally about an eighth of an inch long, with soft, globular bodies. Some have wings and others are wingless. On the whole, they are slow-moving and fragile.

Their complicated life-cycle makes them very difficult to control, for they are reproduced in large numbers and in several different ways. Eggs laid in early winter on the woody branches of peach trees, for example, hatch out in spring into wingless females. These produce living young, which in turn give birth to both winged and wingless forms. These fly about and produce living young all through summer and autumn. Early in winter these adults lay eggs again on woody branches where they

shelter during the cold weather. In places with mild winters, where foliage does not disappear completely, the aphids do not lay eggs, but shelter in the live state on plants like Cabbages, Rambler roses and other herbaceous plants, including weeds.

Aphids injure plants by sucking out the plant juices or sap. This damages plants in many ways, causing wilting, especially of vegetables, distortion of leaves such as the curling of the young foliage of Peaches and Citrus, as well as stunting of flowers like Chrysanthemums. Some aphids cause galls to form on Poplars and Elm trees, while a woolly aphis causes pseudo-galls to form on Apple trees. Aphids are very harmful in that they carry virus diseases, such as mosaics, to healthy plants, by inoculating them after sucking the sap from a diseased plant. Honeydew, often seen glistening on leaves, is excreted by aphids and is sought after by ants.

Control. It is important to control ants wherever possible in order to reduce aphis infestation (see under "Ants"). Most aphids can be killed easily by spraying them with nicotine sulphate mixed with soft soap as a spreader. They must be sprayed directly so that the spray comes in contact with their bodies. Always choose a calm day and spray during the hottest part of the day, as heat helps the nicotine to be more effective. Spray as soon as the first aphids are noticed in spring and keep a watch for the second generation about ten days later, spraying again if necessary. Pyrethrum dust is a contact insecticide that will kill aphids, but has very little residual value.

The effects of some of the modern insecticides last longer than nicotine sulphate, which dissipates in a few hours. Malathion is effective against aphids and lasts for two or three days. Metasystox is a systemic insecticide which remains effective for up to three weeks. Farmers use dangerous poisons like Parathion, HETP and TEPP, which are not recommended for the home garden.

Some types of aphis may require special treatment. The grey Cabbage aphis, which clusters under the leaves, is best controlled by Lindane (the pure form of BHC), while Malathion and Metasystox may also be used. Cease spraying with Malathion one week before harvest and with Metasystox one month before harvest. The woolly aphis on Apples and Pears can be sprayed with BHC while the trees are dormant. Spraying with BHC during the growing season may cause the fruit to have a tainted odour, so that it is best to use Lindane then, but not later than a month before harvesting. The best control of the woolly aphis is its natural parasite (*Aphelinus mali*), all too often killed when spraying with DDT against Codling Moth. BHC is very effective when spraying aphids on ornamental shrubs in place of nicotine sulphate. Summer oils kill aphids on Citrus.

SCALE INSECTS (Family *Coccidae*)

Scale insects are tiny and usually look like shell-like incrustations on the twigs of woody plants or on leaves. They attach themselves to the plants and suck out the juices. Some are as small as a pin's head while others are larger, but they all cause great damage to crops.

The "scale" is a protective covering for a soft insect underneath. Some types, like the rose and red scale, are called "armoured" scale insects, for they are tiny helpless creatures sheltering under a scale-like shield formed by a previous moult. Unarmoured scale insects are those which have the scale attached to their backs as part of their bodies. Some scale insects (*Ceroplastes*) are soft, white and waxy.

Scale insects reproduce by laying eggs or by producing living young. There is only one generation a year. When the female lays eggs, she shrinks and fills the hollow under the scale with eggs. Some living young escape from beneath the parent scale. The young are known as "crawlers", which crawl about and settle down to feed on its host. The wind often disperses them to other plants. Scale insects seldom move unless they are proceeding to a woody twig to moult, which they do twice. They excrete honeydew on which a black sooty mould fungus will grow, especially on neglected Citrus trees, and render the plant unsightly. Soft Wax Scale, which attacks Jacarandas, excretes honeydew even more copiously, resulting in a disfiguring sooty mould.

Scale insects affect plants differently, but generally cause the death of twigs, branches or whole trees. Infestation results in disfigurement to trees and fruit. Scale attacks plants of economic importance such as fruit trees, grapes and berries, but is also present on ornamentals like Camellia, Holly, Jacaranda, Laurel, Ochna, Oleander, Cape Honeysuckle (*Tecomaria capensis*), Pepper-tree (*Schinus molle*) and Palms. Certain types of scale affect Asparagus, Cucumber, Ferns, Brinjals, Granadillas, Orchids, other hot-house plants and house plants.

Control. As a preventative measure against scale and mealybugs, practise ant control, for ants increase scale infestation (see under "Ants"). Most types of scale can be kept down on fruit trees, rosebushes and berries by spraying them in winter, while they are dormant, with 1 part of Lime Sulphur to 15 parts of water. Wet the branches thoroughly. This can be repeated in early spring when there are crawlers present, but should not be used after the buds have opened. Very heavily infested branches should be pruned out and burned. Mineral

oil sprays can also be used in winter on dormant fruit trees, but not on peach trees. If the insects are still about during spring, Malathion wettable powder or emulsion can be used when the weather is too warm for Lime Sulphur. Parathion can be used by farmers.

Ornamental trees should be watched carefully for infestations of scale. They should be sprayed in early summer with Malathion or with light mineral oil. Scale which is present on house plants or hot-house plants may be removed by regular applications of soapy water. Otherwise Malathion should be used.

Soft Wax Scale on Jacarandas can be controlled by Malathion or by a mineral oil spray mixed with nicotine sulphate.

Scale on Citrus Trees. There are several different types of scale which infest citrus trees. Light mineral oil sprays may be used on citrus trees during summer when the scale insects are seen. One spray is generally sufficient if it is thoroughly done. The scale must be cleaned off thoroughly by January or February so as to prevent it from spreading on to the ripening fruit, when it will be too late to use oil sprays. The trees should be thinned carefully so that the spray can reach all parts of it. Malathion is also effective against citrus scale and farmers can use Parathion.

Soft Brown Scale on citrus should be sprayed with a mineral oil spray mixed with nicotine sulphate. Malathion may also be used and is even more effective when mixed with Parathion. Gusathion is also recommended for Soft Scale.

Citrus psylla is a scale insect on citrus trees which is more disfiguring than destructive. It causes little blisters or depressions on the leaves after the tiny insect has already sucked the juices from that spot and moved on. By spraying with Malathion on new foliage one could possibly prevent further disfigurement.

Australian Bug. (*Icerya purchasi.*)

This is a scale insect called the Cottony-cushion scale in New Zealand. The insect itself is a reddish-brown oval scale edged with short woolly hairs. The female shrinks as she lays eggs by developing a large cottony ribbed sac, nearly ⅛ inch long, at the end of her body. Many people think that this white, fluted, rounded part is the insect, but if it is opened, it will be found to contain a mass of pinkish eggs. The female remains attached by its suckers at one end of the scale to the host plant. The young crawlers are reddish and covered with a cottony secretion.

The eggs take a fortnight to hatch in summer and the crawlers take from three to five months to mature. A second generation is produced each year. The Australian bug troubles Citrus and has been found on Acacias, Roses, Dahlias, Grape-vines, Tung-nut trees, Pears and Fir trees.

Control. The Vedalia ladybird eats Australian bugs and will keep them down so that they are not of economic importance to farmers. Practise ant control, for ants reduce the ladybird population (See under "Ants"). In the garden, the insects should be removed by hand as soon as even one is seen on a tree, preferably before the young ones are released from the egg sac. They can be sprayed with Malathion or a mineral oil spray (1 part to 60 parts of water). Farmers may use Parathion.

MEALYBUGS (Various species).

These insects belong to the same family as the scale insects and Australian bug. They grow up to about a quarter-inch in length and have a flattened body covered with white woolly powder. There is a fringe of threads around the edges of the body. One type of mealybug has two longer filaments at the back and is called the Long-tailed Mealybug. Its body is only an eighth of an inch long. It is found mainly on grapes.

Mealybugs attack Citrus, Grape-vines, Pears, Granadillas, Figs, Guavas, Plums, Oleanders, Wistaria, Fuchsias, Palms and plants like Orchids, Cineraria, Ferns, Saintpaulias and other indoor or glass house plants.

Control. In the case of house-plants, the insects can be dabbed with methylated spirits, applied by touching them with a piece of cottonwool wrapped around a match tip. They shrivel immediately. Colonies on Fuchsias can also be dabbed with methylated spirits. A strong jet of water, if the plants can stand it, will dislodge small infestations.

In the case of large plants and trees, one should not spray if ladybirds are present. Practise ant control, for ants reduce the ladybird population. (See under "Ants".) Mealybugs are killed by Malathion. Parathion can be used by farmers. The long-tailed Mealybug is also killed by Malathion, Parathion or by spraying plants with nicotine sulphate (1 teaspoon to 1 gallon of water mixed with 4 teaspoons of summer oil).

THRIPS

Thrips are tiny insects which can only be seen properly under a magnifying glass, being one-twenty-fifth of an inch in length. On examination, they have 2 pairs of wings fringed with long hairs. They rasp the surfaces of the leaves and suck up sap, so that their presence can be seen when the leaves have a silvered or whitened appearance. They excrete tiny blots of glistening fluid like varnish. Thrips do not have a true life cycle. The eggs

are laid in the leaf tissue and hatch into yellowish nymphs in about a week. These become adults in from two to four weeks, moulting four times. There are several generations a year.

Thrips are common pests on Gladioli, Onions and Citrus. Onion thrips also attack Potatoes, Peas, Tomatoes, Cabbage, Bean, Cucumber and other garden plants. Gladiolus thrips sometimes attack Iris and Lily. Citrus thrips also attack Guava, Rhododendron, Azalea, Feijoa, Cyclamen and other plants, both in the garden and in the greenhouse. Greenhouse thrips cause a corky silvered area on citrus fruits that develops cracks later. Gladiolus thrips whiten the flowers as well as the foliage and often distort these or prevent them from developing. Badly infested corms become sticky or corky and may not produce plants at all.

Control. All thrips can be controlled with Malathion. DDT and BHC wettable powders or emulsions are also used, but BHC is not used on edible crops. Lime-sulphur spray when deciduous trees are dormant in winter will control thrips, and sulphur dust can be used on some plants. Weeds harbour the pests and should be kept down.

Gladiolus Thrip. Do not plant infested corms. They can be dusted when dormant during storage with DDT or BHC dust. Commercial growers spray corms once a fortnight with Parathion. The corms can be soaked in hot water (112°F. to 120°F.) to kill all thrips.

Gladiolus plants must be sprayed regularly with a DDT emulsion. The applications vary with the climate. During hot summers, they should be sprayed once a week. In cooler places, once a fortnight is sufficient. In excessively hot places the spraying may be increased to once in five days.

Onion Thrip. This may be controlled by spraying regularly between the leaves with 20 per cent DDT emulsion or DDT wettable powder, every three or four weeks from early summer until within a fortnight of harvest.

Citrus Thrips can be controlled by Malathion. Farmers use Parathion.

Greenhouse Thrips can be controlled by a DDT or BHC spray or by spraying with Malathion.

SPIDERS AND MITES

Ordinary spiders have four pairs of legs as distinct from true insects which have three. They have two body segments. Some are poisonous to humans but none injure plants. Spiders are thought to be beneficial, in fact, for they ensnare many a possibly harmful insect in their webs.

Mites belong to the same class of insect as spiders and usually also have four pairs of legs, but only one body segment. They are usually so small that they must be examined under a magnifying glass. Some mites feed on leaves and cause "blisters" on Pear leaves or "bronzing" on the stems and fruits of Tomato. Others cause galls on plants. Insecticides used for the control of mites are called acaricides or miticides.

RED SPIDER MITE (*Tetranychus telarius*).

Although known as "Red Spider", this is not a true spider, but a mite. It is so tiny that it can only be examined under a magnifying glass. It can be noticed when the foliage becomes discoloured, usually turning lighter in colour. Whole colonies of mites feed on the underside of the leaves and spin a very fine reddish-brown web over themselves as a protection. This can be noticed on close examination.

Infestations of red spider cause the plant to be severely stunted. Those plants bearing fruit become worthless. The plants commonly infected are Strawberries (in these the leaves may turn purplish), Beans, Peas, Apples, Gooseberries, Cucumber, Tomato, Violet, Foxglove, Carnation, Clematis and many other ornamental plants.

Control. Red Spider is effectively controlled with Malathion, the acaricide Kelthane or the systemic insecticide Metasystox. Lime-sulphur sprays on dormant trees in winter help to keep down mites. Summer and winter oils suffocate citrus mites. Ovotran kills the eggs during winter and may also be applied at other times. Dusting sulphur or Malathion are used to control mites on low-growing crops like Strawberries. A careful watch for mites should be kept during warm, dry weather.

BRYOBIA MITE

This tiny black mite spends its life on deciduous fruit trees. It causes discoloration of the leaves when sucking the plant juices in the same way as Red Spider mite. It can be seen moving on the underside of the leaves only with the aid of a magnifying glass.

Control. Like Red Spider, Bryobia Mite can be controlled with Malathion, Kelthane or Metasystox. Lime-sulphur should be used as a dormant winter spray. Ovotran will kill the eggs during winter.

BUGS

STINKBUGS (Twig Wilters or Tip Wilters).

The adult insects are shaped like a shield and there are many species. The green stinkbug (*Antestia*) and the large black stinkbug (*Holopterna volga*) are probably the best known. They are sucking insects and suck the juices from tender young shoots, causing wilting, blackening and collapse of the succulent shoots of plants like Dahlias or the developing kernels of Sweet Corn. Bean pods become distorted and do not produce seed, while Tomatoes become corky beneath the skin where they have been punctured by the insects. The pests also attack Peas, Beets, Cabbages, Cauliflower, Pumpkin, Marrow, Rhubarb, Tree Tomato, Grapes and shrubs, grasses and weeds of many kinds.

Stinkbugs lay their eggs in clusters or rafts on the underside of leaves in spring. The adults fly about and produce three generations a year. They shelter in hedges or on weeds and long grass during winter. Stinkbugs owe their common name to the fact they emit an unpleasant odour when disturbed or crushed. The eggs hatch into nymphs which moult five times before reaching the adult stage in about three months.

Control. The Green Stinkbug should be dusted, while feeding, with DDT dust or sprayed with DDT wettable powder. Repeat this a fortnight later. Where DDT must not be used, as on plants of the Cucumber family or on Cauliflowers after the flowers are formed, Malathion may be used instead. BHC can also be used, but not on edible crops because of its musty odour. Parathion can be used by farmers. The Black Stinkbug is best controlled by BHC, Malathion or Parathion.

One should handpick all Stinkbugs as soon as a few are seen in a garden, dropping them into a tin of paraffin. Destroy egg rafts and keep weeds down in order to provide fewer hiding places in winter.

BAGRADA BUG (*Bagrada hilaris*).

This is a small, brownish type of stinkbug with a tiny yellow cross on its back. One must dust under the leaves and on the ground with 5 per cent DDT dust as soon as the bugs are noticed. 5 per cent BHC dust and Malathion may also be used.

BEETLES

Beetles have biting mouth-parts and destroy plant foliage. Most beetles have a complete life cycle and their larvae also damage plants, for they also have biting mouth-parts. Beetles generally have horny wing-cases on their backs and three pairs of legs. Many of them are large in size and easily noticed.

Some beetles are harmless to plants such as carnivorous ground beetles, while other ground-beetles damage germinating maize seed and are a problem to farmers. Ladybirds are beneficial beetles, for they feed on aphids and scale insects and are regarded as the most important natural control of these pests. Ants disturb ladybirds and their larvae, reducing their numbers. (See under "Ants"). Ladybirds may be recognised by their usually rounded bodies and spotted wing-cases. A few ladybird beetles, like the Pumpkin Beetle, are plant feeders.

CHAFER BEETLE (*Adoretus* and others).

This is also known as the Brown Beetle or Bronze Beetle. It is the best known and most destructive beetle in the garden. The shiny brown adults, about ½ inch long, fly about at night during summer and chew the leaves of roses, stone fruit trees and ornamental shrubs. They sometimes tear pieces out of young apples and berries. They often fly indoors, being attracted by the light. The larva, a white grub with a brown head, remains deep in the soil and chews at the roots of annual plants and grasses, doing almost as much damage as a cutworm, with which it is frequently confused.

Control, Adult. When the beetles chew holes in leaves in summer, spray the foliage with DDT wettable powder. BHC (not on edible crops) or arsenate of lead are also effective. Repeat the spray after a fortnight. It does not help very much to collect the beetles after dark with the aid of a torch.

Grubs. In order to protect one's seedlings from the white grubs, stir DDT powder into the top few inches of soil before planting or between the seedlings after planting. Dieldrin 50 per cent wettable powder can be sprayed over the seedbeds after planting or stirred into the top soil. Chlordane or BHC can be stirred into the soil, but do not use BHC on root crops.

It is important to cultivate the soil as much as possible and to clear the soil of weeds, especially between fruit trees, so that the adults cannot lay their eggs on these, which they do from October to January. Kill all exposed grubs while digging the soil.

ASTYLUS BEETLE (*Astylus atromaculatus*)

Also called the Spotted Maize Beetle, this small beetle looks like an elongated ladybird and has distinctive yellow markings against a black background on its wings. The adult is primarily a pollen feeder and disfigures the flowers of the Daisy family (*Compositae*) and plants with plenty of pollen like Celosias and the tops of Maize plants. The larva is a hairy grub which feeds on seeds in the soil, particularly Maize seed, and also eats ripening Strawberries. The larva is more troublesome than the adult.

The eggs are laid in late summer under leaves or sod in the soil. They hatch within a fortnight. The larva spends winter in the soil and the adult emerges in the following summer. There is only one generation a year.

Control, Adult. The adults fly about in swarms and are not easy to control. DDT dust, BHC dust or Malathion dust can be applied to the feeding insects. They should be collected by hand if possible.

Grub. If the grubs are found feeding on Strawberries, make a weak solution of dieldrin (8 level teaspoons of 25 per cent wettable powder to 2 gallons of water) and pour this on to the ground between the plants. Lift the leaves and do not allow the poison to touch the stems. The grub is more of a pest to the farmer than the gardener. Farmers should dust Maize seed with BHC or dieldrin dust before planting.

C.M.R. BEETLES. (*Mylabris oculata*)

These large beetles are strongly marked with yellow bands across their backs. Their common name refers to the uniform of the Cape Mounted Rifles. When they attack flowers, they should be dusted with DDT dust or Malathion dust.

LADYBIRD BEETLES ON PUMPKINS AND POTATOES (*Epilachna dregei*)

The majority of Ladybirds are beneficial insects, but a few are plant feeders such as the Potato Ladybird Beetle and the Pumpkin Ladybird Beetle. They can be controlled with DDT dust or sprays. Malathion dust can be used on the dry foliage of pumpkin plants, which are Cucurbits and are injured by DDT. Lead arsenate is an old remedy that can also be used.

FRUIT EATING BEETLES (*Pachnoda* species)

These yellow and black beetles damage ripe fruit, flying both by day or by night. They are about ¾ inch long.

Control. As one cannot spray the ripe fruit, these beetles should be hand-collected as much as possible. A mixture of sugar and water in small pots hanging amongst the branches will attract the beetles, which fall into the liquid and drown.

MOTHS AND BUTTERFLIES
(*Lepidoptera*)

Moths and butterflies have a complete life cycle and their larvae or caterpillars do a great deal of damage, possibly more damage than any other order of insects. Some are night-flying and some day-flying in the adult stage. The only record of an adult troubling plants is the Fruit-sucking Moth.

FRUIT-SUCKING MOTH (*Achaea* species).

The Moth flies about at night and damages fruit. If fruit is damaged at night, one may suspect that the moth is about and use the same bait for it that is used for Fruit-fly. (See page 257.) Baits that can be used are sugar and water mixed with Malathion or Dipterex. The larvae feed on Acacias and indigenous bush. If they can be seen, spray with DDT, BHC or Arsenate of lead. Derris powder may also be used.

CATERPILLARS

These are the larvae of moths or butterflies. They vary in size, shape and colour and may be small or large, white, green, banded or speckled with beautiful markings. They may also be smooth or hairy and some have stinging hairs as a means of protection.

Caterpillars all have biting mouth-parts and can do irreparable harm to crops and garden plants. There are too many to be listed here, but a few of the better known are described separately below.

Control. All caterpillars of butterflies and moths, except Codling moth, need only be sprayed when they are first seen. Most of them can be controlled effectively by spraying with DDT. Toxaphene is used as an alternative for spraying Bollworm. BHC dust can be used on lawn caterpillars. BHC is as effective as DDT, but should not be used on edible crops because of its musty odour. Arsenate of lead can be used on hairy caterpillars as an alternative. Derris powder is a perfectly safe insecticide and should be used wherever there is a small outbreak of caterpillars in a garden. Repeat the spray to kill the second generation.

ARMY WORM. (*Laphygma exempta*)

This pest has captured the imagination of the public as its appearance on farm lands, where it is very destructive, is often announced in the press. It also appears sometimes on lawns and golf courses in the cities. Contrary to popular belief, the adult is not a white butterfly, but a brownish, night-flying moth which is seldom seen. It lays eggs on grasses and the larvae hatch out from midsummer onwards. The larvae march together in the mass, eating only grasses, maize and other members of the grass family, causing rapid destruction. In the mass the "worms" appear to be green with black stripes, but solitary caterpillars are pale in colour.

Control. As soon as the young caterpillars are seen, they should be sprayed with DDT emulsion. DDT dust or wettable powder may also be used, but are less effective than the emulsion. Endrin emulsion and Diazinon emulsion or wettable powder are also recommended.

CUTWORMS (*Euxoa segetis*)

The adult is a moth which flies at night and lays eggs on weeds and on the bare ground. The larva emerges at the beginning of summer and attacks mainly summer seedlings of annual flowers and vegetables like Tomatoes, as well as perennials like Dahlias, which have succulent stems. As these pests remain underground, emerging only at night to nip off the stalks of young seedlings at ground level, they are difficult to control.

Cutworms are blackish caterpillars, up to 1½ inches in length, which may be found curled up near the soil surface particularly in the evening. If one scratches the soil surface near a damaged plant with a small stick, one can often find the culprit waiting to attack the other plants that night and destroy them.

Control. Cultivation of the soil helps to keep the pests down. One can dig around one's annuals regularly in a small garden and hunt out the cutworms. Weeds should be eradicated and the soil should remain bare for a week or two before planting out summer seedlings. The laborious task of placing a paper collar to a depth of 1½ inches into the soil around each seedling protects the plant, but does not kill the cutworm.

DDT, Toxaphene or dieldrin may be sprayed on to the surface of the soil around seedlings and on to the base of the young plants. A light dressing of BHC powder may be worked into the ground before planting, but should not be used where root crops are to be grown for fear of tainting. Excessive use of BHC may cause growth to be retarded.

Cutworms may be completely eradicated by using several poisoned baits, but great care must be taken in preparing them and they should not be used where pets might get at them. Dieldrin can be mixed with mealie-meal and enough water to make a porridge, then scattered over the soil at sunset. It remains effective for a long time. A small area can be baited at first and, if a few dead cutworms are found, the whole area can then be treated. Other baits are made by mixing 1 lb. of sugar and 5 lb. of bran with 4 oz. of Sodium fluosilicate, 4 oz. of Calcium arsenate, or 6 oz. of Paris green. The last two contain arsenic which is highly poisonous.

CODLING MOTH (*Cydia pomonella*)

This scourge attacks mainly Apple trees, but may also affect Pears, Walnuts and Quinces. If it were not controlled it would mean no Apple harvest in most years, so that anyone who has Apple trees should be prepared to spray them according to a regular programme.

The life-history of the Codling moth should be known so that the method of control can be understood. The adult is a greyish moth which flies about at night and lays its eggs on the blossoms, foliage or tiny fruit clusters of the apple tree. These eggs hatch in from ten to fourteen days and the pinkish white larva bores into the fruit mainly through the calyx end, but also through the side. It feeds on the inside core of the apple and when fully mature, after about six weeks, crawls out again and seeks a place under a piece of loose bark in which to spin a cocoon. The larvae usually descend in midsummer. The adult moth usually emerges from the cocoon in late winter or early spring and lays its eggs once more. The apple is, of course, ruined by the holes inside the fruit. A caterpillar might "sting" the fruit and spoil its market value by biting a tiny hole in the skin before being killed by the poison sprayed on the apples. This may callus over, but remains as a blemish.

Control. Once the caterpillar has entered the fruit it is too late to save it, so that one must be quick to try to prevent this happening. It is no use spraying the blossom, as this will kill the pollinating bees and probably prevent the fruit from "setting". As soon as the blossoms have three-quarters dropped their petals, one should commence spraying with DDT 50 per cent wettable powder and cover the trees completely. The spraying must continue at ten-day intervals until the beginning of December and then at fortnightly intervals until the end of January. Four sprays are usually sufficient for Walnuts.

DDT spray should not be applied later than about three weeks before harvesting. It has the disadvantage that it kills *Aphelinus mali*, the natural parasite on the woolly apple aphis, so that the latter pest may become a problem. It will then be necessary to spray with Gusathion or another insecticide, such as Sevin, but not within a month of harvest. (See under Control of Aphids above.)

Banding the trees with sacking to trap the cocoons which may hibernate in its warmth is a good practice, but is not a control on its own, and should not take the place of spraying.

At one time lead arsenate was used alone and then alternately with DDT, but since 1947, DDT has been used alone. If the caterpillars build up resistance in time, and they are already showing signs of doing so, particularly in the western Cape, it might be necessary to supplement with other insecticides such as Malathion or Parathion. This is one of the important commercial pests subjected to constant experimentation by the Department of Agriculture.

FALSE CODLING MOTH (*Argyroploce leucotreta*)

This is a pest of citrus trees mainly in large orchards. The adult is a moth and the larvae enters and destroys oranges.

Control. There is no real chemical control. One must pick up and destroy all infested fruit in orchards once a week. Drop them into a tin of paraffin.

LAWN CATERPILLARS (*Spodoptera abyssinia*)

The adult is a moth which lays its eggs on certain lawns and grasses. The caterpillar lives in the soil under the grass mat. It comes out at night and feeds on the undergrowth of the lawn. White patches form where the grass dies off. If one digs underneath, the larva can generally be found.

Control. Dust the lawn with DDT or BHC dust and water it in.

CABBAGE CATERPILLAR (*Plutella maculipennis*)

This is the larva of the Diamond-Backed Moth. It is a slim, smooth, pale green caterpillar, just over an inch in length, which feeds on the underside of cabbage leaves and other succulent green leaves, making a lacy patch at first and later eating the leaves into holes.

Control. Handpick caterpillars if there are only a few. Spray with DDT wettable powder or Malathion. Do not spray cabbages with DDT after the heads have formed because of residues which remain in the cabbages. Cabbage seedlings may be dipped into a solution of lead arsenate (3 oz. in 4 gallons of water) when transplanting.

AMARYLLIS CATERPILLAR (*Brithys pancrattii*)

Also known as the CRINUM BORER, LILY BORER or LILY TIGER, this is one of the chief pests of bulbs in the garden. The adult is a moth, which lays its eggs on the leaves. The larva is a striped black and white caterpillar which eats into the leaves and bores down into the bulbs, destroying them. It creates havoc with Nerines, *Crinum*, Daffodils, *Haemanthus*, *Amaryllis belladonna*, *Zephyranthus*, *Cyrtanthus* and other members of the *Amaryllis* family. It generally appears from November to the end of February and there are several generations during that time.

Control. Dust with DDT powder or spray with 50 per cent DDT wettable powder as soon as the first caterpillar is seen. Repeat once a week if necessary. Destroy all caterpillars individually and remove leaves infested with the caterpillars under the tissue. As a preventative, dust plants like Nerines, which are readily infested, at weekly intervals from December until February, with DDT powder.

MAIZE STALK BORER (*Busseola fusca*)

This is more a pest of farmers than of gardeners, but if an 18-inch high Mealie plant has speckled leaf markings, the caterpillar may be eating the inside of the stalk. In this case a teaspoon of DDT $2\frac{1}{2}$ or 5 per cent dust can be poured inside the leaf funnels of each plant. Dipterex and Endrin in powder or emulsion form can also be poured down or sprayed into the funnels. Old Mealie-stalks should never be left in the ground after harvesting as this provides a home for the caterpillars in winter.

BOLLWORM (Called EARWORM on Maize) (*Heliothis obsoleta*)

These are caterpillars that burrow into Tomatoes, Oranges and Cotton plants, mainly on farmlands. Bollworm also eats its way into young ears of Maize (Mealies) and is then called an Earworm. It also attacks Snapdragons.

Control. As soon as the caterpillars are seen on the plants they should be dusted with DDT 5 per cent powder or sprayed with DDT 50 per cent wettable powder. The spray should not be used on Tomatoes after the fruit has set. Orange trees are mainly attacked in spring as the fruit is setting. Toxaphene may also be used to control Bollworm.

In order to prevent the Earworm from infesting the tops of Mealies, one should dust the silk and cobs with DDT 5 per cent dust before the Mealies are ripe. Keeping the soil free from weeds will keep down the pests.

POTATO TUBER MOTH (*Phthorimaea operculella*)

The adult moth lays eggs on the tubers and the larvae burrow into the potatoes and spoil them. This is a pest which usually only troubles the large grower of potatoes.

Control. One can prevent the adult from laying eggs on the tubers by hilling up the soil around the plants as they grow. About a fortnight after the shoots have appeared above ground, the plants can be sprayed with DDT 50 per cent wettable powder. It is important to purchase clean seed potatoes.

BORERS

These are the larvae of moths or beetles. The adult of the Apple-and-Quince borer is a moth, while the adults of the Fig Borer and Hibiscus Borer are beetles. One can examine the holes in the bark and the sawdust or frass at the entrance to determine whether or not these holes are made by borers. The Apple-and-Quince borer attacks the tree at any spot, but the Fig Borer generally lays eggs in the trunk about 3 feet from the base. It is a serious pest of figs in places with hot climates like Pretoria and also affects willow trees.

Once the borer is inside the tree there is little that one can do to control it. Do not grow Figs or Quinces in hedges in order to prevent infestation from one tree to another.

FIG BORER (*Prynetra spinata*)

The only method of control is prevention. The trees must be pruned with a single stem up to at least 3 feet in height and should not be allowed to branch out at ground level. Tie a band of fine wire gauze at least 2 feet wide or preferably 3 feet wide, around the base of the trunk. This prevents the female from laying its eggs, which it always does in the bottom 3-foot portion of the tree. Once the borer has infested the tree, the tree cannot be saved and will probably die. One could cut the borer out of the bark, but usually by the time one notices it, the damage has gone too far.

APPLE-AND-QUINCE BORER (*Coryphodema tristis*)

This is not such a serious pest as the Fig Borer. If the frass is seen, scrape it away to expose the holes and prod them with a long wire to impale the insect or squirt DDT into the holes. Plug the holes with mud or putty. Other than that, one can only burn infested branches and examine the loose bark for caterpillars in summer, destroying them individually. There is little that can be done to prevent borers from entering apple or quince trees.

HIBISCUS BORER (*Pseudagrilus sp.*)

This is an important pest on the south coast of Natal, where the larva of the Hibiscus Borer tunnels into the stems and branches of large bushes and destroys them within about two years. The adult, which is an iridescent green beetle, about $\frac{1}{4}$ of an inch in length, feeds on the leaf edges, but does no appreciable damage. No method of control is known at the present time, but experiments are in progress at the Natal Department of Agriculture in Pietermaritzburg.

WHITEFLIES
(*Trialeurodes natalensis*)

Whitefly is not a serious pest in gardens and is mainly a sporadic pest in greenhouses. It is usually found on Begonia, Cineraria, Calceolaria and Ferns, but can also infest Abutilon, Chrysanthemum, Dahlia, Beans, Cucumbers and Tomatoes.

Whiteflies are very tiny, delicate insects, one twenty-fifth of an inch in length, which have a white powdery

A greenhouse will enable one to grow orchids like these magnificent Cattleyas and Laeliocattleyas. *Columnea microphylla* is a good companion plant, seen here with large flame flowers on its dainty trailing stems. (See Chapter 35.)

Fountain Grass (*Pennisetum ruppelii*) will grow on poor, dry soil, but makes an excellent background plant near a pond or in a rockery.

Ivy has countless uses. Here a miniature-leaved variety of *Hedera helix* softens the edges of brick steps.

Astylus Beetles (natural size) swarm particularly on flowers of the daisy family during summer. (See Chapter 37.)

The Amaryllis Caterpillar (*Brithys pancrattii*) destroys a Crinum flower (natural size).

Aphids (magnified) infesting the stems of Asclepias. (See Chapter 37.)

Australian Bug (*Icerya purchasi*), showing the scale-like insect and the white, ribbed egg sac (magnified 3 times).

Incrustation of White Scale on an Aloe leaf (greatly magnified).

Rose leaves showing Black Spot disease. (See Chapter 38.)

covering. They flutter about the plants on hot days, but usually remain on the underside of foliage. They lay tiny yellowish eggs on the leaves, which hatch out into nymphs in about a fortnight. These remain on the leaves and suck out the juices, causing yellowing and wilting of the plant. At this stage the nymphs resemble scales. After about a month the nymphs moult and leave their transparent cases on the leaves, emerging as adults. There are several generations in a season. They excrete sticky honeydew, and sooty mould grows on this, making the plants unsightly.

Control. BHC and Malathion sprays are recommended. Nicotine sulphate with soft soap may also be used.

GRASSHOPPERS

The Elegant Grasshopper (*Zonocerus elegans*) nips off the tops of tender young plants like germinating Sweet-peas and other succulent growth.

Control. As this insect flies about rapidly it is difficult to spray it directly. The plants they feed on can be sprayed with BHC or Chlordane.

CRICKETS

These large black insects are well known because of their shrill chirping at night and are chiefly a pest of tobacco farmers. They may cause damage in the garden by severing the grass on lawns or by dragging young plants down into their burrows.

Control. Where they are present in sufficient numbers to cause damage to lawns, especially after long, dry summers, water BHC, DDT or dieldrin onto the lawns or around their holes to kill them.

FLIES, FRUIT-FLY

The household fly does not injure plants, but there are several members of the same order which do, notably the Fruit-fly, which is regarded as one of the worst pests in horticulture. Flies have a complete life cycle, but the legless larva is usually called a maggot. The flies which attack plants all have biting mouth-parts and the maggot usually has a pair of rasping hooks.

FRUIT-FLY

The Mediterranean fruit-fly (*Ceratitis capitata*) and the Natal fruit-fly (*Pterandrus rosa*) affect the fruit in nearly every orchard in the country and threaten the harvest in commercial fruit-growing areas. The damage is increasing and everyone who has Peach, Nectarine or Guava trees should spray according to a programme in order to try to destroy the pests.

The adult fruit-fly "stings" the fruit and lays its eggs beneath the skin. When they hatch, the maggots eat the fruit and destroy it inside, often making it rot. When the fruit falls, the maggots pupate in the ground and develop into adults.

Control. Preventative measures such as collecting all fallen fruit, dropping it into a bucket of water and crushing it so that the maggots cannot pupate, will help to reduce the fly population. A few fruit-flies survive the winter on evergreen fruits such as Loquat, Citrus, Avocadoes and Guavas, feeding on honeydew secreted by aphids and scale insects. If such trees grow near deciduous fruit orchards, they should be sprayed once or twice during winter. When using bait, one must try to kill the adult before it can sting the fruit. The old method of killing the adult is to trap it with a poisoned bait spray, as follows.

As soon as the young fruit is half-grown and reaches the size of a walnut, the spray must be prepared and applied. It must be applied weekly until ripening time on deciduous fruit trees and again immediately after rain. Guavas should be sprayed twice during winter, since they are evergreen. The spray should be placed in a coarse syringe and allowed to fall in large droplets on the foliage of the trees. The bait can also be placed in special terracotta pots and hung amongst the branches, so that it may not be necessary to spray too often. These baits are poisonous and should not be used where children can reach them.

Several poisons may be used as bait and must be mixed with water and sugar to attract the fruit-flies. Staleysauce may be mixed with the poisons instead of sugar. This is a protein bait attractant which is a yeast product and is said to attract fruit-flies for several miles. The recommended poisons are Malathion wettable powder, Dipterex wettable powder (this is a form of Tugon). Parathion is used by farmers.

Two new chemicals, Lebaycid and Rogor E are now recommended. See page 274 and 275 for use.

GLADIOLUS FLY (*Epimidiza hirta*)

This tiny fly lays its eggs on Gladiolus leaves and the tiny maggots hatch out in two days, burrowing into the surface and destroying the foliage.

Control. If one can spray a protective film over the foliage, it will kill the maggots and also kill the females by contact when they alight to lay their eggs. Regular spraying every week or ten days with DDT emulsion such as E 27, will control this pest. Repeat the spray after rain.

As this is the same spray used for thrip in Gladiolus, it simplifies the control of both pests.

CARNATION BUD FLY (*Epimidiza nigra*)

This fly lays eggs in Carnation buds and the maggots destroy the bud.

Control. Spray every ten days with DDT emulsion as for Gladiolus fly. Dipterex wettable powder mixed with water may also be used as a weekly spray.

PUMPKIN AND MELON FLY (*Dacus ciliatus*)

These flies sting the fruit like Fruit-fly, laying their eggs inside, and the resulting maggots spoil the fruit. They infest Pumpkins, Marrows, Watermelons, Cucumbers, Papaws and Granadillas.

Control. Use a baited spray in the same way as for fruit-flies, spraying the foliage once a week from flowering time until the recommended precautionary period before harvesting. To make the baited spray, mix sugar and water with Malathion powder, Dipterex or Sodium fluosilicate as described above. Farmers may use Parathion.

ANTS

ARGENTINE ANTS, RED ANTS, BLACK ANTS, ETC.

Ants do not injure plants directly, but do so indirectly by causing greater infestation by aphids and scale insects, including mealybugs. Experiments in South Africa have shown that wherever there are ants in orchards and vineyards, the population of pests like red scale, soft brown scale and mealybugs is increased. When ants are controlled, the infestation by aphids and scale insects is considerably reduced.

Aphids and scale insects secrete honeydew which is sought after by ants and it has been popularly supposed that the ants carry the pests from tree to tree in order to provide them with fresh nourishment. Ants, however, do not do this, for the winged aphis starts colonies of aphids on other plants and scale insects crawl about or are dispersed by wind. The ant disturbs the natural enemies of these pests, such as ladybirds and wasps, and makes it difficult for them to grow to maturity. Ants come in greater numbers than ladybirds and will chase away the ladybird or its tiny larva that feeds on the aphis or scale insect. When the helpless larva is disturbed, it will not have the best conditions for growth and will often die. This means that there are fewer mature ladybirds, fewer eggs laid and fewer predators and parasites on aphids and scale insects.

One should make every effort to eliminate ants from rose-gardens and the soil around fruit-trees, if not from all over the garden.

Control. Ants can be controlled by trapping or by the use of insecticides, used during summer and autumn. One can tie 4-inch-wide bands of hessian, spread with sticky materials, around tree-trunks, so as to trap ants which are climbing up. This sticky material can be purchased and should not be painted directly on to the bark or it may injure it. The bands can be kept on throughout summer and replaced from time to time.

One can water the soil around trees, as well as ant-holes, with insecticides containing dieldrin emulsion or wettable powder, Chlordane or BHC. Dieldrin is recognised as one of the best insecticides for the control of ants in general. The insecticides can also be mixed with dampened soil and then worked into the top soil in autumn. If dieldrin is used, the treatment need not be repeated for three or four years, but if Chlordane is used, it should be repeated annually. Both poisons should be handled with great care. Pugnacious Ants require more frequent treatment.

Sprays made with these chemicals can also be painted on to the trunks of trees near the base or sprayed directly on to the bark near the base. Spray paths and benches in greenhouses to control ants. Shallow containers of poisoned bait made with Sodium arsenite and sugar can be placed at the base of trees, but this is not advisable where children or pets are about as this is a highly poisonous chemical.

TERMITES (WHITE ANTS)

Termites are distinguished from true ants by their white colour and thicker waists. There are many different types of termites, of which the Harvester Termites (or Forage Ants) do the most damage in gardens. These eat holes in lawns by severing the grass and taking it down into their large nests below ground. *Hodotermes mozambicus* occurs over most of southern Africa and the brown workers are slightly smaller than the well-known flying ant, which flies into the air to mate. *Microhodotermes* occurs in the S.W. Cape and Karoo and is easier to control as it has a smaller nest.

The Wood-eating Termites, also called Fungus-growing termites (Odontotermes, Macrotermes, Microtermes, etc.), normally live on dead wood in nature, but where there is no dead wood as in a garden, they turn their attention to the living bark of young shrubs and rose bushes, particularly before these have become established. At the same time, they damage wooden benches, trellises, rustic wooden steps and other structures in the garden made of wood, which has not been treated with wood preservatives to withstand their onslaught. Paint the wood with proprietary products containing 5 per cent Pentachlorophenol. These termites will also destroy dormant dahlia bulbs in the soil, being attracted by the woody stalks; eat woody cuttings before they have taken root or even undermine the interior of weak growing plants. They are also attracted by fibrous compost.

Both groups of termites must be controlled in different ways owing to their different reactions towards poisons.

Control of Harvester Termites or Forage Ants. Dieldrin is now recommended for the elimination of the true Harvester Termite. It is usually sprayed on to the surface where the ants feed, and they take the grass down to their nest, or it may be used as a bait mixed with ground-nut hulls. Aldrin kills specific termites such as the Karoo Harvester Termite and the Snouted Harvester Termite. The Harvester Termite colony will also be destroyed by the use of poison bait made with Sodium fluosilicate. The termites take this down their burrows and the whole colony can be poisoned. The narrow subterranean passages extend so far from the nest that the ants emerge in many neighbouring properties, so that it is helpful to ask one's neighbours to join in the task of administering the bait at the same time. If it is adequately applied, one application of poisoned bait will probably be enough, especially if it is put down in early winter. In small gardens, the bait can be scattered around the holes each day until the ants are no longer active. It will take up to about a month to eliminate the colony in this way.

Preparation of Bait. Soak dry grass cuttings, about $\frac{1}{2}$ an inch in length, in a tin containing a solution of $\frac{1}{4}$ lb. of Sodium fluosilicate and 2 gallons of water. The solution must be stirred all the time. Lift out the grass cuttings with a wire strainer and allow the excess liquid to drain off. Dry the bait on newspaper and rake it about until it is bone dry. Use it immediately and store the remainder in a strong paper bag, aiming to use it all within the next two or three weeks. Store the poisonous solution away from children or animals. Sodium fluosilicate is safe to handle, but the hands should be scrubbed after preparing the bait.

Control of Wood-eating Termites. (Also called Fungus-growing Termites.) These termites will not take poisoned bait, so that they are very difficult to control. One can discourage them from attacking susceptible plants during their early stages of growth. If one can protect young trees and shrubs for the first three years then it is almost certain that they will withstand the onslaught of termites.

(I) To Repel Wood-eating Termites. Five per cent DDT dust should be worked into the top 6 or 12 inches of soil, using 4 oz. of powder to a cubic foot of soil. It is best to mix this evenly into the soil over an area of 18 inches wide and 18 inches deep, before planting the tree if possible. Otherwise, work it into the top soil as deeply as possible. One application of DDT will be sufficient for the three-year period. This treatment can also be used to protect rose bushes in infested areas. BHC may be used on lawns. Calcium arsenate powder can also be used in the same way, but as arsenic compounds are cumulative in the soil, it should never be used in flower or vegetable beds. Be aware of its highly poisonous contact properties. It can be incorporated into the soil when planting new lawns to poison the top 6 inches of soil and repel the termite. One can also spike an established lawn thoroughly, sprinkle the calcium arsenate dust over it and water it in well. This may also be done with the 5 per cent DDT dust. One treatment should be enough. In order to protect the straw mulch around Strawberries one should spray it with a solution of 10 per cent wettable DDT powder before spreading it.

Whenever the wood-eating termites attack large trees like Jacarandas, the mud blanket that these creatures place over the trunk as a cover must be scraped away and one should destroy all mud tunnels and dig away the soil for a short distance from the trunk. Cavities in trees should be cleaned out and filled. (See Care of Trees, Chapter 29.) Water and feed the tree to build up its vigour.

Termites generally attack plants and trees that are not in the best of health and have dead branches on them. Prune out all dead wood and destroy old stumps. Remove all dead wood in the vicinity. In established large orchards in virgin soil, it has been found that one should leave twiggy débris between the young trees, although not too near the trunks, so that the termites will have something to live on and not attack the trees. Remove all plants that are sickly as a result of disease, lack of moisture, poor feeding or insect attack or try to remedy these conditions. Regular cultivation around trees and on flower beds breaks up the termite passages and discourages attack.

(II) Complete eradication of the wood-eating or fungus-growing termites can only take place by asking a specialist to smoke them out with a white-arsenic-and-sulphur toxic smoke treatment. This requires specialised knowledge and equipment. Other fumigants, such as petrol and extraction-naphtha, may be used if applied expertly and directly to the nest cavity. The removal of the queen and the nest (except in the case of Carton-nest-building Termites) does not eradicate colonies of termites. Useless measures are flooding the nests with water, the introduction of motor exhaust fumes and fumigation with calcium cyanide.

SLUGS AND SNAILS

The snail, with his curly shell on his back, is too well-known to need description. A slug has a soft, shiny body like a snail, but has no shell. Both do tremendous damage to ornamental foliage or vegetables like Lettuce and will eat the succulent stems of young plants right through. They gather in moist places and will destroy a whole crop of germinating seedlings overnight. They cling to the moist surface of pots, climbing up to destroy leafy plants. Slugs and snails are particularly active during rainy spells. They lay masses of gelatinous eggs in moist soil and under rocks. These hatch into tiny replicas of the adult.

Control. The eggs should be destroyed whenever found and cultivation of the soil will help to expose them. The best snail and slug-killer is Metaldehyde. This is a powder which is also obtainable in solid form. It is usually mixed with mealie-meal or bran (1 oz. to 2 lb. of bran) to make a bait that is scattered around one's plants in the early evening when it is cool and the snails come out to feed. Ready-made snail bait in the form of pellets or powder can be purchased. The mixture may be scattered dry on to moist soil or moistened very slightly. Rain will dissolve and wash away the metaldehyde, so that one should try to prevent this during rainy weather by placing it in little heaps under a tilted metal lid or an overturned broken flower pot.

When planting out a bed of young seedlings or dahlia tubers in summer, one should encircle the whole bed with an inch-wide trail of powdered bait which will act as a barrier against snails, which emerge from under leafy clumps made by Agapanthus, Watsonias and other bushy plants. The empty snail shells will be found the following morning. Hide the pellets under foliage so as to take care that pets do not eat them, as they are poisonous. Snails collect under rocks and the rockery should be kept clear of them. It is best to be extravagant and use a great deal of snail bait all over the garden at the same time, in an attempt to eliminate them together, rather than bait little areas and allow them to breed in other parts. Always scatter snail bait near potted plants, for both slugs and snails are attracted to the moisture beneath and around them. Snails can also be gathered by hand at dusk and dropped into a pail of salt water.

WORMS

Earthworms, centipedes and millipedes are common in gardens and while the first two are beneficial creatures the other is not.

EARTHWORM. This is a beneficial creature, for it digests soil and passes it through its body. It is found in damp soil which is usually rich in organic matter and improves the texture of the soil. In its burrowing it might pull down very young seedlings, but this is not usual. The only people who do not regard earthworms with favour are the makers of golf courses or bowling greens where the small mounds of soil (called casts) interfere with the passage of balls and render the greens unsightly. They are destroyed on greens by watering with a solution of ammonium sulphate or Derris powder. Copper sulphate is effective, but may injure the grass.

CENTIPEDES are also classed as beneficial worms for they are carnivorous, feeding on slugs, insects and, often, earthworms. They have segmented, wormlike bodies which are usually flattened, each segment bearing one pair of legs.

MILLIPEDES. These are types of centipedes that feed on decaying vegetable matter and frequently damage the roots of plants and potato tubers. They have segmented bodies like centipedes, but millipedes are round in cross-section, each segment bearing two pairs of legs. Some millipedes are quite large and may be seen easily, especially after rains.

Control. Destroy large millipedes individually when seen. Well-drained soil and frequent digging keeps down millipedes. DDT dust and sprays are effective. Sprinkle 5 per cent DDT dust in drills with newly planted seed in infested soils. Malathion will kill millipedes if it hits them directly and it may be sprayed on the area which they traverse.

CUTWORMS. See Beetles and Chafer Beetles.

EEL-WORM (Nematodes).

These are tiny parasitic worms which can only be seen under a microscope, so that they can only be recognised by the damage that they do to plants. They cause swellings on the roots of infested plants.

(I) THE BULB EELWORM. If these are present on Narcissi they appear when the bulbs are dormant as cottony tufts at the base of the bulb scales. These are the larvae which either attack the dormant bulb or enter the soil when the bulb is replanted and will infect healthy bulbs. Never plant bulbs which appear to be partly decayed or have soft, cottonwool-like tufts at the base. Eelworm causes blister-like swellings on the foliage of Narcissi. The eelworm lays hundreds of eggs in the bulb in one season.

(II) Root-Knot Eelworm. When plants are not making good progress and show signs of wilting, the roots should be examined for signs of small swellings. Do not confuse these swellings with the nitrogenous nodules on roots of plants of the legume family. The Root-knot Eelworm is a pest of Tomatoes, Potatoes, Carrots, Onions, Strawberries, Lettuce, Delphinium, Scabious and Cyclamen as well as a host of other plants. Eelworm seems to occur in light soils and is an important pest in greenhouses where temperatures are high.

Control. A practical preventative is not to grow susceptible crops in the same soil for two successive years. Eelworm does not usually infect grasses, so that farmers often plant grass in infested lands for about three years. Other resistant crops are being developed. Peanuts are said to be immune to attack, amongst others. The following vegetables are fairly tolerant and are grown as alternative crops: Asparagus, Cabbage, Cauliflower, Celery, Sweet Corn, Radish, Rhubarb, Spinach and Turnip. Otherwise, one could let the ground lie fallow and keep it free of weeds.

Once a crop has been infested, it cannot be saved. Infested plants should be dug out and burnt. Do not put these in the compost. Eelworm can even be spread by implements and shoes, so that the soil should be cleaned off and they should be disinfected. Cyclamen corms may be dipped into hot water at 110°F. for 30 minutes, to kill all eelworm. Grow your own Tomato seedlings to prevent infestation from other gardens.

Eradication of eelworm before planting can only be effected by soil fumigation with D-D or E.D.B. 4.5. This usually requires special equipment, like an injector gun, which will probably be beyond the scope of the small home gardener. Although not ideal, the soil can also be fumigated in a simpler way. One can mark the area to be fumigated into lines one foot apart, drawn from north to south and from east to west. Where the lines intersect, one should place sticks to mark the spots which will then be exactly one foot from each other. (A 3-foot wooden plank with long nails at 12-inch intervals is an aid to marking the area.) With an iron rod, make a 9-inch deep hole at each intersection. Apply 1 teaspoon of E.D.B. 4.5 or D-D into the hole through a funnel. Seal the hole immediately with the heel of one's shoe. After all the holes have been sealed the ground can be lightly watered. Gases will form below ground and destroy the eelworm. After two weeks take a handful of soil and smell it. If it smells of the fumigant dig the soil and aerate it. Do not plant anything until all the odour has dis-

appeared or the plants will die. Wet soils hold the gas longer.

As D-D and E.D.B. 4.5 are highly toxic liquids, great care must be taken when using them and it is advisable to wear protective clothing. One should not inhale the fumes or allow the liquid to spill on the skin or clothing.

OTHER GARDEN PESTS
MOLES

Moles generally trouble gardeners who live on the outskirts of the town or near the open veld. There are several methods of trapping moles, all of which require patience and vigilance. Gardeners have many pet ways of combating moles, including growing special plants such as *Euphorbia lathyrus*, Kidney Beans and Castor Beans, which are thought to repel them.

There are two types of Mole which belong to different groups. The greyish Rodent Mole or Mole-Rat eats plants and destroys bulbs and garden produce. The Golden Mole or "Kruipmol" only destroys plants and raises lawns while burrowing along beneath the surface in search of insects. Both are treated differently.

The Golden Mole or surface mole is destroyed by inserting a pronged spring trap over the burrow. Lawns may be watered with an arsenate of lead solution (1 oz. per square yard). This is highly poisonous and need only be done again after one or two years if necessary.

The Rodent Mole requires more patience to eradicate. It may be dug out when burrowing or trapped at the entrance to a burrow. Conceal the trap by digging out a square of earth so that the trap lies level with the bottom of the tunnel. Close the top completely by covering it over with a metal sheet and a layer of soil. Prepare the trap in the afternoon and examine it the next day. Poisoned bait in the form of a piece of potato smeared with strychnine can be pushed well into the entrance and the opening plugged with grass and earth. Do not handle the bait and remove it if it is ejected with a mound of soil. Poisonous Castor-oil Beans may be pushed down into the holes. Some people lie in wait and shoot the mole at the entrance of the burrow.

If these methods fail one can call in a specialist to gas out the moles with cyanide powders, which must be applied with a special pump. Fumigation tablets containing phosphorus may be pushed into burrows, but release poisonous gases and should be handled with caution. They should be used when opened and not kept in storage or near buildings.

CHAPTER THIRTY-EIGHT

COMMON DISEASES OF PLANTS AND THEIR CONTROL

The fight against disease in the garden is rather a heart-breaking one, for so many diseases are caused by adverse weather conditions over which the gardener has no control. An experienced gardener will learn not to grow plants that are susceptible to disease in his own climatic area, although this is a negative outlook. If, by proper attention to soil and situation requirements, as well as good cultural practices, he can grow plants which were disease-ridden in former years, then he will have gained practical knowledge of how to conquer the disease. If the disease attacks year after year, in spite of good husbandry, however, then it is best to avoid growing that particular plant.

One can help to prevent disease from spreading in a garden by scrupulously sweeping up and burning diseased or spotted fallen leaves as well as burning infected plants. Never add these to the compost or the spores will remain over to the next season and infect the following year's plants.

When removing a disease-ridden tree or plant, never put another of the same kind in its place without checking whether conditions of growth need improving or the same trouble will recur. Remember that fungus attack nearly always comes as a result of poor conditions of growth—poor soil, waterlogged soil with poor drainage, lack of fertility or even the excess use of nitrogenous fertilizer, as well as wrong situations, such as a shady position for a sun-loving plant. If these conditions can be improved, then replace the soil with fresh soil, as in the case of planting another rose in place of a diseased one. It may be that neighbouring trees have grown so big as to shade the area formerly considered suitable for a fruit tree and one must now reluctantly eliminate the fruit tree from the garden.

Spraying with the fungicides offered for sale in the shops is largely a preventative measure, where previous knowledge has shown that the disease is likely to occur. This is worthwhile doing on ornamental trees and shrubs, particularly roses, or fruit trees, even if it does not prevent the disease from occurring altogether. Some leaf diseases, like Black Spot, do not necessarily kill the rose bush, although it will become weakened and prone to other diseases if it becomes defoliated too often. Pre-

ventative spraying, at the beginning of the rainy season, as well as other practical measures, like watering by irrigation only and destroying fallen leaves and petals continuously, will help to lessen the disease.

Leaf diseases in general are only harmful when they cause defoliation and the plant's resistance is lowered to other diseases. They are caused by fungi or bacteria and are spread during humid weather when there is little wind to dry foliage. In the case of deciduous trees and shrubs, one always has the opportunity to make a fresh start at the beginning of spring by using preventative fungicides when the leaves unfold. Once one has treated a tree for disease, pay attention to watering and fertilization to increase its resistance. Vigorous, healthy and well-cared-for plants will resist disease in many cases.

In the case of small annual crops of flowers and vegetables, it is only worth spraying at the first sign of the disease in order to prevent it from spreading to all the plants. One should remove and destroy any seriously infected plants immediately. If the disease appears to be widespread, it is best to pull up and burn the plants in order to prevent further spread of the disease. Do not grow susceptible crops in a situation where a diseased crop has been grown.

Many insect pests carry disease, particularly virus diseases, to plants, so that the elimination of pests like aphids will help to keep down disease.

One should always buy healthy plants so as not to introduce disease into one's garden. Never plant seedlings that have spots on their leaves or appear to be sickly in other ways. Inspect tubers of potatoes and dahlias or bulbs to see whether they are clean and firm. Do not plant a bulb that feels soft or has white fungal fluff at its base. Take advantage of the plant-breeder's work in producing disease-resistant strains and purchase the best seed from reliable sources.

Modern research is discovering more and more aids against plant disease. Antibiotics are being tried against bacteria and some fungi. Some materials are harmful and cause plant injury. Experiments may one day enable us to combat plant disease as easily as we combat insect pests. Meanwhile we must endeavour to recognise the common diseases that attack our plants and do our best to protect them with the means that we have at our disposal.

The advantage of using fungicides is that they are easily handled and not as harmful (except for the mercury compounds) to human beings as many modern insecticides. Crops can be harvested a short time after spraying. A list of the fungicides in use today follows in the next chapter.

Spraying programmes for fruit trees are complicated, but must be done frequently if any success is to be attained. These are more easily followed by the commercial grower than by the gardener, but an attempt should be made to spray regularly for the more important diseases.

There are so many plant diseases that it is quite impossible to give a list of these or even all the details of the common diseases in a short book. An attempt will be made to describe some of the most common diseases which trouble gardeners, giving an indication of many susceptible plants and suggested methods of control.

Plant diseases are usually divided into fungus diseases, bacterial and virus diseases. These will be dealt with in turn. There are also several physiological diseases caused by high temperature and frost, or by lack of light or shortage of water. Mineral deficiencies cause some diseases known as deficiency diseases. A knowledge of practical gardening and of what one's plants require will help to right many of these physiological diseases.

FUNGUS DISEASES

The vast majority of plant diseases are caused by fungi. A fungus is a living plant which is reproduced by spores. The parasitic fungi exist on living plants and cause their injury or death. Some fungi, called saprophytes, live only on dead organic matter and cause its decay, but do not injure living plants.

Parasitic fungi, like all fungi, require warmth and moisture for growth. They are prevalent during summer and develop during warm, rainy weather. They multiply rapidly by ejecting spores into the air which settle on the leaves of plants and grow into new plants inside the host, drawing nourishment from it. Disease spores are spread by the wind, rain, insects or birds. They are also spread by using infected tools and boxes which have stored infected bulbs.

In order to check the entry of fungus diseases into plants, one sprays with chemicals called fungicides. These aim to place a protective film over the leaf surface so that the spores are destroyed. Once they grow into the leaves there is little that one can do to stop the disease. If one has not sprayed as a preventative at the beginning

of the rainy season and notices the first sign of a disease like Black Spot on roses or Mildew on cucurbits one should spray immediately, nevertheless, in order to attempt to prevent further infection which will cause severe defoliation of the plant.

BLACK SPOT (*Actinonema rosae*)

This is a common disease in the garden and affects Roses in particular. The leaves have one or two black spots, up to ¼ inch in diameter, on them. After a short time the leaves turn yellow and drop off. Some roses are more tolerant than others and will resist Black Spot more. Yellow and copper-coloured roses are said to be particularly susceptible. If roses are allowed to become defoliated continuously, there will be more and more dieback and eventually the whole bush may die.

Control. As the rose is continuously infected by spores from old leaves, these should be swept up regularly. A mulch in early summer will reduce the danger of spores rising up from the soil. Penetration of Black Spot takes place when the leaves have been wet for over 6 hours. In gardens where the foliage is not splashed while watering there is little Black Spot except in rainy periods or heavy dews. Never water roses with an overhead sprinkler later than noon and water preferably by irrigation.

Dusting and spraying with fungicides from the time the leaves uncurl or from the beginning of the rainy period until late summer will help to protect roses from Black Spot. Weekly spraying is satisfactory, but this may have to be done more often during wet weather. The copper sprays are considered better for Black Spot than the sulphur sprays. These include fixed copper or copper oxychloride. A very effective organic fungicide against Black Spot is Maneb.

MILDEWS

There are two types of mildew, the more common and conspicuous, though perhaps not so serious, being powdery mildew and the other being downy mildew, which causes more damage even though it is not so common. Wherever mildew is mentioned by itself, it is powdery mildew that is generally meant.

POWDERY MILDEW

This group of common diseases is caused by a fungus which forms a white, felted covering on the leaves and young shoots, drawing nourishment by means of small suckers which penetrate the top layer of cells. They eventually stunt growth and cause death by smothering as the felt layer becomes thicker, as well as by taking food from the plant. Powdery mildew is common on roses, apple and peach trees, flowers like delphinium and Sweet-peas, and also on grapes, cucumber, marrow and pumpkin. It has caused defoliation of papaw trees on the Natal coast. The spores are wafted by wind currents which die if the air is dry, but germinate if humidity is high.

Control. Remove and burn badly infected shoots, especially before spraying. Thin out plants during wet seasons and allow them plenty of ventilation. Avoid excessive use of nitrogenous fertilizer which results in too much succulent growth during rainy periods. Dust with sulphur or Karathane at the first sign of mildew or spray with wettable sulphur or wettable Karathane. Sulphur tends to burn foliage during hot weather so that it should be thinly applied at such times.

DOWNY MILDEW

These are not such easily noticed fungus diseases, nor so common, but are much more serious as they have a more deep-seated growth. Yellowish patches appear on the top surface of the leaves, while the underneath surface is coated with a whitish-grey down. Downy mildew infects plants like onion, radish, melon, antirrhinum (in S.W. Cape), mesembs in the Cape, seedling cabbages and cauliflower.

Control. It is best to remove and destroy any of these infected plants or portions of them and to spray the remainder with sulphur sprays, Bordeaux mixture or one of the new organic fungicides like Zineb.

RUST

Rust on plants is usually so-called because of the presence of rusty brown dots on the foliage and stems. These are caused by several fungi, the best known being *Puccinia* and *Uromyces*. The rust fungus penetrates the small opening on the leaf or stem and grows in the spaces between the cells, appearing as a tiny rusty spot around the point of entry, sometimes causing distortion of the leaves. Rust fungi have a complicated life cycle and the spores are carried over to the following season by other special spores.

The peculiarity of rust fungi is that each species attacks a different type of plant or even a special portion of a plant. The same species can infect a few closely related plants. *Puccinia pruni-spinosae*, for example, which attacks the leaves of the almond, apricot, nectarine and peach, causes them to drop off prematurely in late summer with subsequent decline in the vigour of the tree.

Rust fungi often attack plants that are growing in unsuitable conditions. Aloes that are overcrowded or are grown in shady, moist places when they prefer sunshine are subject to rust, caused by a species of *Uromyces. Uromyces* species also cause rust on dwarf beans, especially during wet weather, and on the less resistant varieties; Scarlet Runner Beans and Beet, and are prevalent and destructive on Carnations, Dianthus, Sweet Williams, Gladiolus, Dierama (Harebell) and Watsonia.

Various species of the *Puccinia* fungus cause rust on Antirrhinum (Snapdragons), Chrysanthemum, Cornflower, Geranium hybrids, Chinkerinchees, Hollyhock (destructive under moist conditions), Iris, Leonotis and on Kweek Grass (*Cynodon dactylon*). Another fungus causes rust on Roses, although this disease is not as common on Roses as Black Spot or Mildew, and others cause rust on Poplar Trees and Figs late in the summer.

Control. When rust is seen to attack annual plants, destroy the badly infected plants and spray the others with a fungicide containing sulphur. The sulphur sprays are found to be better for rusts than copper sprays, but rusts are difficult to control. Repeat the spray according to weather conditions and the severity of infection. Spray susceptible plants with sulphur sprays at the beginning of the rainy season. Try to grow rust-resistant strains of plants whenever possible. Grow these plants well in good soil, a sunny situation, and water regularly. Grow susceptible plants like Snapdragons during the dry winter months in the summer rainfall area, for they are more prone to rust attack during the rainy period in summer.

DIE-BACK

One hears a great deal about Die-back on Roses. This is due to several reasons. Bad pruning generally causes die-back, while poor soil conditions, especially where roots are waterlogged in winter, encourage it. Some die-back is due to Canker, but die-back is also caused by several fungi. They are generally weak fungi that only attack plants and trees that are not growing vigorously or have been injured. The fungus *Cytospora* causes die-back on neglected Peach and Plum trees.

Control. Prune the dead branches off carefully to vigorous wood and paint the open cuts. Burn the prunings. Fertilize and water the tree in order to restore its vigour. If the tree is too misshapen and old it is probably better to replace it with a new one.

SOOTY MOULD (*Capnodium salicinum*)

This is a fungus disease which comes as a result of insect attack. It mainly affects citrus trees and is found in neglected orchards where the trees have not been tended.

One type of mould has also been found on apple trees in the eastern Cape. Insects like scale exude copious amounts of honeydew and the mould grows on this sticky substance. It will cover the plant with a black sooty coating and exclude sunlight, preventing food production from taking place in the green part of the plant. If sooty mould is unchecked, the plant will lose vigour and die.

Control. Sooty mould can be removed by washing off by hand or with a strong jet. Fruit can be washed off and eaten with safety. Spray with an insecticide like Malathion to kill the scale insects.

LEAF SPOT

Leaf spot diseases first appear as numerous, tiny, irregular, brownish spots on the leaves. These spread rapidly over leaves and stems, the spots grow larger and eventually the whole leaf turns brown and dies. Spores may ooze out of small black fruiting bodies on the leaves and spread the disease in wet weather.

These diseases spread mainly during wet seasons and in misty areas. They are caused by a number of fungi, such as *Septoria* species. These affect many garden flowers, such as Arum, Barberton Daisy, Shasta Daisy, Chrysanthemum (in the summer rainfall area), Pelargonium (in S.W. Cape) and vegetables such as beet, celery, tomato and lettuce. Other leaf-spot fungi often destroy carnations and iris in wet seasons and affect dahlias, cyclamen, gaillardia, iceland poppy, lupin (in S.W. Cape), primrose (on Witwatersrand), violet, strawberry, bean (in Natal), pea (called Leaf and Pod Spot), Hibiscus (in S.W. Cape), Wistaria and trees like Cherry, Mulberry, Protea, Silver Tree, Poplar and Lemon (especially in the mist belt where trees may become defoliated).

Control. One should not save one's own seed from infected plants, but purchase fresh seed. Copper sprays and the new organic fungicides are recommended for leaf spot and should be applied at the first sign of the disease. The susceptible plants mentioned above should be sprayed with a fungicide in the seedling stage if one lives in areas of high humidity. This protective spraying should be continued every fortnight during the growing season. This is particularly necessary in the summer rainfall area. Susceptible plants growing in the winter rainfall area should be sprayed during the winter months as well.

Burn all annual and perennial plants that have been infected and do not add these to the compost. Do not grow susceptible plants in the same spot in the following year.

PEACH LEAF-CURL (*Taphrina* species)

This is a fungus disease, also formerly known as Leaf Blister, which affects mainly Peach trees as well as Nectarines, Apricots and Poplar trees (in the western Cape and Natal). It follows certain moist climatic conditions. Long periods of wet weather while the new leaf buds are opening favour infection. The fungus penetrates the leaves soon after the buds unfold and they appear to be curled and blistered. The leaves become distorted and discoloured, turning yellow and red, sometimes with a bloom on the surface. These generally die and fall, and, if the wet weather persists, the second crop of leaves may be infected as well. Shoots may become stunted with a crowded rosette of twisted leaves and fruit may become scabbed, cracked, or bear disfiguring wrinkled, swollen areas.

Aphids feeding on leaves of peach trees often cause curling and distortion of the leaves and these can be destroyed by spraying promptly with nicotine sulphate or Malathion.

Control. Spray thoroughly with a fungicide like lime-sulphur, freshly made Bordeaux mixture or a copper-containing spray, as soon as the dormant buds begin to swell. If very thoroughly done, one spray should be sufficient, but it is probably best to spray again ten days later. Prune out obviously infected shoots when these are noticed. Pick up and burn all fallen leaves to prevent re-infection of new growth.

LEAF BLIGHT
(Late Blight, etc.)

Blight is a term used to describe the death of leaves from almost any cause. It is used mainly to describe particular diseases like Potato Leaf Blight, also known as Late Blight or Irish Blight, which is caused by the fungus *Phytophthora infestans*. It affects potatoes and tomatoes. Late Blight affects potatoes particularly in cold wet areas, such as the southern Cape and misty, mountainous areas of the northern Transvaal and Natal, but it also occurs on the highveld and in the Orange Free State.

The disease attacks tomatoes or potatoes any time after they have begun to grow, when black patches appear on the leaves and stems. During wet weather the leaf becomes white and downy beneath and the whole leaf is blackened rapidly. The plants may be killed in a few days. Tomato fruits may be infected on mature plants by developing greenish-brown, water-soaked areas which enlarge to cover the whole surface, turning brown. The surface becomes corrugated yet firm. Late Blight is particularly severe during autumn when the nights are colder. The fungus remains in diseased potato tubers and is carried over to the next season.

Different fungi cause Leaf Blight on Quinces, Carrots, Peas, and on Mulberry trees during wet seasons. Leaf and Flower Blight of *Mesembryanthemum* (Vygies) occurs on cultivated plants in the Cape.

Control. Late Blight of Tomatoes can be controlled by spraying the seedlings with a copper fungicide or one of the new organic fungicides like Zineb. Repeat this treatment regularly at 14-day intervals during the growing season, depending on the weather. Spray weekly during wet weather.

Late Blight of Potatoes can be arrested by spraying the shoots with a fungicide as soon as they emerge from the soil and at regular intervals thereafter, as with tomatoes. If infection develops in a small garden, dig out the tubers immediately, using whatever healthy tubers one can and destroying the others. All the diseased stems should be collected and burnt. Be careful to plant only healthy tubers or the disease will spread. Do not plant tomatoes in the same area which has formerly grown potatoes.

Annual plants like Peas should be treated like Tomatoes. It is best to take healthy cuttings of Mesembs before the disease spreads and to destroy the old plants. Plant them in a well-drained, sunny position. Removal of infected shoots, if it is noted quickly, together with the use of a fungicidal spray, may save the mature plant.

DAMPING-OFF FUNGI (*Pythium* and others)

Damping-off describes the collapse and death of seedlings caused by fungi, such as *Pythium*, entering the stem at ground level so that they fall over. This generally occurs when conditions are too wet and seedlings too overcrowded. Seedlings of stocks and tomatoes suffer from damping-off during hot weather and rainy conditions. Pine tree seedlings in the northern Transvaal have been known to damp off because of excessively moist conditions.

Control. Avoid overcrowding of seedlings in seedboxes and cover them when it rains so that they do not become too wet. They should not be watered while they are still wet. The seedlings can be watered with a weak fungicide if damping-off recurs repeatedly, but it is best to build a raised, perfectly drained seedbox with a fitted cover and to plant one's seed sparsely.

Spores of damping-off fungi remain in the soil, so that one should use sterilized soil for seed-raising if the trouble occurs in the following season. It is always best to change the soil each time one plants seeds.

WILT

Wilt normally describes the flagging of plant foliage due to lack of water, but this is not a disease and plants recover if they are watered immediately. Wilt, however, is also the name given to fungus disease which is closely associated in many ways with damping-off, for the plants also collapse and die. One of the same fungi (*Pythium*) that causes damping-off also causes the wilt of Pea plants in the eastern Transvaal.

Wilt often occurs where conditions for growth are unfavourable, such as too hot a soil for plants that prefer a cool soil. It is thought that the fungus is a weak parasite that only attacks when the plant vigour is lessened by poor conditions of growth. *Pythium* species cause Crown Rot or Wilt of Asters in hot soil and Foot or Stem Rot of Stapelia in rockeries. Wilt diseases of mature plants in this country are caused by other important fungi, such as *Fusarium*, *Rhizoctonia* and *Sclerotinia*. The fungus parasite enters the plant through the root or lower stem and spreads through the tissues, cutting off the food and water supply. The leaves at the growing point usually show signs of wilting first, then the older leaves commonly turn yellow and drop, while the plant becomes stunted. Infected plants may recover partially, but generally they collapse and die.

Fusarium Wilt Diseases are especially common on Tomatoes in the eastern Transvaal, where one is compelled to grow resistant varieties. Asparagus and Potato are also susceptible, particularly in hot soils. *Fusarium* wilt also affects garden flowers like Aster; Salpiglossis (in the Transvaal); Snapdragon and Sweet-pea, especially where soils are too warm; Carnations, especially in Natal and the eastern Transvaal, as well as fruits like Watermelon in the Transvaal and Cape.

Fusarium fungi also cause Rots such as Crown Rot of Iceland Poppy (especially with rising temperatures), Shirley Poppy, Stocks in warm soil, Statice (in the Transvaal) and Rhubarb; Crown, Stem and Root Rot of Carnations; Root Rot of Zinnia on the south coast and Root Rot of Lupin in the S.W. Cape.

Other Wilt fungi cause wilting of Delphinium, Sweet Sultan and Verbena (Transvaal), as well as Root Rot of Cornflower and many other plants in the eastern Transvaal and Cape.

Control. There is no cure for wilt, but practical measures can be taken to prevent the spread of the disease. Remove infected plants immediately and burn them. Do not add them to the compost. Practise rotation of crops and do not grow the same plant in the same soil for a period of at least three years. In theory the soil could be disinfected, but this is not really practical and it is better to grow other crops in the soil, to improve growing conditions or to avoid growing susceptible crops altogether. Do not use an excess of nitrogenous manure, as this tends to aggravate the disease. Make sure that you obtain healthy tubers and seedlings for planting in the garden.

ANTHRACNOSE (RIPE ROT)

This describes a group of widespread and common fungus diseases which cause dark sunken areas where the fungus grows in the tissues of plants. Anthracnose affects Papaw, Guava, Banana and Mango, causing the fruit to rot. It may affect Walnuts. It is common on cucurbits and beans. The fungi attack mainly after rains, especially when rain falls out of season.

Control. As these diseases affect commercial fruit-growers mainly, they are not really a gardener's problem. There is no real cure and it is too unpractical for the gardener to spray large trees thoroughly in the hope of preventing the disease. In areas where such trees are prone to the disease, it is best to avoid growing them. Grape vines can be sprayed regularly with a copper fungicide in order to combat the disease in areas where it is prevalent, but this has not been proved conclusively. Small annual crops like beans should be destroyed if they are attacked by anthracnose. As this disease develops during moist periods, there is little one can do to prevent its advent. Correct methods of cultivation on sunny, well-drained soil will be the best preventative.

FUSICLADIUM DISEASE OF APPLES AND PEARS

This fungus disease is also known as Scab or, in other countries, as Black Spot of Apples. It occurs mainly in the fruit-growing districts of the south-western Cape.

Control. This is a disease of commercial importance and requires an intensive spraying programme, advised by the local Department of Agriculture. Several fungicides are used in the control of this disease, including the new organic fungicides like Thiram.

FUNGUS DISEASES ON LAWN

Brown Patch. Lawns are often troubled during summer by large, irregular brown patches, indicating dying grass, which appear almost overnight in some cases. This is thought to be a result of the fungus *Rhizoctonia*. The fungus attack comes as a result of wet soil and poor drainage. This may happen when a lawn is heavily watered during its normally dormant period. If the brown patch is caused by a fungus then one must first

improve the aeration of the soil by spiking it with a hollow-tined fork and brushing in sand. The affected portions can then be watered with a fixed copper fungicide, Captan or mercurial fungicides. The latter are very poisonous, so that they should be used with great care.

Brown patch is not always caused by a fungus, however, and is more often the result of too little water or an uneven water supply. The use of nitrogenous fertilizers which promote growth aggravates brown patch if the lawn is not cut regularly and frequently. (See under Lawns, Chapter 24.)

Dollar Spot. Small round, whitish patches may appear on lawns during late summer as a result of fungus disease. It is not common, but occurs on compacted soil with poor drainage which becomes very wet during rainy weather. Treat as for Brown Patch.

BACTERIAL DISEASES

Bacteria are microscopic organisms that are distributed mainly by water, insects, animals and man. They multiply rapidly by cell division and bring about decay in organic substances, playing a part in the making of humus. There are not many bacterial diseases of plants and this is fortunate since there is nothing to be done but to destroy diseased plants.

Bacteria can overrun a plant within a matter of hours, causing death and decay. Such diseases are Bacterial Wilt and Bacterial Blight (Fire blight or Vlamsiekte), which affect a few plants of commercial importance in this country. When plants like Tomato, Potato or Brinjal wilt suddenly and appear blackened and decayed, they may suffer from a Bacterial Wilt and should be pulled out and burnt immediately. In the case of Grape Vines which may be attacked by Bacterial Blight in the Western Province, the twigs at the tips become blackened and look as if they have been scorched by fire. One should immediately notify the local Department of Agriculture which will adopt quarantine measures.

CROWN GALL

This is possibly the best known and most easily recognised bacterial disease that occurs in the garden. It is caused by *Bacterium tumefaciens*, which causes tumours or globular swellings on the roots or on the trunk near the base of trees and shrubs like Roses, Almond, Cherry, Nectarine, Peach, Apricots on Peach Stock, Pear, Pecan, Poplar, Quince, Walnut and, occasionally, on Grape Vines, Apples and Blackberries in the winter rainfall area. The bacteria gain entrance to the tree through wounds in the bark. The tissues are not killed, but become irritated and abnormally large, forming a gnarled ugly mass called a "gall". It later resembles a cauliflower. As a result, growth may be retarded, foliage turns yellow, roots and branches may die and trees may die altogether.

Control. Prevention is the only method of control. Inspect new trees on receipt from the nursery for signs of galls or swellings on the stems or roots and do not plant them in your garden. Avoid wounding tender bark on new trees by scraping it with the lawnmower or when cultivating the soil around the roots.

Crown gall is not as destructive in the garden as it was once thought to be and it is not necessary to uproot a tree suffering from the disease unless it shows signs of dying. If a rose bush, for example, dies and is found to have a large gall at the crown, then one must dig out and replace the soil with fresh soil, as the bacteria live in the soil for several years and might infect the new rose bush. The disease is more likely to spread on wet soils.

Do not confuse crown gall with burls or insect galls.

Burls or Burr knots occur on Apple trees and other trees as a result of wounding. Swellings appear on the trunk, often near the bottom or even on the larger branches, and the twisted grain which develops inside is valued by cabinet makers. Burls are not harmful.

Insect galls are also not destructive to the tree although they look unsightly. Insects like chalcids pierce leaves or twigs and lay their eggs inside. The tissues grow over this intrusion and become enlarged, forming a globular swelling or gall which increases in size as the larva hatches and develops. Eventually the insect breaks open the gall, emerges and flies away. The insect simply uses the tree as a protection for its young, but does not kill the tree. Eventually the tree may die as a result of having too many galls on it, but there is no point in cutting down or pruning back the tree for these insect galls cannot infect other trees. It is impossible to spray the trees in order to prevent the insects from laying eggs and, once the egg is inside, spraying is ineffective. One must simply regard insect galls as harmless and ignore them. They are common on Willow trees.

Galls on trees are sometimes referred to as **cankers,** but a canker is a sunken area on a branch, often bleeding but sometimes dry. A canker interferes with the food supply to the tissues, causing the wilting and death of the branch. Cankers on tree trunks will cause the whole top to wilt and die back. Fungi causing cankers enter through old stubs, cavities, split branches and unpainted pruning cuts.

Cankers are not common on trees in South Africa. Many wounds made carelessly on trees by children will rot and so become cankers. The whole tree must be destroyed if the disease is severe. Otherwise, affected branches can be cut off and burned. The cankers can be cut out and the area painted with Bordeaux paste or other fungicide.

VIRUS DISEASES

Viruses are so tiny that they cannot be seen under a microscope, so that we mainly know them by the harm they do. Healthy plants are infected with virus diseases by means of insects, chiefly aphids, which have visited diseased plants and inoculate the healthy ones while sucking out the sap. One can spread a virus disease by handling or cutting an infected plant and then touching a healthy one without washing the hands or sterilising the knife. Many virus diseases are spread during budding or grafting.

Virus diseases usually show up as a discoloration of the leaves in various types of chlorosis, meaning yellowing of the leaves. Streak virus diseases show stripes on the leaves and even on flowers. Some do not affect the vigour of the plant and have led to interesting "breaks" in tulips. The best-known virus diseases are, possibly, the Mosaics, showing mottled leaves which may be accompanied by distortion. Spotted Wilt virus is an important virus disease of tomatoes. Virus diseases do not always kill the plant quickly, but it becomes weaker and weaker, a perennial sometimes lasting for several years, while it acts as a source of infection for other plants.

Control of Virus Diseases. An infected plant cannot be cured, so that it must be destroyed as soon as the virus disease is noticed. Spraying against insect pests like aphids will help to prevent the spread of diseases like Mosaic and others.

CHAPTER THIRTY-NINE

CHEMICALS USED IN PLANT PROTECTION

The following chemicals are in use today as insecticides and fungicides, although some are making way for others. If a gardener finds that an old-fashioned remedy that he has used for years is still effective, then he will not want to change to the latest discovery, even though it has been proved to give better results. Many of the chemicals will kill the same insects, so that it may simply be a matter of convenience to use whatever one has in one's spray cupboard.

The word Compatibility appears at the end of each chemical described. This does not only mean that the suggested chemicals can be mixed together in a receptacle without losing their identity, but also that they will not cause spray injury to the plant if applied within a short time after one another.

As a general rule, it is not advisable to mix together the chemicals used in plant protection. Spraying with fungicides goes on constantly as a preventative, while one only sprays for insects when these are seen. It is wasteful, therefore, to incorporate an insecticide with a fungicide, except on special occasions. To do this once or twice in a season may be considered a time-saver by some, but it requires more trouble in mixing and is not economical. To do this as a matter of course is a complete waste of money. Combination sprays can be purchased ready-made and may be used by the inexperienced gardener, but these are not necessarily cure-alls and their active ingredients should be noted.

Some chemicals enhance each other if they are mixed together, such as nicotine sulphate and lime sulphur. Lead arsenate is less injurious to plant foliage if combined with Bordeaux mixture. Malathion is more effective when mixed together with Parathion for the control of soft scale in citrus. This is a specialised study, however, and its use is more for the farmer than for the gardener, so that one cannot generalise.

Haphazard mixtures of two chemicals may ruin the efficacy of one or both of these, while some mixtures may even cause plant injury and burning of foliage or browning of fruit. Some spray materials form poisonous substances which injure plants. If sulphur is mixed with summer oils, for example, a toxic sulphur compound is produced. A wetting agent or spreader normally used with one ingredient may cause excessive penetration of the second.

It is best to treat each insect on its own and spray it with the easiest and quickest means at one's disposal. Fungus diseases must be understood and sprayed with fungicides as a preventative only if the disease is not incurable.

Study the attributes of the chemicals described below. Note whether some sprays are best used in the hottest part of the day, like nicotine sulphate, or whether they should be used during cooler conditions for fear of causing spray injury. A spray designed for the dormant period will injure the buds once they have begun to swell or unfold. Some chemicals should not be sprayed on to foliage which is wet with dew, or when conditions are humid, or there may be excessive penetration and plant injury. Avoid spraying on extremely hot sunny days or on windy days. Always use the chemicals in the amounts specified by the manufacturer. An increase in dosage may damage the plants.

A summary in table form will follow at the end of this chapter as a guide to the gardener who has already read this and the preceding chapters on insect pests and diseases.

I. INSECTICIDES
FOR THE CONTROL OF GARDEN PESTS

ARSENATE OF LEAD

Until recent years, lead arsenate has been one of the most commonly used stomach poisons for chewing insects. It has been largely superseded by DDT or other modern chemicals and is considered outmoded, but can be used on occasion.

Arsenate of lead is highly poisonous and should be kept locked away. It should not be used where there is any danger of children chewing leaves sprayed with it. Lead arsenate can be used mainly on ornamental shrubs and trees when beetles or caterpillars are active. It must not be used on edible crops within a month of harvesting and is not recommended for use on citrus trees or it may destroy the acid content of the fruit. It is no longer used as a bait for fruit-fly. It may be used as a bait for termites (white ants), but Sodium fluosilicate is better.

Arsenate of lead has one advantage over DDT in that it kills only the harmful insect that chews the leaves and not the beneficial insect like a ladybird which may be present. The disadvantage of arsenical sprays is that they are cumulative and build up residues in the soil or wherever they fall.

Compatibility. Arsenate of lead can be mixed with lime sulphur.

CALCIUM ARSENATE

This powder is not used much today, as arsenical sprays are not generally recommended. Its chief use is as a repellant against Wood-eating Termites. It may be watered in around young ornamental trees and shrubs or on to lawns. Only one application is required. DDT 5 per cent dust is as effective and not so poisonous.

PARIS GREEN

This is no longer used as an insecticide as it is a highly poisonous arsenical compound and causes plant injury. It may be prepared as a bait for cutworms.

METALDEHYDE
(Trade names, Meta, Sluggem Pellets, Snail Bait).

Metaldehyde is the best remedy for slugs and snails. It is supplied in tablet or powder form and is mixed with bran or mealie-meal to make a bait, which can also be bought ready mixed. It should be slightly moistened or applied to moist soil after rain or watering. It may be placed under an overturned broken flower pot or a tin so as to keep its efficacy during rainy weather, as it dissolves easily.

LIME SULPHUR

This is really a fungicide, but can also be used as a contact insecticide in order to kill scale insects, particularly white peach scale. It is used in winter on dormant fruit trees and rose bushes and is commonly known as a cleansing spray. Lime sulphur helps to keep down mites on fruit trees, like Bryobia Mite, as well as citrus mites, if used at three-quarter petal drop and again ten days later. Lime sulphur also acts on fungus spores in winter. It should not be used in hot weather as it may injure foliage.

Compatibility. Do not mix Lime sulphur with Bordeaux Mixture or other copper compounds or with Malathion. It can be used together with DDT powder, arsenate of lead, nicotine sulphate and wettable sulphur.

SODIUM FLUOSILICATE

This is a stomach insecticide which is recommended for killing Fruit-fly, Pumpkin or Melon fly, Harvester Termites and Cutworms. It is a very effective poisonous dust which must be prepared as a solid bait or a baited spray. Avoid inhaling the dust while mixing and store, labelled, in a locked cupboard.

To control and attract Fruit-fly or Melon-fly, mix Sodium fluosilicate with sugar and water and spray it as a coarse droplet spray on to the foliage of fruit trees or on to the leaves of Marrows, Cucumbers, Melon or Pumpkin. Spraying should cease three to four weeks before harvesting.

As a bait for cutworms, Sodium fluosilicate must be mixed with sugar and chopped green vegetables such as cabbage. Sprinkle this bait on to seedling beds at sunset or even on to bare soil before planting seedlings. Keep pets away from this as it is poisonous.

To eradicate Harvester Termites, mix $\frac{1}{2}$-inch-long grass cuttings into a solution of Sodium fluosilicate and water, drain, dry and scatter over lawns where termites are working. (See under Termites, Chapter 37.) Prepare sufficient bait for immediate use and try not to keep it for more than a week or two.

CARBAMATES

These fall into the intermediate group of poisons and are fairly safe to use.

CARBARYL
(Trade name: Sevin)

This has a wide scope and is recommended for the control of Codling Moth, Cotton Aphid, Leafrollers on deciduous fruit, especially in late summer, Pear Bud Mite, Army Worm, Maize Chafer Beetle and Maize Stalk Borer.

MESUROL

This is of especial use to farmers and is used as a cover spray for Codling Moth, Long-tailed Mealybugs and Vine Mealybugs.

ACARICIDES

These are chemicals used especially for the control of mites. They are sometimes called miticides.

KELTHANE

This chemical is an acaricide recommended for the control of Red Spider Mite, Bryobia Mite and Red Citrus Mite on deciduous fruit trees and citrus trees. It is a conventional contact insecticide. Kelthane must not be used on edible crops within one week of harvesting. It is fairly safe to handle but contact and inhalation should be avoided.

Compatibility. Kelthane can be combined with most insecticides and fungicides, but not with Lime Sulphur.

One can add a wetting agent to enable it to spread further and adhere to the plant.

Ovotran

(Trade names, Ovotran and Ovex.)

This is an acaricide which can be used at any time, summer or winter, to kill the eggs of mites.

Acricid

This is recommended for Citrus Red Mite, Brobia Mite on deciduous fruit—peaches, apples and pears—and Red Spider on apples only.

Tedion

This is used for Red Spider on deciduous fruit, ornamental shrubs and cotton, as well as on Citrus Red Mite.

OILS

Oils for garden use are refined petroleum oils. Summer oils or "white" oils are light emulsions while winter oils or "red" oils are denser and have a greater sticking powder. Oils are used to destroy aphids, scale insects and mites (as well as their eggs) by suffocating them with a fine covering film. Although they are safe to handle, the need for oils in the garden is somewhat redundant in view of the many insecticides available to kill these pests.

Summer Oils

(Trade name: Alboleum.)

Summer oil can be applied to citrus and evergreen trees preferably in the cool part of the day. Do not spray citrus trees in flower, but only when the fruit is the size of a walnut. Cease spraying two months before harvest. Summer oils are no longer recommended on deciduous fruit trees by the Department of Agriculture.

Compatibility. Summer oils must never be mixed with a sulphur spray or they will cause severe fruit and foliage injury. If sulphur sprays have been used, wait ten days before spraying with summer oil. Summer oils can be mixed with nicotine sulphate (especially for soft brown scale), Bordeaux mixture, DDT, arsenate of lead or Parathion.

Winter Oil

(Trade names: Pestridol, Capsine.)

Winter oils are recommended for winter use on Apples and Pear trees in order to correct delayed foliation. The addition of D.N.O.C. (dinitro compounds, as in Capsine) improves its efficiency in this direction, but one must use protective clothing while using it. Winter oils may also be used on ornamental deciduous shrubs, but are not recommended on Peach trees or Citrus.

Compatibility. Winter oils must not be combined with Lime Sulphur or Bordeaux Mixture. Sulphur should not be used on the trees until two or three weeks after spraying with winter oils.

PLANT EXTRACTS

Nicotine Sulphate

This is a very poisonous liquid derived from tobacco leaves and is also obtainable in dust form, called nicotine dust. Although poisonous to human beings, it is easy to handle and has been popular for many years. It is an effective contact poison against aphids and can be used in combination with summer oil against soft brown scale.

Nicotine sulphate is not always recommended as its effects are dissipated in a few hours. It must actually hit the insect to be effective. Many modern insecticides have longer residual qualities and are used in preference, particularly as some are effective against scale and other insects at the same time. Unless one wishes only to destroy aphids, nicotine sulphate may be redundant. It is not used very often.

Nicotine sulphate must be mixed with soft soap as a spreader and must wet the plant thoroughly. The mixture becomes volatile and asphyxiates the insect by entering its body openings as a gas. This is aided by high temperatures, so that nicotine sulphate spray should be used in the heat of the day and on calm days. It is not so effective on cold days. It can be used in hot-houses with good effect.

Nicotine sulphate is harmless to plants but should not be used on tomatoes and potatoes. It can be absorbed through the skin in enclosed spaces and a respirator and protective clothing should then be worn. Cease spraying within two days of harvesting edible crops.

Compatibility. Nicotine sulphate can be mixed with all commonly used insecticides and fungicides. The soft soap, however, is not always compatible with other sprays.

Derris

(Trade names: Katakilla and Cubor Derris.)

This is a chemical found in a plant root (*Derris elliptica*). The insecticide is made by grinding the root into a powder which is used as a dust or a wettable powder. It is safe to use and does not cause plant injury. This is a stomach and contact insecticide which is used mainly for caterpillars.

Derris is not very popular nowadays as it acts slowly and must be repeated at weekly intervals until the pests have disappeared. It has been replaced by numerous modern insecticides.

Rotenone

This is the same as Derris and not used much in this country.

PYRETHRUM

This is the dust ground from the flower of *Chrysanthemum cinerariaefolium*. It needs an activator to enhance its value. Pyrethrum is a contact poison used in the garden to kill aphids, but it is more generally used for house flies. It has little residual value in the garden and must be kept in an airtight container. It is usually harmless and non-irritating to the skin. Pyrethrin i and ii are the active principles of Pyrethrum.

CHLORINATED HYDROCARBONS

These are modern insecticides which are very poisonous, but also very effective.

DDT

This is a powerful contact and stomach insecticide which is used to kill many types of garden insects, including caterpillars, thrips, stinkbugs, Chafer Beetles, Gladiolus Fly and Codling Moth. DDT will not kill all aphids, mites or scale insects. It is available as an insoluble dusting powder of different strengths (at $2\frac{1}{2}$ per cent, 5 per cent or 10 per cent), as a 50 per cent wettable powder which can be made into a liquid spray and also as an oil emulsion. (Trade names of emulsions are Birsol, Sillortox DDT emulsion, DDT-Sol and Grenade E.27 Emulsion, etc.) DDT powder is packed under several trade names by different firms, but the strength always appears on the labels. The dusts and wettable powder are comparatively simple to handle, but are poisonous and one must wash carefully after use and not inhale the dust.

Two and a half per cent DDT dust is used mainly to place in leaf funnels of young mealie plants against Maize Stalk Borer and to dust on Tomatoes before the setting of the fruit as a protection against Bollworm, or the tomato caterpillar. Five per cent DDT dust and 10 per cent DDT dust will kill thrips, many beetles, stinkbugs, larvae of moths and butterflies, as well as soil pests like ants, grubs, and cutworms. Dusting should be done on calm, dry days, preferably in the early morning or late evening. The dust can be mixed and worked into the soil for soil pests. It will discourage Wood-eating Termites. DDT wettable powder does the same work but lasts a little longer than the powder and penetrates more evenly. It is used in a spray programme for Codling Moth.

DDT dusts and sprays must not be used on members of the cucumber family (Cucurbits) or they will burn the foliage. It should not be used on Cabbages after the heads have formed, nor on Tomatoes after the fruit has set. Spraying must cease on edible crops within 30 days of harvesting. Never spray plants in flower with DDT or bees will be killed. DDT will not kill mites but the insects which feed on them, so that excessive use of DDT may cause mite infestation. Its use on apple trees against Codling Moth kills the parasite (*Aphelinus mali*), that feeds on the woolly apple aphid, and causes this to become a pest. DDT is not recommended as a spray on citrus trees as it kills ladybirds which feed on aphids.

Compatibility. DDT may be mixed with most insecticides and fungicides, but not with hydrated lime and other alkaline materials. It should not be mixed with lime-sulphur or Bordeaux mixture.

DDD (or TDE)
(Trade name: Rothane.)

This is similar to DDT and can be used as an alternative, but is not as widely used. It is less toxic, but must also not be used on crops within 30 days of harvest.

BHC

Available as dust or wettable powder, this chemical is used in much the same way as DDT and controls many of the same insects. It may be combined with DDT in proprietary insecticides, such as Aldet, Koperin and Pyagra Garden Insect Dust. BHC attacks aphids, caterpillars, thrips, white flies, bugs, beetles, white grubs, and repels termites on lawns. It can be used as a soil treatment for wireworms and may be watered into the soil against ordinary ants. It is sprayed on crickets and grasshoppers and is more effective than DDT for control of the latter. A light dressing of BHC can be mixed with maize seed to prevent attack on the germinating maize by the Maize beetle.

Too much BHC in the soil can retard growth. It is not recommended for edible crops, particularly root vegetables, for it has a musty odour which lingers and taints the harvest. It can even taint apples when sprayed on to the foliage, so that these trees must be sprayed with BHC only in the dormant season. Like DDT, it should not be applied to cucurbits. It must not be used on cabbages after the heads have formed. Do not use on edible crops within a month of harvest. Wash well after using BHC spray.

Compatibility. BHC can be mixed with most insecticides and fungicides, but not with hydrated lime or other alkaline materials.

LINDANE

This is a purified form of BHC, known as the pure gamma isomer of BHC. It attacks the same insects. It is said not to taint edible crops and can be applied up to one month of harvesting. Lindane is just as safe as BHC and DDT in handling. Wash well after use. Lindane dust (available as Terralind) can be used as a soil treatment on vegetable or flower beds by working into the topsoil to repel cutworms, white grubs, wireworms and soil beetles. It is obtainable as an oil emulsion (Lindane 20 M or Lindasol) to control aphids, thrip, beetles, stinkbugs, white flies and grasshoppers. It can be used on vegetables, but not on Cabbages after the heads have formed and it is best to avoid using it on root crops.

Compatibility. It can be combined with other insecticides and fungicides in the same way as BHC.

CHLORDANE

This is a stomach and contact poison which is mainly used as a soil poison against ants, termites and soil pests and will also kill lawn caterpillars. As a general insecticide it acts more slowly than BHC or DDT.

RHOTHANE

This is an intermediate poison, recommended for Leaf-rollers on deciduous fruit, C.M.R. Beetles, Bagrada Bug and American Bollworm on tomatoes only.

TOXAPHENE

This is quite a commonly used chlorinated hydrocarbon. It is generally used for the same purposes as DDT, which is more widely used, and is about as toxic, although it acts more slowly. It is recommended for C.M.R. Beetles, Bagrada Bug and American Bollworm. It is not suitable for Cucurbits or Peach trees. It can be sprayed on to the surface of the soil and the base of seedlings to kill cutworms.

METHOXYCHLOR

This chlorinated hydrocarbon is less effective than DDT against certain pests, but is safer to handle. Its use may be recommended on vegetable crops.

THIODAN

This is an intermediate poison packed by several firms and is a chlorinated sulphur compound with a wide range. It is recommended for Aphids, Thrips, Citrus Psylla—when new leaves appear—Army Worm, American Bollworm, Maize Stalk Borer, Orange Dog Caterpillar on Citrus and on Cutworms as a bait.

DIELDRIN

This is a highly poisonous chlorinated hydrocarbon which is especially useful for the control of ants and cutworm. It is incorporated into dieldrin-containing insecticides with trade names such as Kynadrin, Ludrex, Killdrin and Agricol. It can be obtained as a wettable powder or as an emulsion. Dieldrin is a stomach and contact insecticide with residual properties, which is very poisonous to fish and mammals. It must not be used on edible crops except when these are seedlings. Dieldrin is used mainly as a soil poison or as a bait.

It can be used as a soil treatment in the garden for controlling cutworm or grubs. The easiest way to use it is to mix the wettable powder (1 oz. to a gallon of water = 4 lb. per acre) in a watering can and water it on to the soil before planting. This mixture can also be sprayed on to the stems of seedlings which have been planted out in spring. The powder can be worked or watered into the soil against soil pests like white grubs and cutworms. Maize seed can be dusted with dieldrin to prevent damage by beetles before germination where these pests are prevalent.

Dieldrin will destroy red or black garden ants. This helps to keep down aphids, scale and mealybugs which are encouraged by ants. It can be watered into the soil around rose trees and fruit trees or vines, or it can be mixed with soil and spread on to the surface. It may not be necessary to repeat this treatment for three years. The wettable powder will not injure plants while the emulsion might burn foliage like grass, so that it is best to use the powder when watering the lawn with dieldrin. It is better to err on the side of a too weak rather than a too strong solution. Mix 1 oz. wettable powder to 1 or 2 gallons of water.

Dieldrin can be made into a cutworm bait by mixing it with mealie-meal and water to make a porridge. This can be scattered between seedlings at sunset. As it may retain its efficacy for three weeks, it should not be used in this way where there is a danger of children, pets or chickens finding and eating it.

Great care should be exercised while preparing or using insecticides containing dieldrin. It is not necessary to wear a respirator, but overalls and rubber gloves should be worn. Dieldrin can be absorbed into the skin and should be washed off immediately if it comes in contact with the skin.

Compatibility. Dieldrin may be mixed with all commonly used insecticides and fungicides.

ENDRIN

This chemical is closely related to dieldrin, but is more toxic. It is also more effective and used chiefly by farmers for Maize Stalk Borer, Army Worm and Cotton Bollworm.

ALDRIN

This is also a wettable powder closely related to dieldrin, which has a shorter residual effect. It is a soil insecticide used by farmers on tobacco crops. It kills specific Harvester Termites, such as the Karoo and Snouted types, and Crickets.

ORGANIC PHOSPHORUS COMPOUNDS

MERCAPTOTHION

(*O, O,-dimethyl dithiophosphate of diethyl mercaptosuccinate*)

(Trade names are Malathion, Kilpest, Pesthion, Datathion, Malatox and others.)

This modern chemical is used to kill the majority of insects in the garden, both sucking and chewing, particularly Aphids, Mealybugs, Mites (Red Spider and Bryobia), Thrip, Citrus Psylla, Soft Brown Scale and Red Scale. It may also be made into a bait with sugar to kill Fruit-Fly and Pumpkin or Melon Fly. It is also used for Army Worm, C.M.R. Beetles and Grasshoppers. It may be used on ants by pouring down ant holes or spraying the soil around these, but only has a residual effect of two to three days.

Malathion can be applied to citrus trees, deciduous fruit trees and vegetables, but not within seven days of harvesting. (Plums may be sprayed within three days of harvest, but Citrus should not be harvested until 10 days after spraying.) Malathion should not be applied to Cucurbits, unless the plants are dry, or to potatoes. It is not recommended for ferns and some succulents like Crassula, but the wettable powder can be used for scale on Aloes.

This is one of the least poisonous of the organic phosphorus compounds and is available as a wettable powder (25 per cent), an emulsified liquid (50 per cent) or a 5 per cent dust. It must be handled with care although protective clothing need not be worn while using it. Avoid skin contact or inhalation and wash thoroughly after use. Store in a safe place out of the reach of children.

Compatibility. Malathion can be mixed with most insecticides and fungicides, but not with Bordeaux mixture, mercurials or lime sulphur.

DIPTEREX (A form of Tugon).

This organic phosphorus compound is more toxic than Malathion, but is still fairly safe to handle and protective clothing need not be worn while using it. It is a wettable powder which is used mainly as a bait for Fruit-Fly, mixed with sugar and water. Cease spraying one week before harvest. Dipterex can be mixed with water without sugar and used as a weekly spray to control Carnation Bud Fly.

DIAZINON

A residual contact and stomach poison, this is also one of the organic phosphorus compounds, more toxic than either Malathion or Dipterex, but not as dangerous as Parathion. Protective clothing should be worn when using it.

It is useful to farmers and is used mainly for aphids and mites, including Red Spider and Bryobia, as well as for Army Worm. Diazinon is available as a wettable powder or as an emulsion. Edible crops should not be sprayed within a fortnight of harvesting. It should not be used for tomatoes or potatoes.

PARATHION

(Trade names: Thiophos, Folidol E.605, Fosferno, Paraphos and Luphos.)

This highly poisonous organic phosphorus compound is a contact insecticide with residual properties lasting from two to four days. It controls a wide range of insects and mites.

This chemical must be handled with extreme caution wearing protective overalls, boots, a proper respirator (not a handkerchief around the mouth and nose), eye-shields and rubber gloves. It is readily absorbed through the skin and exposure to the fumes and spray mist can cause serious illness, if not death. Several deaths have already occurred through careless handling. This poison is extremely useful to the farmer who has the facilities to use it properly and it is not recommended for the home gardener, particularly as Malathion controls the same pests and is safer to handle. Parathion must not be used on Cucurbits, Tomatoes or Potatoes and one must cease spraying edible crops three weeks before harvesting.

Compatibility. It is compatible with most sprays.

GUSATHION

This very poisonous chemical is useful for the control of soft brown scale on citrus and may also be used for red spider, aphids and codling moth. Mix with Parathion for the control of Red Scale. It should not be applied within three weeks of harvest. Protective clothing must be worn while using it and one should observe the same precautions as when using Parathion. It is recommended for farmers rather than for the home gardener.

HETP AND TEPP

These are highly toxic organic phosphorus compounds in the same class as Parathion. Although crops may be harvested 48 hours after using the sprays, the operator must be just as careful in handling them. These chemical are, therefore, not recommended for the home gardener. Their use requires specialised knowledge, for they cause injury to the foliage of some plants.

LEBAYCID

This organic phosphate is used as a full cover spray for the control of Fruit-Fly on peaches, apples and plums, as well as on sub-tropical fruits. It is an improvement on the chemicals which have to be mixed with a protein bait as it is prepared more easily and may be used less frequently. Three applications are considered sufficient for use on

Fruit-Fly in the home garden. Use 1 tablespoon to 4 gallons of water. Apply the first spray about 7 weeks before the fruit ripens, the second 4 weeks and the third 1 week before harvesting. The fruit may be eaten 7 days after spraying.

Lebaycid is also used for Pumpkin Fly, for Aphids on Cucurbits, on Woolly Apple Aphid and on Bryobia Mite. The emulsion is used for Codling Moth on apricots only and the wettable powder on Codling Moth on apples and pears. Lebaycid is an intermediate poison, but normal precautions should be taken when using it.

DISYSTON

This is a highly poisonous chemical, mainly of use to farmers, and it is not recommended for home gardens. Its special value is that it is recommended for Gladiolus Fly and Gladiolus Thrip. It is also used against Aphids on cabbages and potatoes.

PHORATE

This is used for Aphids on cabbage, cauliflower and potatoes. Although used for the same purpose as Disyston, it is not recommended for Gladiolus Fly or Thrip.

VAMIDOTHION

This organic phosphorus compound is used as a specific poison for the Woolly Apple Aphid.

SYSTEMIC INSECTICIDES

These are new insecticides which are absorbed through the leaves and roots of the plant into the sap. The whole plant becomes poisonous for about three weeks and any aphids or mites (including red spider) which suck the juices will be killed during this period. These systemic insecticides only affect the smaller sucking insects, but as the many types of aphids and red spider are among the chief garden pests and carriers of virus diseases, they are valuable. They have the advantage of being more selective in action and less harmful to the beneficial insects than many other insecticides. It is always best not to spray blossom while it is being visited by bees. Whereas nicotine sulphate must actually hit the aphids, the systemic insecticide remains effective for about three weeks and one application may be sufficient to control the pest in the garden for the remainder of the season.

Unfortunately, most systemic insecticides are dangerous to the operator when spraying, for they can be absorbed into the bloodstream if they contact the skin. In general, fully protective clothing should be worn, as well as a respirator, face shield and rubber gloves. Systemic insecticides can be watered on to the soil at the base of ornamental plants so that they are absorbed by the roots. This makes them safer and easier to handle. Do not use them in this way on edible crops because of the danger of residues.

There are several systemic insecticides, some so dangerous that they are not recommended in the home garden, such as Systox and Schradan (Pestox 3 and O.M.P.A.). Metasystox, Ekatin and Rogor E are regarded as much safer, especially the latter.

METASYSTOX (Previously called Metaisosystox)

This systemic insecticide is packed by several firms and produced as an emulsion. It is also sold as "Metasystox i". It attacks aphids and mites, including Red Spider and Bryobia, penetrating by absorption and being effective for three weeks.

Metasystox must be used with care, wearing a face shield while mixing, but it is not necessary to wear a respirator or special clothing while spraying with it. Do not spray on a windy day or allow the wind to waft the spray on to the operator. Wash immediately if any is spilt on the skin. Metasystox is recommended for use on deciduous fruit trees, roses, carnations and ornamental plants. Up to the present time its use has been registered on the following vegetables: Potatoes, Cabbage, Cauliflower, Beans and Brussels Sprouts. Further tests on vegetables are being made. Spraying with Metasystox must not be done within four weeks of harvesting edible crops.

Compatibility. Metasystox can be mixed with DDT, fixed coppers and carbamates (protective fungicides), but not with Bordeaux mixture, captan, lime sulphur or any deficiency spray containing lime.

ROGOR E (Previously called Rogor 40)

Regarded as one of the safest of the systemic insecticides, this is recommended for Aphids, especially on beans, cabbage and cauliflower; cucurbits, deciduous fruit trees and strawberries, but must not be used on *Begonia, Chrysanthemum, Ficus, Lagerstroemia* (Pride of India) or *Zinnia*. It is also used as a cover spray for Red Spider on strawberries and other plants, as well as on Bryobia Mite.

It is used with Parathion on Red Scale on Citrus trees and on Citrus Psylla, but not when the lemons are formed or on rough lemons. It is also recommended for Circular Purple Scale on Citrus. Rogor E is used as a cover spray on Fruit-Fly, and may be used with a protein bait against Fruit-Fly on deciduous fruit. It is recommended against Long-tailed Mealybugs and assists in Codling Moth control.

EKATIN

This is used as a full cover spray for Aphids on peaches, cabbages and beans, as well as for Red Spider.

FORMOTHION

(Trade name: Anthio.)

This systemic insecticide is used for Red Spider.

SOIL FUMIGANTS

D.D. and E.D.B., (also packed as Terrafume).

These are liquids which are inserted into the soil and vaporise upwards into a gas which destroys eelworm, especially the Root knot eelworm. Once the crop has been infested it cannot be saved, so that the use of soil fumigants is a preventative measure.

They must be administered to bare soil at least two weeks before planting, as they are toxic to plant life. They should be applied to the soil with the aid of an injector gun. Although not ideal, they can also be poured through a funnel into a hole drilled in the soil with a rod. (See under Eelworm in Chapter 37 on Insect Control.)

Soil fumigants must be handled with care as they are toxic to humans and animals. Avoid skin contact and wear an eye shield and respirator if possible. Do not inhale the fumes. Wash immediately with soap and water if the chemicals are spilt on to skin or clothing.

Compatibility. Soil fumigants are not used in combination with any other chemical.

D.B.C.P.

This is recommended for Banana Eelworm, applied to irrigation water. It is not fully tested on Citrus Nematode.

II. FUNGICIDES
FOR THE CONTROL OF FUNGUS DISEASES

SULPHUR FUNGICIDES

SULPHUR

This is a yellow powder which can be used as a dust, commonly called dusting sulphur, or as a wettable powder in suspension for spraying. Colloidal sulphur is sulphur in a very fine form and is available under various proprietary brands.

Sulphur is used as a protective fungicide, mainly against powdery mildew and rust. Sulphur tends to cause burning of foliage during very hot weather and should be dusted on very thinly at such periods.

LIME-SULPHUR

Lime-sulphur is used both as an insecticide to control scale on dormant, deciduous trees and roses and as a fungicide. It will destroy all overwintering disease spores. It should be sprayed on when the buds first begin to swell during winter. Lime-sulphur may be spoilt on exposure to air and should be used within two hours after mixing with water.

Compatibility. Lime-sulphur is safe to handle, but may cause plant injury if it is mixed with oil sprays, Bordeaux mixture or copper sprays. It may be mixed with nicotine sulphate or wettable sulphur powder. It can also be mixed at weak strength with lead arsenate or Parathion, but should then be used immediately or it loses its efficacy.

COPPER FUNGICIDES

BORDEAUX MIXTURE

This is a long-established copper fungicide which is very effective if it is made correctly. It is used to control leaf diseases of fruit trees, vegetables and flowers, such as Leaf Spot, Black Spot of Roses and Blights. It adheres well to foliage and is not easily washed off by rain.

Bordeaux mixture is becoming less popular in gardens of today as there are several disadvantages in using it. In the first place, both factory-made and home-made Bordeaux mixtures are apt to stain foliage a little and one can substitute with many good modern fungicides that leave no residues such as fixed coppers, Captan and Karathene (for Mildew). Secondly, Bordeaux mixture causes a certain amount of leaf injury if it is not made correctly or if the lime used in mixing it is not of good quality. Fresh, home-made Bordeaux mixture is economical and is considered to be the best copper-containing fungicide, yet the busy gardener seldom has the time or patience to prepare it correctly. As it cannot be kept, it has to be made freshly each time it is used. Bordeaux mixture must be agitated continuously while spraying or it may settle in the bottom half of the container and become too strong, causing leaf injury. It is apt to block the spray-nozzles.

Factory-made Bordeaux mixture, in powder form to be mixed with water, can save the gardener some trouble, but it must be fresh. If the powder is greyish instead of blue, it must be discarded. In spite of the above-mentioned disadvantages, home-made Bordeaux mixture is recommended, especially when larger quantities are needed.

Bordeaux mixture must be used within an hour or two of mixing, for it loses its efficacy within three hours of being made. One should prepare only as much as one can use and throw away the remainder. It must be stirred while spraying in order to keep it in suspension.

To make Bordeaux Mixture. Bordeaux mixture is made by mixing together copper sulphate (bluestone) and hydrated (slaked) lime (calcium hydroxide) with water. This forms a complex mixture consisting largely of a copper hydroxide suspension. It is important to purchase fresh hydrated lime of good quality.

Bordeaux mixture must be made in wooden, plastic or porcelain containers, but not in metal containers. In order to make 4 gallons of the spray, dissolve 5 oz. of copper sulphate in 2 gallons of water. In a separate, larger container, mix 5 or 6 oz. of fresh, hydrated lime with 2 gallons of water to form a suspension. Mix the two liquids together and stir well. Use immediately and stir while spraying. One can mix equal quantities of copper sulphate and lime, but there is less chance of plant injury if the mixture is kept more alkaline and one adds more lime.

Compatibility. Bordeaux mixture can be combined with lead arsenate, nicotine sulphate and DDT, as well as with colloidal sulphur, but not with Lime-sulphur.

CUPROUS OXIDE
(Trade name: Perenox.)

This is a copper spray, obtainable as a powder, which must simply be mixed with water. It does not scald the leaves as easily as Bordeaux mixture.

This chemical controls mainly leaf-spot diseases. It should be applied at least once a week during rainy periods.

COPPER OXYCHLORIDE—A Fixed Copper Spray
(Trade names: Oxychlor, Coprochlor, Coppesan, Cupravit, Protane, Blitox and others.)

This is a bluish-green, insoluble copper compound known as a fixed copper, which is prepared as a wettable powder. It can be used under most conditions where Bordeaux mixture is used and has the advantage that it can be mixed with water whenever it is needed. Whether Bordeaux mixture or copper oxychloride is better for controlling some diseases more than others is largely a matter for experiment.

Copper oxychloride is used to control the Black Spot diseases of Roses, Citrus and Mangoes; Downy Mildew diseases of Onions and Cucumber; Late Blight on Tomatoes and Potatoes; Leaf-Spot diseases on Celery, Tomatoes, Potatoes; Peach Leaf Curl; Anthracnose diseases on Bananas, Grapes, Mangoes, and other fungus diseases of commercial importance.

Compatibility. Copper oxychloride may be mixed with nicotine sulphate, DDT and Parathion, but not with Lime-sulphur.

NEW ORGANIC FUNGICIDES

During the Second World War, when copper was at a premium, experiments were made to find a copper substitute and the new organic fungicides were produced as a result. These are known as carbamates, dinitro com-

pounds, mercury compounds and others. Most of them have long scientific names which have recognised abbreviations like Zineb and Captan, which have been accepted as coined common names.

I. CARBAMATES

These are protective fungicides derived from dithiocarbamic acid. They are fairly specific chemicals which are used more for some plant diseases than for others. They cause less injury to foliage than sulphurs during hot weather. The best known in this country are as follows:

Zineb
(This is sold under the Trade name of Dithane – Z 78.)

Zineb, which contains zinc, is used generally for leaf-spotting diseases and in the control of Late Blight of Tomatoes and Potatoes. During rainy weather, it must be applied regularly every ten days. Potatoes or Tomatoes sprayed with Zineb usually give higher yields than when sprayed with Bordeaux mixture.

Maneb
(Trade name: Dithane M-22)

Maneb contains manganese in place of zinc. It is used for the control of Late Blight in the same way as Zineb. It is recommended especially for Black Spot of Roses.

Thiram (or T.M.T.D.)
(Trade names: Pomarsol, Fernide.)

This is a greyish-white wettable powder used at 50 per cent strength as a seed disinfectant in South Africa. At 80 per cent strength, it is used as a spray for the control of Fusicladium disease of Apples and Pears in the southwestern Cape. The spray may also be used for Late Blight of Tomatoes and must be applied weekly.

II. CAPTAN
(Trade names Kaptan, Flit 406 and Orthocide)

Captan is a protective organic sulphur fungicide which is used on a wide range of Leaf-spot diseases, such as Black Spot (of Roses), Rust (on Carnations), Leaf-spot (on Carnations, Tomatoes, Potatoes), Late Blight (on Tomatoes and Potatoes) and Fusicladium disease of Apples. It is also used to control Brown Patch of lawns, Damping-off of seedlings, Root-Rot and Bulb-Rot.

Captan is safe to use in handling, but the makers advise that spraying on edible crops should cease fifteen days before harvesting. One should not spray during very hot dry weather.

Compatibility. Captan may be mixed with all non-alkaline sprays, but not with lime or oil sprays.

III. GLYODIN
(Trade name: Gly-kop)

This organic fungicide is recommended especially to control Leaf-spot of Chrysanthemum, Black Spot of Roses, Rust of Snapdragons, as well as Fusicladium disease of Apples. It is not recommended for Pear trees. Glyodin is relatively safe to use.

Compatibility. Glyodin must not be mixed with summer oils, DDT, BHC, Malathion, Parathion or dieldrin.

IV. DINITRO COMPOUNDS
(Trade name: Karathane)

This powder is available as a 2 per cent or 3 per cent dust or as a wettable powder. It is used especially for powdery mildew on Roses, Apples, members of the Cucumber family (Cucurbits) and for garden flowers. Start using at the first sign of mildew and repeat at ten-day intervals if necessary. One should cease treating edible crops two weeks before harvest. Do not use it during hot dry weather. It is best to dust towards evening when the sun is weak and to dust thoroughly on the upper and lower surfaces of the leaves.

V. ORGANIC MERCURY COMPOUNDS
(Trade names: Agallol, Agrosan, Aretan, Ceresan, Merfusan, Frodin, Mercane and others.)

These are extremely poisonous compounds which are chiefly for the use of the farmer or commercial grower. They are used as seed dressings for crops or for treating flower bulbs in storage in case of bulb-rot. They may also be used as a dressing on lawns to control Brown Patch. One hears of the work done with mercury compounds in combating Black Spot, but their use is not general and is likely to be limited because of the poisonous residues on harvested crops.

TABLE I

INSECT AND PEST CONTROL IN A NUTSHELL

Pest	Insecticide	Remarks
Aphids.	Malathion spray or dust.	Not on cucurbits unless plants are dry. Cease one week before harvest.
	Rogor E.	Not on Chrysanthemum, Zinnia, Begonia, Ficus, Jacobinia or Lagerstroemia.
	BHC—sprays or dust.	Not for cucurbits or root crops.
	Ekatin.	On peaches, cabbages and beans.
	Lindane—sprays or dust. (especially grey aphids).	Cease 30 days before harvest.
	Disyston.	On cabbages, potatoes.
	Metasystox.	Cease one month before harvest.
	Lebaycid.	On Cucurbits and Woolly Apple Aphid.
	Nicotine sulphate and soft soap.	Use during heat of the day. Not on tomatoes, potatoes.
	Phorate.	On cabbages, cauliflowers, potatoes.
	Summer oils.	On citrus in cool conditions.
	Thiodan.	
	Gusathion.	
	(Parathion, HETP and TEPP).	For farmer's use.
	Sevin.	On cotton.
	Vamidothion.	On Woolly Apple Aphid.
Scale Insects.	Lime sulphur in winter.	On dormant deciduous fruit trees and roses.
	Mineral oil sprays.	Use preferably during winter.
	Malathion.	During spring, summer and autumn when infested.
	(Parathion).	For farmers.
Soft Brown Scale.	Mineral oil and nicotine sulphate.	Mainly on citrus.
	Gusathion.	Soft brown scale and red scale.
	Malathion.	On soft brown scale and citrus psylla.
Soft Wax Scale.	Malathion. Nicotine sulphate and mineral oil.	On Jacarandas or citrus.
Circular Purple Scale.	Rogor E.	On citrus.
Red Scale.	Rogor E.	On citrus.
	Gusathion with Parathion.	
Australian Bug.	Malathion.	Handpick before eggs are released.
	Mineral oil spray.	Spray if plant is infested.
	(Parathion).	For farmers' use.

279

TABLE I—(*Continued*)

INSECT AND PEST CONTROL IN A NUTSHELL

Pest	Insecticide	Remarks
Mealybugs.	Methylated spirits.	For houseplants apply with matchstick and cottonwool—also hothouse plants.
	Rogor E.	Long-tailed Mealybugs.
	Malathion sprays.	
	(Parathion).	For farmers' use.
	Mesurol.	Long-tailed and Vine Mealybugs.
Citrus Psylla.	Thiodan.	When new leaves appear.
	Rogor E.	Not when lemons are formed or on rough lemons.
Thrips.	DDT emulsions and wettable powders.	Use DDT emulsion regularly for Gladiolus thrip.
	BHC emulsions and wettable powders.	Not on edible crops. Greenhouse thrips.
	Malathion.	For citrus thrip.
	Lime sulphur in winter.	On dormant deciduous trees.
	Disyston.	Gladiolus Thrip.
	Sulphur dust.	
	(Parathion).	For farmers' use.
	Thiodan.	
Spider mites. (Red spider and Bryobia mite.)	Lime sulphur in winter.	On deciduous trees, roses and ornamentals.
	Ovotran for eggs in winter.	Can be applied in winter and at other times.
	Rogor E.	For Red Spider on strawberries and other plants.
	Kelthane spray.	For deciduous fruit and citrus. Cease one week before harvest.
	Ekatin.	
	Malathion spray.	Cease 1 week before harvesting edible crops.
	Formothion (Anthio).	
	Metasystox spray.	Cease 4 weeks before harvesting edible crops.
	Sevin.	For Pear Bud Mite.
	Dusting sulphur.	On strawberries.
	Lebaycid.	For Bryobia Mite.
	(Parathion and TEPP).	For farmers' use.
	Tedion.	For Red Spider on deciduous fruit and Citrus Red Mite.
	Acricid.	For Citrus Red Mite, Bryobia Mite on deciduous fruit and for Red Spider on apples only.
	Gusathion.	
Bugs. Green Stinkbug.	DDT dust or wettable powder.	Dust while feeding. Repeat after two weeks. Not on cucurbits.
	BHC dust or wettable powder.	Not on edible crops.
	Malathion (Parathion).	Parathion for farmers' use.

TABLE I—(*Continued*)

INSECT AND PEST CONTROL IN A NUTSHELL

Pest	Insecticide	Remarks
Large Stinkbug.	BHC.	Handpick. Destroy egg rafts. Spray insects by contact.
	Malathion (Parathion).	Parathion for farmers' use.
Bagrada Bug.	5% DDT dust. 5% BHC dust. Malathion.	Dust ground and under foliage as soon as noticed.
	Rhothane.	
	Toxaphene.	
Beetles. Chafer Beetle. Adult.	DDT wettable powder.	When seen during summer.
	BHC.	Not on edible crops.
	Arsenate of lead.	On ornamental trees and shrubs.
Grubs.	DDT powder on soil surface.	Before planting or between seedlings.
	Dieldrin 50% wettable powder.	Before planting.
	Chlordane.	Stir into soil.
	BHC.	Not on root crops.
Maize Chafer Beetle.	Sevin.	
Astylus Beetle.	DDT dust, BHC dust, Malathion dust.	Dust on to feeding insects.
Astylus Grub.	Dieldrin, BHC dust or Lindane.	Dust maize seed before sowing. Pour weak dieldrin solution on to soil between strawberry plants, if necessary.
CMR Beetle.	DDT dust, Malathion dust, Lindane,	Dust feeding beetles.
	Rothane, Toxaphene.	
Ladybird Beetles.	DDT dust or sprays.	Not on cucurbits.
	Malathion dust.	On pumpkins when plants are dry.
	Lead arsenate.	
Fruit-eating Beetle.	No chemical control.	Hand collect.
	Sugar and water bait in pots among branches.	
Moths and Butterflies. Fruit-sucking Moth.	Bait of Malathion or Dipterex with sugar and water.	Spray on to foliage or hang in pots amongst branches.

Caterpillars.
  (Larvae of moths,
  etc. These are
  chewing insects).
	DDT, BHC, Toxaphene,
	Thiodan on Orange Dog Caterpillar
	on citrus,
	Arsenate of lead.
		Handpick. Spray when seen. Repeat spray for second generation.

Army Worm.	DDT emulsion, Thiodan, Sevin, Endrin emulsion, Diazinon emulsion or wettable powder.	Spray on to lawns as soon as seen.
Cutworms.	DDT spray, Toxaphene or dieldrin spray.	Spray on to surface of soil and base of seedlings.
	BHC powder in soil.	Not on root crops.
	Dieldrin bait, Thiodan bait, Dipterex bait, Baits of calcium arsenate, Paris Green or sodium fluosilicate.	Take great care when scattering poison baits because of danger to pets.
Codling Moth.	DDT spray, Sevin, Mesurol, Rogor E, Gusathion.	Follow a regular spraying programme.
	Lebaycid.	Emulsion on apricots; wettable powder on apples, pears.

TABLE I—(*Continued*)

INSECT AND PEST CONTROL IN A NUTSHELL

Pest	Insecticide	Remarks
False Codling Moth.	No chemical control.	Destroy infested oranges.
Lawn Caterpillar.	DDT or BHC dust, Chlordane (Rhothane, methoxychlor).	Dust lawn and water in.
Cabbage Caterpillar.	DDT wettable powder. Malathion spray, Thiodan.	Handpick. Spray when seen. Do not spray cabbages with DDT after the heads have formed.
Amaryllis Caterpillar.	DDT 5% or 10% dust or wettable powder.	Keep a watch for the first one in November and spray or dust susceptible plants weekly until February.
Maize Stalk Borer.	DDT dust, Sevin, Thiodan, Dipterex or Endrin powders or emulsions.	Pour these insecticides down the leaf funnels of maize.
Bollworm (ear-worm on Maize).	DDT dust or spray, Thiodan, Toxaphene.	Dust silk and cobs of maize before ripening. Spray tomatoes as soon as pests are seen. Do not spray tomatoes after the fruit has set.
	Rhothane.	On tomatoes only.
Potato Tuber Moth.	DDT wettable powder, Thiodan.	As soon as shoots appear.
Borers. (Larvae of Moths or Beetles.)	No chemical control.	Protect trees with gauze against Fig borer. Keep watch for sawdust of Borers. Destroy by probing holes with wire and plug with mud or putty.
Whiteflies. (Sucking insects).	Malathion spray, (Parathion). Nicotine sulphate and soft soap.	Spray when seen, usually in greenhouses.
Grasshoppers.	BHC or Chlordane.	Spray the plants they feed on.
Crickets.	BHC, DDT or dieldrin, Lindane.	Water on to lawns or around their holes if troublesome.
Flies. Fruit-fly.	Poisoned bait spray for adults. Sugar and water or a protein attractant added to: Malathion wettable powder. Dipterex wettable powder. Parathion (for farmers' use.)	See instructions on labels for harvesting.
	Rogor E.	Cover spray on deciduous and sub-tropical fruit.
	Lebaycid.	Cover spray on deciduous and sub-tropical fruit.
Gladiolus Fly.	Disyston.	Mainly for farmers' use.
	DDT emulsion.	Spray fortnightly throughout summer.
Carnation Bud Fly.	DDT emulsion.	Use as for Gladiolus Fly.
	Dipterex and water.	Spray once a week.
Pumpkin & Melon Fly.	Bait sprays as for fruit-fly. Lebaycid.	Spray foliage weekly from flowering time to recommended period before harvesting.
Ants.	Dieldrin, chlordane or BHC.	Water into soil or spray base of trees. Mix with soil and spread on surface.
	Sticky bands on trees.	Do not paint directly on to bark.
	Bait of sodium arsenite.	Highly poisonous. Not where children or pets are about. Not recommended in general.

TABLE I—(Continued)

INSECT AND PEST CONTROL IN A NUTSHELL

Pest	Insecticide	Remarks
Termites. Harvester.	*Eradicate* with bait made with sodium fluosilicate.	Scatter on lawns in winter.
	Dieldrin.	On some species—Snouted Harvester Termite.
	Aldrin.	Kills specific species—Karoo Harvester Termite and Snouted Harvester Termite.
Wood-eating.	*Repel* with DDT dust, BHC dust, or calcium arsenate dust.	Work into soil. Do not use BHC on edible crops. Only use calcium arsenate on soil before planting lawn.
	To eradicate, specialist control with BHC smoke treatment or white arsenic and sulphur toxic smoke treatment.	
Snails and Slugs.	Metaldehyde—in the form of baits.	Scatter bait between seedlings in the evening.
Millipedes.	DDT dust or dieldrin dust.	Dust seed in infested soil.
	Malathion spray.	Spray area or hit directly.
Eelworm. (Nematodes).	Eradicate with soil fumigation using D-D or E.D.B. 4.5.	Best applied with special equipment. Apply 2–3 weeks before planting where eelworm has been troublesome in the previous season. Practise rotation of crops.
	D.B.C.P.	On banana Eelworm.
Other Pests. **Moles.** Golden Mole.	Repel on lawns with arsenate of lead.	Trap.
Rodent Mole.	Bait with strychnine.	Trap. Shoot.
	Fumigation tablets (phosphorus)	Handle with extreme caution.
	Specialist control with cyanide powders.	

TABLE II

CONTROL OF FUNGUS DISEASES IN A NUTSHELL

Disease	Main Plants Affected	Fungicide or Treatment	Remarks
Black Spot.	Roses.	Copper sprays. Copper oxychloride. Captan. Maneb. Glyodin.	Apply to foliage once a week from beginning of rainy season, more often during wet weather.
Mildew (Powdery).	Roses. Apple, Peach. Flowers, like delphinium. Vegetables like peas.	Sulphur dust. Wettable sulphur sprays. Karathane spray.	At weekly intervals at the first sign of mildew. Check ventilation of plants.
Mildew (Downy).	Onion, pea, melon. Seedling cabbages and cauliflowers. Snapdragons in S.W. Cape.	Lime sulphur (summer strength). Zineb (Dithane Z 78). Maneb (Dithane M 22).	Spray healthy plants after removing diseased plants or portions of them.
Rust.	Fruit trees. Vegetables. Flowers. Roses (not common).	Sulphur dust. Wettable sulphur sprays.	Destroy infected annuals. Spray susceptible plants at beginning of rainy season. Check growing conditions. Grow rust-resistant varieties.
Die-Back.	Fruit trees in poor condition. Injured trees.	Prune and fertilize.	A weak fungus that only attacks plants that are not growing vigorously.

TABLE II—(Continued)

CONTROL OF FUNGUS DISEASES IN A NUTSHELL

Disease	Main Plants Affected	Fungicide or Treatment	Remarks
Sooty-Mould.	Citrus (following insect infestation).	Remove mould with water. Spray with an insecticide to kill insects (scale and aphids).	Usually only in neglected orchards where insects have not been controlled.
Leaf-Spot Diseases.	Garden flowers, vegetables in wet seasons and misty areas. Trees in misty areas.	Copper sprays. New organic fungicides.	Spray at first sign of Leaf-Spot. In misty areas and winter rainfall area, spray susceptible plants from seedling stage throughout growing season. Destroy infected plants.
Peach Leaf-Curl.	Peach, nectarine, apricot.	Lime-sulphur in winter. Freshly made Bordeaux mixture or a copper containing spray. Also destroy aphids with an insecticide.	Aggravated by wet weather and humidity. Apply as soon as buds begin to swell. Repeat 10 days later.
Leaf-Blight.	Tomatoes, potatoes, peas, carrots, quinces, mulberry (wet seasons). Mesembs (vygies) in Cape.	Cuprous oxide or new organic fungicides like Zineb, Captan, Maneb or Thiram.	Apply from seedling stage in places where disease is common. Apply weekly or fortnightly. See special spray programme in Chapter 38.
Damping-off Fungi.	Seedlings, where conditions are too wet or overcrowded.	Water with a weak fungicide.	Build a raised, well-drained seedbed and sow seed thinly.
Wilt.	Unfavourable growth conditions, e.g. Asters in hot soil.	No control. Prevent spread of disease by practical measures.	Common.
(a) Fusarium Wilt.	Tomatoes (E. Tvl.). Garden flowers where soil is too warm. Causes crown and stem rot of many plants.	Remove and burn infected plants. Do not grow tomatoes in same place for 3 seasons.	Grow resistant varieties. Avoid excess use of nitrogenous fertilisers.
Anthracnose (Ripe Rot).	Vegetables. Tropical fruit (of commercial importance).	Regular spraying programmes with copper fungicides may help, but are not practical on large trees.	Attacks after rain, especially if unseasonable. Correct cultivation is best prevention.
Fusicladium Disease (Scab).	Apples and pears (in the S.W. Cape).	Regular spraying programme. Consult Local Department of Agriculture.	A disease of commercial importance.
Brown Patch.	Lawns, with wet soil and poor drainage.	Aerate soil with hollow-tined fork. Add coarse sand. Water with a fixed copper fungicide or Captan. Use mercurial fungicides with great care.	Brown patch often appears as a result of uneven water supplies. Mow frequently, removing a little top growth at a time.
Dollar Spot.	Lawns—not common. Occurs on compacted soil and during rainy weather.	Aerate soil as above. Water affected patches with a fixed copper fungicide, Captan or mercury compounds (with care).	Prepare soil well before planting. Attend to drainage.

TREATMENT TABLE FOR BACTERIAL AND VIRUS DISEASES

Crown Gall Bacterial.	Deciduous fruit trees, Roses.	Prevention is only control. Plant healthy trees. Do not injure young trees or destroy trees if growing satisfactorily. Replace soil if tree dies.	Do not confuse Crown gall with insect galls which are comparatively harmless. Cankers (sunken areas) on trees are destructive, but not common.
Virus Diseases: (a) Mosaic, (b) Streak diseases, (c) Spotted Wilt Virus.	Vegetables and flowers of many kinds. Tomatoes, flowers and vegetables.	No cure or chemical preventative. Destroy infected plants. Keep down insect pests like aphids.	Eliminate susceptible plants for a season.

INDEX

Scientific names appear in italics. Numbers in heavy type indicate more detailed descriptions.